D1566660

Measuring Entrepreneurial Businesses

Studies in Income and Wealth
Volume 75

National Bureau of Economic Research
Conference on Research in Income and Wealth

Measuring Entrepreneurial Businesses
Current Knowledge and Challenges

Edited by **John Haltiwanger, Erik Hurst, Javier Miranda, and Antoinette Schoar**

The University of Chicago Press

Chicago and London

The University of Chicago Press, Chicago 60637
The University of Chicago Press, Ltd., London
© 2017 by the National Bureau of Economic Research
Published 2017
Printed in the United States of America

26 25 24 23 22 21 20 19 18 17   1 2 3 4 5

ISBN-13: 978-0-226-45407-8 (cloth)
ISBN-13: 978-0-226-45410-8 (e-book)
DOI: 10.7208/chicago/9780226454108.001.0001

LCCN: 2017003529

♾ This paper meets the requirements of ANSI/NISO Z39.48–1992
(Permanence of Paper).

Relation of the Directors to the
Work and Publications of the
National Bureau of Economic Research

1. The object of the NBER is to ascertain and present to the economics profession, and to the public more generally, important economic facts and their interpretation in a scientific manner without policy recommendations. The Board of Directors is charged with the responsibility of ensuring that the work of the NBER is carried on in strict conformity with this object.

2. The President shall establish an internal review process to ensure that book manuscripts proposed for publication DO NOT contain policy recommendations. This shall apply both to the proceedings of conferences and to manuscripts by a single author or by one or more co-authors but shall not apply to authors of comments at NBER conferences who are not NBER affiliates.

3. No book manuscript reporting research shall be published by the NBER until the President has sent to each member of the Board a notice that a manuscript is recommended for publication and that in the President's opinion it is suitable for publication in accordance with the above principles of the NBER. Such notification will include a table of contents and an abstract or summary of the manuscript's content, a list of contributors if applicable, and a response form for use by Directors who desire a copy of the manuscript for review. Each manuscript shall contain a summary drawing attention to the nature and treatment of the problem studied and the main conclusions reached.

4. No volume shall be published until forty-five days have elapsed from the above notification of intention to publish it. During this period a copy shall be sent to any Director requesting it, and if any Director objects to publication on the grounds that the manuscript contains policy recommendations, the objection will be presented to the author(s) or editor(s). In case of dispute, all members of the Board shall be notified, and the President shall appoint an ad hoc committee of the Board to decide the matter; thirty days additional shall be granted for this purpose.

5. The President shall present annually to the Board a report describing the internal manuscript review process, any objections made by Directors before publication or by anyone after publication, any disputes about such matters, and how they were handled.

6. Publications of the NBER issued for informational purposes concerning the work of the Bureau, or issued to inform the public of the activities at the Bureau, including but not limited to the NBER Digest and Reporter, shall be consistent with the object stated in paragraph 1. They shall contain a specific disclaimer noting that they have not passed through the review procedures required in this resolution. The Executive Committee of the Board is charged with the review of all such publications from time to time.

7. NBER working papers and manuscripts distributed on the Bureau's web site are not deemed to be publications for the purpose of this resolution, but they shall be consistent with the object stated in paragraph 1. Working papers shall contain a specific disclaimer noting that they have not passed through the review procedures required in this resolution. The NBER's web site shall contain a similar disclaimer. The President shall establish an internal review process to ensure that the working papers and the web site do not contain policy recommendations, and shall report annually to the Board on this process and any concerns raised in connection with it.

8. Unless otherwise determined by the Board or exempted by the terms of paragraphs 6 and 7, a copy of this resolution shall be printed in each NBER publication as described in paragraph 2 above.

Contents

Prefatory Note

This volume contains revised versions of the papers presented at the Conference on Research in Income and Wealth entitled "Measuring Entrepreneurial Businesses: Current Knowledge and Challenges," held in Washington, DC, on December 16–17, 2014.

We gratefully acknowledge the financial support for this conference provided by the Bureau of Economic Analysis and the Kauffman Foundation. Support for the general activities of the Conference on Research in Income and Wealth is provided by the following agencies: Bureau of Economic Analysis, Bureau of Labor Statistics, Census Bureau, Board of Governors of the Federal Reserve System, Internal Revenue Service, and Statistics Canada.

We thank John Haltiwanger, Erik Hurst, Javier Miranda, and Antoinette Schoar, who served as conference organizers and as editors of the volume.

Introduction

John Haltiwanger, Erik Hurst, Javier Miranda, and
Antoinette Schoar

The contribution of entrepreneurial businesses to economic growth is an often debated topic among the academic and policy-making communities and the subject of much discussion in the business and popular press. That there are high-growth entrepreneurial businesses that have made a substantial impact on the US economy, particularly in the high-tech sectors of the economy, is self-evident. High-tech start-ups from the last few decades, including Apple, Facebook, Google, and Microsoft, are now among the largest and most influential companies in the world. The entrepreneurs who founded these businesses have been the subject of much attention with in-depth profiles and popular movies about their lives and how they achieved such enormous success.

However, the high-profile, high-growth entrepreneurs are small in number relative to the hundreds of thousands of new start-ups in the United States every year. Many of the latter fail soon after they start up or do not grow. In spite of this, recent evidence suggests that start-ups and young businesses make important contributions to job creation, innovation, and productivity growth. It is now understood, for example, that the job-creating prowess of

John Haltiwanger is a Distinguished University Professor of Economics at the University of Maryland and a research associate of the National Bureau of Economic Research. Erik G. Hurst is the V. Duane Rath Professor of Economics at the University of Chicago Booth School of Business and a research associate of the National Bureau of Economic Research. Javier Miranda is principal economist in the Center for Economic Studies, US Census Bureau. Antoinette Schoar is the Michael Koerner '49 Professor of Entrepreneurial Finance at MIT Sloan School of Management, a research fellow of the Center for Economic Policy Research, and a research associate and director of the Entrepreneurship Working Group at the National Bureau of Economic Research.

For acknowledgments, sources of research support, and disclosure of the authors' material financial relationships, if any, please see http://www.nber.org/chapters/c13491.ack.

small businesses is better attributed to the job-creating prowess of start-ups and young businesses. However, since many start-ups fail and don't grow, it is apparent that any job-creating prowess is not shared equally among young businesses.

Understanding the enormous heterogeneity across entrepreneurs is an ongoing area of active research. Some of this heterogeneity may reflect differences in aspirations and abilities across entrepreneurs. Alternatively, it may reflect differences in economic circumstances and business conditions facing entrepreneurs. Our ability to accurately track how businesses perform in a complex economic and financial environment is hampered by difficult measurement challenges. The US statistical agencies have traditionally focused on large, mature businesses in their measurement of business activity. The logic is that large, mature businesses account for most activity so this focus facilitates obtaining precise measures of the level of US economic activity (e.g., employment or gross domestic product [GDP]). This has implied that there has been less information and data collected for tracking entrepreneurial business activity. However, as it has become apparent that entrepreneurial businesses are critical for understanding the growth in US business activity, there is increased attention to measuring and tracking entrepreneurial businesses. The increased attention to entrepreneurial businesses has been made easier by the increased use of administrative data in tracking business activity.

In December of 2014 the Conference on Research in Income and Wealth (CRIW) of the National Bureau of Economic Research (NBER) held a conference in Washington, DC, to provide a forum where economists, data providers, and data analysts could present research on the state of entrepreneurship and to address the challenges we face in understanding this dynamic part of our economies. The conference invited participants to present papers from a theoretical and empirical perspective and to set an agenda for the future of entrepreneurial research. The conference drew participants from academia, government, and nonacademic research institutions. This volume includes the papers presented at the conference. The papers have undergone review and, in some cases, substantial revision since their presentation at the conference.

The themes of the conference address the challenges of measuring entrepreneurship and the contribution of entrepreneurial firms to our economies and ultimately our standards of living. The most basic questions are still under investigation. What characterizes an entrepreneur? What are their goals and motivations? How do they bring them about? Where do their ideas originate from? What is the role of founding teams? How do entrepreneurs finance their operations? What types of employees do they hire? What is their contribution to innovation and productivity growth? How is the entrepreneur and the entrepreneurial firm changing over time? How did entrepreneurs fare during the Great Recession?

Addressing these questions requires progress both conceptually and in terms of economic measurement. The chapters in this volume tackle these conceptual and measurement questions from a variety of different perspectives. Chapters in the volume fit into three broad themes but with substantial overlap, especially given the focus on economics measurement. The first broad theme is to explore entrepreneurial heterogeneity. Some chapters explore the role of high-growth, high-impact entrepreneurs while others explore the vast majority of entrepreneurs that don't grow. Another component of this theme is to explore how differences in individual backgrounds are important for understanding entrepreneurial heterogeneity. The second broad theme is the challenges that entrepreneurs face and how this has varied over time, including over the business cycle. The chapters in the volume that address these issues focus on what we know based on existing evidence and the measurement gaps. The third broad theme is found in chapters that focus on core data and measurement issues and gaps. Some of these chapters discuss new data infrastructure projects under development that have the promise to improve our understanding of the contribution of entrepreneurship to the economy substantially. Others highlight that, in some cases, we know even less than we think we know about entrepreneurship given data limitations that are not well recognized or understood.

Entrepreneurial Heterogeneity

The first few chapters in the volume address one of the key challenges of entrepreneurship research: understanding heterogeneity in the nature of entrepreneurs. The first two chapters focus on high-growth, high-impact entrepreneurs. In "High-Growth Young Firms: Contribution to Job, Output, and Productivity Growth," John Haltiwanger, Ron S Jarmin, Robert Kulick, and Javier Miranda investigate the contribution of high-growth firms in the United States to economic performance. As they note, most of the recent evidence on the contribution of high-growth firms has been to job creation. The authors build on the Census Bureau Longitudinal Business Database (LBD) to create a universe file of employer businesses that incorporate gross output (real revenue) measures. This permits their exploring the contribution of high-growth firms to output and productivity growth. The authors define high-growth firms as those that grow in excess of 25 percent from one year to the next. The authors find that the patterns for high-output-growth firms largely mimic those for high-employment-growth firms. High-growth firms (whether in terms of jobs or output) are rare but contribute disproportionately to overall economic growth. The share of activity accounted for by high-growth output and employment firms varies substantially across industries. High-growth industries include the high-tech and energy-related industries. Firms in small business-intensive industries are less likely to be high-output growth, but small business-intensive industries do not have significantly smaller shares of either employment or output activity accounted for by high-growth firms. The authors also find that high-growth businesses contribute disproportionately to productivity growth.

In "Nowcasting and Placecasting Entrepreneurial Quality and Performance," Jorge Guzman and Scott Stern propose a method to identify high-quality, high-growth firms at time of inception, well before they have demonstrated successful outcomes. The authors focus on incorporated businesses from public-use records linked to business outcome measures, including achieving an initial public offering (IPO) or a significant acquisition. The authors estimate entrepreneurial quality or the probability of high-growth outcome as a function of start-up characteristics observable at or near the time of initial business registration, such as firm name or filing for a trademark/patent. Guzman and Stern implement this approach using data from the state business registry of Massachusetts from 1988 to 2014. The authors find that more than 75 percent of growth outcomes occur in the top 5 percent of their estimated quality distribution. The authors propose two new economic statistics for the measurement of entrepreneurship: the Entrepreneurship Quality Index (EQI) and the Regional Entrepreneurship Cohort Potential Index (RECPI). They find a high correlation between an index that depends only on information directly observable from business registration records and that can be calculated in real time with an index that allows for a two-year lag that allows the estimate of entrepreneurial quality to incorporate early milestones of success. The authors argue these indices are of substantial policy relevance in that they allow for the characterization of entrepreneurial attitude and quality at any arbitrary level of geographic granularity and over time.

The first two chapters focus on the high-growth, high-impact firms. Both of those chapters emphasize that such firms are rare. A third chapter turns toward describing the incentives and dynamics of the vast majority of start-ups that do not grow. In "Wealth, Tastes, and Entrepreneurial Choice," Erik G. Hurst and Benjamin W. Pugsley argue the nonpecuniary benefits of managing a small business are a first-order consideration for many entrepreneurs. The authors develop a model of occupational choice based on heterogeneous taste for entrepreneurship. In this model, individuals differ in their utility from owning a business but are otherwise equal; the model abstracts away from differences in entrepreneurial ability, entrepreneurial luck, or binding liquidity constraints. The authors are able to predict several features of the data with this simple model, including the observation that there are many small businesses in industries with low entry costs. The model also predicts that owning a business is a relative luxury good and that small business subsidies are regressive.

Another set of chapters investigate the characteristics and nature of entrepreneurs. In "Are Founder CEOs Good Managers?" Victor Manuel Bennett, Megan Lawrence, and Raffaella Sadun investigate the management practices adopted by firms where the founders are also the CEOs using data from the World Management Survey. The authors find that founder CEO firms have the lowest management scores of any owner-manager pair type and that this difference is associated with significant performance differentials. The authors argue the managerial gap of founder CEO firms is likely due to either informational problems leading to suboptimal managerial practices or to nonpecuniary returns to inefficient but power-preserving practices.

A related set of questions are about who becomes an entrepreneur and how the heterogeneous characteristics of entrepreneurs impact outcomes. One important question in this context is the connection between immigration and entrepreneurship. In "Immigrant Entrepreneurship," Sari Pekkala Kerr and William R. Kerr examine immigrant entrepreneurship and the survival and growth of immigrant-founded businesses over time relative to native-founded companies. The analysis quantifies immigrant contributions to new firm creation in a wide variety of fields and using multiple definitions. A theme of the chapter is that it is difficult to assemble comprehensive data for assessing the contribution of immigration to entrepreneurship in the United States. These authors seek to overcome this limitation by combining several restricted-access US Census Bureau data sets to create a unique longitudinal data platform that covers the time period 1992–2008 and many states. They describe differences in the types of businesses initially formed by immigrants and their medium-term growth patterns. One core challenge they face is that data on the characteristics of founders, including their immigration status is limited, especially in the context of the databases that have been assembled to track new businesses and their dynamics in the United States. The authors discuss how they have overcome this limitation and also make constructive suggestions about improvements that need to be made to explore this and related questions about the characteristics of entrepreneurs.

Challenges Facing Entrepreneurs: Finance and Business Conditions

There is accumulating evidence that entrepreneurs are hit hard during economic downturns, especially those that involve a financial crisis like the Great Recession. In "How Did Young Firms Fare during the Great Recession? Evidence from the Kauffman Firm Survey," Rebecca Zarutskie and Tiantian Yang examine the evolution of several key firm economic and financial variables in the years surrounding and during the Great Recession using the Kauffman Firm Survey, a large panel of young firms founded in 2004 and surveyed for eight consecutive years. The authors find that young firms experienced slower growth in revenues, employment, and assets and faced tighter financing conditions during the recessionary years. The authors also find some evidence that firm growth picked up following the recession, but not to previous levels. They also find financial constraints continued in the period immediately following.

Related themes are explored in the chapter "Small Businesses and Small Business Finance during the Financial Crisis and the Great Recession: New Evidence from the Survey of Consumer Finances," by Arthur B. Kennickell, Myron L. Kwast, and Jonathan Pogach. The authors use multiple years of the Federal Reserve's Survey of Consumer Finances (SCF) to examine the experiences of small businesses owned and actively managed by households during the Great Recession and its aftermath. This is the first chapter to use the SCF to study small business. The authors provide a road map for using the SCF for this purpose. The data contain a broad cross section of firms and their owners. The authors find the majority of small businesses were severely credit constrained during the financial crisis and the Great Recession. The authors document complex interdependencies between the finances of small businesses and their owners with an important role for housing real estate assets.

Due to the perceived importance of entrepreneurial ventures for economic growth, it is not surprising that governmental policies often attempt to facilitate the creation and growth of young businesses. The next two chapters explore government programs intended to encourage entrepreneurial activity. In "Does Unemployment Insurance Change the Selection into Entrepreneurship?" Johan Hombert, Antoinette Schoar, David Sraer, and David Thesmar explore entrepreneurial performance in response to a reform of the unemployment insurance system in France that lead to a 25 percent increase in the supply of newly created firms. The authors explore whether the predictive ability of different markers of entrepreneurial success such as the presence of a growth plan changed with the reform. They find they did not, suggesting entrepreneurial quality did not decline with this policy stimulating entrepreneurship.

In "Job Creation, Small versus Large versus Young, and the SBA," J. David Brown, John S. Earle, and Yana Morgulis analyze a list of all Small Business Administration (SBA) loans between 1991 and 2009 linked with annual information on all US employers from the Census Bureau. The authors estimate the variation in SBA loan effects on job creation and firm survival across firm age and size groups. They find the estimated number of jobs created per million dollars of loans within the small business sector generally increases with size and decreases in age. They also find young firms are particularly vulnerable to exit and benefit the most in this regard from the loans. The authors argue this is consistent with small, mature firms being least financially constrained in their growth while young, faster-growing firms experience the greatest financial constraints to growth.

Data Gaps and Promising Avenues for the Future

One of the core questions about entrepreneurship is the role of financing. For high-growth, high-impact firms, obtaining venture capital funding is often part of the path to success. While this market and its impact on entrepreneurial activity has been the focus of active study, Steven N. Kaplan and Josh Lerner raise a variety of questions about the quality of the data commonly used for this purpose in their chapter, "Venture Capital Data: Opportunities and Challenges." The chapter carefully reviews commercial and private data sources and research on venture capital investments and performance. After careful review of the primary data and the research using that data, the authors conclude that the availability of data as well as the consistency of the academic findings using these data are still lacking. The authors also see and are careful to highlight opportunities for data improvement. The authors briefly discuss the efforts by a new nonprofit research institute to create a high-quality database that will be accessible to researchers under conditions that will ensure the protection and confidentiality of VC's data.

In the final chapter, "The Promise and Potential of Linked Employer-Employee Data for Entrepreneurship Research," Christopher Goetz, Henry Hyatt, Erika McEntarfer, and Kristin Sandusky describe newly available (and early prototypes of) public-use statistics from the Longitudinal Employer Household Dynamics program of the US Census Bureau. These data provide additional detail about the structure and workforce of entrepreneurial firms and about the dynamics of entrepreneurial employment. The new data include new quarterly workforce dynamic indicators by firm age, worker flows across firms, and a proposed new series describing sole proprietors' businesses that includes owner information. These new public-use statistics fill some gaps in the available data on entrepreneurship. They provide researchers with a rich set of new data to explore the early workforce dynamics of entrepreneurial firms, where they draw their workers from, as well as movements from self-employment to sole proprietor. The microdata on entrepreneurs underlying this effort also offers great promise for future research.

Conclusions

It is an exciting time for the field of entrepreneurship. There is increased attention on the role of entrepreneurs in the economy from the academic, statistical, and policy-making communities. In academia, programs of study focusing on entrepreneurs are increasingly common. Developments of administrative data tracking businesses as well as private data sources are providing new opportunities for the study of entrepreneurship. However, as emphasized by the chapters in this volume, there are many core open questions about entrepreneurship that involve both conceptual and measurement issues. It is our hope that the community developing and studying the data on entrepreneurship can use the accumulated knowledge and wisdom embodied in the chapters in this volume to make progress on these issues in the years to come.

The conference organizers and attendees thank those who made this conference a success and the NBER and CRIW volume possible: the NBER and CRIW for financial support and the NBER, especially Helena Fitz-Patrick, for assistance in compiling this volume.

I

Entrepreneurial Heterogeneity

1

High-Growth Young Firms
Contribution to Job, Output, and Productivity Growth

John Haltiwanger, Ron S. Jarmin, Robert Kulick, and Javier Miranda

1.1 Introduction

Business start-ups and high-growth young firms disproportionately contribute to job creation in the United States. In a typical year, start-ups account for about 10 percent of firms and more than 20 percent of firm-level gross job creation. Less well known is that most US business start-ups exit within the first ten years, and the median surviving young business does not create jobs but remains small. A small fraction of young firms create jobs rapidly and contribute substantially to job creation. These high-growth young firms are the reason that start-ups make a long-lasting contribution to net job creation.[1]

Most of the limited evidence on high-growth firms has been about their contribution to job creation. Less is known about the nature of their contribution to output and productivity growth due primarily to data limitations.

John Haltiwanger is a Distinguished University Professor of Economics at the University of Maryland and a research associate of the National Bureau of Economic Research. Ron S Jarmin is the Assistant Director for Research and Methodology at the US Census Bureau. Robert Kulick is a PhD candidate in economics at the University of Maryland. Javier Miranda is principal economist in the Center for Economic Studies, US Census Bureau.

We thank David Brown, Tim Dunne, participants of the NBER/CRIW Conference on Measuring Entrepreneurial Businesses, and participants of the 2015 ASSA meetings for helpful comments. We thank the Kauffman Foundation for financial support. Any opinions and conclusions expressed herein are those of the author(s) and do not necessarily represent the views of the US Census Bureau. All results have been reviewed to ensure that no confidential information is disclosed. For acknowledgments, sources of research support, and disclosure of the authors' material financial relationships, if any, please see http://www.nber.org/chapters/c13492.ack.

1. This discussion is based on Haltiwanger, Jarmin, and Miranda (2013) and Decker et al. (2014). Note that the statistic that start-ups account for more than 20 percent of firm-level job creation is based on gross job creation by firms, not establishments. Start-ups account for slightly less than 20 percent of establishment-level job creation.

For the United States, substantial progress has been made in developing longitudinal business databases that permit tracking growth and survival of businesses in terms of jobs. Studies of the role of business dynamics in output and productivity growth are largely limited to the manufacturing sector with some limited analysis of the retail trade sector where the data are most suitable.

In this chapter, we describe our efforts to extend the data infrastructure on business dynamics to permit tracking real output and labor productivity growth at the firm level for the entire US private sector on an annual basis. To our knowledge, this is the first database at the firm level that tracks both output and employment outcomes for all types of firms in the private sector on an annual basis.[2] This enables us to study the contribution of young high-growth firms to real output and productivity growth (i.e., real output per worker).

High-growth firms are part of the ongoing dynamics of real output and input reallocation that characterize economic growth in the United States and other market economies. Since at least the work of Dunne, Roberts, and Samuelson (1989) and Davis and Haltiwanger (1990, 1992), we have known that underlying net growth in the United States is a high pace of job reallocation. Early work focused on decomposing net employment growth into gross job creation and destruction. More recent work has shown that there is a high pace of real output and capital reallocation that accompanies the employment reallocation (see, e.g., Foster, Haltiwanger, and Krizan 2001; Becker et al. 2006), at least for selected sectors. One of the earliest findings in this literature is that young businesses exhibit a high pace of reallocation relative to more mature businesses. A second key finding in the early literature is that most of the job reallocation reflects reallocation within industry. While early work focused on US manufacturing, recent work has extended the analysis to the entire US private sector (e.g., Haltiwanger, Jarmin, and Miranda 2013; Decker et al. 2014).[3]

The high pace of within-industry reallocation has been interpreted through the predictions of the canonical firm dynamics models of Jovanovic (1982), Hopenhayn (1992), and Ericson and Pakes (1995), among others. In these models and in the subsequent literature, firms in the same industry differ in their productivity and the reallocation dynamics reflect moving resources away from less productive to more productive businesses. Such productivity differences can be endogenous given the role of endogenous innovation and research and development (R&D) activities. Entrants and

2. For publicly traded firms, COMPUSTAT provides a rich source of output, asset, and other data. The quinquennial economic censuses can be used to provide output data for most sectors every five years. Annual surveys of specific sectors can be used to generate samples of firms for most sectors but they are less well suited for longitudinal analysis at the firm level.
3. Hereafter we often refer to these as HJM (2013) and DHJM (2014).

young businesses play a critical role in these dynamics. They put competitive pressure on incumbents, and in some models they are critical for innovation (see, e.g., Acemoglu et al. 2013).

The high pace of real output and input reallocation of young businesses is interpreted as part of the learning and selection dynamics as well as the endogenous innovation dynamics that are present in this class of models. Jovanovic (1982) argues that entering firms initially do not know their type, but learn about it over time. In that model, high-growth young firms are those that learn that they are high productivity or high demand. In contrast, high-decline young firms are those that learn that they are low productivity or demand. Ericson and Pakes (1995) extended these learning ideas to environments where all firms engaging in some new form of activity have to learn whether they are profitable in that activity. Moreover, with endogenous innovation such as in Acemoglu et al. (2013), productivity evolves based on the amount and success of innovative activity. In these models with more active learning and endogenous innovation, high-growth young firms are those that innovate and learn successfully.

While some theoretical models highlight the potentially critical role of high-growth young firms to growth, it is increasingly understood that the contribution of high-growth young firms is likely to be much more important in some sectors than others. For example, the recent work of Hurst and Pugsley (2012) highlights the heterogeneity in the motivation for starting a business and hence their potential growth. They point to sectors dominated by small businesses that reflect occupational and lifestyle choices of business owners (such as wanting to be their own boss) rather than an entrepreneurial desire to innovate and grow. In such sectors it may be the case that high-growth firms do not play a significant role in contributing to job creation and productivity growth.

Most previous efforts to analyze the role of high-growth firms focused only on one single dimension of growth—employment. We create a revenue-enhanced version of the Census Bureau's Longitudinal Business Database that has been the workhorse of much research on firm dynamics. These data permit us to examine high-growth firms along both the employment and output dimensions, as well as to examine their role in productivity growth as in the models discussed above.

We find that the patterns for high-growth-output firms largely mimic those for high-employment-growth firms. High-growth-output firms are disproportionately young and these firms make outsized contributions to output and productivity growth. The share of activity accounted for by high-growth-output- and employment firms varies substantially across industries—in the post-2000 period the share of activity accounted for by high-growth firms is significantly higher in the high-tech- and energy-related (for the latter, the share of output) industries. A firm in a small business-intensive industry is less likely to be a high-growth-output firm, but small business-intensive industries do not have significantly smaller shares of activity accounted for by high-growth firms for either output or employment.

The chapter proceeds as follows. Section 1.2 presents a description of the data developed and used in this chapter. Section 1.3 presents our main empirical findings. Our findings are mostly descriptive findings about the joint distribution of employment, real output, and productivity growth. Given our interest in entrepreneurship, in section 1.4 we focus considerable attention on the role of young firms in these dynamics. Concluding remarks that summarize our main findings and discuss next steps are in section 1.5.

1.2   Business Dynamics Data

We use two core-related databases in this chapter. Both are based on the Census Business Register (BR). We use the Census Bureau's Longitudinal Business Database (LBD) to construct measures of firm employment growth and firm age. We then append to these core business dynamics data firm-level revenue data contained in the BR and sourced from administrative records. First, we discuss the basic LBD data and then describe our work to enhance the LBD with revenue information.

1.2.1   Business Dynamics Measurement with the LBD

Like the BR, the LBD covers the universe of establishments and firms in the US nonfarm business sector with at least one paid employee. The LBD includes annual observations beginning in 1976 and currently runs through 2013. It provides information on detailed industry, location, employment, and parent firm affiliation for every establishment. Employment observations in the LBD are for the payroll period covering the 12th day of March in each calendar year. The LBD's high-quality longitudinal establishment and firm-ownership information make possible the construction of our measures of firm growth and firm age. In what follows, we first discuss the key features of the LBD and then return to discussing the data we use from the BR to measure real output.

A unique advantage of the LBD is its comprehensive coverage of both firms and establishments. Firm activity is captured in the LBD up to the level of operational control instead of being based on an arbitrary taxpayer ID.[4] The ability to link establishment and firm information allows firm characteristics such as firm size and firm age to be tracked for each establishment.

---

4. A closely related database at the BLS tracks quarterly job creation and destruction statistics (Business Employment Dynamics). The BED has advantages in terms of both frequency and timeliness of the data. However, the BED only can capture firm dynamics up to the level of establishments that operate under a common taxpayer ID (EIN). There are many large firms that have multiple EINs—it is not unusual for large firms operating in multiple states to have at least one EIN per state.

Firm-size measures are constructed by aggregating the establishment information to the firm level using the appropriate firm identifiers. The construction of firm age follows the approach adopted for the BDS and based on our prior work (see, e.g., Becker et al. 2006; Davis et al. 2007; Haltiwanger, Jarmin, and Miranda 2013). Namely, when a new firm ID arises for whatever reason, we assign the firm an age based on the age of the oldest establishment that the firm owns in the first year in which the new firm ID is observed. The firm is then allowed to age naturally (by one year for each additional year it is observed in the data), regardless of any acquisitions and divestitures as long as the firm continues operations as a legal entity. This permits defining start-ups as new firms with all new establishments and shutdowns as firms that cease operations and all establishments shut down.

We utilize the LBD to construct annual establishment-level and firm-level employment growth rates. The measures we construct abstract from net growth at the firm level due to mergers and acquisitions (M&A) activity. We use Davis, Haltiwanger, and Schuh (1996) net growth-rate measures that accommodate entry and exit.[5] We refer to this as the DHS growth rate.

Computing establishment-level growth rates is straightforward, but computing firm-level growth rates is more complex given changes in ownership due to mergers, divestitures, or acquisitions. In these instances, net growth rates computed from firm-level data alone will reflect changes in firm employment due to adding and/or shedding continuing establishments. This occurs even if the added and/or shed establishments experience no employment changes themselves. To avoid firm growth rates capturing changes due to M&A and organization change, we compute the period $t-1$ to period t net growth rate for a firm as the sum of the appropriately weighted DHS net growth rate of all establishments owned by the firm in period t, including acquisitions, plus the net growth attributed to establishments owned by the firm in period $t-1$ that it has closed before period t. For any continuing establishment that changes ownership, this method attributes any net employment growth to the acquiring firm. Note, however, if the acquired establishment exhibits no change in employment, there will be no accompanying change in firm-level employment induced by this ownership change. The general point is that this method for computing firm-level growth captures only "organic" growth at the establishment level and abstracts from changes in firm-level employment due to M&A activity (see supplementary data appendix to Haltiwanger, Jardin, and Miranda [2013] for an example).

The LBD permits us to characterize the comprehensive distribution of firm employment growth rates including the contribution from firm entry, firm exit, and continuing firms.[6] We begin our analysis with the LBD to

---

5. This growth-rate measure has become standard in analysis of establishment and firm dynamics because it shares some useful properties of log differences, but also accommodates entry and exit (See Davis, Haltiwanger, and Schuh 1996; Törnqvist, Vartia, and Vartia 1985).
6. By continuing firms we mean firms that continue between $t-1$ and t.

characterize the distribution of firm net employment growth rates for both continuing and exiting firms. Much of our analysis focuses on firms that are age 1 and older so that we do not focus on start-ups in their first year. Our recent work (see Haltiwanger, Jarmin, and Miranda 2013) highlights the contribution of start-ups to job creation in their first year. As we noted in the introduction, start-ups account for slightly more than 20 percent of firm-level gross job creation (and slightly less than 20 percent of establishment-level job creation). The focus of the current chapter is postentry dynamics.

1.2.2   Enhancing the LBD with Firm-Level Measures of Revenue

A key innovation of this chapter is that we introduce real output and productivity-growth measures to the analysis of high-growth firms. Our measure of output is a gross-output measure derived from revenue data from the Census Bureau's Business Register (BR), which also provides the source data for the LBD. The BR's revenue measure is based on administrative data from annual business income tax returns. Unlike payroll and employment, which are measured at the establishment level going back to 1976, the nominal output data are available at the tax reporting or employer identification number (EIN) level only and then only starting in the mid-1990s. The tax reporting unit is equivalent to a particular physical location (an establishment) only in the case of single-unit firms. In the case of multiunit firms, the administrative data does not apportion output to particular establishments. Thus, in the BR, revenue is only measured at the establishment level for single-location firms. Constructing a comprehensive revenue measure is further complicated by the fact that the content of the receipts fields on the BR vary substantially by type of activity and the legal structure of the firm according to different tax treatments.

For sole proprietorships, business income taxes are filed on the business owner's individual income taxes. Administrative data enable linking these individual income tax returns to the payroll EINs for sole proprietors, but these links are imperfect (see Davis et al. 2009). Corporations and partnerships file their business income taxes with an EIN but a challenge is that firms may have multiple EINs. Information from the Economic Censuses, Company Organization Survey, and administrative records are used to develop high-quality links between all the payroll EINs of a firm and the parent firm ID. This implies that for most corporations and partnerships, we link the business income tax EIN to one of the payroll EINs. Given the links of the payroll EINs to the parent firm identifier, this enables us to construct a consistent measure of employment and output at the firm level. However, multiple EIN firms are not required to report income using the same EIN they use to report quarterly payroll. As a result, income EINs can become "detached" from their payroll EINs. We discuss these issues in more detail in appendix A, but overall we successfully added nominal revenue measures to over 80 percent of the firm records in the LBD in our sample period. We denote this as the revenue enhanced subset of the LBD.

We find that the pattern of missingness of revenue is only weakly related to observable indicators in the full LBD like firm age, firm size, broad industry, the employment growth rate, or multiunit status. Consistent with this finding, the relationship between the distribution of firm employment growth rates and firm age for the revenue enhanced subset of the LBD and the full LBD are very similar. However, to mitigate possible selection issues we weight our subset data with inverse propensity score weights (IPW). These weights are based on estimation of propensity score models separately for continuers, deaths, and births from the full LBD. The propensity score models use logistic regressions with the dependent variable equal to one if the firm has revenue and zero otherwise. Observable firm characteristics from the full LBD used in the models include firm size, firm age, employment growth rate, industry, and a multiunit status indicator. The propensity score-weighted data yields patterns of employment growth rates, employment-weighted entry, and employment-weighted exit that are quite similar to those obtained from the full population of continuers, entrants, and exiters. Additional details are provided in the data appendix.[7]

We deflate the nominal revenue measures with a general price deflator (the GDP Implicit Price Deflator). As such, our measures of real gross output will reflect both real output changes and changes in relative prices across industries. Revenue fields in the BR can be noisy so we adopt filters to clean out unreasonable values. These filters are discussed further in the data appendix and include minimum and maximum productivity value cutoffs, maximum revenue cutoffs, and maximum revenue-growth values. Subsequent references to output in what follows should be interpreted as real revenue or equivalently real gross output.

A limitation of our real gross output measure is that it does not capture the contribution of intermediate inputs. In many of our exercises, we control for interacted industry and year effects. Doing so effectively controls for industry-specific deflators. Moreover, this also acts as a control for industry-specific variation in intermediate input shares.[8] Controls for industry and year effects is especially important when we examine labor productivity, since cross-industry variation in gross output per worker are difficult to interpret. We also note that for output growth we use DHS measures of growth. Another limitation of our output growth measures is that since we do not have the underlying establishment-level output growth we cannot abstract from the contribution of M&A activity to output growth.

7. We note that we exclude 2001 and 2002 from our statistics since the 2001 data are problematic (which impacts the growth-rate distributions in both 2001 and 2002).

8. Most of our analysis focuses on the distribution of growth rates of gross output. Growth rates abstract from any industry-level differences in gross output from differential intermediate input shares.

The filters we design partly take care of this as M&A activity can lead to spurious large flows of output. We have checked and found that the broad patterns we find for employment growth largely hold when we do not adjust for M&A growth—but still we regard this as a limitation that should be acknowledged (and also as an area for future research).

1.3   The Role of High-Growth Firms for Job Creation, Real Output Growth, and Productivity Growth

1.3.1   The Up or Out Dynamics of Young Firms in the United States

Employment Dynamics

We begin by comparing results we obtain with the output-enhanced subset of the LBD with prior findings from HJM and DHJM that make use of the full LBD. Those papers emphasized two features of the employment-growth dynamics of young firms in the United States: (a) the up or out dynamic of young firms, and (b) differential patterns of dispersion and skewness of firm-growth distribution by firm age.

As highlighted in HJM, decomposing overall net growth into the net growth from continuers and the contribution from exit reveals the up or out pattern of young firms. Figures 1.1A and 1.1B show the net employment growth rate for surviving firms as well as the job destruction rate from firm exit by firm age. Figure 1.1A shows results from the full LBD and figure 1.1B from the output-enhanced subset adjusted using inverse propensity score weights. We exclude years not covered by the output-enhanced subset.[9] Firm exit is defined as discussed above. All statistics are employment weighted. Figures 1.1A and 1.1B focus on the postentry dynamics of firms; in our nomenclature, age one is the year after entry. We exclude entrants in these figures since age zero businesses only create jobs in their year of entry.[10] The weighted sum of net job creation yields overall net employment growth for a given age group.[11] Conditional on survival, young firms have much higher growth rates than more mature firms. Young firms also have a substantially

9. In particular, the statistics are based on tabulations of pooled data from 1996 to 2013 from the Longitudinal Business Database (LBD), excluding the 2001 and 2002 years. We exclude those years here since the output data for 2001 has been partially lost. As we discuss below, the focus on the 1996–2013 period implies that our statistics are influenced by the Great Recession.

10. See HJM (2013) and DHJM (2014) for an extensive analysis of the contribution of start-ups to job creation. We have noted their average contribution. Those papers highlight that there has been a declining pace of entry in the United States. They also note that entry rates vary substantially across sectors and geographic regions. But interestingly, the papers note that even with variation in the entry rates the postentry dynamics are similar across sectors in terms of up or out dynamics.

11. Overall net growth is the sum of the weighted net-growth rate for continuers plus job destruction from exit. The weight is the share of employment for continuing firms. See HJM (2013) for details.

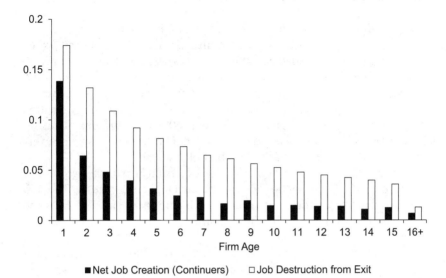

Fig. 1.1A   Up or out dynamics of firms, 1996–2013, LBD

Source: Statistics computed from the Longitudinal Business Database and the revenue-enhanced subsets 1996–2000 and 2003–2013.

Notes: Figures 1.1A and 1.1B show patterns of net employment growth for continuing firms and job destruction from firm exit for firms age one and older.

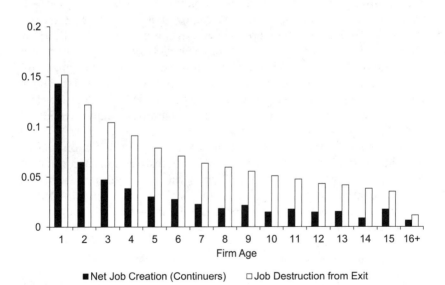

Fig. 1.1B   Up or out dynamics of firms, 1996–2013, revenue-enhanced subset of LBD

Source: Statistics computed from the Longitudinal Business Database and the revenue-enhanced subsets 1996–2000 and 2003–2013.

Notes: Figures 1.1A and 1.1B show patterns of net employment growth for continuing firms and job destruction from firm exit for firms age one and older.

higher (employment-weighted) exit rate than more mature firms. Slightly over 50 percent of an entering cohort of firms in figure 1.1A will have exited by age five (on an employment-weighted basis). The very high failure rate of young firms is partially offset by the contribution of the surviving firms. For the sample period in figure 1.1A, five years after the entry of an average cohort, the employment is about 70 percent of the original contribution of the cohort. This is in spite of losing over 50 percent of employment to business exits.[12] Figure 1.1B shows very similar patterns for our propensity score-weighted, revenue-enhanced subset of the LBD.

Figures 1.2A and 1.2B examine job creation from firm births by size class for both the LBD population and the revenue-enhanced subset. The job-creation rate from births is particularly high among the smallest firms and decreases monotonically with the firm size. Patterns are again very similar across figures 1.2A and 1.2B.

One implication of figures 1.1A and 1.1B is that the overall net employment growth rate is negative for all firm age groups for age greater than firm age equal to zero. This pattern is evident from the job destruction rate from exit exceeding the net employment growth rate for continuing firms for all firm age groups. This pattern partly reflects our sample period, which includes the sharp contraction and slow recovery of 2007–11. But it also reflects the more general pattern that even in a typical year of overall positive net growth, continuing firms tend to be mildly contracting on average with overall (economy-wide) net employment growth being positive because of the contribution of firm start-ups (depicted in figures 1.2A and 1.2B). HJM show that this pattern holds for the sample period 1992–2005.[13] A related implication of figures 1.1A and 1.1B is that overall net employment growth rates are increasing with firm age.[14] Again, this partly reflects our sample period since young firms were hit especially hard in the Great Recession (see Fort et al. 2013), but is also a common pattern more generally (see figure 4 of HJM).

The second finding, highlighted in DHJM, highlights the dispersion and skewness of the employment growth rate distribution of continuing young firms. Figures 1.3A and 1.3B show the 90th, 50th (median), and 10th percentiles of the net job-growth distribution of surviving firms by firm age. As before, figures 1.3A and 1.3B show the LBD population and the revenue-enhanced subset, respectively. Percentiles are from the

---

12. These calculations of the five-year contribution of each cohort are low relative to those reported in HJM (2013) or in DHJM (2014). These differences reflect differences in sample periods and, in particular, whether the years of the Great Recession are included. HJM (2013) use the period 1992–2005. They find that for five years after the entry of an average cohort, the employment is about 84 percent of the original cohort. DHJM (2014) use the period 1992–2011 and find the same calculation yields 80 percent.

13. The BDS shows that in the years of most robust net growth, both very young and very old firms tend to have positive overall net growth inclusive of the contribution of exit.

14. This can be inferred by computing the overall net growth implied by figure 1.1.

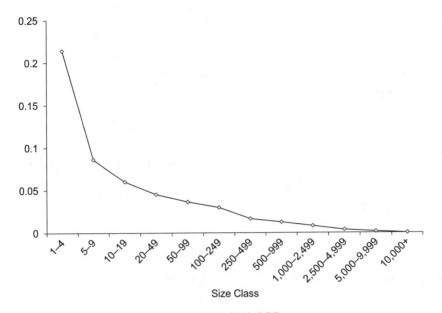

Fig. 1.2A   Job creation from births, 1996–2013, LBD

Source: Statistics computed from the Longitudinal Business Database and the revenue-enhanced LBD subsets 1996–2000 and 2003–2013.

Notes: Figure 1.2A shows the pattern of job creation from firm births by size class.

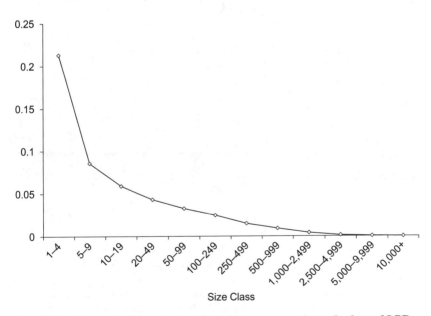

Fig. 1.2B   Job creation from births, 1996–2013, revenue-enhanced subset of LBD

Source: Statistics computed from the Longitudinal Business Database and the revenue-enhanced LBD subsets 1996–2000 and 2003–2013.

Notes: Figure 1.2B shows the pattern of job creation from firm births by size class.

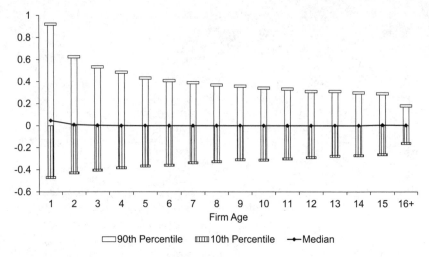

Fig. 1.3A   Net employment growth, 1996–2013, LBD

Source: Statistics computed from the Longitudinal Business Database and revenue-enhanced LBD subsets 1996–2000 and 2003–2013.

Notes: The 90th, 10th, and median are all based on the employment-weighted firm-level employment growth rate distribution for each firm.

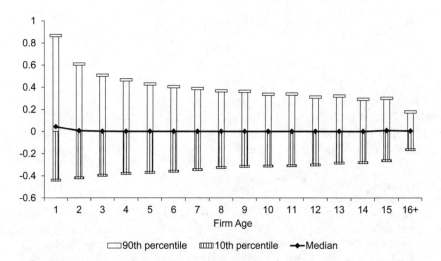

Fig. 1.3B   Net employment growth, 1996–2013, revenue-enhanced subset of LBD

Source: Statistics computed from the Longitudinal Business Database and revenue-enhanced LBD subsets 1996–2000 and 2003–2013.

Notes: The 90th, 10th, and median are all based on the employment-weighted firm-level employment growth rate distribution for each firm.

employment-weighted distribution, which mitigates the impact very small firms have on these statistics. We discuss dispersion by examining the patterns of the 90–10 differential and skewness by comparing the difference between the 90–50 and the 50–10 differentials.

Results from the full LBD and the propensity-weighted, revenue-enhanced sample are again very similar. Young continuing firms have very high dispersion of employment growth, and also very high positive skewness. The median employment growth rate for young firms is close to zero (and for that matter the median is close to zero for all firms) so the positive skewness is seen in the relative magnitudes of the 90th and 10th percentiles where the employment growth rates of younger firms are much more skewed to the right (positive) compared to more mature firms. This accounts for the high mean net employment growth rate of young firms relative to older firms from figures 1.1A and 1.1B. Taking figures 1.1A and 1.1B and 1.3A and 1.3B together, the typical young continuing firm (as captured by the median) exhibits little or no employment growth, even conditional on survival; however, among all the young firms, a small fraction exhibit very high rates of growth.

Our results thus far show that the full LBD and the revenue-enhanced subset yield very similar patterns for continuing firms, for entrants, as well as exiters. Comparison of figures 1.1A through 1.3B, and more extensive analysis contained in appendix A, indicate that by using propensity-score matching we are able to capture the basic patterns of firm behaviour from the LBD, giving us the confidence to proceed with our revenue-enhanced subset of LBD firms for the remainder of the analysis.

Output Dynamics

Keeping the pattern in figures 1.1A, 1.1B, 1.2A, and 1.2B in mind, we now characterize the distribution of output growth rates. We again use inverse propensity-score weights in calculations with the revenue-enhanced subset that permits measuring real gross output.

Figures 1.4A and 1.4B examine the output dynamics from continuers and from births, respectively. We first note that the patterns depicted in figures 1.4A and 1.4B are very similar to those in figures 1.1A and B and 1.2A and B. Young continuing firms experience on average high output growth rates relative to more mature firms. Young firms also experience higher rates of output destruction from exit. However, there are also some notable differences. We find output growth by continuers exceeds output destruction from exit for all age classes. Indeed, for most age classes, output growth for continuers exceeds destruction from exit. Comparing figures 1.1A and 1.4A, we find that young business exits generate larger percentage job losses than output losses. This is consistent with young business exits having relatively low productivity—a result emphasized in Foster, Haltiwanger, and Krizan (2001, 2006) for selected sectors. Turning to figure 1.4B, we can examine

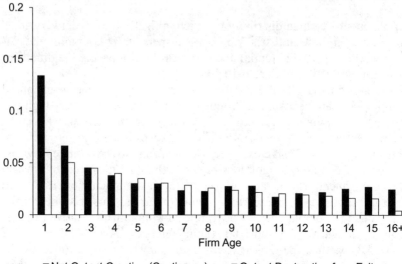

■ Net Output Creation (Continuers)   **□ Output Destruction from Exit**

Fig. 1.4A   Up or out output dynamics for firms, 1996–2013, revenue-enhanced LBD
Source: Statistics computed from the revenue-enhanced LBD subsets 1996–2000 and 2003–2013.
Notes: Figure 1.4A shows patterns of net output growth for continuing firms and output destruction from firm exit for firms age one and older.

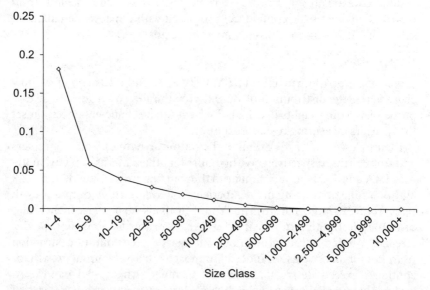

Fig. 1.4B   Output creation from births, 1996–2013, revenue-enhanced subset of LBD
Source: Statistics computed from the revenue-enhanced LBD subsets 1996–2000 and 2003–2013.
Notes: Figure 1.3B shows the pattern of output creation from firm births by size class.

the contribution of start-ups to output in their size classes. We see that the smaller start-up firms account for 18 percent of overall output in their size class. This is smaller when compared to their job contribution in figures 1.2A and 1.2B, but still a considerable amount.

1.3.2 Real Output versus Net Employment Growth Rate Distributions by Firm Age

Figure 1.5 characterizes the distribution of firm output growth rates by firm age for continuing firms. Depicted are the 90th, 50th, and 10th percentiles of the output-weighted distribution. As before, activity weighting mitigates the impact that very small firms have on these statistics since they account for only a small fraction of output. Comparing figures 1.3 and 1.5 yields many similarities, but also some notable differences. Output growth rates exhibit high dispersion and positive skewness for young firms in a similar manner to employment growth rates. However, while net employment growth for the median surviving firm is close to zero (except for age one firms), we find that real output growth for the median continuing firm is in excess of 4 percent per year in each of the first four years and in excess of 3 percent in all years.

The skewness of firm growth for young firms is less pronounced for output growth than for employment growth. However, we find that this is driven in part by cyclical dynamics.[15] Our revenue-enhanced subset of the LBD is only available from 1996–2013 so that the Great Recession plays a potentially important role. Figures 1.6A and 1.6B depict the 90–50 and 50–10 differentials for output growth (1.6A) and net employment growth (1.6B) for the subperiods 1996–06 (prior to the recession), 2007–10 (the recession), and 2011–13 (postrecession). The cycle clearly influences the skewness patterns, especially for output growth. In figure 1.6A, we find that the 90–50 exceeds the 50–10 for output growth for all firm ages at or below 5 and that the 90–50 is about the same as the 50–10 for firm ages greater than 5 for the period 1996–06.[16] However, in the recession period the 50–10 differential increases substantially for all ages so that rather than positive skewness, the output growth distribution exhibits negative skewness for most ages, and especially for older firms. In the postrecession period, we again see a pattern resembling that for the years 1996–06, although some of this may be the cyclical recovery. Figure 1.6B shows similar but more muted patterns when

---

15. Decker et al. (2015) emphasize that skewness of employment dynamics exhibits a negative trend. We have not investigated that pattern in the current chapter. Our sample is less well suited for examining changing trends since it starts in 1996 compared to 1981 for Decker et al. (2015). Still, the latter analysis emphasizes that the post-2000 period is a period of rapid decline in skewness in employment growth rates with differential patterns across sectors. Investigating these patterns using the output data would be of great interest.

16. The exclusion of 2001 and 2002 from our 1998–06 sample period may be playing a role here as well. However, we note that the full LBD shows substantial positive skewness in the employment growth-rate distribution using all years from 1998–06.

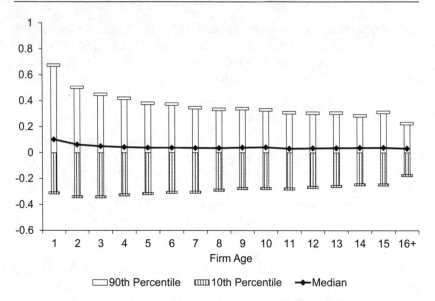

Fig. 1.5   **Output growth distribution for continuing firms, 1996–2013**

Source: Statistics computed from the revenue-enhanced LBD subsets 1996–2000 and 2003–2013.

Notes: The 90th, 10th, and median are all based on the output-weighted, firm-level output growth rate distribution for each firm.

employment growth is considered as opposed to output growth. In short, we find that the positive skewness for young firms exhibited in terms of both output and net employment growth is procyclical. In what follows, for the sake of brevity, we will mostly present results for our entire sample period but we will note when patterns are especially sensitive to the business cycle.

Turning to figure 1.6C, we find that the mean output and net employment growth rates for surviving firms exhibit very similar patterns that decline sharply with firm age. Based on figures 1.3A, 1.3B, 1.5, 1.6A, and 1.6B, we know that underlying these quite similar mean patterns are differences in the shapes of the underlying distributions. For net employment growth, the high mean for young firms is driven by the positive skewness for young firms. Or put more simply, the high average is driven by high growth firms. For output growth, the high mean for young firms reflects both the high median for young firms and the greater positive skewness for young firms.

In either case, figures 1.3A, 1.3B, and 1.5 highlight the very high net employment and output growth of the 90th percentile firms, particularly for young firms. We quantify their importance in Table 1.1A where we decompose output and employment growth. We find that 12 percent of continuing firms have output growth in excess of 25 percent accounting for about

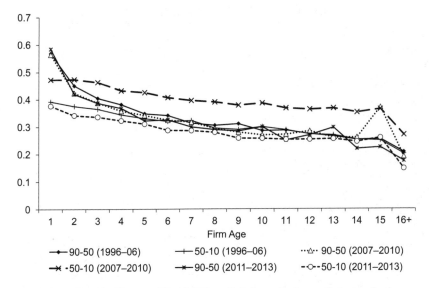

Fig. 1.6A   The 90–50 versus 50–10 differentials for output growth for continuing firms by subperiods

Source: Statistics computed from revenue-enhanced LBD subsets 1996–2000 and 2003–2013.

Notes: The 90th, 10th, and median are all based on the output-weighted firm-level output growth rate distribution for each firm.

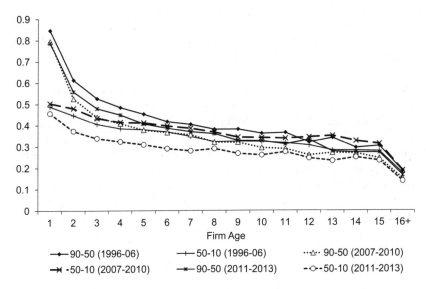

Fig. 1.6B   The 90–50 versus 50–10 differentials for employment growth for continuing firms by subperiods

Source: Statistics computed from the revenue-enhanced LBD subsets 1996–2000 and 2003–2013.

Notes: The 90th, 10th, and median are all based on the employment-weighted firm-level employment growth rate distribution for each firm.

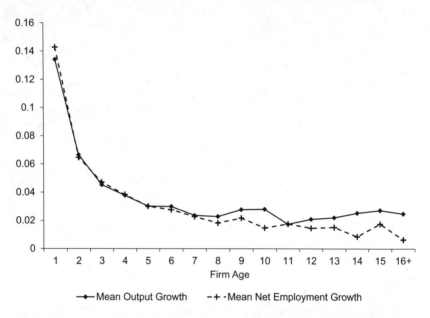

Fig. 1.6C   Mean output and employment growth for continuing firms, 1996–2013
Source: Statistics computed from the revenue-enhanced LBD subsets 1998–2000 and 2003–2011.
Notes: The mean net employment growth is the employment-weighted average firm-level employment growth rate for each firm age. The mean output growth is the output-weighted average firm-level output growth rate for each firm age.

50 percent of the gross output creation for continuing firms.[17] Analogously, about 17 percent of continuing firms have net employment growth in excess of 25 percent accounting for close to 60 percent of gross job creation for continuing firms. Start-ups and exiting firms also contribute to employment and output growth. Table 1.1B looks at the contribution to output and employment growth from the entry and exit margins. Start-ups contribute disproportionately to employment and output growth. The contribution to employment growth is particularly large, accounting for an additional 25 percent of gross job creation versus 15 percent for output creation. Exiting firms account for a disproportionate share of employment, but this is less true for output.

In what follows, we explore the characteristics of high-growth firms on a number of margins. In particular, we consider not only firm age, but firm size, industry, and geographic location. We turn to that analysis below. Before doing so, we provide evidence on the connection between output and net employment growth rates.

17. By this we mean the output creation from growing firms.

Table 1.1A   **The share of output and job creation accounted for by high-growth firms**

	High-growth firms	
	Output (%)	Employment (%)
Share of gross creation	49.8	58.5
Share of firms	12.3	16.7

Source: Tabulations from revenue-enhanced LBD subsets 1996–2000, and 2003–2013.

Table 1.1B   **The share of output and job creation accounted for by births and deaths**

	Firms (%)	Output (%)	Employment (%)
Births	10.2	14.8	24.8
Deaths	8.8	10.7	26.1

Source: Tabulations from revenue-enhanced LBD subsets 1996–2000 and 2003–2013.

1.3.3 The Joint Distribution of Real Output and Net Employment Growth Rates

Theoretical models of firm adjustment in response to shocks suggest a positive correlation between output and employment growth. This correlation may depend on the nature of the adjustment costs and frictions. We find that output and net employment growth rates for surviving firms are positively correlated but the contemporaneous correlation is not high (about 0.218). Further analysis shows that this reflects in part the pattern that output growth rates tend to lead employment growth rates. Table 1.2A shows the estimates from a simple reduced form one-lag vector autoregression (VAR) model relating firm-level net employment growth and output growth for continuing firms.[18] Net employment growth estimates reported in the first column show there is negative serial correlation reflecting the well-known regression to the mean in employment growth rates. Interestingly, however, lagged output growth is associated with higher net employment growth in the current period. The same is not true (to the same extent) for the relationship between lagged net employment growth and current period output growth shown in column (2), suggesting first that the output shock leads the employment adjustment, and second that output growth is only weakly correlated with prior growth shocks.

The patterns in table 1.2A are consistent with standard adjustment cost models for employment dynamics (see, e.g., Cooper, Haltiwanger, and

---

18. We weight the regressions with the LHS employment growth with employment weights and the regressions with the RHS output growth output weights. We have tried common weights and obtain similar results.

Table 1.2A   VAR relating net employment and output growth

	Dependent variable	
Explanatory variables:	Net employment growth	Output growth
Lagged net employment growth	–0.103	0.023
	(0.000)	(0.000)
Lagged output growth	0.125	–0.003
	(0.000)	(0.000)

Source: Estimated specifications using revenue-enhanced LBD subsets 1996–2000 and 2003–2013.
Note: Standard errors in parentheses. Specifications are weighted by employment and output, respectively.

Table 1.2B   VAR relating probability of being high-growth-output and high-growth-employment firms

	Dependent variable	
Explanatory variables:	High-growth-employment firms	High-growth-output firms
Lagged high-growth-employment firms	0.066	0.071
	(0.000)	(0.000)
Lagged high-growth-output firms	0.131	0.123
	(0.000)	(0.000)

Source: Estimated specifications revenue-enhanced LBD subsets 1996–2000 and 2003–2013.
Note: Standard errors in parentheses. Specifications are weighted by employment and output, respectively.

Willis 2007).[19] In such models, firms facing a positive profit (e.g., demand or productivity) shock exhibit immediate increases in output but a delayed adjustment for factors such as capital and labor.

We now explore whether the patterns at the mean of the growth rate distributions carry over to the upper tails of the joint growth rate distribution. Table 1.2B shows results for similarly estimated simple one-lag VAR models for indicators for high-growth episodes firms. For this purpose, a firm experiences a high-output (employment) growth episode in a particular year if the firm's output (net employment) growth rate is greater than 25 percent.

Table 1.2B shows that having a high-growth output episode in the previous year is positively associated with having both high-output and employment growth episodes in the current year. Interestingly, in spite of the overall negative serial correlation for employment growth in table 1.2A, there is

19. This likely also reflects the timing of the data. Employment growth from $t-1$ to t represents a March-to-March change, while output growth represents annual output changes during the calendar year from $t-1$ to t. Our primary focus is not on dynamics so we do not explore this issue further.

Table 1.3   Distribution of high-growth and high-decline events for
                   five-year-old firms

Number of events	Output		Employment	
	High decline	High growth	High decline	High growth
0	61.30	39.42	50.69	32.69
1	25.99	28.01	33.47	32.73
2	9.57	18.67	12.94	21.78
3	2.66	9.41	2.62	9.40
4	0.41	3.42	0.27	2.86
5	0.06	1.07	0.01	0.54

Source: Tabulations from revenue-enhanced subset of LBD. Shares are percentages of columns.

some positive persistence in high employment growth episodes. These patterns are consistent with high-growth-output (employment) events extending beyond a single year, with high-growth-output events tending to precede high-growth-employment events.

Table 1.2B implies high-growth events exhibit positive persistence. But this simple VAR does not tell how often high-growth events are reversed. Table 1.3 provides insights for this latter question. For each five-year-old firm, we count the number of high-growth and high-decline events that the firm has experienced. A five-year-old firm can have between 0 and 5 high-growth and high-decline events. Table 1.3 shows the distribution of high-growth and high-decline events for both employment and output. The skewness highlighted earlier for young firms is self-evident in the much higher share of five-year-old firms having N high-growth compared to high-decline events.

Conditional probabilities are also easily computed from the joint distribution of high-growth and high-decline events.[20] The probability that a five-year-old firm with one, two, three, and four high-output growth events has zero high-decline events is 54 percent, 50 percent, 59 percent, and 74 percent, respectively.[21] Thus, most five-year-old firms with one or more high-output growth events have no high-decline events. Similar remarks apply to conditional probabilities for high-employment growth events compared to high-employment decline events.

1.3.4   The Characteristics of High-Growth Firms: By Firm Age, Firm Size, and Industry

Our objective in this section is to provide descriptive statistics about the characteristics of firms in the top of the growth-rate distribution. To this

20. The joint distributions are depicted in figures 1B.1 and 1B.2 of appendix B.
21. The (output weighted) probability that a firm with zero high-growth events has zero high-decline events is about 70 percent. This is not surprising since most output is at firms with zero high-decline events.

end, we estimate linear probability regressions pooling across firm years. We consider discrete dependent variables that take on a value of one if the firm is a high-growth output (employment) firm. As before, we define high-growth firms as those with annual growth in excess of 25 percent.[22] For the specifications with high-growth-output indicators, we weight by output (averaged in period $t - 1$ and t) and for the specifications with high-growth-employment indicators we weight by employment (averaged in $t - 1$ and t).

We first focus on firm age and firm size characteristics. For firm age, we consider firm age classes between one and sixteen and older. For firm size, we use within-industry deciles of the size distribution. In the case of the output-growth specifications, these are output-weighted deciles of output size. For the employment-growth specifications, we use employment-weighted deciles of employment size. For calculating these deciles, we use two alternative measures of size for output and employment. We use base year size (e.g., output or employment in period $t - 1$) and current average size (i.e., the average of output or employment in period $t - 1$ and t). We consider both, since as discussed in HJM, using base year size yields regression to the mean effects (i.e., given transitory shocks a firm classified as small in the prior period is more likely to grow). The use of current average size is a compromise between using base year and current year size (where the latter suffers from the opposite problem from base year size). We present our estimated firm size and firm age coefficients via a series of graphs. We do not report standard errors, but note given the very large sample size (in excess of 30 million) all of the standard errors for the reported size and age effects are less than 0.001. The same remarks apply to the state and industry effects that we report below.

Figures 1.7 and 1.8 report the estimated firm age effects for high-growth employment and output firms, respectively, with and without size controls. The likelihood of being a high-growth employment and output firm is decreasing with firm age even with firm size controls. The latter have relatively little influence on the patterns. It is apparent that our earlier findings in figures 1.3 and 1.5 are robust to controlling for firm size effects. We note that in unreported results we also find that these patterns are robust to controlling further for industry and year effects.

Figures 1.9 and 1.10 report the analogous estimated firm size effects for high-growth employment and output firms with and without age controls. For the firm size effects, we report results using both base year and current average size categories. If we do not control for firm age, there is an inverse relationship between firm size and the likelihood of being a high-growth firm using both the base year and current average size approaches. But once we control for firm age, these patterns are substantially mitigated. For high-growth-employment firms, the relationship between the likelihood of being

---

22. There is nothing inherently special about the 25 percent cutoff. We have found our results are robust to using alternative cutoffs.

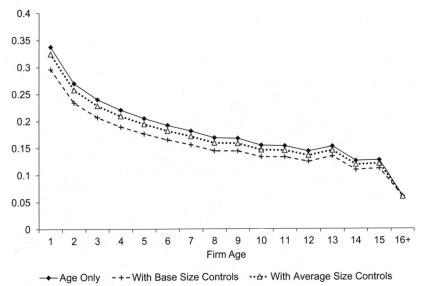

Fig. 1.7   Employment high-growth firms by firm age, 1996–2013

Source: Statistics computed from the revenue-enhanced LBD subsets 1996–2000 and 2003–2013.

Note: Reported are estimated effects of linear probability models on controls as listed. All coefficients are reported relative to unconditional mean for 16+.

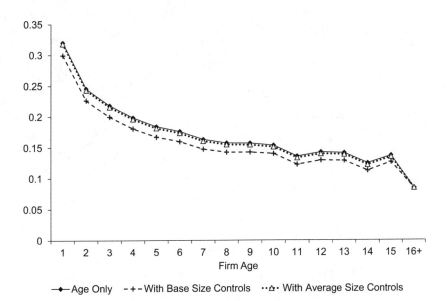

Fig. 1.8   Output high-growth firms by firm age, 1996–2013

Source: Statistics computed from the revenue-enhanced LBD subsets 1996–2000 and 2003–2013.

Note: Reported are estimated effects of linear probability models on controls as listed. All coefficients are reported relative to unconditional mean for 16+.

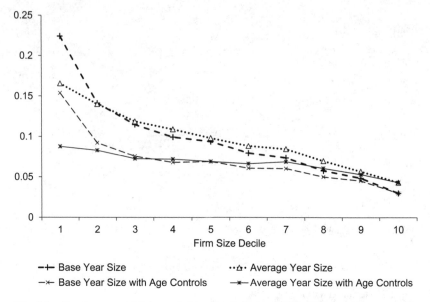

Fig. 1.9 Employment high-growth firms by firm size, 1996–2013

Source: Statistics computed from the revenue-enhanced LBD subsets 1996–2000 and 2003–2013.

Note: Reported are estimated effects of linear probability models on controls as listed. All coefficients are relative to unconditional means for top size decile.

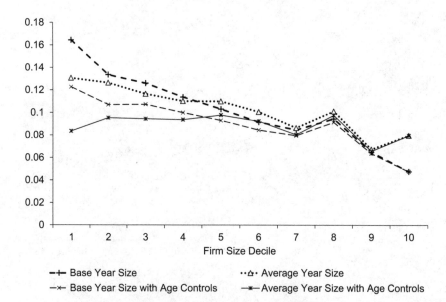

Fig. 1.10 Output high-growth firms by firm size, 1996–2013

Source: Statistics computed from the revenue-enhanced LBD subsets 1996–2000 and 2003–2013.

Note: Reported are estimated effects of linear probability models on controls as listed. All coefficients are relative to unconditional means for top size decile.

a high-growth firm and size is relatively flat using current year average size and age controls. For high-growth-output firms, the relationship becomes partly positive.

The inference we draw from figures 1.7–1.10 is that firm age is a robust and key determinant of the likelihood of being a high-growth firm. In contrast, once we control for firm age, firm size has relatively little influence. The role of firm age as opposed to firm size is reminiscent of the findings in HJM that found that young firms grow faster than more mature firms, but that small firms do not grow faster than large firms once firm age is taken into account. We note, however, that while firm age is a key determinant that the adjusted R-squared (see table 1.4) from age effects alone is 2 percent for the output growth distribution and 5 percent for the employment growth rate distribution. With size, industry, state, and year effects the adjusted R-squared rises to about 8 percent for output growth (using either base year or current average year size) and between 8 and 9 percent for employment growth. Industry effects alone yield 5 percent and 4 percent, respectively, in terms of adjusted R-squared. These patterns imply that the factors that determine which firm is a high-growth firm largely are factors within firm age, firm size, industry, and year cells that we do not observe in our data. Still there is systematic variation by industry to which we turn to now.

Figure 1.11A shows the top fifty industries and figure 1.11B shows the bottom fifty industries for high-growth-output firms. Figures 1.12A and 1.12B show the analogous patterns for high-growth-employment firms. Reported are the regression estimates with industry effects alone. Regressions are either employment or output weighted. We begin by noting that all four-digit North American Industry Classification System (NAICS) sectors have some high-growth firms. The top-ranked industries have high-growth firms that account for as much as 39 percent of industry output and 29 per-

Table 1.4	Adjusted R-squared for effects accounting for high-growth firms	
	High-growth-output firms	High-growth-employment firms
Industry	0.050	0.041
Age	0.021	0.053
Base year size	0.011	0.033
Average size	0.004	0.015
Year	0.010	0.004
State	0.007	0.002
All effects (base year size)	0.082	0.092
All effects (average size)	0.078	0.081

Source: Estimated adjusted R-squared with dependent variable using the revenue-enhanced LBD subsets 1996–2000 and 2003–2013. Specifications are weighted by output (column [1]) and employment (column [2]), respectively.

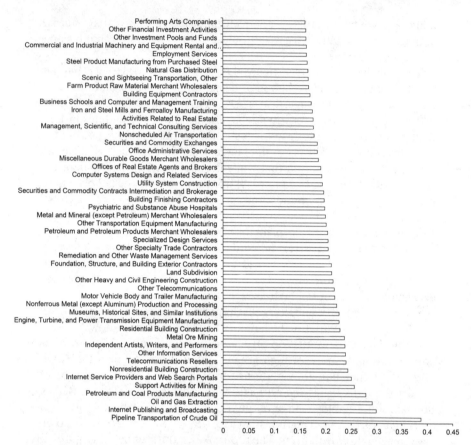

Fig. 1.11A   Top fifty high-growth firms industry effects: Output

Source: Statistics computed from the revenue-enhanced LBD subsets 1996–2000 and 2003–2013.

Note: Reported are estimated effects of linear probability models on industry effects.

cent of industry employment. In contrast, the bottom-ranked industries have high-growth firms that account for less than 1 percent of industry output and employment.

Table 1.5A reports analysis of whether there are industry clusters that are more or less likely to have high-growth firm activity. The industry clusters we consider are sectors that can be classified as tradable, construction, high tech, bio tech, and energy related. We also include a small business-intensive sector dummy. This dummy is equal to 1 for the forty industries with the largest share of activity accounted by small firms where small is defined as having twenty employees or less.[23] Hurst and Pugsley (2012) suggest these

23. This follows Hurst and Pugsley (2012).

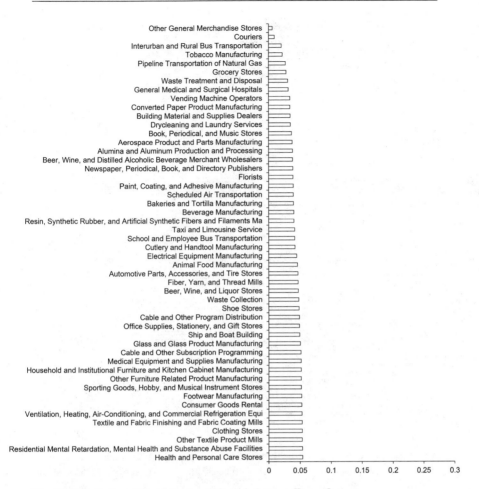

Fig. 1.11B   Bottom fifty high-growth firms industry effects: Output
Source: Statistics computed from the revenue-enhanced LBD subsets 1996–2000 and 2003–2013.
Note: Reported are estimated effects of linear probability models on industry effects.

industries are disproportionally dominated by entrepreneurs with little interest or motivation for growth.

The dependent variable in table 1.5A is the share of either output or employment accounted by high-growth firms. We find that the energy-related sectors have greater high-growth firm activity in terms of output, but not employment. High-tech sectors have greater high-growth firm activity in terms of both output and employment. Tradeable sectors have lower high-growth activity, especially in terms of employment. The latter is consistent with the view that employment gains from high-growth firms in the tradable sectors have largely been offshored during our sample period. The construc-

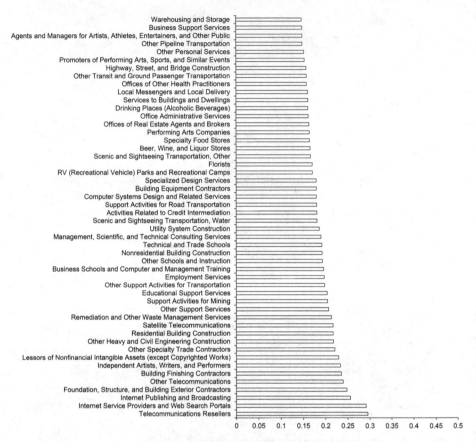

Fig. 1.12A   Top fifty high-growth firms industry effects: Employment

Source: Statistics computed from the revenue-enhanced LBD subsets 1996–2000 and 2003–2013.

Note: Reported are estimated effects of linear probability models on industry effects.

tion sector also has especially high output-growth activity. This likely reflects the housing boom in the first decade of the twenty-first century. We find that the biotech sectors do not have significantly higher or lower high-growth activity. This contrast with the high-tech sectors is interesting and deserves further investigation. It may be that this is due to the way innovation takes place in this sector. One view is that successful biotech firms are much more likely to be bought up by large, mature firms rather than grow internally, since the process of bringing new pharmaceuticals from testing to the market (with all of the required approvals) favors the large firms.

We also find that small business-intensive sectors do not have significantly higher or lower high-growth activity in terms of output or employment. This finding might seem to be at odds with the hypothesis of Hurst and Pugsley

Fig. 1.12B   Bottom fifty high-growth firms industry effects: Employment

Source: Statistics computed from the revenue-enhanced LBD subsets 1996–2000 and 2003–2013.

Note: Reported are estimated effects of linear probability models on industry effects.

(2012) that these are sectors where the typical firm is not growth oriented. That is, based on this hypothesis, we might have anticipated statistically significant negative effects. As we show in table 1.5B, there is an important and subtle difference between investigating what the typical firm is doing in a sector versus what share of activity is accounted for by high-growth firms. The key issue here is the role of activity weighting. The weighted rows in table 1.5B use the same dependent variables as in table 1.5A (namely, the share of industry activity accounted for by high-growth firms). The unweighted rows in table 1.5B use the share of firms that are high-growth firms (on either an output or employment basis) as the dependent variable.

When we examine what the average firm is doing on an unweighted basis we find some evidence in support of Hurst and Pugsley's hypothesis. Specifi-

Table 1.5A   The role of industry groupings in accounting for high-growth firms

Explanatory variables:	Dependent variable: High-growth firm industry effects	
	Output	Employment
Tradable	–0.017	–0.053
	(0.008)	(0.007)
Construction	0.036	0.020
	(0.013)	(0.011)
High tech	0.033	0.037
	(0.016)	(0.013)
Bio tech	–0.042	–0.016
	(0.034)	(0.028)
Energy	0.044	–0.010
	(0.014)	(0.012)
Small business intensive	–0.008	0.015
	(0.010)	(0.009)

Note: Dependent variables are the estimated industry effects on high-growth firms.

Table 1.5B   Small business-intensive dummy variable coefficients by dependent variable

Dependent variable	Small business-intensive dummy coefficient
Employment HGF weighted	0.036
	(0.009)
Employment HGF unweighted	0.004
	(0.005)
Output HGF weighted	0.006
	(0.010)
Output HGF unweighted	–0.022
	(0.008)

Note: Dependent variables are the estimated industry effects on high-growth firms.

cally, the probability that a firm is a high-output growth firm is lower in small business-intensive sectors; however, that same relationship does not hold for high-employment growth firms. But these findings do not imply there is less overall activity accounted for by high-growth firms in these industries. Weighted results show small business-intensive sectors do not have lower shares of activity accounted for by high-growth firms.

These results help reconcile the alternative perspectives in Hurst and Pugsley (2012) and our work. The average firm in these small business-intensive sectors is unlikely to grow (at least in terms of output). But even in these sectors, there are on an activity-weighted basis sufficient high-growth firms that these sectors have no less activity than other sectors in high-growth activity. Looking back at figures 1.3 and 1.5, recall that overall the median firm exhibits little growth, so it is not surprising that in small business-intensive sectors the typical or average firm exhibits lower than average propensity to grow rapidly. But even in these sectors there are enough high-growth firms in the tail of the activity-weighted growth rate distribution that small business-intensive sectors have broadly similar levels of high-growth firm activity.

1.3.5   Sensitivity Analysis

We now briefly discuss the results of a number of sensitivity analyses we conducted and that are described more fully in appendix A. The rankings of industries in terms of high-growth output and high-growth employment events exhibit substantial positive correlation (see figure 1B.3). We also find that the industry rankings for high-growth firms are reasonably stable over time (see figure 1B.4). We also investigated the relationship between the first three moments of the growth-rate distribution by industry. We find that industries exhibiting greater high-growth firm activity also tend to have high overall mean growth on both an output and employment basis (see table 1B.1). But industries with a large fraction of high-growth activity also have a large fraction of high-decline activity and greater volatility as captured by the 90–10 differential. High-growth activity is also associated with greater positive skewness in the respective growth-rate distribution (as measured by the difference between the 90–50 and 50–10 differentials in net output and employment growth rates). These patterns are also exhibited in scatter plots (see figures 1B.5 and 1B.6).

Appendix B shows related types of exercises for state variation in the share of high-growth firm activity (see figures 1B.11, 1B.12, and table 1B.2). We find that states with a larger share of output in high-growth-output firms are also states with a larger share of employment in high-growth-employment firms. States at the top on the basis of output growth are energy-intensive states such as Oklahoma, South Dakota, Texas, and North Dakota. For the ranking by high-growth firms by employment, Oklahoma is toward the top but Texas and North Dakota are not. There is a very strong correlation in high-growth output and employment states compared to industries. There is somewhat less stability of state rankings relative to industry rankings. We find that high-growth firm effects for a state are positively related to overall growth, dispersion, and skewness.

1.4   Firm Age and Productivity Dynamics: The Role of High-Growth Young Firms?

We now turn to the relationship between high-growth young firms and productivity dynamics. The revenue-enhanced LBD is the first economy-wide database to include measures of output and productivity on an annual basis. We are especially interested in the contribution that high-growth young firms have on the reallocation components of productivity growth. As such, we focus on continuing firms in this section. We use the output and employment measures to construct a labor productivity measure for each firm. Since we use gross output and not value added, these statistics are not comparable across industries so we focus on within-industry patterns. This controls for industry-specific differences in intermediate input shares. In addition, since we do not have industry-specific output deflators for all industries, we always control for industry by year effects in this section. This is equivalent to controlling for industry-specific deflators.

Figures 1.13A and 1.13B show the mean and standard deviations of the within-industry (log) labor productivity measure by firm age. We construct these figures as follows. First, we compute the within-industry means and standard deviations within each detailed six-digit industry for each firm age group. In figure 1.13A we generate these means on an unweighted basis, and in figure 1.13B we use employment weights to weight up to the industry level. Then, in both figures, we take an average across all industries where we use gross output weights following the procedures used in Foster, Haltiwanger, and Krizan (2001) and Baily, Hulten, and Campbell (1992). For the mean calculation we index the average productivity of sixteen-year-olds and older at 1 so that the reported effects reflect differences from that oldest group.

Figure 1.13A shows that, relative to other firms in the same industry, mean (log) labor productivity rises with firm age whether we use the unweighted or weighted approach within industries. However, the differences by firm age are much larger in magnitude using the weighted approach. When we weight by employment, the patterns reflect both the unweighted mean within the industry, firm age cell, and the covariance between size and productivity within the cell as per the Olley and Pakes (1996) decomposition.[24] The weighted mean patterns show a more dramatic increase with firm age. By construction, this pattern reflects a sharp rise in the covariance between size and productivity within an industry by firm age cell. The latter pattern is not surprising, since for young firms the relationship between size and productivity is likely weak as firms have not sorted themselves out in terms of the relationship between relative size and productivity. Another possible factor is that measurement error is greater for young firms, but this should be less problematic in this setting given the use of administrative data.

Figures 1.13A and B also show that the within-industry dispersion of productivity declines monotonically with firm age. For both the unweighted

---

24. The Olley-Pakes (1996) decomposition of the level of productivity is given by:

$$P_{it} = \sum_{e \in i} \omega_{et} P_{et} = \widetilde{P_{et}} + \sum_{e \in i} (\omega_{et} - \widetilde{\omega_{et}})(P_{et} - \widetilde{P_{et}}),$$

where a tilde represents the simple average across all plants in the same industry. When we compute the weighted average productivity for each age group and compare it to the unweighted average, the difference is the Olley-Pakes covariance term for the age group.

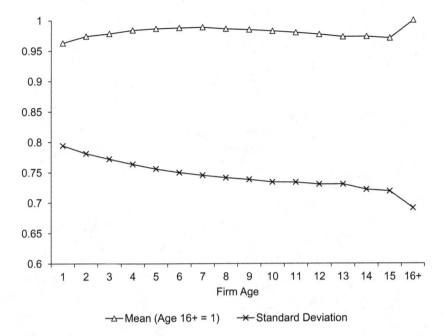

Fig. 1.13A   Mean and standard deviation of within-industry labor productivity by firm age (unweighted within industries)

Source: Statistics computed from the revenue-enhanced LBD subsets 1996–2000 and 2003–2013.

and weighted results, we find similar patterns. The patterns are consistent with our findings of much greater dispersion in both output and net employment growth for young firms.

To explore the contribution of high-growth firms, we turn to examining within-industry decompositions of industry-level productivity growth for continuing firms.[25] We control for industry and time effects via the decomposition itself. We define an index of industry-level productivity as given by:

$$P_{it} = \sum_{e \in i} \omega_{et} P_{et},$$

where e indexes firms, i indexes industry, P is log labor productivity, and ω is the share of employment. Note that for the purposes of a labor productivity index the appropriate weight is employment, since then the index is the geometric mean of firm-level labor productivity. Then the change in this index at the industry level (which is log based so that it can be interpreted

25. From the existing literature (see, e.g., Foster, Haltiwanger, and Krizan 2001, 2006), we know that net entry contributes disproportionately to within-industry productivity growth as exiting businesses are much lower in productivity than entering businesses. We are focusing on continuing firms given the limitations of our output-restricted database.

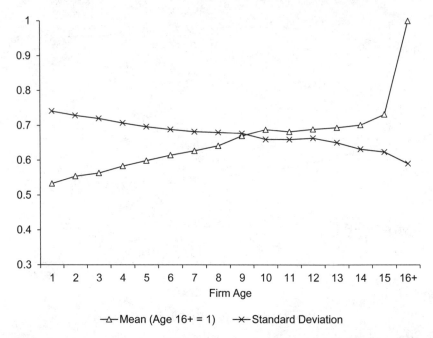

─△─Mean (Age 16+ = 1)   ─✕─Standard Deviation

Fig. 1.13B   Mean and standard deviation of within-industry labor productivity by firm age (weighted within industries)

Source: Statistics computed from the revenue-enhanced LBD subsets 1996–2000 and 2003–2013.

as an index of industry-level productivity growth) can be decomposed into within and between effects as given by:

$$\Delta P_{it} = \sum_{e\in i}\bar{\omega}_e\Delta P_{et} + \sum_i(\bar{P}_e - \bar{P}_i)\Delta\omega_{et},$$

where a bar over a variable represents the average over $t - 1$ to t. The first term on the right-hand side (RHS) is the within term and the second term is the between term. The within term captures the weighted average of within-firm productivity growth, while the between term captures the contribution of changes in employment shares. A firm contributes positively to the between term if it has labor productivity higher than the industry average. In this decomposition, we focus on within-industry patterns by using an industry-specific decomposition.

We calculate this decomposition for every industry/year pair in our data. To compute an aggregate average we use average gross output weights following the approach of Foster, Haltiwanger, and Krizan (2001) and Baily, Hulten, and Campbell (1992). Figure 1.14 shows the results of this decomposition for the average (output weighted) industry for all years and for the subperiods 1996–06, 2007–10, and 2011–13. We find that the within term

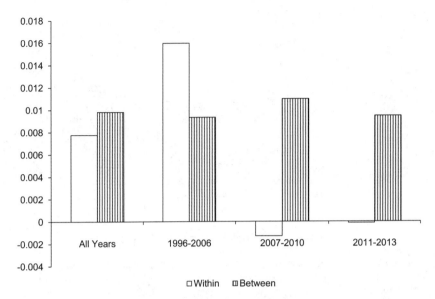

Fig. 1.14   Within versus between components of within-industry labor productivity growth

Source: Statistics computed from the revenue-enhanced LBD subsets 1996–2000 and 2003–2013.

is highly procyclical. It is positive for the overall period, much higher in the 1996–06 period, negative in the 2007–10 period, and almost zero for the 2011–2013 period. This is consistent with within-firm productivity being procyclical—likely for reasons associated with varying capacity utilization and the adjustment costs discussed earlier. In contrast, the between term is more stable over time and is always positive. It is not surprising then that the between term accounts for much of the overall increase for the full period and about half the increase for the period 1996–06.

To explore the role of high-growth firms we focus on the between term, since it is both more stable but also captures the reallocation dynamics where high-growth firms play such a critical role. Figure 1.15A shows the contribution of each of the output growth rate classes, and figure 1.15B shows employment growth rate classes by time period. Interestingly, we find that it is especially high-growth and high-decline businesses that account for the between term and the patterns are roughly similar for both output- and employment-growth rate classes. For the growth-rates classes with relatively modest increases or decreases we find little contribution of the between component. Since the between term is only positive for a group of growing (shrinking) firms if they have productivity that is on average higher (lower) than the overall average, these findings imply rapidly growing firms have above average productivity, while rapidly shrinking firms have

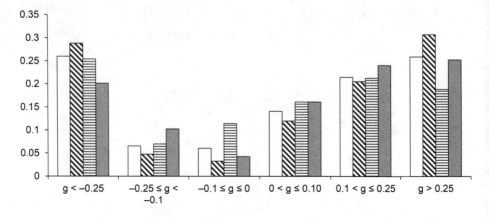

□ All Years ◪ 1996–2006 ⊟ 2007–2010 ▨ 2011–2013

Fig. 1.15A   Share of between accounted for by output growth rate classes

Source: Statistics computed from the revenue-enhanced LBD subsets 1996–2000 and 2003–2013.

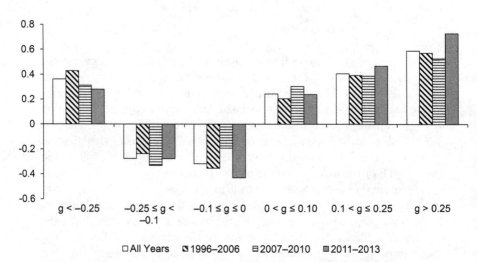

□ All Years ◪ 1996–2006 ⊟ 2007–2010 ▨ 2011–2013

Fig. 1.15B   Share of between accounted for by employment growth rate classes

Source: Statistics computed from the revenue-enhanced LBD subsets 1996–2000 and 2003–2013.

below average productivity. In this respect, Figures 1.15A and 15B remind us that the high-growth firms are part of the overall dynamic contributing to productivity-enhancing reallocation with an equally important role for rapidly shrinking low-productivity firms.

Where do young high-growth firms fit into this picture? First, we note that young firms that are less than ten years old only account for about 13 percent of output and 19 percent of employment. But we find that young firms contribute about 50 percent to the between term—much higher than their share of activity. Also, high-growth young firms contribute about 40 percent to the high-growth component of the between term. Thus, we find that young firms disproportionately contribute to the between term overall, and that high-growth young firms contribute disproportionately to the between-term contribution of high-growth firms.

1.5   Concluding Remarks

We find that high-growth young firms contribute disproportionately to job creation, output, and productivity growth. Young firms are very heterogeneous. Many fail in their first few years, and even among those that survive there is considerable dispersion in the growth patterns they experience. Conditional on survival, young firms have higher average net employment growth and output growth than their more mature counterparts. For employment growth, this is especially striking since median net employment growth for young firms is about zero. As such, the higher mean reflects the substantial positive skewness with a small fraction of very fast-growing firms driving the higher mean net employment growth. For output growth, young firms have higher median growth than their more mature counterparts. Still, young firms exhibit more positive skewness in growth rates than their mature counterparts on both an employment and output growth basis—although the positive skewness of output growth for young firms is highly procyclical.

Given these findings, we explored the characteristics of the high-growth firms further. Consistent with the above, we find that high-growth firms are more likely to be young than mature, even controlling for firm size. We also found that there is considerable variation across industries and states in the fraction of activity accounted for by young firms. The range across industries is substantial. Industries at the top of the ranking have as much as 40 percent of activity in high-growth firms, while industries at the bottom of the ranking have close to zero. In the post-2000 period, the share of activity accounted for by high-growth firms is significantly higher in the high tech and energy-producing (for the latter the share of output) industries. A firm in a small business-intensive industry is less likely to be a high-growth-output firm, but small business-intensive industries do not have significantly smaller shares of activity accounted for by high-growth firms for either output or employment. These findings are not in conflict with each other, but rather emphasize the importance of distinguishing between the typical (median or even average firm) and the activity accounted for by high-growth firms. Small business-intensive sectors often still have a small but highly influential contribution of high-growth firms.

We find that the ongoing reallocation dynamics of which high-growth young firms play a critical part contributes substantially to within-industry labor productivity growth. Our findings suggest that at least half of within-industry labor productivity growth for continuing firms is attributable to employment being reallocated from less productive to more productive firms within the industry. Young firms contribute disproportionately to this contribution from reallocation. But in this respect both high-growth and high-decline firms contribute substantially to the productivity-enhancing reallocation.

Industries and states with a greater fraction of high-growth firms exhibit high overall net growth, higher volatility, and also higher positive skewness. In this respect, a propensity for high growth is an indicator related to first, second, and third moments of the growth-rate distribution.

We interpret our findings as being consistent with models of innovation and growth that impact the first, second, and third moments. A rough storyline that we think fits the patterns we observed is as follows: firms with positive productivity realizations (exogenously or through endogenous innovative activity) leads to growth that contributes to both dispersion and positive skewness in the firm growth-rate distribution. The latter reflects the rareness of being a successful innovator (i.e., being in the right tail of the productivity distribution), and those that do succeed exhibit rapid growth. Those rare rapidly growing firms contribute substantially to net job creation, output growth, and labor-productivity growth. But often accompanying growth are those that do not succeed, so that volatility accompanies growth.

This storyline is obviously incomplete on many dimensions. It may be that (and we have presented some evidence of this) shocks and innovation in some sectors do not involve this complex dynamics of entry, exit, volatility, and skewness. Another set of issues relate to industry life cycle; that is, what do the dynamics of industries and locations in decline look like. They may also involve volatility. Similarly, there may be shocks that induce reallocation without much productivity growth or even adverse consequences for growth. For example, uncertainty shocks of the type emphasized by Bloom (2009) may have this character.

Our analysis has been intentionally descriptive. We think the data infrastructure we have developed and the basic facts we have presented provide a framework for more direct analysis of the process of innovation and growth. Our findings suggest that exploring patterns by firm age and examining first, second, and third moment effects will be important for detecting and understanding periods of growth and innovation. Moreover, we think our data infrastructure and approach should be helpful to explore factors that distort innovation and growth. The recent findings of Hsieh and Klenow (2014) that show that young firms grow rapidly in the United States relative to their counterparts in India and Mexico is highly relevant in this context. Our findings show that the rapid growth of young firms in the United States involves substantial skewness and dispersion. As such, distortions that may be adversely impacting the growth of young firms in India and Mexico (among other countries) may be impacting many of the different margins that underlie the patterns we have detected.

Appendix A
Data Appendix

In this appendix, we describe the construction of the firm-level revenue variable that serves as the basis for our analysis. We then describe how this variable is used to construct a revenue-enhanced subset of the LBD that includes continuers, births, and deaths, and discuss our methodology for cleaning the data. Finally, we describe our implementation of propensity-score matching to control for potential selection effects. In presenting our propensity-score models, we compare propensity-score-adjusted job creation and job destruction statistics from the revenue-enhanced subset to the results for the full LBD to indicate the effectiveness of our strategy.

Construction of the Revenue Variable

The US Census Bureau Business Register files contain revenue data sourced from business administrative income and payroll filings. These data are used for statistical purposes, including the Economic Census program and the Nonemployer Statistics program. There are a number of different tax forms and different revenue items within those forms that are relevant for calculating firm-level revenue depending on the sector that a firm operates in (or more specifically, the particular reporting tax unit, the EIN, within a firm), as well as the legal form of organization of the firm (nonprofits, partnerships, corporations, or sole proprietors). In an effort to build revenue measures reasonably comparable across firms, starting in 2002 the census developed an algorithm that takes these differences in tax forms and revenue concepts into account.[26] Within the census, this "best receipts" variable has previously been applied to single-unit firms only. Thus, we extended the

---

26. Algorithms are available to Census Bureau employees and RDC researchers that have an approved project and a need to know. Depending on the form and industry these algorithms may include total revenue, net receipts, gross revenue, receipts from interest, receipts from gross rents, total income, cost of goods sold, and direct as well as rent expenses.

original methodology in two ways. First, we apply the Census Bureau methodology to multiunit firms. Multiestablishment firms can report different parts of their operations under different and independent EIN filings. There are many possible reasons firms organize across multiple EINs including geographic, tax status, or business considerations. Given these within-firm sources of variation, we apply the algorithm at the EIN level first, using the EIN's self-reported NAICS classification to assign an industry to the EIN. The taxable revenue items that are included in the EINs total revenue are determined by this industry designation. We then compute a firm-level revenue measure by summing up all of the EINs associated with a particular firm.

Second, we developed an analog of the algorithm for years prior to 2002. The Business Register went through a complete redesign in 2002, which made it possible to keep additional fields that had been combined in prior years. We modify the pre-2002 algorithm to adjust for the different revenue items available before 2002. For any given year of revenue, we use prior-year revenue variables from the following year's BR. Previous research from the census has indicated that due to extended filing schedules, late filing, and other factors, these prior-year revenue variables provide significantly improved revenue information. Thus, in applying our algorithms we always use revenue for a given year from the BR file for the following year. Figure 1A.1 shows the results of applying these algorithms on the BR revenue measures and after filtering. Revenue is deflated using the GDP Implicit Price Deflator. Real revenue is in 2009 dollars.

The Revenue-Enhanced LBD Subset

Based on the revenue variable describe above, each observation in the LBD falls into one of four revenue categories: revenue continuers with revenue data in both year $t - 1$ and year t, revenue deaths with revenue in year $t - 1$ but no revenue in year t, revenue births with no revenue in year $t - 1$ and revenue in year t, and observations with no revenue data at either time. Observations in the fourth category are dropped in their entirety from the sample, while the subsets represented by the first three categories are cleaned to ensure that the observations are suitable for analysis.

Inspection of the revenue data reveals a number of outliers. These can come about for a number of reasons including typographical errors, OCR errors, units errors, and even denomination errors. Outliers are also common among commodity and energy-trading entities, as well as businesses organized in terms of holding companies. To address these issues, for the revenue continuers subset we apply the following filters:

1. We drop observations with labor productivity (revenue divided by employment) above the 99.9th percentile and below the 0.1th percentile for both years $t - 1$ and t.

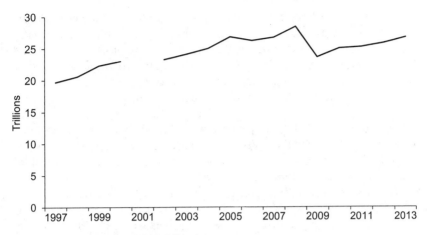

Fig. 1A.1   Real revenue (2009 dollars)

2. We drop observations reporting over $1 billion in average revenue and a DHS revenue growth rate of less than –0.5 or greater than 0.5.

3. We drop observations reporting over $100 million in average revenue and a DHS revenue growth rate of less than –1.5 or greater than 1.5.

4. We drop any observations reporting $1 trillion in average revenue or more.

These filters are designed to narrowly target specific problems such as unusually high or low labor-productivity values, unusually high revenue values, and unusually high changes in revenue, all the while minimizing the number of records we exclude from the data. Overall, this procedure excludes 0.14 percent of the total universe of revenue continuers.

For the revenue deaths and births we apply the same labor productivity filter for the relevant year of revenue. Because all revenue deaths and births have DHS revenue growth rates of –2 or 2, application of the additional filters amounts to a restriction on the DHS revenue denominator of $100 million. Overall, this procedure excludes 0.08 percent and 0.13 percent of the total universe of revenue deaths and births, respectively. Then, so that only true employment deaths and births are counted, the revenue death and revenue birth files are restricted to observations that represent employment deaths for the former and employment births for the latter. The remaining observations from each subset are then combined to form the revenue-enhanced LBD subset.

Missing Observations, Selection, and Propensity-Score Matching

Firms typically use the same EINs when filing payroll and income tax reports. This facilitates linking employment and revenue activity for a given firm at the Census Bureau. However, this is not always the case. About 20 percent of businesses file their payroll and income reports under different EINs. When this happens, the Census Bureau has no direct way of linking the two records. These revenue EINs become orphan records to payroll EINs, although they are never identified as such. Revenue records without a corresponding payroll record are considered nonemployer EINs.[27] The practical consequence of this is that for 21.8 percent of the revenue-enhanced LBD subset, we are missing revenue data. Further, it is often the case that employers will consistently use different EINs when filing their payroll and income, so many of these firms are missing all of their revenue data, making it difficult to impute their records. In addition to potential selection resulting from the examination of only observations that have revenue data, the additional filters and restrictions placed on the data may create problematic selection effects, particularly in the case of deaths and births.

Given that selection effects may differ for continuers, deaths, and births, we developed separate propensity-score models for employment continuers with revenue data, employment deaths with revenue data, and employment births with revenue data. Each of these partitions constitutes the set of firms for which the dependent variable equals 1 in a propensity score model that is run on the universe of LBD employment continuers, LBD employment deaths, and LBD employment births, respectively. For the employment continuers, the propensity score is inverse probability-weight calculated from the predicted values from a logistic regression including firm size, firm size squared, firm age, firm age squared, an indicator variable for firms of age sixteen and older, employment growth rate (seven classes), broad industry (twenty classes), and a multiunit status indicator. For deaths, we employ the same model, except we exclude the growth-rate classes. Finally, for births the model includes firm size, firm size squared, broad industry, and the indicator for multiunit status. Figures 1A.2, 1A.3, and 1A.4 examine the performance of our propensity-score model in terms of total net job creation, job destruction from exit, and job creation from births. Although these figures indicate some modest selection effects present in the revenue-enhanced LBD subset, the propensity-score model yields patterns of employment growth dynamics for continuers, births, and deaths for the enhanced-revenue subset of the LBD that closely mimic those for the full LBD. Figures 1A.2–1A.4 also show that even without weighting the enhanced-revenue subset does a reasonable job of capturing the employment dynamics from the full LBD.

27. For example, corporations file Form 1120 for their income taxes and Form 941 for their employment taxes (http://www.irs.gov/Businesses/Small-Businesses-&-Self-Employed/Corporations).

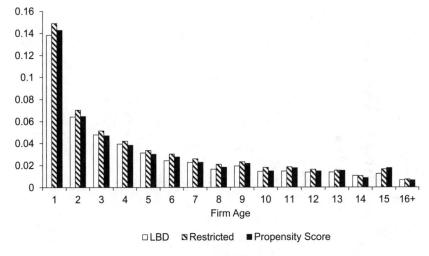

Fig. 1A.2   Net employment growth for surviving firms by sample, 1996–2013

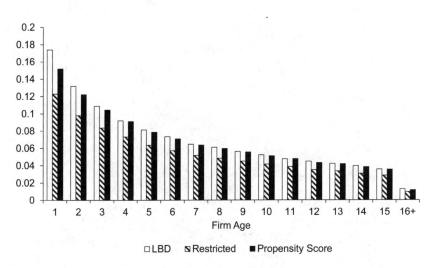

Fig. 1A.3   Job destruction from exit by sample, 1996–2013

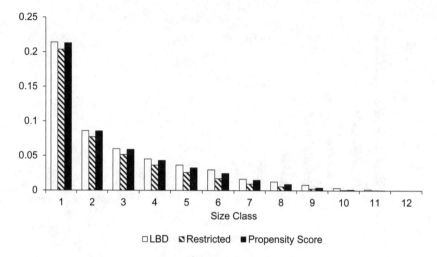

Fig. 1A.4   Job creation from births by sample, 1996–2013

Appendix B
Supplemental Results

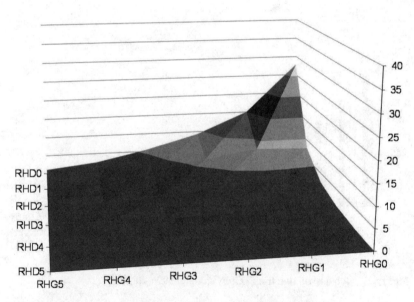

Fig. 1B.1   Percentage of RHG and RHD events for five-year-old firms (revenue weighted)

Source: Statistics computed from the revenue-enhanced LBD subsets 1996–2000 and 2003–2013.

Note: RHG = revenue high growth; RHD = revenue high decline. Reported shares are revenue weighted.

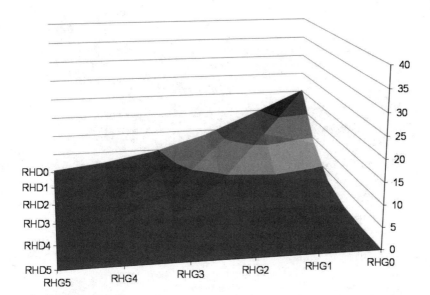

Fig. 1B.2   Percentage of EHG and EHD events for five-year-old firms (employment weighted)

Source: Statistics computed from the revenue-enhanced LBD subsets 1996–2000 and 2003–2013.

Note: EHG = employment high growth; EHD = employment high decline. Reported shares are employment weighted.

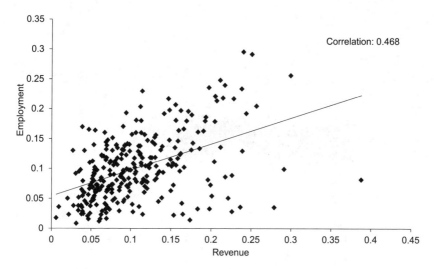

Fig. 1B.3   Industry effects revenue versus employment

Source: Statistics computed from the revenue-enhanced LBD subsets 1996–2000 and 2003–2013.

Note: Reported are estimated effects of linear probability models on industry effects.

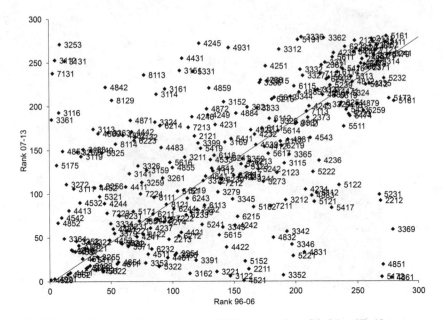

Fig. 1B.4   Industry rankings in revenue HGF, change from 96–06 to 07–13

Source: Statistics computed from the revenue-enhanced LBD subsets 1996–2000 and 2003–2013.

Note: The rankings for 1996–06 use the estimates from the 1996–06 period (except for 2001 and 2002) and the rankings of 2007–13 use the estimates from the 2007–13 period. Reported are estimated effects of linear probability models on industry effects.

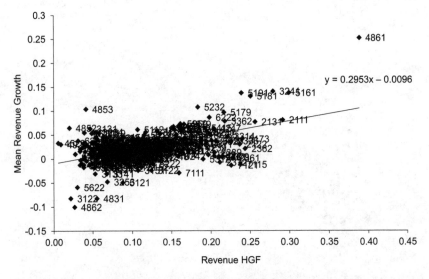

Fig. 1B.5   Revenue HGF versus revenue growth by industry

Source: Statistics computed from the revenue-enhanced LBD subsets 1996–2000 and 2003–2013.

Note: Reported revenue HGF are estimated effects of linear probability models on industry effects. Mean revenue growth is revenue-weighted mean revenue growth for firms.

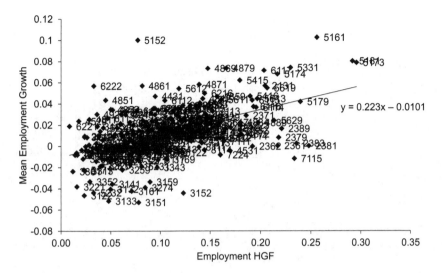

Fig. 1B.6   Employment HGF versus employment growth by industry

Source: Statistics computed from the revenue-enhanced LBD subsets 1996–2000 and 2003–2013.

Note: Reported employment HGF are estimated effects of linear probability models on industry effects. Mean employment growth is employment-weighted mean employment growth for firms.

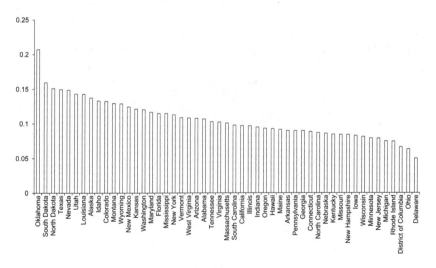

Fig. 1B.7   High-growth firm state effects (revenue)

Source: Statistics computed from the revenue-enhanced LBD subsets 1996–2000 and 2003–2013.

Note: Reported are estimated effects of linear probability models on industry effects.

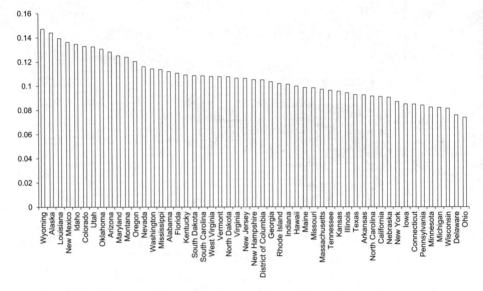

Fig. 1B.8   High-growth firm state effects (employment)

Source: Statistics computed from the revenue-enhanced LBD subsets 1998–2000 and 2003–2011.

Note: Reported are estimated effects of linear probability models on industry effects.

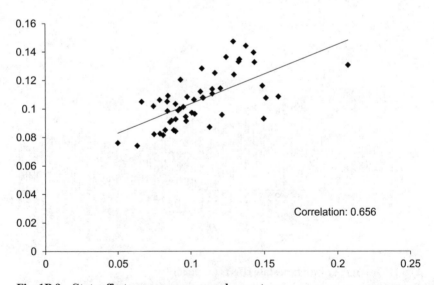

Correlation: 0.656

Fig. 1B.9   State effects revenue versus employment

Source: Statistics computed from the revenue-enhanced LBD subsets 1996–2000 and 2003–2013.

Note: Reported are estimated effects of linear probability models on state effects.

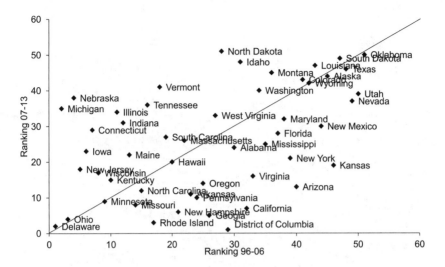

Fig. 1B.10   State rankings in revenue HGF, change from 96–06 to 07–13

Source: Statistics computed from the revenue-enhanced LBD subsets 1996–2000 and 2003–2013.

Note: The rankings for 1996–06 use the estimates from the 1996–06 period (except for 2001 and 2002) and the rankings of 2007–13 use the estimates from the 2007–13 period. Reported are estimated effects of linear probability models on state effects.

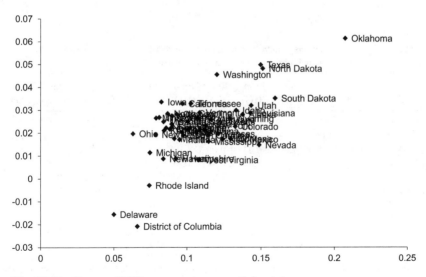

Fig. 1B.11   Revenue HGF versus revenue growth by state

Source: Statistics computed from the revenue-enhanced LBD subsets 1996–2000 and 2003–2013.

Note: Reported revenue HGF are estimated effects of linear probability models on state effects. Mean revenue growth is revenue-weighted mean revenue growth for firms.

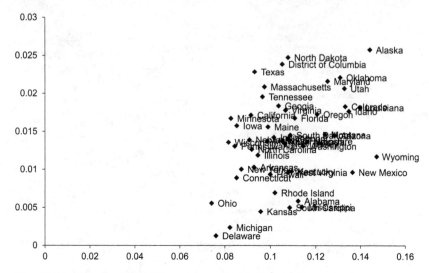

Fig. 1B.12 Employment HGF versus employment growth by state

Source: Statistics computed from the revenue-enhanced LBD subsets 1996–2000 and 2003–2013.

Note: Reported employment HGF are estimated effects of linear probability models on state effects. Mean employment growth is employment-weighted mean employment growth for firms.

Table 1B.1   Correlations of high-growth industry effects with summary measures of first, second, and third moments of industry distributions

	Rev. (GR)	Rev. (HG)	Emp. (GR)	Emp. (HG)	Rev. (HD)	Emp. (HD)	Rev. (90–10)	Emp. (90–10)	Rev. (skew)	Emp. (skew)
Rev. (GR)	1.00	0.52	0.39	0.06	−0.40	−0.16	−0.02	−0.07	0.40	0.16
Rev. (HG)		1.00	0.28	0.47	0.43	0.36	0.76	0.44	0.15	0.15
Emp. (GR)			1.00	0.52	−0.05	0.03	0.08	0.25	0.24	0.54
Emp. (HG)				1.00	0.44	0.81	0.54	0.92	−0.02	0.35
Rev. (HD)					1.00	0.53	0.81	0.52	−0.44	−0.02
Emp. (HD)						1.00	0.57	0.94	−0.15	−0.07
Rev. (90–10)							1.00	0.61	−0.24	0.05
Emp. (90–10)								1.00	−0.11	0.13
Rev. (skew)									1.00	0.16
Emp. (skew)										1.00

Note: Rev. = revenue, Emp. = employment, GR = net growth, HG = high-growth industry effect, HD = high-decline industry effect, 90–10 = activity-weighted 90–10 differential (employment weights for Emp. and revenue weights for Rev.). Skew = (90–50) –(50–10) (activity weighted).

Table 1B.2   **Correlations of high-growth state effects with summary measures of first, second, and third moments of state distributions**

	Rev. (GR)	Rev. (HG)	Emp. (GR)	Emp. (HG)	Rev. (HD)	Emp. (HD)	Rev. (90–10)	Emp. (90–10)	Rev. (skew)	Emp. (skew)
Rev. (GR)	1.00	0.64	0.46	0.21	−0.36	0.06	0.20	0.17	0.61	0.15
Rev. (HG)		1.00	0.45	0.66	0.37	0.54	0.82	0.63	0.43	0.31
Emp. (GR)			1.00	0.33	−0.05	0.02	0.20	0.22	0.28	0.61
Emp. (HG)				1.00	0.58	0.91	0.75	0.98	0.07	0.35
Rev. (HD)					1.00	0.63	0.79	0.60	−0.46	0.22
Emp. (HD)						1.00	0.73	0.97	−0.01	0.05
Rev. (90–10)							1.00	0.77	0.01	0.25
Emp. (90–10)								1.00	0.05	0.19
Rev. (skew)									1.00	0.01
Emp. (skew)										1.00

Note: Rev. = revenue, Emp. = employment, GR = net growth, HG = high-growth industry effect, HD = high-decline industry effect, 90–10 = activity-weighted 90–10 differential (employment weights for Emp. and revenue weights for Rev.). Skew = (90–50) –(50–10) (activity weighted).

References

Acemoglu, Daron, Ufuk Akcigit, Nicholas Bloom, and William R. Kerr. 2013. "Innovation, Reallocation, and Growth." NBER Working Paper no. 18993, Cambridge, MA.

Baily, Martin Neil, Charles Hulten, and David Campbell. 1992. "Productivity Dynamics in Manufacturing Plants." In *Brookings Papers on Ecnomic Activity: Microeconomics*, edited by Clifford Winston and Martin Neil Baily. Washington, DC: Brookings Institution Press.

Becker, Randy A., John Haltiwanger, Ron S. Jarmin, Shawn D. Klimek, and Daniel J. Wilson. 2006. "Micro and Macro Data Integration: The Case of Capital." In *A New Architecture for the US National Accounts*, Studies in Income and Wealth, vol. 66, edited by Dale W. Jorgenson, J. Steven Landefeld, and William D. Nordhaus, 541–609. Chicago: University of Chicago Press.

Bloom, Nicholas. 2009. "The Impact of Uncertainty Shocks." *Econometrica* 77 (3): 623–85.

Cooper, Russell, John Haltiwanger, and Jonathan Willis. 2007. "Search Frictions: Matching Aggregate and Establishment Observations." *Journal of Monetary Economics* 54:56–78.

Davis, Steven J., and John Haltiwanger. 1990. "Gross Job Creation and Destruction: Microeconomic Evidence and Macroeconomic Implications." In *NBER Macroeconomics Annual 1990*, edited by Olivier Jean Blanchard and Stanley Fischer, 123–68. Cambridge, MA: MIT Press.

———. 1992. "Gross Job Creation, Gross Job Destruction, and Employment Reallocation." *Quarterly Journal of Economics* 107:819–64.

Davis, Steven J., John Haltiwanger, Ron Jarmin, C. J. Krizan, Javier Miranda, Alfred Nucci, and Kristin Sandusky. 2009. "Measuring the Dynamics of Young and Small Businesses: Integrating the Employer and Nonemployer Universes." In *Producer Dynamics: New Evidence from Micro Data*, edited by Timothy Dunne, J. Bradford Jensen, and Mark J. Roberts. Chicago: University of Chicago Press.

Davis, Steven J., John Haltiwanger, Ron Jarmin, and Javier Miranda. 2007. "Volatility and Dispersion in Business Growth Rates: Publicly Traded versus Privately Held Firms." In *NBER Macroeconomics Annual 2006*, edited by Daron Acemoglu, Kenneth Rogoff, and Michael Woodford, 107–80. Cambridge, MA: MIT Press.

Davis, Steven J., John C. Haltiwanger, and Scott Schuh. 1996. *Job Creation and Destruction*. Cambridge, MA: MIT Press.

Decker, Ryan, John Haltiwanger, Ron Jarmin, and Javier Miranda. 2014. "The Role of Entrepreneurship in US Job Creation and Economic Dynamism." *Journal of Economic Perspectives* 28 (3): 3–24.

———. 2015. "Where Has All the Skewness Gone? The Decline of High Growth (Young) Firms in the US." NBER Working Paper no. 21776, Cambridge, MA.

Dunne, Timothy, Mark Roberts, and Larry Samuelson. 1989. "Plant Turnover and Gross Employment Flows in the US Manufacturing Sector." *Journal of Labor Economics* 7 (1): 48–71.

Ericson, Richard, and Ariel Pakes. 1995. "Markov-Perfect Industry Dynamics: A Framework for Empirical Work." *Review of Economic Studies* 62 (1): 53–82.

Fort, Teresa, John Haltiwanger, Ron S Jarmin, and Javier Miranda. 2013. "How Firms Respond to Business Cycles: The Role of the Firm Age and Firm Size." *IMF Economic Review* 61:520–59.

Foster, Lucia, John Haltiwanger, and C. J. Krizan. 2001. "Aggregate Productivity Growth: Lessons from Microeconomic Evidence." In *New Developments in Productivity Analysis*, Studies in Income and Wealth, vol. 63, edited by Charles R. Hulten, Edwin R. Dean, and Michael J. Harper, 303–72. Chicago: University of Chicago Press.

———. 2006. "Market Selection, Reallocation and Restructuring in the US Retail Trade Sector in the 1990s." *Review of Economics and Statistics* 88 (4): 748–58.

Haltiwanger, John, Ron S Jarmin, and Javier Miranda. 2013. "Who Creates Jobs? Small vs. Large vs. Young." *Review of Economics and Statistics* 2013:347–61.

Hsieh, Chang-Tai, and Peter Klenow. 2014. "The Life Cycle of Plants in India and Mexico." *Quarterly Journal of Economics*. doi: 10.1093/qje/qju014.

Hopenhayn, Hugo A. 1992. "Entry, Exit, and Firm Dynamics in Long Run Equilibrium." *Econometrica* 60 (5): 1127–50.

Hurst, Erik, and Benjamin Pugsley. 2012. "What Do Small Businesses Do?" *Brookings Papers on Economic Activity* 43 (2): 73–142.

Jovanovic, B. 1982. "Selection and the Evolution of Industry." *Econometrica* 50 (3): 649–70.

Olley, G. Steven, and Ariel Pakes. 1996. "The Dynamics of Productivity in the Telecommunications Equipment Industry." *Econometrica* 64 (6): 1263–97.

Törnqvist, Leo, Pentti Vartia, and Yrjö O. Vartia. 1985. "How Should Relative Changes be Measured?" *American Statistician* 39 (1): 43–6.

2

Nowcasting and Placecasting Entrepreneurial Quality and Performance

Jorge Guzman and Scott Stern

> When any estimate is examined critically, it becomes evident that the maker, wittingly or unwittingly, has used one or more criteria of productivity. The statistician who supposes that he can make a purely objective estimate of national income, not influenced by preconceptions concerning the "facts," is deluding himself; for whenever he includes one item or excludes another he is implicitly accepting some standard of judgment, his own or that of the compiler of his data. There is no escaping this subjective element in the work, or freeing the results from its effects.—Simon Kuznets (1941, 3)

A central challenge of economic measurement arises from the inevitable gap between the theoretical rationale for an economic statistic and the phenomena being measured. Not simply an abstract concern, the ability to reliably and systematically link economic phenomena closely to productivity or economic growth is central to the ability of policymakers and researchers to evaluate policy or understand the drivers of economic performance.

These concerns are particularly salient in the measurement of entrepreneurship. Though entrepreneurship is often cited by economists and policymakers as central to the process of economic growth and performance (Schumpeter 1942; Aghion and Howitt 1992; Davis and Haltiwanger 1992),

Jorge Guzman is a PhD student in the Technological Innovation, Entrepreneurship, and Strategic Management Group at MIT Sloan School of Management. Scott Stern is the *David Sarnoff Professor of Management* and Chair of the Technological Innovation, Entrepreneurship, and Strategic Management Group at the MIT Sloan School of Management and a research associate and director of the Innovation Policy Working Group at the National Bureau of Economic Research.

This chapter was prepared for the NBER/CRIW Measuring Entrepreneurial Businesses: Current Knowledge and Challenges conference, Washington, DC, December, 2014. We are thankful to David Audretsch, Pierre Azoulay, Erik Brynjolfsson, Georgina Campbell, Christian Catalini, Iain Cockburn, Mercedes Delgado, Catherine Fazio, Joshua Gans, Karen Mills, Fiona Murray, Abhishek Nagaraj, Ramana Nanda, Hal Varian, Ezra Zuckerman, Sam Zyontz, and the conference organizers John Haltiwanger, Erik Hurst, Javier Miranda, and Antoinette Schoar for comments and suggestions. We would also like to thank participants in NBER/CRIW preconference, the MIT Regional Entrepreneurship Acceleration Program, and seminar participants at the MIT Initiative on the Digital Economy, Micro@Sloan, the 2014 NBER-AIEA conference, and the 2014 DRUID meetings. We thank Raymond J. Andrews for his measuring the "type" of entrepreneurship that seems likely to be associated with overall economic performance has been challenging. While studies of high-performance ventures primarily rely on samples that select a population of firms that have already achieved relatively rare milestones such as the receipt of venture capital, broader population studies of entrepreneurs and small businesses emphasize the low-growth prospects of the average self-employed individual (Hamilton 2000; Hurst and Pugsley 2011). As emphasized by Schoar (2010) in her synthesis of entrepreneurship on a global basis, there is a gap between the small number of transformative entrepreneurs whose ambition and capabilities are aligned with scaling a dynamic and growing business and the much more prevalent incidence of subsistence entrepreneurs whose activities are an (often inferior) substitute to low-wage employment.

It is important to emphasize that, though luck and unobserved ability undoubtedly play an important role in the entrepreneurial process, the gap in the outcomes and impact of different ventures also reflect ex ante fundamental differences in the potential of those ventures. While most "Silicon Valley"-type start-ups fail, their intention at the time of founding is to build a company with a high level of equity and/or employment growth (and often are premised on exploiting new technology or serving an entirely new customer segment). At the same time, the ambition and potential for even a "successful" local business is often quite modest, and might involve building a firm of a small number of employees and yielding income comparable to that which would have been earned through wage-based employment. In other words, as emphasized by Hurst and Pugsley (2011), though policymakers and theory often treat entrepreneurs as a homogenous group (at least from an ex ante perspective), entrepreneurs seem to be very heterogeneous in terms of the ambition and potential of their ventures. For the purposes of measurement, then, it is critical that we not only capture variation in entrepreneurial outcomes but also develop the capability to measure variation in the quality of entrepreneurial ventures from the time of founding.

Building on Guzman and Stern (2015),[1] this chapter develops a novel approach to the estimation of entrepreneurial quality that allows us to char-

superb development of the visualizations in figures 2.3, 2.6, and 2.8. Carlos Garay provided RA support, and Alex Caracuzzo and MIT Libraries provided important data support. We are thankful to Patrick Fennelly and the Massachusetts Corporation Division for their help getting this data. We also acknowledge and thank the Jean Hammond (1986) and Michael Krasner (1974) Entrepreneurship Fund and the Edward B. Roberts (1957) Entrepreneurship Fund at MIT for financial support. All errors and omissions are, of course, our own. For acknowledgments, sources of research support, and disclosure of the authors' material financial relationships, if any, please see http://www.nber.org/chapters/c13493.ack.

1. Guzman and Stern (2015) introduce the distinction between entrepreneurial quality and quantity and the broad methodology in this chapter of predicting growth outcomes from start-up characteristics available at or around the time of founding for a population sample of business registrants. At some points in describing the methodology and data, we draw from

acterize regional clusters of entrepreneurship at an arbitrary level of granularity (placecasting), and examine the dynamics of entrepreneurial quality over time on a near real-time basis (nowcasting). Our approach combines three interrelated insights. First, because the challenges to reach a growth outcome as a sole proprietorship are formidable, a practical requirement for any growth-oriented entrepreneur is business registration (as a corporation, partnership, or limited liability company). We take advantage of the public nature of business registration records (in this chapter, from the state of Massachusetts from 1988 to 2014) to define a population sample of entrepreneurs observed at a similar (and foundational) stage of the entrepreneurial process. Second, moving beyond simple counts of business registrants (Klapper, Amit, and Guillen 2010), we are able to measure characteristics related to entrepreneurial quality *at or close to the time of registration*. For example, we can measure start-up characteristics such as whether the founders name the firm after themselves (eponymy), whether the firm is organized in order to facilitate equity financing (e.g., registering as a corporation or in Delaware), or whether the firm acquires or develops measurable innovations (e.g., a patent or trademark). Third, we leverage the fact that, though rare, we observe meaningful growth outcomes for some firms (e.g., those that achieve an initial public offering [IPO] or high-value acquisition within six years of founding), and are therefore able to estimate the relationship between these growth outcomes and start-up characteristics.

We apply our approach in the context of Massachusetts from 1988 to 2014.[2] First, consistent with Guzman and Stern (2015) (which uses our approach on California data), we find that a small number of characteristics allow us to develop a robust predictive model that distinguishes firm quality. In an out-of-sample test, we find that 77 percent of realized growth outcomes occur in the top 5 percent of our estimated quality distribution (and nearly 50 percent in the top 1 percent of the estimated quality distribution). Importantly, we find that there is significant benefit in predictive accuracy from including multiple start-up characteristics (relative to, say, exclusively relating quality to a single characteristic such as applying for a patent), and, at the same time, the quantitative significance of different start-up charac-

---

that paper to accurately describe our procedures and sample. This chapter significantly extends and expands upon Guzman and Stern (2015) in several respects, including the formal definition and proposal for two new economic statistics (EQI and RECPI), the inclusion of additional start-up characteristics variables such as media mentions and a measure for serial founders, extending the method to a second state (Massachusetts), evaluating the dynamics over time at both the state level as well as at more granular regional levels, and explicitly comparing an index that can be computed in real-time versus one that incorporates information from early milestones over the first two years of the venture.

2. Our current results depend on a cross section of firms using the locations listed as of November 2014, rather than their founding location. In a series of tests, we find the probability of changing location to be low—for example, for cohorts from 2008 to 2012, the probability of changing ZIP Codes is 0.12. We are currently undertaking a data effort to account, to the extent feasible using public data, for the full history of location changes for all firms.

teristics are roughly similar in our sample here and our sample of California firms in Guzman and Stern (2015).

We then use these estimates to propose two new economic statistics for the measurement of entrepreneurship: the Entrepreneurship Quality Index (EQI) and the Regional Entrepreneurship Cohort Potential Index (RECPI). The EQI is a measure of *average quality* within any given group of firms, and allows for the calculation of the probability of a growth outcome for a firm within a specified population of start-ups. The RECPI multiplies EQI and the number of start-ups within a given geographical region (e.g., a town or even the state of Massachusetts). Whereas EQI compares entrepreneurial quality across different groups (and so facilitates apples-to-apples comparisons across groups of different sizes), RECPI allows the direct calculation of the expected number of growth outcomes from a given start-up cohort within a given regional boundary.

We use these indices to offer a novel characterization of changes in entrepreneurial quality across space and time. We start with an overall assessment of Massachusetts, where RECPI increased dramatically during the second half of the 1990s, and then falls dramatically in the wake of the dot-com crash. The RECPI then increased by more than 25 percent from its low in 2003 through 2012. We find that RECPI has predictive power: while there is no meaningful relationship between the pattern of growth outcomes and the *number* of new firms (i.e., a measure of quantity), RECPI at the county-year level has a strong quantitative and statistical relationship with the number of realized growth outcomes.

We then turn to our placecasting applications, where we characterize entrepreneurial quality at different levels of geographic granularity (but do not directly use information about the location itself). We document striking variation in the level of average entrepreneurial quality across different Massachusetts towns: the area around Boston has a much higher average level of entrepreneurial quality than the rest of the state, and there is striking variation within the Boston metro area, with Kendall Square, the northeast Route 128 corridor, and the Boston Innovation District registering a very high level of average entrepreneurial quality. Over time, we document a striking change in entrepreneurial quality leadership as the Route 128 corridor has ceded EQI leadership to Cambridge. We are also able to offer more granular assessments, including comparing the areas immediately surrounding the Massachusetts Institute of Technology (MIT)/Kendall Square versus Harvard Square, and illustrating the microgeography of entrepreneurial quality with an address-level visualization of the area immediately surrounding MIT.

We then examine the potential for nowcasting entrepreneurial quality, where we evaluate whether it is possible to make timely entrepreneurial quality predictions in advance of observing the ultimate growth outcomes associated with any cohort of start-ups. We specifically compare an index that relies only on start-up characteristics immediately observable at the time of business registration (name, Delaware registration, etc.) with an index that allows for a two-year lag in order to incorporate early milestones such as patent or trademark application or being featured in local newspapers. Our results suggest that, though there is information that is gleaned from allowing for a lag, a nowcasted EQI is feasible and closely correlated with a more patient index.

Finally, we begin to consider the relationship between our measures and issues of theoretical or policy interest. Specifically, we find that the most significant "gap" between our index and the realized growth outcomes of a given cohort seem to be closely related to investment cycles: while the most successful cohort of Massachusetts start-ups was founded in 1995, the year 2000 cohort registered the highest estimated quality. This finding is particularly important in the light of recent work on capital market cycles, the need for follow-on financing, and innovative entrepreneurship (Nanda and Rhodes-Kropf 2013, 2014). Though we are cautious in interpreting our results, our results are consistent with the idea that an important loss from variation in the level of risk capital financing is the lack of follow-on investment for precisely the cohort of ventures that actually registered the highest overall potential impact. More generally, consistent with earlier studies of the concentration of innovation such as Audretsch and Feldman (1996) and Furman, Porter, and Stern (2002), our findings highlight the idea that, relative to the overall level of entrepreneurial activity, entrepreneurial quality is highly clustered in both space and time. Uncovering why entrepreneurial quality is concentrated remains an important topic for future research.

The rest of this chapter proceeds as follows. We motivate our approach by discussing the need for a measure of entrepreneurial quality in section 2.1, and then present a methodology for constructing such a measure in section 2.2. Section 2.3 introduces the data, and sections 2.4 and 2.5 present our key findings. Section 2.6 concludes.

2.1 Why is the Measurement of Entrepreneurial Quality Important?

Our motivation for developing an index of entrepreneurial quality stems from a growing agreement among entrepreneurship scholars that while new firms seem to have a positive effect in regional economic growth *on average* (Davis and Haltiwanger 1992; Decker et al. 2014; Kortum and Lerner 2000; Glaeser, Kerr, and Kerr 2014), there is very significant heterogeneity across firms from the time of their founding, and only a very small fraction of start-ups seem to be driving the economy-wide benefits from entrepreneurship (Kerr, Nanda, and Rhodes-Kropf 2014). As emphasized by Schoar, even if entrepreneurship has a net positive effect, policy efforts that aim to increase the supply of entrepreneurship without regard to quality could have a negative economic effect: "I argue that unless we understand the differences between those two types of entrepreneurs more clearly, many policy interventions may have unintended consequences and may even have an adverse impact on the economy." (Schoar [2010], 57; for further discussion, also see Hurst and Pugsley [2010], Kaplan and Lerner [2010], and Decker et al. 2014).

While there is increasing understanding of the importance of accounting for heterogeneity among entrepreneurs in the measurement of entrepreneurship, developing systematic measures of entrepreneurial quality has been challenging. In the area of entrepreneurial finance, researchers have often proceeded by simply examining samples of firms that have reached relatively rare milestones such as venture capital. While this facilitates the examination of the dynamics of high-potential firms, it nonetheless creates a disconnect between these small samples of selected firms and the overall population of start-up firms.[3] One notable and insightful exception is the positive relationship between organizing a firm as a corporation and entrepreneurial income, highlighted by Levine and Rubinstein (2013). At the same time, researchers have attempted to use publicly available data to develop specific indices of entrepreneurship, often at the regional level. Most of these indices have focused either on measures of entrepreneurial quantity (e.g., the Kauffman Index of Entrepreneurial Activity measures the rate of start-ups per capita using data from the Current Population Survey, and work by Leora Klapper and coauthors has provided benchmarking data for the rate of business registration across countries and time [Klapper, Amit, and Guillen 2010]), or on surveys that measure entrepreneurial attention, attitudes, or entrepreneurial activity (with the Global Entrepreneurship Monitor being the most influential and systematic effort based on surveys on a global basis [see Amorós and Bosma 2014]). While these efforts have provided significant insight into the overall rate and attitudes toward entrepreneurial activity, these approaches have yet to directly address the interplay between the heterogeneity among entrepreneurs and the process of economic growth. Finally, research exploiting establishment-level data such as the Longitudinal Business Data (or the more aggregated Business Dynamics Statistics) have been able to document the role of entrepreneurship in job creation (e.g., emphasizing the importance of young firms rather than small firms in that process), and also highlighting an observed reduction in the rate of business dynamism in the United States over time (Haltiwanger 2012; Decker et al. 2014; Hathaway and Litan 2014a). But, as emphasized by Hathaway and Litan, the challenge in directly incorporating heterogeneity is a measurement problem: "The problem is that it is very difficult, if not impossible, to

---

3. Self-selection into the sample can result in a different type of selectivity. For example, the Startup Genome Project is a private effort to characterize regional start-ups aiming to address challenges of measuring the nature of start-up activity (Reister 2014). However, the data they have gathered through self-submission and curated methods is very far from comprehensive. For example, in the Cambridge Innovation Center at 1 Broadway, in Cambridge, MA, Startup Genome identifies only nine (presumably active) firms at the time of writing, while business registration records show 229 *new* firms at this address between 2007 and 2012.

know at the time of founding whether or not firms are likely to survive and/ or grow." (Hathaway and Litan 2014b, 2).

Establishing a measurement framework for entrepreneurial quality would not simply be of interest for policymakers, but would also allow for the direct assessment of key questions in entrepreneurship. For example, while clusters of entrepreneurship such as Silicon Valley or Boston are associated with a disproportionate share of companies that achieve a meaningful growth outcome (e.g., an IPO or acquisition), is this due simply to the fact that these areas are home to higher-quality ventures or is there a separate impact of being located in a fertile entrepreneurial ecosystem? How does the quality of entrepreneurship vary across different types of founders (e.g., men versus women, or other demographic distinctions)? Finally, how does entrepreneurial quality vary with investment cycles (i.e., how does the level of entrepreneurial quality change during an investment boom, and what happens to high-quality entrepreneurial ventures that are founded just before an investment slowdown)? A measure of entrepreneurial quality could also be used to evaluate the impact of specific policy changes and programs, and also evaluate the role of institutions that impact some start-ups but not others. More generally, systematic measurement of entrepreneurial quality has the potential to serve as a tool for a broad range of questions relating to the causes and consequences of entrepreneurship.

2.2 Methodology

Building on this motivation, we now develop a novel methodology for estimating entrepreneurial quality for a population sample of start-ups at the time of founding, and propose preliminary candidates for two novel economic statistics to track and evaluate regional entrepreneurial performance: an Entrepreneurial Quality Index (EQI), a measure of the average quality of new firms, and a Regional Entrepreneurship Cohort Potential Index (RECPI), equal to the average quality of new firms multiplied by the number of new firms within a given cohort-region. Our approach combines three interrelated elements: the ability to observe a population sample of entrepreneurs, a procedure to estimate entrepreneurial quality for each start-up at the firm level, and a procedure to aggregate across quality into regional indices.

Data Requirements. A first requirement for a timely and granular index of entrepreneurial quality is an unbiased (ideally population) sample of new firms, and the ability to identify the quantity and quality of entrepreneurship of new cohorts on a timely basis.[4] As discussed further in section 2.3,

---

4. Limiting the sample to firms having achieved a meaningful intermediate outcome (e.g., the receipt of venture capital) will inevitably conflate the process of selection into the intermediate outcome (which itself is likely to be changing over time and location) with the variation in underlying quality of ventures across time and location.

we exploit publicly available business registration records to satisfy this first requirement. Since business registration is a practical (and straightforward) requirement for growth, the sample of business registrants in a given time period composes a meaningful cohort of start-ups for which one could evaluate quantity (the number of business registrants, or the number of business registrants of a certain type) as well as quality (by assessing the underlying quality of each business registrant in a standardized way).

Estimating Entrepreneurial Quality. To assess quality (at any level of granularity), we must first be able to estimate entrepreneurial quality for any given firm. To do so, we take advantage of the fact that, both directly within business registration records as well as through other publicly available data sources (such as the patent and trademark record, the news media, etc.), we are able to potentially observe a set of "start-up characteristics." The central challenge is to develop a systematic approach that allows one to rank different start-ups based on these start-up characteristics. We do so by creating a mapping between a meaningful growth outcome (observed, of course, with a lag) and the characteristics observable at or near the time of founding. More precisely, for a firm i born in region r at time t, with start-up characteristics $X_{i,t,t}$, we observe a growth outcome $g_{i,r,t+s}$ s years after founding and estimate:

$$(1) \qquad \theta_{i,r,t} = 1{,}000 \times P(g_{i,r,t+s}|X_{i,r,t}) = 1{,}000 \times f(\alpha + \beta X_{i,r,t}).$$

Using this predictive model, we are able to *predict* quality as the probability of achieving a growth outcome given start-up characteristics at birth, and so estimate entrepreneurial quality as $\hat{\theta}_{i,r,t}$.[5] To operationalize this idea, we draw on standard approaches in predictive modeling and divide our sample into three separate elements: a training sample, a test sample, and a prediction sample. The training sample is composed of the majority of observations for which we can observe both start-up characteristics and the growth outcome (i.e., the observable growth sample ends s years prior to the present) and is the sample we use to estimate equation (1).[6] We are then able to use the remaining data from the observable growth sample to conduct out-of-sample validation of our estimates (and, of course, are able to draw these samples multiple times to evaluate the robustness of our results to alternative draws of both samples). Finally, we are able to construct a prediction sample in which we observe start-up characteristics but have not yet observed the growth outcome. As long as the process by which start-up characteristics map to growth remain stable over time (an assumption which is itself test-

5. While there exist several data mining methods to build a predictive model (including linear regression, binary regression, and neural networks), our methodology uses a logit regression, which performs well in quality of predictions (relative to a linear probability model) while still allowing interpretability of the economic magnitudes and significance of the coefficients for the measures used (Pohlman and Leitner 2003).
6. We reserve 30 percent of the sample for which we observe both the growth outcome and start-up characteristics for the test sample.

able), we are able to then develop an estimate for entrepreneurial quality, even for very recent cohorts. In particular, we can examine the trade-off between relying exclusively on start-up characteristics immediately observable at the time of business registration (which will allow one to create real-time statistics) with estimates that allow for a lag in order to incorporate early milestones such as patent or trademark application or being featured in local newspapers.

Calculating an Entrepreneurial Quality Index. To create an index of entrepreneurial quality for any group of firms (e.g., all the groups within a particular cohort or a group of firms satisfying a particular condition), we simply take the average quality within that group. Specifically, in our regional analysis, we define the Entrepreneurial Quality Index (EQI) as an aggregate of quality at the region-year level by simply estimating the average of $\theta_{i,r,t}$ over that region:

$$(2) \qquad EQI_{r,t} = \frac{1}{N_{r,t}} \sum_{i \in \{I_{r,t}\}} \theta_{i,r,t},$$

where $\{I_{r,t}\}$ represents the set of all firms in region r and year t, and $N_{r,t}$ represents the number of firms in that region-year. To ensure that our estimate of entrepreneurial quality for region r reflects the quality of start-ups in that location rather than simply assuming that start-ups from a given location are associated with a given level of quality, we exclude any location-specific measures $X_{r,t}$ from the vector of observable start-up characteristics.

Three particular features of EQI are notable. First, while the general form of $EQI_{r,t}$ is a panel format, it is possible to construct a cross-sectional distribution of quality at a moment in time (i.e., EQI_{r,t_0}) to facilitate analyses such as spatial mapping. Second, the level of geographical aggregation is arbitrary: while the discussion of a "region" may connote a large geographic area, it is possible to calculate EQI at the level of a city, ZIP Code, or even individual addresses. Finally, we can extend EQI in order to study an arbitrary grouping of firms (i.e., we do not need to select exclusively on geographic boundaries). For example, we can examine start-ups whose founders share a common demographic characteristic (e.g., gender), or firms that undertake a specific strategic action (e.g., engage in crowdfunding).

The Regional Entrepreneurship Cohort Potential Index (RECPI). From the perspective of a given region, the overall potential for a cohort of start-ups requires combining both the quality of entrepreneurship in a region and the number of firms in such region (a measure of quantity). To do so, we define RECPI as simply $EQI_{r,t}$ multiplied by the number of firms in that region-year:

$$(3) \qquad RECPI_{r,t} = EQI_{r,t} \times N_{r,t}.$$

Since our index multiplies the *average* probability of a firm in a region-year to achieve growth (quality) by the number of firms, it is, by definition, the expected number of growth events from a region-year given the start-up characteristics of a cohort at birth. Under the assumption of excluding regional effects (e.g., agglomeration economies) or time-based effects (e.g., changes in available financing), our index can be interpreted as a measure of the "potential" of a region given the "intrinsic" quality of firms at birth, which can then be affected by the impact of the entrepreneurial ecosystem, or shocks to the economy and the cohort between the time of founding and a growth outcome.

Assessing the Merit of our Quality Estimates. Our methodology estimates the quality of new firms through a predictive model of probability of achieving a growth outcome, and as such the predictive accuracy of the model must be evaluated before relying on its estimates to draw economic inference. Specifically, given concerns about the potential for overfitting (Taddy 2013), we reserve 30 percent of the observable growth outcome sample in order to conduct out-of-sample validation. In particular, we conduct the analysis multiple times to evaluate the robustness of our estimates to the sample from which it is drawn, and also plot the share of realized outcomes (in the test sample) associated with different percentiles of our estimated quality distribution. Robustness of the coefficients to different samples and a model with strong predictive accuracy in out-of-sample testing suggest stronger candidates as economic statistics.

2.3   Data

As mentioned earlier, our analysis leverages publicly available business registration records, a potentially rich and systematic data for entrepreneurship and business dynamics. Business registration records are public records created when individuals register a business. This analysis focuses on the state of Massachusetts from 1988 to 2014 (see appendix table 2A.1 for a short description and discussion of these records). During the time of our sample, it was possible to register several types of businesses: corporations, limited liability companies, limited liability partnerships, and general partnerships. While it is possible to found a new business without business registration (e.g., a sole proprietorship), the benefits of registration are substantial, including limited liability, protection of the entrepreneur's personal assets, various tax benefits, the ability to issue and trade ownership shares, credibility with potential customers, and the ability to deduct expenses. Furthermore, all corporations, partnerships, and limited liability must register with the state in order to take advantage of these benefits: the act of *registering* the firm triggers the legal creation of the company. As such, these records form the *population* of Massachusetts businesses that take a form that is a practical prerequisite for growth.[7]

---

7. This section draws on Guzman and Stern (2015), where we introduce the use of business registration records in the context of entrepreneurial quality estimation.

Concretely, our analysis draws on the complete population of firms satisfying one of the following conditions: (a) a for-profit firm whose jurisdiction is in Massachusetts or (b) a for-profit firm whose jurisdiction is in Delaware but whose principal office address is in Massachusetts. In other words, our analysis excluded nonprofit organizations as well as companies whose primary location is external to Massachusetts. Applied over the years 1988–2014, the resulting data set is composed of 541,666 observations.[8] For each observation we construct variables related to (a) the growth outcome for each start-up, (b) start-up characteristics based on business registration observables, and (c) start-up characteristics based on external observables that can be linked directly to the startup. Table 2.1 reports the summary statistics, both for the overall sample (divided out by our estimation and prediction sample periods) and conditional on whether the firm achieved a growth outcome or not.

Growth. Our methodology allows for different types of growth outcomes, both continuous and binary. For the purposes of this chapter, we focus on a binary measure *Growth*, which is a dummy variable equal to 1 if the start-up achieves an initial public offering (IPO) or is acquired at a meaningful positive valuation within six years of registration.[9] In future work, we intend to move beyond this measure to include other outcomes such as employment or sales. Both IPO and acquisition outcomes are drawn from Thomson Reuters SDC Platinum.[10] We observe 462 positive growth outcomes for the 1988–2005 start-up cohorts (used in all our regressions), yielding a mean of *Growth* of 0.0014. The median acquisition price is $77 million (ranging from a minimum of $11.9 million at the 5th percentile to $1.92 billion at the 95th percentile).[11]

Start-Up Characteristics. The core of the empirical approach is to map growth outcomes to observable characteristics of start-ups at or near the time of business registration. We develop two types of measures: (a) mea-

8. The number of firm births in our sample is substantially higher than the US Census Longitudinal Business Database (LBD), done from tax records. For Massachusetts in the period 2003–2012, the LBD records an average of 9,450 new firms per year and we record an average of 24,066 firm registrations. While the reasons for this difference are still to be explored, there are at least two reasons that we expect will be in part causing this difference: (a) partnerships and LLCs who do not have income during the years they do not file a tax returns and are thus not included in the LBD, and (b) firms that have zero employees are not included in the LBD.

9. Our results are robust to changes in the time allowed for a firm to achieve growth. See Guzman and Stern (2015, Supplementary Materials) for a subset of those robustness tests.

10. While the coverage of IPOs is likely to be nearly comprehensive, the SDC data set excludes some acquisitions. However, though the coverage of significant acquisitions is not universal in the SDC data set, previous studies have "audited" the SDC data to estimate its reliability, finding a nearly 95 percent accuracy (Barnes, Harp, and Oler 2014).

11. In our main results, we assign acquisitions with an unrecorded acquisitions price as a positive growth outcome, since an evaluation of those deals suggests that most reported acquisitions were likely in excess of $5 million. All results are robust to the assignment of these acquisitions as equal to a growth outcome.

Table 2.1   Summary statistics for Massachusetts firms[a]

| | 1988 to 2005 | | | | | | | | | 2006 to 2014 | | |
| | All firms | | | Growth = 0 | | | Growth = 1 | | | All firms | | |
	N	Mean	Std. dev.	N	Mean	Std. dev.	N	Mean	Std. dev.	N	Mean	Std. dev.
Year	319,011	1997.4110	5.298	318,549	1997.412	5.300	462	1996.842	4.130	197,501	2009.6	2.353
Business registration information												
Corporation	319,011	0.736	0.441	318,549	0.736	0.441	462	0.942	0.235	197,501	0.374	0.484
Short name	319,011	0.474	0.499	318,549	0.473	0.499	462	0.810	0.393	197,501	0.475	0.499
Eponymous	319,011	0.150	0.357	318,549	0.150	0.357	462	0.011	0.104	197,501	0.143	0.350
Delaware	319,011	0.059	0.236	318,549	0.058	0.235	462	0.738	0.440	197,501	0.058	0.235
Intellectual property												
Trademark	319,011	0.002	0.039	318,549	0.001	0.038	462	0.043	0.204	197,501	0.003	0.052
Patent	319,011	0.005	0.070	318,549	0.005	0.067	462	0.236	0.425	197,501	0.004	0.065
Media mentions												
Mentioned in *Boston Globe*	319,011	0.003	0.053	318,549	0.003	0.052	462	0.069	0.254	197,501	0.004	0.065
Founder effects												
Repeat entrepreneur	319,011	0.011	0.104	318,549	0.011	0.104	462	0.015	0.122	197,501	0.014	0.117
Repeat entrepreneur in high tech	319,011	0.001	0.027	318,549	0.001	0.027	462	0.004	0.066	197,501	0.001	0.027
Cluster groups[b]												
Local	319,011	0.191	0.393	318,549	0.191	0.393	462	0.037	0.188	197,501	0.220	0.414
Traded	319,011	0.530	0.499	318,549	0.530	0.499	462	0.578	0.494	197,501	0.482	0.500
Traded high technology	319,011	0.056	0.231	318,549	0.056	0.230	462	0.199	0.400	197,501	0.041	0.199
Traded resource intensive	319,011	0.135	0.342	318,549	0.136	0.342	462	0.080	0.272	197,501	0.102	0.302

[a]All nonprofit firms, firms whose jurisdiction is not Delaware or Massachusetts, and firms in Delaware with a main office address outside of Massachusetts are dropped from our sample.

[b]Cluster groups are calculated by grouping industry clusters in the US Cluster Mapping Project into five large categories.

sures based on business registration observables, and (b) measures based on external indicators of start-up quality that are observable at or near the time of business registration. We review each of these in turn.

Measures Based on Business Registration Observables. We construct ten measures based on information observable in the business registration records. Four are measures that we anticipate are associated with firm potential, four are dummy variables based on the industry cluster most closely linked to the start-up, and two are associated with measures of serial entrepreneurship to capture the underlying quality of the founder.

We first create two binary measures that relate to how the firm is registered, *Corporation*, whether the firm is a corporation rather than an LLC or partnership, and *Delaware Jurisdiction*, whether the firm is registered in Delaware. *Corporation* is an indicator equal to 1 if the firm is registered as a corporation and 0 if it is registered either as an LLC or partnership.[12] In the period of 1988 to 2005, 0.19 percent of corporations achieve a growth outcome versus only 0.03 percent of noncorporations.[13] *Delaware jurisdiction* is equal to 1 if the firm is registered under Delaware, but has its main office in Massachusetts (all other foreign firms are dropped before analysis). Delaware jurisdiction is favorable for firms which, due to more complex operations, require more certainty in corporate law, but it is associated with extra costs and time to establish and maintain two registrations. Between 1988 and 2005, 5.8 percent of the sample registers in Delaware; 74 percent of firms achieving a growth outcome do so.

We then create two additional measures based directly on the name of the firm. Drawing on the recent work of Belenzon, Chatterji, and Daley (2014; hereafter BCD), we use the firm and founder name to establish whether the firm name is eponymous (i.e., named after one or more of the founders). *Eponymy* is equal to 1 if the first, middle, or last name of the top managers is part of the name of the firm itself.[14] Fifteen percent of the firms in our training sample are eponymous (an incidence rate similar to BCD), though only 1.08 percent for whom *Growth* equals 1. It is useful to note that, while we draw on BCD to develop the role of eponymy as a useful start-up characteristic, our hypothesis is somewhat different than BCD: we hypothesize that eponymous firms are likely to be associated with lower entrepreneurial quality. Whereas BCD evaluates whether serial entrepreneurs are more likely to invest and grow companies that they name after

12. Previous research highlights performance differences between incorporated and unincorporated entrepreneurs (Levine and Rubinstein 2013).

13. It is important to note that the share of corporations in Massachusetts has moved dramatically after limited liability companies were introduced in 1995, from around 92 percent in 1994 to 36 percent in 2013.

14. We consider the top manager any individual with one of the following titles: president, CEO, or manager. We require names be at least four characters to reduce the likelihood of making errors from short names. Our results are robust to variations of the precise calculation of eponymy (e.g., names with a higher or lower number of minimum letters).

themselves, we focus on the cross-sectional difference between firms with broad aspirations for growth (and so likely avoid naming the firm after the founders) versus less ambitious enterprises, such as family-owned "lifestyle" businesses.

Our second measure relates to the length of the firm name. Based on our review of naming patterns of growth-oriented start-ups versus the full business registration database, a striking feature of growth-oriented firms is that the vast majority of their names are at most two words (plus perhaps one additional word to capture organizational form, e.g., "Inc."). Companies such as Akamai or Biogen have sharp and distinctive names, whereas more traditional businesses often have long and descriptive names (e.g., "New England Commercial Realty Advisors, Inc."). We define *Short Name* to be equal to 1 if the entire firm name has three or less words, and zero otherwise. Forty-seven percent of firms within the 1988–2005 period have a short name, but the incidence rate among growth firms is more than 80 percent.[15]

We then create four measures based on how the firm name reflects the industry or sector within which the firm is operating. To do so, we take advantage of two features of the US Cluster Mapping Project (Delgado, Porter, and Stern 2015), which categorizes industries into (a) whether that industry is primarily local (demand is primarily within the region) versus traded (demand is across regions) and (b) among traded industries, a set of fifty-one traded clusters of industries that share complementarities and linkages. We augment the classification scheme from the US Cluster Mapping Project with the complete list of firm names and industry classifications contained in Reference USA, a business directory containing more than 10 million firm names and industry codes for companies across the United States. Using a random sample of 1.5 million Reference USA records, we create two indices for every word ever used in a firm name. The first of these indices measures the degree of localness, and is defined as the relative incidence of that word in firm names that are in local versus non-local industries (i.e., $\rho_i = (\sum_{j=\{\text{local firms}\}} \mathbb{1}[w_i \subseteq \text{name}_j] / \sum_{j=\{\text{nonlocal firms}\}} \mathbb{1}[w_i \subseteq \text{name}_j])$). We then define a list of Top Local Words, defined as those words that are (a) within the top quartile of ρ_i and (b) have an overall rate of incidence greater than 0.01 percent within the population of firms in local industries (see Guzman and Stern 2015, table S10, for the complete list). Finally, we define *local* to be equal to 1 for firms that have at least one of the Top Local Words in their name, and zero otherwise. We then undertake a similar exercise for the degree to which a firm name is associated with a traded name. It is important to note that there are firms that we cannot associate either with traded or local and thus leave out as a third category. Just more than 15 percent of

---

15. We have also investigated a number of other variants (allowing more or less words, evaluating whether the name is "distinctive" in the sense of being both noneponymous and also not an English word). While these are promising areas for future research, we found that the three-word binary variable provides a useful measure for distinguishing entrepreneurial quality.

firms have local names, though only 3.7 percent of firms for whom *growth* equals 1, and while 53 percent of firms are associated with the traded sector, 57 percent of firms for whom *growth* equals 1 do.

We additionally examine the type of traded cluster a firm is associated with, focusing in particular on whether the firm is in a high-technology cluster or a cluster associated with resource-intensive industries. For our high-technology cluster group (*Traded High Technology*), we draw on firm names from industries included in ten sets of clusters from the US Cluster Mapping Project: Aerospace Vehicles, Analytical Instruments, Biopharmaceuticals, Downstream Chemical, Information Technology, Medical Devices, Metalworking Technology, Plastics, Production Technology and Heavy Machinery, and Upstream Chemical. From 1988 to 2005, while only 5.6 percent of firms are associated with high technology, this rate increases to 20 percent within firms that achieve our growth outcome. For our resource-intensive cluster group, we draw on firms names from fourteen USCMP clusters: Agricultural Inputs and Services, Coal Mining, Downstream Metal Products, Electric Power Generation and Transmission, Fishing and Fishing Products, Food Processing and Manufacturing, Jewelry and Precious Metals, Lighting and Electrical Equipment, Livestock Processing, Metal Mining, Nonmetal Mining, Oil and Gas Production and Transportation, Tobacco, and Upstream Metal Manufacturing. While 14 percent of firms are associated with resource-intensive industries, the rate drops to 8 percent among growth firms.

Finally, we sought to develop measures that would link entrepreneurial quality to the quality and potential of the firm founders. Specifically, we construct two measures based on whether the individuals connected to the firm have been associated with start-up activity in the past. *Repeat Entrepreneurship*, equals 1 if the president, CEO, or manager of a firm is also listed as a president, CEO, or manager in a deceased firm that became inactive before the current firm was registered. To guarantee we match the same individual, we require an exact match on both name and address. We then interact *Repeat Entrepreneurship* with the *High Tech* cluster dummy to create *High Tech. Repeat Entrepreneurship*, a measure of serial entrepreneurship in high technology start-ups.[16]

Measures Based on External Observables. We construct two measures related to start-up quality based on information in intellectual property data sources and one measure related to media presence close to birth.[17]

16. While we only use these two founder measures in this chapter, we have explored other measures including estimating gender and ethnicity and plan to investigate these types of social and demographic variables in future work.

17. While this chapter only measures external observables related to intellectual property and media, our approach can be utilized to measure other externally observable characteristics that may be related to entrepreneurial quality (e.g., measures related to the quality of the founding team listed in the business registration such as through LinkedIn profiles, or measures of early investments in scale such as a Web presence).

Building on prior research matching business names to intellectual property (Balasubramanian and Sivadasan 2010; Kerr and Fu 2008), we rely on a name-matching algorithm connecting the firms in the business registration data to external data sources. Importantly, since we match only on firms located in Massachusetts, and since firms' names legally must be "unique" within each state's company registrar, we are able to have a reasonable level of confidence that any "exact match" by a matching procedure has indeed matched the same firm across two databases. Our main results use "exact name matching" rather than "fuzzy matching"; in small-scale tests using a fuzzy-matching approach (the Levenshtein edit distance; Levenshtein [1965]), we found that fuzzy matching yielded a high rate of false positives due to the prevalence of similarly named but distinct firms (e.g., Capital Bank vs. Capitol Bank, Pacificorp Inc. vs. Pacificare Inc.).[18]

We construct two measures related to start-up quality based on intellectual property data sources from the US Patent and Trademark Office. *Patent* is equal to 1 if a firm holds a patent application within the first year and 0 otherwise. We include patents that are filed by the firm within the first year of registration and patents that are assigned to the firm within the first year from another entity (e.g., an inventor or another firm). While only 0.6 percent of the firms in Massachusetts have a patent application, 7.2 percent of growth firms do. Our second measure, *Trademark*, is equal to 1 if a firm applies for a trademark within the first year of registration. While only 0.2 percent of firms have a trademark, 3.7 percent of growth firms do.

Finally, we construct a measure based on the firm's presence in media outlets. *Media Mentions* is equal to 1 if a firm has a news story with its name in the business section of the *Boston Globe* within a year of its founding date. To do so, we search for all firms' names in the historical records of the *Boston Globe*, allowing a one-year window before and after the founding date and finding those that have articles on the business section.[19] While we can identify an early media mention for only 0.14 percent of firms, this number increases to 3.6 percent when considering growth firms.[20]

---

18. Our matching algorithm works in three steps: First, we clean the firm name by: (a) expanding eight common abbreviations (Ctr., Svc., Co., Inc., Corp., Univ., Dept., and LLC.) in a consistent way (e.g., Corp. to Corporation); (b) removing the word "the" from all names; (c) replacing "associates" for "associate"; and (d) deleting the following special characters from the name: . | ' " — @ _ . Second, we create three variables that hold (a) the organization type (e.g., Corporation, Incorporated, Limited Liability Company), (b) the firm name without the organization type, and (c) the firm name without the organization type and without spaces. Finally, we proceed to do the actual matching of data sets. First on firm name and organization type, then only on name, and finally on collapsed name. Our companion paper contains further tests on the name-matching procedure and all our scripts are available in the online appendix.

19. We identify articles in the business section by using the journalist's name and only keeping those that often report business-related news.

20. While this result might lead to some bias due to the geographic nature of the *Boston Globe*, the state of Massachusetts is sufficiently small that we expect high potential firms to be

2.4   Estimating Entrepreneurial Quality and Performance

We undertake our analysis in several stages. First, we examine the relationship between our growth outcome and various start-up characteristics, identify a candidate set of start-up characteristics from which to estimate entrepreneurial quality, and evaluate the performance of our estimator in an out-of-sample test. We then turn to the calculation of our two proposed indices, EQI and RECPI, implement and evaluate our key placecasting and nowcasting applications, and consider the overall performance of our estimator and indices as well as the interpretation of our results in the context of the broader literature.

We begin in table 2.2 with a series of univariate logit regressions of *Growth* on each of our measured start-up characteristics. As mentioned earlier, these regressions (and all subsequent regressions) are conducted on a random 70 percent training sample of the complete 1988–2005 data set, reserving 30 percent of the 1988–2005 data as a test sample. To facilitate the interpretation of our results, we present the results in terms of the odds-ratio coefficient and the pseudo-R^2.

These univariate results are suggestive. Various simple measures directly captured from the registration record (such as whether the firm is a corporation or registered in Delaware, or is named after the founder or using less than two words) are each highly significant and associated with a large increase in the probability that a given firm achieves a growth outcome. For example, corporations are associated with a more than five times increase in the probability of growth, and those that register in Delaware are associated with more than a forty times increase in the probability of growth. Conversely, firms named after their founders have only a 5 percent chance of a growth outcome relative to those with a noneponymous name. Equally intriguing results are associated with measures of the degree of innovativeness and novelty of the start-up: *Patent* is associated with nearly a sixty times increase in the probability of growth, and *Trademark* and *Mentioned in Boston Globe* are each associated with more than a thirty times increase in the probability of growth. Importantly, not all candidate measures are associated with a meaningful statistical relationship: both of our founder measures are associated with much smaller and statistically insignificant effects on the probability of growth.

It is, of course, important to emphasize that each of these coefficients must be interpreted with care. While we are capturing start-up characteristics that are associated with growth, we are not claiming a causal relationship between the two: if a firm with low growth potential changes its legal juris-

---

mentioned in the *Boston Globe* regardless of specific locations. Furthermore, all of our results are robust to excluding this measure.

Table 2.2   Univariate logit from predictors on growth

	Univariate regression coefficient	Pseudo-R^2 (%)
Corporation	5.834***	1.9
	[1.379]	
Short name	4.901***	3.3
	[0.695]	
Eponymous	0.052***	1.7
	[0.030]	
Delaware	44.795***	20.2
	[5.591]	
Patent	58.528***	8.3
	[8.092]	
Trademark	38.689***	1.9
	[9.616]	
Mentioned in *Boston Globe*	30.843***	2.4
	[6.541]	
Repeat entrepreneurship	1.117	0
	[0.563]	
High tech. repeat entrepreneurship	4.031	0
	[4.049]	
N	223,307	

Note: Incidence ratios (odds ratios) reported. Robust standard errors in brackets.
***Significant at the 0.1 percent level.
**Significant at the 1 percent level.
*Significant at the 10 percent level.

diction to Delaware, that is unlikely to have any impact on its overall growth prospects.[21] Instead, Delaware registration is an informative signal, based on the fact that external investors often prefer to invest in firms governed under Delaware law, of the ambition and potential of the start-up as observed at the time of business registration. Reliance on a univariate measure makes inference particularly tricky: in isolation one cannot evaluate whether any particular start-up characteristic is more or less important than others.

21. One important concern in policy applications of this methodology is that our measures might change incentives of firms such that they try to "game" the result by selecting into high-quality measures they previously did not care about (e.g., changing its name from long to short). We note that this possibility, though real, is bounded by the incentives of the founders. For example, it is unlikely that a founder with no intention to grow would incur the significant yearly expense required to keep a registration in Delaware (which we estimate around $1,000). Similarly, firms that signal in their name as being a local business (e.g., "Taqueria") are unlikely to change their names in ways that affect their ability to attract customers. Finally, we also note that any effects from gaming would be short-lived since, as low-quality firms select into a specific measure the correlation between such measure and growth—and therefore the weight our prediction model would assign to it—weakens.

We therefore proceed in table 2.3 to consider these effects in tandem. We begin by simply examining the impact of three measures directly observable from the business registration record: Corporation, Short Name, and Eponymous. Each are statistically and quantitatively significant: while corporations and short names are each associated with a more than four times increase in the probability of growth, eponymy reduces the probability of growth by nearly 95 percent. When we introduce cluster dummies in column (2), the results for these business registration measures remains similar; at the same time, the results suggest that businesses whose names are associated with a traded high-technology cluster are more than three times more likely to grow, and local businesses register a 64 percent growth probability penalty. In column (3), the inclusion of a dummy for whether the firm registers in Delaware has several effects. First, and most importantly, Delaware registration is associated with more than forty times increase in the probability of growth (we once again caution that this effect is not causal, but instead helps identify firms whose underlying potential both makes them more likely to register in Delaware and more likely to realize a growth outcome). At the same time, the inclusion of the Delaware dummy reduces the measured penalty associated with eponymy and being associated with a local business name, and reduces the boost associated with being in a high-technology cluster. Interestingly, the pseudo-R^2 increases from 11 percent to 31 percent with the inclusion of the Delaware dummy. The specification in column (3) is particularly interesting since these data rely only on information directly observable from the registration record, and so in principle can be observed on a nearly real-time basis for the purposes of a nowcasting version of EQI.

In column (4), we move toward incorporating measures that capture key early milestone achievements for a start-up that might serve as informative signals for their likelihood of entrepreneurial success. Events such as the assignment of a patent, a patent or trademark application, or mention in the media can only occur once the venture has been launched, but might occur in a timely enough manner to still provide information for the purposes of entrepreneurial quality estimation (particularly for EQI applications in which we would like to examine particular regions and places on an historical basis). Model 4 includes two measures of intellectual property. Since the patent and Delaware indicators are highly correlated (62 percent of patenting firms are also registered in Delaware), we separate the effect into distinct interaction components. Having a patent increases the likelihood of growth forty times, and Delaware firms are forty times more likely to achieve growth. Interestingly, the combined effect (131.9) is smaller than the joint product of the individual effects. Finally, a firm with an early trademark is more than three times more likely to grow. Importantly, the business registration coefficients remain similar in magnitude and statistical significance to the results in column (3). Model 5 includes one additional measure,

Table 2.3   Logit regression on growth (IPO or acquisition in six years or less)

	Firm business registration data			Lagged measures		Other measures	
	1	2	3	4	5	6	7
Corporation	5.471***	5.155***	8.863***	8.065***	7.872***	7.880***	7.885***
	[1.288]	[1.222]	[2.174]	[1.994]	[1.948]	[1.952]	[1.953]
Short name	4.207***	3.840***	2.693***	2.454***	2.373***	2.372***	2.372***
	[0.595]	[0.539]	[0.393]	[0.365]	[0.355]	[0.355]	[0.355]
Eponymous	0.0568***	0.0639***	0.132***	0.145**	0.143***	0.143***	0.143***
	[0.0330]	[0.0371]	[0.0776]	[0.0850]	[0.0826]	[0.0826]	[0.0826]
Delaware			42.63***				
			[5.876]				
Delaware patent interactions							
Patent only				40.36***	39.98***	40.00***	40.00***
				[13.48]	[13.26]	[13.26]	[13.26]
Delaware only				40.38***	38.33***	38.33***	38.33***
				[6.100]	[5.864]	[5.861]	[5.860]
Patent and Delaware				131.9***	116.3***	116.2***	116.3***
				[26.20]	[23.84]	[23.79]	[23.79]
Trademark				3.369***	3.383***	3.382***	3.386***
				[0.990]	[1.005]	[1.004]	[1.006]
Mentioned in *Boston Globe*					5.742***	5.747***	5.738***
					[1.518]	[1.516]	[1.508]

Founder effects							
Repeat entrepreneurship						0.931	0.855
						[0.507]	[0.533]
High tech. repeat entrepreneurship							1.496
							[1.972]
US Cluster Mapping Groups							
Local		0.323***	0.636	0.718	0.726	0.726	0.726
		[0.0884]	[0.181]	[0.206]	[0.209]	[0.209]	[0.209]
Traded		1.119	1.033	1.115	1.133	1.134	1.134
		[0.145]	[0.137]	[0.150]	[0.154]	[0.153]	[0.154]
Traded resource intensive		0.415***	0.642*	0.655*	0.640*	0.640*	0.638*
		[0.0863]	[0.135]	[0.137]	[0.133]	[0.133]	[0.134]
Traded high technology		3.971***	2.197***	1.748***	1.783***	1.782***	1.773***
		[0.606]	[0.349]	[0.286]	[0.293]	[0.293]	[0.292]
Observations	223,307	223,307	223,307	223,307	223,307	223,307	223,307
Pseudo-R^2	0.064	0.090	0.277	0.302	0.310	0.310	0.310
Log-likelihood	−2,320.6	−2,258.1	−1,792.7	−1,731.7	−1,712.1	−1,712.1	−1,712.0

Note: Exponentiated coefficients; standard errors in brackets.

***Significant at the 0.1 percent level.

**Significant at the 1 percent level.

*Significant at the 5 percent level.

Mentioned in Boston Globe, which captures whether the start-up was mentioned in the business section of the primary Massachusetts newspaper within the first year after registration. Media is associated with more than a five times increase in the probability of growth, and the coefficients associated with the other variables remains similar.

Finally, columns (6) and (7) include two measures to capture the impact of serial entrepreneurship—one based on whether at least one of the founders has ever been associated with a Massachusetts start-up before, and the other interacting that measure with our high-technology cluster variable. Though the direction of each of these measures is as predicted, neither is significant nor large (relative to many of the other coefficients in these regressions). We should emphasize that, since we require that the serial entrepreneur maintains their address between the two ventures, we may be not yet capturing and tracking serial entrepreneurship in a meaningful way. Identifying more precise and nuanced information from founders is an important agenda for future research using this methodology.

Overall, these regressions offer striking indicators of the relationship between observable start-up characteristics and the realization of growth. There is dramatic variation in the estimated probability of growth for individual firms. For example, using the estimates from column (5), comparing the growth probability of a Delaware corporation with a patent and trademark (116.3 * 3.4 * 7.9) to a Massachusetts LLC without intellectual property yields an odds-ratio of 3,097:1.[22] Importantly, the overall results accord well with Guzman and Stern (2015), which uses the same methodology on California data: if supported by further evidence from other states and jurisdictions going forward, the stable nature of the markers of entrepreneurial quality provide an important foundation for the creation of robust economic statistics in this area.

Candidate Specification Choice and Evaluation. Before turning to the calculation of our indices and exploration of our nowcasting and placecasting applications, we first investigate whether it is possible to identify a preferred benchmark candidate specification that we can use as our basis for entrepreneurial quality estimation going forward. To do so, we first compare models that include or exclude specific sets of regressors using a standard likelihood ratio test. Specifically, in each row of table 2.4, we compare the likelihood function (as well as differences in pseudo-R^2; McFadden [1974]) between two models, one of which (M) is nested in the other (N). For the first five rows (where we introduce different combinations of restricted and unrestricted specifications), we can reject the null hypothesis associated with the restricted model. In other words, regardless of which variables we include

22. More dramatically, at the (near) extreme, comparing the growth probability of a Delaware corporation with a patent (7.8 * 116.3), trademark (3.4), media mention (5.7), and noneponymous short name (6.9 * 2.4) with an eponymous partnership or LLC with a long name but no intellectual property or media mentions, the odds-ratio is 295,115 to one!

Table 2.4   Likelihood ratio test comparing different models

Restricted model		Unrestricted model		$R_{M,N}$ (%)	Critical $p <$ .01 value	LR value
Model (M)	Log-likelihood	Model (N)	Log-likelihood			
Business registration information without Delaware	−2,258.1	Business registration information	−1,792.7	20.61	6.63	930.80***
Business registration information	−1,792.7	Intellectual property and business registration	−1,731.7	3.40	13.28	122.00***
Business registration information without Delaware	−2,258.1	Intellectual property and business registration without Delaware	−2,094.01	7.27	9.21	328.18***
Intellectual property and business registration	−1,731.7	Media, IP, and business registration	−1,712.1	1.13	6.63	39.20***
Only Delaware registration	−1,978.9	Media, IP, and business registration	−1,712.1	13.48	23.21	533.54***
Media, IP, and business registration	−1,712.1	Media, IP, business registration, and founder effects	−1,712.0	0.01	9.21	0.20

***Significant at the 0.1% level.

first, we find significant explanatory effects from the Media, IP, and full range of Business Registration measures. However, regardless of specification, we find no robust effects associated with our founder measures. As such, for the remainder of our analysis, we adopt (table 2.3, column [5]) as our preferred specification in evaluating our estimator.

We then evaluate our estimates using the 30 percent test sample of observations, which have not been used in the estimation but for which we observe both the growth outcome and start-up characteristics. In particular, using only data from the test sample (but relying on the estimates from table 2.3, column [5] to estimate entrepreneurial quality), figure 2.1 presents the relationship between the distribution of realized growth events versus the distribution of firm-level entrepreneurial quality. The results are striking; 77 percent of all growth firms are in the top 5 percent of our estimated growth probability distribution, and 49 percent are within the top 1 percent (interestingly, these results are extremely similar to the findings for California from Guzman and Stern [2015]). To be clear, growth is still a relatively rare event even among the elite: the average firm within the top 1 percent of estimated entrepreneurial quality has only a 14 percent chance of realizing a growth outcome.

As well, we evaluate whether our results are driven by the particular sample that was drawn for the training sample. This is particularly relevant as growth is rare in our data set (only 462, or 0.14 percent) and several of our measures are also relatively rare (e.g., less than 1 percent of all firms patent or receive a trademark). To evaluate whether our sampling matters, we repeat the process of separating out the sample into a training and test sample 100 times, implement table 2.3, column (5) with each draw to estimate entrepreneurial quality for each firm in that draw's test sample, and then calculate a test statistic that is equal to the number of realized growth outcomes in the test sample, which we estimate to be in the top 5 percent of the estimated quality distribution. Relative to our baseline sample result of 77 percent, the mean of this test statistic is 79 percent (with a 95 percent confidence interval between 73 percent and 84 percent). At least within the overall Massachusetts sample in this chapter, our estimates of entrepreneurial quality are robust to the sample that we draw.

2.5   Calculating Entrepreneurial Quality and Performance Indices

We now turn to the centerpiece of our analysis: the calculation of EQI and RECPI at different levels of geographic agglomeration and across time in order to evaluate a number of different placecasting and nowcasting applications. We now incorporate the full sample of Massachusetts firms from 1988 through 2012, and so include the part of the prediction sample for which we can observe the full set of start-up characteristics (recall that our

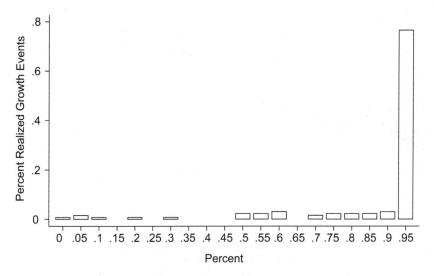

Fig. 2.1   Estimated entrepreneurial quality percentile versus incidence of realized growth outcomes (30 percent 1988–2005 test sample)

baseline candidate, table 2.3, column [5], involves a two-year lag between founding date and the incorporation of early patenting, trademark, and media data).

We begin with the calculation of RECPI for the state of Massachusetts for each year between 1988 and 2012. In figures 2.2A and 2.2B, we compare the realized level of growth events (per start-up cohort) with two different entrepreneurship indices: a simple measure of entrepreneurial quantity (the number of newly registered businesses for that cohort) versus RECPI, which scales the number of registered businesses by the EQI for those businesses for each cohort year. While there appears to be no correlation between the realized growth events from a cohort and entrepreneurial quantity, there is a much closer relationship with RECPI, where we are incorporating entrepreneurial quality. RECPI grows at a rapid rate from 1991 to 2000 (with a very large spike in 1999–2000) and then falls dramatically (along with the realized level of exits between 2001 and 2004). From 2004 to 2012, Massachusetts RECPI has increased by approximately 17 percent. Intriguingly, as we discuss in the conclusion (and consistent with the emphasis on investment cycles and start-up dynamics by Nanda and Rhodes-Kropf 2013), the notable divergence between realized growth events and RECPI is coincident with the rapid rise and collapse of the early stage risk capital market in the late 1990s: realized growth events were much "higher" than predicted for the 1995–1998 cohorts, essentially on target for the 1999 cohort, and much lower for all subsequent cohorts.

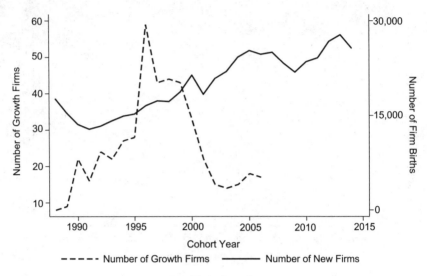

Fig. 2.2A   Growth firms versus firm births by cohort

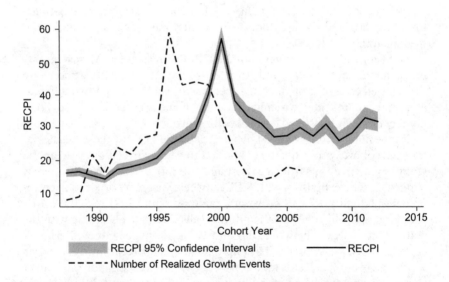

Fig. 2.2B   Regional Entrepreneurship Cohort Potential Index (RECPI)
Note: The RECPI standard error estimated through Penrose square root law (i.e., $\sigma_{RECPI} = \sigma_{EQI} * \sqrt{(N)}$).

2.5.1   Placecasting Entrepreneurial Quality

We now turn to a set of placecasting applications where we calculate EQI and RECPI for different regions in Massachusetts (and during different time periods); in order to illustrate the range of potential applications with these tools, we begin at a relatively aggregate level of geographic scope and then focus in on much more granular analyses (i.e., we move from the state to the city to the neighborhood to the individual address level). We begin in figure 2.3, where we calculate EQI for all firms registered in each of 351 distinct municipalities in Massachusetts from 2007 to 2012. Though this map completely abstracts away from quantity (EQI is simply the average quality for each town), there is a striking concentration of quality around the Boston metropolitan area. Relative to an average EQI for the state of 0.8, Cambridge records the highest level of average quality at 5.7 (i.e., the average firm founded in Cambridge has a 5 in 1,000 chance in realizing growth, which is nearly eight times higher than an average firm in Massachusetts). Cambridge is followed by a cluster of cities around the northwest section between the Route 128 and 495 corridors, including Bedford, Waltham, Burlington, Lexington, and Woburn. Maynard (the founding town for DEC Computers) ranks seventh with an EQI of 3.4. Though by far the largest city in Massachusetts (and the clear leader in the total number of business registrations), Boston ranks 23rd in the state with an EQI of 2.0 between 2007 and 2012. Though quality is highly concentrated around Boston, there are clusters of entrepreneurial quality around different parts of the Commonwealth, including Amherst, Foxborough, and Beverly. Importantly, quality is in the bottom half of the distribution in several former industrial cities, including Worcester. Finally, quality is consistently low in popular vacation destinations such as Cape Cod, Martha's Vineyard, and the Berkshires.

These overall patterns of concentrated quality hold more generally over time. In figure 2.4, we calculate EQI for the five largest counties in Massachusetts (associated with more than 95 percent of all growth outcomes) between 1988 and 2012. Over the past twenty-five years, Middlesex County (which includes both Cambridge and many of the key Route 128 towns) has held a distinctive advantage in EQI, with a more recent period of convergence with Suffolk County (i.e., Boston). Within this broad pattern, there are striking dynamics among entrepreneurial clusters within Boston. In figure 2.5, we plot RECPI for three distinct areas: the Route 128 corridor (which we define as Waltham, Burlington, Lexington, Lincoln, Concord, Acton, and Wellesley), Cambridge, and Boston. During the 1990s, Route 128 contained the highest level of RECPI, even though the combined populations of the Route 128 cities are only 29 percent of the total population of Boston. Over the past decade, there has been a dramatic shift in overall entrepreneurial leadership in the Boston area. Cambridge now outpaces both Boston and the Route 128 corridor, though both Boston and Cambridge experienced

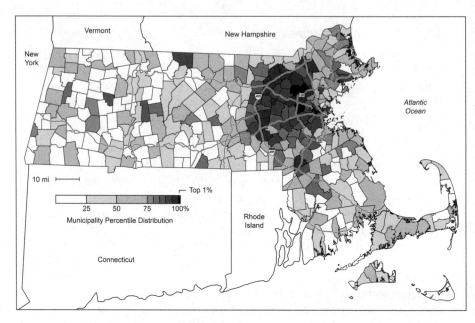

Fig. 2.3 Entrepreneurial quality in Massachusetts by municipality (2007–2012)

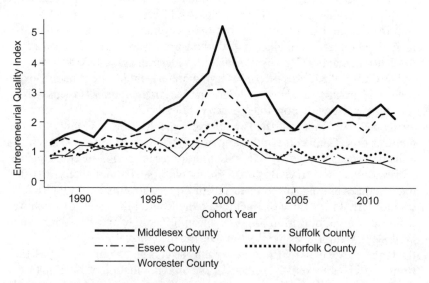

Fig. 2.4 Entrepreneurship Quality Index (EQI) by county (top five counties of thirteen total [95 percent of growth outcomes])

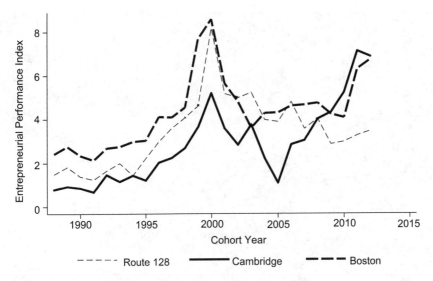

Fig. 2.5   RECPI for select cities (Route 128 versus Cambridge versus Boston)

a significant estimated increase in RECPI between 2009 and 2012. These changes are consistent with more qualitative accounts: a range of media and academic commentators have highlighted the rise of Cambridge as a hub of high-growth entrepreneurship (Katz and Wagner 2014), and our estimates provide direct evidence for this phenomena and also suggest that this rise is not simply the result of a localized expansion of risk capital, but instead reflects an increase in the intrinsic quality of start-ups within Cambridge relative to more suburban locations.

We further enhance the granularity of our analysis in figure 2.6, where we calculate EQI for each ZIP Code in the Boston metropolitan area for the 2007–2012 period. Here we can see that, even within cities such as Cambridge or Boston, there is considerable heterogeneity: Kendall Square (02142) registers the single-highest level of EQI in the state, followed by the ZIP Code associated with the Harvard Business School (02163). Other notable areas of entrepreneurial quality include the area surrounding the Boston Innovation District (02210), as well as a set of ZIP Codes along the Route 128 corridor surrounding Lincoln Laboratories, as well as the remaining ZIP Codes within Cambridge. Wealthy residential districts such as Newton, Brookline, and Weston are associated with lower levels of average entrepreneurial quality.

Looking over time at a comparison between MIT/Kendall Square (02142), the area surrounding Harvard University (02138 and 02163) and the Boston Seaport area (which now includes the Boston Innovation District [02210]), we see that each of these areas registered a similar level of entrepreneurial

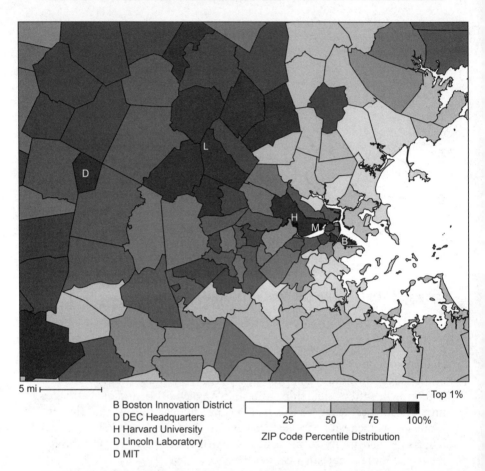

Fig. 2.6   Entrepreneurial quality in the greater Boston area by ZIP Code (2007–2012)

quality in the late 1980s and early 1990s. However, beginning around 1994, the MIT/Kendall Square area began to experience a significant and sustained rise in average entrepreneurial quality, and (contra the overall pattern of risk-capital financing) actually reached its highest level (in terms of an average) in 2003. The average for the MIT/Kendall Square area again increased over the second half of the last decade and experienced a very sharp increase in 2011 and 2012. A higher level of stability is observed in the Harvard and Seaport District, though the Seaport District registers a significant rise starting in 2010, coincident with the establishment of the Boston Innovation District in this area by Mayor Thomas Menino. While the rise of the MIT/Kendall Square area has been much discussed (Katz and Wagner 2014), it is nonetheless striking to see the impact of this sustained pattern of economic on the geography of entrepreneurial quality (see figure 2.7).

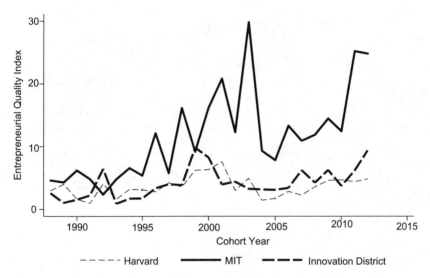

Fig. 2.7 Boston-area growth neighborhoods (MIT, Harvard, and Boston Innovation District)

We further refine our analysis and illustrate the potential of our approach by examining the microgeography of entrepreneurial quality at the level of individual addresses. Figure 2.8 shows the complete set of new business registrants between 2008 and 2012 in the three ZIP Codes adjacent to MIT: 02139, 02141, and 02142. For each address where at least one start-up registers, we include a circle whose radius is proportional to the number of business registrants, and whose color is determined by the average level of entrepreneurial quality at that location. The results are striking, with a very significant level of variation across individual addresses. Across these two square miles, the average level of entrepreneurial quality (weighted by address) is 6.0 but the median is 0.1, reflecting a highly skewed distribution. On the one hand, the area around Central Square and Cambridgeport (to the north and west of MIT) are characterized by a large number of addresses with a very small number of start-up events, each of which is estimated to have a low level of quality (with EQI registering at 0.1 and lower for the majority of individual addresses). While there are some addresses in Central Square and Cambridgeport registering significant levels of entrepreneurial quality (particularly along Massachusetts Avenue), these are dwarfed by the intensive concentration of entrepreneurial quality (both in terms of EQI and RECPI at each location) that immediately surrounds the Kendall Square area (to the east of MIT). One Broadway, the home of the Cambridge Innovation Center, is home to 229 business registrants, with an average entrepreneurial quality score of 15. The Atheneum (215 1st Street, a space that includes dedicated wet lab space for life sciences companies) hosted fifteen

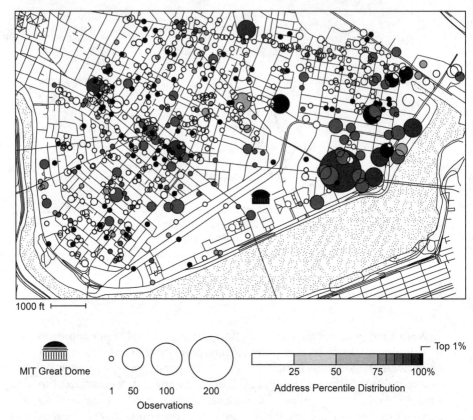

1000 ft ┝━━━━┥

MIT Great Dome

○ ◯ ◯ ◯

1   50   100   200
Observations

Address Percentile Distribution

25   50   75   100%

┌─ Top 1%

Fig. 2.8   Entrepreneurial quality and quantity in the MIT vicinity by individual address (2007–2012)

firms with an average entrepreneurial quality score of more than 70. While entrepreneurship is distributed across the MIT ecosystem, the cluster of world-class entrepreneurial quality surrounding MIT is concentrated in an even smaller geographic area.

2.5.2   Nowcasting Entrepreneurial Quality

While our placecasting applications offer significant insight into the geography or entrepreneurial quality and change in entrepreneurial quality over longer time periods, the development of a measurement approach for entrepreneurial quality for policymakers must be able to be calculated in a timely manner in order for it to be relevant and useful for policy decision making. Indeed, a contribution of our method is the ability to *predict* entrepreneurial quality for recent start-up cohorts (that have not yet realized growth outcomes or not) based on observable start-up characteristics. However, in our discussion of an estimation model in section 2.5, we prioritized the inclusion of start-up characteristics that allow us to differentiate between start-ups in nuanced ways rather than prioritizing the timeliness and ease of calculating entrepreneurial quality. Most notably, our key measures associated with intellectual property (either patents or trademarks) as well as our measure of media mentions are only observed with a lag. For example, in the case of patents, inclusion of a measure of whether a firm files a patent within one year after business registration necessitates a 2.5 year lag between business registration and the inclusion of that firm in an entrepreneurial quality estimate (since patent applications are not disclosed until eighteen months after filing). Alternatively, one could prioritize being able to calculate a perhaps more noisy estimate of entrepreneurial quality with real-time data that could be directly estimated from data available within the business registration record itself. In figures 2.9A, 2.9B, and 2.9C, we compare the patterns of indices that are based on EQI estimates that depend only on information directly observable from business registration records (i.e., based on table 2.3, column [3]) with our baseline index that allows for a two-year lag that allows the estimate of entrepreneurial quality to incorporate early milestones such as patent or trademark application or being featured in local newspapers (i.e., table 2.3, column [5]). In figure 2.9A, we simply compare the overall RECPI for Massachusetts based on our baseline index versus an index that explicitly prioritizes nowcasting. The results are intriguing: there is a very close relationship between the two through 2000, and, while there is divergence over time, the correlation between the two indices is very high through the end of 2012. Interestingly, Massachusetts continues to register an improving level of RECPI in 2013 and through November 24, 2014.[23]

We then turn in figures 2.9B and 2.9C to evaluate how our more granular analyses fare when comparing the baseline and nowcasting indices. In figure 2.9B, we revisit the comparison between Route 128, Cambridge, and Boston. On the one hand, nowcasting advantages Boston over these two other areas in terms of an overall ranking (presumably because Cambridge and Route 128 are associated with firms that are more focused on formal intellectual property). At the same time, beyond this level effect for Boston, the historical patterns are quite similar, with a clear transition of entrepreneurial leadership from Route 128 to Cambridge over time. Indeed, this gap sees to have only increased in the last two years. Finally, figure 2.9C compares three neighborhood clusters: MIT/Kendall Square, Harvard, and the Boston Innovation District. As in figure 2.9B, the overall historical patterns are similar, though the absolute size of the gap between the MIT area and the others is smaller. From a nowcasting perspective, the use of more recent data

23. For the sake of comparison, we scale the measure for 2014 by estimating the number of firms that will register from November 24 to December 31 in 2014 through an adjustment equivalent to the share of firms that were registered over these dates in 2013 (i.e., we multiply our estimate by 1.09).

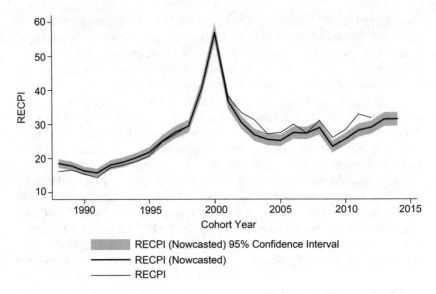

Fig. 2.9A   Nowcasted Massachusetts RECPI (RECPI standard error estimated through Penrose square root law [i.e., $\sigma_{RECPI} = \sigma_{EQI} * \sqrt{(N)}$])

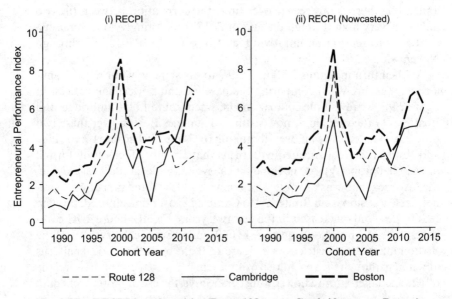

Fig. 2.9B   RECPI for select cities (Route 128 versus Cambridge versus Boston)

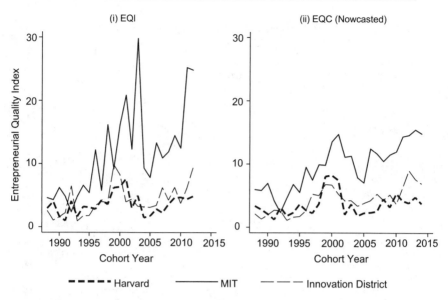

Fig. 2.9C   Nowcasted Boston-area growth neighborhoods (EQI) (MIT, Harvard, and Boston Innovation District)

documents the rise of the Boston Innovation District in a more sustained way, and only suggests that the rate of *new* firm formation may have slowed after a dramatic rise between 2010 and 2011 (presumably because the initial firms within the district created an bump during 2011).

2.5.3   Evaluating Entrepreneurial Quality and Performance

As a final exercise, we examine how our proposed measures perform in terms of predicting the number of realized growth events associated with a given regional cohort. In table 2.5, we perform a series of regressions in which the dependent variable is the number of Growth events per county-year, and examine various measures of entrepreneurship (and include county fixed effects to account for differences in county overall size and composition). In table 2.5, column (1), we simply examine a measure of quantity (ln [# of births]): the coefficient is small, noisy, and negative. In table 2.5, column (2), we employ churn, a standard measure of business dynamism (Decker et al. 2014) to examine the impact of this measure on the number of growth events within a county. Though positive, the coefficient is small and remains insignificant. Even taken at face value, the effect would be modest: doubling the level of churn would be associated with just an 8 percent increase in the total number of expected growth events. Turning to EQI, we find a far more encouraging result: EQI is not only statistically significant, but also associated with a meaningful increase in the realized number of growth events. Finally, RECPI is associated with a very large

Table 2.5   OLS regression on ln(growth) by cohort year and county

	1	2	3	4
Ln(# of births)	−0.0137 [0.0494] (−0.277)			
Ln(churn) *Churn = births + deaths*		0.0851 [0.0522] (1.629)		
Quality × *1,000 for readability*			0.234** [0.0609] (3.837)	
Ln(RECPI) *RECPI = quality × no. of births*				0.514** [0.168] (3.059)
County fixed effects	Yes	Yes	Yes	Yes
N	266	266	266	266
R^2	0.794	0.796	0.809	0.808

Note: Robust standard errors in brackets; *t*-statistics in parenthesis.
**Significant at the 1 percent level.
* Significant at the 5 percent level.

increase in the overall elasticity: doubling RECPI is associated with more than a 50 percent increase in the number of expected growth events in a region-cohort-year. Though we caution that we need to investigate this result further, it points to an important potential additional lens through which to utilize these tools: an important share of realized growth events are due to "intrinsic" factors observable at the time of founding, with other factors such as regional ecosystems, timing, and idiosyncratic factors playing separate roles. The variance decomposition of entrepreneurial growth remains an important topic for future research.

2.6   Conclusion

Motivated by the need to account directly for heterogeneity among entrepreneurial ventures, this chapter has developed and applied a methodology that allows for the estimation of entrepreneurial quality that facilitates both placecasting (identifying clusters of entrepreneurial quality without direct use of location information in the prediction) and nowcasting (forecasting the realized entrepreneurial quality of recent cohorts based on start-up characteristics, but in advance of realizing growth outcomes). We specifically introduce very preliminary exemplars for two new economic statistics—an Entrepreneurial Quality Index (EQI) and a Regional Entrepreneurship Cohort Potential Index (RECPI).

We believe that the general methodology offered here has the potential for application by policymakers and analysts. Given the possibility that entrepreneurial quality is a leading indicator for other outcomes in regional performance, tracking EQI would allow government analysts to measure and manage entrepreneurial quality, and so track entrepreneurial dynamics in a more proactive and informed way. Not simply a tool for direct measurement, our methodology further allows government organizations (e.g., the Small Business Administration) to design and evaluate interventions that focus on the quality of entrepreneurship rather than only increasing rates of firm formation, thus facilitating an approach that could potentially increase the impact of such interventions substantially.

While our approach is general in nature, both the nature of our approach and our specific implementation come with important limitations and assumptions. First, in terms of selectivity, our analysis assumes that entrepreneurs register their businesses (in some way) in a systematic way constant across time and locations (or at least within a state). While it is likely that some businesses are registered at different stages of their life cycle than others, we leave the timing of registration itself to future work. Second, we have focused entirely on an equity growth outcome, and we have not yet extended our analysis systematically to explore alternative growth outcomes, such as those associated with employment or revenue. Finally, while our start-up characteristics are highly informative (in the sense of prediction), we nonetheless do not have access to important (and potentially observable) measures such as precise industry codes or background information about the founders. Integrating our public data business registration approach with data covering individuals and establishments such as the Longitudinal Business Database (LBD) and Longitudinal Employer-Household Dynamics (LEHD) can provide a much more fine-grained assessment of the interplay between initial conditions and subsequent growth and is an important priority for future research.

Our approach also highlights the significant potential of business registration records, a data source that has been used sparingly and only in an aggregated form by economists. It is possible that the promise of business registration records for economic policy analysis would be significantly improved if these records required somewhat more granular information about the objectives of an enterprise (e.g., industry codes or founder addresses). From a more pedantic view, the lack of standardization and the uneven level and scope of digitization of business registration records remains a barrier to scaling business registration analysis across the entire United States.

While our focus in this chapter has been in the development and preliminary application of our methodology to address key challenges in the measurement of entrepreneurship, our results also highlight potential linkages with areas of theoretical or policy interest. For example, RECPI, our quantity-adjusted index, estimates the expected number of growth events from a cohort given its start-up characteristics, without accounting for regional effects or financial cycles. Thus, RECPI can be interpreted as the "potential" of a cohort of new firms given their intrinsic qualities. In close interplay with recent theory that relates changes in the *demand* for quality entrepreneurship to investment cycles dynamics (Nanda and Rhodes-Kropf 2013), our index documents substantial year-to-year changes in the *supply* of quality of entrepreneurship. The relationship is procyclical—cohorts increase in quality as the investment opportunities improve and the market gets "hotter." However, the realized performance of a cohort is affected by two opposing effects from the investment cycle: while later cohorts in the cycle have more intrinsic potential to generate growth, earlier cohorts have more time *in* the "hot" market (before a recession like the dot-com bust) to achieve it. The changing time dynamics of the *supply* of entrepreneurial quality and its interplay with regional outcomes is an open area of research.

Spatially, in similarity to previous results that find substantial agglomeration of innovation relative to overall industrial activity (Furman, Porter, and Stern 2002; Audretsch and Feldman 1996), we find entrepreneurial quality is substantially more concentrated than entrepreneurial quantity or population. While there are several potential reasons for this pattern, we find no reason to conclude any a priori, and thus suggest this as an interesting finding with potential for future research.

Finally, our results highlight the microgeography of the quality of entrepreneurship and suggest that clusters of entrepreneurial quality may benefit from being analyzed at a very low level of aggregation. In the spirit of recent work emphasizing the highly local nature of knowledge spillovers and the nuanced shapes of entrepreneurial clusters (Arzaghi and Henderson 2008; Kerr and Kominers 2014), examining the factors that shape the boundaries of high-quality entrepreneurship is an important area for future research.

Appendix

Massachusetts Business Registration Records

Business registration records are a potentially rich and systematic data source for entrepreneurship and business dynamics. While it is possible to found a new business without business registration (e.g., a sole proprietorship), the benefits of registration are substantial, including limited liability, protection of the entrepreneur's personal assets, various tax benefits, the ability to issue and trade ownership shares, credibility with potential customers, and the ability to deduct expenses. Among business registrants, there are several categories, and the precise rules governing each category vary by jurisdiction and time. This study focuses on the state of Massachusetts from 1988 to 2014, at which point one could register the following: corporations, limited liability companies, limited liability partnerships, limited partnerships, professional limited liability partnerships, and general partnerships.

The data in this chapter comes from the Secretary of the Commonwealth of Massachusetts, Corporations Division[24] containing four files: a master file, containing a master record for all firms ever registered in Massachusetts at the moment of extraction; an individuals' file, containing all the directors and titles of each firm; a name history file, with previous names of each firm; and a merger history file, with all mergers that have occurred in Massachusetts. The master file includes the following fields: firm ID, tax status (nonprofit or for profit), firm type (corporation, limited liability company, etc.), firm status (active, deceased, merged, etc.), jurisdiction (Massachusetts or another US state), address, firm name, Massachusetts incorporation date, jurisdiction incorporation date (for foreign firms), address of the principal office (for firms foreign to Massachusetts), and Doing Business As names. The individual file includes the following fields: firm ID, title, first name, middle name, last name, business address, and residential address.

After combining these files, we generate unique firm identifiers. For this chapter, we select a data set of the for-profit firms first registered in Massachusetts from January 1, 1988, to November 25, 2014, satisfying one of the following two conditions: for-profit firms whose jurisdiction is Massachusetts and for-profit Delaware firms whose main office is in Massachusetts. Table 2A.1 lists the number of observations in our data set for each annual cohort year from 1988 to 2014. It is useful to note that, for those firms registered in Delaware we use the year they register in Delaware, not in Massachusetts, as their founding date. Both the links to the underlying data and the program files used to construct the data set are available as requested from the authors.

As a final note, this chapter uses a subset of the business registration records we have now gathered from several states, including California, Texas, Florida, Washington, and New York. Though our evaluation of Texas, Florida, Washington, and New York is at a more preliminary stage, we have found very similar qualitative findings in terms of the impact of factors observable at or near the time of registration on subsequent growth outcomes, and the ability of these models to offer detailed characterization of growth entrepreneurship clusters.

---

24. http://www.sec.state.ma.us/cor/coridx.htm; data received on November 27, 2014.

Table 2A.1   **Number of observations per year**

Year	N^a	Share of total (%)	Cumulative share (%)
1988	17,613	3.3	3.3
1989	15,390	2.8	6.1
1990	13,601	2.5	8.6
1991	12,838	2.4	11.0
1992	13,333	2.5	13.4
1993	14,173	2.6	16.1
1994	14,903	2.8	18.8
1995	15,242	2.8	21.6
1996	16,575	3.1	24.7
1997	17,320	3.2	27.9
1998	17,220	3.2	31.1
1999	18,742	3.5	34.5
2000	21,374	3.9	38.5
2001	18,351	3.4	41.8
2002	20,852	3.8	45.7
2003	21,962	4.1	49.8
2004	24,238	4.5	54.2
2005	25,284	4.7	58.9
2006	24,692	4.6	63.5
2007	25,014	4.6	68.1
2008	23,262	4.3	72.4
2009	21,841	4.0	76.4
2010	23,505	4.3	80.7
2011	24,120	4.5	85.2
2012	26,745	4.9	90.1
2013	27,787	5.1	95.3
2014[b]	25,689	4.7	100.0

[a]N is the number of observations after limiting the sample to for-profit firms registered in Massachusetts and for-profit firms registered in Delaware with their main office in Massachusetts.

[b]The year 2014 only includes firms up to those registered on November 24 of 2014.

Table 2A.2   **Share of entrepreneurship performance by region**

County	Share of entrepreneurship performance (%)	Share of firm births (%)
Middlesex County	49.0	29.3
Suffolk County	17.9	13.6
Norfolk County	10.2	13.4
Essex County	7.6	11.3
Worcester County	5.6	9.5
Plymouth County	3.0	7.1
Bristol County	2.3	5.1
Hampden County	1.7	4.4
Berkshire County	0.8	1.6
Hampshire County	0.7	1.4
Barnstable County	0.7	1.9
Nantucket County	0.2	0.6
Franklin County	0.1	0.5
Dukes County	0.1	0.4

Table 2A.3   Ranking of entrepreneurial quality by city

Rank	City	Quality	Rank	City	Quality	Rank	City	Quality
1	CAMBRIDGE	5.772	62	TAUNTON	1.080	123	COHASSET	0.721
2	BEDFORD	4.666	63	NEWBURYPORT	1.071	124	GEORGETOWN	0.721
3	WALTHAM	4.448	64	SOUTHBRIDGE	1.068	125	MARION	0.719
4	BURLINGTON	4.320	65	WEST BRIDGEWATER	1.053	126	RUSSELL	0.716
5	LEXINGTON	4.051	66	PAXTON	1.049	127	WESTMINSTER	0.709
6	WOBURN	3.397	67	SHERBORN	1.044	128	STURBRIDGE	0.705
7	MAYNARD	3.392	68	SHARON	1.024	129	NORTHAMPTON	0.697
8	BOXBOROUGH	2.936	69	TOPSFIELD	1.020	130	ROCKPORT	0.695
9	FOXBOROUGH	2.707	70	PELHAM	1.017	131	LAKEVILLE	0.688
10	LINCOLN	2.617	71	CHESTER	1.016	132	BARNSTABLE	0.688
11	HOPKINTON	2.574	72	NORWELL	1.005	133	SHEFFIELD	0.682
12	ANDOVER	2.470	73	ROCKLAND	1.004	134	WASHINGTON	0.679
13	LITTLETON	2.448	74	MEDWAY	0.998	135	SCITUATE	0.675
14	SOUTHBOROUGH	2.433	75	NEW BRAINTREE	0.996	136	LEOMINSTER	0.674
15	BILLERICA	2.433	76	AYER	0.978	137	CHELSEA	0.670
16	MARLBOROUGH	2.422	77	MEDFORD	0.974	138	WAREHAM	0.668
17	CHELMSFORD	2.400	78	NEWBURY	0.964	139	ESSEX	0.663
18	WESTFORD	2.351	79	WORTHINGTON	0.951	140	HARDWICK	0.660
19	WESTBOROUGH	2.259	80	WINCHESTER	0.938	141	CHICOPEE	0.657
20	ACTON	2.219	81	ALFORD	0.938	142	WEST TISBURY	0.655
21	BOLTON	2.023	82	BRAINTREE	0.930	143	SWAMPSCOTT	0.653
22	WAKEFIELD	2.022	83	LUNENBURG	0.926	144	GROVELAND	0.652
23	BOSTON	1.984	84	MARBLEHEAD	0.920	145	IPSWICH	0.644
24	WILMINGTON	1.913	85	PEABODY	0.917	146	WRENTHAM	0.640
25	HOLLISTON	1.896	86	BOXFORD	0.916	147	PLAINVILLE	0.639
26	WELLESLEY	1.879	87	GRAFTON	0.912	148	RANDOLPH	0.634
27	NEWTON	1.852	88	AMESBURY	0.911	149	CONWAY	0.632
28	CONCORD	1.852	89	ADAMS	0.895	150	SALEM	0.620
29	SUDBURY	1.811	90	LENOX	0.893	151	NEW BEDFORD	0.619
30	CARLISLE	1.798	91	DEDHAM	0.888	152	STONEHAM	0.618

31	NATICK	1.782	92	NORTH ANDOVER	0.888	153	AUBURN	0.615
32	WATERTOWN	1.620	93	LEYDEN	0.881	154	GARDNER	0.615
33	BEVERLY	1.592	94	SAVOY	0.878	155	HALIFAX	0.614
34	ROYALSTON	1.591	95	WALPOLE	0.874	156	HAVERHILL	0.614
35	STOW	1.581	96	ASHLAND	0.874	157	MIDDLETON	0.609
36	NEEDHAM	1.578	97	MILLIS	0.871	158	ORLEANS	0.604
37	GOSHEN	1.573	98	WILLIAMSTOWN	0.867	159	WINCHENDON	0.601
38	MANSFIELD	1.535	99	HUBBARDSTON	0.861	160	SHREWSBURY	0.601
39	HUDSON	1.527	100	TYRINGHAM	0.861	161	FALL RIVER	0.600
40	WENHAM	1.475	101	YARMOUTH	0.854	162	NORTON	0.599
41	AMHERST	1.442	102	SANDISFIELD	0.849	163	HANOVER	0.599
42	FRAMINGHAM	1.433	103	GLOUCESTER	0.845	164	WILBRAHAM	0.599
43	NORTHBOROUGH	1.418	104	LOWELL	0.839	165	TOWNSEND	0.598
44	CANTON	1.417	105	UPTON	0.839	166	ASHBURNHAM	0.597
45	BROOKLINE	1.380	106	MILFORD	0.836	167	PLYMOUTH	0.597
46	WESTWOOD	1.371	107	DUXBURY	0.829	168	NORTH READING	0.596
47	BELMONT	1.370	108	AVON	0.815	169	STOUGHTON	0.595
48	WAYLAND	1.333	109	PITTSFIELD	0.809	170	RAYNHAM	0.591
49	WESTON	1.328	110	CHARLEMONT	0.808	171	MALDEN	0.587
50	TEWKSBURY	1.320	111	ATTLEBORO	0.807	172	WEST STOCKBRIDGE	0.585
51	HARVARD	1.316	112	READING	0.802	173	MELROSE	0.584
52	ARLINGTON	1.302	113	BELCHERTOWN	0.798	174	MASHPEE	0.582
53	SOMERVILLE	1.285	114	NORTHFIELD	0.786	175	MILLBURY	0.579
54	DALTON	1.262	115	LYNNFIELD	0.786	176	EASTON	0.576
55	DANVERS	1.227	116	BRIMFIELD	0.776	177	DUDLEY	0.575
56	NORWOOD	1.194	117	LAWRENCE	0.764	178	NORFOLK	0.573
57	DOVER	1.151	118	FITCHBURG	0.755	179	ROWLEY	0.572
58	FRANKLIN	1.085	119	WORCESTER	0.736	180	METHUEN	0.567
59	GROTON	1.085	120	AGAWAM	0.736	181	CLINTON	0.565
60	MEDFIELD	1.082	121	QUINCY	0.733	182	PALMER	0.565
61	BERLIN	1.081	122	HINGHAM	0.728	183	NEW ASHFORD	0.563

(continued)

Table 2A.3   (continued)

Rank	City	Quality	Rank	City	Quality	Rank	City	Quality
184	STERLING	0.560	240	WEBSTER	0.434	296	DARTMOUTH	0.311
185	SANDWICH	0.552	241	PETERSHAM	0.432	297	MONTEREY	0.310
186	WEYMOUTH	0.549	242	MERRIMAC	0.431	298	DIGHTON	0.310
187	HOPEDALE	0.545	243	DUNSTABLE	0.430	299	FLORIDA	0.309
188	MILTON	0.542	244	BARRE	0.429	300	NEW MARLBOROUGH	0.307
189	FALMOUTH	0.541	245	LANCASTER	0.429	301	CHESHIRE	0.306
190	LEE	0.539	246	WARE	0.428	302	BLACKSTONE	0.305
191	SUNDERLAND	0.538	247	MANCHESTER-BY-THE-SEA	0.422	303	LEVERETT	0.302
192	WESTFIELD	0.538	248	EAST LONGMEADOW	0.421	304	ORANGE	0.301
193	KINGSTON	0.538	249	BERNARDSTON	0.417	305	BUCKLAND	0.299
194	HULL	0.534	250	NEW SALEM	0.408	306	ACUSHNET	0.297
195	WEST SPRINGFIELD	0.533	251	GREAT BARRINGTON	0.406	307	WELLFLEET	0.293
196	LONGMEADOW	0.532	252	WESTPORT	0.406	308	SHUTESBURY	0.293
197	DOUGLAS	0.525	253	TYNGSBOROUGH	0.403	309	CLARKSBURG	0.291
198	MILLVILLE	0.523	254	CHILMARK	0.402	310	BECKET	0.290
199	HOLYOKE	0.523	255	LUDLOW	0.401	311	AQUINNAH	0.287
200	HOLBROOK	0.517	256	BROCKTON	0.401	312	CHESTERFIELD	0.284
201	SPRINGFIELD	0.516	257	SUTTON	0.400	313	BROOKFIELD	0.284
202	HANSON	0.515	258	LYNN	0.399	314	HINSDALE	0.281
203	OXFORD	0.514	259	HARWICH	0.398	315	PRINCETON	0.278
204	WESTHAMPTON	0.511	260	DRACUT	0.398	316	EAST BRIDGEWATER	0.277
205	ROCHESTER	0.511	261	SOUTH HADLEY	0.397	317	PHILLIPSTON	0.271
206	MONTAGUE	0.509	262	HADLEY	0.390	318	COLRAIN	0.265
207	REHOBOTH	0.509	263	FAIRHAVEN	0.389	319	NORTH ATTLEBOROUGH	0.264
208	WEST BROOKFIELD	0.506	264	CARVER	0.389	320	RICHMOND	0.262
209	SOUTHWICK	0.502	265	CHARLTON	0.389	321	ERVING	0.256
210	MARSHFIELD	0.494	266	PLYMPTON	0.388	322	EGREMONT	0.256

#	Name	Value	#	Name	Value	#	Name	Value
211	EASTHAMPTON	0.490	267	BRIDGEWATER	0.387	323	HUNTINGTON	0.253
212	BOURNE	0.488	268	WARREN	0.386	324	OAKHAM	0.252
213	WEST NEWBURY	0.487	269	EASTHAM	0.382	325	OAK BLUFFS	0.252
214	BELLINGHAM	0.485	270	WHITMAN	0.382	326	MOUNT WASHINGTON	0.249
215	MENDON	0.484	271	NANTUCKET	0.382	327	BERKLEY	0.246
216	TRURO	0.480	272	EVERETT	0.382	328	GILL	0.245
217	SALISBURY	0.479	273	LEICESTER	0.379	329	LANESBOROUGH	0.243
218	RUTLAND	0.478	274	NAHANT	0.378	330	WHATELY	0.241
219	DENNIS	0.477	275	UXBRIDGE	0.374	331	TEMPLETON	0.235
220	BOYLSTON	0.477	276	MATTAPOISETT	0.370	332	NORTH BROOKFIELD	0.235
221	PEPPERELL	0.476	277	CHATHAM	0.368	333	BLANDFORD	0.234
222	REVERE	0.471	278	HAWLEY	0.367	334	WARWICK	0.234
223	ATHOL	0.469	279	WINTHROP	0.364	335	ASHFIELD	0.232
224	PEMBROKE	0.467	280	SOUTHAMPTON	0.357	336	CUMMINGTON	0.228
225	SAUGUS	0.466	281	GREENFIELD	0.353	337	OTIS	0.228
226	DEERFIELD	0.464	282	HAMILTON	0.348	338	PLAINFIELD	0.227
227	NORTH ADAMS	0.462	283	STOCKBRIDGE	0.348	339	WINDSOR	0.218
228	TISBURY	0.460	284	HATFIELD	0.347	340	TOLLAND	0.218
229	MONSON	0.457	285	WILLIAMSBURG	0.339	341	GRANVILLE	0.215
230	ABINGTON	0.454	286	WENDELL	0.339	342	SHELBURNE	0.212
231	SOMERSET	0.449	287	NORTHBRIDGE	0.335	343	HEATH	0.211
232	SHIRLEY	0.449	288	WALES	0.328	344	MONTGOMERY	0.210
233	PROVINCETOWN	0.448	289	BREWSTER	0.328	345	HANCOCK	0.204
234	SWANSEA	0.446	290	SEEKONK	0.326	346	ROWE	0.199
235	EAST BROOKFIELD	0.446	291	ASHBY	0.324	347	PERU	0.193
236	HOLDEN	0.444	292	WEST BOYLSTON	0.322	348	FREETOWN	0.189
237	SPENCER	0.442	293	GRANBY	0.316	349	MIDDLEFIELD	0.146
238	MIDDLEBOROUGH	0.437	294	HAMPDEN	0.316			
239	EDGARTOWN	0.437	295	HOLLAND	0.315			

References

Aghion, Philippe, and Peter Howitt. 1992. "A Model of Growth through Creative Destruction." *Econometrica* 60 (2): 323–51.

Amorós, José E., and Neils Bosma. 2014. "Global Entrepreneurship Monitor: 2013 Executive Report." Babson College and London Business School. http://www .babson.edu/Academics/centers/blank-center/global-research/gem/Documents /GEM%202013%20Global%20Report.pdf.

Arzaghi, Mohammad, and J. Vernon Henderson. 2008. "Networking of Madison Avenue." *Review of Economic Studies* 75 (4): 1011–38.

Audretsch, David B., and Maryann P. Feldman. 1996. "R&D Spillovers and the Geography of Innovation and Production." *American Economic Review* 86 (3): 630–40.

Balasubramanian, Natarajan, and Jagadeesh Sivadasan. 2010. "NBER Patent Data-BR Bridge: User Guide and Technical Documentation." CES Working Paper no. 10-36, Center for Economic Studies, US Census Bureau.

Barnes, Beau, Nancy Harp, and Derek Oler. 2014. "Evaluating the SDC Mergers and Acquisitions Database." Available at SSRN: https://ssrn.com/abstract=2201743.

Belenzon, Sharon, Aaron Chatterji, and Brendan Daley. 2014. "Eponymous Entrepreneurs." Working Paper, Duke University. https://sites.duke.edu/ronniechatterji /files/2014/07/EE_Full_June27_Final_wAuthors.pdf.

Davis, Steven, and John Haltiwanger. 1992. "Gross Job Creation, Gross Job Destruction, and Employment Reallocation." *Quarterly Journal of Economics* 107 (3): 819–62.

Decker, Ryan, John Haltiwanger, Ron Jarmin, and Javier Miranda. 2014. "The Role of Entrepreneurship in US Job Creation and Economic Dynamism." *Journal of Economic Perspectives* 28 (3): 3–24.

Delgado, Mercedes, Michael Porter, and Scott Stern. 2015. "Defining Clusters in Related Industries." *Journal of Economic Geography* 16 (5). http://joeg.oxford journals.org/content/early/2015/06/02/jeg.lbv017.

Furman, Jeffrey, Michael Porter, and Scott Stern. 2002. "The Determinants of National Innovative Capacity." *Research Policy* 31:899–933.

Glaeser, Edward L., Sari Pekkala Kerr, and William R. Kerr. 2014. "Entrepreneurship and Urban Growth: An Empirical Assessment with Historical Mines." *Review of Economics and Statistics* 97 (2): 498–520.

Guzman, Jorge, and Scott Stern. 2015. "Where is Silicon Valley?" *Science* 347 (6222): 606–09.

Haltiwanger, John. 2012. "Job Creation and Firm Dynamics in the United States." *Innovation Policy and the Economy* 12 (April): 17–38.

Hamilton, Barton. 2000. "Does Entrepreneurship Pay? An Empirical Analysis on the Returns to Self-Employment." *Journal of Political Economy* 108 (3): 604–31.

Hathaway, Ian, and Robert Litan. 2014a. "Declining Business Dynamism in the United States: A Look at States and Metros." Economic Studies at Brookings, Brookings Institution. https://www.brookings.edu/research/declining-business -dynamism-in-the-united-states-a-look-at-states-and-metros/.

———. 2014b. "Declining Business Dynamism: It's For Real." Economic Studies at Brookings, Brookings Institution. https://www.brookings.edu/research/declining -business-dynamism-its-for-real/.

Hurst, Erik, and Benjamin Pugsley. 2011. "What Do Small Businesses Do?" *Brookings Papers on Economic Activity* 2011 (2): 73–118.

Kaplan, Steven N., and Josh Lerner. 2010. "It Ain't Broke: The Past, Present, and Future of Venture Capital." *Journal of Applied Corporate Finance* 22 (2): 36–47.

Katz, Bruce, and Julie Wagner. 2014. "The Rise of Innovation Districts: A New Geography of Innovation in America." Brookings Institution, Metropolitan Policy Program. https://c24215cec6c97b637db6-9c0895f07c3474f6636f95b6bf3db 172.ssl.cf1.rackcdn.com/content/metro-innovation-districts/~/media/programs /metro/images/innovation/innovationdistricts2.pdf.

Kerr, William, and Shihe Fu. 2008. "The Survey of Industrial R&D—Patent Database Link Project." *Journal of Technology Transfer* 33 (2): 173–86.

Kerr, William, and Scott Kominers. 2015. "Agglomerative Forces and Cluster Shapes." *Review of Economics and Statistics* 97 (4): 877–99.

Kerr, William, Ramana Nanda, and Matthew Rhodes-Kropf. 2014. "Entrepreneurship as Experimentation." *Journal of Economic Perspectives* 28 (3): 25–48.

Klapper, Leora, Raphael Amit, and Mauro Guillen. 2010. "Entrepreneurship and Firm Formation across Countries." In *International Differences in Entrepreneurship*, edited by Josh Lerner and Antoinette Schoar. Chicago: University of Chicago Press.

Kortum, Samuel, and Josh Lerner. 2000. "Assessing the Contribution of Venture Capital to Innovation." *RAND Journal of Economics* 31 (4): 674–92.

Kuznets, Simon. 1941. *National Income and Its Composition, 1919–1938*, vol. I. New York: National Bureau of Economic Research.

Levenshtein, V. I. 1965. "Binary Codes Capable of Correcting Deletions, Insertions, and Reversals." *Doklady Akademii Nauk SSSR* 163 (4): 845–48.

Levine, Ross, and Yona Rubinstein. 2013. "Smart and Illicit: Who Becomes an Entrepreneur and Does it Pay?" NBER Working Paper no. 19276, Cambridge, MA.

McFadden, Daniel. 1974. "Conditional Logit Analysis of Qualitative Choice Behavior." *Frontiers in Econometrics*, chapter 4, 105–42. Amsterdam: Academic Press.

Nanda, Ramana, and Matthew Rhodes-Kropf. 2013. "Investment Cycles and Startup Innovation." *Journal of Financial Economics* 110 (2):403–18.

———. 2014. "Financing Risk and Innovation." HBS Working Paper no. 11–013, Harvard Business School, Harvard University. http://www.hbs.edu/faculty/Pages /item.aspx?num=49551.

Pohlman, John, and Dennis Leitner. 2003. "A Comparison of Ordinary Least Squares and Logistic Regression." *Ohio Journal of Science* 103 (5): 118–25.

Reister, Shane. 2014. "Why We Should Actively Track and Measure Startup Communities." In *Kauffman Thoughtbook 2015—Entrepreneurship: New Directions for a New Era*. Accessed December 2014. http://www.kauffman.org/thoughtbook2015 /paths-to-entrepreneurship#startupcommunities.

Schoar, Antoinette. 2010. "The Divide between Subsistence and Transformational Entrepreneurship." *Innovation Policy and the Economy*, vol. 10, edited by Josh Lerner and Scott Stern. Chicago: University of Chicago Press.

Schumpeter, Joseph A. 1942. *Capitalism, Socialism, and Democracy*. New York: Harper.

Taddy, Mathew. 2013. "Big Data Analysis." Lecture on NBER Summer Institute: Econometric Methods for High-Dimensional Data. http://www.nber.org /econometrics_minicourse_2013/bigecon.pdf.

Wealth, Tastes, and Entrepreneurial Choice

Erik Hurst and Benjamin W. Pugsley

3.1 Introduction

What drives small business entry? Why do most firms stay small while only a few grow fast? What explains the distribution of firm size within a country? There is a large and active literature trying to answer these questions. The canonical models of business formation segment the population into "entrepreneurs" and "workers" where entrepreneurs are often equated with either small business owners or the self-employed. Most of the existing research attributes differences across entrepreneurs with respect to ex post performance to either differences in financing constraints facing the firms (e.g., Evans and Jovanovic 1989; Clementi and Hopenhayn 2006),

Erik Hurst is the V. Duane Rath Professor of Economics at the University of Chicago Booth School of Business and a research associate of the National Bureau of Economic Research. Benjamin W. Pugsley is an economist in the Macroeconomic and Monetary Studies Function at the Federal Reserve Bank of New York.

We would like to thank Fernando Alvarez, Jaroslav Borovicka, Patrick Kline, Augustin Landier, Josh Lerner, E. J. Reedy, Jim Poterba, Sarada, Andrei Shleifer, Mihkel Tombak, and seminar participants at Boston College, the 2011 Duke/Kauffman Entrepreneurship Conference, the Federal Reserve Bank of Minneapolis, Harvard Business School, the Institute for Fiscal Studies, 2011 International Industrial Organization Conference, London School of Economics, MIT, NBER 2010 Summer Institute Entrepreneurship Workshop, Penn State, Stanford University, University of Chicago, and the 2014 NBER/CRIW Conference on Entrepreneurship for their comments on an earlier version of this chapter. Hurst gratefully acknowledges financial support from the Ewing Marion Kauffman Foundation. Pugsley gratefully acknowledges financial support from the Ewing Marion Kauffman Foundation dissertation fellowship. Any opinions and conclusions expressed herein are those of the author(s) and do not necessarily represent the views of the US Census Bureau, the Federal Reserve Bank of New York, or the Federal Reserve System. All results have been reviewed to ensure that no confidential information is disclosed. For acknowledgments, sources of research support, and disclosure of the authors' material financial relationships, if any, please see http://www.nber .org/chapters/c13498.ack.

differences in ex post productivity draws across the firms (e.g., Simon and Bonini 1958; Jovanovic 1982; Pakes and Ericson 1998; Hopenhayn 1992), or differences in entrepreneurial ability of the firms' owners (e.g., Lucas Jr. 1978). These models, however, assume no heterogeneity in preferences for either small business ownership or small business growth.

Even though the canonical models of entrepreneurship assume away preference heterogeneity in the population, recent empirical work suggests that such heterogeneity is an important feature of the data. For example, Hurst and Pugsley (2011) document that roughly 50 percent of small business owners within the United States report that nonpecuniary benefits were one of the primary reasons that they started their business.[1] These self-reported nonpecuniary benefits included responses such as "wanting to be my own boss," "tired of working for others," "wanting flexibility to set my own hours," or "wanting to pursue my passion." Hurst and Pugsley (2011) also show that most small business owners report having no desire to grow their business. When asked about their ideal firm size, the median response of new business owners is that they desire their business to only have at most a few employees. Moreover, those reporting that they started their business for nonpecuniary reasons were much more likely than a group motivated by a new business idea to report that their ideal firm size was small. This is not surprising given that the overwhelming majority of small business owners in the United States are skilled craftsmen (e.g., plumbers, electricians, painters), skilled professions (e.g., lawyers, dentists, accountants, insurance agents), or small shopkeepers (e.g., dry cleaners, gas stations, restaurants).

Additionally, there is a large literature showing that the median small business owner earns less as a business owner than she would have earned had she remained a wage or salary worker. Using data from the Survey of Income and Program Participation, Hamilton (2000) documents that the median small business owner receives lower accumulated earnings over time than otherwise comparable wage and salary earnings. Pugsley (2011) expands on Hamilton's findings, showing that these patterns persist for both newly formed businesses as well as older small businesses (those in existence for at least a decade). Moskowitz and Vissing-Jørgensen (2002) document that the returns to investing in private equity (predominantly business ownership) are no higher than the returns to investing in public equity, despite the additional undiversifiable risk.[2] Collectively, these papers suggest that

1. Respondents in the Panel Study of Entrepreneurial Dynamics were asked to report the top two reasons they started their business. Hurst and Pugsley classified these responses into five broad categories: nonpecuniary benefits was one of the categories.

2. Measurement issues surrounding income reports by the self-employed complicate such analyzes. Hurst, Li, and Pugsley (2014), for example, show that the self-employed underreport their income by roughly 25 percent to household surveys. Moskowitz and Vissing-Jørgensen (2002) incorporate the fact that business owners underreport their income when computing the differential returns to private equity.

nonpecuniary benefits may explain why the total compensation for running a small business (risk-adjusted) is much lower for the median small business owner relative to remaining a wage/salary worker.

In this chapter, we craft a simple static model of small business entry with selection on the nonpecuniary benefits of small business ownership. The key element in the model is that individuals differ in their preference for owning a small business, and these preferences are the sole drivers of small business entry within the model. To highlight the mechanism, we assume away the standard forces that researchers usually use to model small business entry and growth. For example, individuals in the model do not differ in either their latent ability to create a new business nor do they differ in their ex post productivity. Furthermore, we assume that capital is not needed to start a new business. As a result, there is no role for liquidity constraints to affect small business entry. In that sense, our model should be viewed as being in a similar style to Evans and Jovanovic (1989), who also develop a deliberately stylized model to study an alternative mechanism for selection of entrants. The difference is that Evans and Jovanovic focused on differences in ability across entrepreneurs and the role of binding liquidity constraints. We, instead, focus solely on preference heterogeneity with respect to nonpecuniary benefits for small business ownership. As we show, many of the key predictions of these two stylized models are identical.

While wanting to highlight the economic effects of nonpecuniary benefits, we do feel there are benefits from adding two additional degrees of heterogeneity to our setup. First, like Evans and Jovanovic (1989), we allow households to differ with respect to their initial wealth. Second, we allow for different industries where each industry is defined by its natural scale. Some industries (e.g., car manufacturing) have large fixed costs and, as a result, a large natural scale. Other industries (e.g., plumbers) have relatively small fixed costs and, as a result, a smaller natural scale. The heterogeneity across sectors in their natural scale will yield predictions about what sectors will be dominated by small businesses within our model. When entrepreneurs form a business they are more likely to do so in sectors with a relatively low natural scale. This is because the key trade-off within the model stems from the benefits the individual gets (in utility terms) from starting her own business relative to the costs imposed from having a small business and losing the benefits of scale.

With these simple features, we show our model yields many key empirical facts without relying on differences in entrepreneurial ability, differences in entrepreneurial luck, or binding liquidity constraints. First, we show that the model predicts that people with large nonpecuniary benefits of small business formation will be concentrated in industries with low natural scale. This results from our assumption that nonpecuniary benefits do not depend on industry or the scale of the business. The intuition is that individuals will want to get their nonpecuniary benefits in the industry with the lowest costs. In these industries small businesses will also have a competitive advantage because of their implicit lower pecuniary marginal costs. This matches evidence showing a strong correlation between an industry's share of small businesses (out of all small businesses) and the fraction of employment within that industry that occurs within small businesses. For example, a large fraction of small businesses (out of all small businesses) are skilled craftsmen. Within the detailed skilled craftsmen industries, most employment occurs within small businesses. There are very few big firms in the plumber, electrician, and painter industries. However, there are many old firms in the plumber, electrician, and painter industries. Reconciling these two facts is the finding that very few firms in the skilled craftsmen industries ever grow beyond being small (conditional on survival).

Second, the model predicts that earnings will be lower for those who run a small business. Equilibrium forces imply that individuals must be indifferent between working for others or starting their own business. Since at the margin there is a utility flow from owning a business, pecuniary earnings must be lower for small business owners. Again, the fact that small business owners earn less than comparable wage/salary workers seems to be a feature of the data for the median small business owner.

We also show that our model predicts a positive correlation between small business ownership and wealth even though there are no binding liquidity constraints, differences in risk preferences, or ex ante correlation of tastes and initial wealth. The reason for this is that we are modeling the utility flow of owning a business as being separable from the rest of the individuals' consumption bundle. As wealth increases, the marginal utility of the rest of the consumption bundle falls. The cost of running a small business in our model is the foregone market wage less the business's pecuniary earnings. This cost must always be positive in an equilibrium with a small business sector. When wealth is higher, the marginal utility loss from the lower pecuniary earnings is lower. This makes the cost of running a business, in utility terms, lower. To put it another way, our model generates that owning a business is a relative luxury good. In a world with nonpecuniary benefits, there could be a strong correlation between wealth (or exogenous changes in wealth) and business ownership that have nothing to do with binding liquidity constraints. This complicates the inferences made in many empirical studies that look for exogenous changes in wealth and subsequent business entry as evidence of binding liquidity constraints.

Related to the above findings, we show that labor productivity within the economy is declining the greater the level of nonpecuniary benefits in the economy. If there are reasons people prefer the small business sector, there are pecuniary costs to a society in that individuals will forego the benefits of scale to enter the small business sector. This can offer one potential reason why measured labor productivity differs dramatically between countries with differing sizes of the small business sector.[3] However, in a world with nonpecuniary benefits of small business ownership, labor productivity differences need not imply utility differences.

Finally, and potentially most provocatively, the model predicts that small business subsidies in this model—funded by lump sum taxes—are regressive. There are no distortions in our model, so it is not surprising that small business subsidies strictly reduce welfare. However, because of the fact that wealthy people are more likely to buy the utility flow of small business ownership, the subsidies are regressive. More wealthy individuals are small business owners than poor individuals. The subsidy on small business ownership just transfers resources to the wealthy from the poor. The net gain to the wealthy relative to the poor is strictly positive if the taxes to fund the subsidy are lump sum. The regressivity could be undone if the taxes paid to fund the subsidy also increase in household wealth.

We are well aware that our model is highly stylized and abstracts from many features we believe to be relevant with respect to small business formation. However, our goal is to highlight how a simple model of nonpecuniary benefits of small business ownership has predictions that are similar to many canonical models used in the literature that rely on heterogeneity in ability, luck, or liquidity constraints to explain small business entry and dynamics. In the last section of the chapter, we set out a road map for researchers by offering some guidance on new moments that can be used to help discipline the various forces within our model. We then talk about how we can improve measurement to better create empirical counterparts to the moments needed to test among the importance of the various potential drivers of small business ownership and growth. For example, a key prediction that distinguishes nonpecuniary benefits from the other stories is the size of the wage difference between wage/salary workers and small business owners. Researchers can use these gaps as additional moments to help calibrate the average size of the nonpecuniary benefits from small business ownership. However, much additional work needs to be done to measure these gaps empirically. In particular, one needs to account for the potential that business owners may underreport their income, the fact that business income is more volatile, and the fact that employers often provide additional fringe benefits to workers.

In summary, we think researchers should take seriously the potential for nonpecuniary benefits of small business ownership when crafting models of small business entry and firm dynamics. There seems to be a belief by some that small businesses would only grow faster if they were not bound by liquidity constraints or government regulations. This is likely true for some small businesses. However, if people are starting small businesses for nonpecuniary reasons, subsidies to small business owners may actually be welfare reducing. We also show that under some conditions, the subsidies

---

3. See, for example, La Porta and Shleifer (2014).

will be regressive. The benefits of the subsidy will go to the wealthier households who were more likely to buy the utility flow of running a business. Understanding the relative importance of different drivers of small business formation and growth will allow researchers and policymakers to assess the potential costs and benefits of different policies.

3.2   Empirical Facts

In this section, we establish a set of facts that will help to guide our modeling choices below.

3.2.1   Heterogeneity in Small Business Propensity across Industries

To establish our first set of facts, we use data from the US Census Longitudinal Business Database (LBD). The LBD is a complete annual census of US business establishments with paid employees that spans the years 1976 to 2011. Establishments are linked to their parent firm through both survey and administrative records within a year. Then the data are longitudinally linked by both establishment and firm identifiers across years in order to measure entry, growth, and exit.[4] While the LBD files are available for each year at the establishment level, we transform the data so the unit of observation is at the year and firm level.

We follow the approach adopted in the US Census Business Dynamic Statistics (BDS) and assign the firm's age as the age of its oldest establishment. For industry information, we assign a four-digit North American Industry Classification System (NAICS) industry code to each firm. For multiunit firms, we assign the firm's "industry" as the modal industry classification across all of the firm's establishments.[5] Our sample pools annual firm-level employment measures from 1992 to 2011 for all firms with nonmissing employment data. Because firm age is left censored in 1976, 1992 is the first year where we can identify firm age through age fifteen.

For the work below, we classify each firm in year t by its size, s, age, a, and four-digit industry, j. We define small firms as those employers with between one and nineteen employees.[6] This category accounts for roughly 20 percent of all US business employment. We then consider three mutually exclusive age groups: "young" firms ages zero to five, "middle" firms ages six to nine, "older" firms ages ten to fifteen, and an additional category for all remaining

4. See Jarmin and Miranda (2002) for details on the construction of the LBD.
5. We used the procedure in Fort and Klimek (2016) to map standard industrial classification (SIC) industry codes to NAICS industry codes. In Fort's procedure, some of the four-digit industries cannot be mapped between the NAICS and SIC categories. These industries are mapped at higher levels of aggregation (two digit or three digit). We collapse these unmatched categories into a single cell.
6. Our results are robust to defining small firms as having less than fifty or less than one hundred employees. We focus on firms with less than twenty employees for consistency with the results in Hurst and Pugsley (2011).

firms over age fifteen. Using the year/firm files, for each year we compute the total number of firms, n_{jast}, and employment, e_{jast}, within each four-digit industry, age, and size group.

We are interested in, at a detailed level, an industry's link with small businesses, and we propose two alternative measures of an industry's small business orientation. First we measure a four-digit industry's firm or employment share of all small businesses or small business employment. To do this, for each industry j we define the following:

$$x_j^m = \frac{1}{T}\Sigma_{t=1}^T \frac{\Sigma_a m_{j,a,\text{small},t}}{\Sigma_j \Sigma_a m_{j,a,\text{small},t}},$$

where m is either a measure of employment, e, or a measure of the number of firms, n. For example, x_j^n is the number of small firms (of any age) in four-digit industry j as a share of the total number of small businesses regardless of age or industry, averaged over the sample period of 1992 to 2011. Analogously, x_j^e is the total number of employees in small firms (of any age) in four-digit industry j as a share of all employment in small businesses regardless of age or industry. Generically, x_j^m provides a measure to identify the most important industries among small businesses. We also define two additional measures computed for only young or older small businesses:

$$x_{j,a=\text{young}}^m = \frac{1}{T}\Sigma_{t=1}^T \frac{m_{j,a=\text{young},s=\text{small},t}}{\Sigma_j m_{j,a=\text{young},s=\text{small},t}}$$

$$x_{j,a=\text{older}}^m = \frac{1}{T}\Sigma_{t=1}^T \frac{m_{j,a=\text{older},s=\text{small},t}}{\Sigma_j m_{j,a=\text{older},s=\text{small},t}}$$

For example, $x_{j,a=\text{young}}^e$ is industry j's share of total young small firm employment.

Whereas our first measure captures the concentration of an industry among small businesses, our second type of measure captures the concentration of small businesses within an industry. We define as y the fraction of employment (firms) in small businesses in industry j out of all employment (firms) in industry j regardless of size. Formally,

$$y_j^m = \frac{\Sigma_a m_{j,a,s=\text{small}}}{\Sigma_s \Sigma_a m_{j,a,s}},$$

where the denominator is total employment, $m = e$, or total number of firms, $m = n$, in industry j across firms of all sizes and ages. As above, we can further define $y_{j,a=\text{young}}^e$ and $y_{j,a=\text{older}}^e$ as the share of employment among small firms ages zero to five and ages ten to fifteen in industry j out of all industry j firms within each respective age group.

These industry measures need not be the same. The first measure identifies the most important industries for the small business sector. The second measure identifies the industries with a high concentration of small businesses. It is possible that large industries, even with a relatively small share of small businesses, may still be important for the small business sector if they are sufficiently large.

Figure 3.1 analyzes the first measure and plots the cumulative distribution of x_j^n (on the y-axis) against the industry rank of x_j^n. For example, the four-digit industry with the largest share of small firms out of all small firms is residential building construction. This industry would get a rank of 1. This four-digit industry comprises roughly 3.5 percent of all firms with less than twenty employees. As seen in figure 3.1, roughly twenty-five four-digit industries in the United States comprise one-half of all firms with less than twenty employees. Hurst and Pugsley (2011) list the top forty four-digit industries that represent over 60 percent of all firms with less than twenty employees. Essentially all of these firms are skilled craftsmen (builder, plumbers, painters, electricians), skill professionals (doctors, dentists, accountants, lawyers, real estate agents, insurance agents) and small shopkeepers (dry cleaners, restaurants, grocery stores, bars, gas stations).

The patterns in figure 3.1 persist with firm age. Figure 3.2, panel A,

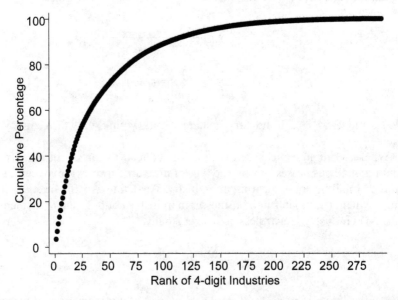

Fig. 3.1   Cumulative distribution of x_j^n (on the y-axis) against the industry rank of x_n^j

Notes: We select all firms with up to twenty employees. These firms are grouped by their four-digit NAICS industry code. There are 295 such industries. Industries are then ranked by the average fraction of small businesses (out of all small businesses) that are in each industry. A rank of 1 means that industry had the largest fraction of small businesses (out of all small businesses). The rank is then plotted against the cumulative percentage of small businesses (out of all small businesses) in an industry of a given rank.

A. Cumulative distribution by age group

B. Industry ranks of young versus old firms

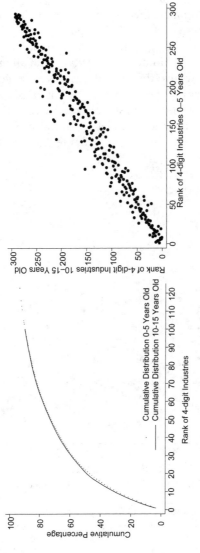

Fig. 3.2 Comparing cumulative distribution and rank of x_j'' by age group

Notes: We select all firms with up to twenty employees. These firms are grouped by their four-digit NAICS industry code and age group (zero to five years old and ten to fifteen years old). For each age group, industries are then ranked by the average fraction of small businesses (out of all small businesses) that are in each industry. A rank of 1 means that industry has the largest fraction of small businesses (out of all small businesses). The rank is then plotted against the cumulative percentage of small businesses (out of all small businesses) in an industry of a given rank. The figure plots the 100 industries with the highest fraction of small businesses ages ten to fifteen years (out of all small businesses ages ten to fifteen years).

replicates figure 3.1 for young firms and older firms separately. The cumulative distributions are nearly on top of each other. Of course in this plot, the industry rank is not held fixed across firm age groups, and one may worry that industry's ranks are shifting as firms age. Figure 3.2, panel B, shows that this is not the case. The figure plots the rank of $x_{j,a=\text{young}}^{n}$ against the rank of $x_{j,a=\text{older}}^{m}$. Industries that dominate the distribution of small young businesses also dominate the distribution of small older businesses.

Figure 3.3 plots the rank of $x_{j,a=\text{young}}^{n}$ (x-axis) against the level of y_{j}^{n} (y-axis), that is, it plots industries that dominate the share of small businesses (out of all small businesses) are also the same industries for which small firms dominate employment within the industry. The relationship is essentially monotonic. Most small businesses are skilled craftsmen, skilled professionals, and small shopkeepers. These industries are also ones where most employment is in small firms. For example, figure 3.3 says that in the ten

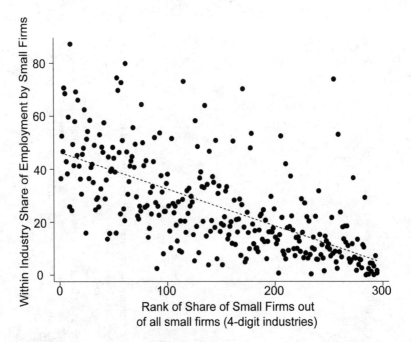

Fig. 3.3   Rank of young firms versus level of y_{j}^{e}

Notes: Firms are grouped by their four-digit NAICS industry code, age group, and size. For each age group (ages zero to five and ages ten to fifteen) we computed the percentage of small firms (up to twenty employees) in a given industry out of all firms in that industry y_{h}^{e} and the percentage of each industry's small firms out of all small firms x_{j}^{e}. For concerns regarding the disclosure rules of the Census Bureau, we trimmed the sample of industries to those with fractions between percentile 2.5 and 97.5. For the sample industries, the figure plots the percentage of small firms (up to twenty employees) in a given industry out of all firms in that industry, for firms ages zero to five years and ages ten to fifteen years. The line represents the 45-degree line.

most prevalent industries among small businesses, small firms account for anywhere from roughly 40 to 90 percent of each industry's employment.

Figure 3.4 compares $y^e_{j,a=\text{young}}$ (x-axis) against $y^e_{j,a=\text{older}}$ (y-axis). In words, the x-axis measures the share of employment in industry j that is in small young firms out of all young firms, while the y-axis measures the share of employment in industry j (this is in small older firms out of all older firms). Again, there is a strong amount of persistence within industries as firms age. For example, the skilled craftsmen have essentially between 60 and 80 percent of employment in small firms when they are young. Those same industries have between roughly 60 and 80 percent of employment in small firms when they are older. These results add to the results in Hurst and Pugsley (2011), showing that most small firms never grow. Put another way, even among older firms, there are still many small firms. In some industries, small firms employ most of the workers in the industry regardless of firm age.

Finally, figure 3.5 plots the log of the average size in the industry when the firm was young (x-axis) against the log difference in industry size between when the industry was older (ten to fifteen years) and young (zero to five

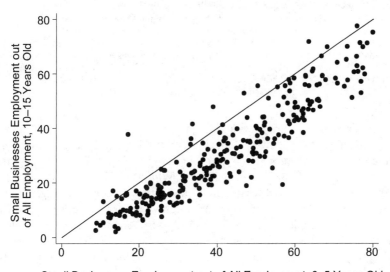

Fig. 3.4   Small business share of total industry employment for young versus old firms

Notes: Firms are grouped by their four-digit NAICS industry code, age group, and size. For each age group (ages zero to five years and ages ten to fifteen years) we computed the percentage of employment by small firms (up to twenty employees) in a given industry out of the employment of all firms in that industry. For concerns regarding the disclosure rules of the Census Bureau, we trimmed the sample of industries to those with fractions between percentile 2.5 and 97.5. For those industries, the figure plots the percentage of employment by small firms (up to twenty employees) in a given industry out of all employment in that industry, for firms ages zero to five years and ages ten to fifteen years. The line represents the 45-degree line.

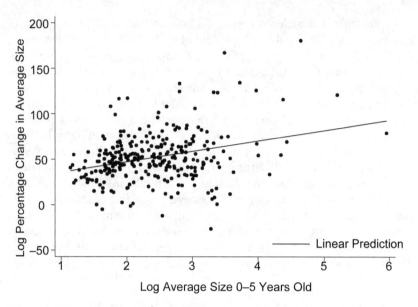

Fig. 3.5   Industry average size and conditional growth rate

Notes: Firms are grouped by their four-digit NAICS industry code, age group, and size. For each age group (ages zero to five years and ages ten to fifteen years) and industry, we computed the average size as total employment divided by total number of firms. The y-axis is the difference in logs between firms ages ten to fifteen years and firms ages zero to five years, multiplied by 100. The x-axis is the average size (logs) of young firms. Each dot represents that relation for each four-digit NAICS industry code. The line represents the linear fit of the log percentage change of size and the average size of young firms (ages zero to five).

years). The relationship shows a slight increasing relationship between initial size and subsequent growth. If the industry had relatively large firms when young it was much more likely to grow than industries with smaller firms when young. This figure is in growth rates. What this also implies is that most industries that are small when young never grow by any meaningful measure. For example, if the industry had roughly seven employees when young (such that log employment was roughly 2), ten years later average employment in that industry was roughly eleven employees (a 50 percent increase in employment). Again, this is consistent with the fact that most small firms do not grow and that these nongrowing small firms are concentrated in a narrow industries.

The results in figures 3.1–3.5 will motivate some of our modeling choices in the next section. In particular, the model will incorporate different industries. Industries will be defined by their natural scale. As a result, some industries will have small natural scale (e.g., plumbers) while other industries will have larger natural scale (e.g., manufacturers). Even though our model is static, the results in figures 3.1–3.5 also suggest that firms in small-scale industries are less likely to grow as they age.

3.2.2   The Importance of Nonpecuniary
Benefits in Small Business Formation

For our second set of facts, we review the work in Hurst and Pugsley (2011). Using data from the Panel Study of Entrepreneurial Dynamics II (PSED), Hurst and Pugsley show that the median small business reports starting their business for nonpecuniary reasons. The PSED started with a nationally representative sample of 31,845 individuals. An initial screening survey in the fall of 2005 identified 1,214 "nascent entrepreneurs." To be considered a nascent entrepreneur, individuals had to meet the following four criteria. First, the individual had to currently consider himself or herself as involved in the firm creation process. Second, he or she had to have engaged in some business start-up activity in the past twelve months. Third, the individual had to expect to own all or part of the new firm being created. Finally, the initiative, at the time of the initial screening survey, could not have progressed to the point that it could have been considered an operating business. The goal was to sample individuals who were in the process of establishing a new business.

In the winter of 2006, after the initial screening interview, these 1,214 respondents were surveyed about a wide variety of activities associated with their business start-up. They were asked detailed questions about their motivations for starting the business, the activities they were currently undertaking as part of the start-up process, the competitive environment in which the business would operate, and their expectations about the desired future size and activities of the business. Follow-up interviews occurred annually for four years, so that the data also have a panel dimension.

As part of the initial survey of the PSED, the business owners were asked, "Why do (or did) you want to start this new business?" Respondents could report up to two motives. The respondents provided unstructured answers, which the PSED staff coded into forty-four specific categories. We took the raw responses to the question and created five broad categories of our own: nonpecuniary reasons, reasons related to the generation of income, reasons related to the desire to develop a new product or implement a good business idea, reasons related to a lack of better job options, and all other reasons. The main responses in the nonpecuniary category include "want to be my own boss," "flexibility/set own hours," "work from home," and "enjoy work, have passion for it/hobby." The main responses in the generating income category include "to make money" or "need to supplement income." The main responses in the new product or business idea category include "satisfy need," "there is high demand for this product/business," "untapped market," and "lots of experience at work."

Hurst and Pugsley (2011) document that roughly 50 percent of all respondents reported nonpecuniary benefits as being one of the primary reasons they started their business. The second most common response (38 percent) was the respondent had a good business idea. The fraction who reported nonpecuniary benefits as the primary reason to start the business was consistent across different subsamples of PSED respondents. For example, for those firms that remained in business through 2010 (four years after the first interview), 52 percent reported that nonpecuniary benefits was a primary reason for starting their business. Hurst and Pugsley show that those that report nonpecuniary benefits as the primary reason for starting a business were less likely to actually grow, were less likely to report ex ante wanting to grow, were less likely to actually innovate along observable mentions, and were less likely to report ex ante wanting to innovate. There was variation in the extent to which nonpecuniary benefits were important across industries. For example, those entering retail trade industries were much more likely to report nonpecuniary benefits as a driver of their entry decision. Conversely, very few individuals who entered the manufacturing sector reported nonpecuniary benefits as a driver of their entry decision.

3.3 A   Model of the Small Business Sector

We propose a highly stylized model of the small business sector that matches key features of the data described in section 3.2 with few additional free parameters. In particular, we introduce nonpecuniary benefits from small business ownership into a static equilibrium model of occupational choice. As shown above, most business owners report nonpecuniary benefits as an important reason as to why they started their business, and in the model as an equilibrium outcome the small business sector will only be populated by people who start their business for nonpecuniary reasons.

To focus on the allocative role of nonpecuniary benefits, we make a number of additional abstractions. First, we ignore the dynamics of small business formation and growth. As discussed in section 3.2 and further in Hurst and Pugsley (2011), most small businesses just do not grow or have any intention to grow.[7] Second, we ignore financial market frictions. Hurst and Lusardi (2004) find that liquidity constraints do not appear to bind and that initial capital requirements for most businesses are quite low. Even without financial frictions, it will become clear that the consumption value of business ownership will imply a strong correlation between wealth and probability of business ownership. Finally, we abstract from differences in skill or comparative advantage. We treat all workers as equally capable employees or proprietors of their own businesses. Rather than as a realistic description of the labor market, we view these simplifications as a stepping off point to see how far we can go before needing to confront the more complex issues of skill sorting in a dynamic frictional labor market.

7. Eliminating dynamics and risk excludes pursuing a number of interesting questions, some of which Pugsley (2011) takes up in a dynamic model of entrepreneurship.

In the model, households differ only in their endowed wealth and their preference (if any) for running a business. They decide whether to use their labor to own and operate a business or instead to work as an employee in the corporate firm sector. If they decide to run a business, they also must decide what goods to sell among the many types of goods sold. Each good is produced using a technology with u-shaped average costs and goods differ by their efficient scale of production. Corporate firms can produce anything small businesses can produce using the same technology, but they are unconstrained in their ability to hire additional labor and may reach their efficient scale. We study an equilibrium where corporate firms and small businesses compete to sell each good and where in equilibrium each good is supplied by the firm offering the lowest price.

3.3.1   Intermediates and the Small Business and Corporate Sectors

There is a continuum of intermediate goods represented by the set $B = [\underline{b}, \overline{b}]$ with $\underline{b} > 0$. Each type of good b is characterized by the technology used to produce it, where b serves both as the good's name and as a parameter governing its minimum efficient scale of production, which increases with b.

Good b may be produced by either a corporate-owned firm or a household-owned small business using the technology

$$(1) \qquad f_b(n) = An^\theta - b.$$

where n represents the employment. With span of control parameter $\theta < 1$, the fixed cost b implies hump-shaped returns to scale, and because labor is the only factor of production, the scale of production may also be expressed in terms of its required employment n.[8] We label the natural scale (expressed in terms of employment) as n_b^*. In an equilibrium with a competitive market for good b, free entry will impose that $n_b = n_b^*$. We can locate this value by solving for the value of n that makes the elasticity of scale $[n f_b'(n) / f_b(n)]$ exactly equal to 1, so for $b > 0$

$$(2) \qquad n_b^* = \left(\frac{b}{A}\frac{1}{1-\theta}\right)^{1/\theta}.$$

If a plant were to operate at its natural scale n_b^*, then its marginal cost of production (and thus its market price) given wage w would be would be $w(b^{1-\theta} / A_\chi)^{1/\theta}$ where $\chi \equiv \theta^\theta (1-\theta)^{1-\theta}$.

The technology described by equation (1) for each b is available to both corporate and small business sectors. They differ only in their flexibility over choosing n.

Small Businesses Sector. If a household produces b as a small business, it

---

8. Here the fixed cost is paid in units of the intermediate good. Results are very similar using an alternative formulation with a fixed cost in terms of labor input $(An - b)^\theta$.

must set $n = 1$. This prevents household-owned and operated small businesses from reaching the minimum efficient scale for any $b > A(1 - \theta)$. Depending on the range of B, households producing goods where $b < A(1 - \theta)$ would be allocating too much time to the business. Although we later rule out this possibility by our choice of A, this situation may be more common than one initially thinks. Sole proprietors who do not pay themselves a market wage may allocate more of their own or family labor to their business than they would have hired at market rates. Regardless, given the requirement that $n = 1$ and facing a price schedule p_b, an entrepreneurial household who produces good b earns $p_b(A - b)$ as proprietor's income. For goods where $b > A$, the required fixed cost exceeds the small business owner's capacity to produce.

Corporate Sector. Corporate-owned plants are distinguished by being unconstrained in their choice of $n \geq 0$. For convenience, we refer to each corporate-owned plant as a corporate firm.[9]

3.3.2 Individual Good Demand

Demand for individual goods b comes from a competitive final good sector that combines intermediate inputs x_b to produce a final good

$$(3) \qquad C = \left(\int_B x_b^{(\sigma-1)/\sigma} db \right)^{\sigma/(\sigma-1)},$$

of the type described by Spence (1976) and Dixit and Stiglitz (1977) where σ represents the elasticity of substitution between inputs. A cost-minimizing final good sector implies conditional input demand functions for each intermediate good b such that:

$$(4) \qquad x_b(p_b) = C p_b^{-\sigma},$$

where p_b represents the price of good b. We use the final good as numeraire to normalize its price (and marginal cost) as 1.

3.3.3 Households and Nonpecuniary Benefits

There is a unit measure of households who differ in their endowed wealth, y, and in their "taste" for small business ownership γ. We label the joint distribution characterizing household heterogeneity as $F(\gamma,y)$. For simplicity, we assume that $\gamma \geq 0$, $y \geq 0$, and that both variables are independently distributed so that:

$$F(\gamma, y) = F(\gamma)F(y),$$

where $F(\gamma)$ and $F(y)$ represent the marginal distributions of taste and wealth heterogeneity. The independence assumption assures there is no relationship between wealth and entrepreneurial taste ex ante.

---

9. While the boundaries of the firm for a household-owned small business are clear, the boundaries in the corporate sector are not well defined. In practice, a corporate-owned firm could operate multiple plants in one or more individual good markets. We only require that there are a sufficient number of corporate firms to ensure individual good markets are competitive.

Households have preferences over consumption of a final good and whether or not they allocate their labor to running a business ordered by:

$$u = \log c + \gamma \mathbf{1}_e,$$

where c represents consumption of the Spence-Dixit-Stiglitz final good and $\mathbf{1}_e$ is an indicator that is 1 if the household runs a business and 0 otherwise.[10] Here γ has the interpretation of a taste for small business ownership or equivalently, in this context, a preference for not having a boss. For simplicity, we have assumed $\gamma \geq 0$, but this is clearly an innocuous assumption.

If a household chooses employment, it earns the market wage w. If instead it chooses to operate a small business and produce a particular good b it earns proprietor's income $p_b(A - b)$. Although households must choose a particular b, in an equilibrium, each entrepreneurial household will be indifferent among the set of goods produced by small businesses, and in anticipation this outcome we label the proprietor's income:

$$z \equiv p_b(A - b),$$

which does not depend on b.

Propensity to Choose Entrepreneurship. An individual household's labor supply is indivisible and equal to 1. Rogerson (1988) shows how the nonconvexity associated with indivisible labor supply produces equilibrium allocations that are not Pareto optimal. To restore optimality, he introduces lotteries over the labor supply decision that may be perfectly insured so that households may equalize consumption over either idiosyncratic outcome. We complete markets using the same procedure so that households of type γ choose a probability of business ownership e. The choice of e will represent both the probability of starting a business and the state-contingent price of consumption should the business start. Then $1 - e$ will represent the probability of the business not starting and the price of consumption for that contingency.[11] As in Rogerson (1988), optimizing households will equalize consumption across idiosyncratic outcomes and the problem is iso-morphic to choosing c and $e \in [0,1]$ to maximize

(5) $\log c + \gamma e$

subject to

---

10. Individuals only get the nonpecuniary benefit from running the business themselves. This is consistent with the fact from section 3.2 that the overwhelming majority of small businesses have very few employees, if any. The extreme form of the nonpecuniary benefits–that they accrue only if the firm has only one employee and that they are diversified completely away among corporately owned firms—is made for simplicity. We could write down a more flexible specification that let the nonpecuniary benefits decay as the number of employees increase without altering the main implications of the model.

11. This setup does not require there be a sufficient number of each type γ households. So long as markets are complete, each type γ household can insure against the idiosyncratic outcome of E.

(6) $c + (w - z)e = w + y.$

We write the budget constraint so w on the right-hand side has the interpretation of the full value of the household's time, and $w - z$ represents the pecuniary opportunity cost (if any) of running a small business. We will later show that $w - z$ is strictly positive in any equilibrium with a small business sector.

3.3.4 A   Competitive Two-Sector Equilibrium

We define an equilibrium where entrepreneurial households compete with firms to supply each good b, and the remaining worker households provide the labor required by the firms. The equilibrium features a cutoff $b^* \in [\underline{b}, \overline{b}]$, dividing B into goods produced by entrepreneur households and goods produced by firms.[12]

Definition 1.   Given a distribution $F(\gamma)F(y)$ of heterogeneous households who differ in taste γ and endowed wealth y, and production technologies described by equations (1) and (3), a two-sector competitive equilibrium consists of the following:

1. Wage w and intermediate good prices p_b for $b \in B$;
2. allocations $c(\gamma,y)$ and $e(\gamma,y)$ that given prices w and p_b for $b \in B$ maximize equation (5) subject to equation (6) for each type γ,y;
3. wealth cutoffs $y_{1\gamma}$ and $y_{2\gamma}$ that depend on γ such that

$$e(\gamma, y) \in \begin{cases} \{0\} & \text{if } y \leq y_{1\gamma} \\ [0,1] & \text{if } y_{1\gamma} < y \leq y_{2\gamma} \\ \{1\} & \text{otherwise;} \end{cases}$$

4. allocations n_b that maximize profits given w and p_b for corporate firms producing good b;
5. a density q_b of operating corporate firms over each good b consistent with free entry;
6. a cutoff $b^* \geq \underline{b}$ where if $b \geq b^*$ then $q_b > 0$ and $q_b = 0$ otherwise;
7. and market clearing;
    (a) final good market

$$\int\int (c(\gamma, y) - y)dF(y)dF(\gamma) = \left(\int_B x_b^{(\sigma-1)/\sigma} db \right)^{\sigma/(\sigma-1)};$$

    (b) intermediate good markets

$$x_b = q_b(An_b^\theta - b) \text{ when } b \geq b^*$$

---

12. In general, the choice of technology implies two cutoffs, b_1 and b_2, that is, there are goods $b < b_1$ where firms are the lowest cost producer. For these goods, entrepreneur households would be operating well beyond the good's natural scale of production. To eliminate this possibility, we restrict $\underline{b} > A(1 - \theta)$ so that the smallest possible natural scale is at least $n = 1$. This ensures that $b_1 < \underline{b}$.

and

$$\int_{\underline{b}}^{b^*} x_b db = \int\int \left(AE(\gamma, y) - \int_{\underline{b}}^{b^*} b db \right) dF(y) dF(\gamma);$$

(c) labor market

(7)
$$\int_B q_b n_b db = 1 - \int\int e(\gamma, y) dF(y) dF(\gamma).$$

The following lemma establishes that intermediate prices for any $b < b^*$ must adjust to make the household indifferent over its choice of b.

Lemma 1.   In an equilibrium where $b^* > \underline{b}$, proprietor's income $z = p_b(A - b)$ does not depend on b.

Proof.   This follows almost immediately from the assumption of access to the same technology. Suppose to the contrary that there exists b' such that $p_{b'}(1 - b') > p_b(1 - b)$ for all other $b < b^*$, then this cannot be an equilibrium since all households that run a business would prefer to produce b'.

To solve for this equilibrium, we first address the marginal households, that is, suppose $y \in (y_{1\gamma}, y_{2\gamma})$ for some household y, γ. From the first order condition for E, an optimal choice of $E(\gamma, y)$ requires

(8)
$$\lambda = \frac{\gamma}{w - z},$$

where λ is the marginal utility of income. For these marginal entrepreneurial households $w - z$ represents the opportunity cost of increasing the probability of running a business. With log preferences over consumption, then

$$c(\gamma, y) = \frac{w - z}{\gamma},$$

and the probability of running a business is

$$e(\gamma, y) = \frac{w + y}{w - z} - \frac{1}{\gamma}.$$

The solution of $e(\gamma, y)$ for the marginal households determines the wealth thresholds as the values of y that make $e(\gamma, y)$ exactly equal to 0 or 1

$$y_{1\gamma} = \frac{w - z}{\gamma} - w \text{ and } y_{2\gamma} = y_{2\gamma} = \frac{w - z}{\gamma} - z.$$

Consumption for households outside of these thresholds will be equal to their endowment y and any earned income, w or z.

It is useful to define two aggregate quantities. We let E represent the total supply of labor allocated to operating small businesses

$$E \equiv \int\int e(\gamma, y) dF(y) dF(\gamma).$$

Likewise, we let C represent aggregate demand for the final good

$$C \equiv \int\int (c(y,\gamma) - y) dF(y) dF(\gamma).$$

In the firm sector (when $b \geq b^*$) free entry ensures that firms operate at their minimum efficient scale $n_b = n_b^*$. This is the only value of n_b at which profits are exactly to zero. With price equal to marginal cost then:

(9)
$$p_b = w \left(\frac{b^{1-\theta}}{A\chi} \right)^{1/\theta}.$$

Given intermediate demand x_b from equation (4) and the required price of b from equation (9), intermediate good market clearing pins down the quantity of firms q

(10)
$$q_b = Cw^{-\sigma} \frac{1-\theta}{\theta} (A\chi)^{\sigma/\theta} b^{[(\theta-1)\sigma-\theta]/\theta}.$$

Recall that we have normalized $P = 1$ so all prices are in units of the final good.

Next we determine the small business sector and firm sector partitions. In a competitive market with free entry, each good b will be supplied by the producer offering the lowest price. We locate the cutoff good b^* that equates the marginal cost of firms with the price charged by small businesses.

Proposition 1.   With $\underline{b} > A(1 - \theta)$, $\bar{b} > A$ and $\underline{b}$ sufficiently below $\bar{b}$, then there is a unique cutoff b^* that defines the corporate sector $B^c = [b^*, b] \cap B \neq \varnothing$ and the small business sector $B^e = B \setminus B^c \neq \varnothing$ where b^* is the larger real root on the interval $[0, A)$ of the following equation

(11)
$$w \left(\frac{b^{*1-\theta}}{A\chi} \right)^{1/\theta} = \frac{z}{A - b^*},$$

Proof.   See appendix.

With all equilibrium objects expressed in terms of the market wage w and equilibrium proprietor's income z, it only remains to identify these prices by clearing the labor and intermediates markets. Since the intermediates markets for $b \in B^c$ has already been cleared to determine q_b, we focus on $b \in B^e$. Market clearing requires that $(A - b)E_{yyb} = Cp_b^{-\sigma}$, and since we have established that entrepreneur households are indifferent over $b \in B^e$ we need only check that this holds for aggregate small business production. By multiplying market clearing through by $(A - b)^{-\sigma}$, since $p_b = [z / (A - b)]$ we can write the equation as $(A - b)^{1-\sigma} E_{yyb} = Cz^{-\sigma}$ for each b. Integrated over all B^e requires

(12)
$$Cz^{-\sigma} \int_{\underline{b}}^{b^*} (A - b)^{\sigma-1} db = E,$$

where b^* is the root defined by Proposition 1. Likewise, after substituting in n_b^* and q_b using equations (2) and (10), labor market clearing may be simplified as

(13) $1 - E = \int_{b*}^{\bar{b}} C(b^{1-\theta} / A\chi)^{(1-\sigma)/\theta} db.$

Unfortunately it is not possible to obtain algebraic solutions for w, z, and $b*$, even when making simplified assumptions for both the distributions of y and γ. However, given parameter values, we can numerically solve for the roots of the three simultaneous equations (11)–(13) where the first equation must be solved for the appropriate root.

3.4   The Importance of Nonpecuniary Benefits

In this section, we show that the introduction of nonpecuniary motives into our simple equilibrium model generates sharp implications for the relationships between earnings, productivity, wealth, and firm size that are consistent with the evidence we present in section 3.2 as well as additional established empirical regularities highlighted in the broader literature. As we highlight throughout this chapter, the inferences drawn from these empirical regularities can be altered significantly if one fails to account for the potential of nonpecuniary benefits to small business formation.

For the remainder of the chapter, we consider an example where y and γ are independently distributed as uniform random variables with supports $[\underline{y}, \bar{y}]$ and $[\underline{\gamma}, \bar{\gamma}]$. Independence imposes no ex ante relationship between wealth y and tastes γ. If both y and γ have independent uniform distributions, then one can simplify the expressions for the aggregates E and C as

$$E = \frac{(1/2)(w + 2\bar{y} + z)(\bar{\gamma} - \underline{\gamma}) - (w - z)\log(\bar{\gamma} / \underline{\gamma})}{(\bar{y} - \underline{y})(\bar{\gamma} - \underline{\gamma})},$$

when $y_{1\gamma}$ and $y_{2\gamma}$ are inside the support of y for all γ and

$$C = \frac{(w - z)^2 \log(\bar{\gamma} / \underline{\gamma}) - (1/2)[w^2 - z^2 + 2(wy - z\bar{y})](\bar{\gamma} - \underline{\gamma})}{(\bar{y} - \underline{y})(\bar{\gamma} - \underline{\gamma})}.$$

3.4.1   Earnings Gaps and Aggregate Productivity

First, consistent with the empirical findings of Hamilton (2000), Moskowitz and Vissing-Jørgensen (2002), and Pugsley (2011) the model generates a gap in earnings between wage workers and business owners. The small business owners are willing to produce the good at a wage lower than they could have earned in the firm sector because they receive some of their compensation in the form of nonpecuniary benefits. The following proposition establishes that the pecuniary opportunity cost of running a small business is always positive in an equilibrium with a small business sector.

Proposition 2.   If $B^c \neq \varnothing$ and $\underline{\gamma} > 0$ then $w - z > 0$.

Proof.   Since B^c is nonempty, at least some household type must be willing to work as an employee. That household is either marginal or an inframarginal employee. If the household is marginal then it satisfies equation (8) with equality. Since $\gamma > 0$ and $\lambda > 0$, then $w - z$ must also be positive. If the household is inframarginal and $E_{\gamma\gamma} = 0$, then $\gamma < \lambda (w - z)$ and again $w - z$ must be positive.

Notice that this result does not rely on that labor is less effective when operating a business instead of employed at a firm.

The existence of nonpecuniary benefits also informs the well-documented relationship between wages and firm size. Many researchers have documented that workers in smaller firms earn less than workers in larger firms (see Brown and Medoff 1989). In figure 3.6, we plot the equilibrium wage gap, normalized by total value added C, over alternative parameterizations of the distribution of γ. We show how the wage gap increases with the average strength of the nonpecuniary benefit. Nonpecuniary compensating differentials for running a business are a key aspect of understanding the relationship between wages and firm size, at least on the low end of the firm-size distribution.

The wage gap is also tied to measured aggregate productivity. If there were no nonpecuniary motives and every household worked in the firm sector so $B^c = B$, average labor productivity AP (total value added/total hours) would equal w. We will continue to refer to this case as the "zero gamma" economy. With a small business sector:

$$AP = w - (w - z)E.$$

To see this we just integrate over all the households' budget constraints. We can think of AP as a weighted average of income from either sector, or as the wage w adjusted for the wage gap $w - z$, as we have written here. Figure 3.7 plots how measured aggregate productivity also declines with the mean of the distribution of γ.[13] For reference we plot aggregate productivity of the zero gamma economy as the dot on the vertical axis.[14] As nonpecuniary motives become more important, the wage gap and the size of the small business sector E both grow, lowering AP. It is true that w also grows as wages adjust for a small firm labor supply, but this effect is always offset by the losses from $(w - z)E$, where both the opportunity cost $w - z$ and the small business sector E growth with $E[\gamma]$, as we establish in the following proposition.

Proposition 3.   If $B^e \neq \varnothing$, and $\underline{\gamma} > 0$, then $(\partial AP / \partial E[\gamma]) < 0$.

The proof relies on a careful application of the implicit function theorem on the system of equations defined by (11)–(13). The resulting algebra is

---

13. We omit the plot for small values of $E[\gamma]$ to avoid complications from corner solutions for the wealth thresholds.

14. With $\gamma = 0$, the equilibrium wage w_0 is easy to work out since $C = w$, you can show that

$$w_0 = [A(1 - \theta)^{1-\theta}\theta^{\theta}]^{1/\theta} \left(\int b^{[(1-\theta)(1-\sigma)]/\theta}db\right)^{1/(\sigma-1)}.$$

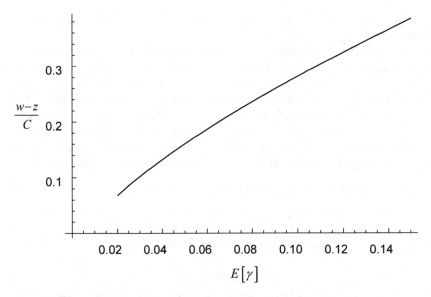

Fig. 3.6 Wage gap (as a fraction of aggregate output)
Note: $\theta = 0.75, \underline{b} = 1, \overline{b} = 5, \sigma = 2, \underline{y} = 0, \overline{y} = 30,$ and $\overline{\gamma} - \underline{\gamma} = 0.02.$

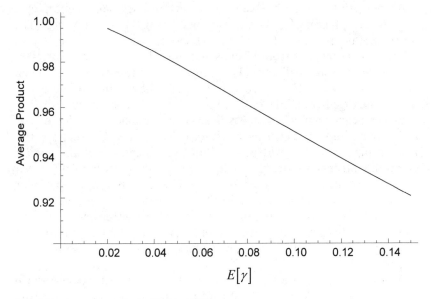

Fig. 3.7 Average product of labor (AP)
Note: $\theta = 0.75, \underline{b} = 1, \overline{b} = 5, \sigma = 2, \underline{y} = 0, \overline{y} = 30,$ and $\overline{\gamma} - \underline{\gamma} = 0.02.$

tedious, but can be verified with symbolic algebra software such as Mathematica.

In summary, the simple model shows that a model with nonpecuniary benefits will result in individuals in the firm sector earning higher pecuniary returns than workers in the self-employed sector. This results in a very discrete relationship that implies a positive firm size/wage relationship. Finally, the extent of nonpecuniary benefits will affect measured labor productivity within the economy. Even though no technology parameters will change, differences in the distribution of nonpecuniary benefits across locations or across time will result in differences in measured labor productivity.

3.4.2   Wealth and Business Ownership

The second important implication of our model is that, without any financial frictions, the model produces an increasing relationship between initial wealth y and the probability of owning a business E.

Proposition 4.   If $B^e \neq \varnothing$ then $(\partial E_{\gamma y} / \partial y) \geq 0$.

Proof.   If the household is a worker, then $E_{\gamma y} = 0$ and $(\partial E_{\gamma y} / \partial y) = 0$. If the household is marginal, then $(\partial E_{\gamma y} / \partial y) = (1 / [w - z]) > 0$ by the previous proposition, and when the household is an inframarginal entrepreneur, then $E_{\gamma y} = 1$ and $(\partial E_{\gamma y} / \partial y) = 0$.

An increasing relationship between wealth and entry is often interpreted as evidence of binding liquidity constraints for small business owners. The presence of nonpecuniary benefits raises questions about relying on such an identification strategy. Figure 3.8 plots the probability of business ownership $E_{y\gamma}$ over the wealth distribution. For each y we average over the conditional distribution $F(\gamma \mid y)$. For a particular value of γ the wealth cutoffs are relatively close together and the probability of entry is increasing linearly in y. However, heterogeneity in γ makes E_y a smooth nonlinear function of y as these thresholds evolve over the entire distribution of γ. The shape of this relationship is consistent with probit estimations of entry on wealth (see, for example, Hurst and Lusardi 2004). In our model, the probability is flat over a segment of the population that is not liquidity constrained. At low levels of initial income, the marginal utility of consumption is large relative to the marginal utility of the nonpecuniary benefits of business ownership. Likewise, the wealthy pay an opportunity cost to run the business in the form of lost wages because they enjoy running a business relative to other forms of consumption.

Again, this result undermines much of the empirical strategy performed by Evans and Leighton (1989), Evans and Jovanovic (1989), Quadrini (1999), Gentry and Hubbard (2004), Cagetti and De Nardi (2006), Fairlie and Woodruff (2005), and Fairlie and Krashinsky (2006). In these models, the relationship between wealth and the probability of starting a business (or

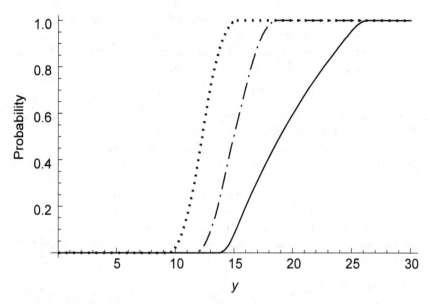

Fig. 3.8   Probability of business ownership for *y* households

Note: $\theta = 0.75$, $\underline{b} = 1$, $\bar{b} = 5$, $\sigma = 2$, $\underline{y} = 0$, $\bar{y} = 30$, $\bar{\gamma} - \underline{\gamma} = 0.02$, and with $E[\gamma] = 0.05$ (solid), 0.10 (dashed), and 0.15 (dotted).

even exogenous changes in wealth and the probability of starting a business) are evidence that liquidity constraints bind. Our model yields the same predictions in a world with no financial frictions. If one takes the nonpecuniary benefits of owning a small business seriously, using the relationship between exogenous changes and wealth and the probability of starting a business as being de facto evidence of liquidity constraints is invalid.

3.4.3   What Do Small Businesses Produce?

Third, the model of nonpecuniary benefits informs the type of goods where we should observe a high concentration of small business owners. In our model, small business owner households only produce goods that would have been produced by small- to medium-scale firms. Recall that the interval $[\underline{b}, b^*]$ defines the small business sector B^e. Then any factor that enlarges the size of the small business sector does so by increasing the equilibrium cutoff b^*. This tells us that if any $b \in B^e$ were to be produced by a firm in a competitive market, the firm would have a smaller efficient scale than any other firm producing in the firm sector $b \in B^c$. This is consistent with the sorting we document in section 3.2, where most household-owned businesses start in a very narrow set of industries that operate at a small scale in the long run. These results suggest that using the concentration of small businesses within a sector can inform researchers about the average returns to scale in that sector. To our knowledge, this approach has never been pursued to estimate the returns to scale across various industries.

Additionally, the magnitude of the distribution of nonpecuniary benefits has a direct impact on the size of the small business sector.

Proposition 5.   The size of B^e increases with $E[\gamma]$.

This follows immediately from applying the implicit function theorem on the system of equations defined by equations (11)–(13) at the equilibrium allocation to determine $(db^* / dE[\gamma])$. To see how the small business sector B^e depends on the distribution of γ, figure 3.9 plots the equilibrium cutoff b^* for various $E[\gamma]$ holding all other moments and parameters fixed. As nonpecuniary motives become more important, the small business sector grows by successfully competing with higher b firms. The firms' costs are higher because of the tighter labor market, and entrepreneur households are willing to bear the additional cost in lost wages in return for the nonpecuniary compensation.

3.4.4   Distribution of Firm Size

Finally, the distribution of γ has important implications for the equilibrium cross-sectional distribution of firms. Entrepreneur households draw business away from the small- to medium-size firms. This is the flip side of the previous point about b^*. Here we use a change of variables to express

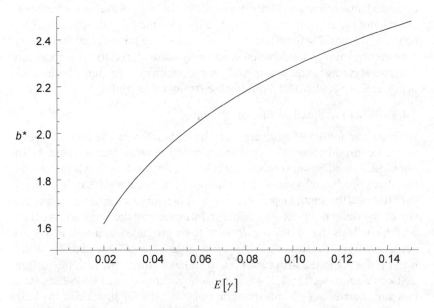

Fig. 3.9   Small business cutoff b^*
Note: $\theta = 0.75$, $\underline{b} = 1$, $\bar{b} = 5$, $\sigma = 2$, $\underline{y} = 0$, $\bar{y} = 30$, and $\bar{\gamma} - \underline{\gamma} = 0.02$.

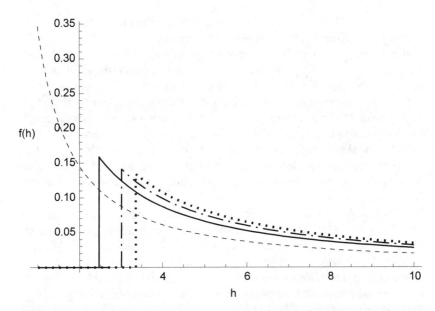

Fig. 3.10   Distribution of firm sizes

Note: θ = 0.75, $\underline{b}$ = 1, $\bar{b}$ = 5, σ = 2, $\underline{y}$ = 0, $\bar{y}$ = 30, $\bar{\gamma} - \underline{\gamma}$ = 0.02, and with $E[\gamma]$ = 0.05 (solid), 0.10 (dashed-dotted), and 0.15 (dotted). The dashed line represents the distribution of firms in the zero gamma economy.

the density of firms as a function of size *n*. After a change of variables the density *q* may be written in terms of employment *n* as

$$q(n) \propto Cw^{-\sigma}n^{\sigma(\theta-1)-\theta}n > 1,$$

where the constant of proportionality is $(A^{\theta}\theta)^{\sigma-1}$ and with a mass point of *E* at *n* = 1. Note that the firm-size distribution for *n* > 1 satisfies Zipf's law when σ > 1, that is, the density for *n* is Pareto with paramter σ(θ − 1) − θ. This is a robust feature of the distribution of firms in the United States.[15] In figure 3.10 we plot this distribution of firm sizes measured by employment *n*. For reference, we also include a dashed line representing the distribution of firms in a zero gamma economy. In this picture it is especially clear that entrepreneur households specialize in the types of goods that would have been produced by smaller-scale firms.

3.5   A Regressive Small Business Subsidy

In this section, we consider how a model of nonpecuniary benefits could inform the costs and benefits of subsidizing small business ownership. Despite their political appeal, the welfare calculus of a small business sub-

15. See Axtell (2001).

sidy is not at all obvious. The importance of nonpecuniary benefits in the decision to become a small business owner makes this especially difficult. To make this point we introduce a very simple subsidy into our model funded by a lump sum tax levied equally across all households. We show that the redistributive role of this subsidy could actually benefit the wealthy at the expense of the poor. We want to stress that our model offers no reason for policymakers to want to subsidize small businesses. Our goal is to highlight (a) the potential costs of subsidies to small business owners and (b) the distributional effects of subsidizing small business owners. We realize that any costs must be weighed against potential benefits. Most of the literature focuses only on the benefit. We feel the model is well suited to highlight some of the costs.

To begin, we introduce a simple proportional subsidy to the model. An unsubsidized small business household producing b earns p_b per unit sold. We let s represent a proportional subsidy to small business households so that small business owners will instead earn $p_b(1 + s)$ per unit sold.[16]

We augment the earlier equilibrium definition to include the subsidy and a new requirement that the government balance its budget through a lump sum tax levied across all households.

Definition 2. With $P = 1$ and small business subsidy $s > 0$, given a distribution of households $F(\gamma,y)$ characterized by preference parameter γ and initial wealth y, and production technologies described by equations (3) and (1), a two-sector subsidized competitive equilibrium consists of the following:

1. A lump sum tax T, paid by all households;
2. wage w and intermediate good prices p_b;
3. allocations $c(\gamma,y)$ and $e(\gamma,y)$ that given prices w and p_b maximize equation (5) subject to equation (6) for households of type γ,y;
4. wealth cutoffs $y_{1\gamma}$ and $y_{2\gamma}$ that depend on γ such that

$$E_{y\gamma} \in \begin{cases} \{0\} & \text{if } y \leq y_{1\gamma} \\ [0,1] & \text{if } y_{1\gamma} < y \leq y_{2\gamma} \\ \{1\} & \text{otherwise;} \end{cases}$$

5. allocations n_b that maximize firm profits given w and p_b for firms producing good b;
6. a density of firms q_b producing b that may freely enter or exit the market;
7. a cutoff $b^* \geq \underline{b}$ where if $b \geq b^*$ then $q_b > 0$ and $q_b = 0$ otherwise;
8. market clearing;
   (a) final good market

16. This subsidy may be interpreted as a $s(A - b)$ reduction in fixed operating costs b for each small business of type b.

$$\iint [c(\gamma, y) - y + T] dF(y) dF(\gamma) = \left(\int_B x_b^{(\sigma-1)/\sigma} db \right)^{\sigma/(\sigma-1)};$$

(b) intermediate good markets

$$x_b = q_b (An_b^\theta - b) \text{ when } b \geq b^*$$

and

$$\int_{\underline{b}}^{b^*} x_b db = \iint \left(Ae(\gamma, y) - \int_{\underline{b}}^{b^*} b \, db \right) dF(y) dF(\gamma); \text{ and}$$

(c) labor market

$$\int_B q_b n_b db = 1 - \iint e(\gamma, y) dF(y) dF(\gamma).$$

9. and the government balances its budget

(14) $$T = \int (A - b) p_b (1 + s) E_b db.$$

We repeat the steps from section 3.3.4 to compute the equilibrium with a subsidy. In this case we must replace proprietor's income z with $(1 + s)z$ in equations (12) and (7), leaving equation (11) (where $[z / (A - b)]$ represents the selling price p_b) unchanged. Since E is linear in y, the government budget balance equation may be solved analytically for T as a function of w, $z(1 + s)$, and b^*. The threshold b^* is now the larger real root on the interval $(0, A)$ of

(15) $$w \left(\frac{b^{*1-\theta}}{A\chi} \right)^{1/\theta} = \frac{z(1 + s)}{A - b^*},$$

with all endogenous quantities as a function of w, $z(1 + s)$, and b^*, then given parameter values, these may be recovered by solving the system of equations defined by (12), (13), and (15).

We take two approaches to quantity the welfare gains or losses from the subsidy. First, we consider aggregate welfare, as measured by a utilitarian planner. Second, because the aggregate measure obscures some interesting redistribution, we look at the households' individual burdens computing an equivalent variation measure of the subsidy's cost.

Using the first approach, the model implies that small business subsidies reduce aggregate welfare. To see this, we define a utilitarian measure of aggregate welfare W_s as the equally weighted sum of each household's utility in equilibrium under subsidy $s \geq 0$.

$$W_s = \iint (\log c_{yy} + \gamma e_{yy}) dF(y \mid \gamma) dF(\gamma).$$

Figure 3.11 plots W_s as a function of s. The overall reduction in welfare is not surprising. In our example there are no market failures that would provide a beneficial role for a subsidy, and the unsubsidized competitive outcome is first best. With equal Pareto weights, the $s = 0$ allocation can be supported as a solution to a planning problem where increasing $s > 0$ simply distorts the allocation of labor across the two sectors. Holding Var[γ] fixed, varying $E[\gamma]$ does not change the rate at which the subsidy trades off aggregate

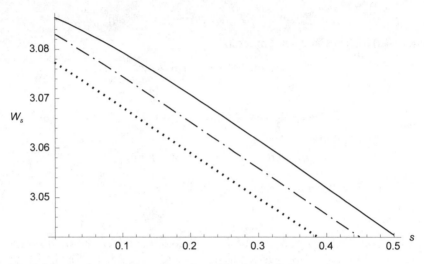

Fig. 3.11   Aggregate welfare effect of small business subsidy $s \geq 0$

Note: $\theta = 0.75$, $\underline{b} = 1$, $\bar{b} = 5$, $\sigma = 2$, $\underline{y} = 0$, $\bar{y} = 30$, $\bar{\gamma} - \underline{\gamma} = 0.02$, and with $E[\gamma] = 0.05$ (solid), 0.10 (dashed-dotted), and 0.15 (dotted).

welfare. The more interesting result is the redistribution hidden behind the aggregate measure.

The existence of non-pecuniary motives makes the individual welfare effects of the subsidy highly nonlinear. To study the household level effects of the subsidy, we introduce a measure of equivalent variation. We compute $EV_{y\gamma}$ as

$$EV_{y\gamma}(s) = c(u_s; w, z) - (w + y),$$

where u_s is household y, γ equilibrium utility under subsidy s, and $c(u_s; w, z)$ is the minimum expenditures required at the unsubsidized equilibrium prices w and z in order to achieve u_s and $(w + y)$ is the unsubsidized equilibrium expenditures (or total wealth). We normalize this measure by $w + y$ and express equivalent variation $EV_{y\gamma} / (w + y)$ as a fraction of the households' total wealth. Using the subsidized and unsubsidized equilibrium allocations, we can compute this measure over the entire joint distribution of households to study the household-level welfare costs of the subsidy.

Using this measure, we find this simple small business subsidy to be regressive, actually benefiting wealthy business owners at the expense of wage employees. Figure 3.12 plots this welfare measure for the baseline case. The left panel plots the normalized EV measure over the entire joint distribution $F(y, \gamma)$ for a small subsidy policy $s = 0.05$. It is a little difficult to read the surface plot, but it is evident that for some households (with $EV / (w + y) > 0$) the subsidy is a net benefit. In the right-hand plot we integrate over γ to recover

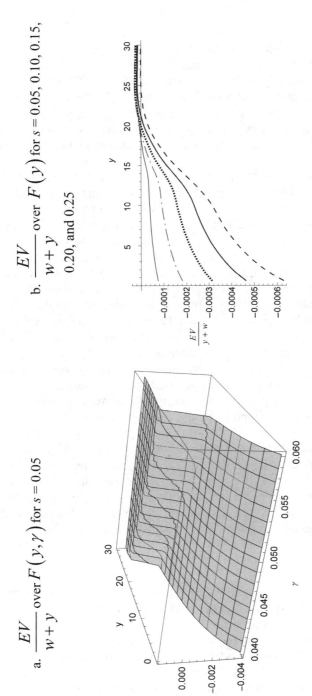

a. $\dfrac{EV}{w+y}$ over $F(y, \gamma)$ for $s = 0.05$

b. $\dfrac{EV}{w+y}$ over $F(y)$ for $s = 0.05, 0.10, 0.15,$ 0.20, and 0.25

Fig. 3.12 Equivalent variation as a fraction of full income ($w + y$) of subsidy s policies

Note: $\theta = 0.75$, $\underline{b} = 1$, $\bar{b} = 5$, $\sigma = 2$, $\underline{y} = 0$, $\bar{y} = 30$, $\bar{\gamma} - \underline{\gamma} = 0.02$, and with $E[\gamma] = 0.05$.

$$EV_y = \int EV_{y\gamma} dF(\gamma \mid y),$$

the total welfare gain or loss for all households with wealth y and plot this measure over the wealth distribution $F(y)$. We plot several policies ranging from a small subsidy $s = 0.05$ to a large subsidy $s = 0.25$. From this graph it is evident that even when summing across high and low γ households, wealthy households stand to benefit from a subsidy. Figure 3.13 makes this point more apparent by considering the three distributions of γ we have studied under a low subsidy in the left-hand panel and a high subsidy in the right-hand panel.

Part of the large welfare cost to the poorer households is driven by the lump sum taxation assumption. This is an extreme example where all households equally share the tax burden regardless of their total wealth $w + y$. To see why, consider the effect of a subsidy. It makes entrepreneurship more lucrative to all households. Many would have run businesses anyway, but some will switch from wage employment to business ownership, constricting the labor supply. The downward-sloping aggregate labor demand curve implies a higher equilibrium wage. In the lump sum taxation example, the modest increase in wages for poorer-worker households is dominated by the additional tax burden needed to fund the subsidy. A more progressive policy where tax rates are based on wealth could reverse this policy, however a proportional income tax would not reverse the result. In fact, a proportional income tax would be even more regressive, since wage income constitutes the majority of consumption for the less wealthy households.

These mechanics also give some intuition for the result that wealthy entrepreneur households stand to benefit from the subsidy. While the subsidy entices some worker households into a higher probability of business ownership, the effect on this margin is relatively small. However, all business-owning households stand to benefit from the subsidy, and the wealthy business owners who would have started their businesses anyway, especially so. The best-case scenario for them is a subsidy with a small group of existing business owners, this way the individual benefit of the subsidy is not diluted by a larger tax needed to pay for a subsidy across a larger small-business sector.

3.6   Implications

The goals of this chapter were twofold. The first goal was empirical. In section 3.2, we expanded on the work in Hurst and Pugsley (2011) using restricted-access administrative data in the census LBD. We document the large amount of heterogeneity across narrow industries in the extent to which small businesses are important. For many narrow industries like dentists or florists, almost all employment within the industry is in small businesses. For other narrow industries like natural gas pipelines and scheduled air transport, essentially none of the employment within the industry

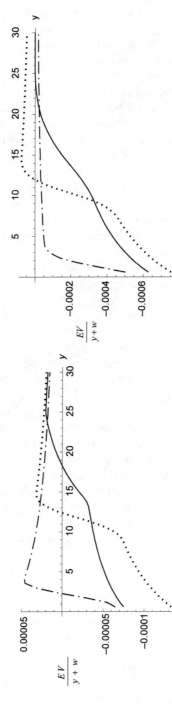

Fig. 3.13 Equivalent variation as a fraction of full income ($w + y$) of high and low subsidy s policies

Note: $\theta = 0.75$, $\underline{b} = 1$, $\bar{b} = 5$, $\sigma = 2$, $\underline{y} = 0$, $\bar{y} = 30$, $\bar{\gamma} - \underline{\gamma} = 0.02$, and with $E[\gamma] = 0.05$ (solid), 0.10 (dashed-dotted), and 0.15 (dotted).

takes place within small businesses. Also, in section 3.2 we highlighted the fact that most young small businesses do not eventually grow, even conditional on survival for ten or more years. Put another way, while most new and young businesses are small, most old businesses also remain small. The facts in section 3.2 are consistent with the facts documented in Haltiwanger, Jarmin, and Miranda (2013) and Hurst and Pugsley (2011).

The second goal of the chapter was theoretical. We developed a highly stylized and static equilibrium model of an economy with a small business sector. The model included three key elements. First, we allow for different industries of the economy to differ in their natural scale of production. In any industry firms may be incorporated or run by small business owners (households), where the only difference is small business owners are limited in their capacity to grow. This modeling choice was motivated by the facts presented in section 3.2 showing that the size of the small business sector differs markedly across industries, and further, that the vast majority of young small businesses become old small businesses conditional on their survival. Second, we allow at least some individuals to have a preference for owning and working in a small business over employment within a corporate firm. The magnitude of the utility flow may vary across the population. With no differences in skill, nonpecuniary benefits generated from a taste for small business ownership are the only source of selection. This modeling choice was motivated by the work of Hurst and Pugsley (2011) documenting that nonpecuniary benefits were a key driver of small business formation. Nevertheless, the relative value of the nonpecuniary versus pecuniary benefits will vary with the marginal utility of consumption. So third and finally, we allow individuals to differ in their initial wealth, generating dispersion in the equilibrium marginal utility of consumption across the population. Collectively, these assumptions yielded a variety of predictions about the small business sector that are consistent with the data. In particular, the model predicts: (a) small businesses are concentrated in a few industries, (b) higher-wealth individuals are more likely to be small business owners, and (c) small business owners earn lower earnings on average relative to what they would have earned if they remained a wage/salary worker.

Our model abstracted from many of the common drivers of small business formation. For example, most of the existing research attributes differences across firms with respect to ex post performance to either differences in financing constraints facing the firms (e.g., Evans and Jovanovic 1989; Clementi and Hopenhayn 2006), differences in ex post productivity draws across the firms (e.g., Simon and Bonini 1958; Jovanovic 1982; Pakes and Ericson 1998; Hopenhayn 1992), or differences in entrepreneurial ability of the firms' owners (e.g., Lucas Jr. 1978). It is not that we do not believe these to be empirically important or that all of the model's predictions are reasonable. For example, the market structure generated adjustment in the quantity if individual goods sold entirely on the extensive margin of firm or small business entry. Instead, we offered a stark model to illustrate that preference heterogeneity alone yields many of the same predictions as models with heterogeneous entrepreneurial ability across individuals and liquidity constraints. It is straightforward to introduce differences in skill and liquidity constraints to the model, and Pugsley (2011) incorporates these features into a dynamic model of the small business sector. One question we think is important going forward, also considered in Pugsley (2011), is what is the relative importance of the different factors in explaining both the mass of small businesses we observe in the data and why some firms grow while others do not? To be concrete, we think it is important to assess the relative importance of (a) nonpecuniary benefits, (b) technological differences in scale across industries, (c) differences in ex ante entrepreneurial ability, (d) differences in ex post luck, and (e) binding liquidity constraints in explaining the distribution of firm size within the economy. It is challenging to robustly differentiate these factors, and as we show, the policy and growth implications of these different factors differ markedly.

3.6.1   Modeling Needs

To facilitate testing among these different drivers of small business growth, new models need be developed and new data brought to bear on the issue. Going forward we believe that traditional models of small business formation and growth should allow for heterogeneous nonpecuniary benefits of owning a small business across individuals in the population. Theoretically, the importance of nonpecuniary benefits can be distinguished from the other factors by examining earnings data. Individuals are willing to take lower pecuniary benefits (earnings) to run a small business if nonpecuniary benefits exist. However, the ability stories, the luck stories, and the liquidity constraints story all predict that earnings for those that remain business owners should be larger (in expectation) than they would be if the individual remained a wage/salary worker. By incorporating nonpecuniary benefits into standard models of firm dynamics, the models could then illustrate how wage data could be used to test among the various drivers of small business entry.

One attempt to do this was Pugsley (2011), which introduces preference heterogeneity to an otherwise standard model of entrepreneurship with credit frictions similar to Cagetti and De Nardi (2006). The preference heterogeneity, similar to the form in this chapter, generates nonpecuniary compensation from business ownership that effectively shifts the productivity and wealth thresholds for which business ownership is viable. He uses the model to determine to what extent the distribution of firm size is driven by selection on tastes, and finds using the structural model that roughly 40 percent of the distribution of firms (all very small firms) would not be viable without some further nonpecuniary compensation from running the business. This helps the model fit the existence of small firms with relatively low exit rates and no growth that are traditionally harder to understand with pure productivity or credit friction-driven distributions of firm size.

Additionally, it would be useful to amend our current models to allow for multiple sectors. As we illustrated in section 3.2, there is a large amount of heterogeneity in the firm-size distribution across industries. By developing models with multiple sectors, richer predictions can be developed. The detailed industry-level data can then be exploited to potentially test among some of the model ingredients.

3.6.2   Data Needs

With the advent of the restricted-use Longitudinal Business Database (LBD), researchers have had access to a wealth of information about firm dynamics. As seen from our work in section 3.2, researchers can track employment at the establishment level for businesses of differing ages across different sectors. Some measures of sales and total payroll can be merged into this data. However, these data do not contain much information about the owner(s) of the businesses. As seen above, one way to distinguish between the importance of nonpecuniary benefits and other factors in driving the firm-size distribution is to measure the wages of the owner as they transition into and out of self-employment. The LBD, in its current form, is not well suited to provide this information.

To examine the earnings movements of individuals as they transition in and out of business ownership, researchers have relied on household surveys. Because of the need to follow an individual as they move in and out of business ownership, panel data is necessary. Also, because business owners represent such a small fraction of the population, large samples are needed. Finally, the panel dimension of the data needs to be long enough to measure an individual's permanent income both before and after owning a business. Very few household surveys within the United States are constructed such that they are nationally representative, have large sample sizes, and have long panel dimensions. The Survey of Income and Program Participation (SIPP) is essentially the only household data set that meets this criteria. Even then, the panel component of the SIPP is relatively short (up to four years). As a result, essentially all work assessing whether individuals earn less as small business owners (or the self-employed) relative to what they would have earned as wage/salary workers is done using the SIPP. For example, both Hamilton (2000) and Pugsley (2011) document that the median small business owner earns about 20–30 percent less than they would have as a wage/salary worker.

Even with the SIPP data, however, there are limitations to what can be done with the SIPP with regard to this question. First, as discussed in Hurst and Pugsley (2011), the self-employed tend to underreport their income to household surveys (relative to wage/salary workers). Second, it is conceptually hard to measure the labor earnings of the self-employed. How much of the reported earnings are the return to labor and how much are the return to capital? Third, household surveys often do not measure fringe benefits provided by the firm. If there are differences in fringe benefits provided by large employers to wage/salary workers relative to what is provided to the small business owner, earnings differences will be further mismeasured. Finally, most of the existing research does not measure well the variability of earnings of small business owners. Ideally, one would want to measure risk-adjusted differences in earnings between the self-employed and wage/salary workers. The work by Hamilton (2000) and Pugsley (2011) abstract from the potential differences in measurement error in earnings between small business owners and wage/salary workers, as well as differences in the variability of the earnings between the two groups.

Going forward, it would be useful to think about ways to better measure the earnings differentials of the self-employed relative to wage/salary workers. Subjective survey questions, like those from the Panel Study of Entrepreneurial Dynamics, suggest that nonpecuniary benefits are an important driver of small business entry. However, it would be nice to quantify their importance. The only way we can see to do this is to measure the earnings differentials that occur as individuals transition into and out of small business ownership.

Finally, and perhaps the most useful, would be to leverage the existing survey and administrative records to create matched databases available for researcher access. It may be technologically feasible to merge covariates of business owners identified in the SIPP into the LBD. Similarly, other Census-run survey instruments, such as the Current Population Survey, which is joint with the Bureau of Labor Statistics, could be linked to existing administrative data. A similar effort is already underway to link the SIPP to Social Security Administration records on lifetime earnings histories. These sorts of projects are cost-effective because they make use of the already existing (and very expensive) fielding of surveys.

3.6.3   Policy Implications

Policymakers on both the Left and the Right often discuss the importance of subsidizing small business formation. For example, the recent health care reform within the United States exempts small business (those with less than fifty full-time equivalent employees) from a mandate to provide their employees with health insurance. The US Small Business Administration (SBA) in 2010 guaranteed over $20 billion in loans to small businesses (primarily those with less than 500 employees).[17] Looney (2011) outlines many other regulatory exemptions and preferential tax treatment provided to small businesses. For example, small businesses are also exempt from some provisions of the Americans with Disabilities Act (ADA) and some rules set forth by the Occupational Safety and Health Administration (OSHA).

Economic arguments for subsidizing small businesses hinge on small busi-

---

17. See Adam Looney's published comments to Hurst and Pugsley (2011).

nesses being important contributors to aggregate innovation and growth where market forces alone fail to allocate sufficient resources to the sector. For example, the social returns from technological spillovers or improving communities may far exceed the private returns to the small business owner. Even absent positive spillovers, financial constraints may limit the scale of small businesses or whether or not they even form. The subject of entrepreneurship and technological spillovers is well studied in the growth literature (e.g., Audretsch, Keilbach, and Lehmann 2006; Acs et al. 2009). If a substantial portion of R&D occurs in small firms, the social returns to entrepreneurship could far exceed the private returns. Jones and Williams (1998), for example, find the optimal level of investment in research and develoment (R&D) to be two to four times the observed level of investment. Additionally, subsidizing small businesses may be appropriate if liquidity constraints or other financial market imperfections prevent small businesses from securing the financing they need to bring their innovations to market (Evans and Jovanovic 1989; Evans and Leighton 1989). While it is hard to think that the government can better allocate funding to small businesses than private lenders, the argument for governments trying to relax small business liquidity constraints is more persuasive if the social return to small business ownership is higher than the private return. Thus, there is some interaction between the two common economic justifications for subsidizing small businesses.

Policymakers, however, also believe that small businesses are the engines of economic growth. Recent research by Haltiwanger, Jarmin, and Miranda (2013) suggest that it is the young firms not the small firms that are likely to grow. The work in Haltiwanger, Jarmin, and Miranda (2013) and our work above documents that most small firms do not grow. Additionally, our findings above, coupled with those in Hurst and Pugsley (2011), document that while it is young firms that contribute disproportionately to growth, most young firms also never grow. This fact remains true even conditional on the business surviving. So while young firms are more likely to grow than older firms, most firms conditional on survival never grow. Collectively, our work shows that in a world with nonpecuniary benefits of owning a small business, subsidies to small businesses may have little effect on business growth. Furthermore, as we document above, these subsidies may be regressive in that the wealthy may be more likely to purchase the consumption flow of small business ownership.

The fact that the nonpecuniary benefits of small business ownership are not taxed results in sectors where nonpecuniary benefits are a larger fraction of total compensation being tax preferred relative to other sectors. To the extent that small business ownership offers larger nonpecuniary benefits relative to owning a larger business or being a wage worker, the small business sector would be tax preferred even if there are no other direct subsidies offered by the government. Additionally, there is a large literature showing that small business owners are much more likely to underreport their income to tax authorities relative to wage and salary workers. Again, if it is easier to underreport income to tax authorities if one owns a small business, the small business sector again would be tax preferred relative to other sectors even if there are no additional direct small business subsidies.

The point we want to emphasize in this subsection is that while policymakers and researchers often invoke the potential benefits of direct small business subsidies, there is very little quantitative research documenting the actual benefits and costs of small business subsidies. The results in our chapter suggest that the potential costs may be nontrivial. To our knowledge, there is no empirical work that evaluates whether subsidizing small businesses is a positive net present value venture. Addressing this question seems like a very important area for future research. Our work in this chapter and the work in Hurst and Pugsley (2011) suggests that subsidies may be less distortionary if they were targeted at growth and innovation as opposed to being mostly linked to firm size. Such policies could address the concerns raised by our results in at least two ways. First, we show that most small businesses operate in industries with potentially smaller natural scales. Business owners with little intention to grow or innovate may select into these industries for that very reason. By focusing the subsidy on the intensive margin, the subsidy is more likely to be taken up by a business owner focused on growth or innovative activity. Subsidies could lower the cost of credit for existing firms, and by increasing their value entice productive entrepreneurs with high-wage employment opportunity costs. Second, if nonpecuniary compensation is independent of the scale of the firm, the incidence of an expansion subsidy would be undistorted by nonpecuniary benefits. If anything, nonpecuniary benefits may help separate businesses that want to grow from businesses that would prefer to remain small. Of course, there may be other social virtues to noninnovative small businesses, such as supporting communities and neighborhoods, which are aided by subsidizing the entry and exit margins. However, when targeting job creation or innovative risk taking, our findings suggest caution when supporting businesses purely by size.

In conclusion, our work suggests that more work is needed both empirically and theoretically to help policymakers assess the costs and benefits of subsidizing small business activity.

Appendix
Omitted Proofs

Proof of Proposition 1.   Given wage w and small business owner income z, the price $p^c(b)$ of good b produced by the corporate sector is $wb^{(1-\theta)/\theta}$ $[A\theta^\theta(1-\theta)^{1-\theta}]^{-1/\theta}$ and the price of the same good when $(b < A)p^e(b)$ produced by the small business sector is $z / (A - b)$. Good b is provided by the lowest-priced sector.

We locate the lowest-price sectors using the solution to equation (11). With $\theta \in (0,1)$, equation (11) has exactly two real roots on the interval $[0,A)$. To see this, first note that $p^e(b)$ is continuous, strictly increasing and convex on this interval with $p^e(0) = (z / A) > 0$ and $\lim_{b \to A} p^e(b) = \infty$. Then, note that $p^c(b)$ is also continuous and strictly increasing on this interval with $p^c(0) = 0$ and $\lim_{b \to A} p^c(b) = p^c(A) < \infty$, and further that for good $b = (1 - \theta)A$ (this is the good with a minimum efficient scale exactly equal to the small business size of 1) that $p^c[(1 - \theta)A] > p^e[(1 - \theta)A]$. This last inequality follows from $z < w$, which is shown in Proposition 2. Since on the interval $[0,A)$, $p^c(b)$ is strictly convex when $\theta > 1 / 2$, strictly concave when $\theta < 1 / 2$ and linear when $\theta = 1 / 2$, it crosses $p^e(b)$ exactly twice: once below $b = (1 - \theta)A$ and once above. Label these roots b_1 and b_2, respectively. Small businesses are the lowest-cost provider when $b \in (b_1,b_2) \cap B$. Values of b below the smaller root b_1 correspond to goods with an efficient scale sufficiently below 1 so that the small business is inefficiently large and not competitive. The restriction $\underline{b} > (1 - \theta)A$ rules out this possibility since $(1 - \theta)A > b_1$, ensuring that small businesses are the lowest-cost provider of all goods below b_2. So, $b^* = b_2$ is the unique cutoff defining the set of goods produced by the corporate sector $B^c = [b^*,b] \cap B$. The restriction $\bar{b} \geq A$ ensures some measure of goods is produced by the corporate sector. So long as $\underline{b} < b^*$ the small business sector $B^e = B / B^c$ is also not empty.

References

Acs, Zoltan J., Pontus Braunerhjelm, David B. Audretsch, and Bo Carlsson. 2009. "The Knowledge Spillover Theory of Entrepreneurship." *Small Business Economics* 32 (1): 15–30.
Audretsch, David B., Max C. Keilbach, and Erik E. Lehmann. 2006. *Entrepreneurship and Economic Growth.* Oxford: Oxford University Press.
Axtell, Robert L. 2001. "Zipf Distribution of US Firm Sizes." *Science* 293 (5536): 1818–20.
Brown, Charles, and James Medoff. 1989. "The Employer Size-Wage Effect." *Journal of Political Economy* 97 (5): 1027–59.
Cagetti, M., and M. De Nardi. 2006. "Entrepreneurship, Frictions, and Wealth." *Journal of Political Economy* 114 (5): 835–70.
Clementi, Gian Luca, and Hugo A. Hopenhayn. 2006. "A Theory of Financing Constraints and Firm Dynamics." *Quarterly Journal of Economics* 121 (1): 229–65.
Dixit, A. K., and J. E. Stiglitz. 1977. "Monopolistic Competition and Optimum Product Diversity." *American Economic Review* 67 (3): 297–308.
Evans, D. S., and B. Jovanovic. 1989. "An Estimated Model of Entrepreneurial Choice under Liquidity Constraints." *Journal of Political Economy* 97 (4): 808.
Evans, D. S., and L. S. Leighton. 1989. "Some Empirical Aspects of Entrepreneurship." *American Economic Review* 79 (3): 519–35.

Fairlie, R. W., and H. A. Krashinsky. 2006. "Liquidity Constraints, Household Wealth, and Entrepreneurship Revisited." Unpublished Manuscript, University of California, Santa Cruz.

Fairlie, R. W., and C. M. Woodruff. 2005. "Mexican Entrepreneurship: A Comparison of Self-Employment in Mexico and the United States." NBER Working Paper no. 11527, Cambridge, MA.

Fort, Theresa, and Sean Klimek. 2016. "The Effects of Industry Classification Changes on US Employment Composition." Working Paper, Dartmouth College, March.

Gentry, W. M., and R. G. Hubbard. 2004. "'Success Taxes,' Entrepreneurial Entry, and Innovation." NBER Working Paper no. 10551, Cambridge, MA.

Haltiwanger, John, Ron S. Jarmin, and Javier Miranda. 2013. "Who Creates Jobs? Small versus Large versus Young." *Review of Economics and Statistics* 95 (2): 347–61.

Hamilton, B. H. 2000. "Does Entrepreneurship Pay? An Empirical Analysis of the Returns to Self-Employment." *Journal of Political Economy* 108 (3): 604–31.

Hopenhayn, Hugo A. 1992. "Entry, Exit, and Firm Dynamics in Long Run Equilibrium." *Econometrica: Journal of the Econometric Society* 60 (5): 1127–50.

Hurst, Erik, Geng Li, and Benjamin Pugsley. 2014. "Are Household Surveys Like Tax Forms? Evidence from Income Underreporting of the Self-Employed." *Review of Economics and Statistics* 96 (1): 19–33.

Hurst, Erik, and A. Lusardi. 2004. "Liquidity Constraints, Household Wealth, and Entrepreneurship." *Journal of Political Economy* 112 (2): 319–47.

Hurst, Erik, and Benjamin Wild Pugsley. 2011. "What Do Small Businesses Do?" *Brookings Papers on Economic Activity* 2011 (2): 73–118.

Jarmin, R. S., and J. Miranda. 2002. "The Longitudinal Business Database." Working Paper no. CES-02–17, Center for Economic Studied, US Census Bureau.

Jones, Charles I., and John C. Williams. 1998. "Measuring the Social Return to R & D." *Quarterly Journal of Economics* 113 (4): 1119–35.

Jovanovic, Boyan. 1982. "Selection and the Evolution of Industry." *Econometrica: Journal of the Econometric Society* 50 (3): 649–70.

La Porta, Rafael, and Andrei Shleifer. 2014. "Informality and Development." *Journal of Economic Perspectives* Summer:109–26.

Looney, Adam. 2011. Comment on "What Do Small Businesses Do?" *Brookings Papers on Economic Activity* Fall:128–37.

Lucas Jr., R. E. 1978. "On the Size Distribution of Business Firms." *Bell Journal of Economics* 9 (2): 508–23.

Moskowitz, T. J., and A. Vissing-Jørgensen. 2002. "The Returns to Entrepreneurial Investment: A Private Equity Premium Puzzle?" *American Economic Review* 92 (4): 745–78.

Pakes, Ariel, and Richard Ericson. 1998. "Empirical Implications of Alternative Models of Firm Dynamics." *Journal of Economic Theory* 79 (1): 1–45.

Pugsley, Benjamin. 2011. "Selection and the Role of Small Businesses in Firm Dynamics." Unpublished Manuscript, University of Chicago.

Quadrini, V. 1999. "The Importance of Entrepreneurship for Wealth Concentration and Mobility." *Review of Income and Wealth* 45 (1): 1–19.

Rogerson, R. 1988. "Indivisible Labor, Lotteries and Equilibrium." *Journal of Monetary Economics* 21 (1): 3–16.

Simon, Herbert A., and Charles P. Bonini. 1958. "The Size Distribution of Business Firms." *American Economic Review* 48 (4): 607–17.

Spence, M. 1976. "Product Selection, Fixed Costs, and Monopolistic Competition." *Review of Economic Studies* 43 (2): 217–35.

Are Founder CEOs Good Managers?

Victor Manuel Bennett, Megan Lawrence, and
Raffaella Sadun

4.1 Introduction

There is remarkable variation in the practices by which seemingly similar firms are managed (Bloom and Van Reenen 2007). Those differences have been attributed to a wide variety of industry, firm, and managerial characteristics including competitive pressure (Hermalin 1994; Bennett 2013), psychological traits (Galasso and Simcoe 2011; Malmendier and Tate 2005) or personal "style" of the CEO who leads the organization (Bertrand and Schoar 2003), and the ownership structure of the firm (Morck, Shleifer, and Vishny 1988).

In this chapter we study the adoption of basic management practices in firms in which the CEO of the firm and its founder are one and the same—which we define as "founder CEO" firms in what follows. While founder CEOs are typically portrayed as highly extrinsically and intrinsically motivated individuals (Jensen and Meckling 1976; Wasserman 2006), it is unclear whether they should necessarily serve as top managers of their firm. There are several reasons why founders may not be the best top managers. First, the skills needed to create a new venture may not necessarily coincide with the capabilities needed to lead the firm through more advanced phases of

Victor Manuel Bennett is assistant professor of strategy at Duke University. Megan Lawrence is assistant professor of strategic management at the Owen Graduate School of Management at Vanderbilt University. Raffaella Sadun is the Thomas S. Murphy Associate Professor of Business Administration in the Strategy Unit at Harvard Business School and a faculty research fellow of the National Bureau of Economic Research.

This chapter has been prepared for the NBER/CRIW conference "Measuring Entrepreneurial Businesses: Current Knowledge and Challenges." Sadun would like to thank Harvard Business School and the Kauffman Foundation for financial support. For acknowledgments, sources of research support, and disclosure of the authors' material financial relationships, if any, please see http://www.nber.org/chapters/c13499.ack.

growth and expansion.[1] Furthermore, founder CEOs might be reluctant to adopt practices that standardize the operations of the firm, since these practices reduce the idiosyncratic and personalized aspects of the entrepreneur's role (Rajan 2012) and the private benefits of control associated with them (Bandiera, Prat, and Sadun 2013).

We investigate these issues using the World Management Survey (WMS), an international data set providing detailed information on the management practices for a large sample of medium and large manufacturing firms (Bloom et al. 2014; Bloom and Van Reenen 2007) in thirty-two countries. The management processes surveyed in the WMS are akin to managerial "best practices" and have been found to be strongly and causally related to superior firm performance (Bloom and Van Reenen 2007; Bloom et al. 2013; Bloom, Sadun, and Van Reenen 2016).

The WMS includes a large number of founder and nonfounder CEOs' firms of similar ages and sizes within the same industries and countries. Although we cannot estimate causal effects of being led by a founder CEO, the richness of the data allows us to examine the conditional correlation between management and the founder CEO status of the company while controlling for a large set of potentially confounding covariates suggested by theory and earlier empirical investigations such as firm age, size, average skills of the workforce, country of operation, and main industry of activity.

We start our analysis by reporting three main stylized facts. First, firms led by founder CEOs have lower management scores relative to other forms of concentrated and dispersed ownership. Second, the association between management and firm performance in founder CEO firms is positive and significant, similar to what is generally found for other ownership types. This positive association suggests both that the lower level of management quality in founder CEO firms is likely to result in worse firm performance and that lower management scores among founder CEO firms are not due to the fact that these firms have lower returns to management. Third, firms led by founder CEOs experience significant improvements in their management practices upon a change of ownership, and these improvements are generally much larger than what is found for other ownership transitions.

A natural question arising from these findings is: Why are firms led by founder CEOs not adopting performance-enhancing managerial processes or replacing themselves with managers who do? We present three not-necessarily-mutually-exclusive possible classes of explanations for the persistence of poor management practices at firms with founder CEOs despite the performance penalty: (a) that founder CEOs are unaware of their managerial gaps; (b) that environmental or institutional variables make it more

---

1. This viewpoint is supported by the fact that venture capital firms and private equity firms frequently replace founders with professional managers (Hellmann and Puri 2002).

costly or less attractive for founder CEOs to hire more capable managers to replace themselves, or to select practices consistent with the process of standardization needed to attract external capital (Rajan 2012); and (c) that the adoption of formalized managerial processes may interfere with the founders' ability to pursue nonpecuniary benefits of control, such as investing in a pet project or hiring people based on personal or family affiliations. The initial findings presented in the chapter provide support for (a) and (c), but we do not find evidence that founder CEO firms are systematically different according to the quality of the institutional environments in which they are embedded.

Our findings face several limitations. First, the nature of the firms included in the WMS data (companies between 50 and 5,000 employees) significantly dampens our ability to analyze the role of founder CEOs on organizations in their early stages of life and/or managers in the early years of their tenure, which may both be more salient to the entrepreneurship literature. Second, the nature of our data does not allow us to estimate the *causal* effect of founder CEOs on management adoption and firm performance; rather, we present simple conditional correlations. Relatedly, the lack of information on CEO skills, preferences, and experiences does not allow us to look in more detail at the heterogeneity within different types of founder CEOs.

The chapter is structured as follows. In section 4.2 we provide a description of the WMS data. In section 4.3 we explore the differences in management practices between firms led by founder CEOs and firms and all other forms of leader-ownership. In section 4.4 we explore the relationship between management and firm performance. In section 4.5 we present the analysis of the possible drivers of the managerial differences across ownership types. Section 4.6 concludes.

4.2   Data

4.2.1   Survey Methodology

To measure the presence of basic management practices, we use the World Management Survey (WMS), which was collected using a methodology first described in Bloom and Van Reenen (2007). The survey is based on an interview-based evaluation tool that defines and scores from 1 ("worst practice") to 5 ("best practice") across eighteen key management practices. Appendix table 4A.1 lists the management questions and also gives some sense of how the responses to each question are mapped onto the scoring grid.[2]

The evaluation tool attempts to measure management practices in three

---

2. For the full set of questions for each sector (manufacturing, retail, schools and hospitals), see www.worldmanagementsurvey.org.

key areas. First, *monitoring*: How well do organizations monitor what goes on inside the firm and use this information for continuous improvement? Second, *targets*: Do organizations set the right targets, track the right outcomes, and take appropriate action if the two are inconsistent? Third, *incentives/people management*: Are organizations promoting and rewarding employees based on performance, prioritizing careful hiring, and trying to keep their best employees?[3]

The methodology gives a firm a low score if it fails to track performance, has no effective targets, does not take ability and effort into account when deciding on promotions (e.g., completely tenure based), and has no system to address persistent employee underperformance. In contrast, a high-scoring organization frequently monitors and tries to improve its processes, sets comprehensive and stretching targets, promotes high-performing employees, and addresses (by retraining/rotating and, if unsuccessful, dismissing) underperforming employees.

The survey design included teams of MBA-type students with business experience conducting the interviews with the plant managers in their native languages. Plant managers were purposely selected, as they were senior enough to have an overview of management practices but not so senior as to be detached from day-to-day operations. The survey is based on a double-blind methodology. First, managers were not told they were being scored or shown the scoring grid. They were told only that they were being "interviewed about their day-to-day management practices." To do this, the interviewers asked open-ended questions[4] and continued with open questions focusing on specific practices and trying to elicit examples until the interviewer could make an accurate assessment of the firm's practices.[5] Second, the interviewers were not told anything in advance about the organization's performance; they were provided only with the organization's name, telephone number, and industry.

The data set includes randomly sampled medium-sized firms (employing between 50 and 5,000 workers) in the manufacturing sector. The sampling

3. These practices are similar to those emphasized in earlier work on management practices, by, for example, Osterman (1994), Ichniowski, Shaw, and Prennushi (1997), and Black and Lynch (2001).
4. For example, on the first monitoring dimension in the manufacturing survey, the interviewer starts by asking the open question "Could you please tell me about how you monitor your production process?" rather than a closed question such as "Do you monitor your production daily [yes/no]?"
5. For example, the second question on that monitoring dimension is "What kinds of measures would you use to track performance?" rather than "Do you track your performance?" and the third is "If I walked around your factory, what could I tell about how each person was performing?" The combined responses to the questions within this dimension are scored against a grid that goes from 1, which is defined as *Measures tracked do not indicate directly if overall business objectives are being met. Tracking is an ad hoc process (certain processes aren't tracked at all)*, to 5, which is defined as *Performance is continuously tracked and communicated, both formally and informally, to all staff using a range of visual management tools.*

frame was drawn in such a way that the firms sampled for each country are representative of the distribution of medium-sized manufacturing firms across a variety of different databases. The survey achieved a response rate of about 50 percent through a combination of government endorsements and internal managerial efforts. Reassuringly, responses were uncorrelated with the (independently collected) performance measures for the firm (see Bloom et al. 2014 for details).

The data set also includes a series of "noise controls" on the interview process itself (such as the time of day and the day of the week), characteristics of the interviewee (such as tenure in firm), and the identity of the interviewer (a full set of dummy variables for the interviewer to account for any interviewer bias). In some specifications we include these variables to control for measurement error. The data was also internally validated through silent monitoring of the interviews (whereby a second person listening in on a phone extension independently scored the interview), and repeat interviews (using a different interviewer and a second plant manager within the same firm). In both cases, the comparisons suggested a high level of consistency across different interviewees and interviewers (see Bloom et al. 2014 for details).

4.2.2 Ownership

Firms are classified in several different ownership categories using information collected during the survey and are subsequently cross checked against public accounts and Web searches. This process first determines whether any individual person, group of individuals, or organization owns more than 25.01 percent of the shares of the company. If this is not the case, the firm is classified as owned by "dispersed shareholders." If a single group of individuals or organization owns more than 25.01 percent of the shares of the company, the firm is subsequently classified in the following categories according to the nature of the controlling individuals/organization: "founder" (the owner coincides with the person who founded the firm); "family" (the owner/s are affiliated with the family of the firm's founder); "private equity"; "private individuals"; "managers"; and "government." The firm is classified in the "other" category if the ownership type does not match any of the above categories (this typically happens for country-specific ownership types, such as foundations in Germany). When a founder or a family owns the firm, we further distinguish between the cases in which the CEO is the founder him/herself or is affiliated with the owning family.

In what follows, we will focus most of the discussion on the difference between firms that are owned and run by a founder CEO, which represent in total 18 percent of the sample, and all the other types of ownership. Table 4.1 presents a detailed breakdown of the frequencies of founder CEO firms included in the sample according to their ownership type across the thirty-two countries included in the sample. Clearly, founder CEO firms are much more likely to be found in developing countries relative to more

Table 4.1   **Firm ownership across countries**

Sample	All	All other ownership	Founder CEO
Argentina	566	471	95
Australia	470	442	28
Brazil	1,145	754	391
Canada	418	368	50
Chile	543	471	72
China	761	601	160
Colombia	170	114	56
Ethiopia	131	90	41
France	610	571	39
Germany	608	592	16
Ghana	107	54	53
Greece	272	222	50
India	921	529	392
Italy	310	252	58
Japan	172	168	4
Kenya	184	134	50
Mexico	524	424	100
Mozambique	85	59	26
New Zealand	149	135	14
Nicaragua	97	77	20
Nigeria	118	55	63
Poland	364	330	34
Portugal	311	252	59
Republic of Ireland	161	127	34
Singapore	373	308	65
Spain	213	194	19
Sweden	377	369	8
Tanzania	150	102	48
Turkey	332	173	159
United Kingdom	1,332	1,225	107
United States	1,393	1,267	126
Zambia	68	46	22
Total	**13,435**	**10,976**	**2,459**

developed economies—the fraction of founder CEO firms across Organisation for Economic Co-operation and Development (OECD) economies is 11 percent versus 30 percent in non-OECD countries.[6] Therefore, in our analysis we will primarily examine within-country comparisons in order to allay the concern that the differences in management practices across firms may capture unobserved country characteristics.

6. This fact is not surprising given that many founder CEO successions are associated with growth milestones (Wasserman 2003), and developing economies have many more small firms (Hsieh and Olken 2014).

Table 4.2   **Summary statistics**

Sample	Total (1)	All other ownership (2)	Founder CEO (3)	(2)–(3), p-value (4)
Management	2.873	2.952	2.518	0.434***
	(0.678)	(0.669)	(0.600)	(29.63)
Operations	2.941	3.037	2.515	0.522***
	(0.764)	(0.750)	(0.678)	(31.70)
People	2.736	2.783	2.524	0.259***
	(0.653)	(0.656)	(0.593)	(18.00)
Firm employment	850.382	952.282	395.753	556.5***
	(3,821.212)	(4,205.027)	(778.492)	(6.53)
Plant employment	270.084	280.909	223.831	57.08***
	(410.197)	(427.679)	(321.067)	(6.09)
Firm age	48.463	52.266	25.297	26.97***
	(42.500)	(44.469)	(11.769)	(20.34)
MNE status	0.404	0.476	0.088	0.388***
	(0.491)	(0.499)	(0.283)	(36.56)
Skills	15.068	15.637	12.644	2.993***
	(16.893)	(17.147)	(15.536)	(7.58)
Observations	13,436	10,977	2,459	

Notes: Table is calculated with simple averages. Column (4) indicates that the differences in raw averages between founder CEOs and all other ownership are significant at the 1 percent level across all variables. MNE status is an indicator variable equal to 1 if the firm is a multinational. Skills measures the proportion of firm employees (managers and nonmanagers) with a college degree. Management is the average management score based on responses to the eighteen categories assessed in the WMS (Bloom and Van Reenen 2007). Operations is the average management score for the set of questions associated with monitoring and target practices. People is the average management score for the set of questions associated with HR practices within the firm.
***Significant at the 1 percent level.

4.3   Management Practices in Founder CEO Firms

4.3.1   Cross-Sectional Analysis

In this section we examine the differences in management practices across different ownership types, focusing, in particular, on firms owned and managed by their founder.

Table 4.2 shows summary statistics for the overall sample and the raw comparisons between founder CEO firms and the rest of the ownership categories. The first three rows of table 4.2 show that founder CEO firms on average appear to be much less likely to have adopted the basic managerial practices included in the WMS. This gap is significant when we consider the overall management score, as well as when we distinguish between the operational questions (*monitoring* and *target setting*) and the *people management*

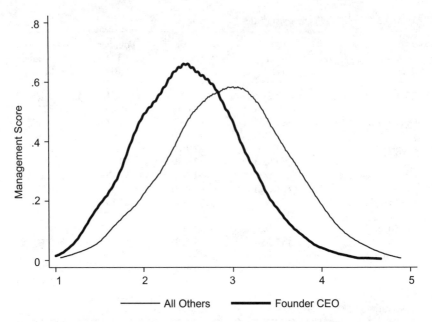

Fig. 4.1   Kernel density plot of management scores for founder CEO firms and all other ownership types

questions asked in the survey.[7] Looking beyond sample means, figure 4.1 presents a kernel density plot of management scores for founder CEO firms and firms with other ownership types. The graph shows that the lower average is not due to a tail of firms with low management bringing down the average, but rather that the entire mass of the distribution is shifted to the left.

Clearly, management is not the only dimension along which founder CEO firms differ from the other ownership types included in the WMS. Although the criteria for inclusion in the management survey skew the distribution toward larger firms, it is still the case that founder CEO firms are smaller and younger than the other firms in the sample. Founder CEO firms are also less likely to be part of a domestic or foreign multinational and have, on average, a smaller fraction of employees with a college degree. To understand the extent to which the differences in management scores between founder CEO

7. The gap in management scores between founder CEO firms and other ownership types is still evident when we use a more granular ownership classification. Figure 4A.1 in the appendix plots the raw average management scores across the finer ownership classifications introduced in section 4.2.2. Founder CEO firms have the lowest average management scores even relative to the second-lowest category, family firms managed by a family CEO. The difference between the two types of ownership is significant at the 1 percent level, and remains so even when we control for country and industry (three-digit SIC) fixed effects.

firms versus other ownership types can be accounted for by these observable firm characteristics—which are typically associated with differences in management practices (e.g., Bloom, Sadun, and Van Reenen 2016)—in table 4.3 we show the conditional correlation between management and the founder CEO dummy controlling for a progressively larger set of controls (standard errors clustered at the firm level are shown in parentheses under the coefficients). To the extent that these differences are endogenous to ownership, the resulting estimates will provide a lower bound to the causal effect of the founder CEO dummy.

The dependent variable in all regressions presented in table 4.3 is the firm-level average management score, aggregated across all questions and standardized. Column (1) shows that the relationship between lower management scores and founder CEOs is significant when comparing firms within countries. The difference is large (0.608 of a standard deviation) and significant at the 1 percent level. Column (2) adds industry (Standard Industrial Classification [SIC] three-digit dummies) and log firm employment to control for size and the different distribution of founder CEO firms across sectors. Since larger firms tend to be better managed on average, adding firm size reduces the magnitude of the coefficient on the Founder CEO dummy from 0.412 to 0.254, but it remains significant at the 1 percent level. In column (3) we add a control for the log of firm age to verify the extent to which the management gap may be driven by firm age, which table 4.2 shows to differ significantly across ownership types. Even looking across firms of a similar age, the founder CEO dummy remains of a similar magnitude and significance. In column (4) we add controls for fraction of employees (managers and nonmanagers) with college degrees and multinational status, two variables that are empirically correlated with higher management scores and are systematically less prevalent in founder CEO firms. As a result, the coefficient on the founder CEO dummy is almost halved, becoming 0.162, but the coefficient remains significant at the 1 percent level. Finally, in column (5), our baseline specification going forward, we add a set of interview noise controls including interviewer identity and length of the interview. In this specification, the magnitude of the coefficient on the founder CEO dummy lowers to 0.138. Finally, because of evidence that developed countries have higher management practices, on average, in columns (6) and (7) we look at differences across non-OECD and OECD countries and find the results to be remarkably similar, and statistically indistinguishable, across the two subsets.

Overall, the multivariate analysis shows the existence of a managerial gap in founder CEO firms relative to other ownership types that is not fully accounted for by differences in firm country of location, industry of activity, firm size, age, or skills. Using the estimates from table 4.3, columns (1) and (5), the analysis reveals that observable firm, industry characteristics, and interview noise are able to account for about 67 percent of the

Table 4.3   Founder CEO management

Sample	All (1)	All (2)	All (3)	All (4)	All (5)	Non-OECD (6)	OECD (7)
Founder CEO	-0.412***	-0.254***	-0.266***	-0.162***	-0.138***	-0.128***	-0.148***
	(0.022)	(0.021)	(0.021)	(0.021)	(0.019)	(0.025)	(0.031)
Ln(firm employment)		0.233***	0.235***	0.194***	0.176***	0.179***	0.175***
		(0.008)	(0.008)	(0.008)	(0.007)	(0.011)	(0.010)
Ln(firm age)			-0.063***	-0.038***	-0.041***	-0.015	-0.043***
			(0.013)	(0.013)	(0.012)	(0.036)	(0.013)
Skills				0.133***	0.120***	0.138***	0.106***
				(0.007)	(0.006)	(0.009)	(0.009)
MNE status				0.364***	0.325***	0.341***	0.319***
				(0.019)	(0.017)	(0.029)	(0.021)
Constant	0.711***	-1.843***	-1.613***	-1.924***	-3.894***	-3.667***	-2.375***
	(0.097)	(0.112)	(0.121)	(0.119)	(0.623)	(0.195)	(0.606)
Observations	13,436	13,436	13,436	13,436	13,436	4,877	8,559
Adjusted R-squared	0.182	0.287	0.289	0.337	0.450	0.477	0.367
Country dummies	Yes	Yes	Yes	Yes	Yes	Yes	Yes
Industry dummies	No	Yes	Yes	Yes	Yes	Yes	Yes
Firm employment	No	Yes	Yes	Yes	Yes	Yes	Yes
Firm age	No	No	Yes	Yes	Yes	Yes	Yes
Skills	No	No	No	Yes	Yes	Yes	Yes
MNE status	No	No	No	Yes	Yes	Yes	Yes
Noise	No	No	No	No	Yes	Yes	Yes

Notes: Dependent variable is the management z-score. All columns estimated by ordinary least squares (OLS) with standard errors clustered at the company level (due to inclusion of a subset of panel firms). Columns (1)–(5) use the entire sample for estimation; columns (6) and (7) repeat specification (5) for non-OECD and OECD countries separately. Country controls are a full set of country dummies for the countries in which the headquarters of each firm is located (which may be different from the country in which the interviewed plant manager is located for the case of multinational firms). Industry controls are SIC three-digit dummies. Firm employment, firm age, skills, and MNE status are included and described in table 4.1. Noise controls include the duration of the interview and an indicator for the specific person conducting the interview.

***Significant at the 1 percent level.

**Significant at the 5 percent level.

*Significant at the 10 percent level.

within-country difference between founder CEO firms and other forms of ownership $((0.412 - 0.138) / 0.412)$, with the rest still being captured by the founder CEO dummy. To further explore the extent to which other unobservable firm characteristics—rather than founder CEO ownership and control—may account for this remaining gap, we turn to analyzing changes in management over time across different types of ownership.

4.3.2   Panel Analysis

About 2,844 firms included in the WMS were interviewed more than once over time and, of these, 905 also experienced a change in ownership type. Of these, 167 (of the 487 total founder CEO firms in the subsample of 2,844 firms) classified as founder CEO firms in their first appearance in the WMS data set transition to a different form of ownership. In this section, we exploit this specific sample with panel management data to further explore the extent to which the managerial gap examined in section 4.3.1 can be traced back to founder CEO ownership, rather than to other unobservable fixed firm characteristics.

More specifically, we examine whether firms that where initially (i.e., at the time of their first appearance in the WMS data) owned and managed by their founder and experienced a change in ownership before their subsequent appearance in the WMS data saw an improvement in their management scores relative to firms that did not experience an ownership change. Ownership changes are likely to be endogenous—firms are typically acquired on the basis of unobservable characteristics, including their productivity or potential for improvement. Therefore, to control for the possibility that the postacquisition management scores might reflect dynamics unrelated to the change in ownership, we set up this comparison using a difference-in-difference approach, comparing the change in management scores experienced by initial founder CEO firms transitioning to other ownership types (167 firms) to the change in management scores experienced by firms that were initially classified in other ownership categories and also experienced a change in ownership (738 firms).

The identification assumption underlying this comparison is that the unobserved factors leading to an ownership change in founder CEO firms are similar to those leading to an ownership change in other types of firms. To gauge the empirical relevance of this assumption, we investigated the relationship between a dummy capturing the ownership change between two distinct waves of the WMS and a basic set of firm-level controls. Reassuringly, the results (presented in table 4A.2) show that changes in ownership are not significantly correlated with the initial level of management in both types of transitions, nor with firm size. However, firm age and multinational enterprise (MNE) status both appear to be positively and significantly correlated with changes in ownership for founder CEO firms, but not for the other ownership types. Therefore, while we do not find evidence that founder CEO firms undergoing an ownership change are differentially selected on the basis of their overall management scores relative to other ownership types, we cannot entirely rule out differential selection based on other observable firm characteristics, which may be associated with future changes in management.

With this caveat in mind, we report the graphic result of the difference-in-difference in figure 4.2. The bars show the change in management score between two periods, t (the first time a firm appeared in the WMS) and $t +$ 1 (the last time a firm appeared in the WMS), for four classes of firms. On the left-hand side of the graph, we focus on firms that at time t were *not* owned by a founder CEO and distinguish between those that at $t + 1$ had not experienced an ownership change (far left bar in the graph, 1,619 firms), and those that had experienced an ownership change (second bar from the left, 738 firms). The left-hand-side comparison indicates that there is no significant change in the management scores for firms initially classified in the nonfounder CEO category, regardless of ownership changes. On the right-hand side of the graph, we repeat the same classification for firms that were at time t classified as founder CEO firms, and distinguish between

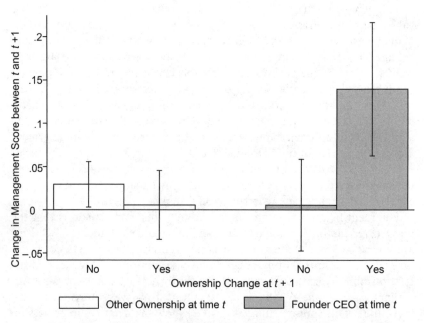

Fig. 4.2   Changes in management score based on ownership changes

Notes: The graph shows average change in management score for each of four categories of ownership observed in the WMS panel data set: nonfounder CEO firms with no change in ownership (1,619 firms), nonfounder CEO firms with a change in ownership (738), founder CEO firms with no change in ownership (320), and founder CEO firms with a change in ownership (167). The error bar values denote 5 percent confidence intervals for each category.

those that remained classified as such at time $t + 1$ (third bar in the graph, 320 firms), and those that instead had transitioned to a different ownership type at time $t + 1$ (far right bar in the graph, 167 firms).

The graph shows that while the average change in management score between t and $t + 1$ is not distinguishable from zero for founder CEO firms that did not experience a change in ownership, those firms that began with a founder CEO and had transitioned to a different ownership type by $t + 1$ experienced a significant increase in their management score.

Although the graph is based on raw data, these results are robust to the inclusion of country and industry dummies, firm characteristics, and interview noise, as shown in table 4.4. Just like in figure 4.2, the dependent variable in all columns of table 4.4 is the raw change in the average management score between t and $t + 1$. In column (1), we include as dependent variables only country dummies and an indicator for whether the ownership status

Table 4.4   **Impact of ownership changes on management scores**

	Change in management score				
Dependent variable	(1)	(2)	(3)	(4)	(5)
Ownership change	0.016	0.015	−0.017	−0.015	−0.001
	(0.028)	(0.028)	(0.031)	(0.032)	(0.032)
(Initial) founder CEO		0.046	−0.016	−0.015	0.011
		(0.031)	(0.038)	(0.040)	(0.041)
Ownership change * (initial)			0.171***	0.153**	0.190***
founder CEO			(0.064)	(0.066)	(0.066)
Constant	−0.060	−0.069	−0.060	−0.083	−0.897***
	(0.047)	(0.048)	(0.048)	(0.051)	(0.225)
Observations	2,844	2,844	2,844	2,844	2,844
Adjusted R-squared	0.008	0.009	0.010	0.016	0.083
Country dummies	Yes	Yes	Yes	Yes	Yes
Industry dummies	No	No	No	Yes	Yes
Firm employment	No	No	No	No	Yes
Firm age	No	No	No	No	Yes
Skills	No	No	No	No	Yes
MNE status	No	No	No	No	Yes
Noise	No	No	No	No	Yes

Notes: Dependent variable is the change in management score between the first and the last time a firm was interviewed for the WMS. Therefore, only firms who have been administered the survey two or more times are included in this estimation. All columns are estimated using OLS and robust standard errors. Ownership change is an indicator variable equal to 1 if an ownership change occurred between the first and last time the focal firm was interviewed for the WMS. (Initial) founder CEO is equal to 1 if the firm had founder CEO ownership the first time the WMS was administered and equal to 0 otherwise.
***Significant at 1 percent.
**Significant at 5 percent.
*Significant at 10 percent.

changed. The results suggest that change in ownership *per se* is not associated with a significant change in management practices. In column (2), we add an indicator for whether the ownership type was founder CEO in period t, and we find that the coefficient is positive but statistically insignificant, suggesting that founder CEO firms overall did not experience large improvements in management between the two time periods. In column (3), we include an interaction between the indicators for having a founder CEO in period t and a change in ownership prior to time $t + 1$. This positive and significant coefficient shows that firms that used to be owned and run by their founder experience large gains in their management score when these firms experience a change in ownership prior to time $t + 1$. The magnitude of the coefficient in the interaction is 0.171, which is 28 percent of the standard deviation in founder CEO score and significant at the 1 percent level. The magnitude and significance of the coefficient is robust to the inclusion of industry dummies (column [4]), and other firm and noise controls (column [5]), including the dummy capturing MNE status and firm age.

Overall, these results suggest that the differences in management scores discussed in section 4.2 are tightly related to the identity of the CEO, rather than being driven by unobserved characteristics of the firms led by founder CEOs. To further illustrate this point, in figure 4.3 we break down the changes observed in founder CEO firms at time $t + 1$ according to the detailed type of ownership at time $t + 1$. The average change in management scores is positive across all transitions. Interestingly, the largest change appears when the founder remains the main owner of the firm but an external manager takes the top position. This suggests that it is the presence of the founder in an active operational role in the company that potentially dampens management adoption, rather than founder ownership *per se*.

4.4   Does Management Matter in Founder CEO Firms?

A growing body of research has documented the presence of large and significant performance implications for the managerial practices investigated in the WMS (Bloom et al. 2013, 2014; Bloom and Van Reenen 2007). However, one possible explanation behind the managerial gap explored in section 4.3 is that formalized managerial processes might be relatively less important for the performance of founder CEO firms. For example, founder CEOs might be able to substitute for formalized practices with other unobservable managerial skills, such as their charisma, connections, or intrinsic motivation.

We investigate this issue in table 4.5, where we estimate a simple production function—log sales as a function of the total number of employees, capital, and materials, all drawn from published accounts drawn from the accounting database ORBIS using the following specification:

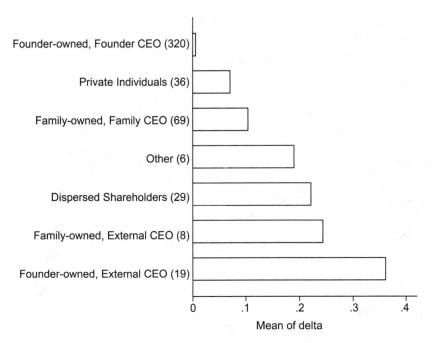

Fig. 4.3   Changes in management score for firms originating with founder CEOs

Notes: The graph shows the change in management score for firms that were surveyed more than once in the WMS data and were owned and managed by founder CEOs in the first survey wave in which they appeared. The bars display the average change in management score for each type of ownership transition, indicated in the last observation in the WMS data (as well as the changes in management score for those founder CEO firms that experienced no transition—the first row). The number of observations of each type of transition (as well as the nontransition group) is shown in parentheses next to the ownership type.

$$y_{itsc} = \alpha \text{FounderCEO}_{it} + \beta \text{Management}_{it}$$
$$+ \gamma \text{FounderCEO}_{it} * \text{Management}_{it}$$
$$+ F_{it}\theta + \delta e_{it} + \vartheta m_{it} + \mu k_{it} + \zeta_s + \tau_t + \rho_c + \varepsilon_{itsc},$$

where y, e, m, k represent the natural logarithm of, respectively, firm-level sales, employment, materials, and capital; F the set of firm-level controls employed in earlier tables; and ζ_s, τ_t, and ρ_c denote industry, time, and country fixed effects. Since we use repeated cross sections for each firm, errors are clustered at the firm level across all columns. The key parameter in this specification is γ, which allows us to evaluate whether the relationship between management and performance is systematically different for founder CEO firms relative to other ownership types.

Column (1) shows that founder CEO firms tend, on average, to be 9.4 percent less productive than other ownership types (the coefficient is significant at the 5 percent level). Column (2) adds to the specification the average man-

Table 4.5   Performance of founder CEO firms

Dependent variable	Ln(sales) (1)	Ln(sales) (2)	Ln(sales) (3)	Change in ln(sales) (4)	ROCE (5)	ROA (7)
Founder CEO	−0.094**	−0.082*	−0.079*	−0.000	−0.174	14.310
	(0.046)	(0.045)	(0.044)	(0.009)	(0.979)	(59.670)
Management		0.093***	0.092***	0.006**	1.035***	52.259**
		(0.015)	(0.015)	(0.002)	(0.356)	(22.746)
Founder CEO * management			0.006	0.001	−0.658	−68.110
			(0.048)	(0.007)	(0.728)	(43.172)
Ln(firm employment)	0.628***	0.616***	0.616***		1.500***	65.538**
	(0.023)	(0.023)	(0.023)		(0.440)	(27.632)
Ln(materials)	0.226***	0.224***	0.224***		1.149***	52.683**
	(0.014)	(0.014)	(0.014)		(0.374)	(24.274)
Ln(capital)	0.246***	0.240***	0.240***		−1.008***	3.456
	(0.016)	(0.015)	(0.015)		(0.336)	(20.129)
Change in ln(firm employment)				0.417***		
				(0.026)		
Change in ln(materials)				0.518***		
				(0.019)		
Change in ln(capital)				0.151***		
				(0.013)		
Constant	2.902***	3.078***	3.076***	−0.068	0.173	−1956.993
	(0.295)	(0.290)	(0.290)	(0.084)	(10.420)	(1684.996)
Observations	9,203	9,203	9,203	8,902	7,677	8,720
Adjusted R-squared	0.807	0.810	0.810	0.388	0.100	0.089
Country dummies	Yes	Yes	Yes	Yes	Yes	Yes
Industry dummies	Yes	Yes	Yes	Yes	Yes	Yes
Firm employment	Yes	Yes	Yes	Yes	Yes	Yes
Firm age	Yes	Yes	Yes	Yes	Yes	Yes
Skills	Yes	Yes	Yes	Yes	Yes	Yes
MNE status	Yes	Yes	Yes	Yes	Yes	Yes
Noise	Yes	Yes	Yes	Yes	Yes	Yes

Notes: The sample used for this table includes only those firms for which sales, employment, capital, ROCE, and ROA data could be found in ORBIS and other databases. All columns are estimated using OLS and standard errors clustered at the firm level.
***Significant at the 1 percent level.
**Significant at the 5 percent level.
*Significant at the 10 percent level.

agement score which, consistent with earlier research, appears to be positive and strongly correlated with productivity (coefficient 0.093, standard error 0.015). This result also shows that, although differences in management are able to account for about 13 percent of this difference (0.094 − 0.082/0.094), the founder CEO dummy remains statistically significant at the 10 percent level. In column (3) we introduce the founder CEO * management interaction to test for differential slopes by ownership types. We find the interaction to be small and positive, though statistically insignificant at conventional levels. This basic finding is confirmed in columns (4), (5), and (6), where we look, respectively, at one-year log changes in sales, ROCE, and ROA as alternative outcome variables.

Overall, we find no support for the hypothesis that management might be a less critical factor in firms led by their founders relative to other ownership types.

4.5   Why do Founder CEO Have Low Management Scores?

The persistence of founder CEOs using weaker management practices in light of the positive performance associated with management is a puzzle. If founder CEOs have a stake in the financial performance of the organization, it seems that they would be better served by either adopting performance-enhancing practices or by replacing themselves with professional managers.

In this section, we explore some of the reasons why we might observe this nonadoption of management practices among founders. First, we investigate whether the managerial gap explored in section 4.3 might be due to *informational* constraints, that is, founder CEOs might simply not know or not be able to recognize the added value of the practices we investigate. Second, founder firms may arise in situations where the incentive to adopt these practices and standardize the business practices of the organization might be dampened by the institutional constraints in which the firms are embedded (Rajan 2012). Third, founders might resist the adoption of formalized management practices because they derive nonmonetary benefits of control (Hamilton 2000; Moskowitz and Vissing-Jørgensen 2002) and perceive these processes as a potential obstacle to the pursuit of possible private benefits. We explore these non-mutually-exclusive arguments below.

4.5.1   Informational Constraints

One potential explanation for the wide heterogeneity in adoption of performance-enhancing management practices across firms might be due to problems of *perception*—that is, founders may underestimate the practices' effect on productivity or overestimate the degree to which they are being implemented in practice (Gibbons and Henderson 2011).

To investigate whether the perception problem might be a possible explanation of the managerial gap documented across founder CEO firms, we exploit a self-reported measure collected at the end of the WMS survey in which managers assess the quality of their own practices on a scale from 1 to 10.[8] Figure 4.4 plots the average standardized WMS scores associated with the manager self-assessed scores (generated using a nonparametric lowess estimator overlaid onto the scatter plot of values) for both founder CEO

---

8. The exact wording of the question is: "Ignoring yourself, how well managed do you think the rest of the company is on scale: 1 to 10, where 1 is worst practice, 10 is best practice, and 5 is average?"

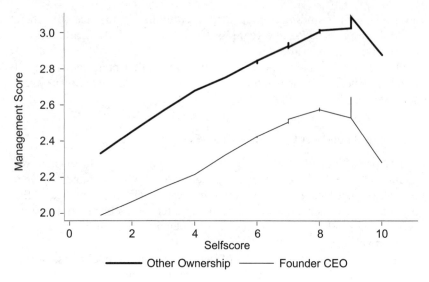

Fig. 4.4   Manager self-score of firm management compared with WMS management score

Note: The graph shows the result of a lowess estimator of self-responses of the interviewed plant manager when asked to indicate his/her impression of firm management (on a scale of 1–10) as compared to the management score derived from the WMS interview.

firms and the other ownership types. The self-assessed own-firm management score and the one obtained through the WMS interviews are positively correlated for all but the highest level of self-assessment, where true score trends down slightly in both cases. Interestingly, however, managers at founder CEO firms tend to systematically overestimate how well managed their firm is—the same level of self-score maps into a systematically lower level of actual management score for founder CEO firms.[9]

To look in more detail at the relationship between actual and self-assessed scores across ownership types, we define an "awareness" metric in the following way. First, we categorize each firm according to its quintile in the actual management score distribution within its country. Second, we do the same for the self-assessed management quality by country. Third, we define a variable taking values as follows: −1 if the difference between the actual and self-assessed quintile is less than −1, indicating that the manager systematically underestimated the relative quality of his or her firm's management quality; 0 if the difference in the quintiles is between −1 and 1 (included), if the self-assessment was relatively accurate; and 1 if the difference between

9. Because the phrasing of the question rules out the manager evaluating his/herself, these results do not seem to be consistent with personal overconfidence. The results may be consistent with hiring policies resulting in less experienced managers or with weak performance monitoring policies that result in managers having a weak idea of what works, however.

Table 4.6   Own-firm management self-assessment by ownership type

	Total	All other ownership	Founder CEO
Underconfidence	3,775	3,448	327
	30.16%	33.90%	13.93%
Realism	7,112	5,608	1,504
	56.81%	55.14%	64.08%
Overconfidence	1,631	1,115	516
	13.03%	10.96%	21.99%
Total	12,518	10,171	2,347
	100%	100%	100%

Notes: Table includes raw number of firms for which underconfidence, realism, and overconfidence were detected in the interviewed plant manager's self-assessment of his/her firm's management. To collect the self-score, managers were asked on a scale of 1–10 how they perceived their firms' management proficiency. This data was subsequently divided into quintiles, as were the WMS management scores, separately. Underconfidence is classified as having a self-assessment quintile value at least 2 quintiles lower than the actual management score of the firm. Realism is assigned to a firm if the interviewed manager's self-score of the firm's management is within 1 quintile (above or below) the actual management score for the firm. Lastly, Overconfidence is a result of a managerial self-score of at least 2 quintiles higher than the firm's WMS management score. Along with the raw number of firms, the percentage of the total firms is included for all firms and, separately, founder CEO firms and firms under all other forms of ownership.

the actual and self-assessed quintile is greater than 1, indicating the manager systematically overestimated the relative quality of his or her firm's own management quality. Table 4.6 summarizes the values of this variable across different ownership types. Overall, about 57 percent of the managers appear to have a relatively good idea of where their firm stands in terms of management. About 30 percent seem to underestimate their firm's relative standing, while 13 percent overestimate their firm's management quality relative to the actual scores. The distribution of the scores across these three categories of managers, however, is systematically different across ownership types. More specifically, founder CEO firms tend to have a larger fraction of firms that overestimate (22 percent vs. 11 percent) or have a realistic assessment (64 percent vs. 55 percent) of their scores and a much smaller fraction that underestimate their scores (14 percent vs. 34 percent).

To see whether these differences in awareness might be able to account for the differences in scores documented in section 4.3, we include the "awareness metric" in the specification calculated in table 4.3, column (5), and test whether the inclusion of this metric has any sizable effect on the coefficient measuring the founder CEO dummy effect. The results of this exercise are shown in table 4.7. We start with a baseline specification in column (2) where we simply show that the coefficient on the founder CEO dummy is still negative and significant and of similar size in the sample of firms for which the

Table 4.7   Accounting for awareness of management quality on management

Sample	All (1)	All (2)	All (3)	Non-OECD (4)	Non-OECD (5)	OECD (6)	OECD (7)
Founder CEO	-0.138***	-0.125***	-0.093***	-0.125***	-0.106***	-0.122***	-0.068**
	(0.019)	(0.019)	(0.017)	(0.025)	(0.023)	(0.030)	(0.026)
Ln(firm employment)	0.176***	0.172***	0.137***	0.180***	0.148***	0.169***	0.132***
	(0.007)	(0.007)	(0.007)	(0.011)	(0.010)	(0.010)	(0.009)
Ln(firm age)	-0.041***	-0.033***	-0.024**	-0.013	-0.015	-0.034**	-0.023**
	(0.012)	(0.012)	(0.011)	(0.037)	(0.032)	(0.013)	(0.012)
Ln(skills)	0.120***	0.123***	0.095***	0.139***	0.114***	0.111***	0.083***
	(0.006)	(0.006)	(0.006)	(0.009)	(0.009)	(0.009)	(0.008)
MNE status	0.325***	0.337***	0.258***	0.342***	0.271***	0.336***	0.259***
	(0.017)	(0.017)	(0.015)	(0.029)	(0.025)	(0.022)	(0.018)
Awareness			-0.650***		-0.563***		-0.698***
			(0.011)		(0.017)		(0.014)
Constant	-3.894***	-4.110***	-3.352***	-3.694***	-2.955***	-2.827***	-2.119***
	(0.623)	(0.712)	(0.540)	(0.196)	(0.180)	(0.623)	(0.445)
Observations	13,436	12,518	12,518	4,827	4,827	7,691	7,691
Adjusted R-squared	0.450	0.467	0.592	0.478	0.579	0.392	0.549
Country dummies	Yes	Yes	Yes	Yes	Yes	Yes	Yes
Industry dummies	Yes	Yes	Yes	Yes	Yes	Yes	Yes
Firm employment	Yes	Yes	Yes	Yes	Yes	Yes	Yes
Firm age	Yes	Yes	Yes	Yes	Yes	Yes	Yes
Skills	Yes	Yes	Yes	Yes	Yes	Yes	Yes
MNE status	Yes	Yes	Yes	Yes	Yes	Yes	Yes
Noise	Yes	Yes	Yes	Yes	Yes	Yes	Yes

Notes: Dependent variable is the management z-score index. All columns estimated by ordinary least squares (OLS) with standard errors clustered at the company level (due to inclusion of a subset of panel firms). Columns (1)–(3) use the entire data set whereas columns (4)–(7) test the effect of managerial awareness in non-OECD and OECD countries, respectively.

***Significant at the 1 percent level.
**Significant at the 5 percent level.
*Significant at the 10 percent level.

self-assessment metric is available (column [2] compared to column [1]).[10] In column (3) we add the awareness metric—which reduces the coefficient on the founder CEO dummy by about 25 percent (from 0.125 to 0.093), but the coefficient is still sizable and significant at the 1 percent level. In columns (4) to (7) we repeat the same experiment for firms in non-OECD (columns [4] and [5]) and OECD countries (columns [6] and [7]). In both cases, the coefficient on the founder CEO dummy remains negative and significant; however, the reduction in its coefficient when the awareness variable in included is much larger in OECD countries (46 percent vs. 15 percent).

Overall, these results suggest that the lower managerial scores of founder CEO firms are associated with managers' systematic lack of awareness of the weakness of their firms' management quality (especially in OECD countries), but this lack of self-awareness does not fully explain the management gap that we find for founder CEOs relative to other ownership types.

4.5.2   Institutions

In this section we explore whether inefficient institutions may be a possible driver of the lower managerial scores of founder CEO firms. The potential role of institutions in shaping the incentive to adopt formalized managerial practices can best be seen in terms of the framework proposed by Rajan (2012) to investigate when and to what extent founders will have the incentive to "standardize" their business practices, that is, to establish processes that "reduce the idiosyncratic and personalized aspects of the entrepreneur's role." This set-up is useful since the processes considered by Rajan encompass several of the managerial practices included in the WMS; for example: (a) formalizing implicit agreements with employees, (b) spreading the allocation of responsibilities across functions so that they can be more easily managed by outsiders, and (c) introducing strategic planning and information systems so that the information that a CEO needs to make decisions is more easily available.

One of the key insights of Rajan's framework is that the standardization decision creates a fundamental tension for the founder. On one hand, standardization might be necessary to attract external capital. Potential backers may see these practices as tools through which the human capital in the firm, particularly the CEO, becomes more replaceable, reducing risk by making the firm more amenable to external control. On the other hand, the founder might resist standardization precisely because it makes his or her personal human capital less critical and more easily substituted by an external CEO. In this setup, the founder is encouraged to adopt these "standardized" practices to gain access to capital markets. If capital markets are not well developed, the rewards associated with standardization will be reduced for

---

10. The smaller sample is due to the fact that the self-assessment question was introduced in the 2006 WMS wave, whereas the whole sample started being collected in 2004.

the founder, hence reducing the incentive to incur the loss of personal rents associated with it. For this reason, institutions that support liquid capital markets may, by extension, support the adoption of superior management practices in founder-owned ventures.

Institutions might also have an impact on the standardization decisions even in absence of the need to raise capital through the market. For example, delegation to other talented managers able to guide the firm through the standardization process might be prohibitively costly in countries with poor contractual enforcement (Bandiera, Pratt, and Sadun 2013). These costs might be based on objective constraints—that is, heightened risk of expropriation—or subjective perceptions of the associated risks—that is, lack of trust (Bloom, Sadun, and Van Reenen 2012). Therefore, institutions that lower the costs of contractual enforcement or foster generalized trust may lower the costs of adopting superior management practices.

To investigate these issues we estimate the following model:

$$\text{Management}_{itsc} = \alpha \text{FounderCEO}_{it} + \beta \text{FounderCEO}_{it}$$

$$* S_c + F_{it}\theta + \zeta_s + \tau_t + \rho_c + \varepsilon_{itsc}.$$

Our coefficient of interest is β, which captures the differential effect of different country-specific institutional variables (measured in the country in which the firms' central headquarters [CHQ] are located)[11] for founder CEO firms. If institutions play any role in shaping the adoption of formalized management practices, we would expect $\beta > 0$, meaning that the gap between founder CEO firms and other forms of ownership would be smaller in more efficient institutional environments.[12]

We also investigate differences across different types of management practices covered by the WMS, by estimating this regression for the overall management score, and separately for the operations (all questions referring to *monitoring* and *target* practices) and *people* (all the questions pertaining to HR management practices) sections of the survey. We are specifically interested in practices related to managing people as they may most directly shape the founder's ability to retain control over the company. For example, introducing more formalized human resources (HR) may limit the founder's ability to promote family and friends to positions of power and, more generally, to use promotions to reward personal loyalty (Bandiera, Prat, and Sadun 2013).

The results of this analysis are shown in table 4.8 (we cluster the standard

11. Headquarters is the level at which the institutional constraints are more likely to influence the decision to adopt management practices (see Bloom et al. [2013] for a similar application). An alternative approach would be to match the plant with the institutional variable measured in the country in which the plants are located. The results shown in this section are virtually unchanged when we use this alternative approach.

12. Note that all regressions include country dummies. Therefore, we do not estimate the linear correlation between country-level institutions and management, but their differential correlation across founder CEO firms and other ownership types.

Table 4.8   Impact of institutional context on founder CEO management

Dependent variable	Management (1)	Operations (2)	People (3)	Management (4)	Operations (5)	People (6)	Management (7)	Operations (8)	People (9)	Management (10)	Operations (11)	People (12)
Founder CEO	-0.131***	-0.120***	-0.020	-0.156***	-0.141***	-0.030**	-0.130***	-0.118***	-0.021	-0.129***	-0.121***	-0.013
	(0.021)	(0.016)	(0.014)	(0.019)	(0.016)	(0.012)	(0.021)	(0.017)	(0.013)	(0.021)	(0.016)	(0.014)
Founder CEO * ln(GDP per capita)	0.006	0.002	0.002									
	(0.009)	(0.009)	(0.005)									
Founder CEO * (accounting standards)				-0.000	-0.001	0.001						
				(0.002)	(0.002)	(0.001)						
Founder CEO * (rule of law)							0.000	0.000	0.000			
							(0.001)	(0.001)	(0.000)			
Founder CEO * trust										0.118	0.008	0.186
										(0.189)	(0.146)	(0.117)
Constant	-3.735***	-2.785***	-1.796***	-3.483***	-2.724***	-1.376***	-3.746***	-2.795***	-1.797***	-3.736***	-2.786***	-1.796***
	(0.347)	(0.261)	(0.205)	(0.382)	(0.304)	(0.231)	(0.342)	(0.259)	(0.203)	(0.347)	(0.261)	(0.204)
Observations	12,386	12,386	12,386	10,888	10,888	10,888	12,386	12,386	12,386	12,386	12,386	12,386
Adjusted R-squared	0.451	0.438	0.332	0.436	0.420	0.328	0.451	0.438	0.332	0.451	0.438	0.333
Country dummies	Yes	Yes	Yes	Yes	Yes	Yes	Yes	Yes	Yes	Yes	Yes	Yes
Industry dummies	Yes	Yes	Yes	Yes	Yes	Yes	Yes	Yes	Yes	Yes	Yes	Yes
Firm employment	Yes	Yes	Yes	Yes	Yes	Yes	Yes	Yes	Yes	Yes	Yes	Yes
Firm age	Yes	Yes	Yes	Yes	Yes	Yes	Yes	Yes	Yes	Yes	Yes	Yes
Skills	Yes	Yes	Yes	Yes	Yes	Yes	Yes	Yes	Yes	Yes	Yes	Yes
MNE status	Yes	Yes	Yes	Yes	Yes	Yes	Yes	Yes	Yes	Yes	Yes	Yes
Noise	Yes	Yes	Yes	Yes	Yes	Yes	Yes	Yes	Yes	Yes	Yes	Yes

Notes: All columns estimated by ordinary least squares (OLS) with standard errors clustered at the level of the country in which the firm's CHQ is located. Each interaction variable is tested in three columns with three different standardized dependent variables: overall management score, operations management score, and people management score. The GDP per capita is drawn from the World Bank Development indicators, measured in the country in which the firm headquarters is located. Similarly, accounting standards is used as a proxy for financial development in the country where the firm headquarters is located (Rajan and Zingales 1998). Rule of law is drawn from the World Bank's Doing Business Survey. Trust is derived from the World Values Survey, and denotes the percent of people answering "yes" to the question "Generally speaking, would you say that most people can be trusted or that you can't be too careful?"

***Significant at the 1 percent level.

**Significant at the 5 percent level.

*Significant at the 10 percent level.

errors at the CHQ country level throughout). We start in columns (1)–(3) by using, as a rough measure of institutional quality, the log of gross domestic product (GDP) per capita (purchasing power parity [PPP] adjusted and expressed in constant 2005 USD). The interaction founder CEO * ln(GDP per capita) is not significant across any of the columns. We obtain similarly insignificant results by following Rajan and Zingales (1998) in using a variable capturing differences in standards of financial disclosures by country as a proxy for the founder's ability to attract external capital, which is necessary to providing the incentive to standardize. Similarly, the interaction between the founder CEO dummy and a variable capturing the overall quality of the Rule of Law (Kaufmann, Kraay, and Mastruzzi 2011) in columns (7)–(9) and a measure of generalized trust developed from the World Values Survey (World Values Survey Association 2008) in columns (10)–(12) are also all statistically insignificant.

In conclusion, we fail to find evidence that development, or more specifically the quality of the institutional environment in which firms operate, has a role in explaining the relative gap in management practices of founder CEO firms. This finding holds for the overall management score, as well as the score relating to people management practices.

4.5.3   Private Benefits of Control

As mentioned above, a possible reason for the lack of adoption of formalized management practices across founder CEO firms is that standardization may directly dissipate the personal rents that the founder enjoys by being at the helm of his or her organization. For example, Hurst and Pugsley (2011) found that over 50 percent of new business owners reported nonpecuniary benefits as a reason for starting their businesses, citing reasons like "wanting flexibility over schedule" and "to be one's own boss" as of first-order importance for their choices.[13]

Unfortunately, we do not have information on the different *individual* preferences of the managers included in the WMS sample. Our approach is to instead investigate whether the adoption of management practices varies according to differences in *societal* preferences. A primary candidate for this type of exercise is the strength of family values in the country where the firm's central headquarters are located. Using an index derived from several questions included in the World Values Survey,[14] Bertrand and Schoar

13. That is consistent with Bennett and Chatterji's (2015) finding that 58 percent of people who considered starting a business did so because they wanted to "be [their] own boss, turn a hobby into a job, or control [their] own schedule."
14. Bertrand and Schoar (2006) used principal component analysis to combine the answers to five family-related questions into a single index. The questions include (a) general importance family in life, (b) parental respect by children, (c) parental duty to their children, (d) importance of obedience as a quality in children, and (e) importance of independence as a quality in children. We use the same index as a proxy for family values.

(2006) show that the strength of family values is highly correlated with the fraction of family firms—including founder CEO firms—in the economy and in general with the organizational structure of firms. In our setting, we hypothesize that strong family values may create an incentive for founder and family CEOs to select and reward employees on the basis of family affiliations rather than through potentially more objective merit-based HR processes, whose adoption is measured in our management index.

We investigate this idea in table 4.9, by including in our baseline regression an interaction between the Family Values Index and the founder CEO dummy. The interaction between the strength of family values and the founder CEO dummy is negative, as expected, but statistically insignificant when we look at the overall management score (column [1]). Interestingly, however, the insignificance is entirely driven by the operations questions of the survey. When we focus the index on the *people* section of the survey— that is, the type of practices that are likely to have a more direct effect on the ability to employ family members as employees—in column (3), we find that stronger family values are associated with significantly lower management scores for founder CEO firms.

In the subsequent columns of table 4.9 we investigate this result further by looking at its sensitivity with respect to the inclusion of additional country controls and examining various subsamples of the data. In column (4) we simply repeat the specification adding as controls other relevant country characteristics (log GDP per capita and trust) and their interaction with the founder CEO dummy, to check whether the proxy for family values might capture other salient country characteristics. The coefficient on founder CEO * family values is reduced by about 30 percent, but it remains large and statistically significant at the 10 percent level.

Because a great deal of research has investigated the impacts of family CEOs (e.g., Villalonga and Amit 2006), and in fact often conflate founder CEOs with family CEOs (Wasserman 2003), in column (5) we add to the specification an interaction between a dummy denoting family CEOs (i.e., CEOs that are affiliated to the founding family, but belong to later generations relative to the founder) and its interaction with family values. While the management scores of family CEO firms also appear to be lower in countries with strong family values, differently from founder CEO firms, the interaction is not statistically significant.

In line with Rajan (2012), we explore whether the relevance of family values varies according to the nature of the industry in which the firm operates. In particular, we would expect family values to play a relatively smaller role in industries with high external financial dependence (defined as in Rajan and Zingales [1998]). It is in these industries where the need to raise external capital is likely to dominate the personal returns to private control. In line with this hypothesis, in columns (6) and (7) we show that founder

Table 4.9   People management in founder CEO firms

Sample	All					Low external capital dependence	High external capital dependence
	Management (1)	Operations (2)	People (3)	People (4)	People (5)	People (6)	People (7)
Founder CEO	-0.131***	-0.123***	-0.012	-0.011	-0.038***	-0.024	-0.004
	(0.022)	(0.018)	(0.011)	(0.013)	(0.013)	(0.017)	(0.023)
Founder CEO * family values	-0.017	0.012	-0.053**	-0.044*	-0.067***	-0.089***	-0.040
	(0.047)	(0.037)	(0.021)	(0.025)	(0.022)	(0.021)	(0.041)
Family CEO					-0.086***		
					(0.015)		
Family CEO * family values					-0.031		
					(0.019)		
Founder CEO * ln(GDP per capita)				0.001			
				(0.005)			
Founder CEO * trust				0.049			
				(0.126)			
Constant	-3.734***	-2.787***	-1.790***	-1.791***	-1.746***	-0.817***	-1.357***
	(0.348)	(0.261)	(0.206)	(0.205)	(0.201)	(0.262)	(0.270)
Observations	12,386	12,386	12,386	12,386	12,386	5,862	5,006
Adjusted R-squared	0.451	0.438	0.333	0.332	0.334	0.292	0.341
Country dummies	Yes	Yes	Yes	Yes	Yes	Yes	Yes
Industry dummies	Yes	Yes	Yes	Yes	Yes	Yes	Yes
Firm employment	Yes	Yes	Yes	Yes	Yes	Yes	Yes
Firm age	Yes	Yes	Yes	Yes	Yes	Yes	Yes
Skills	Yes	Yes	Yes	Yes	Yes	Yes	Yes
MNE status	Yes	Yes	Yes	Yes	Yes	Yes	Yes
Noise	Yes	Yes	Yes	Yes	Yes	Yes	Yes

Notes: The dependent variable in columns (1) and (2) are, respectively, the overall management z-score and the operations z-score. The dependent variable in columns (3)–(7) is the people management z-score. All columns estimated by ordinary least squares (OLS) with standard errors clustered at the level of the country in which the firm's CHQ is located. Columns (6) and (7) split the sample according to the Rajan and Zingales financial dependence variable (below and above the sample median). Family values is derived from the World Values Survey as described in Bertrand and Schoar (2006) and measured in the country in which the firm headquarters is located. The GDP per capita is drawn from the World Bank Development indicators, measured in the country in which the firm headquarters is located. Rule of law is drawn from the World Bank's Doing Business Survey. Trust is derived from the World Values Survey, and denotes the percent of people answering "yes" to the question "Generally speaking, would you say that most people can be trusted or that you can't be too careful?"
***Significant at the 1 percent level.
**Significant at the 5 percent level.
*Significant at the 10 percent level.

CEO * family values interaction is significant only in industries with low external financial dependence.[15]

While these measures are proxies, rather than direct measures of non-pecuniary benefits, overall, these results provide suggestive evidence that different considerations besides pure profit maximization—for example, the value provided by foregoing objective HR processes to hire a family member or a friend in the firm—may play a role in explaining the relatively low adoption of management practices across founder CEO firms, especially with respect to processes aimed at formalizing HR processes for employee selection, reward, and retention.

4.6   Conclusion

We find evidence that firms led by founder CEOs are significantly less likely to implement basic management practices, even if these practices are associated with better firm performance. We explore the reasons for the differential adoption. Specifically, we investigate three potential causes: (a) that founders do not perceive their firms to have a management gap, (b) that the institutional environment dampens the incentive to implement superior practices, and (c) that nonpecuniary benefits from control counterbalance the lost rents from those worse practices. We find support for both (a) and (c).

The results shown in this chapter are broadly consistent with an emerging literature emphasizing the heterogeneity in growth and motivation of entrepreneurial firms (Hurst and Pugsley 2011; Mullins and Schoar 2013; Bennett and Chatterji 2015) and with managerial studies focusing on the positive association between structured management practices and performance across start-ups (Dávila, Foster, and Jia 2010). We extend this literature by providing additional evidence of the managerial practices adopted by founder CEO firms and their relationship with country-specific cultural norms, such as family values, across a wide range of countries and industries.

This chapter contributes to the existing literature on the performance of founder CEO firms. In contrast to our chapter, several studies report a positive effect of founder CEOs on firm performance (Adams, Almeida, and Ferreira 2009; Fahlenbrach 2009). One possible reason for this discrepancy results from the type of firms used in the analysis. While this chapter includes a wide range of private and public firms across several countries, the positive effect of founder CEOs is typically derived from the analysis of samples of public US enterprises, which may have implemented standardized manage-

15. We also investigated whether the presence of strong family values could affect the returns to management practices by repeating the performance regressions from table 4.5, including an interaction term management * family values. We find no evidence of a lower return associated with management practices in countries where family values are higher (see table 4A.3 in the appendix).

ment practices in order to be able to raise external capital (Rajan 2012) or, more generally, be positively selected relative to representative founder CEO firms.

The persistent managerial gap of founder CEO firms described in this chapter suggests that government-sponsored programs aimed at fostering entrepreneurial activity may face significant challenges in delivering growth. In particular, our results suggest that—in order to be effective—financial support provided to new enterprises may need to be coupled with effective policies aimed at improving the managerial capabilities of founders and a better understanding of their motivations.

Unfortunately, a paucity of data on key differences in CEO skills, experience, preferences, and ability prevent us from exploring in further detail the mechanisms through which founder CEO status affects management practice adoption. We see this as a promising area for further research.

Appendix

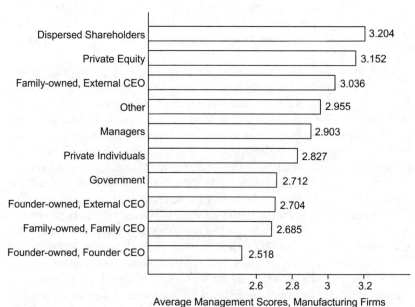

Fig. 4A.1   **Management scores across ownership types**

Table 4A.1   **Survey questions**

Practices	What we are measuring?
Operations management and performance monitoring	
Introducing lean (modern) techniques	Measures how well lean (modern) manufacturing management techniques have been introduced
Rationale for introducing lean (modern) techniques	Measures the motivation/impetus behind changes to the operational processes, and whether a change story was well communicated, turning into company culture
Continuous improvement	Measures attitudes toward process documentation and continuous improvement
Performance tracking	Measures whether firm performance is measured with the right methods and frequency
Performance review	Measures whether performance is reviewed with appropriate frequency and follow-up
Performance dialogue	Measures the quality of review conversations
Consequence management	Measures whether differing levels of firm performance (not personal but plan/process based) lead to different consequences
Target setting	
Target balance	Measures whether targets cover a sufficiently broad set of metrics and whether financial and nonfinancial targets are balances
Target interconnection	Measures whether targets are tied to the organization's objectives and how well they cascade down the organization
Time horizon of targets	Measures whether the firm has a "three-horizons" approach to planning and targets
Target stretch	Measures whether targets are based on a solid rationale and are appropriately difficult to achieve
Clarify and comparability of targets	Measures how easily understandable performance measures are and whether performance is openly communicated to staff
Talent management	
Managing talent	Measures what emphasis is put on overall talent management within the organization
Rewarding high performers	Measures whether there is a systematic approach to identifying good and bad performers and rewarding them proportionately
Removing poor performers	Measures how well the organization is able to deal with underperformers
Promoting high performers	Measures whether promotion is performance based and whether talent is developed within the organization
Retaining talent	Measures whether the organization will go out of its way to keep top talent
Creating a distinctive employee value proposition	Measures the strength of the employee value proposition

Note: Survey instruments with full set of questions asked are available at: www.worldmanagement survey.org.

Table 4A.2   **Factors correlated with ownership changes**

Dependent variable	Dummy = 1 if firm experiences a change in ownership between two survey waves, t and $t + 1$		
Sample	All (1)	Firms classified as founder CEO at time t (2)	Firms classified as different ownership at time t (3)
Management score (t)	–0.018	–0.055	–0.008
	(0.014)	(0.036)	(0.015)
Ln(firm employment) (t)	0.013	0.034	0.014
	(0.008)	(0.025)	(0.008)
Ln(firm age) (t)	–0.009	0.139**	–0.003
	(0.013)	(0.062)	(0.013)
Skills (t)	–0.006	0.022	–0.011
	(0.008)	(0.018)	(0.009)
MNE status (t)	0.008	0.229***	–0.009
	(0.019)	(0.070)	(0.020)
Constant	0.118	–0.052	0.024
	(0.116)	(0.334)	(0.145)
Observations	2,844	493	2,351
Adjusted R-squared	0.131	0.143	0.156
Country dummies	Yes	Yes	Yes
Industry dummies	Yes	Yes	Yes
Noise	Yes	Yes	Yes

***Significant at the 1 percent level.
**Significant at the 5 percent level.
*Significant at the 10 percent level.

Table 4A.3   Returns to management for different strength of family values

Dependent variable	Ln(sales) (1)	ROCE (2)	ROA (3)
Family Values Index	−0.190*	−0.329	−362.284
	(0.104)	(3.626)	(242.689)
Management	0.077***	0.700*	27.214
	(0.019)	(0.392)	(25.130)
Family Values Index * management	−0.023	−0.226	−9.652
	(0.026)	(0.532)	(33.069)
Ln(firm employment)	0.636***	1.270**	54.603*
	(0.024)	(0.505)	(30.905)
Ln(materials)	0.207***	0.859*	30.412
	(0.015)	(0.440)	(28.882)
Ln(capital)	0.226***	−0.625	19.019
	(0.016)	(0.385)	(22.390)
Constant	3.108***	−14.062	155.132
	(0.290)	(9.580)	(836.400)
Observations	7,760	6,327	7,281
Adjusted *R*-squared	0.808	0.084	0.080
Industry dummies	Yes	Yes	Yes
Firm employment	Yes	Yes	Yes
Firm age	Yes	Yes	Yes
Skills	Yes	Yes	Yes
MNE status	Yes	Yes	Yes
Noise	Yes	Yes	Yes

Notes: The sample used for this table includes only those firms for which sales, employment, capital, ROCE, and ROA data could be found in ORBIS and other databases. All columns are estimated using ordinary least squares (OLS) and standard errors clustered at the firm level. The Family Values Index is taken from Bertrand and Schoar's (2006) survey of family values by country of CHQ location.

***Significant at the 1 percent level.
**Significant at the 5 percent level.
*Significant at the 10 percent level.

References

Adams, R., H. Almeida, and D. Ferreira. 2009. "Understanding the Relationship between Founder-CEOs and Firm Performance." *Journal of Empirical Finance* 16 (1): 136–50.

Bandiera, O., A. Prat, and R. Sadun. 2013. "Managing the Family Firm: Evidence from CEOs at Work." NBER Working Paper no. 19722, Cambridge, MA.

Bennett, V. M. 2013. "Organization and Bargaining: Sales Process Design at Auto Dealerships." *Management Science* 59 (9): 2003–18.

Bennett, V. M., and A. K. Chatterji. 2015. "The Entrepreneurial Process." Working Paper, Duke University.

Bertrand, M. and A. Schoar. 2003. "Managing with Style: The Effect of Managers on Firm Policies." *Quarterly Journal of Economics* 118 (4): 1169–208.

————. 2006. "The Role of Family in Family Firms." *Journal of Economic Perspectives* 20 (2): 73–96.

Black, S. E., and L. M. Lynch. 2001. "How to Compete: The Impact of Workplace Practices and Information Technology on Productivity." *Review of Economics and Statistics* 83 (3): 434–45.

Bloom, N., B. Eifert, A. Mahajan, D. McKenzie, and J. Roberts. 2013. "Does Management Matter? Evidence from India." *Quarterly Journal of Economics* 128 (1): 1–51.

Bloom, N., R. Lemos, R. Sadun, D. Scur, and J. Van Reenen. 2014. "The New Empirical Economics of Management." *Journal of the European Economic Association* 12 (4): 835–76.

Bloom, N., R. Sadun, and J. Van Reenen. 2012. "The Organization of Firms across Countries." *Quarterly Journal of Economics* 127 (4): 1663–705.

————. 2016. "Management as a Technology?" NBER Working Paper no. 22327, Cambridge, MA.

Bloom, N., and J. Van Reenen. 2007. "Measuring and Explaining Management Practices across Firms and Countries." *Quarterly Journal of Economics* 122 (4): 1351–408.

Dávila, A., G. Foster, and N. Jia. 2010. "Building Sustainable High Growth Startup Companies: Management Systems as Accelerators." *California Management Review* 52 (3): 75–109.

Fahlenbrach, R. 2009. "Founder-CEOs, Investment Decisions, and Stock Market Performance." *Journal of Financial and Quantitative Analysis* 44 (02): 439–66.

Galasso, A., and T. S. Simcoe. 2011. "CEO Overconfidence and Innovation." *Management Science* 57 (8): 1469–84.

Gibbons, R., and R. M. Henderson. 2011. "Relational Contracts and Organizational Capabilities." *Organization Science* 23 (5): 1350–64.

Hamilton, B. H. 2000. "Does Entrepreneurship Pay? An Empirical Analysis of the Returns of Self-Employment." *Journal of Political Economy* 108 (3): 604.

Hellmann, T., and M. Puri. 2002. "Venture Capital and the Professionalization of Start-Up Firms: Empirical Evidence." *Journal of Finance* 57 (1): 169–97.

Hermalin, B. E. 1994. "Heterogeneity in Organizational Form: Why Otherwise Identical Firms Choose Different Incentives for Their Managers." *RAND Journal of Economics* 25 (4): 518.

Hsieh, C-T., and B. A. Olken. 2014. "The Missing 'Missing Middle.'" *Journal of Economic Perspectives* 28 (3): 89–108.

Hurst, E., and B. W. Pugsley. 2011. "What Do Small Businesses Do?" Brookings Papers on Economic Activity, no. 2. https://www.brookings.edu/bpea-articles /what-do-small-businesses-do/.

Ichniowski, C., K. Shaw, and G. Prennushi. 1997. "The Effects of Human Resource Management Practices on Productivity: A Study of Steel Finishing Lines." *American Economic Review* 87 (3): 291–313.

Jensen, M. C., and W. H. Meckling. 1976. "Theory of the Firm: Managerial Behavior, Agency Costs and Ownership Structure." *Journal of Financial Economics* 3 (4): 305–60.

Kaufmann, D., A. Kraay, and M. Mastruzzi. 2011. "The Worldwide Governance Indicators: Methodology and Analytical Issues. *Hague Journal on the Rule of Law* 3 (02): 220–46.

Malmendier, U., and G. Tate. 2005. "CEO Overconfidence and Corporate Investment." *Journal of Finance* 60 (6): 2661–700.

Morck, R., A. Shleifer, and R. W. Vishny. 1988. "Management Ownership and Market Valuation: An Empirical Analysis." *Journal of Financial Economics* 20:293–315.

Moskowitz, T. J., and A. Vissing-Jørgensen. 2002. "The Returns to Entrepreneurial Investment: A Private Equity Premium Puzzle?" *American Economic Review* 92 (4): 745–78.

Mullins, W., and A. Schoar. 2013. "How Do CEOs See Their Role? Management Philosophy and Styles in Family and Non-Family Firms." NBER Working Paper no. 19395, Cambridge, MA.

Osterman, P. 1994. "How Common is Workplace Transformation and Who Adopts It?" *Industrial and Labor Relations Review* 47 (2): 173–88.

Rajan, R. G. 2012. "The Corporation in Finance." *Journal of Finance* 67 (4): 1173–217.

Rajan, R. G., and L. Zingales. 1998. "Financial Dependence and Growth." *American Economic Review* 88 (3): 559–86.

Villalonga, B., and R. Amit. 2006. "How Do Family Ownership, Control and Management Affect Firm Value?" *Journal of Financial Economics* 80 (2): 385–417.

Wasserman, N. 2003. "Founder-CEO Succession and the Paradox of Entrepreneurial Success." *Organization Science* 14 (2): 149–72.

———. 2006. "Stewards, Agents, and the Founder Discount: Executive Compensation in New Ventures." *Academy of Management Journal* 49 (5): 960–76.

World Values Survey Association. 2008. *World Values Survey*. Ann Arbor: University of Michigan.

Immigrant Entrepreneurship

Sari Pekkala Kerr and William R. Kerr

5.1 Introduction

Immigrant entrepreneurship is of central policy interest and a frequent hot point in the popular press. Many policymakers believe that immigrant founders are an important and underutilized lever for the revival of US job growth and continued recovery from the Great Recession. Several local and national policy initiatives have been launched to attract immigrant entrepreneurs (e.g., the Thrive competition in New York City, the Office of New Americans in Chicago, and the White House Startup America initiative). Some of the policy initiatives focus on specific issues that have been found to limit immigrant entrepreneurs from starting or growing their businesses (e.g., language barriers, difficulty navigating the legal steps to start a company, or lack of capital to pilot projects), while others are generally focused on attracting more new businesses into the country. Policies vary

Sari Pekkala Kerr is an economist and senior research scientist at the Wellesley Centers for Women (WCW) at Wellesley College. William R. Kerr is the Dimitri V. D'Arbeloff-MBA Class of 1955 Professor of Business Administration at Harvard Business School and a research associate of the National Bureau of Economic Research.

This is a revised version of a paper prepared for the Conference on Research in Income and Wealth (CRIW) NBER meeting on December 16–17, 2014, in Washington, DC. We thank our discussant Ethan Lewis, the editors, and CRIW-NBER participants for very helpful comments. We thank the Alfred P. Sloan Foundation, National Science Foundation, Harvard Business School, and the Ewing Marion Kauffman Foundation for financial support that made this research possible. The research in this chapter was conducted while the authors were Special Sworn Status researchers of the US Census Bureau at the Boston Census Research Data Center. Research results and conclusions expressed are the authors' own and do not necessarily reflect the views of the Census Bureau or the NSF. This chapter has been screened to ensure that no confidential data are revealed. For acknowledgments, sources of research support, and disclosure of the authors' material financial relationships, if any, please see http://www.nber.org/chapters/c13502.ack.

in the immigrant group that they target, ranging from a specific focus on high-skilled immigrant entrepreneurship with venture capital (VC) backing to broad-based measures that potentially touch many diverse immigrant communities.

Academic research, unfortunately, possesses only a small voice in this debate or policy design. For example, advocates of greater immigrant entrepreneurship mainly cite a few extreme examples of success such as Sergey Brin, one of the founders of Google, and extrapolate information from some exceptionally influential case studies regarding Silicon Valley and large high-tech companies (e.g., Saxenian 1999; Wadhwa et al. 2007). While each of these supporting pieces has its merits and liabilities, it is important for rigorous trends and statistics to also inform this debate. For example, even with respect to Silicon Valley and high-tech companies, it is not immediately clear what the oft-cited statistics mean—it is likely true that more than half of the entrepreneurs in Silicon Valley are of immigrant origin, as the surveys suggest, but the exact same could be said of the undergraduate student populations at most schools in the San Francisco area. Second, given the substantial heterogeneity in immigrant entrepreneurship, which comes in just as many flavors as native entrepreneurship, it is unsatisfying to focus on such a narrow population of high-tech entrepreneurs for contemplating possible initiatives.

For economists to be able to aid the policy process, and ultimately improve economic performance in this arena, we need better-grounded estimates on the importance of immigrant groups for the creation of new firms, the business activities and growth profiles of created firms, and so on. This study constructs a data platform using Census Bureau administrative data to assist in this process. The purpose of this chapter is to detail the platform's components and provide some early views of the trends for immigrant entrepreneurs and the patterns in their behavior. We have several audiences in mind. First, we are able to offer some new facts to the discussion of immigrant entrepreneurship that can be useful for policy discussions, although we do not examine any specific policy actions or recommendations about encouraging immigrant entrepreneurship in this study. Second, we hope that others find this discussion encouraging for making progress on this front and that they too seek access to these data through the Census Bureau. Ideally, our chapter can provide them a one-stop-shop for what is feasible in the data and how to build the platform, and this chapter goes into greater depth than is normal for academic papers on how the platform is built and its traits. Finally, we speak to future efforts to enhance these data. In terms of representative statistics, this platform is likely as good as it gets with today's data collection. We describe below a wish list for future data development efforts.

Section 5.2 provides a brief review of the previous empirical literature on immigrant entrepreneurs and their traits. Fairlie and Lofstrom (2014) provide a comprehensive recent review of this literature strand and statistics from the 2007 Survey of Business Owners (SBO). In this chapter, relative to prior academic work, we make three contributions. First, our data platform provides consistent estimates of immigrant entrepreneurship over a long time period (1995–2008) and across skill levels (e.g., all entrepreneurs, VC-backed firms). Existing work, even when using representative national samples, tends to be cross-sectional at a given point in time and focused on a specific skill population, whereas for most purposes the comparisons across time and groups would be very important. Second, we study the different dynamics of employment and growth among immigrant-led businesses compared to those founded by natives. Fairlie and Lofstrom (2014) conclude that a central research goal for immigrant entrepreneurship is to identify the dynamics of employment growth among these firms, and our constructed platform makes progress in this domain. Third and related, we provide a first breakdown of these growth dynamics by the age of immigration to the United States. This last analysis is preliminary and mostly undertaken to show the potential of the data for observing differences along traits identifiable from the 2000 Census match, but striking nonetheless.

Section 5.3 details the construction of our data platform. The strength of our study lies in the ability to use and combine several restricted-access US Census Bureau data sets to create a unique longitudinal data platform with millions of observations. Indeed, a key purpose of this chapter is to report on the potential of these data and describe their traits for research purposes. The backbone for our work is the employer-employee data in the Longitudinal Employer-Household Dynamics (LEHD) database. The LEHD provides firm-worker information collected from unemployment insurance records. From this information, one can observe the birth of new firms and their employee composition, including immigration status. We also utilize other data: (a) the Longitudinal Business Database (LBD) to assess the employment growth dynamics of new firms, (b) the long-form records of the 2000 Decennial Census to collect additional person- and household-level traits (e.g., year of arrival to the United States), and (c) external data sets to identify companies that have VC backing or achieve an initial public offering (IPO). The resulting data platform can describe many forms of entrepreneurship, ranging from general patterns to "growth entrepreneurs" described in the VC literature. These detailed new data allow us to study person- and firm-level patterns in a way that has not been possible to date, and this section also depicts the variations and limits on the definitions of entrepreneurship in the LEHD.[1]

Section 5.4 provides our trend estimates. Most of our work focuses on eleven states present in the LEHD since 1992, which include California and

---

1. In a broad review of the immigration literature, Lewis (2013b) raises immigrant entrepreneurship as one of the key areas requiring further study and notes the key ingredient of employer-employee data for this purpose. The LEHD is the source of this type of administrative information for the United States.

Florida. We estimate 24 percent of entrepreneurs in these states from 1995 to 2008 are immigrants, which broadly corresponds with other studies. As important, this immigrant entrepreneurship share rises from 17 percent in 1995 to 27 percent in 2008. Our sample, by coincidence, draws from heavy immigration states. Looking at a sample of twenty-eight states present in the LEHD by 2000, we estimate these numbers may be 3 percent higher than the total population, with the growth trend being similar. Returning to our focal set of states, the immigrant share among entrepreneurs receiving VC financing is modestly higher, reaching 30 percent in 2005 compared to 27 percent for all firms. In terms of entrepreneurship rates, roughly 2 percent of immigrants start a business over a three-year period; 0.1 percent start a firm backed by VC financing. These rates are higher than those we estimate for natives, which is reflected in the fact that immigrants constitute 19 percent of the LEHD workforce in our sample, less than the entrepreneurship shares reported above.

Section 5.5 documents basic patterns related to entry, survival, and growth of immigrant versus native businesses. On the whole, the businesses started by immigrant entrepreneurs perform better than native businesses with respect to employment growth over three- and six-year horizons. This is evident in the raw data and mostly persists when comparing immigrant- and native-founded businesses started in the same city, industry, and year. By contrast, immigrant-founded businesses show no advantages with respect to payroll growth, and may in fact generate lower-wage job growth. Combining business survival with growth dynamics, immigrants tend to be engaged in more volatile, up-or-out type dynamics, along the lines described by Halti-wanger, Jarmin, and Miranda (2013) for young businesses and job creation. Most of this effect is captured by the city-industry-year choices made for businesses, versus variation in growth patterns within these cells. Breaking down these aggregate results, the strongest employment growth impacts for immigrants are found in high-wage businesses and high-tech sectors. Conditional on receiving VC investment, however, we do not observe greater business survival, better employment outcomes, or higher likelihood of going public for firms founded by immigrant entrepreneurs. Businesses founded by immigrants who came to the United States by age eighteen have stronger growth patterns than those founded by immigrants migrating as adults.

Section 5.6 concludes with a discussion of these findings in the larger context of immigration and entrepreneurship policy. This section also describes enhancements to the platform that would enable better research efforts going forward. Immigration policy is designed and administered at the national level, with few restrictions on the location choices of immigrants within the United States. A methodological conclusion from this study is that the LEHD-based platform can consistently describe immigrant entrepreneurship across many industries, geographies, and skill levels. This is an important ingredient for delivering systematic advice about how immigrant entrepreneurs impact the US economy and where the effects of expansion in admission levels might be felt. We also find that the detail of the LEHD can aid more effective policy advice for subgroups of immigrants. The surveys most cited in the public discourse are actually quite crude in this regard. For example, although Sergey Brin is often used as the showcase example for immigration reform on high-skilled H-1B policies, he came to the United States as a child, while the H-1B program is focused on temporary admissions of adults with college-level education. Our disaggregation by the age at arrival for immigrants indicates this assembled platform can help begin to disentangle these important details. To be clear, our study stops well short of making a direct input to immigration policy design on this or other dimensions, but we do find that these data elements are of sufficient strength and depth that they can serve as an effective foundation for future research efforts to inform the economic consequences of selection strategies based upon certain immigrant traits.

On the other hand, we note that there are many places where the LEHD has limits, some of which may be addressable. For example, here we define entrepreneurship status through initial wage profiles of firm employees, which is certainly incomplete. Over short-term horizons, it would be useful to consider linking LEHD workers to SBO-type data to evaluate the accuracy and bias of derived entrepreneurship definitions with greater detail. Similarly, we describe how links of LEHD workers to external data sources at the individual level would be powerful (e.g., entrepreneurs/CEOs contained in the Venture Xpert data, inventors contained in United States patent data). More challenging, while we are able to make progress toward some of the important traits of immigrants, we miss completely with the LEHD the essential questions of immigration visa type (e.g., H-1B, green card), which is strongly emphasized by Hunt (2011) as a key predictor for choices by immigrants with respect to entrepreneurship. For the evaluation and design of effective policy, the inclusion of visa status and transitions over time must be at the top of any wish list.

5.2   Previous Literature on Immigrant Entrepreneurs

This section provides some background for our study from the academic literature, with Fairlie and Lofstrom (2014) reviewing the immigrant entrepreneurship literature in a more comprehensive manner. There is a large body of literature showing that general rates of business ownership are higher among the foreign born than natives in many developed countries, including the United States, United Kingdom, Canada, and Australia.[2] Fairlie (2012) and Fairlie and Lofstrom (2014) also observe that trends in

2. Studies include Borjas (1986), Lofstrom (2002), Clark and Drinkwater (2000, 2006), Schuetze and Antecol (2007), and Fairlie, Zissimopoulos, and Krashinsky (2010).

self-employment rates and new business formation are increasing among immigrants but decreasing among natives in the United States. In closely related work to the current analysis, Hunt (2011, 2015) focuses on skilled immigrants and finds that they are more likely to start firms with more than ten employees than comparable natives. Hunt uses the National Survey of College Graduates (NSCG), which provides a nationally representative sample of persons with a college degree and interesting information about the initial visa status of immigrants. She finds that the probability of starting a firm was highest for those initially arriving on a study visa or a work visa versus family reunification. While the level of detail on the specific degrees and entry visas in the NSCG is impressive, the major issues for researchers trying to describe national trends in immigrant-founded firms are the small sample sizes, the lack of longitudinal dimension, and the absence of firms as a data element.

In parallel to these general patterns, a second research stream focuses specifically on immigrant entrepreneurship in the high-tech sector. Saxenian (1999, 2002) documents that up to a quarter of the high-tech firms in Silicon Valley in the 1980s and 1990s were founded or being run by immigrants. Wadhwa et al. (2007) extends this survey analysis to the rest of the country and other industries to study firms founded in 1995–2005. They document similar shares of immigrant-founded companies across the country, although elements of their study are difficult to generalize.[3] Table 5.1 provides a summary of several related studies on immigrant entrepreneurs. These efforts connect into a broader line of work showing the overrepresentation of skilled immigrants among certain extreme outcomes in US science and engineering: for example, US-based Nobel Prize winners (Peri 2007), high-impact companies (Hart and Acs 2011), patent applications (Wadhwa et al. 2007), members of the National Academy of Sciences and the National Academy of Engineering (Stephan and Levin 2001), and biotech companies undergoing initial public offerings (Stephan and Levin 2001). It is these kinds of factors that likely drive the current policy enthusiasm toward immigrant entrepreneurs. On the other hand, with respect to immigrant high-tech contributions, Hart and Acs (2011) suggest that although immigrants play an important role, "most previous studies have overstated the role of immigrants in high-tech entrepreneurship."

---

3. The sample with responses covers 7 percent of the approximately 30,000 firms in the Dunn & Bradstreet data that were founded in 1995–2005, had sales greater than $1 million, and employed at least fifty persons. Despite the extensive efforts of their research team to reach a subset of companies listed in the Dunn & Bradstreet data, the study faces a lower response rate, selectivity in terms of which firms choose to respond, and perhaps limits regarding the ability of the surveys to reach the right person to answer the questions related to the founders' origin (as an HR or a PR person might not know whether one of the founders moved to the United States as a child). Therefore, the researchers extrapolate from their sample to produce nationally representative numbers for revenue and employment generation. Monti, Smith-Doerr, and MacQuaid (2007) provide related evidence from Massachusetts high-tech firms.

Table 5.1   Previous studies on immigrant entrepreneurship

Study (1)	Data sources (2)	Sample design (3)	Period (4)	Immigrant entrepreneur share (%) (5)	Founding rate among immigrants (%) (6)	Founding rate among natives (%) (7)
Saxenian (1999)	Dun & Bradstreet, surveys	Silicon Valley tech firms	1980–1998	24	n/a	n/a
Anderson & Platzer (2006)	Thomson Financial, survey, Internet	340 publicly traded, venture capital-backed firms, independent in 1990–2005	1990–2005	25	n/a	n/a
Wadhwa et al. (2007)	Dun & Bradstreet, surveys	US tech firms with > $1m sales and > 20 employees	1995–2005	25	n/a	n/a
Reynolds & Curtin (2007)	Panel Study of Entrepreneurial Dynamics	New founders who plan to grow firm to 50+ employees	1999	15	n/a	n/a
Monti, Smith-Doerr, and MacQuaid (2007)	MA Biotech Council member list	New England biotech firms	2006	26	n/a	n/a
Fairlie (2008)	Census IPUMS 2000, Current Population Survey 1996–2007	Working-age business owners, work > 15 hours per week	2000, 1996–2007	17	0.4	0.3
Hart & Acs (2011)	Survey	"High-impact" high-tech companies	2002–2006	16	n/a	n/a
Robb et al. (2010)	Kauffman Firm Survey	High- and medium-tech firms founded in 2004	2004	10.3	n/a	n/a
Hunt (2011)	NSCG 2003	Firms founded in 2004 that survived until to 2008	2008	9.4	n/a	n/a
Fairlie (2012)	Survey of Business Owners 2007, Current Population Survey 1996–2010	College degree holders, working in 2003	1998–2003	n/a	0.8	0.6
		Owners of businesses in 2007, workforce in 2010	2007, 2010	13	0.6	0.3

Notes: The immigrant share of entrepreneurs in Saxenian (1999) covers only Chinese and Indian ethnic groups, based on the CEO surnames. The founding rate in Hunt (2011) covers firms founded between 1988 and 2003 that have at least ten employees in 2003. The founding rates in Fairlie (2008, 2012) are monthly. Fairlie (2008) defines the immigrant entrepreneur share as the percentage of new companies that had at least one immigrant founder (of all business owners, 12.5 percent are immigrants). Hart and Acs (2011) use Corporate Research Board's American Corporate Statistical Library (ACSL) listings to identify the set of "high-impact" companies and obtain survey responses from 29 percent of them.

Statistics with respect to immigrant entrepreneurship among VC-backed firms are harder to assemble. Fairlie (2012) calculates from the 2007 SBO that equally few native and immigrant business owners rely on any VC funding; more generally, the study finds that immigrants are less likely to start a business with no capital and just as likely as natives to start a business with more than $1 million of capital. Hegde and Tumlinson (2014) and Bengtsson and Hsu (2015) are recent examples of studies of immigrant entrepreneurship among VC-backed firms using ethnic names to distinguish the likelihood of a founder being an immigrant. In an advocacy piece, Anderson and Platzer (2006) identify the higher immigrant entrepreneur share among publicly listed VC-backed US companies.

Related to our focus on entrepreneurs and how immigration influences the supply of these individuals, prior studies show that more educated business owners run more successful businesses, generate more innovations, and grow their firms faster over time (e.g., Unger et al. 2011). There is an overall positive relationship between education and business ownership, although the evidence is somewhat mixed as highlighted in the meta-analysis of van der Sluis, van Praag, and Vijverberg (2008). Lofstrom, Bates, and Parker (2014) postulate that this may be due to sorting into industries based on entry barriers. They find that educational credentials of highly educated potential entrepreneurs are associated with lower probability of small-firm ownership in less financially rewarding industries, while they increase entry into higher-barrier industries offering higher returns.

Immigrants can take a variety of paths into firm ownership in the United States. Many skilled immigrants enter the United States for study or paid work and found their company after several years in the country, while a smaller number enter for the specific purpose of opening a business. Kerr, Kerr, and Lincoln (2015a, 2015b) describe in greater detail how US immigration law and corporate sponsorship of visas contribute to this career trajectory. Akee, Jaeger, and Tatsiramos (2007) find that premigration self-employment in home countries increases the probability of self-employment by immigrants in the United States and boosts self-employment earnings. Lofstrom (2002) finds that self-employment probabilities and earnings for immigrants increase with time spent in the United States, perhaps even reaching earnings parity with observationally similar US-born entrepreneurs after about twenty-five years in the country. The use of repeated cross sections of censuses, however, limits the degree to which the role of assimilation can be separated from selective out-migration. Blau and Kahn (2016) describe cultural factors influencing gender-based rates of assimilation for work by immigrants.

The spillover effects to native opportunities for opening a business have been examined by several research teams. Fairlie and Meyer (2003) find some evidence that immigration may negatively affect native self-employment probabilities using the 1980 and 1990 Census records. Other researchers suggest skilled immigrants generate positive spillover effects in local areas. For example, recent work points toward positive spillover effects for cities or states when measured in terms of innovation, publications, and productivity (e.g., Kerr and Lincoln 2010; Hunt and Gauthier-Loiselle 2010; Peri, Shih, and Sparber 2015). Lewis and Peri (2015) provide a theoretical framework and review of literature on the effects of immigration on local areas. Evidence from more historical contexts is mixed (e.g., Borjas and Doran 2012; Moser, Voena, and Waldinger 2014). Kerr (2013) provides an extended review of literature on skilled immigration and notes the particular gap around the empirics of immigrant entrepreneurship specifically.

Another line of work documents how immigrant entrepreneurs appear to specialize in a narrower range of industries or occupations compared to native entrepreneurs. Very common examples from the United States include Korean entrepreneurs for dry cleaners, Vietnamese entrepreneurs for nail care salons, Gujarati Indian entrepreneurs for the motel industry, and Punjabi Indian entrepreneurs for convenience stores. Chung and Kalnins (2006) provide a first analysis of this specialization for US Indian entrepreneurs, and Patel and Vella (2013) document patterns more broadly and show earning consequences. Fairlie, Zissimopoulos, and Krashinsky (2010) provide cross-country comparisons for some groups. Kerr and Mandorff (2015) provide a theoretical model and empirical evidence of how small group sizes and social isolation can provide comparative advantages for ethnicities in self-employed sectors where the entrepreneurs benefit from the tight networking of their social group.

Compared to this earlier literature, the LEHD-based platform has the capacity to provide critical and novel information for the enhanced understanding of immigrant entrepreneurship and the effective calibration of immigration policy. Indeed, even though earlier work has tackled many important issues, there remain unfortunate gaps in both the big-picture study of immigrant entrepreneurship and in the depth of insights feasible.

Starting with the big picture, immigrant entrepreneurship is often greatly hyped in both policy and media circles, and a number of newspaper and business press articles (e.g., *Forbes*, *New York Times*) tout immigrant founders as the solution to the sluggish recovery from the Great Recession. Similarly, current local and national policy efforts seek to attract and support new firm formation by immigrants, as noted in the introduction. Many of the studies in table 5.1 are limited by sample designs that are not broadly representative of the economy, or they are cross-sectional in nature if representative. This creates a credibility challenge for the work, even when undertaken with the utmost objectivity; the gap gets extremely large with advocacy pieces or those concentrating only on the most prominent high-tech clusters. Building directly upon administrative data, an LEHD-based platform can provide a substantially stronger foundation for its covered states and the credibility necessary for grounding debates around common facts.

The depth is also essential. Some studies, such as Fairlie (2008, 2012) and Fairlie et al. (2015), provide attractive estimates from the Current Population Survey (CPS) that are the current best practice for longitudinal series. The CPS is in many respects a solid platform, given its stable data collection and long series, and we compare some of our work to the CPS later. The difficulty with the CPS is the ultimate depth that it can provide. Its sample sizes of about 500,000 adults are large enough to provide annual estimates for states or industries, but the cell counts become too small when attempting to jointly view these traits. Moreover, the CPS records cannot be linked to future growth trajectories of the firms, the use of venture-capital funding, and so on. The CPS relies on founders declaring themselves to be self-employed and yet also does not measure if other employment is being generated. Thus, while the CPS is an important and publicly available resource, the development of an LEHD-based platform that includes every business in covered states will provide much deeper capacity for statistical and analytical work. As we describe below, there is no question that the LEHD is far from perfect in terms of what it can do; on the other hand, if these limitations are acceptable, then the scope of follow-on work becomes extraordinary. This depth is true in terms of potentially publishable statistics of entry rates, and also in terms of more complex academic questions (e.g., how many prior employers do immigrants typically have before starting a firm and how does this prior job history impact entrant performance).

Reading the anecdotal accounts and collected statistics regarding immigrants being very involved in high-growth entrepreneurship, it seems natural from a policy perspective to want to encourage this development. Encouraging immigrant entrepreneurs seems like an essential prong of science policy, and its mandate reaches the highest levels of government. Yet, the earlier research has developed only partial data needed to effectively evaluate these policies or enhance their design. Research based upon case studies or small surveys may identify the trend, but they fail to build the empirical foundation necessary for confidence in the design of proposed legislation and the likely impact of reforms. The data platform introduced here makes significant headway in that respect as it will utilize and combine universal and unique microdata sets on individuals and firms (LEHD, LBD, and the Decennial Censuses). In short, this provides a unique platform for the study of immigration and entrepreneurship.

5.3   Census Bureau Data and Measurement

5.3.1   Data Platform

The LEHD is the centerpiece of our platform, in combination with the LBD and a person-level match to the 2000 Decennial Census of Population (census). These data sets are confidential, housed by the US Census Bureau, and accessible via research data centers. Built from quarterly worker-level filings by employers for the administration of state unemployment insurance (UI) benefit programs, the LEHD identifies the employees of each private-sector firm in the United States and their quarterly compensation. It is longitudinally linked at both the firm and employee levels, allowing one to model how firm employment structures adjust over time, how new entrepreneurial firms form, and how individuals transition from wage work into entrepreneurship. This rich data source is currently available for thirty-one states for research purposes, and it will eventually cover the whole country.

The initial LEHD dates vary by state, and we focus on two samples in this chapter. The first is the eleven states that have LEHD records that begin by 1992 or earlier: California, Colorado, Florida, Idaho, Illinois, Louisiana, Maryland, North Carolina, Oregon, Washington, and Wisconsin. Our data extend through 2008, and the newest vintage of the LEHD continues coverage until 2011. Certain analyses are also conducted on a larger set of twenty-eight states present in the LEHD by 2000, as shown in appendix table 5A.1 and figure 5.1. The larger sample can only be followed over a short time span, but it helps us understand the impact of state-level variation in immigration and entrepreneurship rates for the trends presented in this chapter, particularly the inclusion of immigrant-heavy California and Florida among our primary sample.

The LEHD Individual Characteristics File (ICF) contains basic information about individuals such as age, gender, race, place of birth, and citizenship status. Through the Employment History Files (EHF), one can also discern earnings and employment histories of each person job-by-job and in aggregate. In addition, unique person identifiers (PIKs) afford matches of the LEHD to the individual-level records contained in the 2000 Census of Populations. The PIKs are anonymous identifiers that match one-for-one with Social Security numbers. The Census long-form responses cover one-sixth of the US population, allowing us to link census responses for roughly 16 percent of our LEHD workers. From the 2000 Census, we extract individual-level characteristics from the Person File and household and housing-unit characteristics from the Household File. Long-form responses contain very detailed person and household characteristics (e.g., year of entry into the United States, level of education, occupation, marital status, family composition, household income by source, etc.). It is important to recognize that while the LEHD covers employees from the early 1990s through 2008—including new immigrants at the end of the end of the sample period—the 2000 Census match requires individuals to be living in the United States by 2000.

We build a tailored data set for the analysis of immigrant status and entry into entrepreneurship, first focusing on the dynamics over time. We take several steps to reduce the set of massive data records into a manageable platform that properly represents the phenomenon of interest, and it

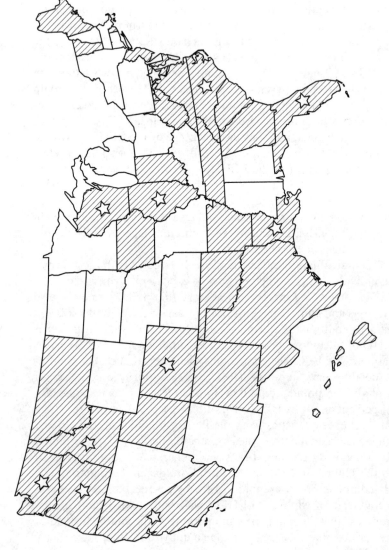

Fig. 5.1 LEHD state coverage

Notes: The figure indicates with shading the states that are covered by the 2008 version of the LEHD used in this study. Alaska is not covered. Stars indicate the eleven states whose coverage begins by 1992. The wider sample used in this study includes all shaded states excepting Arkansas. Coverage for all states ends in 2008.

is important to describe these steps as they have some bearing on our measurements. We begin by retaining for each individual his or her main job during the year (i.e., the job from which the person obtains the majority of their LEHD earnings). We also only retain persons for whom the average quarterly earnings from the main job are at least $2,000 per quarter. We further restrict our sample in each year to individuals age twenty-five to fifty. This age restriction is such that we stay reasonably far away from retirement decisions—and, in particular, the formation of small-scale businesses as a form of semiretirement—and concentrate on entrepreneurial activity in the peak employment years of each person's working life. Moreover, we require individuals be present in the LEHD at least three quarters that span two calendar years.

Immigrants are simply identified as those persons born outside of the United States. This information is available for all LEHD individuals and is based on the Social Security Administration (SSA) Statistical Administrative Records System (i.e., StARS database). Some of these immigrants may have later been naturalized and become citizens, but that information is not utilized in this study. This is partly due to our focus and also due to uncertainty about the updating procedures for this information. By defining immigration status through the ICF files, we can depict immigrant entrepreneurship consistently over the sample period, including new arrivals. We separately consider information from the match with the 2000 Census, which records the year when the immigrant arrived into the United States.

5.3.2   Defining Firm Entry and Entrepreneurs

Our evaluation of entry into entrepreneurship also utilizes the LBD, a business registry that contains annual employment and payroll for all private-sector establishments in the United States since 1976. The LBD and the LEHD use several levels of establishment and firm identifiers: (a) State Employer Identification Numbers (SEIN), (b) federal Employer Identification Numbers (EIN), and (c) the overall company identifier (ALPHA) that the Census Bureau uses to link the establishments of multiunit companies together. Following Haltiwanger, Jarmin, and Miranda (2013), we identify for each establishment the first year during which the firm that the establishment belongs to was observed to be in operation within the LBD. We also create for each firm the number of employees that the LBD reports were working for this firm in the initial year.[4] Approaching entrant definition in this way accomplishes several things—it builds off of the national LBD database to avoid issues related to the partial LEHD state coverage, connects SEINs as appropriate into parent firms, and ensures a consistent

---

4. The data structure of the LEHD and LBD allow for establishments within each firm to have different industries and locations. In rare cases where required in this study, we define the main industry and main location of a multiunit firm through the facility with the largest number of employees.

definition of entry with prior academic work using the Census Bureau data. As two examples, this approach ensures our entrepreneurship definition does not include the formation of a new SEIN by an existing multiunit firm expanding into an LEHD state, nor the development of new SEINs for tax purposes by existing businesses. With respect to the broader literature, our approach focuses on the formation of employer establishments, whereas the commencement of Schedule C self-employment activity is unmeasured and not considered to be entrepreneurship in this sample.[5]

A very important issue, and the weakest link of these data for the study of entrepreneurship, is that the LEHD does not designate the founders or owners of firms. Similarly, compensation data includes bonus pay but not equity ownership of individuals. We use the term "entrepreneur" to describe anyone present in the data who satisfies three criteria: (a) in an entering single-unit firm per the Haltiwanger, Jarmin, and Miranda (2013) definition, (b) present in the LEHD in the first year that the new firm entered, and (c) among the top three initial earners in the firm. With respect to the first condition, we require the new firm be a single-unit firm in its start year to ensure that we have complete employment records from the LEHD. By itself, the second condition focuses on the initial employees of the firm and will in many cases include early hires. The third condition then associates entrepreneurship with the top initial earners in the firm. This will clearly be inaccurate in some cases, and some entrepreneurs deliberately take low salaries or no compensation from their firms early on to conserve funds. On the other hand, as we describe below, most firms in our sample are small and are likely reasonably well modeled by this approach. We also show results that drop the third condition and thereby provide statistics related to all initial employees in the firm.

Terms like "entrepreneurship" are also vague with respect to the time dimension. For example, a strict application of our three-part definition would declare the founder of a new firm to be a wage worker starting in the second year of a firm's life, yet many still consider Mark Zuckerberg to be an entrepreneur a decade after the founding of Facebook. For most of our trend statistics, we accordingly use a three-year window that declares an individual to be an entrepreneur if the firm was founded in the prior three years. We still require that the individual had been present in the year of founding and a top initial earner, the second and third conditions. In fact, we do not require the individual remain necessarily associated with the firm, simply that the firm and individual persist. We present results that alternatively use a strict one-year definition. Overall, an unfortunate trade-off exists in that longer windows for keeping track of entrepreneurs result in shorter sample durations, due to the greater number of preperiod years that must

5. There is scope for further work on this regard using the Integrated LBD that contains nonemployer firms.

be devoted to determining the initial values. Said differently, if we wanted to declare individuals to be entrepreneurs if they have founded a business over the prior ten years, the earliest start date for the LEHD-based sample series is 2001, after the 1990s high-tech boom period that is so interesting to study.

5.3.3 Benchmarks for Definitions

We can use the public-use Survey of Business Owners (SBO) data from 2007 to help benchmark these choices with respect to the top three earners and their limits. The file contains over two million observations on employer and nonemployer firms, and the data contain detailed information about the firm and its owners. We focus on employer firms that mirror the LEHD-based sample built upon UI data, and we drop a small number of firms where the firm does not report whether the first-listed owner is a native or immigrant or no ownership data are present at all. Throughout, we use sample weights to provide population-level statistics.[6]

We first analyze the likelihood that the business represents the owner's primary source of personal income. For the full cross-section of single-owner businesses in 2007, this is true for 81.8 percent of businesses with an immigrant owner and 81.4 percent of businesses with a native owner. Similarly, when incorporating businesses with multiple owners, at least one owner reports the business as the primary income source in 81.9 percent of firms where an immigrant owner is present, very similar to the 81.3 percent rate in firms where no immigrant owner is present. When looking at the most recent entrants (i.e., business founded in 2007), the overall fraction of businesses being the primary income source unsurprisingly declines due to transition issues, but remains at two-thirds. It also tilts modestly toward immigrants— across all 2007 entrants, 70.3 percent and 64.7 percent of immigrant- and native-owned entering businesses constitute the primary ownership source, respectively, and this difference is statistically significant (t-stat = 4.03). Nonetheless, these general patterns are supportive of the use of LEHD records for identifying entrepreneurs, compared to an environment where most owners only derived very modest sums from businesses (e.g., businesses set up for tax purposes, hobby entrepreneurship, or to employ household workers).

We next consider calculations that help evaluate our focus on up to three owners. The news is again mostly supportive. Across all SBO firms in 2007, the average number of owners is 1.8, while for the newest 2007 entrants it is 1.7 owners. With our approach in the LEHD data, the average owner

---

6. This is the first-ever SBO Public Use Microdata Sample and it allows researchers to create their own tabulations and analyses on entrepreneurial activity, including the relationships between firm characteristics such as sources of capital, number of owners, firm size, and firm age. Going forward, a main data objective is to unite our LEHD platform with the confidential version of the SBO. (Data and descriptions are available at: https://www.census.gov/econ /sbo/pums.html.)

number is 2.16. This difference comes mostly from underestimating the share of firms with a single founder, and in some cases we are including an extra person in some of our assignments. On the other hand, a nontrivial share of SBO businesses report four or more owners compared to our cap at three entrepreneurs. Without more information, we must draw the line at some founder count, and we believe three founders provides the best balance.

This trade-off suggests that we need to examine closely how immigrant owners are distributed over the owner count distribution to see if scope for bias exists. Focusing on the 2007 entrants, we find relatively uniform rates of an immigrant owner being present: 23.4 percent, 22.4 percent, 27.0 percent, and 27.3 percent for firms with one, two, three, and four or more owners, respectively. A rising share on this dimension is to be expected, given our focus on any owner being an immigrant, and the differences are very modest. This suggests a rather small scope for issues emerging with counting too few or many owners with our three-person definition. This does not resolve the possibility of confusing employees with owners, to which we return shortly. Among the largest ownership teams for entering firms, we do not find immigrants being substantially different in terms of order listed. For four or more person teams, the immigrant shares are 20.3 percent, 14.4 percent, 13.8 percent, and 14.2 percent for the first through fourth positions (max reported) of listed owners. These structures again do not suggest very substantial issues likely to emerge with a three-person focus compared to using two- or four-person cut-offs.[7]

As a final step, the SBO contains some employment information that we can compare against the owner counts. As advanced warning, however, two significant issues exist in the analysis to follow. First, how each firm chooses to count owners toward employment is unclear. Second, the public-use SBO files intentionally introduce noise into the employment data to protect the identity of firms. Thus, while we believe the following analysis is quite informative for whether our definition creates a bias for immigrant versus native businesses, we need to be cautious about the exact figures reported. Our approach is simply to define an indicator variable for cases where we know we would have added an extra employee to our owner/entrepreneur definition because the employment count exceeds the owner count and the owner count was less than three owners; this is not comprehensive for all possible errors in our definition, but it is the most worrisome. Among the 2007 SBO entrants, this condition is met in 39.4 percent of cases. This number seems high to us, but we also do not know really how to evaluate it in light of the

7. In our regression sample, our mean immigrant entrepreneur share is 22.6 percent, with a 2005/1995 growth ratio of 1.31 (column [2] of table 5.3 that is discussed below). We find comparable means and very similar growth ratios when examining firms that start with one entrepreneur (23.6 percent, 1.32) or two entrepreneurs (21.4 percent, 1.29).

noisy data, and so forth. What we do take great comfort in, however, is that this fraction is 40.3 percent for immigrant-owned businesses and 39.1 percent for native-owned businesses, with the differences not statistically significant (t-stat = 0.74). This suggests that we while we may modestly mismeasure levels (e.g., identifying too many entrepreneurs), we are unlikely to have a bias by immigration status in this regard.

Overall, we take comfort in the SBO comparison. Any single rule like our three-person definition will face liabilities, and these tabulations appear to say our calibration is reasonably balanced. We also note one feature that helps isolate our technique from potential biases where we may identify an employee as an entrepreneur. Empirical studies of the hiring patterns by immigrant owners emphasize the strong degree to which they hire from their own ethnic group (e.g., Garca-Pérez 2012; Andersson, Burgess, and Lane 2012; Andersson et al. 2014; Åslund, Hensvik, and Skans 2014). Thus, our "false positive" for an immigrant-owned business is most likely to be an immigrant, and vice versa for a native-owned business. As an extreme example, our definition would be fully robust to unpaid owners or the inclusion of too many wage earners if the immigrant status of the employees exactly mirrored that of the true owners. This extreme condition does not hold, of course, but the quite high rates of concentration among small employers documented in Andersson et al. (2014) and similar studies are comforting for our design.

A second point of comparison comes from individuals to whom we can link LEHD records to their responses to the 2000 Census. The long form collects whether or not an individual declares themselves to be primarily self-employed in an incorporated firm, primarily self-employed in an unincorporated firm, an employee in a private-for-profit firm, or other categories. Looking at 2000 for individuals working in an SEIN created since 1995, we find that we label as an entrepreneur 66 percent of those declaring themselves to be self-employed in an incorporated firm. By contrast, we only label as an entrepreneur 29 percent of those declaring themselves to be self-employed in an unincorporated firm. Thus, our definition clearly tilts toward incorporated firms and those oriented toward employment and possibly growth, capturing a large portion of this group. The larger deviation, which is not surprising, is that about two-thirds of the overall set of people we declare to be entrepreneurs are listing themselves as an employee in a private-for-profit firm. Specifically, the composition of our entrepreneurial pool breaks down as 68 percent saying they are employed in private-for-profit firms, 28 percent self employed, and a small residual in other categories. In many of these new firms, no one is declaring themselves to be self-employed, which is a limitation of this approach to defining entrepreneurship. We thus find it difficult to benchmark this form of the metric compared to the self-employment breakdown.

5.3.4   Measuring Firm Dynamics

Our analyses consider the survival and growth of new businesses, which we measure exclusively through the LBD. This choice, which was not obvious to us at the start of this project, is important. By measuring outcomes through the LBD, we capture the full employment and payroll growth that the firm experiences (domestically in the United States). Alternative metrics based upon SEINs alone can miss substantial firm adjustments that occur within LEHD states when they open up new SEIN codes. Moreover, by definition, LEHD-based definitions of growth are subject to the state coverage limitations of the database. Thus, in combination with the discussion above, our strategy can be summarized as follows: (a) find single-unit firm entrants from 1992 to 2008 in the LBD that are in a covered LEHD state, (b) collect the initial employment records that are contained in the LEHD to describe the immigrant-native composition of initial employees and founders, and (c) return to the LBD for subsequent growth outcomes. This strategy allows us to retain all entrants and consistently measure growth; fortuitously, it also lets us use the LBD outcome data to 2011 for growth dynamics, even though our version of the LEHD ends in 2008. The only potential biases will relate to the specific set of states that we observe and how they compare nationally. On the other hand, this strategy would not necessarily be optimal in cases where one wanted to observe the employment composition of firm growth (e.g., the year-on-year subsequent hiring of immigrants or natives).

Our platform describes immigrant entrepreneurship in general and across subpopulations. We split the sample by low- and high-wage firms using the median quarterly earnings during the year of entry. We also define firms as high-tech if the majority of their employment is in a three-digit Standard Industrial Classification (SIC) code listed as a high-tech industry in Hecker (1999). Separate characterizations are also provided by one-digit SIC codes. Given the specific academic interest and policy focus on VC-backed firms, we identify entrants that receive VC funding by 2005, as recorded in the Venture Xpert database, using name- and geographical location-matching algorithms (Kerr, Nanda, and Rhodes-Kropf 2014). As we do not have matches beyond this point, we only study VC-backed entrepreneurship rates through 2005. Finally, we provide some tentative notes about whether firms go public by 2005. This information is collected by observing whether the new firm is later present in the Census Bureau's Compustat Bridge File, which was last updated for the 2005 public firm cohort.

5.3.5   Additional Discussion

A central goal of this project is the compilation of information and best practices necessary for using the LEHD for studies of immigrant entrepreneurship. To this end, a detailed data appendix provides specific instructions and commentary for researchers regarding the LEHD, with a special focus on the firm-level dimensions and the longitudinal aspect of the LEHD data. This appendix information extends beyond the present study to also document issues noted in the Kerr, Kerr, and Lincoln (2015b) study of large firms. Additional restricted-access materials are available upon request. The appendix also provides thoughts about other data sets that could improve upon the entrepreneurship definitions developed here.

5.4   Entrepreneurship Trends

5.4.1   LEHD Statistics

Table 5.2A presents our core trends using all LEHD workers and a three-year definition for entrepreneurship. For these initial tabulations that regard all workers, we do not impose the single-unit firm restrictions or similar, keeping a very broad set of data. Column (2) considers immigrant participation rates in new firms relative to the total immigrant workforce in the LEHD. Approximately 6.0 percent of immigrants in the LEHD are working in new firms born over the prior three years, with some evidence for a decline in the rate over time. Appendix table 5A.2A provides the observation counts that underlie these estimates, which cover 3.2 and 4.6 million immigrants in 1995 and 2008, respectively. Throughout this chapter, observation counts are approximate and rounded per Census Bureau disclosure requirements. This appendix table also shows that immigrants constitute 19.3 percent of the LEHD sample from 1995 to 2008, growing from 16.4 percent to 21.2 percent, and the native rate of employment in new firms averages 4.6 percent (versus 6.0 percent for immigrants). The native rate is similarly declining after 2005.[8]

Column (3) documents that 2.2 percent of immigrants are among the top earners in a new business and thus declared to be an entrepreneur by our definition. Parallel to Fairlie and Lofstrom (2014) and in contrast to column (2), this share grows substantially to 2005 before declining some. Features of the data initialization process for identifying entrepreneurship are more difficult for 1995 and 1996 for some states, and we are required to use some minor extrapolation for these initial years for column (3) in tables 5.2A and 5.2B. These initialization challenges impact entrepreneurial rate calculations mostly, with upcoming share-based calculations in columns (4)–(10) being substantially less sensitive and unadjusted. Similarly, we report the trend statistics through 2008, but we hesitate to make too much of the declines observed after 2005. Through 2005, the entry rates are overall stable, and we believe some, if not all, of the decline after 2005 can be traced to declines in

8. While the eleven states are present in the LEHD by 1992, the statistics begin in 1995 to allow full initiation of all of our data and definitions. For example, while we can identify from the LBD the full set of young firms in 1992 (i.e., those born in 1989–1992), we do not know the immigration status of all of their top earners in the first year of the firm's life.

Table 5.2A   Trends in immigrant entrepreneurship and participation in new firms

Year (1)	Immigrant rate of employment in new firms (2)	Immigrant entrepreneur rate, defined as top three initial earners in business (3)	Immigrant share of employment in new firms (4)	Immigrant entrepreneur share, defined as top three initial earners in business (5)	Column (5) restricted to top quartile of entrepreneurial income in start year (6)	Share of entering LEHD SEINs with one or more immigrant (7)	Share of entering LBD firms with one or more immigrant (8)	Immigrant share of workers in entering LBD firms (9)	Column (9) weighted by employment (10)
1995	6.3	1.6	20.6	16.7	15.6	29.8	31.1	19.3	18.8
1996	6.4	2.0	21.0	19.3	15.5	30.9	33.1	20.3	19.4
1997	6.2	2.1	21.5	21.0	16.3	31.7	33.0	20.5	19.8
1998	6.1	2.1	21.9	22.1	16.9	32.4	33.8	20.8	20.0
1999	6.2	2.1	22.0	22.6	16.9	33.5	34.3	21.3	20.2
2000	6.1	2.1	22.7	23.2	18.5	34.2	35.9	22.1	20.9
2001	6.0	2.1	23.5	24.3	18.8	35.6	36.6	23.6	22.6
2002	5.9	2.2	24.7	25.6	20.0	36.7	38.5	25.1	23.4
2003	6.1	2.3	25.2	26.6	19.4	36.0	38.6	25.7	24.0
2004	6.3	2.4	25.7	27.0	20.3	35.8	36.8	24.9	24.1
2005	6.3	2.5	25.7	27.1	20.7	35.9	37.4	25.3	24.0
2006	6.0	2.4	25.6	27.2	19.8	35.9	37.8	26.3	24.4
2007	5.5	2.3	25.4	26.9	19.7	34.2	36.0	25.2	24.4
2008	4.9	2.0	25.6	27.1	20.1	35.6	37.0	26.2	24.8
Mean	6.0	2.2	23.7	24.1	18.5	34.2	35.7	23.3	22.2
Ratio 08/95	0.78	1.24	1.24	1.62	1.29	1.19	1.19	1.36	1.32
Ratio 05/97	1.02	1.22	1.20	1.29	1.27	1.13	1.13	1.23	1.21

Notes: Table provides broad trends related to employment in new firms by natives and immigrants in the LEHD and LBD. The sample includes eleven states present in the LEHD by 1992: CA, CO, FL, ID, IL, LA, MD, NC, OR, WA, and WI. Columns (2) and (3) consider immigrant participation rates in new firms relative to the total immigrant workforce in the LEHD. Columns (4)–(10) consider immigrant shares of activities relative to natives. New firms are defined through the LBD as described in the text and retain their entering status for the first three years of the firm's life. Caution should be exercised with column (2) and (3)'s trends from 2006 onward due to declines in match rates for the Business Registry Bridge between the LEHD and LBD late in the sample. Caution should also be used for column (3)'s entry rates in 1995 and 1996 due to ongoing initialization that required minor extrapolation. Share-based calculations in columns (4)–(10) are substantially less sensitive to these issues. The appendix provides complementary statistics: (a) considering shorter series for twenty-eight states present in the LEHD by 2000, (b) adjusting the definition of new firms to apply to the first year of business entry only, and (c) separating one-digit SIC industries.

match rates of new firms in the Business Registry Bridge between the LEHD and LBD. That said, to the extent that the trends are real, they would match the broad secular decline in employment in young US firms documented by Decker et al. (2014). Most of our focus is on the share of entrepreneurs who are immigrants, which is not materially influenced by these issues.

Columns (4)–(10) consider immigrant shares of activities relative to natives. Columns (4) and (5) repeat the previous two analyses on a relative basis. We estimate immigrants account for about 24 percent of entrepreneurs and the new employees of firms in our sample. The immigrant share of new entrepreneurs rises dramatically in our sample from 16.7 percent in 1995 to 27.1 percent in 2008, while the trend for immigrant shares of initial employees is more modest. Figure 5.2 graphs these trends. In column (6), we isolate the top quartile of the initial earnings distribution of start-ups (measured as quarterly averages). Immigrants tend to create firms with lower initial earnings, and the upward trend in immigrant shares for this top quartile is a bit weaker. Some of this pattern resurfaces below when looking at payroll growth regressions.

A number of studies report the share of firms with at least one immigrant founder. This often appears motivated by a desire to have the highest share possible for advocacy pieces, but it may also stem from a genuine

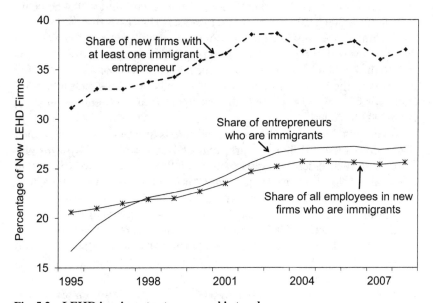

Fig. 5.2 LEHD immigrant entrepreneurship trends

Notes: See table 5.2A. Sample includes eleven states present in the LEHD by 1992: CA, CO, FL, ID, IL, LA, MD, NC, OR, WA, and WI. New firms are defined through the LBD and retain their entering status for the first three years of the firm's life. Entrepreneurs are defined as top three initial earners in business.

desire to capture the number of businesses touched in some way by immigrant entrepreneurship. By contrast, our baseline estimates are implicitly allowing fraction immigrant entrepreneurship in firms with several starting employees and weighting larger initial teams more (up to three employees). Columns (7) and (8) show that about 35 percent of entering SEINs or LBD firms have an initial immigrant employee, with column (7) also implicitly showing that our LEHD-LBD match is not introducing a bias. Columns (9) and (10) show patterns defined over larger LBD samples. While the results vary somewhat depending on these definitions used, the main message from table 5.2A is that the overall time-series pattern of our findings remains largely unchanged—immigrants are accounting for roughly a quarter of entrepreneurs and their share is increasing with time.

Appendix table 5A.2A provides complementary statistics for the twenty-eight states present in the LEHD by 2000. The wider state panel allows us to assess the potential impact of focusing on just eleven states, including two of the nation's most immigrant-heavy states, California and Florida. Considering the overlapping 2002–2008 period, our longer panel has an average immigrant worker share of 20.6 percent compared to 17.3 percent in the wider sample; likewise, the immigrant share of entrepreneurship is 25.4 percent versus 21.6 percent. Thus, our "levels" statistics are on the order of 3 percent higher. On the other hand, rates of immigrant and native entry are extremely close (5.9 percent vs. 5.8 percent, 4.5 percent vs. 4.4 percent), and all of the 2002–2008 trends are very close to each or even stronger in the wider sample. We thus conclude that our longer state sample may overstate national levels slightly, but is otherwise quite representative. This is due in part to the larger average state sizes in the longer panel (despite the addition of Texas in the larger set of twenty-eight states), with the eleven baseline states constituting 57 percent of the employment in the twenty-eight states from 2002 to 2008.

Appendix table 5A.2B shows that the results are robust to defining new firm employment through the first year of business entry only. This narrower definition essentially cuts the rate of firm entry by two-thirds. The one-year employment rate in new firms for immigrants is now 2.0 percent, compared to 1.5 percent for natives, a sizable differential remaining. The immigrant share of employment in new firms grows from 17.6 percent in 1992 to 24.9 percent in 2008, parallel to our baseline results in table 5.2A.

Appendix tables 5A.3A and 5A.3B report results for one-digit industries. Rates of immigrant entry are highest in mining and construction (SIC1), wholesale and retail trade (SIC5), and services (SIC7). Splitting industries at the three-digit level, entry rates tend to be higher for low-tech sectors, but this pattern is inverted around 2000 during the high-tech boom. A similar pattern is evident for VC-backed entry. Some of these patterns reflect inherent differences in entry rates across sectors and over time, common to immigrants and natives. In terms of share of initial employment, immigrants have higher relative representation in manufacturing (SIC2–3), wholesale and retail trade (SIC5), and services (SIC7).

Table 5.2B repeats table 5.2A for the part of our sample of firms that are backed by VC investors. About 0.11 percent of immigrants are starting top earners in VC-backed firms from 1995 to 2005. This share is naturally substantially less than the 2.2 percent in table 5.2A due to the relatively small number of ventures receiving VC investment. Reflecting the VC bubble that peaked in 2000, this rate is hump-shaped over time with a peak in 2000. Immigrants constitute about 28 percent of VC-backed founders, with this fraction increasing over time. The substantial majority of entering VC-backed firms have at least one initial immigrant employee, with the more similar results regarding overall fractions of founders coming from the fact that VC-backed firms tend to have larger counts of initial employees and larger founding teams. On the whole, immigrant entrepreneurship is somewhat stronger for VC-backed firms than generally, with 30 percent of the former being immigrants compared to 27 percent overall in 2005.

Our data platform allows us to compare initial immigrant and native employees by (a) their LEHD characteristics for the full sample, and (b) the Census long-form responses for the matched sample. Appendix tables 5A.4 and 5A.5 provide these results that we quickly summarize here. On average, immigrant employees in new firms tend to be slightly older and more likely to be male, with lower average LEHD quarterly earnings before, during, and after the founding of the firm. By contrast, the average quarterly earnings for immigrants before, during, and after the founding of VC-backed firms tends to be higher than their native peers. Looking at respondents matched to the 2000 Census, immigrants employed in young firms are more likely to be older, male, married, and have more children. While less likely to own a home, immigrants are more likely to own a higher-priced home and rent more expensive properties. This is partially connected to immigrants being more likely to live in high-priced gateway cities. The average year of arrival for our 2000 cross section is 1984, so that the average tenure in the United States in 2000 is sixteen years. These statistics are reasonable and comforting for our match, although we focus most of our analytical attention elsewhere. We return later to the year of arrival when considering differences between adult arrivals and those migrating as children.

Fairlie (2013) documents from the 2007 SBO that immigrant-owned businesses represent 13.2 percent of all businesses in the United States, with $434,000 in average annual sales (compared to non-immigrant-owned firm sales of $609,000). Only 28 percent of immigrant-owned businesses in the SBO hire outside employees, while the share is even smaller (26 percent) among the non-immigrant-owned businesses. For those that do hire employees, the average number of employees is eight in the immigrant-owned businesses and twelve in the native-owned businesses. Among our sample, the average initial employment for firms founded by immigrants exclusively

Table 5.2B Table 5.2A for firms backed by venture capital

Year (1)	Immigrant rate of employment in new firms (2)	Immigrant entrepreneur rate, defined as top three initial earners in business (3)	Immigrant share of employment in new firms (4)	Immigrant entrepreneur share, defined as top three initial earners in business (5)	Column (5) restricted to top quartile of entrepreneurial income in start year (6)	Share of entering LEHD SEINs with one or more immigrant (7)	Share of entering LBD firms with one or more immigrant (8)	Immigrant share of workers in entering LBD firms (9)	Column (9) weighted by employment (10)
1995	1.1	0.06	28.3	24.7	20.1	50.8	61.6	23.6	18.6
1996	1.4	0.08	28.4	24.7	25.1	49.6	73.3	25.5	22.7
1997	1.8	0.09	24.3	25.6	25.1	53.7	64.4	23.6	20.8
1998	1.6	0.12	24.3	27.0	24.0	55.5	74.1	28.9	24.4
1999	2.0	0.14	24.2	27.1	27.4	57.5	76.1	28.4	26.1
2000	2.2	0.17	23.5	27.8	26.4	62.0	87.9	31.7	27.4
2001	2.1	0.16	26.0	30.5	38.5	57.2	76.1	33.6	31.0
2002	1.7	0.13	26.1	32.9	31.5	59.1	83.0	37.7	35.7
2003	1.4	0.11	27.2	31.2	33.1	54.8	77.7	35.4	36.0
2004	1.3	0.10	24.6	30.4	31.3	59.9	79.3	35.7	33.9
2005	1.9	0.10	28.5	30.0	29.1	57.9	79.4	34.9	33.3
Mean	1.7	0.11	25.9	28.4	28.3	56.2	75.7	30.8	28.2
Ratio 05/95	1.73	1.71	1.01	1.21	1.45	1.14	1.29	1.48	1.79
Ratio 05/97	1.06	1.08	1.17	1.17	1.16	1.08	1.23	1.48	1.60

Notes: See table 5.2A Companies backed by venture capital investors are identified through firm names and locations as described in the text. Venture capital matching is available through 2005. Inclusion in the venture capital group occurs if venture capital financing is ever received, rather than being specific to the first years of the firm.

is 4.4 workers, compared to 7.0 workers for firms launched exclusively by natives. When both types of founders are present, the average is 16.9 workers. Thus, in general, our data appears to match the broad levels and patterns of the employer firms in the SBO sample, as well as differences in the typical sizes between immigrants and natives. Our overall numbers are naturally lower given the focus on the initial year of the firm (versus a cross section of employment patterns in existing firms).

5.4.2   CPS Comparison

To check our LEHD-based approach against publicly available survey data, we derive entrepreneurship trends using the Current Population Survey (CPS) Merged Outgoing Rotation Group (MORG) data from the NBER.[9] The data include details about the respondent's place of birth starting in 1994, and also report the class of worker where one of the categories is "self-employed in an incorporated business." We prepare a CPS sample that matches the traits of our LEHD work, starting with individuals age twenty-five to fifty who live in one of our core eleven states and work in the private sector. We further limit the data to those persons who are in the labor force and have a known level of education and potential labor market experience of at least one year. To stay consistent with the LEHD, we include as immigrants all those who are born outside of the United States.

Figure 5.3A first compares the immigrant workforce shares evident in the two data sources. The levels are very comparable, and the trends quite similar, with the CPS trend being modestly sharper. Figure 5.3B next compares the immigrant share of the entrepreneurial groups. The CPS trend includes as new entrepreneurs those who are newly self-employed in an incorporated business. The levels are more different here, with the LEHD being consistently at least 3 percent–4 percent higher. Perhaps more important, while both are upwardly sloping, the timings are different. The LEHD shows stronger growth during the 1990s, while the CPS picks up more in the middle to late first decade of the twenty-first century. We do not have a strong hypothesis regarding the source of these differences, although some of it may connect to the CPS redesign in 2002–2003. Unreported tabulations include unincorporated self-employed workers into the CPS entrepreneurial definitions, finding that the resulting trend sits in between the two series shown in figure 5.3B, with the augmented CPS series retaining its trend differences from the LEHD.

Figure 5.3C finally compares various metrics regarding rates of entrepreneurship for immigrants. Relative to the immigrant entrepreneurial shares shown in figure 5.3B, entrepreneurial rate calculations are substantially more sensitive to definitional decisions that can have large impact on their levels (regardless of data source). From the CPS, we provide at the top of

9. We thank Ethan Lewis for his guidance on this work. (Data available at: http://www.nber .org/data/morg.html.)

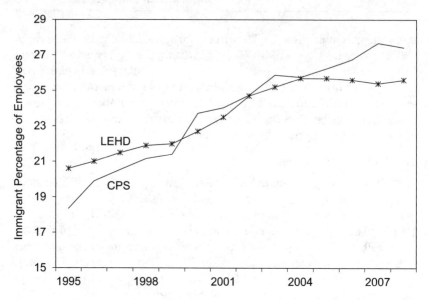

Fig. 5.3A   LEHD-CPS comparison for immigrant worker shares (workers in the private sector in eleven focal LEHD states)

Notes: Samples from both data sources include eleven states present in the LEHD by 1992: CA, CO, FL, ID, IL, LA, MD, NC, OR, WA, and WI. Included individuals are age twenty-five to fifty, employed in the private sector, and meet certain educational and work history restrictions. An immigrant is defined as a person born outside of the United States.

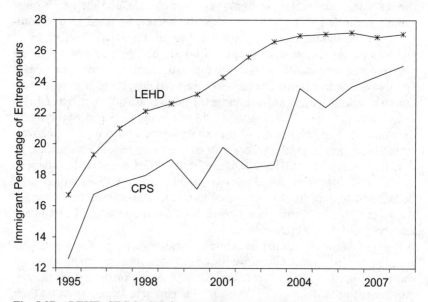

Fig. 5.3B   LEHD-CPS for immigrant entrepreneurial shares (entrepreneurship and self-employment in the private sector in eleven focal LEHD states)

Notes: See figure 5.3A. LEHD entrepreneurs are defined as top three initial earners in business and retain this status for the first three years after the firm's start. CPS entrepreneurs are defined as those entering incorporated self-employment.

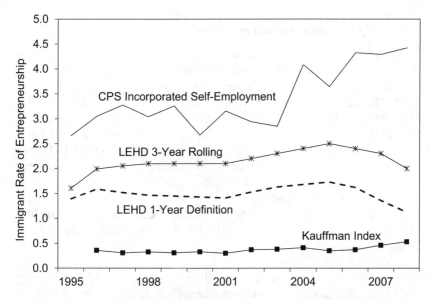

Fig. 5.3C   LEHD-CPS for immigrant entrepreneurial rates (comparison of immigrant entrepreneurial measures to immigrant population)

Notes: CPS measures include the overall incorporated self-employment rate for immigrants in the sample, which retains self-employed owners who have held their business for many years, and the Kauffman Foundation's Index that is derived from the CPS through new entry into self-employment. LEHD measures are provided with one- and three-year windows for comparison.

figure 5.3C a measure of the incorporated self-employment rate for immigrants in the sample. This includes self-employed owners who have held their business for many years, and thus provides a higher estimate of about 3.5 percent for the years; this share would exceed 10 percent if including unincorporated self-employment. At the bottom of figure 5.3C is the Kauffman Foundation Index that is derived from the CPS through entry into self-employment (Fairlie et al. 2015); due to its focus on entrepreneurial transitions, the rate is much smaller at about 0.4 percent. For the LEHD we show our core measure, where we use a three-year window for counting entrepreneurs and the one-year version that is most comparable to the Kauffman Foundation Index. It is clear that our metrics fall in between the extremes of CPS-based approaches. We tend to see comparable stability, and both data sources speak to a growing rate for immigrants compared to natives in terms of entrepreneurial transitions (which is mostly implied by figure 5.3B).[10]

---

10. The one-year rolling definition of entrepreneurship in the LEHD provides an entry rate that is about two-thirds of the three-year basis in figure 5.3C. This limited gap is due to the high rate of business failure in the first three years of operation. By contrast, employment in new ventures shows a greater difference, as described above for appendix table 5.2B. This is because employment counts capture the growth and scaling of surviving ventures through their first

5.5   Analysis of Firm Survival and Growth

We next consider differences in the performance of firms founded by immigrants versus natives. Table 5.3 first provides descriptive statistics for the sample of firms used for analytical work comparable to tables 5.2A and 5.2B. The analytical sample includes firms founded 1992–2005 in a Primary Metropolitan Statistical Area (PMSA) within a state present in the LEHD since 1992. Relative to tables 5.2A and 5.2B, several data preparation steps are undertaken to exclude entrants that are multiunit LBD entering firms and entrants lacking complete information for the considered LBD and LEHD metrics (e.g., reported payroll). The metrics focus on the immigrant-native composition of the top three initial earners. The sample ends with 2005 entrants to allow observation of LBD outcomes until 2011 and to circumvent any issues with the LEHD-LBD match (Business Registry Bridge) in later years.

Table 5.4A shows a basic tabulation of the data over a three-year growth horizon. We include in this analysis all entering cohorts of firms during the 1992–2005 period, with outcomes measured after three years for each entrant (e.g., 2004 employment for a 2001 entrant). In panel A, each row represents a separate starting size category in terms of employment. We then tabulate the share of entrants for each starting size category that grow to the level indicated by column headers by the third year, with rows summing to 100 percent. Thus, column (2) shows that over one-third of firms close across this time span, while column (7) shows that very few firms reach or exceed 100 employees, especially when starting from the smallest size category. The cells in bold represent the least moment from initial employment levels, which is the most likely outcome other than business closure.[11]

Panel B provides for each cell the average initial immigrant entrepreneurship share for the firms in that group. Entrepreneur definitions use the top three initial earners, independent of whether these individuals remain top earners in the firm across the three years. The Total rows and columns provide the weighted average immigrant entrepreneurship rates for their groups. The shares in column (8) decline across starting levels reflective of the lower sample average initial employment for immigrant-started businesses noted above. Panel C similarly provides the average initial immigrant employment share for grouped firms independent of initial earnings.

The intriguing initial pattern in the data points to a greater volatility of immigrant entrepreneur outcomes. The immigrant shares are frequently lowest among the bolded cells that represent static employment levels. In all cases, immigrants are more represented among closed firms in column (2)

---

three years, in addition to business failure effects. As our identification of entrepreneurs is fixed from the first year of each venture and with a maximum of three founders, this latter effect is not present and the differences based upon windows is smaller in figure 5.3C.

11. The majority of closed businesses are failed companies, but closures also include acquired companies should the LBD identifiers change, some of which may be quite successful outcomes.

Table 5.3   Trends for samples used in analytical work

Year (1)	Full sample			Firms backed by venture capital		
	Immigrant entrepreneur share, defined as top three initial earners in business (2)	Column (2) with employment weights (3)	Share of entering firms with one or more immigrant entrepreneur (4)	Immigrant entrepreneur share, defined as top three initial earners in business (5)	Column (2) with employment weights (6)	Share of entering firms with one or more immigrant entrepreneur (7)
1995	19.2	18.1	23.7	22.3	15.2	35.6
1996	20.2	18.4	25.1	21.9	17.4	42.6
1997	20.5	19.3	25.5	25.2	23.3	39.4
1998	20.7	19.2	25.9	28.1	17.0	44.0
1999	21.2	19.4	26.7	28.0	25.1	48.5
2000	22.2	20.6	28.1	28.7	21.6	49.4
2001	23.6	21.9	29.4	30.1	24.5	53.8
2002	25.0	22.3	30.8	34.4	26.8	58.0
2003	25.6	23.3	31.3	30.9	25.1	52.1
2004	24.9	23.5	30.3	32.0	22.7	57.5
2005	25.2	23.2	30.6	31.2	27.0	49.5
Mean	22.6	20.8	27.9	28.4	22.3	48.2
Ratio 05/95	1.31	1.28	1.29	1.40	1.78	1.39
Ratio 05/97	1.23	1.20	1.20	1.24	1.16	1.26

Notes: Table provides descriptive statistics for the sample of firms used for analytical work. The sample includes firms founded 1992–2005 in a PMSA within a state present in the LEHD since 1992. Relative to tables 5.2A and 5.2B, several data preparation steps are undertaken to exclude entrants that are multiunit LBD entering firms and entrants lacking complete information for considered LBD and LEHD metrics (e.g., reported payroll). Metrics focus on the immigrant-native composition of the top three initial earners. The sample ends with 2005 entrants to allow observation of LBD outcomes to 2011 and to circumvent issues with the LEHD-LBD match in later years. Employment weights are capped at fifty initial employees.

Table 5.4A   Growth tabulations and immigrant entrepreneurship share, three-year horizon

Row headers group by initial employment: (1)	Employment after three years:						
	Closed (2)	1–4 empl. (3)	5–9 empl. (4)	10–19 empl. (5)	20–99 empl. (6)	100+ empl. (7)	Total (8)
A. Distribution of outcomes by initial firm size, full sample (rows sum to 100 percent)							
1–4 employees	0.392	**0.448**	0.110	0.034	0.014	0.001	
5–9 employees	0.356	0.167	**0.281**	0.144	0.049	0.003	
10+ employees	0.385	0.040	0.087	**0.209**	0.246	0.033	
B. Starting immigrant entrepreneurship share in new firms by outcome distribution							
1–4 employees	0.226	**0.220**	0.205	0.200	0.205	0.212	0.220
5–9 employees	0.208	0.206	**0.180**	0.182	0.213	0.187	0.196
10+ employees	0.200	0.207	0.202	**0.179**	0.181	0.166	0.190
Total	0.220	0.219	0.196	0.187	0.191	0.173	0.212
C. Starting immigrant employment share in new firms by outcome distribution							
1–4 employees	0.230	**0.224**	0.209	0.205	0.213	0.240	0.224
5–9 employees	0.213	0.209	**0.183**	0.187	0.221	0.218	0.200
10+ employees	0.215	0.217	0.203	**0.182**	0.197	0.232	0.203
Total	0.226	0.222	0.199	0.191	0.204	0.232	0.217

Notes: Table describes transition/growth properties over three-year horizon for entering cohorts 1992–2005, with outcomes measured after three years for each entrant (e.g., 2004 for a 2001 entrant). Panel A tabulates the share of entrants for each starting size category that grow to the level indicated by column headers, with rows summing to 100 percent. Panel B provides for each cell the average initial immigrant entrepreneurship share for grouped firms. Entrepreneur definitions use top three initial earners, independent of whether these individuals remain with the firm or as a top earner in the firm. Panel C provides for each cell the average initial immigrant employment share for grouped firms.

compared to the bolded cells. Moreover, among the firms that begin with 5–9 or 10 or more employees, immigrant shares are lowest in the bolded cells compared to any other movement. In the smallest category, which panel A shows is the most stagnant of the initial size categories, immigrant shares among those firms remaining at 1–4 employees closely mirrors the overall share. Table 5.4B similarly considers a six-year growth horizon for cohorts, which uses the LBD data up to 2011 for our 2005 entrants. Over half of entrants fail by year six, which reflects typical start-up life expectancies. The patterns are mostly repeated here, especially in panel C. In panel B, there is less evidence of upside growth outcomes.

While intriguing, these tabulations do not account for general differences in when immigrant versus native firms are founded or their other measurable attributes. To address these issues, table 5.5A considers regressions of the three-year outcomes that take the form,

$$Y_{f,t+3} = \eta_t + \beta \text{ImmigrantEntrepreneurShare}_{f,t} + \gamma X_{f,t} + \varepsilon_{f,t},$$

where f and t index firms and entering cohorts. We include a vector of cohort fixed effects η_t and control for the initial attributes of the firms $(X_{f,t})$ in terms of their starting log employment and log payroll. Regressions are unweighted and report robust standard errors. Panel A presents the summary statistics for outcome variables. Panel B provides the baseline regression, with the last row giving the relative effect of increasing the immigrant entrepreneur share from zero to one compared to the sample mean.

Column (1) considers firm survival until the third year. On average, 64 percent of firms survive this long, with immigrant-founded firms being 0.3 percent less likely to survive compared to similar firms with only native founders. Columns (2)–(7) consider traits of firms conditional on surviving to their third year. We first look at employment growth, measuring changes relative to the firm's average in two periods following Davis, Haltiwanger, and Shuh (1996): $[Y_{f,t+3} - Y_{f,t}] / [(Y_{f,t+3} + Y_{f,t}) / 2]$. This measure is bounded by $[-2, 2]$, prevents outliers, and symmetrically treats positive and negative shifts. Conditional on survival, firms founded by immigrants show greater growth. Columns (3) and (4), by contrast, show no difference in terms of growth of payroll or establishment counts. The lower payroll growth may indicate lower wage growth, additional jobs being lower wage, or that partial employment is in greater use. Column (5) alternatively models employment growth through indicator variables for the firm achieving more workers than its initial level, while columns (6) and (7) are similarly defined for the firm reaching 100 workers or being among the top 10 percent of firms in terms of employment in its specific industry. These approaches confirm the employment growth observed in column (2). The final regression shows immigrant-started firms are much more likely to receive VC financing.

Panel C takes a more stringent approach that controls for cohort-PMSA-industry fixed effects, with industry being defined at the two-digit

Table 5.4B   Table 5.4A with a six-year horizon

Row headers group by initial employment: (1)	Employment after six years:						
	Closed (2)	1–4 empl. (3)	5–9 empl. (4)	10–19 empl. (5)	20–99 empl. (6)	100+ empl. (7)	Total (8)
A. Distribution of outcomes by initial firm size, full sample (rows sum to 100 percent)							
1–4 employees	0.571	**0.299**	0.082	0.032	0.015	0.001	
5–9 employees	0.536	0.130	**0.180**	0.105	0.046	0.003	
10+ employees	0.566	0.037	0.065	**0.136**	0.171	0.024	
B. Starting immigrant entrepreneurship share in new firms by outcome distribution							
1–4 employees	0.226	**0.215**	0.203	0.198	0.201	0.221	0.220
5–9 employees	0.208	0.192	**0.178**	0.174	0.203	0.178	0.196
10+ employees	0.198	0.199	0.206	**0.175**	0.173	0.155	0.190
Total	0.220	0.213	0.196	0.183	0.186	0.170	0.212
C. Starting immigrant employment share in new firms by outcome distribution							
1–4 employees	0.230	**0.219**	0.206	0.203	0.209	0.241	0.224
5–9 employees	0.212	0.195	**0.179**	0.180	0.209	0.220	0.200
10+ employees	0.214	0.205	0.204	**0.177**	0.189	0.215	0.203
Total	0.225	0.216	0.198	0.188	0.198	0.221	0.217

Notes: See table 5.4A. Outcome distributions use a six-year horizon for each entrant (e.g., 2007 for a 2001 entrant).

Table 5.5A   Regressions of three-year outcomes using LBD firms

	Fraction alive in third year (1)	Traits of surviving firms in the third year						
		Employment growth relative to firm's average (2)	Payroll growth relative to firm's average (3)	Establishment count growth relative to firm's average (4)	(0,1) third-year employment exceeds initial level (5)	(0,1) third-year employment exceeds 100 workers (6)	(0,1) third-year employment is in top decile of industry (7)	(0,1) received venture capital support (8)
A. Summary statistics								
Mean	0.6418	0.2726	0.2449	0.0033	0.5133	0.0086	0.0848	0.0027
SD	0.4866	0.6823	0.7216	0.0567	0.4998	0.0921	0.2787	0.0515
Observations	535,580	329,260	329,260	329,260	329,260	329,260	329,260	535,580
B. Estimation with cohort fixed effects and controls for initial traits								
Firm's immigrant entrepreneur share	−0.00335	0.03130	0.00037	−0.00025	0.01919	0.00159	0.00362	0.00232
	(0.00186)	(0.00301)	(0.00356)	(0.00022)	(0.00241)	(0.00036)	(0.00109)	(0.00020)
β/mean of DV	−0.005	0.115	0.002	−0.076	0.037	0.185	0.043	0.872
C. Estimation with cohort-PMSA-industry fixed effects and controls for initial traits								
Firm's immigrant entrepreneur share	0.01851	0.00190	−0.02375	−0.00024	0.00656	0.00047	0.00298	0.00045
	(0.00247)	(0.00483)	(0.00569)	(0.00036)	(0.00384)	(0.00064)	(0.00184)	(0.00031)
β/mean of DV	0.029	0.007	−0.097	−0.073	0.013	0.055	0.035	0.169

Notes: See tables 5.3 and 5.4A. Table quantifies how the outcomes of new firms vary by the share of the top three initial earners who are immigrants. The sample includes firms founded 1992–2005 in a PMSA within a state present in LEHD since 1991. Outcome variables are measured through 2011 using the LBD. Columns (2)–(4) measure growth by comparing the change during the period to the average of the start and end values for the firm. Regressions are unweighted, report robust standard errors, and control for the initial traits of starting log employees and log payroll of the venture. Observation counts are approximated per Census Bureau requirements.

level of the SIC classification. This approach removes any differences between immigrants and natives to found firms in certain cities or sectors, which can be important for outcomes, and instead compares immigrant outcomes to natives within these narrow cells. We do not view either approach as an inherently better way to describe the data, as differences in the choices of locations and industries are as relevant as differences in within-cell outcomes (e.g., due to different management practices). In some cases, this choice has material impacts, while in other cases the results are robust across the variation employed in the estimates.[12]

In panel C, we see that immigrant entrepreneurs are more likely to survive for three years compared to their closest native peers. The baseline employment growth is substantially diminished in column (2) compared to panel A, while some of the binary employment growth outcomes in columns (5)–(7) retain more strength. The most robust outcome is achieving the top decile of industry employment, which already has a degree of industry-level benchmarking built into it. Payroll growth is now significantly less than native peers, while establishment count growth is again flat.

Table 5.5B repeats table 5.5A for the six-year outcomes. The relationships in panel B are quite comparable to the three-year outcomes, with payroll and establishment count growth now more evident. Payroll growth is again noticeably smaller than employment growth. In general, there is greater statistical precision for the results with six-year outcomes, and the relative magnitudes are larger in size compared to the US average outcomes than earlier. The introduction of cohort-PMSA-industry fixed effects in panel C of table 5.5B has a similar effect to what it did for the three-year outcomes. Appendix tables 5A.6A and 5A.6B repeat these outcomes using simply the initial immigrant employee share as the explanatory variable, finding comparable results. Perhaps the key difference is that the employment growth outcomes are now more robust to the inclusion of the cohort-PMSA-industry fixed effects.

On the whole, the data paint some interesting differences, albeit tentative and noncausal, between firms founded by immigrants versus natives. When incorporating industry and city choice into the variation, immigrant founders have a greater volatility that somewhat mimics the up-or-out dynamics of young firm growth described in Haltiwanger, Jarmin, and Miranda (2013). They fail more frequently, but generate greater employment growth if they manage to stay in business. Over a six-year horizon they become more associated with higher payroll and establishment counts, but these are second

---

12. Our analysis uses the geocoding for the initial PMSA for the business. In a separate context, Kerr, Kerr, and Nanda (2015) describe the geographic information in much greater detail for the LEHD and the LEHD-Decennial match. There is capacity within the LEHD to observe movements over cities for all individuals; for those matched to the Decennial Census, there is further power to look very closely at the locations of residence versus business. These dimensions would be very interesting to consider in the immigrant context.

Table 5.5B   Table 5.5A with a six-year horizon

	Fraction alive in sixth year (1)	Traits of surviving firms in the sixth year					
		Employment growth relative to firm's average (2)	Payroll growth relative to firm's average (3)	Establishment count growth relative to firm's average (4)	(0,1) sixth-year employment exceeds initial level (5)	(0,1) sixth-year employment exceeds 100 workers (6)	(0,1) sixth-year employment is in top decile of industry (7)
A. Summary statistics							
Mean	0.4350	0.3097	0.3643	0.0034	0.5362	0.0102	0.0842
SD	0.4958	0.7403	0.7984	0.0591	0.4987	0.1003	0.2776
Observations	535,580	233,000	233,000	233,000	233,000	233,000	233,000
B. Estimation with cohort fixed effects and controls for initial traits							
Firm's immigrant entrepreneur share	−0.01365	0.04678	0.00876	0.00047	0.02899	0.00233	0.00386
	(0.00188)	(0.00393)	(0.00468)	(0.00029)	(0.00290)	(0.00048)	(0.00134)
B/US mean	−0.031	0.151	0.024	0.138	0.054	0.228	0.046
C. Estimation with cohort-PMSA-industry fixed effects and controls for initial traits							
Firm's immigrant entrepreneur share	0.01795	0.00760	−0.02769	−0.00032	0.01326	0.00157	0.00029
	(0.00243)	(0.00665)	(0.00794)	(0.00038)	(0.00489)	(0.00087)	(0.00245)
B/US mean	0.041	0.025	−0.076	−0.094	0.025	0.154	0.003

Notes: See table 5.5A

order to employment outcomes. However, much of this action appears to come through the way in which immigrant entrepreneurs chose locations and industries. Conditional on these features, they are more likely to survive than their native peers and modestly more likely to experience employment growth, with payroll growth underperforming comparable firms founded by natives.

Unreported estimations consider whether the industry or geography controls are more important for the differences observed across panels in tables 5.5A and 5.5B. The intriguing answer is that geography plays the central role—especially one state. This can be expressed in two ways. First, where a reversal of coefficient direction occurs across panels, the same pattern usually occurs when just introducing state fixed effects, while this is not true when introducing industry fixed effects. Second, adjustments in sample composition around the one state's inclusion or exclusion can achieve similar shifts as well. We are not able to show these tabulations directly or name the state due to the requirement that LEHD samples (or differences across two related samples) contain three or more states. Our internal files record the state breakout. Thus, in some respect, the unconditional results evident in panel B are the perspective taken when one allows for much of immigrant entrepreneurship to be in one location. This can include possibly endogenous flows of immigrants for opportunities, and it may reflect how immigrant entrepreneurship impacts the state's economic dynamics. By contrast, the patterns in panel C of these two tables are observations that control for these overall regional differences. Both perspectives are quite important to consider.

To look a little further behind these results, we also conduct several sample splits in tables 5.6A and 5.6B for estimations with and without conditioning on cohort-PMSA-industry fixed effects. Each coefficient in the tables is from a separate regression. The top row repeats the baseline specification, followed by splits between low- and high-wage firms, low- and high-tech sectors, and then VC backing (non-VC-backed results are not reported since they are so close to the baseline outcomes). We mostly focus on table 5.6B, where several intriguing differences are present. First, variation among low-wage and low-tech groups is generally responsible for our conditional survival relationship. Second, employment growth is generally associated with high-wage and high-tech sectors. Third, payroll growth compared to natives is never present. Fourth, while immigrant-founded ventures are more likely to access VC financing, they do not display stronger outcomes conditional on this financing. This is in many respects a parallel finding to our observation that city-industry choice accounts for much of the observed differences in the general sample. Finally, where employment growth occurs, it is usually about achieving any employment expansion relative to the initial level or reaching the top deciles of an industry, rather than surpassing the threshold of 100 employees (a benchmark that few newly started firms make). This is true for

Table 5.6A Split sample regressions for estimations with cohort fixed effects

				Traits of surviving firms in the third year			
	Fraction alive in third year (1)	Employment growth relative to firm's average (2)	Payroll growth relative to firm's average (3)	Establishment count growth relative to firm's average (4)	(0,1) third-year employment exceeds initial level (5)	(0,1) third-year employment exceeds 100 workers (6)	(0,1) third-year employment is in top decile of industry (7)	(0,1) received venture capital support (8)
			Estimation with cohort fixed effects and controls for initial traits					
Full sample	-0.00335 (0.00186)	0.03130 (0.00301)	0.00037 (0.00356)	-0.00025 (0.00022)	0.01919 (0.00241)	0.00159 (0.00036)	0.00362 (0.00109)	0.00232 (0.00020)
Low-wage firms	0.01380 (0.00247)	0.00410 (0.00394)	-0.00157 (0.00478)	-0.00045 (0.00024)	0.00320 (0.00331)	0.00000 (0.00038)	-0.00285 (0.00125)	0.00006 (0.00006)
High-wage firms	-0.02681 (0.00280)	0.06039 (0.00463)	0.00316 (0.00531)	-0.00023 (0.00038)	0.04215 (0.00353)	0.00273 (0.00064)	0.00848 (0.00180)	0.00484 (0.00045)
Low-tech firms	-0.00015 (0.00193)	0.03169 (0.00312)	-0.00220 (0.00368)	-0.00018 (0.00023)	0.01994 (0.00252)	0.00169 (0.00037)	0.00271 (0.00112)	0.00092 (0.00014)
High-tech firms	-0.02383 (0.00627)	0.02898 (0.01116)	0.02307 (0.01346)	-0.00126 (0.00083)	0.01794 (0.00822)	-0.00021 (0.00145)	0.01088 (0.00422)	0.00988 (0.00160)
VC-backed firms	0.03990 (0.03374)	-0.11521 (0.05524)	-0.11576 (0.07042)	-0.00624 (0.01009)	-0.01279 (0.02701)	-0.07686 (0.02287)	-0.09093 (0.04436)	n/a

Notes: See panel B of table 5.5A. Each entry in table is a coefficient from a separate regression with the indicated sample.

Table 5.6B   Split sample regressions for estimations with cohort-PMSA-industry fixed effects

		Traits of surviving firms in the third year						
	Fraction alive in third year (1)	Employment growth relative to firm's average (2)	Payroll growth relative to firm's average (3)	Establishment count growth relative to firm's average (4)	(0,1) third-year employment exceeds initial level (5)	(0,1) third-year employment exceeds 100 workers (6)	(0,1) third-year employment is in top decile of industry (7)	(0,1) received venture capital support (8)
		Estimation with cohort-PMSA-industry fixed effects and controls for initial traits						
Full sample	0.0185 (0.0025)	0.0019 (0.0048)	-0.0238 (0.0057)	-0.0002 (0.0004)	0.0066 (0.0038)	0.0005 (0.0006)	0.0030 (0.0018)	0.0005 (0.0003)
Low-wage firms	0.0280 (0.0037)	-0.0337 (0.0076)	-0.0186 (0.0093)	-0.0002 (0.0005)	-0.0209 (0.0064)	0.0003 (0.0008)	-0.0027 (0.0026)	0.0000 (0.0001)
High-wage firms	0.0000 (0.0039)	0.0464 (0.0076)	-0.0216 (0.0087)	-0.0007 (0.0006)	0.0370 (0.0058)	-0.0005 (0.0011)	0.0089 (0.0031)	0.0009 (0.0007)
Low-tech firms	0.0222 (0.0027)	0.0001 (0.0051)	-0.0271 (0.0060)	-0.0003 (0.0004)	0.0062 (0.0041)	0.0008 (0.0007)	0.0018 (0.0019)	0.0002 (0.0002)
High-tech firms	-0.0022 (0.0085)	0.0258 (0.0180)	-0.0084 (0.0221)	-0.0001 (0.0016)	0.0254 (0.0135)	-0.0021 (0.0027)	0.0133 (0.0071)	0.0023 (0.0025)
VC-backed firms	0.0319 (0.0871)	-0.2620 (0.1549)	-0.3500 (0.1868)	0.0101 (0.0138)	-0.0709 (0.0792)	-0.0311 (0.0557)	-0.1061 (0.1163)	n/a

Notes: See panel C of table 5.5A. Each entry in table is a coefficient from a separate regression with the indicated sample.

the general and VC-backed samples, suggesting that employment effects due to immigrant entrepreneurship are more likely to come from accumulated contributions of many firms compared to the extreme outcomes of a few high-growth entities that are often emphasized in the popular debate.

In unreported estimations, we also look at the probability of achieving an IPO by 2005, both in the whole sample and among firms backed by VC investors. We do not observe differences for immigrant entrepreneurs in this regard, but we also hesitate to emphasize this result given the early end date of the Compustat Bridge File for our sample.

While this study does not identify why immigrants might choose riskier city-industry cells, some preliminary candidates can be listed. One is that the self-selection process of international migration leads to a pool of foreign-born individuals in the United States who have a greater tolerance for risk and uncertainty than the average US native. This could lead to differences in the distributions of businesses started by the two groups with respect to potential growth outcomes. A second possibility is that immigrants have weaker wage-based options, due to some combination of factors like limited language skills, reduced acceptance of education credentials, spatial isolation in ethnic enclaves, social exclusion, or similar (e.g., Lewis 2013a). These reduced outside options may make immigrants willing to launch a business of any form and venture into riskier domains. A third, more positive, possibility is that the tight social structures for some immigrant groups allow them a group-based capacity to enter into riskier domains and rely on each other, similar to the studies of immigrant entrepreneurial specialization (e.g., Kerr and Mandorff 2015). This comparative advantage could be consistent with benefits of immigrant-generated diversity documented by Ottaviano and Peri (2006), Mazzolari and Neumark (2012), Nathan (2015), and similar. Another possibility, to complete a first and incomplete list, is that illegal immigration and undocumented workers in immigrant-led firms have somehow led us to mismeasure some of the growth/survival properties. We believe the LEHD-based platform provides power going forward to investigate these questions, for example, by taking advantage of the observation of wage histories before and after entrepreneurial spells to understand outside options. Similarly, the detailed information on country of birth can aid analyses of social isolation, group concentration on entrepreneurship in certain industries, and similar features.

Table 5.7 provides our final analysis, which is fairly brief. One goal of this project is to evaluate whether the 2000 Census traits can be incorporated systematically into the immigrant entrepreneurship analysis. Given the policy interest on the age at arrival of immigrants, we choose this dimension and show some initial tabulations in the transition framework of tables 5.4A and 5.4B. We restrict the sample to start-ups that have immigrant founders, and sample sizes require that we combine the final growth outcomes in column (6) to achieving twenty or more employees. The cells now represent the share

Table 5.7   Distributions of child immigrant entrepreneurship

Row headers group by initial employment: (1)	Employment after three or six years:					
	Closed (2)	1–4 empl. (3)	5–9 empl. (4)	10–19 empl. (5)	20+ empl. (6)	Total (7)
A. Share of immigrant entrepreneurs who migrated as children, three-year distribution						
1–4 employees	0.344	**0.366**	0.450	0.462	0.333	0.372
5–9 employees	0.329	0.455	**0.329**	0.438	0.410	0.373
10+ employees	0.493	0.455	0.343	**0.337**	0.503	0.464
Total	0.391	0.379	0.394	0.403	0.469	0.400
B. Share of immigrant entrepreneurs who migrated as children, six-year distribution						
1–4 employees	0.348	**0.379**	0.449	0.426	0.419	0.372
5–9 employees	0.349	0.368	**0.361**	0.478	0.424	0.373
10+ employees	0.484	0.211	0.375	**0.358**	0.504	0.464
Total	0.392	0.368	0.410	0.418	0.477	0.400

Notes: See tables 5.4A and 5.4B. Values document the share of immigrant entrepreneurs in each cell that migrated to the United States by age eighteen. The sample is restricted to immigrant entrepreneurs age twenty to fifty-four in 2000 who are surveyed by the long form of the Decennial Census.

of immigrant founders in the cell who came to the United States as children. At starting employment levels of nine workers or less, immigrants coming to the United States as children are generally associated with better outcomes in terms of lower closure rates and higher representation among the larger size categories. Immigrants coming to the United States as children are also more likely to start larger firms, and among this largest category they tend to be overrepresented among business closures and the firms that achieve the largest employment outcomes. As important, we form a general conclusion from this exercise that researchers will be able to split the samples sufficiently along traits available in the 2000 Census match to explore outcomes associated with different traits of immigrant entrepreneurs. Tabulations of growth by two or more dimensions (e.g., education and age of arrival) will quickly become strained, requiring multivariate regression analysis instead.

5.6   Conclusions and Future Research

The constructed data platform provides new statistics regarding the patterns of business formation by immigrant entrepreneurs and the medium-term success of those businesses. The definition of an entrepreneur used in this study is in many ways dictated by the coverage of the LBD and the LEHD, and hence it is useful to compare our calculations and estimates to those derived from other data sources. Looking back at table 5.1, our results tend to fall in the upper end of the estimates for the immigrant entrepreneur share. There are several factors potentially at work. First, the LEHD data does not identify the actual founders of businesses, and we may be over- or underinclusive in our definition using the top three initial earners. We have yet to identify a technique to quantify this effect relative to other definitions possible for founders. One of the most feasible comparisons may be business ownership records in the SBO (e.g., Fairlie 2008, 2012). Ownership estimates will be higher than entrepreneurship estimates due to the larger existing stock of native small business owners compared to new firm formation, and so we do not expect this difference to close. But through the study of new entrants captured in the SBO, perhaps the entrepreneurship metrics can be enhanced or their properties better defined.

Beyond immigrant shares of entrepreneurs, rates of entry are more difficult to reconcile due to many alternatives for both the numerator (who is an entrepreneur?) and the denominator (what population are we comparing this to?). Our data have some distinct traits. First, the LEHD only includes employer firms that file UI records, and thus excludes nonemployer firms and self-employment. Addition of these individuals will most likely alter the estimated rates by mainly boosting the numerator. That said, most of the policy focus and academic interest centers on attracting "growth entrepreneurs" that create jobs, in which case a restriction of the analysis to employer firms is actually desired. Second, our denominator focuses on private-sector workers in the LEHD. This denominator could be also more inclusive by incorporating the entire public sector or by being expanded to be all working-age adults in the covered states (e.g., drawn from the Current Population Survey). Using a larger population for the denominator will obviously reduce our measured rate of entrepreneurship. In general, our calculations seek to provide a new, longitudinal view into the patterns of immigrant entrepreneurship and not directly replicate nor necessarily displace findings from earlier studies. Our platform sacrifices on some dimensions (e.g., state coverage, ownership data) and gains on others (e.g., universal samples, longitudinal depth, homogeneity across skills).

While there has been considerable recent interest in immigrant entrepreneurship, as surveyed by Fairlie and Lofstrom (2014), the state of the field in terms of academic studies is still mostly wide open. Even establishing the basic facts has been hampered by the availability of large scale, nationally representative longitudinal data that would capture both firm founders and their firms. Below we describe several promising areas for further research, many of which would benefit from greater data availability from administrative sources.

First, it would be helpful to build a more solid research foundation for quantifying the magnitudes of immigrant contributions to the creation of new entrepreneurial firms in the Science, Technology, Engineering and Mathematics (STEM) fields. Many immigration policies specifically target this area—for example, the longer Optional Practical Training (OPT) period for STEM-degree holders—and much of the concern over encouraging immigrant entrepreneurship focuses here. In doing so, researchers could utilize the employer-employee panel data developed here and ideally also engage in a more causal analysis of policy changes affecting high-skilled immigration in general and poststudy immigration of STEM graduates from US universities in the first decade of the twenty-first century and thereafter.

Second, a better understanding of how the existing immigrants in the United States can more effectively engage in starting new businesses requires careful study of the choices and policy constraints faced by immigrants in their decisions to build and grow new firms versus being workers in a larger corporation. We also lack a clear picture of how the successful immigrant founders enter the United States, which can be for reasons as diverse as schooling, employment, family reunification, and more. A study of the transitions or the sequence of events explaining entry by immigrant entrepreneurs and the role of policies in allowing/blocking this transition would be a helpful start. For example, a frequent policy misconception is that the H-1B immigrants are responsible for lots of start-ups, and expanding the H-1B cap would boost entrepreneurship. While it might indeed do so over some horizon, we would anticipate a significant time lag because H-1B workers are tied to their sponsoring employers until a green card is approved, often taking six or more years. A specific evaluation could focus on the transitions of H-1B holders into entrepreneurship. While the current data platform can provide reasonable approximations of H-1B holders—for example, isolating immigrant computer programmers age twenty-five to thirty who were born in India via the 2000 Census match—a better scenario would be to gain access to the United States Citizenship and Immigration Services (USCIS) records on H-1B visa holders and match them to the LEHD and other Census Bureau data sources. Other visa categories lend themselves to similar evaluations, including the OPT visas for F-1 students. A less intensive alternative is to link smaller sets of individuals like the H-1B visa lotteries studied by Doran, Gelber, and Isen (2015). Accomplishing such linkages may be difficult, but better-quality data ingredients will result in substantially better advice for policymakers.

Continuing on these themes, it is widely thought that immigrant entrepreneurs contribute disproportionately to innovation and technological advancement in the United States (similar to the more established facts about the role of immigrants for innovation generally). One way to quantify immigrant entrepreneur contributions in the science and innovation arena is the United States Patent and Trademark Office (USPTO) patent data (Hall, Jaffe, and Trajtenberg 2001) matched to the person- and firm-level data sources available from the Census Bureau. Indeed, while there exist recent studies on the effect of high-skilled immigration on US innovation, we lack a systematic evaluation of how the creation of new firms by immigrant founders contributes to the overall pace and direction of US innovation and whether these firms produce different types of innovations compared to native-founded firms (e.g., exploration versus exploitation work). Several studies have made progress on the firm-level matching using name-matching techniques (e.g., Kerr and Fu 2008; Balasubramanian and Sivadasan 2011; Akcigit and Kerr 2010). These studies typically find record matching to be easier for larger firms than small start-ups. It would be terrific to have a match of LEHD workers to the inventor records in the USPTO database. Such a match would enable detailed studies of technological trajectories for workers (how start-ups relate to the innovative work of their prior employer), provide greater assurance about the quality of the matches overall, and facilitate interesting work on immigration and other related labor market policies (e.g., noncompete clauses).

In a very similar vein, we have also made significant headway toward identifying firms backed by VC investors in the Census Bureau data (e.g., Chemmanur, Krishnan, and Nandy 2011; Puri and Zarutskie 2012). Subsequent work in entrepreneurial finance frequently focuses on individual entrepreneurs and/or their specific VC investors. Individual-level connections of the LEHD workers to these data would provide a very powerful platform for the study of VC-backed entrepreneurial outcomes.

While the current study provides some descriptive analyses for a broader set of geographic areas, a more detailed analysis of the impact of immigrant entrepreneurship on local job growth and economic development is warranted. Feldman and Kogler (2010) and Carlino and Kerr (2015) review the literature on the geography of innovation that has come since Audretsch and Feldman (1996). Glaeser, Kerr, and Kerr (2015) consider the general link of entrepreneurship to city employment growth, and Samila and Sorenson (2011) consider the specific case of VC-backed start-ups. It would be useful to build on this past work to understand the specific case of immigrant entrepreneurship. Many cities and local areas are attempting to leverage immigrant entrepreneurship directly, and we need to know more about the potential efficacy of such efforts and how any stimulus actually accrues. Kerr (2010) finds that ethnic entrepreneurs are particularly important in the reallocation of inventive activity to be near sources of breakthrough innovations and their scaling process (e.g., Duranton 2007); study of these phenomena within the LEHD data family is quite promising. Similarly, we skip in this study the ethnicity and immigration status of hired employees due to data features noted above (e.g., the expansion of firms across LEHD state lines), and such features would be very natural to incorporate in a local growth context given the complete definitions of employee traits.

Appendix

Data Appendix: LEHD, Immigration, and Firms

This appendix explains in more detail how the LEHD data are structured and what types of issues are likely to arise when attempting to follow persons and firms over time within the LEHD. It is meant to provide guidance and useful suggestions for researchers interested in utilizing these data to study immigration and entrepreneurship at the firm level. Our analysis files for the current study and some previous studies (Kerr and Kerr 2013; Kerr, Kerr, and Lincoln 2015b) are available for researchers within the Census Research Data Center (RDC) network. We can also provide any SAS and Stata programs that have been redacted for any company identification to researchers who do not have access to the Census RDC network, although these files are likely to be of limited use without access to the raw data.

LEHD File Structure and Key Identifiers

The LEHD is available for researchers at the Census Research Data Centers. Access to the LEHD requires an approved project and security clearance. This section gives an outline of the LEHD and is geared toward building a firm sample using the LEHD and auxiliary Census Bureau data sets. The LEHD structure is described in greater technical detail in three Census Bureau documents: McKinney and Vilhuber (2008, 2011) and Abowd et al. (2009). We provide here a short description of the relevant data files and variables for the construction of a firm panel, omitting details of other LEHD structure files and variables for brevity. Prospective users of the LEHD are highly encouraged to review the full technical documentation, as well as any previous studies utilizing the LEHD, since the database has complications and issues for which researchers are building codified and tacit knowledge.

The LEHD data are currently available for research purposes for a total of thirty-one states. All states have signed the Memorandum of Understanding (MOU) to include their data in the LEHD, and once entered into the LEHD they will also retroactively include the data series as far back in time as their state's information and records permit. It is not yet clear when the remaining states will be included in the database. Discussion below includes more details on the partial state coverage and practical concerns that it raises.

The LEHD covers all private companies operating in the United States, and it allows researchers to analyze these companies and their workers at a very detailed level over a long period of time. Firms and their business units are identified in the LEHD by three main variables: SEIN, EIN, and ALPHA. The SEIN is a state tax identifier, the EIN is a federal tax identifier, and ALPHA is the Census Bureau's identifier of overall firms. In addition, as firms can have multiple establishments within a state, the LEHD also provides the SEINUNIT number that corresponds to the SEIN reporting unit (i.e., establishment). These variables uniquely identify a firm and its establishments within a calendar quarter and state. The person identifier (PIK) uniquely identifies a worker across all jobs that the individual holds, is derived from Social Security numbers, and is anonymized to protect the person's identity.

The LEHD consists of several separate files describing the firm, worker, and job that the person holds within the firm. These files are organized separately by state, and they have a uniform structure across all states. First, data contained in the employer characteristics file (ECF) and the employment history file (EHF) are essentially provided at the establishment level (i.e., by SEIN and SEINUNIT). As SEINs are only uniquely associated to a specific firm during a given calendar quarter within a given state, creating a firm-level panel requires first assigning each SEIN to a single ALPHA that can then be linked to a single firm entity. This process is discussed in detail below. The person-level information contained in the individual characteristics file (ICF) can then be easily linked to the EHF using the PIK.

The Business Register Bridge (BRB) files are the key for creating firms that combine all multiunit entities into a single company across all states. The BRB consists of two separate files: the BR list and the ECF list.[13] The former contains the full list of EINs belonging to each ALPHA and is organized by year, EIN, state, county, four-digit SIC, and Census File Number (CFN). The ECF list reports all SEINs belonging to each EIN, and each record is identified by SEIN, SEINUNIT, year, and calendar quarter. The dual nature and differing record structures of the BRB files make them somewhat cumbersome to use, and creating a full mapping of SEINs for each company name in our sample requires several data cleaning steps and additional research for unclear cases. These steps are documented in more detail later in this appendix.

The individual-level information contained in the ICF includes person characteristics such as the date of birth, gender, race, place of birth, and citizenship status. Similarly, the firm-level information in the ECF describes location, industry, payroll, and other firm characteristics at the SEIN and SEINUNIT levels. In turn, each job that a person holds in any of the companies covered by the LEHD is recorded in the EHF. The EHF tells for each calendar quarter how much the person earned while employed in each company that they worked for. The EHF (merged with the ICF) is crucial for calculating statistics on the company workforce over time.

The key ICF variables for identifying immigrants are the place of birth (POBST)[14], the indicator for foreign place of birth (POBFIN), and the indicator for ever being an alien (ALIEN). These variables allow us to construct a "country of birth" variable.[15] On the other hand, the LEHD is missing

13. The BRB files are further separated into two vintage files. The older vintage files cover years until 2001, and the newer vintage files cover years 1997–2004. While data for the overlapping years should be mostly identical, there are instances where the linkage information differs between the two files. We prioritize the later vintage information where conflict exists.

14. The LEHD country codes are based on the official country codes used, for example, by the Department of Defense. They require some additional processing due to the fact that countries have changed over time and the LEHD records the country as written down by the person in their application for a Social Security number. For example, Germany can show up as GM, BZ, GC, or GE depending on the time of application. In unclear cases we used the city of birth variable (POBCITY) to resolve conflicts.

15. Kerr, Kerr, and Lincoln (2015b) further aggregates these into ten country groups: (a) China, Hong Kong, and Macao; (b) India, Pakistan, and Bangladesh; (c) other Asian coun-

some information that would be relevant for a study of high-skilled immigration, or indeed for many other economic topics. First, it does not contain information on the job characteristics such as occupation, position held, hours worked, or hourly wage. The employment data do not identify reporting relationships or similar attributes of the corporate hierarchy. Second, the ICF does not report the person's actual education (an imputed version is provided) or their immigrant status (e.g., green card, H-1B visa), or changes in these characteristics. We would ideally like to know the person's initial year of entry into the United States, as well as any changes that have occurred in their immigrant status over time.

Other Census Data Required for Firm Identification

The LEHD can be used (and is perhaps most naturally used) at the SEIN level, which for most companies roughly corresponds to an establishment, and for single-unit firms contains the entire firm. In theory, researchers can construct larger "Census firms" by using the BRB to identify all SEINs that belong to a single ALPHA, and then consider the ALPHA to be the unique company identifier. This approach often works fine if one is primarily interested in looking at the cross section of firms at a specific point in time, but the approach does not work well when one needs to track large, multiunit companies over time. It is true that most large firms have one core ALPHA under which most of their employment falls within any given year, and this identifier is mostly fixed over time. However, a more careful look at the larger, multiunit firms studied in Kerr, Kerr, and Lincoln (2015b) finds corporate events such as mergers, acquisitions, spin-offs, and so forth substantially weaken the exclusive use of ALPHAs for longitudinal analyses. In other words, an ALPHA with a large number of employees may temporarily disappear, switch to a different ALPHA, or lose (or gain) a very large number of employees from one year to the next as a result of corporate restructuring.

This is undesirable if one is interested in describing changes in a firm's workforce related to a specific phenomenon, such as high-skilled immigration. Some of our prior work (Kerr, Kerr, and Lincoln 2015b; Kerr and Kerr 2013) thus pursues the creation of composite firm entities.[16] Such steps require identifying all of the ALPHAs from the company's workforce during the period of study. With that objective, we find the best approach to be to (a) identify the relevant firms by their names as recorded in the LBD/SSEL

---

tries; (d) English-speaking countries; (e) Russia and former member states of the Soviet Union; (f) other European countries; (g) Middle East; (h) Africa; (i) Central and South America; and (j) other countries. A detailed breakdown of the country codes is available from the authors by request.

16. There can also be conceptual concerns. For example, if the research goal is to study whether immigrants are displacing natives in firms, corporate restructurings need to be very carefully considered. Strictly speaking, an acquisition includes the simultaneous hiring of many immigrant and native workers from the acquired firm, which would have substantial effects on the estimated relationship, but this is not conceptually what studies are after. Kerr, Kerr, and Lincoln (2015b) pursues the creation of composite firms to remove these biases.

and (b) use the LBD/SSEL to identify all ALPHAs that are ever associated with the company name. In other words, the company name becomes the unique firm identifier, and this approach works best when building records for large companies present across the full time period. The most reliable process of identifying ALPHAs for target companies involves a careful review of company histories to identify significant mergers, acquisitions, and spin-offs that take place during the period of interest. The review of company histories is likely to result in a long list of such events. In addition, one should conduct additional research around cases where there is, based on the LBD, a very large shift in the firm employment from one year to the next. These cases often turn out to be mass layoffs, firms going out of business, or other normal events in the firm life cycle. In some cases, however, one finds overlooked corporate events that should again be accounted for in the compiling of composite firms.

Researchers should further search the LBD by company name and name variations, including the companies that have merged into the original sample companies. For each company and its acquisitions, one needs to collect all ALPHAs that are contained in the LBD under any of the name variations. For example, if company AAA has acquired companies BBB and CCC, we would find three (or more) separate ALPHAs in the LBD and group these with a composite company identifier that is used in subsequent work. This process produces a unique company name, along with the full list of ALPHAs that should be combined together in the LEHD for each company. Kerr, Kerr, and Lincoln (2015b) further describes the application of this manual process for the study's group of 319 large firms and major patenting firms. These firm lists and associated identifiers are available to researchers with appropriate approvals and data access.

Identification of Firms in the LEHD

Once the full list of company names and the various ALPHAs belonging to each of the companies are obtained from the LBD, the next step is to use the BRB to identify all EINs ever belonging to those ALPHAs. While the BRB uniquely associates EINs to an ALPHA within a calendar quarter and state, EINs are not necessarily stable over time, potentially creating abrupt changes in the firm employment series that will cause measurement error. The same is true for the SEINs that need to be linked to the ALPHAs via the EIN using the ECF list. Indeed McKinney and Vilhuber (2008) note that the EIN and SEIN exist for tax administrative purposes, and warn that no straightforward method exists for linking multiple SEINs into a single firm. Our preferred approach is described in greater detail below.

As LEHD identifiers do not uniquely capture a complete firm entity, we suggest using the cleaned version of a company name from the LBD as a unique firm identifier. As explained above, each of these firms may contain one or more ALPHAs, and almost certainly contain more than one EIN and SEIN. Using the BR list, one can create a list of ALPHAs that are ever associated with each EIN. Similarly, using the ECF list, one can create for each SEIN the full list of EINs that the SEIN was ever associated with. Combining these two lists provides the full list of SEINs that ever appeared with an ALPHA. Using the groupings of ALPHAs derived from the LBD, one assembles the full list of SEINs that ever belonged to a composite company. At this point, there are a number of SEINs that appear to belong to multiple companies, and this multiplicity requires careful attention. Also, as some of the company restructuring takes place at the establishment level (e.g., the sale of a plant or division), there are also cases where a specific EIN or SEIN belongs to multiple companies during the sample period. These cases require some additional research and data cleaning that is also described below.

Cleaning up EIN and SEIN Associations

The data thus far contain unique SEINs for which the LEHD data needs to be collected. Before proceeding, one needs to check whether each SEIN in the company sample is a unique match or requires special attention. In the latter cases, researchers are best served prioritizing cases for review through the employment levels of SEINs. Reviewing the employment series is also helpful when verifying whether the SEIN overlap is caused by a corporate event that had not been recognized in the initial firm sample construction. The cleaning process at this stage is fairly manual, and may involve searches for company events. Our preferred method in residual, unclear cases is to assign the SEIN based on the number of years that it is associated with companies.

Partial LEHD State Coverage

Appendix table 5A.1 provides a breakdown of the states included in the LEHD by the year in which their data series begins. As the aim of Kerr, Kerr, and Lincoln (2015b) and similar work is to study the evolution of companies and their employment structures, it is problematic if large shifts in company workforce result simply from the fact that new business units are added into the data when a large state enters the LEHD. We often utilize balanced panels of states that begin at one of three points: 1992 (once Florida joins), 1995 (once Texas joins), or 2000 (once the bulk of states enter). Second, one should consider dropping firms for which the included states do not meet a certain threshold in terms of included employment. For example, one may want to exclude finance firms that have much of their employment in New York, even if they have establishments present in covered states, as one cannot reliably represent the firm and its employment patterns using the LEHD states. These coverage ratios can be determined using the LBD.

Merging External Firm-Level Data into the LEHD

There are many firm-level data sources that are of interest for the analysis of firms and immigration. For example, researchers may want to incorporate

Table 5A.1   **Initial year of state inclusion in the LEHD**

Year (1)	States entering LEHD (2)	Cumulative state count (3)
1991 or before	CA, CO, ID, IL, LA, MD, NC, OR, WA, WI	10
1992	FL	11
1993	MT	12
1994		12
1995	HI, NM, RI, TX	16
1996	ME, NJ	18
1997	WV	19
1998	GA, IA, IN, SC, TN, VA	25
1999	UT	26
2000	OK, VT	28
2001		28
2002	AR	29

Notes: The LEHD files for states run through 2008 in the version used in this study. The start year differs by state and is tabulated in this table. Parts of the records for Georgia and Indiana (EHF, ECF) start earlier than 1998.

Labor Condition Application (LCA) data from the Department of Labor (DOL), which is a first step in the application for an H-1B visa from the United States Citizenship and Immigration Services (USCIS). While the USCIS does not release systematic data on the number of H-1B applications and granted visas by firm, microdata on LCAs are available by firm from the DOL.[17] These data contain all LCAs starting from 2001 and include the employer name, address, the number of jobs they wish to fill, and the specific job characteristics (title, occupation, proposed wage, etc.).

The firm names in the LCA database are entered as they appear on the original application. Since the applications are sent separately by different company locations, there may be variations of the company name that need to be dealt with before aggregating the LCAs under the overall company name. For example, 7-Eleven may submit LCAs under slight name variations such as "7-Eleven," "7 Eleven," "7-Eleven Inc," and "7-Eleven Incorporated." Also, the issues related to corporate restructurings resurface here as well. Once the names in the LCA data are cleaned and aggregated, we create a crosswalk for the company names to merge the LCA data into the LEHD data. The aggregated LCAs can then be easily merged into the LEHD by the clean firm name.

A second example is the merger of patent data into the LEHD-LBD to study innovation outcomes. Again, as firm-naming conventions vary between the LBD and the USPTO data, another name-cleaning step is required. Researchers also must aggregate multiple USPTO assignees into parent firms. Finally, for many purposes it would be useful to know more about

17. The data can be retrieved from http://www.flcdatacenter.com/CaseH1B.aspx.

the actual firms than is reported in the LEHD. One example of an external firm-level data set is the Compustat company database. Compustat provides standardized company financials for publicly traded companies. These data are merged via bridge files or crosswalks similar to those described. All bridge files are available to approved Census projects, but should be explicitly requested in initial research proposals to the Census Bureau.

Merging Internal Person-Level Data into the LEHD

While merging the company-specific data into our LEHD platform is relatively easy using the company name, person-specific data matches require the use of the PIK created by the Census Bureau. Three internal data sources can be directly linked to the LEHD: (a) long-form responses from the 1990 and 2000 Decennial Censuses, as well as the related American Housing Surveys, (b) the Current Population Survey (CPS), and (c) the Survey of Income and Program Participation (SIPP). For the purposes of our study, the census and the CPS contain some very relevant information that is not present in the LEHD, including occupation and actual education. As the LEHD contains the CPS person and household identification numbers, as well as the years during which the PIK matches the CPS identifier, it is relatively straightforward to combine CPS data into the LEHD. The CPS does not provide a time series of observations for each respondent, and the occupation is a point-in-time snapshot for each person that does not necessarily correspond to the actual job that the person is doing in the LEHD. Similarly, the census data is easy to link into the LEHD using the PIKs. Household characteristics can be linked to each of the matched persons using the household identifiers that are internal to the Census Bureau data.

Most person-level records in the LEHD have a one-to-one match to the CPS and census. We exclude the few cases where we find multiple CPS or census observations (e.g., in different states). As such persons make up less than 0.01 percent of the sample, including them either multiple times or randomly allocating the information from one of the CPS or census observations makes no difference in terms of the results of the statistical analysis.

Possible LEHD Interfaces

We close this appendix by describing potential future interfaces between the LEHD and other data products. The weakest dimension of the LEHD for entrepreneurship research relates to the identification of business founders/owners, and our approach in this study is not perfect. Indeed, we envision that future work can greatly expand and improve on the current approach by linking in founder/owner data from additional sources. These include, for example, the business ownership data from the Internal Revenue Service (IRS) Form K-1, the Doing Business As (DBA) filings from state secretaries, data on the Legal Form of the Organization (LFO) that could identify sole proprietorships, and perhaps also the forthcoming longitudinal Survey of Business Owners (SBO-X) as well as the existing 2007 and 2012 cross-sectional SBOs.

More specifically, the IRS collects data on business ownership by US individuals via the K-1 form (http://www.irs.gov/pub/irs-pdf/f1120ssk.pdf). Provided that the Census Bureau could assign each of the K-1 owners a PIK to merge into the LEHD, these tax records would provide one avenue for linking the owner information from the K-1 data to the LEHD. The second potential data effort is related to the state secretaries' corporate information that comes from the DBA registration process (http://www.secstates.com/). Each state collects these data, and they are held by the secretaries of state. The registration data generally contain the name and address of the business and the name and other details of the owner, and could in principle be brought into the Census Bureau for the purpose of assigning of company and person identifiers.

The SBO data also contain details of business owners, including their age, gender, race, and whether they are born in the United States. This level of detail would be sufficient for linking the SBO ownership percentages into the LEHD for better identification of whether the owner is among the persons who are on the company payroll. This of course would not cover the entire LEHD, given the survey design of the SBO, but it would help validate/refine definitions and enable analysis of interesting data on the company's start-up and expansion capital.

As unincorporated businesses are not included in the LEHD, we envision utilizing the Integrated Longitudinal Business Database (ILBD) to also cross-verify the status of the owner. The ILBD can be then used to provide descriptive details of the unincorporated businesses, while the census and American Community Survey (ACS) provide a description of the characteristics of the entrepreneurs/owners.

For employer sole proprietors, our approach of identifying firm founders is likely not satisfactory as the business owner will not be on the payroll. Indeed, some fraction of new employer businesses start as sole proprietorships and may later change their legal form of organization. Recent research using the Kauffman Firm Surveys found that about one in three firms begin as a proprietorship, while almost as many begin as limited liability companies and as corporations. Of course, not all sole proprietorships are among employer firms. Cole (2011) provides data that suggests that the share of firms that start as employer sole proprietorships is smaller than one-third; the average sole proprietorship has 0.6 employees. That provides some guidance as to the error that may be introduced by ignoring the LFO in the LEHD context. We hope that future research continues to bring together these data elements to provide ever sharper metrics for entrepreneurship and the role of immigrants.

Table 5A.2A LEHD trends using all earners and three-year new firm definition

Year (1)	Count of immigrants in new firms (2)	Count of other immigrant wage workers (3)	Count of natives in new firms (4)	Count of other native wage workers (5)	Total share of immigrants in LEHD workforce (%) (6)	Immigrant rate of employment in new firms (%) (7)	Native rate of employment in new firms (%) (8)	Immigrant share of employment in new firms (%) (9)
				A. LEHD states present by 1992				
1995	203,480	3,036,760	785,550	15,790,590	16.4	6.3	4.7	20.6
1996	223,590	3,293,330	839,190	16,570,810	16.8	6.4	4.8	21.0
1997	238,330	3,624,270	870,560	17,448,260	17.4	6.2	4.8	21.5
1998	254,720	3,901,610	908,040	18,140,570	17.9	6.1	4.8	21.9
1999	272,660	4,155,360	964,550	18,732,440	18.4	6.2	4.9	22.0
2000	289,120	4,435,670	986,950	19,356,100	18.8	6.1	4.9	22.7
2001	299,620	4,665,730	975,540	19,723,010	19.3	6.0	4.7	23.5
2002	299,430	4,735,170	915,030	19,397,310	19.9	5.9	4.5	24.7
2003	309,820	4,753,190	918,170	19,079,330	20.2	6.1	4.6	25.2
2004	326,070	4,847,310	943,290	19,095,630	20.5	6.3	4.7	25.7
2005	332,780	4,940,650	960,510	19,146,990	20.8	6.3	4.8	25.7
2006	319,490	5,004,690	926,830	19,177,940	20.9	6.0	4.6	25.6
2007	275,820	4,755,270	808,390	18,114,770	21.0	5.5	4.3	25.4
2008	226,920	4,419,640	659,940	16,640,660	21.2	4.9	3.8	25.6
				B. LEHD states present by 2000				
2002	441,390	6,934,120	1,707,180	35,645,500	16.5	6.0	4.6	20.5
2003	445,890	6,992,490	1,684,910	35,077,100	16.8	6.0	4.6	20.9
2004	467,010	7,158,580	1,691,990	35,131,620	17.2	6.1	4.6	21.6
2005	480,550	7,321,280	1,706,910	35,252,440	17.4	6.2	4.6	22.0
2006	463,750	7,449,540	1,636,550	35,356,850	17.6	5.9	4.4	22.1
2007	406,860	7,046,720	1,430,920	33,340,470	17.7	5.5	4.1	22.1
2008	337,480	6,546,090	1,188,780	30,801,120	17.7	4.9	3.7	22.1

Notes: Table provides counts and statistics related to employment in new firms by natives and immigrants in the LEHD. Panel A presents statistics for eleven states present in the LEHD by 1992. Panel B presents statistics for twenty-eight states present by 2000. Table 5A.1 lists states. New firms are defined through the LBD as described in the text and retain their new firm status for the first three years of the firm's life. Caution should be exercised with trends from 2006 onward due to declines in match rates for the Business Registry Bridge between the LEHD and LBD late in the sample. Observation counts are approximated per Census Bureau requirements.

Table 5A.2B   LEHD trends using all earners and one-year new firm definition

Year (1)	Count of immigrants in new firms (2)	Count of other immigrant wage workers (3)	Count of natives in new firms (4)	Count of other native wage workers (5)	Total share of immigrants in LEHD workforce (%) (6)	Immigrant rate of employment in new firms (%) (7)	Native rate of employment in new firms (%) (8)	Immigrant share of employment in new firms (%) (9)
				A. LEHD states present by 1992				
1992	44,770	2,138,260	210,120	12,714,680	14.4	2.1	1.6	17.6
1993	51,640	2,333,490	229,890	13,581,600	14.7	2.2	1.7	18.3
1994	59,350	2,523,290	253,490	14,236,840	15.1	2.3	1.7	19.0
1995	69,060	3,171,180	262,370	16,313,760	16.4	2.1	1.6	20.8
1996	78,990	3,437,930	289,720	17,120,320	16.8	2.2	1.7	21.4
1997	79,920	3,782,690	285,110	18,033,710	17.4	2.1	1.6	21.9
1998	89,420	4,066,900	320,520	18,728,090	17.9	2.2	1.7	21.8
1999	96,200	4,331,820	338,820	19,358,170	18.4	2.2	1.7	22.1
2000	99,720	4,625,080	326,510	20,016,540	18.8	2.1	1.6	23.4
2001	97,340	4,867,410	289,260	20,409,280	19.3	2.0	1.4	25.2
2002	98,290	4,936,300	278,210	20,034,130	19.9	2.0	1.4	26.1
2003	107,280	4,955,730	311,420	19,686,080	20.2	2.1	1.6	25.6
2004	113,290	5,060,100	322,450	19,716,470	20.5	2.2	1.6	26.0
2005	108,710	5,164,720	312,650	19,794,860	20.8	2.1	1.6	25.8
2006	89,640	5,234,540	268,900	19,835,880	20.9	1.7	1.3	25.0
2007	69,370	4,961,720	220,510	18,702,570	21.0	1.4	1.2	23.9
2008	53,730	4,592,830	161,870	17,138,720	21.2	1.2	0.9	24.9
				B. LEHD states present by 2000				
2000	145,660	6,725,760	603,720	36,644,220	15.6	2.1	1.6	19.4
2001	142,060	7,105,810	538,650	37,404,240	16.0	2.0	1.4	20.9
2002	143,950	7,231,560	510,020	36,842,660	16.5	2.0	1.4	22.0
2003	145,430	7,292,940	542,420	36,219,590	16.8	2.0	1.5	21.1
2004	163,690	7,461,900	570,290	36,253,320	17.2	2.1	1.5	22.3
2005	159,460	7,642,370	559,920	36,639,440	17.3	2.0	1.5	22.2
2006	131,500	7,781,790	471,920	36,521,490	17.6	1.7	1.3	21.8
2007	100,410	7,353,160	385,290	34,386,140	17.7	1.3	1.1	20.7
2008	79,880	6,803,680	299,580	31,690,320	17.7	1.2	0.9	21.1

Notes: See table 5A.2A. Table adjusts the definition of new firms to apply to the first year of business entry only.

Table 5A.3A   Immigrant rate of employment in new firms by SIC group

Year (1)	SIC1 (2)	SIC2 (3)	SIC3 (4)	SIC4 (5)	SIC5 (6)	SIC6 (7)	SIC7 (8)	SIC8 (9)	Low tech (10)	High tech (11)	VC funded (12)
					A. LEHD states present by 1992						
1995	9.4	5.2	3.2	5.2	8.2	4.5	8.4	5.3	6.4	5.4	1.1
1996	9.2	5.3	3.3	5.3	8.2	4.7	8.5	5.6	6.4	5.7	1.4
1997	8.5	5.3	3.4	5.1	8.1	4.8	8.0	5.5	6.2	5.7	1.8
1998	8.4	5.4	3.1	4.8	8.0	5.2	8.0	5.1	6.2	5.4	1.6
1999	8.2	5.5	3.0	5.2	7.8	5.4	8.0	5.2	6.2	6.0	2.0
2000	7.9	5.3	2.8	5.0	7.7	5.4	8.3	5.1	6.0	6.7	2.2
2001	7.5	4.3	2.7	5.3	7.5	5.2	8.3	5.1	6.0	6.5	2.1
2002	7.5	4.5	2.6	5.4	7.6	5.3	7.5	5.0	6.0	5.9	1.7
2003	7.7	3.9	2.9	5.7	7.7	6.1	7.5	5.1	6.2	5.8	1.4
2004	8.0	4.6	2.9	5.9	7.6	6.4	7.5	5.2	6.5	5.1	1.3
2005	8.4	4.7	2.9	5.4	7.6	6.6	7.6	5.0	6.5	4.9	1.9
2006	8.1	4.5	2.6	5.0	7.3	6.2	7.1	4.6	6.2	4.6	1.4
2007	7.4	4.1	2.2	5.4	6.8	5.2	6.3	4.2	5.7	3.9	0.9
2008	6.3	3.2	1.9	4.8	6.2	4.3	5.8	4.1	5.1	3.4	0.3
					B. LEHD states present by 2000						
2002	7.6	4.0	2.9	5.4	7.8	5.0	7.6	4.8	6.0	6.0	1.5
2003	7.5	3.6	3.0	5.4	7.8	5.6	7.5	4.7	6.0	5.7	1.2
2004	7.8	4.0	3.0	5.5	7.7	5.8	7.4	4.9	6.2	5.2	1.2
2005	8.1	4.1	2.9	5.2	7.7	6.1	7.6	4.7	6.3	4.9	1.6
2006	7.7	4.0	2.7	4.8	7.4	5.6	7.2	4.4	6.0	4.7	1.2
2007	7.3	3.6	2.3	5.2	7.0	4.8	6.6	4.1	5.6	4.2	0.8
2008	6.4	2.9	2.2	4.7	6.3	4.1	6.0	3.9	5.1	3.8	0.3

Notes: The one-digit SIC codes cover the following industries. SIC1: metal mining, coal mining, oil & gas extraction, nonmetal minerals (except fuels); general building contractors, heavy construction (excl. building), special trade contractors; SIC2: food & kindred products, tobacco products, textile mill products, apparel & other textile products, lumber & wood products, furniture & fixtures, paper & allied products, printing & publishing, chemicals & allied products, petroleum & coal Products; SIC3: rubber & misc. plastics products, leather & leather products, stone & clay & glass products, primary metal industries, fabricated metal products, industrial machinery & equipment, electronic & other electric equipment, transportation equipment, instruments & related products, misc. manufacturing; SIC4: railroad transportation, local & interurban passenger transit, trucking & warehousing, water transportation, pipelines (except natural gas), transportation services, communications, electric, gas & sanitary services; SIC5: wholesale trade-durable goods, wholesale trade-nondurable goods, building materials & garden supplies, general merchandise stores, food stores, automotive dealers & service stations, apparel & accessories stores, furniture & home furnishings stores, eating & drinking places; SIC6: depository institutions, nondepository institutions, security & commodity brokers, insurance carriers, holdings & other investment offices; SIC7: hotels & other lodgings places, personal services, business services, auto repair & services & parkings, miscellaneous repair services, motion pictures, amusement & recreation services; SIC8: health services, legal services, educational services, social services, museums & botanical & zoological gardeners, membership organizations, services NEC. The high-tech industries are based on the three-digit SIC classification as shown in Hecker (1999).

Table 5A.3B Immigrant share of employment in new firms by SIC group

Year (1)	SIC1 (2)	SIC2 (3)	SIC3 (4)	SIC4 (5)	SIC5 (6)	SIC6 (7)	SIC7 (8)	SIC8 (9)	Low tech (10)	High tech (11)	VC funded (12)
					A. LEHD states present by 1992						
1995	13.7	33.2	27.9	16.8	24.5	14.1	20.0	16.0	20.4	22.9	28.3
1996	14.1	33.8	25.7	16.8	25.7	14.8	21.2	16.6	20.9	22.5	28.4
1997	14.2	32.6	26.7	17.1	26.6	15.3	21.8	16.8	21.3	22.9	24.3
1998	14.9	34.4	26.5	17.5	26.8	16.0	22.4	16.8	21.8	22.8	24.3
1999	15.6	34.9	25.8	19.1	26.8	16.0	22.9	17.0	22.0	22.0	24.2
2000	16.6	33.4	28.0	20.8	26.8	16.4	24.0	17.5	22.5	23.6	23.5
2001	17.3	33.0	28.7	21.4	27.5	16.6	25.8	18.4	23.3	24.6	26.0
2002	18.2	33.6	28.2	23.3	29.7	17.7	26.8	19.4	24.6	25.4	26.1
2003	19.3	31.6	26.3	23.6	30.1	19.1	26.3	20.8	25.2	25.4	27.2
2004	19.6	31.0	25.9	23.1	31.3	19.7	27.0	21.9	25.8	24.8	24.6
2005	19.7	30.9	25.9	23.3	31.8	19.9	26.9	21.9	25.6	24.6	28.5
2006	19.9	30.4	25.5	23.0	31.4	20.1	27.0	22.0	25.7	24.7	26.9
2007	19.9	30.4	25.7	21.0	31.1	19.6	26.7	22.1	25.5	24.7	26.3
2008	19.6	28.9	24.6	21.6	30.8	19.4	27.0	22.8	25.7	24.4	28.1
					B. LEHD states present by 2000						
2002	16.1	25.3	22.1	17.3	25.5	14.5	22.9	15.9	20.4	21.9	22.7
2003	16.6	23.7	21.5	16.9	26.3	15.6	22.6	16.8	20.8	22.0	23.4
2004	17.0	24.3	21.8	17.4	27.1	16.3	23.4	18.0	21.6	21.5	21.0
2005	17.1	24.7	21.6	18.3	27.9	16.6	23.7	18.2	22.0	21.7	24.6
2006	17.2	24.7	20.9	18.8	28.0	16.8	24.1	18.3	22.1	21.5	23.7
2007	17.5	24.4	20.5	18.4	28.3	16.5	24.1	18.4	22.2	21.5	23.1
2008	17.5	23.3	20.2	18.3	27.9	16.4	24.0	18.8	22.2	21.2	25.3

Notes: See appendix table 5A.3A.

Table 5A.4   LEHD comparisons of immigrant and native employees in new firms

| Trait | Immigrants | | Natives | | Immigrant/ native ratio | Difference p-value |
(1)	Mean (2)	SD (3)	Mean (4)	SD (5)	(6)	(7)
A. Traits of initial employees in new firms, full sample						
Age	37.6	9.2	36.2	9.9	1.037	0.000
Male	61.8	48.6	57.7	49.4	1.071	0.000
Average quarterly earnings in year before founding	$7,335	$25,140	$9,028	$29,878	0.812	0.000
Average quarterly earnings in year of founding	$9,305	$155,301	$10,236	$31,949	0.909	0.000
Average quarterly earnings in year after founding	$10,199	$23,236	$11,339	$33,915	0.899	0.000
N	1,605,970		5,700,570			
B. Panel A for firms backed by venture capital						
Age	34.8	8.2	34.6	8.9	1.008	0.000
Male	0.71	0.46	0.64	0.48	1.100	0.000
Average quarterly earnings in year before founding	$21,160	$102,666	$19,516	$134,875	1.084	0.089
Average quarterly earnings in year of founding	$20,137	$20,603	$18,525	$21,456	1.087	0.000
Average quarterly earnings in year after founding	$24,957	$23,524	$23,503	$28,566	1.062	0.000
N	18,650		48,910			

Notes: Descriptive traits are developed from LEHD.

Table 5A.5   2000 census comparisons of immigrant and native employees in new firms

Trait (1)	Immigrants Mean (2)	Immigrants SD (3)	Natives Mean (4)	Natives SD (5)	Immigrant/ native ratio (6)	Difference p-value (7)
	Traits of employees in new firms, full sample					
Age	38.1	9.2	36.9	10.0	1.032	0.000
Male	60.0%	49.0%	56.5%	49.6%	1.064	0.000
Married	66.4%	47.3%	53.7%	49.9%	1.235	0.000
Number of children	1.40	1.39	0.98	1.17	1.429	0.000
Bachelor's education and higher	25.2%	43.4%	22.7%	41.9%	1.109	0.000
Home owner	56.6%	49.6%	65.3%	47.6%	0.868	0.000
Home value (max = $1 million)	$188,172	$169,972	$163,722	$152,863	1.149	0.000
Implied rental value	$165,472	$84,305	$154,054	$88,127	1.074	0.000
Move-in date	1994.2	5.7	1992.7	7.7	1.001	0.000
Household income (max = $2.5 million)	$65,737	$74,124	$69,286	$72,430	0.949	0.000
Year of arrival to United States	1984.0	9.7				

Notes: Descriptive traits are developed from 2000 Decennial Census match to LEHD. Implied rental value of dwelling is twenty times monthly rent.

Table 5A.6A Table 5.5A with immigrant share of all initial employees

	Fraction alive in third year (1)	Traits of surviving firms in the third year					
		Employment growth relative to firm's average (2)	Payroll growth relative to firm's average (3)	Establishment count growth relative to firm's average (4)	(0,1) third-year employment exceeds initial level (5)	(0,1) third-year employment exceeds 100 workers (6)	(0,1) third-year employment is in top decile of industry (7)
A. Summary statistics							
Mean	0.6418	0.2726	0.2449	0.0033	0.5133	0.0086	0.0848
SD	0.4866	0.6823	0.7216	0.0567	0.4998	0.0921	0.2787
Observations	535,580	329,260	329,260	329,260	329,260	329,260	329,260
B. Estimation with cohort fixed effects and controls for initial traits							
Firm's immigrant employee share	−0.01017	0.03382	−0.00062	−0.00047	0.01913	0.00479	0.00881
	(0.00182)	(0.00295)	(0.00350)	(0.00019)	(0.00238)	(0.00032)	(0.00097)
B/mean of DV	−0.016	0.124	−0.003	−0.142	0.037	0.557	0.104
C. Estimation with cohort-PMSA-industry fixed effects and controls for initial traits							
Firm's immigrant employee share	0.01753	0.00298	−0.02772	−0.00039	0.00629	0.00454	0.01103
	(0.00244)	(0.00479)	(0.00566)	(0.00033)	(0.00383)	(0.00054)	(0.00167)
B/mean of DV	0.027	0.011	−0.113	−0.118	0.012	0.528	0.130

Notes: See table 5.5A.

Table 5A.6B Table 5.5B with immigrant share of all initial employees

	Fraction alive in sixth year (1)	Traits of surviving firms in the sixth year					
		Employment growth relative to firm's average (2)	Payroll growth relative to firm's average (3)	Establishment count growth relative to firm's average (4)	(0,1) sixth-year employment exceeds initial level (5)	(0,1) sixth-year employment exceeds 100 workers (6)	(0,1) sixth-year employment is in top decile of industry (7)
A. Summary statistics							
Mean	0.4350	0.3097	0.3643	0.0034	0.5362	0.0102	0.0842
SD	0.4958	0.7403	0.7984	0.0591	0.4987	0.1003	0.2776
Observations	535,580	233,000	233,000	233,000	233,000	233,000	233,000
B. Estimation with cohort fixed effects and controls for initial traits							
Firm's immigrant employee share	−0.02096	0.05274	0.01198	−0.00012	0.02953	0.00552	0.00967
	(0.00183)	(0.00386)	(0.00461)	(0.00023)	(0.00286)	(0.00043)	(0.00122)
ß/US mean	−0.048	0.170	0.033	−0.035	0.055	0.541	0.115
C. Estimation with cohort-PMSA-industry fixed effects and controls for initial traits							
Firm's immigrant employee share	0.01591	0.01240	−0.02835	−0.00039	0.01319	0.00484	0.00779
	(0.00236)	(0.00663)	(0.00789)	(0.00038)	(0.00490)	(0.00078)	(0.00228)
ß/US mean	0.037	0.040	−0.078	−0.115	0.025	0.475	0.093

Notes: See table 5.5B.

References

Abowd, J.M., B. E. Stephens, L. Vilhuber, F. Andersson, K. L. McKinney, M. Roemer, and S. Woodcock. 2009. "The LEHD Infrastructure Files and the Creation of the Quarterly Workforce Indicators." In *Producer Dynamics: New Evidence from Micro Data*, edited by Timothy Dunne, J. Bradford Jensen, and Mark J. Roberts, 149–230. Chicago: University of Chicago Press.
Akcigit, U., and W. Kerr. 2010. "Growth through Heterogeneous Innovations." NBER Working Paper no. 16443, Cambridge, MA.
Akee, R. K. Q., D. A. Jaeger, and K. Tatsiramos. 2007. "The Persistence of Self-Employment across Borders: New Evidence on Legal Immigrants to the United States." IZA Discussion Papers no. 3250, Institute for the Study of Labor.
Anderson, S., and M. Platzer. 2006. "American Made: The Impact of Immigrant Entrepreneurs and Professionals on US Competitiveness." National Venture Capital Association Report. http://www.contentfirst.com/AmericanMade_study.pdf.
Andersson, F., S. Burgess, and J. Lane. 2012. "Do as the Neighbors Do: The Impact of Social Networks on Immigrant Employment." IZA Discussion Papers no. 4423, Institute for the Study of Labor.
Andersson, F., M. Garca-Pérez, J. Haltiwanger, K. McCue, and S. Sanders. 2014. "Workplace Concentration of Immigrants." *Demography* 51 (6): 2281–306.
Åslund, O., L. Hensvik, and O. Skans. 2014. "Seeking Similarity: How Immigrants and Natives Manage in the Labor Market." *Journal of Labor Economics* 32 (3): 405–41.
Audretsch, D., and M. Feldman. 1996. "R&D Spillovers and the Geography of Innovation and Production." *American Economic Review* 86:630–40.
Balasubramanian, N., and J. Sivadasan. 2011. "What Happens When Firms Patent? New Evidence from US Manufacturing Census Data." *Review of Economics and Statistics* 93 (1): 126–46.
Bengtsson, O., and D. Hsu. 2015. "Ethnic Matching in the US Venture Capital Market." *Journal of Business Venturing* 30 (2): 338–54.
Blau, F., and L. Kahn. 2016. "Immigration and Gender Roles: Assimilation vs. Culture." NBER Working Paper no. 21756, Cambridge, MA.
Borjas, G. 1986. "The Self-Employment Experience of Immigrants." *Journal of Human Resources* 21:487–506.
Borjas, G., and K. Doran. 2012. "The Collapse of the Soviet Union and the Productivity of American Mathematicians." *Quarterly Journal of Economics* 127 (3): 1143–203.
Carlino, G., and W. R. Kerr. 2015. "Agglomeration and Innovation." In *Handbook of Urban and Regional Economics*, vol. 5, edited by G. Duranton, V. Henderson, and W. Strange, 349–404. Amsterdam: North Holland.
Chemmanur, T., K. Krishnan, and D. Nandy. 2011. "How Does Venture Capital Financing Improve Efficiency in Private Firms? A Look beneath the Surface." *Review of Financial Studies* 24 (12): 4037–90.
Chung, W., and A. Kalnins. 2006. "Social Capital, Geography, and the Survival: Gujarati Immigrant Entrepreneurs in the US Lodging Industry." *Management Science* 52 (2): 233–47.
Clark, K., and S. Drinkwater. 2000. "Pushed Out or Pulled In? Self-Employment among Ethnic Minorities in England and Wales." *Labour Economics* 7 (5): 603–28.
———. 2006. "Changing Patterns of Ethnic Minority Self-Employment in Britain: Evidence from Census Microdata." IZA Discussion Papers no. 2495, Institute for the Study of Labor.
Cole, R. 2011. "How Do Firms Choose Legal Form of Organization?" SBA Release

no. 383, United States Small Business Administration. https://www.sba.gov/sites
/default/files/files/rs383tot.pdf.

Davis, S., J. Haltiwanger, and S. Schuh. 1996. *Job Creation and Destruction.* Cambridge, MA: MIT Press.

Decker, R., J. Haltiwanger, R. Jarmin, and J. Miranda. 2014. "The Role of Entrepreneurship in US Job Creation and Economic Dynamism." *Journal of Economic Perspectives* 28 (3): 3–24.

Doran, K., A. Gelber, and A. Isen. 2015. "The Effects of High-Skill Immigration on Firms: Evidence from H-1B Visa Lotteries." NBER Working Paper no. 20668, Cambridge, MA.

Duranton, G. 2007. "Urban Evolutions: The Fast, the Slow, and the Still." *American Economic Review* 97:197–221.

Fairlie, R. W. 2008. "Estimating the Contribution of Immigrant Business Owners to the US Economy." Small Business Research Summary no. 332, Small Business Administration, Washington, DC.

———. 2012. "Immigrant Entrepreneurs and Small Business Owners, and their Access to Financial Capital." US Small Business Administration Report. https:// www.sba.gov/sites/default/files/rs396tot.pdf.

———. 2013. "Minority and Immigrant Entrepreneurs: Access to Financial Capital." In *International Handbook on the Economics of Migration,* edited by A. F. Constant and K. F. Zimmermann. Cheltenham, UK: Edward Elgar.

Fairlie, R. W., and M. Lofstrom. 2014. "Immigration and Entrepreneurship." In *Handbook on the Economics of International Migration,* edited by B. R. Chiswick and P. W. Miller. Amsterdam: Elsevier.

Fairlie, R. W., and B. D. Meyer. 2003. "The Effect of Immigration on Native Self-Employment." *Journal of Labor Economics* 21 (3): 619–50.

Fairlie, R. W., A. Morelix, E. J. Reddy, and J. Russell. 2015. "The Kauffman Index 2015." Kauffman Foundation Report. http://www.kauffman.org/~/media/kauffman _org/research%20reports%20and%20covers/2015/05/kauffman_index_startup _activity_national_trends_2015.pdf.

Fairlie, R. W., J. Zissimopoulos, and H. A. Krashinsky. 2010. "The International Asian Business Success Story: A Comparison of Chinese, Indian, and Other Asian Businesses in the United States, Canada, and United Kingdom." In *International Differences in Entrepreneurship,* edited by J. Lerner and A. Schoar, 179–208. Chicago: University of Chicago Press.

Feldman, M., and D. Kogler. 2010. "Stylized Facts in the Geography of Innovation." In *Handbook of the Economics of Innovation,* vol. 1, edited by B. Hall and N. Rosenberg, 381–410. Oxford: Elsevier.

Garca-Pérez, M. 2012. "A Matching Model on the Use of Immigrant Social Networks and Referral Hiring." Economics Faculty Working Paper no. 21, Saint Cloud State University. http://repository.stcloudstate.edu/cgi/viewcontent.cgi ?article=1017&context=econ_wps.

Glaeser, E., S. P. Kerr, and W. R. Kerr. 2015. "Entrepreneurship and Urban Growth: An Empirical Assessment with Historical Mines." *Review of Economics and Statistics* 97 (2): 498–520.

Hall, B., A. Jaffe, and M. Trajtenberg. 2001. "The NBER Patent Citation Data File: Lessons, Insights and Methodological Tools." NBER Working Paper no. 8498, Cambridge, MA.

Haltiwanger, J., R. Jarmin, and J. Miranda. 2013. "Who Creates Jobs? Small vs. Large vs. Young." *Review of Economics and Statistics* 95 (2): 347–61.

Hart, D. M., and Z. J. Acs. 2011. "High-Tech Immigrant Entrepreneurship in the United States." *Economic Development Quarterly* 25 (2): 116–29.

Hecker, D. 1999. "High-Technology Employment: A Broader View." *Monthly Labor Review*, June. http://www.bls.gov/opub/mlr/1999/06/art3full.pdf .

Hegde, D., and J. Tumlinson. 2014. "Does Social Proximity Enhance Business Relationships? Theory and Evidence from Ethnicity's Role in US Venture Capital." *Management Science* 60 (9): 2355–80.

Hunt, J. 2011. "Which Immigrants are Most Innovative and Entrepreneurial? Distinctions by Entry Visa." *Journal of Labor Economics* 29 (3): 417–57.

———. 2015. "Are Immigrants the Most Skilled US Computer and Engineering Workers?" *Journal of Labor Economics* 33 (S1): S39–77.

Hunt, J., and M. Gauthier-Loiselle. 2010. "How Much Does Immigration Boost Innovation?" *American Economic Journal: Macroeconomics* 2 (2): 31–56.

Kerr, S. P., and W. R. Kerr. 2013. "Immigration and Employer Transitions for STEM Workers." *American Economic Review Papers and Proceedings* 103 (3): 193–97.

Kerr, S. P., W. R. Kerr, and W. F. Lincoln. 2015a. "Firms and the Economics of Skilled Immigration." In *Innovation Policy and the Economy*, vol. 15, edited by W. R. Kerr, J. Lerner, and S. Stern, 115–52. Chicago: University of Chicago Press.

———. 2015b. "Skilled Immigration and the Employment Structures of US Firms." *Journal of Labor Economics* 33 (S1): S109–45.

Kerr, S. P., W. R. Kerr, and R. Nanda. 2015. "House Money and Entrepreneurship." NBER Working Paper no. 21458, Cambridge, MA.

Kerr, W. R. 2010. "Breakthrough Inventions and Migrating Clusters of Innovation." *Journal of Urban Economics* 67 (1): 46–60.

———. 2013. "US High-Skilled Immigration, Innovation, and Entrepreneurship: Empirical Approaches and Evidence." NBER Working Paper no. 19377, Cambridge, MA.

Kerr, W. R., and S. Fu. 2008. "The Survey of Industrial R&D—Patent Database Link Project." *Journal of Technology Transfer* 33 (2): 173–86.

Kerr, W. R., and W. F. Lincoln. 2010. "The Supply Side of Innovation: H-1B Visa Reforms and US Ethnic Invention." *Journal of Labor Economics* 28 (3): 473–508.

Kerr, W. R., and M. Mandorff. 2015. "Social Networks, Ethnicity, and Entrepreneurship." NBER Working Paper no. 21597, Cambridge, MA.

Kerr, W. R., R. Nanda, and M. Rhodes-Kropf. 2014. "Entrepreneurship as Experimentation." *Journal of Economic Perspectives* 28 (3) 25–48.

Lewis, E. 2013a. "Immigrant Native Substitutability: The Role of Language." In *Immigration, Poverty, and Socioeconomic Inequality*, edited by D. Card and S. Raphael. New York: Russell Sage Foundation.

Lewis, E. 2013b. "Immigration and Production Technology." *Annual Review of Economics* 5:165–91.

Lewis, E., and G. Peri. 2015. "Immigration and the Economy of Cities and Regions." In *Handbook of Urban and Regional Economics*, vol. 5, edited by G. Duranton, V. Henderson, and W. Strange. Amsterdam: North Holland.

Lofstrom, M. 2002. "Labor Market Assimilation and the Self-Employment Decision of Immigrant Entrepreneurs." *Journal of Population Economics* 15 (1): 83–114.

Lofstrom, M., T. Bates, and S. Parker. 2014. "Why Are Some People More Likely to Become Small-Businesses Owners than Others: Entrepreneurship Entry and Industry-Specific Barriers." *Journal of Business Venturing* 29 (2): 232–51.

Mazzolari, F., and D. Neumark. 2012. "Immigration and Product Diversity." *Journal of Population Economics* 25 (3): 1107–37.

McKinney, K., and L. Vilhuber. 2008. "Longitudinal Employer-Household Dynamics. LEHD Infrastructure Files in the Census RDC-Overview: Revision 219." US Census Bureau.

————. 2011. "LEHD Infrastructure Files in the Census RDC: Overview of S2004 Snapshot." CES Working Paper no. 11-13, Center for Economic Studies, US Census Bureau.

Monti, D. J., L. Smith-Doerr, and J. MacQuaid. 2007. "Immigrant Entrepreneurs in the Massachusetts Biotechnology Industry." Immigrant Learning Center, Boston, MA. http://www.ilctr.org/wp-content/uploads/2011/08/immigrants_in _biotechnology-updated.pdf.

Moser, P., A. Voena, and F. Waldinger. 2014. "German Jewish Emigres and US Invention." *American Economic Review* 104 (10): 3222–55.

Nathan, M. 2015. "Same Difference? Minority Ethnic Inventors, Diversity and Innovation in the UK." *Journal of Economic Geography* 15 (1): 129–68.

Ottaviano, G., and G. Peri. 2006. "The Economic Value of Cultural Diversity: Evidence from US Cities." *Journal of Economic Geography* 6 (1): 9–44.

Patel, K., and F. Vella. 2013. "Immigrant Networks and their Implications for Occupational Choice and Wages." *Review of Economics and Statistics* 95 (4): 1249–77.

Peri, G. 2007. "Higher Education, Innovation and Growth." In *Education and Training in Europe*, edited by G. Brunello, P. Garibaldi, and E. Wasmer, 56–70. Oxford: Oxford University Press.

Peri, G., K. Shih, and C. Sparber. 2015. "STEM Workers, H-1B Visas and Productivity in US Cities." *Journal of Labor Economics* 33 (S1): S225–55.

Puri, M., and R. Zarutskie. 2012. "On the Lifecycle Dynamics of Venture-Capital- and Non-Venture-Capital-Financed Firms." *Journal of Finance* 67 (6): 2247–93.

Reynolds, P. D., and R. T. Curtin. 2007. "Business Creation in the United States in 2006: Panel Study of Entrepreneurial Dynamics II Initial Report." Boston: nowPublications.

Robb, A., E. J. Reedy, J. Ballou, D. DesRoches, F. Potter, and Z. Zhao. 2010. "An Overview of the Kauffman Firm Survey: Results from the 2004 to 2008 Data." Kaufmann Foundation Report, May. http://www.kauffman.org/~/media /kauffman_org/research%20reports%20and%20covers/2010/05/kfs_2010_report .pdf.

Samila, S., and O. Sorenson. 2011. "Venture Capital, Entrepreneurship and Economic Growth." *Review of Economics and Statistics* 93:338–49.

Saxenian, A. 1999. *Silicon Valley's New Immigrant Entrepreneurs*. San Francisco: Public Policy Institute of California.

————. 2002. "Silicon Valley's New Immigrant High-Growth Entrepreneurs." *Economic Development Quarterly* 16:20–31.

Schuetze, H. J., and H. Antecol. 2007. "Immigration, Entrepreneurship and the Venture Start-Up Process. The Life Cycle of Entrepreneurial Ventures." In *International Handbook Series on Entrepreneurship*, vol. 3, edited by S. Parker. New York: Springer.

Stephan, P., and S. Levin. 2001. "Exceptional Contributions to US Science by the Foreign-Born and Foreign-Educated." *Population Research and Policy Review* 20 (1): 59–79.

Unger, J. M., A. Rauch, M. Frese, and N. Rosenbusch. 2011. "Human Capital and Entrepreneurial Success: A Meta-Analytical Review." *Journal of Business Venturing* 26 (3): 341–58.

Van der Sluis, J., M. van Praag, and W. Vijverberg. 2008. "Education and Entrepreneurship Selection and Performance: A Review of the Empirical Literature." *Journal of Economic Surveys* 22 (5): 795–841.

Wadhwa, V., A. Saxenian, B. Rissing, and G. Gereffi. 2007. "America's New Immigrant Entrepreneurs." Duke Science, Technology, and Innovation Paper no. 23, Duke University.

II

Challenges Facing Entrepreneurs: Finance and Business Conditions

How Did Young Firms Fare during the Great Recession? Evidence from the Kauffman Firm Survey

Rebecca Zarutskie and Tiantian Yang

6.1 Introduction

While aggregate statistics on the dynamics of the US economy and its firms around the Great Recession of 2007–2009 are widely published by federal agencies such as the Bureau of Economic Analysis and Bureau of Labor Statistics, we have fewer statistics on the economic activity subsets of firms comprising aggregate economic activity over this time period, and even less empirical microeconomic evidence on the dynamics of subsets of firms, particularly young firms.

Such statistics and data are important to consider if certain firms, such as new firms, may have been disproportionately affected or respond differently to macroeconomic and policy shocks. Indeed, recent studies document that a disproportionate share of job creation can be attributed to young firms (Haltiwanger, Jarmin, and Miranda 2013), and that small and young firms may be more sensitive to the business cycle and monetary policy (e.g., Fort et al. 2013; Gertler and Gilchrist 1994; Hancock and Wilcox 1998). These

Rebecca Zarutskie is chief of the Banking and Financial Analysis Section at the Board of Governors of the Federal Reserve System. Tiantian Yang is assistant professor of sociology at Duke University.

We thank Howard Aldrich, Shai Bernstein, John Haltiwanger, and Antoinette Schoar, participants in the NBER/CRIW conference on Measuring Entrepreneurial Businesses, and the volume editors and reviewers for comments and suggestions. We acknowledge the Kauffman Foundation and NORC data enclave for providing secure and remote access to the data used in this research. We thank Daniel Lee with the NORC data enclave for assistance in clearing the statistical output. The analysis and conclusions in this chapter are those of the authors and do not indicate concurrence by other staff or members of the Board of Governors of the Federal Reserve System. For acknowledgments, sources of research support, and disclosure of the authors' material financial relationships, if any, please see http://www.nber.org/chapters/c13501.ack.

studies highlight the importance of measuring a broad set of outcomes for young firms to gain a better understanding of entrepreneurial activity and young firms and their contribution to aggregate economic activity over the business cycle.

In this chapter we use the Kauffman Firm Survey (KFS), a large panel of young firms founded in 2004 and surveyed for eight consecutive years, to examine the dynamics of several key firm-level economic and financial variables in the years surrounding and during the Great Recession. We find that during the Great Recession, particularly 2008 and 2009, firms in the KFS were smaller than otherwise predicted in terms of employment, assets, and revenues. In particular, we find that firm-level employment was about 10 percent lower than otherwise predicted during these years. This translates to each firm having on average 0.5 fewer employees—a meaningful estimate if aggregated across all young firms in the US economy at the time. We also find that firm-level assets were around 20 percent lower and revenues around 30 percent lower at the depths of the recession, all else equal. Including firm fixed effects in our regression analysis does not reduce these estimates by much, suggesting that the reduction in firm size and growth experienced by young firms happened within individual firms during the recession and were not primarily driven by firm attrition.

We also examine whether the wages paid per employee at the firms varied during the recession. We find that wage per employee decreased in the cross section of firms during the recession. However, when we include firm fixed effects, we find that within firms that survived over the recession, wages increased, while employment decreased. This suggests that surviving firms may have kept their most skilled employees during the recession, as well as that firms that paid higher wages on average may have been more likely to shut down during the recession.

We next examine whether financing conditions tightened and may have contributed to the decline in economic activity and growth experienced by these young firms during the recession. To do so, we use special questions added to the KFS that directly ask about whether a firm applied for external credit and whether firms did not apply for a new loan because they anticipated being turned down. We find that a greater percentage of firms did not apply for a loan because they anticipated being denied in 2008, 2009, and 2010 relative to 2007 and 2011. Indeed, firms were 20 percent more likely to report that they did not apply for a loan in these years because they would be denied, indicating that financing conditions were perceived as being much tighter during the recession and in the period immediately following it.

Finally, we examine whether the firms that reported that they were financially constrained experienced different economic outcomes. We find that firms that reported they would be denied for a loan experienced lower asset growth and revenue growth in the year following their report. Moreover, these same firms reported that their owners worked more hours and that they employed a greater share of full-time employees, suggesting that these firms may have used labor as a substitute for purchasing assets using external financing.

Overall, our empirical analysis indicates that young firms were adversely affected by the Great Recession, both from diminished demand and economic activity and from tighter financing conditions. Our analysis also provides some direct estimates of the impact of the recession on firm employment, revenues, assets, and wages and the role of financing constraints in these estimates for very young firms. Existing research on the firm-level impact of the Great Recession, such as Chodorow-Reich (2014) and Duygan-Bump, Levkov, and Montoriol-Garriga (2015), suggests that such large estimates would not be observed if older firms were included in the KFS. Our estimates are an important component to understanding how business cycle shocks may translate to real effects in a particular segment of the economy— young entrepreneurial firms, their owners, and their employees—and how these shocks may spill over into broader measures of economic activity over the business cycle.

We conclude with a discussion of the drawbacks of the design of the KFS in addressing our main questions, in particular the difficulty of the survey design in allowing one to distinguish between firm age effects and time effects and in the limited ability to exploit geographical variation in local economic conditions due to small sample sizes of firms surveyed within each particular geography in the United States. We also consider some features of future data collection and measurement efforts that would be useful in studying entrepreneurial activity and young firms over the business cycle and the impact of economic and financial shocks on young firms and their founders.

6.2   The Kauffman Firm Survey

The KFS is a longitudinal survey of US businesses that began their operations in 2004. Intended to examine new business characteristics, the financing and operating strategy used by new businesses, and how these businesses subsequently evolved, the KFS questionnaire focuses on the four major aspects of businesses: business characteristics, financing and economic outcomes, owner and worker demographics, and business strategy and organization.[1]

To obtain a representative sample of new businesses, KFS used the businesses listed in the Dun and Bradstreet (D&B) database in 2004 as the sampling frame. In particular, firms are considered as candidates for inclusion in the sample if they meet at least one of the following five criteria: (a) payment of state unemployment taxes, (b) payment of Federal Insurance Contribu-

---

1. See http://www1.kauffman.org/kfs/KFSWiki/Data-Dictionary.aspx for detailed data dictionary as well as downloadable questionnaires. See also Farhat and Robb (2014) for more detail on the KFS questionnaire and survey design.

tions Act (FICA) taxes, (c) presence of a legal status for the business, (d) use of an Employer Identification Number (EIN), or (e) use of Schedule C to report business income on a personal tax return. The KFS includes both employer firms and nonemployer firms in its base sample. The D&B database was partitioned into six sampling strata defined by a classification of the firm's high-technology status and the gender of the firm's owner or CEO (based on the D&B data element). There were 32,469 businesses sampled to achieve 4,928 completed questionnaires.

The data collection process began with a mailed advance letter to prospective businesses inviting them to participate using the KFS self-administered Web questionnaire. Following the invitation, business owners who did not complete the questionnaire on the Web received telephone calls from trained interviewers to determine their eligibility and to complete an interview with those that were eligible. Overall, 77 percent of the baseline survey questionnaires were completed in telephone interviews, and 23 percent were completed using the self-administered Web questionnaire. (For a more detailed discussion of the design and sampling methodology underlying the KFS, see DesRoches et al. [2007], Robb et al. [2010], and Farhat and Robb [2014].)

Since the initial interview in 2004, KFS conducted follow-up interviews with businesses selected in the sample annually, and completed seven annual interviews in 2011. Because the 2008 economic recession happened four years later after the initial or baseline interview, KFS permits an empirical analysis of business growth and job creation over this time period. In 2008, KFS added some questions about the challenges that the economic recession imposed on new businesses, including the extent to which business owners think their businesses were affected by the financial crisis and recession. We use some of these questions in our analysis below to examine the impact of the recession on the KFS firms' financing and economic outcomes.

The KFS is the only panel data set of young firms spanning the Great Recession that includes both information on firm-level financial and economic outcomes. However, as Reynolds and Curtin (2009) note in a recent review, only seven out of twenty-six data sets that they identified as relevant for research on entrepreneurship provided longitudinal information on new venture creation, but none of the seven data sets applied selection criteria that would lead to a representative sample of new businesses. Some data sets were designed to examine innovative firms, and thus intentionally excluded less innovative ones, and vice versa. An example of the latter is the Longitudinal Research Database (LRD) maintained by the US Census Bureau. This data set oversamples manufacturing companies with sizable numbers of employees, but does contain information on capital and revenues (McGuckin and Pascoe 1988). There are other databases, such as the US Census Bureau's Longitudinal Business Database (LBD) and the Bureau of Labor Statistics' Longitudinal Database (LDB), that contain a representative sample of new employer firms every year, in the case of the LBD, and every quarter, in the case of the LBD, but these databases do not track nonemployer firms, nor do they contain information on assets, revenues, or financing (Jarmin and Miranda 2002; Searson, Robertson, and Clayton 2000). Likewise, data from the Business Employment Dynamics (BED), maintained by the Bureau of Labor Statistics, are derived from quarterly reports submitted by private-sector employers (BED 2011). Recent efforts at the US Census Bureau have been undertaken to combine information on nonemployer businesses and employer business in the form of the Integrated Longitudinal Database (ILBD), but even so, this database does not contain detailed information on important firm characteristics such as revenues, assets, and financing (Davis et al. 2007).

6.3 Estimating the Impact of the Great Recession on Young Firms Using the KFS

To examine the question of how young firms fared in the years leading up to, during, and following the Great Recession, we employ two empirical strategies using the KFS. First, we examine the changes in the weighted sample averages in our outcome variables of interest. In particular, we examine weighted means of firm-level revenues, profits, employment, assets, and wages, as well as amounts and types of financing used. We also present weighted means for key firm-level conditioning variables, such as whether the firm has intellectual property and whether the firm is in a high-tech industry, as well as several owner demographic characteristics. These population averages allow a first look at how young firm performance may have changed in the recession years and how this may have also affected the firms' owners and employees.

Second, we employ regression and other statistical model estimation to examine the evolution of firm-level outcome variables over time conditional on firm-specific characteristics, and in some cases, geographical characteristics. Doing so allows us to refine our estimates of the impact of the economic and financial shocks experienced by the United States on the firms represented in the KFS by controlling for other factors that may have also influenced the evolution of these firm-level variables.

6.3.1 Weighted Sample Average Dynamics

Tables 6.1A, 6.1B, and 6.1C present weighted averages and standard errors in italics below each average value for the entire panel time frame of 2004 to 2011. Table 6.1A presents weighted averages for our firm-level economic outcome variables of interest—employment outcomes (including wages, full-time employment, and owner hours), assets, revenues, profits, and likelihood of shutting down. We see that the firms in the KFS grow rapidly in terms of employment size between 2004 and 2005, when average employment increases from 1.87 to 3.20. Employment size further increases

Table 6.1A   Firm-level economic variables

	2004–2011	2004	2005	2006	2007	2008	2009	2010	2011
Total employees	3.36	1.87	3.20	3.53	3.69	3.73	3.70	3.92	4.57
	0.16	*0.09*	*0.14*	*0.16*	*0.23*	*0.25*	*0.28*	*0.32*	*0.46*
Percent full-time employees	65.6	67.1	66.3	68.2	64.7	63.7	64.3	62.6	64.9
	0.7	*1.0*	*1.0*	*1.0*	*1.1*	*1.2*	*1.3*	*1.4*	*1.4*
Wage per employee	36,740	15,281	31,241	40,844	30,784	32,735	35,906	49,086	75,159
	2,837	*749*	*6,823*	*8,138*	*1,766*	*1,701*	*2,496*	*11,133*	*19,467*
Hours worked per week	41.0	42.6	43.0	42.4	40.8	39.8	39.0	38.1	38.4
by primary owner	*0.37*	*0.40*	*0.41*	*0.47*	*0.50*	*0.53*	*0.56*	*0.56*	*0.59*
Total assets (dollars)	1,037,596	346,338	721,356	791,815	1,163,242	774,371	1,360,510	1,048,598	3,169,027
	212,057	*132,284*	*330,397*	*250,713*	*408,710*	*254,457*	*598,936*	*403,375*	*1,267,405*
Revenues (dollars)	726,622	157,915	411,720	624,541	717,468	643,055	1,078,788	1,142,535	1,901,893
	81,481	*21,350*	*75,814*	*138,828*	*130,032*	*112,547*	*315,555*	*279,879*	*578,752*
Profits (dollars)	64,627	–3,906	19,005	27,264	47,140	14,505	21,459	31,954	535,490
	41,407	*2,800*	*7,879*	*17,042*	*21,182*	*18,333*	*22,927*	*15,343*	*480,441*
Percent shut down	9.5	0.0	7.5	11.5	13.8	14.6	12.3	12.3	11.4

Note: Statistics are based on the Kauffman Firm Survey using the stratified sample weights. Sample means are reported; standard errors are reported in italics. Please see section 6.4 of the text for variable descriptions.

over the 2005 to 2007 period, reaching 3.69 employees, on average. Over the period 2007 to 2009, the recessionary years, average employment remains flat, even slightly dipping in 2009. Average employment begins to rise again in 2010, reaching 4.57 employees in 2011. These averages suggest that the recession weighed on the employment growth of young firms.

The yearly averages for wage per employee follow a similar pattern as total employment over the survey time frame. Average wage per employee rises from $15,281 to $40,844 between 2004 and 2006 (in nominal dollars). In 2007, nominal wage per employee drops to an average of $30,784, and rises by a small amount in both 2008 and 2009. Wage per employee exhibits more robust growth in 2011, averaging $75,159. In contrast, neither the percentage of employees who are full time nor the number of hours worked by the primary owner-operator per week exhibit a pronounced decline during the recessionary years. Rather, both variables exhibit a steady decline over the sample period, making it difficult to distinguish to what extent the declines are due to the recession or other factors related to firm age. Thus, the population averages suggest that employment and wage per employee may have suffered declines due to the economic and financial shocks arising from the Great Recession.

Turning to total assets, the other main firm input, we also see that, like employment, firms' assets grow quite rapidly in the first year, rising from $346,388 to $721,356 between 2004 and 2005.[2] Assets continue to rise into 2007, reaching over $1 million on average, but decline to around $774 million in 2008 and hover around $1 million dollar level into 2009 and 2010, until rising sharply to over $3 million on average in 2011. Firm revenues and profits display a similar dynamic pattern, growing into 2007, then decreasing in 2008, the height of the recession, and only regaining their growth in 2011.

Finally, turning to the percentage of firms that shut down in a given year, we see that the highest percentage of firms, 14.6 percent go out of business in 2008, and that the percentage hovers around 12 percent for the remainder the following two years, and declines to 11.4 percent in 2011. Overall, the averages presented in table 6.1A suggest that the economic and financial shocks associated with the Great Recession affected the employment, assets base, revenues, profits, and probability of survival of young firms.

Table 6.1B shows weighted means and standard errors for firm-level financing variables. The first two rows show the percentage of firms that have bank debt taken out by the business and that have bank debt taken out by the owners. The two variables display different dynamics. The percentage of firms having a bank loan on behalf of the business increases over time, peaking in 2008, and then declines in 2009 and 2010. The percentage of firms having a bank loan taken out by their owners is at its highest in 2004

---

2. Total assets include physical assets reported by firms such as property, plant, and equipment, as well as cash and other investment assets.

Table 6.1B   Firm-level financing variables

	2004–2011	2004	2005	2006	2007	2008	2009	2010	2011
Has business bank debt (%)	16.4	12.7	15.3	17.4	18.8	18.9	17.8	16.5	16.4
Has personal bank debt (%)	12.5	18.6	14.4	13.8	11.2	11.0	9.7	7.3	6.0
Business debt/total assets	0.219	0.261	0.169	0.211	0.227	0.283	0.214	0.165	0.210
	0.011	*0.022*	*0.015*	*0.021*	*0.027*	*0.031*	*0.025*	*0.021*	*0.037*
Personal debt/total assets	0.442	0.673	0.394	0.398	0.394	0.419	0.422	0.388	0.351
	0.017	*0.035*	*0.024*	*0.028*	*0.034*	*0.035*	*0.037*	*0.040*	*0.048*
Owner-operator equity	0.601	1.680	0.503	0.406	0.376	0.393	0.294	0.310	0.492
Invested/total assets	*0.037*	*0.138*	*0.040*	*0.069*	*0.087*	*0.098*	*0.043*	*0.066*	*0.147*
Non-owner-operator equity	0.214	0.505	0.142	0.156	0.061	0.280	0.259	0.142	0.128
Invested/total assets	*0.057*	*0.131*	*0.026*	*0.074*	*0.015*	*0.230*	*0.219*	*0.098*	*0.059*

Note: Statistics are based on the Kauffman Firm Survey using the stratified sample weights. Sample means are reported; standard errors are reported in italics. Please see section 6.4 of the text for variable descriptions.

and falls steadily over the sample period. These different patterns likely reflect the fact that firms become more able to obtain bank loans backed by the business itself as revenues and assets grow and the firms establish track records. This cycle of financing has been documented in prior studies and in several time periods. See, for example, Berger and Udell (1998) and Robb and Robinson (2014).

The dynamics of the percentage of firms having a business bank loan suggest that financing conditions may have become tighter in 2009 for many firms. This notion is confirmed in the dynamics of the ratio of business debt to total assets, which rises steadily from 2005 to 2008, and then drops sharply in 2009 and 2010. In contrast, the ratio of personal debt to total firm assets hovers around 0.40 after an initial high of around 0.50 in 2004.[3] These averages suggest that the supply of debt backed by business assets was more sensitive to the recessionary shock that was the supply of debt backed by the personal assets of the firms' owners.

Both the ratio of equity invested by owner-operators to total assets and the ratio of equity invested by non-owner-operators to total assets are at their peak when firms first begin, consistent with most theories of firm capital structure. However, we see a slight uptick in the ratio of owner-operator equity invested to total assets in 2010 and 2011, and an uptick in ratio of non-owner-operator equity invested to total assets in 2008 and 2009, suggesting that perhaps these sources of funds were used to partially offset the tighter credit market conditions faced by many firms during and following the recession.

Table 6.1C presents weighted averages for firm characteristics, which will serve as controls in the regression analysis. The number of owners remains fairly constant over the sample period at around 1.8. The percentage of the firm's equity owned by the primary owner rises slightly over the sample period from 80.4 percent to 83.4 percent. Firms' primary owners are around 44.5 years old when they start their firms and they age with their firms until 2010, when more firms with older primary owners exit the panel, lowering the average primary owner age to 45.4. Around 70 percent of firms' primary owners are male, and between 82 and 83 percent are white. Around 6 percent of firms are in high-tech industries over the sample period, and around 19 percent have intellectual property.[4]

---

3. Business debt includes bank loans, credit card balances, and other forms of debt taken out at the level of the firm. Personal debt includes bank loans, credit card balances, and other forms of debt taken out personally by the firm's owners (and often backed by the owners' personal assets).

4. The KFS defines high-tech industries as those with two-digit SIC codes: 28 chemicals and allied products, 35 industrial machinery and equipment, 36 electrical and electronic equipment, and 38 instruments and related products. The KFS defines medium-tech industries with those as three-digit SIC codes: 131 crude petroleum and natural gas operations; 211 cigarettes; 229 miscellaneous textile goods; 261 pulp mills; 267 miscellaneous converted paper products; 291 petroleum refining; 299 miscellaneous petroleum and coal products; 335 nonferrous rolling

Table 6.1C   **Firm owner characteristics**

	2004–2011	2004	2005	2006	2007	2008	2009	2010	2011
Number of owners	1.81	1.69	1.83	1.84	1.79	1.89	1.90	1.76	1.88
	0.07	*0.05*	*0.08*	*0.08*	*0.08*	*0.12*	*0.13*	*0.12*	*0.13*
Percent equity owned by	81.4	80.4	80.3	81.2	81.2	81.9	82.2	82.8	83.4
primary owner	*0.46*	*0.46*	*0.51*	*0.55*	*0.59*	*0.62*	*0.65*	*0.69*	*0.69*
Primary owner age	46.8	44.5	45.7	46.8	48.0	49.1	50.1	45.4	46.3
	0.20	*0.18*	*0.20*	*0.22*	*0.23*	*0.25*	*0.25*	*0.27*	*0.28*
Primary owner is male (%)	69.5	68.5	69.0	70.3	70.2	69.4	69.5	69.9	69.6
Primary owner is white (%)	82.0	81.0	81.4	81.9	82.2	82.8	82.8	82.7	82.7
High-tech industry (%)	5.8	5.6	4.9	5.6	5.7	5.9	6.3	6.9	6.5
Firm has intellectual property (%)	19.4	19.1	19.7	20.6	19.9	19.9	18.4	19.0	18.1

Note: Statistics are based on the Kauffman Firm Survey using the stratified sample weights. Sample means are reported; standard errors are reported in italics. Please see section 6.4 of the text for variable descriptions.

6.3.2 Regression Analysis

We next turn to our regression analysis to examine any differences in the dynamics of firms' economic outcome and financing choices during the recession years, conditional on firm characteristics and past outcomes.

We model firm economic outcomes in log levels as a linear function of lagged log employment and log assets (the two main inputs to production) plus a random error term that reflects variation in the demand for the firm's product or service as well as productivity shocks, as in equation (1) below:

$$\ln(\text{FirmOutcome}(i,t)) = \varphi + \alpha \ln(\text{Employment}(i, t-1))$$
$$(1) \qquad\qquad + \beta \ln(\text{Assets}(i, t-1)) + \gamma \ln(\text{Revenues}(i, t-1))$$
$$+ \delta X(i, t-1) + \theta(t) + \mu(i) + \varepsilon(i,t).$$

When the firm outcome measure is employment, equation (1) states that the firm's choice of employment input in the current year will be a function of last year's employment and last year's assets, as well as last year's revenues, which reflect the lagged error term in the production function stemming from changes in the demand for the firm's goods or services or the firm's productivity, for example. Likewise, when the firm outcome measure is assets, equation (1) states that the firm's current choice of assets in the current year will be a function of last year's employment and assets choices as well as last year's revenues. Equations (1) and (2) also contain a matrix, X, of firm-level controls, which include owner characteristics, past financing choices, and firm sector and industry characteristics. Year and firm fixed effects are also specified, though in some specifications we exclude firm fixed effects in order to estimate the cross-sectional variation in employment and assets over time, conditional on firm characteristics. In all cases, we estimate the regressions using the population weights according to the stratified sample design of the KFS. We begin our estimation sample in 2006, rather than 2005, the first year in the KFS, since many firms report missing or zero values for many of the control and dependent variables in the first year of the KFS. Including this first year does not change the flavor of our results, but does make the comparative coefficients on the year fixed effects harder to interpret when the base year is 2005 instead of 2006.

In addition to estimating the impact of the recession years on firms' employment levels, the KFS also allows us to estimate how many employees

---

and drawing; 348 ordnance and accessories, not elsewhere classified; 371 motor vehicles and equipment; 372 aircraft and parts; 376 guided missiles, space vehicles, parts; 379 miscellaneous transportation equipment; 737 computer and data processing services; 871 engineering and architectural services; 873 research and testing services; 874 management and public relations; and 899 services, not elsewhere classified. Firms are coded as having intellectual property if they report owning copyrights, trademarks, or patents.

are full-time employees, the number of hours worked by owner-operators in the firm, and the wages paid per employee. Firms may have responded to reduced demand for the products and services during the recession by reducing the hours worked by employees in the firm or by lowering the wages they paid their employees. We, therefore, also estimate the following three regression specifications in which the firm outcome measure is a fraction of employees working full time, hours worked by the primary owner, and wage per employee

We also examine the impact of the recession on the probability a firm shuts down. To do so we estimate a Probit model as in equation (2) below:

$$\text{Pr(Firm Exit}(i,t)) =$$

$$(2) \quad \text{NormalCDF}(\alpha \ln(\text{Revenues}(i,t-1)) + \beta \ln(\text{Employment}(i,t-1))$$

$$+ \gamma \ln(\text{Assets}(i,t-1)) + \delta X(i,t-1) + \theta(t) + \varepsilon(i,t)).$$

After estimating the residual effect of the recession years and the evolution of firm outcome variables in the years preceding and following the recession, we examine whether firms' use of financing changed during the recession. We are interested in changes in the use of the types and amounts of financing to better understand whether shocks to the financial markets, in addition to economic shocks, may have also affected how the young firms fared during and after the recession. We estimate regressions that examine whether firms use external debt backed by the assets of the business or by the personal assets of the owners, as well as the amounts of external debt and equity financing outstanding, as a function of firm characteristics and year fixed effects. In particular, we estimate regressions of the following form:

$$\text{Financing}(i,t) = \varphi + \alpha \ln(\text{Revenues}(i,t-1))$$

$$+ \beta \ln(\text{Employment}(i,t-1))$$

$$(3)$$

$$+ \gamma \ln(\text{Assets}(i,t-1)) + \delta Y(i,t-1)$$

$$+ \theta(t) + \mu(i) + \varepsilon(i,t).$$

Equation (3) estimates the types and amounts of financing used as a function of past employment, assets, and revenues and the firm characteristics considered in the previous regression. In addition, the matrix, Y, of firm-level controls contains county-level variables on the structuring of banking markets, as well as other factors that might influence the supply of financing available to firms and underlying economic conditions. These variables matter more in estimates of equation (3) that exclude firm fixed effects. Equation (3) shows the overall changes in financing choices by firms in the years during and surrounding the recession. The independent variables included are meant to help us better understand whether changes in financing reflect changes in underlying demand for financing by the firms versus reduced supply of financing or financing constraints.

Finally, we consider whether we can isolate plausibly exogenous variation in the supply of external financing to firms to estimate the relation between being turned down for financing and our main firm outcomes of employment, assets, and revenues. To do so, we estimate regression equations similar to equations (1) and (2), but use special questions asked during and after the recession on availability of external debt financing as additional control variables and also include the geographic controls measuring the financing supply factors and local economic conditions included the matrix Y in equation (3).

Firm-Level Economic Outcomes

Table 6.2 presents estimates of equation (1) without firm fixed effects; hence, the identifying variation is largely cross-sectional. For each of the four firm employment outcome variables, we estimate three specifications: The first specification only includes year fixed effects. The second specification adds lagged log employment, asset, and revenues. The third specification adds additional controls for owner characteristics and firms' use of debt and equity financing. We begin our estimation sample in 2006, so the base year in the regression is 2006, and the coefficients on the year dummies use year 2006 as the benchmark. Our focus in the discussion of the estimates will be on the coefficients on the year dummies, since these coefficients tell us the impact of the particular year conditional on what we would have expected given the firm's characteristics and past performance.

First, focusing on log employment, column (1) shows us that log employment grew in all years relative to year 2006, but that growth as slowest in 2007. Adding lagged log employment, assets, and revenues in column (2), we see that growth in employment was slower in all years relative to year 2006, but was slowest in 2008 and 2009, both recession years. The coefficients on the year 2008 and 2009 indicators are –0.110 and are significantly different than the coefficients on the other year indicator variables. Translating to nonlogged values, employment at the firm level was on average almost half an employee lower in these recessionary years. Adding further controls for owner characteristics and firm financing in column (3) does not change the nature of the results. Firm-level employment growth in all years looks similar to 2006 once we control for firm characteristics, except in 2008 and 2009, when employment is about 10 percent lower.

Columns (4), (5), and (6) examine log wage per employee. We see that wage per employee is on average lower in 2009 and 2010 relative to 2006 and other years controlling for firm industry and past assets, employment, and revenues. However, adding additional controls for owner characteristics in column (5) eliminates the statistical significance of the negative coefficients on the year 2009 and 2010 dummies. As suggested, when we examined the dynamics of estimated population averages of the fraction of

Table 6.2   **Regression analysis of firm employment outcomes**

	Ln(employment)			Ln(wages/employment)		
	(1)	(2)	(3)	(4)	(5)	(6)
Ln(employment($t-1$))		0.824**	0.816**		−0.314**	−0.328**
		58.79	47.99		−10.40	−9.50
Ln(assets($t-1$))		0.023**	0.021**		0.058**	0.027
		3.22	2.60		2.71	1.00
Ln(revenues($t-1$))		0.038**	0.035**		0.494**	0.506**
		5.15	4.28		17.62	15.10
High-tech industry		0.020	−0.008		0.531**	0.469
		0.84	−0.27		8.49	6.62
Has intellectual property		0.033	0.020		0.029	−0.048
		1.56	0.85		0.50	−0.66
Constant	1.10**	−0.437**	0.025	9.72**	3.44**	4.14**
	42.71	−5.84	0.14	232.08	12.76	6.92
Year 2007	0.100**	−0.063*	−0.040	0.015	−0.074	−0.032
	3.84	−2.02	−1.22	0.30	−1.28	−0.49
Year 2008	0.072*	−0.110**	−0.105**	0.089	−0.065	0.002
	2.45	−4.02	−3.44	1.65	−1.08	0.04
Year 2009	0.117**	−0.110**	−0.134**	−0.037	−0.184**	−0.086
	3.61	−3.42	−3.86	−0.57	−2.74	−1.12
Year 2010	0.166**	−0.043	−0.049	−0.043	−0.201**	−0.147
	4.68	−1.52	−1.54	−0.65	−2.62	−1.50
Year 2011	0.197**	−0.062*	−0.054	0.099	−0.083	0.017
	5.14	−2.15	−1.52	1.38	−1.20	0.20
R^2	0.004	0.759	0.758	0.001	0.330	0.346
F-statistic	—	—	—	—	—	—
Other controls?	No	No	Yes	No	No	Yes
Number of observations	8,457	4,811	3,701	7,203	4,452	3,420
Number of firms	2,752	1,739	1,522	2,328	1,591	1,392
Dependent variable mean	1.20	1.35	1.32	9.74	9.90	9.90
Estimation method	OLS	OLS	OLS	OLS	OLS	OLS

	Full-time employment/ employment			Ln(primary owner weekly hours worked)		
	(7)	(8)	(9)	(10)	(11)	(12)
Ln(employment($t-1$))		−0.072**	−0.073**		−0.021	−0.012
		−3.23	−2.89		−1.03	−0.58
Ln(assets($t-1$))		0.020	0.025		0.010	0.025
		1.56	1.49		0.69	1.59
Ln(revenues($t-1$))		0.099**	0.098**		0.128**	0.133**
		7.00	5.80		9.32	8.28
High-tech industry		0.095*	0.070		−0.022	−0.012
		2.03	1.45		−0.48	−0.25
Has intellectual property		−0.074*	−0.111*		−0.004	−0.003
		−1.95	−2.51		−0.09	−0.07

(*continued*)

Table 6.2   (continued)

	Full-time employment/ employment			Ln(primary owner weekly hours worked)		
	(7)	(8)	(9)	(10)	(11)	(12)
Constant	0.894**	−0.446**	0.151	3.49**	2.12**	2.33**
	36.78	−3.11	0.39	192.20	14.63	7.88
Year 2007	−0.083**	−0.122**	−0.115**	−0.059**	−0.074**	−0.066*
	−2.90	−3.52	−3.06	−3.47	−2.85	−2.29
Year 2008	−0.109**	−0.183**	−0.167**	−0.071**	−0.094**	−0.088**
	−3.52	−4.80	−3.91	−3.75	−3.32	−2.74
Year 2009	−0.103**	−0.211**	−0.170**	−0.104**	−0.122**	−0.103**
	−3.09	−5.17	−3.64	−4.94	−3.92	−2.90
Year 2010	−0.148**	−0.212**	−0.183**	−0.126**	−0.095**	−0.095**
	−4.33	−5.35	−3.86	−5.45	−3.13	−2.62
Year 2011	−0.094**	−0.186**	−0.166**	−0.120**	−0.130**	−0.110**
	−2.68	−4.63	−3.42	−4.92	−4.06	−3.14
R^2	—	—	—	0.002	0.132	0.149
F-statistic	4.30	11.96	5.98	—	—	—
Other controls?	No	No	Yes	No	No	Yes
Number of observations	8,065	4,639	3,573	14,579	5,553	4,424
Number of firms	2,673	1,696	1,479	3,610	2,106	1,878
Dependent variable mean	0.65	0.66	0.66	3.42	3.68	3.69
Estimation method	Tobit	Tobit	Tobit	OLS	OLS	OLS

Notes: Estimates are based on the Kauffman Firm Survey years 2006–2011 using the stratified sample weights. Coefficients are reported followed by t-statistics accounting for clustering at the firm level. Other controls include business debt($t − 1$)/assets($t − 1$), personal debt($t − 1$)/assets($t − 1$), equity invested($t − 1$)/assets($t − 1$), ln(number of owners($t − 1$)), ln(primary owner age($t − 1$)), and indicators for whether the primary owner is male and white. Please see section 6.4 of the text for variable descriptions.
**Significant at the 1 percent level.
*Significant at the 5 percent level.

full-time employees and the number of hours worked by the primary owner in table 6.1A, we see a general decline in both variables over time, as evidenced by the negative coefficients on the year dummies in columns (7) and (10). These coefficients do not change very much when we add controls for past firm performance and owner and financing characteristics in columns (8) and (9) and columns (11) and (12).

Overall, the estimates in table 6.2 show that firms experienced significantly slower growth in employment in 2008 and 2009 relative to other years in the 2006 to 2011 period. However, evidence on whether wages and usage of full-time workers and owner labor changed significantly during the recession is inconclusive.

Table 6.3 presents estimates for the regressions specified in equations (1) and (2). As in table 6.2, we estimate three specifications for each dependent variable. Focusing first on log assets, we see that when we control for lagged

Table 6.3   Regression analysis of firm assets, revenues, and probability of shutting down

	Ln(assets)			Ln(revenues)			Firm shuts down		
	(1)	(2)	(3)	(4)	(5)	(6)	(8)	(9)	(10)
Ln(employment($t-1$))		0.122**	0.091**		0.192**	0.188**		0.001	0.003
		5.40	*3.58*		*7.90*	*6.68*		*0.35*	*0.66*
Ln(assets($t-1$))		0.729**	0.725**		0.154**	0.153**		-0.005*	-0.002
		27.37	*23.61*		*8.32*	*6.65*		*-2.48*	*-0.85*
Ln(revenues($t-1$))		0.146**	0.146**		0.713**	0.701**		-0.004*	-0.005*
		7.15	*6.55*		*23.59*	*18.90*		*-2.00*	*-2.52*
High-tech industry		-0.025	-0.046		0.063	0.032		-0.026**	-0.018*
		-0.51	*-0.76*		*1.68*	*0.74*		*-3.44*	*-2.15*
Has intellectual property		0.042	0.020		0.072*	0.045		0.008	0.005
		1.06	*0.47*		*2.19*	*1.12*		*1.27*	*0.76*
Constant	10.73**	1.25**	1.44**	11.41**	1.75**	2.36**			
	240.84	*7.28*	*3.99*	*226.31*	*8.38*	*5.85*			
Year 2007	0.015	-0.118*	-0.083	0.123**	-0.138*	-0.105	0.024**	0.009	0.005
	0.34	*-2.21*	*-1.40*	*2.67*	*-2.42*	*-1.63*	*3.21*	*1.15*	*0.64*
Year 2008	-0.079	-0.142*	-0.100	0.111*	-0.218**	-0.177**	0.032**	-0.011	-0.018*
	-1.55	*-2.59*	*-1.63*	*2.16*	*-3.85*	*-2.75*	*4.00*	*-1.31*	*-2.03*

(continued)

	(1)	(2)	(3)	(4)	(5)	(6)	(7)	(8)	(9)
Year 2009	-0.085	-0.205**	-0.181**	-0.008	-0.348**	-0.310**	0.009	-0.007	-0.009
	-1.62	*-3.35*	*-2.84*	*-0.14*	*-6.27*	*-4.78*	*1.04*	*-0.77*	*-0.96*
Year 2010	-0.081	-0.093	-0.085	0.040	-0.188**	-0.130	0.009	-0.011	-0.020*
	-1.42	*-1.48*	*-1.21*	*0.69*	*-3.08*	*-1.77*	*1.00*	*-1.27*	*-2.08*
Year 2011	0.010	-0.077	-0.083	0.131*	-0.155**	-0.153*	0.000	-0.030**	-0.034**
	0.16	*-1.21*	*-1.26*	*2.09*	*-2.74*	*-2.40*	*-0.05*	*-3.50*	*-3.47*
R^2/pseudo-R^2	0.000	0.709	0.703	0.001	0.760	0.759	0.002	0.030	0.034
Other controls?	No	No	Yes	No	No	Yes	No	No	Yes
Number of observations	13,052	5,267	4,095	12,232	5,269	4,065	17,975	6,260	4,830
Number of firms	3,531	2,027	1,779	3,325	1,995	1,733	4,427	2,365	2,071
Dependent variable mean	10.7	11.4	11.3	11.5	12.4	12.3	0.13	0.05	0.05
Estimation method	OLS	OLS	OLS	OLS	OLS	OLS	Probit	Probit	Probit

Notes: Estimates are based on the Kauffman Firm Survey years 2006–2011 using the stratified sample weights. Columns (1) through (6) report estimated coefficients followed by *t*-statistics accounting for clustering at the firm level. Columns (7), (8), and (9) report marginal probabilities calculated at the sample mean, rather than coefficients, followed by *z*-statistics accounting for clustering at the firm level. Other controls include business debt(t – 1)/assets(t – 1), personal debt(t – 1)/assets(t – 1), equity invested(t – 1)/assets(t – 1), ln(number of owners(t – 1)), ln(primary owner age(t – 1)), and indicators for whether the primary owner is male and white. Please see section 6.4 of the text for variable descriptions.

**Significant at the 1 percent level.

*Significant at the 5 percent level.

firm outcomes in column (2), firms' assets levels were significantly smaller in 2007, 2008, and 2009 compared to 2006. In these three years, firm-level assets were between 10 to 20 percent lower, all else equal. Evaluated at the weighted sample mean, the estimated coefficient on the year 2009 indicator implies a reduction in the firm assets from around $88,000 to around $74,000. The statistical significance on the year 2007 and 2008 dummies disappears when we control for firm financing and owner characteristics in column (3), but we still see that in 2009 firms' asset levels were still around 2 percent lower than in 2006.

Focusing on firm revenues in columns (4), (5), and (6), we see that revenues were higher in 2007, 2008, and 2011 relative to those in 2006 (column [4]). However, when we control for lagged firm outcomes in column (5), and for financing and owner characteristics in column (6), we see that revenues were lower in all years relative to 2006, especially in the recessionary years of 2008 and 2009, in which firm-level revenues were between 20 and 30 percent lower than otherwise predicted. Translated into dollars, these estimates imply that instead of around $240,000, average firm revenues were $194,000 and $170,000 in 2008 and 2009, all else equal.

Finally, turning to the probability of firms shutting down estimated in columns (7), (8), and (9), we see that without controlling for firm characteristics and past outcome (column [7]), firms are 2.4 percentage points (18 percent) more likely to shut down in 2007 and 3.2 percentage points (25 percent) more likely to shut down in 2008 compared to the probability of failure in 2006.[5] Adding controls for past outcomes in column (8), however, eliminates the statistical significance and magnitudes of estimated coefficients on the yearly indicator variables, suggesting that these greater probabilities of shutting down in the recession years observed in column (7) may be explained by lower firm performance in those years. Adding controls for financing and owner characteristics in column (9) shows that conditional on these characteristics the probability of shutting down was actually lower in 2008, 2010, and 2011 compared to 2006. These results are consistent with prior studies that document that the likelihood of firm failure diminishes as firms age (e.g., Puri and Zarutskie 2012).

The regression analysis in tables 6.2 and 6.3 are panel regressions that primarily use both cross-sectional variation in the independent and dependent variables to estimate the displayed coefficients. In table 6.4, we include firm fixed effects in the panel regressions to only allow within-firm variation to identify the estimated coefficients. Including firm fixed effects allows us to hold constant firm-specific determinants of the dependent variables. Doing so means that selection effects driven by firms exiting the sample will not affect our estimated coefficients.

5. Note that marginal probabilities, rather than coefficients, are reported for the probit models in table 6.3.

In table 6.4, we estimate regressions for each of the dependent variables considered in tables 6.2 and 6.3. For each dependent variable we estimate two specifications—one with only year dummies and one with lagged firm controls. Note that because many of the firm characteristic controls we used in tables 6.2 and 6.3 do not vary at the firm level over the sample period, we exclude them from the second specification in table 6.4.[6]

Focusing first on the employment variables—log employment, log wage per employee, full-time employment ratio, and log owner hours worked—we find similar results to those observed in table 6.2, with the exception of log wage per employee. In particular, we find that controlling for past outcomes (column [2]) that firm-level employment is 6.5 percent lower in 2008 and 9.6 percent lower in 2009, all else equal. These estimates translate to the number of firm-level employees falling by one-quarter to one-third of any employee, all else equal. Full-time employment declines over the sample period (column [5]), but after controlling for firm characteristics, we see that it declines more in 2009 and 2010 (column [6]). We also see that hours worked by owners decline fairly steadily over the sample period (columns [7] and [8]), similar to the pattern observed in table 6.2. Interestingly, we see that once we include firm fixed effects log wage per employee actually increases in the recessionary years 2008 and 2009 (columns [3] and [4]). This stands in contrast to the negative coefficients estimated on these year dummies in table 6.2. These differences in the overall and within-firm panel estimates suggest that firms that exited the sample in 2008 and 2009 paid their employees higher average wages but firms that did survive paid higher wages over the recession, perhaps because their lower-wage and lower-skilled employees left the firm, consistent with the reduced employment levels we observe in these same years in both tables 6.2 and 6.4.

Turning to log firm assets, we see that firms experience a decline in assets in years 2009 to 2011 relative to 2006 (column [10]). Controlling for firm characteristics and past outcomes, we see that decline remains statistically significant only in 2009 and 2010 (column [11]) with firms having 17 percent lower assets in 2010, all else equal. Turning to log firm revenues, we see that firms experience a decline in their revenues in 2009 and 2010 relative to 2006, but the decline is not statistically significant (columns [12] and [13]).

The results in table 6.4 are broadly consistent with those in tables 6.2 and 6.3, indicating that the decline in employment, asset, and revenues during the recession years was experienced at the firm level, and not just cross-sectional differences driven by firms exiting the sample. Overall, the empirical results in this section suggest that the economic and financial shocks stemming from the Great Recession adversely affected young firms, such as those surveyed

---

6. We also exclude the controls for financing in the second specification in table 6.4. There is modest firm-level variation for these variables. Including them does not change our results, but does reduce our sample size and statistical power.

Table 6.4   Panel regression analysis with firm fixed effects

	Ln(employment)		Ln(wages/employment)		Full-time employment/employment	
	(1)	(2)	(3)	(4)	(5)	(6)
Ln(employment($t-1$))		0.228**		0.022**		0.006
		4.24		*2.80*		*0.33*
Ln(assets($t-1$))		0.022		0.034		0.004
		1.38		*1.13*		*0.67*
Ln(revenues($t-1$))		0.026		0.012		0.008
		1.93		*0.44*		*1.09*
Has intellectual property		−0.012		0.153		−0.003
		−0.23		*1.51*		*−0.12*
Constant	1.17**	0.490*	9.68**	9.01**	0.700**	0.552**
	70.99	*2.53*	*279.84*	*20.28*	*81.84*	*5.49*
Year 2007	0.007	−0.020	0.046	0.088	−0.500**	−0.040*
	0.35	*−0.69*	*0.94*	*1.51*	*−3.98*	*−2.39*
Year 2008	−0.005	−0.065*	0.116*	0.146*	−0.068**	−0.046*
	−0.22	*−2.16*	*2.34*	*2.20*	*−4.92*	*−2.50*
Year 2009	−0.033	−0.096**	0.113*	0.190**	−0.063**	−0.062**
	−1.15	*−2.63*	*1.99*	*2.79*	*−4.24*	*−3.24*
Year 2010	0.009	−0.040	0.036	0.044	−0.081**	−0.076**
	0.29	*−1.11*	*0.55*	*0.55*	*−5.22*	*−3.82*
Year 2011	0.021	−0.035	0.141*	0.140*	−0.066**	−0.057**
	0.63	*−0.95*	*2.42*	*2.05*	*−4.20*	*−2.85*
R^2 (within)	0.002	0.079	0.004	0.022	0.015	0.012
Number of observations	6,282	3,848	5,354	3,565	5,947	3,695
Number of firms	1,850	1,266	1,543	1,157	1,788	1,230
Dependent variable mean	1.17	1.35	9.9	10.0	0.66	0.68
Estimation method	OLS	OLS	OLS	OLS	Tobit	Tobit

	Ln(primary owner weekly hours worked)		Ln(assets)		Ln(revenues)	
	(8)	(9)	(10)	(11)	(12)	(13)
Ln(employment($t-1$))		0.014		0.177**		0.356**
		1.06		*2.60*		*5.28*
Ln(assets($t-1$))		0.009		0.041		0.086**
		1.19		*0.91*		*3.10*
Ln(revenues($t-1$))		0.008		0.086**		−0.047
		0.83		*3.58*		*−1.00*
Has intellectual property		0.010		0.026		0.028
		0.51		*0.24*		*0.38*
Constant	3.52**	3.57**	10.71**	9.71**	11.47**	11.56**
	349.29	*31.58*	*396.59*	*20.69*	*455.83*	*23.42*
Year 2007	−0.071**	−0.060**	0.003	−0.052	0.060	0.074
	−5.24	*−3.21*	*0.09*	*−1.00*	*1.90*	*1.50*
Year 2008	−0.094**	−0.095**	−0.056	−0.056	0.057	0.015
	−6.00	*−4.66*	*−1.35*	*−0.89*	*1.58*	*0.23*

(*continued*)

Table 6.4   (continued)

	Ln(primary owner weekly hours worked)		Ln(assets)		Ln(revenues)	
	(8)	(9)	(10)	(11)	(12)	(13)
Year 2009	−0.139**	−0.129**	−0.109*	−0.148*	−0.064	−0.061
	−8.13	−5.71	−2.56	−2.20	−1.62	−0.93
Year 2010	−0.165**	−0.125**	−0.126*	−0.170*	−0.048	−0.065
	−9.01	−5.39	−2.52	−2.20	−1.08	−0.88
Year 2011	−0.209**	−0.171**	−0.123*	−0.078	0.005	0.021
	−10.79	−6.69	−2.55	−1.02	0.12	0.30
R^2 (within)	0.027	0.036	0.003	0.027	0.004	0.056
Number of observations	11,357	4,533	10,179	4,260	9,595	4,291
Number of firms	2,458	1,581	2,414	1,523	2,287	1,503
Dependent variable mean	3.36	3.66	10.6	11.4	11.4	12.4
Estimation method	OLS	OLS	OLS	OLS	OLS	OLS

Notes: Estimates are based on the Kauffman Firm Survey years 2006–2011 using the stratified sample weights. Coefficients are reported followed by t-statistics accounting for clustering at the firm level. Please see section 6.4 of the text for variable descriptions.
**Significant at the 1 percent level.
* Significant at the 5 percent level.

in the KFS, by reducing their employment and asset bases as well as their revenues.

Figure 6.1 plots the year fixed effects for the regressions of employment, revenues, and assets in the third specifications of tables 6.2 and 6.3 (without firm fixed effects) and the second specification of table 6.4 (with firm fixed effects). The graphs show that firms experienced a decline in all three measures, but also experienced a significant recovery. Including firm fixed effects mutes the dynamics of the changes in these three variables, as one would expect given that cross-sectional variation in performance and recovery across firms is eliminated. The graphs in figure 6.1 look similar if we limit our sample to firms that survive until 2011. The dip in performance and strength of the recovery is slightly muted in the case of including firm fixed effects if we eliminate firms that exit the panel before 2011. These results suggest that the decline in performance subsequent recovery were experienced at the firm level rather than being driven by attrition of firms during the recession.

Which Firms Survive?

A related question is, Which firms survive and which firms were more likely to recover after the recession? The answer to this question can be partly seen in the estimated coefficients on the covariates in specifications (9) and (10) in table 6.4. Across all years in the KFS panel, firms are more likely to survive if they are larger, in terms of revenues and assets. In addition, firms

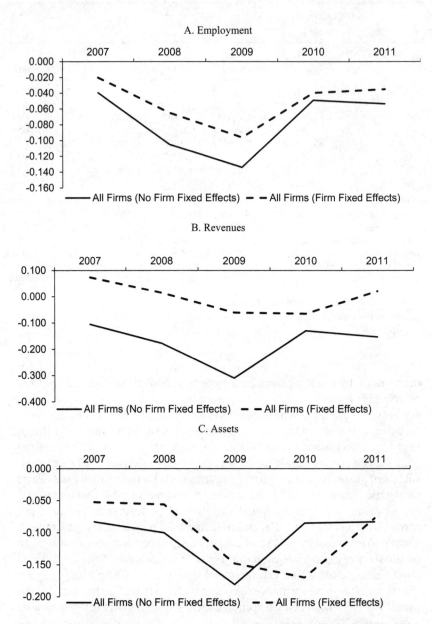

Fig. 6.1   Change in employment, revenues, and assets 2007 to 2011 relative to 2006
Note: Coefficients on the year fixed effects (relative to year 2006) are plotted for regressions using KFS panel data in the form of equations (1), (2), and (6) with covariates in the third specification of tables 6.2 and 6.3 (no firm fixed effects) and the second specification of table 6.4 (firm fixed effects).

in high-tech industries are more likely to survive. In comparing summary statistics of surviving and nonsurviving firms (not shown), we see that surviving firms are more likely to have business debt, but conditional on having business debt, surviving firms have lower leverage ratios. This suggests that financial conditions have an impact on which firms survive. We also find evidence, discussed in the next section, that firms that are less dependent on external debt finance recover more quickly.

Firm Financing

The decline in firm growth during the recession and in the few years after could stem from reduced demand and fewer investment opportunities, as well as financial constraints that limited firms' ability to obtain funds necessary to expand and invest. In this section, we examine how firms' use of financing changed during the recession to shed light on to what extent financial constraints may have contributed to the decline in firm growth during the recession and in the following years.

We begin by noting that when we controlled for lagged debt ratios, both business and personal debt, in the firm outcome regressions in tables 6.2 and 6.3 that these variables did not bear a statistically significant relation with the primary firm outcomes of employment, assets, and revenues. The amount of equity invested in the prior year was positively related to firm assets. These results suggest that firms are choosing their capital structures in a way that is not correlated with their outcomes, after controlling for lagged outcomes. This could suggest that financing or its availability in general did not influence firm outcomes during the sample period. Or it could be the case financial constraints did impact firm outcomes, but that these financial constraints did not affect the debt ratios of the firms, just firms' overall size.

We first examine whether the probability that firms have a bank loan, backed either by the business or the personal assets of the owners, changed during the recession. In table 6.5, we estimate probit models of the probability that a firm has a bank loan of either type as a function of firm characteristics and year dummies. The estimates are reported in columns (1) through (4). In columns (1) and (2), we see that the probability that a firm has a business bank loan does not vary significantly by year. In contrast, the probability of having a personal bank loan to finance the firm declines each year from 2006.

We then estimate the relation between year dummies and firm characteristics to both business and personal debt ratios as well as the ratio of equity invested to total assets in columns (5) through (11) in table 6.5. In column (5), we see that the ratio of business debt to total assets is significantly lower in 2009 onward compared to its level in 2006. However, controlling for firm characteristics in column (6), the statistical significance of these coefficients is reduced, suggesting that it may have been changing firm characteristics, rather than supply constraints, that lowered firms' business debt ratios.

Table 6.5   Regression analysis of firm financing

	Has business bank loan		Has personal bank loan		Business debt/total assets		Personal debt/total assets		Equity invested/total assets	
	(1)	(2)	(3)	(4)	(5)	(6)	(8)	(9)	(10)	(11)
Ln(employment(t − 1))		0.038** *3.78*		0.003 *0.48*		0.086 *1.94*		0.041 *0.84*		0.213* *2.22*
Ln(assets(t − 1))		0.022** *3.31*		0.019** *4.76*		0.044 *1.36*		−0.002 *−0.08*		0.104 *1.67*
Ln(revenues(t−1))		0.054** *7.92*		−0.002 *−0.42*		0.080* *2.33*		−0.021 *−0.65*		−0.419** *−4.60*
High-tech industry		0.034 *1.38*		−0.035* *−2.46*		−0.091 *−0.80*		−0.405** *−3.10*		0.489 *1.29*
Has intellectual property		−0.006 *−0.32*		0.018 *1.42*		0.162 *1.76*		0.176* *2.08*		0.526** *2.62*
Constant					−1.26** *−12.75*		−0.675** *−11.05*	−0.680 *−0.52*	−3.89** *−5.83*	−0.920 *−0.40*
Year 2007	0.012 *1.67*		−0.017** *−3.01*		0.005 *0.06*	−0.160 *−1.73*	−0.029 *−0.42*	−0.017 *−0.15*	−0.795** *−3.07*	−0.176 *−1.03*
Year 2008	0.017* *2.24*		−0.020** *−3.48*		0.130 *1.62*	0.082 *0.83*	0.055 *0.74*	0.067 *0.60*	−0.919** *−3.42*	−0.047 *−0.25*
Year 2009	0.007 *0.88*		−0.030** *−4.63*		−0.088 *−1.02*	−0.129 *−1.07*	−0.027 *−0.34*	−0.251* *−1.99*	−1.93** *−5.87*	−0.485* *−2.03*

(continued)

Year 2010	-0.003	-0.029	-0.051**	-0.047*	-0.256**	-0.141	-0.151	-0.240	-2.23**	-0.817*
	-0.29	*-1.00*	*-7.81*	*-2.54*	*-2.82*	*-0.95*	*-1.75*	*-1.46*	*-5.15*	*-2.45*
Year 2011	-0.005	-0.062*	-0.056**	-0.049*	-0.210*	-0.044	-0.347	-0.310	-2.15**	-0.726*
	-0.49	*-2.14*	*-8.25*	*-2.58*	*-1.99*	*-0.25*	*0.00*	*-1.64*	*-4.58*	*-2.11*
Pseudo-R^2	0.000	0.115	0.010	0.032						
F-statistic	—	—	—	—	3.67	6.20	3.27	6.92	8.21	2.53
Other controls?	No	Yes	No	Yes	No	Yes	No	Yes	No	Yes
Number of observations	15,388	5,565	15,388	5,561	10,662	3,879	11,977	4,533	12,868	4,920
Number of firms	3,704	2,114	3,703	2,118	3,198	1,675	3,380	1,838	3,515	1,948
Dependent variable mean	0.18	0.27	0.10	0.12	0.22	0.22	0.40	0.35	0.45	0.23
Estimation method	Probit	Probit	Probit	Probit	Tobit	Tobit	Tobit	Tobit	Tobit	Tobit

Notes: Estimates are based on the Kauffman Firm Survey years 2006–2011 using the stratified sample weights. Columns (1) through (4) report marginal probabilities calculated at the sample mean rather than coefficients, followed by *z*-statistics accounting for clustering at the firm level. Columns (5) through (6) report estimated coefficients followed by *t*-statistics accounting for clustering at the firm level. Other firm-level controls include business debt($t-1$)/assets($t-1$), personal debt($t-1$)/assets($t-1$), equity invested($t-1$)/assets($t-1$), ln(number of owners($t-1$)), ln(primary owner age($t-1$)), and indicators for whether the primary owner is male and white. Other geography-level controls include unemployment rate($t-1$), ln(labor force($t-1$)), ln(banking institution offices($t-1$)), ln(banking institution deposits($t-1$)), and ln(new house construction($t-1$)). Please see section 6.4 of the text for variable descriptions.

**Significant at the 1 percent level.

*Significant at the 5 percent level.

Turning to the ratio of personal debt to total assets in columns (7) and (8), we likewise see a substantial decline in the ratio beginning in 2009 but only the coefficient on 2009 is significant in the specification including firm controls. Finally, in columns (9) and (10) we see that the ratio of equity invested to total assets declines steadily over the sample period, suggesting that firm age effects, rather than the effects of the recession, may be partly responsible for the decline in equity to asset ratios.

Overall the evidence in table 6.5 suggests that use of external debt financing became less frequent and less intense toward the end of the recession in 2009, when many financial institutions were still experiencing stresses. However, it is difficult to disentangle to what extent this reduction is due to firms' aging, fewer investment opportunities, or financing supply constraints.

Note that in the second specification for each dependent variable in table 6.5 we include a number of geographical controls, which we match to the KFS based on a firm's county. In particular, we include county-level unemployment rate and labor-force size as controls for underlying economic conditions. We include total savings institution deposits and number of offices to control for supply-side conditions in the banking market. We also include the number of new single-family houses as a gauge of how affected a county may have been by the housing crisis that occurred during this time. While we find some evidence that having more banks in a firm's county is positively associated with greater use of bank financing, we do not have the power to use these county-level variables as instruments for the availability of financing to further investigate to what extent financing constraints may have affected firm outcomes.

In addition to the regressions presented in table 6.5, we also divide firms based on dependence on debt financing, measured at the two-digit industry level, and explore whether the dynamics of employment, revenues, and assets changes based on whether firms are financially dependent. We define financially dependent firms as those in industries for which the average ratio of business debt to total assets is above the population average, as measured in 2006. Figure 6.2 plots the year fixed effects for regressions of the form in the second specifications in table 6.4 (with firm fixed effects). We see that firms in financially dependent industries experience steeper declines in employment and assets during the recession and do not recover as quickly. There is no discernable difference in the dynamics of revenues, however. These results suggest that financial conditions affected firms' experience during the recession and subsequent recovery.

The KFS added special questions starting in 2007 about whether firms applied for new loans and whether they did not apply for new loans because they anticipated being turned down. We use these variables to gauge to what extent firm financing may have been driven by demand conditions versus supply conditions. In table 6.6, we estimate probit models (marginal probabilities are reported instead of coefficients) for whether a firm applied for a

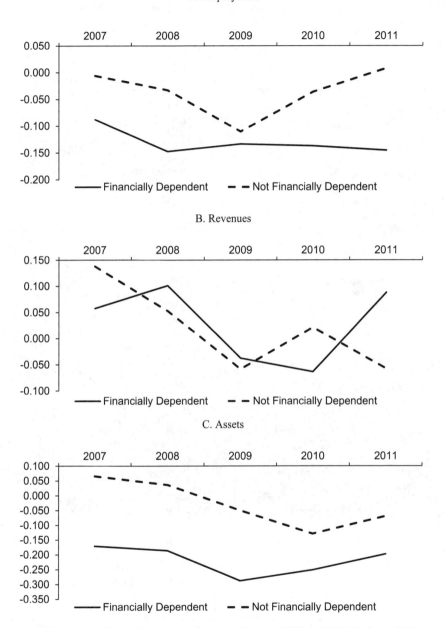

A. Employment

B. Revenues

C. Assets

Fig. 6.2   Change in employment, revenues, and assets 2007 to 2011 relative to 2006, by financial dependence

Note: Coefficients on the year fixed effects (relative to year 2006) are plotted for regressions using KFS panel data in the form of equations (1), (2), and (6) with covariates in the second specification of table 6.4 (firm fixed effects). Firms are classified as being financially dependent if they are in an industry with a debt-to-asset ratio above the population average in 2006.

Table 6.6   **Probit analysis of whether a firm applied for a new loan, 2007–2011**

	Applied for a new loan			Did not apply because would be denied		
	(1)	(2)	(3)	(4)	(5)	(6)
Ln(employment($t-1$))		0.009	0.005		0.013	0.010
		1.07	0.53		1.44	1.01
Ln(assets($t-1$))		0.020**	0.030**		0.001	0.008
		3.67	4.84		0.15	1.30
Ln(revenues($t-1$))		0.035**	0.030**		–0.016**	–0.016*
		5.98	4.69		–2.83	–2.53
Business debt($t-1$)/assets($t-1$)			0.030**			0.013
			3.71			1.39
Personal debt($t-1$)/assets($t-1$)			0.012			0.028**
			1.73			4.35
Equity invested($t-1$)/assets($t-1$)			–0.001			–0.001
			–0.51			–0.38
Ln(number of owners($t-1$))		0.008	0.010		0.021	0.025
		0.72	0.82		1.48	1.69
Ln(primary owner age($t-1$))		–0.018	–0.024		–0.050	–0.053
		–0.52	–0.65		–1.37	–1.33
Primary owner male		–0.027	–0.027		–0.040	–0.052*
		–1.46	–1.40		–1.86	–2.27
Primary owner white		0.033	0.037		–0.115**	–0.104**
		1.59	1.63		–4.73	–3.91
High-tech industry		0.028	0.028		–0.035	–0.034
		1.40	1.34		–1.51	–1.37
Has intellectual property		–0.043	–0.054**		0.063**	0.051*
		–2.70	–3.19		3.46	2.54
Year 2008	0.007	–0.003	–0.005	0.023**	0.046**	0.044*
	0.90	–0.22	–0.29	2.85	2.99	2.53
Year 2009	0.003	0.000	0.004	0.041**	0.046**	0.042*
	0.44	0.03	0.23	4.68	2.67	2.13
Year 2010	–0.012	–0.021	–0.029	0.028**	0.062**	0.054**
	–1.54	–1.30	–1.54	2.99	3.46	2.63
Year 2011	–0.016	–0.052**	–0.055**	0.011	0.023	0.024
	–1.91	–3.20	–2.89	1.18	1.24	1.15
Pseudo-R^2	0.001	0.082	0.091	0.002	0.028	0.034
Number of observations	12,035	4,402	3,446	12,036	4,400	3,441
Number of firms	3,234	1,786	1,550	3,236	1,787	1,549
Dependent variable mean	0.12	0.19	0.19	0.17	0.19	0.19
Estimation method	Probit	Probit	Probit	Probit	Probit	Probit

Notes: Estimates are based on the Kauffman Firm Survey years 200–2011 using the stratified sample weights. The table reports marginal probabilities calculated at the sample mean, rather than coefficients, followed by z-statistics accounting for clustering at the firm level. Please see section 6.4 of the text for variable descriptions.

**Significant at the 1 percent level.
*Significant at the 5 percent level.

new loan and for whether a firm wanted to apply but did not because they anticipated being turned down.

Columns (1) through (3) of table 6.6 estimate probits for whether a firm applied for a new loan. Column (1) just includes year dummies, while columns (2) and (3) include other firm controls. In all specifications, we see that the probability that a firm applied for a loan did not significantly change from during the recession years, but did drop in 2011.[7] However, in columns (4) through (6), we do find evidence that a greater percentage of firms did not apply for loans because they anticipated being denied over the period 2008 to 2010. In particular, over this period, firms were between 4 and 5 percentage points more likely to not apply for loans because they anticipated being turned down compared to 2007. There is no statistically significant difference between the estimated probability in 2011 and 2007.

The evidence in table 6.6 suggests that financing conditions were tighter during the recession. We next turn to an investigation of whether firms that anticipated being denied a loan experienced worse outcomes in the following year, to gain a better sense of how financing constraints arising during the Great Recession may have amplified the response in firm outcomes. Table 6.7 estimates regressions similar to those in tables 6.2 and 6.3, but includes the lagged indicator variable for whether a firm did not apply for a loan because they thought they would be denied.

Of our main outcome variables—employment (column [1]), assets (column [5]), and revenues (column [6])—the indicator variable for anticipation of loan denial only enters significantly and negatively for assets, making a connection between financing constraints and firm asset size. The indicator variable enters negatively for revenues as well, but is not statistically significant. Interestingly, we also find that firms that anticipate being denied a loan have more full-time employees (column [3]) and their owners work more hours (column [4]), suggesting that these firms may compensate by being able to obtain more assets or employees by having their existing employee base work more hours.

Overall the evidence presented in table 6.7 provides some evidence that financing constraints do negatively affect firm growth and may have contributed to the dampened growth they experienced during the recession and in the years following it.

6.4 Discussion

In this section we discuss our analysis of the impact of the Great Recession on young firm outcomes in the context of the existing empirical literature. We then discuss the limitations of the KFS in addressing our main

---

7. Unfortunately, it is difficult to know which of these applications were approved or denied. While the KFS asks this question, the response rate is too low to run a regression including all of the control variables.

Table 6.7   **Relation between anticipated loan denial and subsequent firm outcomes**

	Ln(employment) (1)	Ln(wages/ employment) (2)	Full-time employment/ employment (3)	Ln(primary owner weekly hours worked) (4)	Ln(assets) (5)	Ln(revenues) (6)
Ln(employment($t-1$))	0.835**	−0.335**	−0.066*	−0.017	0.127**	0.179**
	46.30	*−8.60*	*−2.56*	*−0.79*	*4.38*	*7.37*
Ln(assets($t-1$))	0.009	0.038	0.011	−0.002	0.742**	0.107**
	1.13	*1.39*	*0.76*	*−0.14*	*19.45*	*5.93*
Ln(revenues($t-1$))	0.037**	0.529**	0.124**	0.14**	0.115**	0.751**
	4.04	*16.25*	*6.97*	*8.06*	*4.07*	*30.42*
Did not apply for loans because would be denied($t-1$)	0.018	−0.009	0.114*	0.165**	−0.133*	−0.054
	0.66	*−0.12*	*2.33*	*4.49*	*−2.02*	*−1.10*
High-tech industry	0.003	0.455**	0.054	−0.02	−0.145*	−0.029
	0.12	*5.47*	*0.96*	*−0.35*	*−2.11*	*−0.59*
Has intellectual property	0.001	0.022	−0.025	−0.029	0.043	0.031
	0.03	*0.30*	*−0.57*	*−0.59*	*0.83*	*0.72*
Year 2009	−0.013	−0.099	−0.03	−0.037	−0.055	−0.113*
	−0.37	*−1.60*	*−0.83*	*−1.35*	*−0.78*	*−2.13*

(continued)

	(1)	(2)	(3)	(4)	(5)	(6)
Year 2010	0.065**	−0.093	−0.016	−0.022	0.034	0.05
	2.30	−1.23	−0.41	−0.77	0.52	0.84
Year 2011	0.048	−0.025	−0.015	−0.042	0.092	0.071
	1.55	−0.37	−0.38	−1.41	1.43	1.32
Constant	−0.305	3.87**	−0.604	2.11**	1.46**	1.63**
	−1.31	5.42	−1.42	5.56	3.27	3.90
R^2	0.786	0.349	—	0.135	0.710	0.768
Other controls?	Yes	Yes	Yes	Yes	Yes	Yes
Number of observations	2,777	2,650	2,686	3,260	2,980	3,081
Number of firms	1,181	1,134	1,152	1,456	1,367	1,380
Dependent variable mean	1.37	9.9	0.64	3.69	11.5	12.5
Estimation method	OLS	OLS	Tobit	OLS	OLS	OLS

Notes: Estimates are based on the Kauffman Firm Survey years 2007–2011 using the stratified sample weights. Coefficients are reported followed by *t*-statistics accounting for clustering at the firm level. Other controls include ln(number of owners(t − 1)), ln(primary owner age(t − 1)), and indicators for whether the primary owner is male and white. Please see section 6.4 of the text for variable descriptions.

**Significant at the 1 percent level.

*Significant at the 5 percent level.

question of how the Great Recession affected young firms and consider ways in which future data collection efforts may address them.

6.4.1   Other Empirical Studies Estimating the Impact of the Great Recession by Firm Age and Size

To our knowledge, there are no papers that systematically estimate the response of firms' assets and investment, employment, wages, and revenues to the Great Recession for very young firms. However, it is instructive to discuss several other recent studies for older and larger firms to help gauge how the Great Recession may have had a differential effect on the youngest firms.

Regarding the employment effects of the Great Recession, Chodorow-Reich (2014), Siemer (2014), and Duygan-Bump, Levkov, and Montoriol-Garriga (2015) each examine the response of employment by different types of firms based on firms' being financially constrained or more dependent on external financing. Each study finds evidence of a credit channel in reducing firm-level employment during the Great Recession. Chodorow-Reich (2014) finds that during the financial crisis and Great Recession lender health had an economically and statistically significant effect on employment at small and medium firms, but that his data cannot reject the hypothesis of no effect at the largest or most transparent firms. The firms in his estimation are much larger than in the KFS; the employment size at the 10th percentile in Chodorow-Reich's sample is seventy-seven employees. Likewise, Siemer (2014) shows that financial constraints reduced employment growth in small relative to large firms by 4.8 to 10.5 percentage points. The effect of financial constraints is robust to controlling for aggregate demand and is particularly strong in small young firms. Siemer (2014) defines small firms as those with fifty or fewer employees, and young firms as those age five years or younger. Siemer (2014) cannot observe financing behavior of the firms in his sample directly, but rather relies on industry measures of financial dependence for his estimates. Finally, Duygan-Bump, Levkov, and Montoriol-Garriga (2015) show that workers in small firms, defined as those with fewer than 100 employees, were more likely to become unemployed during the 2007–2009 recession than comparable workers in large firms, but only if they were employed in industries with high financing needs.

These three recent empirical studies suggest that the estimates found in our study for very young firms would not likely be observed if the KFS also surveyed older firms and support the notion that young firms were disproportionately affected by the Great Recession, partially through financial constraints, as well as through the demand channel, as measured by employment. These studies cannot comment on assets or other measures of investment due to the nature of the data they examine. Edgerton (2012) examines whether the Great Recession affected investment in machines by smaller businesses and finds that firms that were dependent on lenders that experienced the most distress during the crisis financed significantly less equipment than average firms after the crisis, consistent with younger and smaller firms being more affected by the Great Recession, in this particular study due to greater financial constraints.

Overall, existing studies on the firm-level effects of the Great Recession indicate that younger firms, particularly those that suffered from greater financial constraints, suffered lower growth in employment and lower investment. These studies cannot, however, examine several economic and financing outcomes at the firm level simultaneously as we do in our study.

6.4.2 Weaknesses of the KFS in Measuring the Impact of the Great Recession on Young Firms

While the KFS provides the largest panel data on the economic and financial outcomes of young firms over the Great Recession, allowing us to examine the evolution of several key firm-level outcomes and financing variables over this time period, there are several limitations imposed on the analysis due to the design of the KFS. In this section, we discuss these limitations and consider ways in which future data collection efforts may address them in the subsequent section.

First, because the KFS tracks only one cohort of firms, those founded in 2004, it is difficult, if not impossible, to disentangle age effect from time effects. Indeed, research on age-period-cohort models has shown that panel data from multiple cohorts best identify the causal effects of periodic changes (Yang and Land 2013). Without multiple cohorts of new businesses, we cannot see the evolution of firm outcomes and financing by young firms as if they never went through an economic crisis during their life cycles. Without reference groups of firms that operate in normal economic conditions, it is difficult to attribute the observed yearly changes in new businesses to the periodic effects of economic recession, because these may reflect the age-dependent pattern of firm growth rather than a response to fluctuations in economic conditions. Further, to form estimates of how the population of young firms as a whole fared during the Great Recession, we need panel data from multiple cohorts of firms to examine how the recession affected young firms of different cohorts and ages.

A second limitation of the KFS data is the overall size of the sample. While the survey begins with 4,928 firms in 2004, the size of the sample diminishes over time as some firms go out of business and others simply do not respond to follow-on surveys. During the Great Recession, the number of firms in the KFS ranges between 2,500 and 3,000. Further, if we condition on these firms having nonmissing values for the variables we analyze, the number drops to around 2,000, less than half the original sample size. While over 2,000 firms is still a nontrivial sample size, it does mean that there is not large variation at the local geographical level. The KFS collects information on the county in which a firm is located, potentially allowing one to use this geographical information to exploit differential changes in the local economic and financial environment of firms. However, with only a couple thousand firms, there are only a few firms from each county at best, not enough businesses from each county in order to support rigorous county-level analysis.

A third limitation of the KFS is that it does not collect many variables on the terms of financing and types of institutions that provide financing. The KFS does not ask what the typical interest rate charged on debt financing is, which is a key variable to trace the business cycle in order to assess the impact of financing on economic outcomes. Moreover, information on the type of institution providing financing and its characteristics would allow for a richer examination of which institutions may have cut back their supply of financing during the economic downturn and for what types of firms. Past studies have shown that financial institution characteristics matter for both the pricing and supply of financing (e.g., Rajan 1992; Petersen and Rajan 1994, 2000; Leary 2009).

Finally, the KFS collects very little information on the personal wealth, income, and finances of the founders of the firms it surveys. Given that the existing literature has established that personal wealth and income is both a determinant of entry into entrepreneurship and a potential source of collateral and financing over the firm's life cycle (Avery, Bostic, and Samolyk 1998; Hurst and Lusardi 2004; Holtz-Eakin, Joulfaian, and Rosen 1994), such variables would be useful to examine in our analysis of the impact of financing constraints on firm outcomes during the Great Recession.

6.4.3   Suggestions for Future Data Collection and Measurement Efforts

The Kauffman Foundation has conducted its final survey in 2011 of the panel of firms in the KFS and is currently engaged in new data collection efforts to measure entrepreneurial activity in the United States. In addition, US government agencies, such as the Census Bureau, are currently considering ways to improve the collection of data and measurement of entrepreneurial activity and the performance of new businesses. Given the limitations of the KFS for our analysis that we considered above, we offer some suggestions for the features of these future data collection efforts that may prove useful in studying the future impact of business cycles on entrepreneurs and their new businesses.

First, while panel data are key to studying firm-level outcomes over time, it is important that multiple cohorts be simultaneously sampled and that one can hopefully disentangle firm age effects from time effects, as well as generate more representative statistics for the population of young firms in the United States. Because it may be costly to sample new firms every year, it might be feasible to adopt a sampling strategy similar to that employed by the Federal Reserve's Survey of Small Business Finances (SSBF) or the Census Bureau's Longitudinal Research Database (LRD), both of which reestablish a representative stratified random sample of firms at a lower frequency—three years in the case of the SSBF and five years in the case of the LRD. The resampling frame of the SSBF may be more desirable in the case of young firms, since these firms fail at a high frequency and enter at a high frequency. The LRD, which focuses on established manufacturing firms, resamples at a relatively lower frequency because such firms exhibit less turnover. However, since the LRD both resamples and tracks a panel of firms over time (McGuckin and Pascoe 1988), adding new firms to the panel after resampling, future data collection efforts for new firms might follow this general approach but with the higher frequency adopted by the SSBF.

Second, in order to ensure a large and representative sample of firms, future data collection efforts should focus on increasing the sample size, perhaps by joining forces with US government agencies also focusing on collecting information on firms. Resampling every several years would serve to maintain the sample size, as firms that enter replace those that exit. However, it might be possible to increase the overall sample size. For example, instead of, or in addition to using the D&B database as the basis for the sample, future efforts might use the standard statistical establishment (SSEL) database maintained by the US Census Bureau (in conjunction with the Internal Revenue Service). Using such administrative records as a basis for generating the survey sample might also serve to generate both a more representative and larger sample. As noted above, a larger sample would give greater geographical coverage. With more businesses from the same county, one would be able to merge the data with census level about counties and then test how county-level environmental conditions amplify or reduce the negative influence of economic recessions. In addition, one might be able to exploit plausibly exogenous shocks to some counties in the local economic environment to better identify the impact of economic and financial shocks on firm outcomes.

Third, future data collection efforts should collect more information on the terms of financing received, the types of institutions providing that financing, as well as the wealth and income of the firms' owners. Such information is needed to assess the interplay between availability and cost of financing and economic outcomes of firms, as distinct from the direct impact of economic shocks. One could envision adding questions to a future survey that are similar to those that have appeared on the SSBF that inquire about the price and sources of financing (e.g., Petersen and Rajan 1994, 2000; Mach and Wolken 2006). Questions could also be added on the income and wealth of the equity owners in the firm. One could also envision special questions asking for more detailed information on the types, pricing, and sources of financing to be asked on a less frequent basis. In addition, future efforts that are joint with US government agencies might try to realize synergies between data sets collected by those agencies by allowing researchers to link firms across data sets.

Currently the Kauffman Foundation is involved in an effort to revitalize the US Census Survey of Business Owners (SBO) by broadening the survey and expanding the set of questions asked of firms surveyed. This expanded version of the SBO is termed the SBO-X. While still in the early stages of planning and implementation, such an effort holds promise for the study of entrepreneurs and their firms, especially if the effort results in the compilation of a representative panel of firms over a number of years implementing some of the suggestions above.

6.5   Conclusion

We use the Kauffman Firm Survey (KFS), the largest survey of a panel of young firms spanning the years around and during the Great Recession, to measure and assess the impact of this economic and financial crisis on the performance of young firms.

We find that young firms experienced much lower employment, assets, and revenue growth than would have been otherwise expected during the primary years of the recession. Moreover, our firm-level estimates that, when aggregated, these effects are economically meaningful. We also find evidence that firms were more financially constrained during the recession and in the period immediately following. More firms reported not applying for loans because they anticipated being turned down. Moreover, such firms experienced lower asset and revenue growth, despite their owners and employees working more hours. This evidence suggests that financing constraints, in addition to demand shocks, played a role in the diminished performance experienced by young firms during the Great Recession.

While the KFS allows a unique view of young firm economic and financing outcomes over the Great Recession, its design makes it difficult in some cases to disentangle firm age effects from time effects. Moreover, the relatively small sample sizes within specific local geographies eliminate the ability to use local geographical variation in economic and financial conditions to better identify the impact of the recession on young firms. We conclude with some suggestions for how future data collection and measurement efforts may overcome these limitations.

References

Avery, Robert B., Raphael W. Bostic, and Katherine A. Samolyk. 1998. "The Role of Personal Wealth in Small Business Finance." *Journal of Banking and Finance* 22:1019–61.

Berger, A. N., and G. F. Udell. 1998. "The Economics of Small Business Finance: The Roles of Private Equity and Debt Markets in the Financial Growth Cycle." *Journal of Banking and Finance* 22: 613_73.

Business Employment Dynamics (BED). 2011. "Frequently Asked Questions." Bureau of Labor Statistics. Accessed June 14, 2011. http://www.bls.gov/Bdm /Bdmfaq.Htm#5.

Chodorow-Reich, Gabriel. 2014. "The Employment Effects of Credit Market Disruptions: Evidence from the Financial Crisis of 2008–2009." *Quarterly Journal of Economics* 129 (1): 1–59.

Davis, Steven J., John Haltiwanger, Ron S Jarmin, C. J. Krizan, Javier Miranda, Alfred Nucci, and Kristen Sandusky. 2007. "Measuring the Dynamics of Young and Small Businesses: Integrating the Employer and Non-Employer Universes." NBER Working Paper no.13226, Cambridge, MA.

DesRoches, David, Tom Barton, Janice Ballou, Frank Potter, Zhanyun Zhao, Betsy Santos, and Jaceey Sebastian. 2007. "Kauffman Firm Survey (KFS) Baseline Methodology Report." Kauffman Foundation. Available at SSRN: https://ssrn .com/abstract=1024045.

Duygan-Bump, Burcu, Alexey Levkov, and Judit Montoriol-Garriga. 2015. "Financing Constraints and Unemployment: Evidence from the Great Recession." *Journal of Monetary Economics* 75:89–105.

Edgerton, Jesse. 2012. "Credit Supply and Business Investment during the Great Recession: Evidence from Public Records of Equipment Financing." Working Paper, Federal Reserve Board.

Farhat, Joseph, and Alicia Robb. 2014. *Applied Survey Analysis Using STATA: The Kauffman Firm Survey*. Kansas City, MO: Ewing Marion Kauffman Foundation.

Fort, Teresa, John Haltiwanger, Ron S Jarmin, and Javier Miranda. 2013. "How Firms Respond to Business Cycles: The Role of the Firm Age and Firm Size." *IMF Economic Review* 61 (3): 520–59.

Gertler, Mark, and Simon Gilchrist. 1994. "Monetary Policy, Business Cycles, and the Behavior of Small Manufacturing Firms." *Quarterly Journal of Economics* 109 (2): 309–40.

Haltiwanger, John, Ron S Jarmin, and Javier Miranda. 2013. "Who Creates Jobs? Small vs. Large vs. Young." *Review of Economics and Statistics* 95 (2): 347–61.

Hancock, Diana, and James A. Wilcox. 1998. "The 'Credit Crunch' and the Availability of Credit to Small Businesses." *Journal of Banking and Finance* 22:983–1014.

Holtz-Eakin, Douglas, David Joulfaian, and Harvey S. Rosen. 1994. "Sticking It Out: Entrepreneurial Survival and Liquidity Constraints." *Journal of Political Economy* 102:53–75.

Hurst, Erik, and Annamaria Lusardi. 2004. "Liquidity Constraints, Household Wealth, and Entrepreneurship." *Journal of Political Economy* 112:319–24.

Jarmin, Ron S., and Javier Miranda. 2002. "The Longitudinal Business Database." CES Working Paper no. 02-17, Center for Economic Studies, US Census Bureau. https://www.census.gov/ces/pdf/CES-WP-02-17.pdf.

Leary, Mark T. 2009. "Bank Loan Supply, Lender Choice, and Corporate Capital Structure." *Journal of Finance* 64 (3): 1143–85.

Mach, Traci, and John Wolken. 2006. "Financial Services Used by Small Businesses: Evidence from the 2003 Survey of Small Business Finances." *Federal Reserve Bulletin* October:167–95.

McGuckin, Robert H., and George A. Pascoe. 1988. "The Longitudinal Research Database (LRD): Status and Research Possibilities." CES Working Paper no. 88-02, Center for Economic Studies, US Census Bureau. ftp://ftp2.census.gov/ces /wp/1988/CES-WP-88-02.pdf.

Petersen, Mitchell, and Raghuram Rajan. 1994. "The Benefits of Lending Relationships: Evidence from Small Business Lending." *Journal of Finance* 49 (1): 3–37.

————. 2000. "Does Distance Still Matter? The Information Revolution in Small Business Lending." NBER Working Paper no. 7685, Cambridge, MA.

Puri, Manju, and Rebecca Zarutskie. 2012. "On the Lifecycle Dynamics of Venture-Capital- and Non-Venture-Capital-Financed Firms." *Journal of Finance* 67 (6): 2247–93.

Rajan, Raghuram G. 1992. "Insiders and Outsiders: The Choice between Informed and Arm's Length Debt." *Journal of Finance* 47:1367–400.

Reynolds, Paul D., and Richard Curtin, eds. 2009. *New Firm Creation in the United States: Initial Explorations with the PSED II Data Set*. New York: Springer.

Robb, Alicia, E. J. Reedy, Janice Ballou, David DesRoches, Frank Potter, and Zhao Zhanyun. 2010. "An Overview of the Kauffman Firm Survey: Results from the 2004–2008 Data." Research Paper, Ewing Marion Kauffman Foundation. Available at SSRN: https://ssrn.com/abstract=1606933.

Robb, Alicia M., and David T. Robinson. 2014. "The Capital Structure Decisions of New Firms." *Review of Financial Studies* 27 (1): 153–79.

Searson, Michael, Kenneth Robertson, and Richard L. Clayton. 2000. "The US Bureau of Labor Statistics Longitudinal Establishment Database." BLS Working Paper, Bureau of Labor Statistics. http://www.bls.gov/ore/pdf/st000060.pdf.

Siemer, Michael. 2014. "Firm Entry and Employment Dynamics During the Great Recession." FEDS Working Paper no. 2014-56, Federal Reserve Board. https://www.federalreserve.gov/pubs/feds/2014/201456/201456pap.pdf.

Yang, Yang, and Kenneth Land. 2013. *Age-Period-Cohort Analysis: New Models, Methods, and Empirical Applications*. New York: Chapmen & Hall.

7

Small Businesses and Small Business Finance during the Financial Crisis and the Great Recession
New Evidence from the Survey of Consumer Finances

Arthur B. Kennickell, Myron L. Kwast, and
Jonathan Pogach

It is widely understood that small businesses, small business formation, and the successful financing of both are critical components of the US economy and vital to strong and sustainable economic growth.[1] In addition, it is generally believed that small businesses are, after their start-up phase, relatively dependent on depository institutions, and especially their "relationships" with commercial banks, for credit and other financial services.[2] Thus, the fates of both established and new small businesses during the recent financial crisis and the ensuing recession have been of intense interest to policymakers, practitioners, academics, and the general public.[3]

Arthur B. Kennickell is assistant director in the Division of Research and Statistics at the Board of Governors of the Federal Reserve System and a board member of the National Bureau of Economic Research. Myron L. Kwast is the CFR Senior Fellow in Residence in the Division of Insurance and Research at the Federal Deposit Insurance Corporation. Jonathan Pogach is chief of the Financial Modeling and Research Section at the Center for Financial Research, Federal Deposit Insurance Corporation.

The authors thank Alicia Robb, our conference discussant, the conference volume editors, and Yan Lee, Philip Ostromogolsky, and Robin Prager for very helpful comments and suggestions and Cody Hyman for excellent research assistance. All errors are the sole responsibility of the authors. The views expressed are those of the authors and do not necessarily reflect those of the Board of Governors or its staff, or of the FDIC or its staff. For acknowledgments, sources of research support, and disclosure of the authors' material financial relationships, if any, please see http://www.nber.org/chapters/c13496.ack.

1. Recent papers supporting this view, but in some cases expressing concerns for the future, include Decker et al. (2014), Haltiwanger, Jarmin, and Miranda (2013), and Neumark, Wall, and Zhang (2011).

2. For a review of the literature supporting this view, see Udell (2008).

3. Thus, virtually at the peak of the crisis Congress demanded testimony by Federal Reserve and other officials regarding the crisis's effects on small businesses (see Kroszner 2008). Of course, policymakers' interest in and concern for small business is far from new—the Small Business Administration was created in 1953.

This chapter uses data from the Federal Reserve Board's Survey of Consumer Finances (SCF) in 2007, 2009, and 2010 to examine the experiences of established and new small businesses owned and actively managed by households during these years. In addition, we distinguish small businesses without employees from those with employees. We believe this is the first chapter to present a comprehensive analysis of small businesses during this period, and the first to use these SCF data on small businesses. Although the SCF has been used by many researchers since its inception in 1983 to study household finances, we know of only one other study that has used its information on small businesses owned and actively managed by households, and the data used in that study ended with the 1995 SCF.[4]

The combination of the three surveys provides a new, unique, and logically consistent data set to examine a wide variety of factors that affected small businesses and their owner's households before, during, and just after one of the most important periods in US economic history.

The analysis of the surveys used here has at least four important advantages over previous work. First, because the SCFs survey households with a focus on wealth and the sources and uses of income, they are well suited to evaluate interactions between small business and household finances. Such interactions have long been considered central to understanding entrepreneurial activity. Moreover, the SCF allows comparisons of households that have a small business with those that do not own a small business. Second, the timing of the surveys allows us to observe small businesses and their owners just before, during the heart of, and just after the financial crisis and the Great Recession. Third, the 2009 survey was a reinterview with participants in the 2007 SCF. This panel structure allows us to study directly how a set of small businesses and their owners were affected in the heart of the financial crisis and Great Recession. Fourth, the information on personal businesses collected in the SCF was expanded considerably in the 2010 survey, and some of that additional information is also available in the 2009 survey. This allows testing a number of findings of precrisis studies and provides a benchmark for future research.

In addition to describing and analyzing small businesses over the crisis and its aftermath, this chapter contributes to four areas of the small business literature:

1. Distinctions between established and new small businesses,
2. interdependencies and other interactions between the finances of small businesses and those of their owner's household,
3. the importance of "relationship finance" for small businesses, and
4. determinants of the probability of success, failure, and creation of a small business.

---

4. See Avery, Bostic, and Samolyk (1998).

By way of preview, we summarize briefly our key findings. The financial crisis and the Great Recession severely affected the vast majority of both established and new small businesses. This includes the fact that many firms faced severe credit supply constraints. While the weak economy was cited as a reason for the actual or expected denial of credit, causes more internal to the firm, such as credit history and a poor balance sheet, were cited much more frequently. We find that the interdependencies and other interconnections between the finances of small businesses and their owner-manager households are numerous and complex. We identify a variety of measures of small business-household interconnections. Some, such as a household's net worth, are common to the literature. Others, such as indications of a more complicated role of housing assets in small business finance, are new. Our results indicate that relatively well-educated households and workers who lost their jobs during the Great Recession responded in part by starting their own small business. Factors correlated with the survival of a small business during the crisis and the Great Recession are, with the exception of a household's ex ante net worth, problematic to identify. Our results strongly reinforce the importance of relationship finance to small businesses and the primary role played by commercial banks in such relationships. The key deposit services for small businesses are business checking and savings accounts, and the core credit services are business lines of credit, business loans, and possibly credit cards. Local banking offices are highly important for small businesses. Comparisons of results found using cross-section data with those found using panel data indicate that both types of information are highly valuable for researching the topics this chapter addresses. Thus, both cross-section and panel data are needed to advance our knowledge about household and small business economics.

The chapter proceeds as follows: The next section reviews the extensive small business literature to distinguish our study and place our work within its context. Section 7.2 describes the SCF small business data, including important differences across the three waves of the survey we use, discusses limitations of the SCF data, and compares SCF small businesses to those found in US Census reports. This section sets the stage for our substantive analysis, which proceeds in four parts. Section 7.3 uses variables available on both the 2007 and 2010 SCFs to compare small businesses and the households that own and actively manage them before and after the financial crisis and the Great Recession. In addition, households that own and actively manage a small business are compared with households that do not own a small business. Section 7.4 uses the 2007 cross-section survey and its 2009 panel reinterview to examine differences between small businesses (and their owner-manager households) that survived and those that failed during the crisis and recession. This section also identifies the key characteristics of households that started a small business during this period. Section 7.5 employs the expanded small business data collected on the 2010 SCF and the more limited new data collected on the 2009 panel (but not the 2007 SCF) to investigate a wide range of small business finance topics during these years. Section 7.6 summarizes the key findings from the previous three sections to provide a unified narrative of the experiences of small businesses owned and actively managed by households over the period covered by the three surveys. The section ends with recommendations for future research and improved data collection.[5]

7.1 Literature Review

While the academic literature on small business is huge, virtually all of it predates the recent financial crisis and the Great Recession. That being said, the literature identified a number of interrelated issues and principles that help our work. First, small business research generally distinguishes between new and established small businesses because the two groups exhibit important differences. These differences derive in part from the skills required of entrepreneurs versus those needed by the managers of a going concern. But the differences are also believed to result from a "life cycle" of small business finance and the likelihood that a business will grow from a start-up to a successful larger firm. Second, the interdependencies and other interactions between small business and household finance at both established and new small businesses are typically seen as important but are still poorly understood. Third, for both groups, the relationships between the firm and its sources of finance, especially commercial banks, are viewed as critical to the success of a small business. Indeed, previous research indicates that the importance of relationship finance is a fundamental difference between small businesses and larger firms that have access to broader capital markets. Last, the probabilities that a small business will succeed, fail, or be created at all derive from the interactions of many characteristics of the founding entrepreneur or current owner, the firm itself, the industry the firm is a part of, and the financial and economic environment in which the firm operates. Each of these topics is discussed below.[6]

7.1.1 The Life Cycle of Small Business Finance

Berger and Udell (1998) reviewed and described the life cycle of small business finance. Initially a new firm is not only young and small, but its risk characteristics are typically opaque to outside investors. Very young firms frequently rely on "inside finance" from the founding entrepreneur

5. Appendix A defines the variables used in this study, and appendix B provides univariate results that form the basis for the multivariate correlations discussed in the main text.

6. There are other core small business issues that we do not address. These include the effects of financial (and especially bank) market structure on small businesses' access to funds, the macroeconomic importance of small businesses, including their role in job creation and the transmission of monetary policy, and the roles of gender and race in small business formation and success. For discussions of the first topic, see Kerr and Nanda (2009), Black and Strahan (2002), and Petersen and Rajan (1995); for the second, see Decker et al. (2014), Haltiwanger,

and possibly friends and family members. As the firm grows and begins to show potential for success, angel and venture capital may become available. Eventually the business may come to rely heavily on "outside finance" as commercial banks and other financial institutions become willing to grant lines of credit and loans, public bonds may be floated, and perhaps public equity markets tapped. Along the way, other financial instruments such as trade credit, commercial paper, and private placements of debt or equity may be used. The fact that the life-cycle paradigm has considerable empirical support means that it provides a useful guide to researching small business finances.

Still, Berger and Udell emphasize that the life-cycle paradigm does not fit all small businesses and should only be used as a rough approximation. A recent paper by Robb and Robinson (2012) reinforces their point.[7] Robb and Robinson find that "in spite of the fact that these firms are at their very beginning of life, they rely to a surprising degree on bank debt."[8] However, more consistent with the life-cycle paradigm, Robb and Robinson find that much of this debt is tied directly to the entrepreneur through a sole proprietorship or personnel assets used as collateral.

Our study contributes to this debate in several important ways. First, we adopt the life-cycle paradigm as an organizing principle and test for differences between established and new firms and for the importance of firm size. Second, we are able to estimate a firm's probability of survival over the crisis, controlling for life-cycle characteristics and other household and firm characteristics. Last, we use the augmented data on small businesses available on the 2010 SCF to investigate whether some of the key findings of the precrisis literature are supported by postcrisis data.

7.1.2   Interdependencies between Small Business and Household Finance

The importance of interdependencies and other interactions between small business and household finance has long been recognized. However, the vast majority of studies have focused only on the relationship between household wealth and the probability of starting a new business. Positive correlations are typically interpreted as supporting the view that liquidity constraints are binding for many start-up businesses, and thus reinforce the importance of inside finance for small businesses.[9]

More recent research has challenged the strength of the wealth/small business formation relationship. In two papers, Hurst and Lusardi (2008 and

Jarmin, and Miranda (2013), and Udell (2008); for the roles of gender and race, see Robb and Robinson (2012) and Hurst and Lusardi (2008).

7. These authors use the Kauffman Firm Survey of businesses founded in 2004 to study the capital structure decisions of small businesses in their initial year of operation. The Kauffman Firm Survey is described in Robb and Robinson (2012) and Robb and Reedy (2011).

8. Robb and Robinson (2012, 25).

9. Evans and Jovanovic (1989) were among the first to find a positive relationship between individual wealth and entrepreneurial activity. Holtz-Eakin, Joulfaian, and Rosen (1994) found

2004) find that "Over most of the distribution of wealth, there is no discernible difference in the propensity to become a business owner. It is only at the very top of the wealth distribution (top 5 percent) that a positive relationship between wealth and business entry can be found."[10] These authors also "find that both past and future inheritances predict current business entry, showing that inheritances capture more than simply liquidity."[11]

In (to our knowledge) the only study of its kind to date, Avery, Bostic, and Samolyk (1998) document that the relationship between small business and household finances is highly complex.[12] For example, in partial support of Hurst and Lusardi, Avery, Bostic, and Samolyk (1998) find "no consistent relationship" between an owner's wealth and the use of personal commitments (personal guarantees and pledges of personal collateral) when a small business seeks credit.[13] Consistent with Robb and Robinson (2012), they find that personal commitments are important credit enhancement tools for those small businesses "that rely heavily on loan financing," and that "loans with personal commitments comprise a majority of small business loans, measured in numbers or dollar amounts."[14] Last, Avery, Bostic, and Samolyk (1998) "find strong evidence that personal commitments are substitutes for business collateral, at least for lines of credit."[15]

Our study expands and updates our knowledge in these areas, both during the crisis and as the economy began to recover. For example, we test the interdependence between household wealth and the probability not only of starting but also of *continuing to run* a small business. Unlike previous studies, we are able to separate the effects of wealth based on home ownership and wealth that is independent of home ownership. Other variables that give insight into small business/household interactions include the business owner's age, education, partnership status, risk preferences, and method of acquiring the small business, and we examine the importance of credit relationships running from the household to the small business.

7.1.3   The Importance of Relationship Finance

The third core issue to which our chapter contributes is the importance of "relationship finance."[16] Relationship lending relies primarily on "soft

---

a positive correlation between the probability of starting a business and receiving a recent inheritance. Schmalz, Sraer, and Thesmar (2013), using French data from before the crisis, found a positive correlation between increases in house prices and the probability of starting a small business.

10. Hurst and Lusardi (2008, 1–2).

11. Hurst and Lusardi (2004, 319).

12. These authors use data from both the National Survey of Small Business Finances and the Survey of Consumer Finances from the late 1980s through the mid-1990s.

13. Avery, Bostic, and Samolyk (1998, 1058).

14. Ibid.

15. Ibid., 1059.

16. Udell (2008) reviews the large body of theoretical and empirical research on relationship banking as it applies to small business lending. A short and clearly selective list of other

information" about a borrower, acquired over time by a lender who often has multiple interactions across a variety of financial services with its customer. Soft information is difficult to transmit both within and across organizations and, in the case of small business lending, typically includes deep knowledge of the business's local market. Indeed, Udell (2008) emphasizes "there is considerable evidence that relationship lending may be best delivered by community banks, where soft information does not have to be communicated across locations or hierarchical structures."[17]

While the importance of relationship finance appears well established, the importance of local banking offices to small businesses remains controversial. Using data from 1993, Petersen and Rajan (2002) argued that technological change altered small business lending markets, weakening the importance of local offices of credit suppliers and increasing the physical distance between small businesses and their sources of credit. Papers that use more recent data challenge this view, albeit with a number of important subtleties. Using data from 1997 through 2001, Brevoort and Hannan (2006) find that rather short distances between borrower and lender (two to five miles) still matter for small business lending, though more so for small banks than for larger organizations. DeYoung, Glennon, and Nigro (2008), using data from 1984 through 2001, find that greater lender/small business borrower distances increase the probability of loan default. And, using data through 2003, Brevoort, Holmes, and Wolken (2009) find that while some distances have increased for some financial products (e.g., asset-backed loans) and some small businesses (higher credit quality or more established firms), "distance increases for relationships involving lines of credit or multiple credit product types (bundles) were effectively zero" from 1993 to 2003.[18]

In contrast to relationship lending, most other lending technologies, often called transactions-based lending, rely more on "hard information." According to Udell (2008), hard information, such as financial statements and credit bureau reports, "is easily quantifiable and easily transmitted within the hierarchy of a large banking organization."[19] Examples of transactions-based lending technologies include financial statement lending, asset-based lending, leasing, and credit scoring. It is notable that Udell's list illustrates that in the real world of commercial lending, there is not a sharp distinction between the lending technologies available to community, medium-sized and very large banks. Community banks may have a comparative advantage in relationship lending, but they also use transactions-based technologies, and vice versa for larger banks.

---

important papers in the relationship banking literature includes Schenone (2010), Berger and Udell (1995, 1998, 2006), Berger et al. (2005), Elyasiani and Goldberg (2004), and Petersen and Rajan (1994).

17. Udell (2008, 94). Black and Strahan (2002) present evidence that challenges this view.

18. Brevoort, Holmes, and Wolken (2009, 26).

19. Udell (2008, 94).

The data on small businesses in the 2010 SCF allow us to examine relationship banking issues at the small business level. We can investigate whether some of the findings of precrisis research on relationship banking have held up over this period and establish benchmarks for future research. Moreover, relationship banking and small business finance issues not only are important for better understanding the nature of relationship finance, they also lie at the core of the methodology used by the US Department of Justice and the federal banking agencies for evaluating the potential competitive effects of proposed bank mergers and acquisitions.[20] Specifically, we contribute to the discussion of three fundamental concepts. First, because we can identify the type of financial institution a small business considers its "primary" financial institution, we can assess the continuing importance of commercial banks, other types of insured depositories, and other classes of financial institutions to small businesses. Second, while we cannot tell the size of a small business's primary financial institution, we do know the distance between a small business and the nearest office of its primary financial institution. Thus, we provide an update on the importance of local bank offices and the local offices of other financial institutions. Third, we can evaluate the continuing importance of credit, deposit, and payments financial services to a small business and the extent to which firms tend to cluster, or bundle, their use of financial services at their primary financial institution.

7.1.4   Small Business Survival, Failure, and Creation

The final issue to which our study contributes is the empirical analysis of small business survival, failure, and creation. This literature is voluminous, dates to at least the 1930s, contains both quantitative and qualitative studies, and extends across many countries.[21] Studies have identified four broad categories of relevant factors: characteristics of the founding entrepreneur or current owner, characteristics of the firm itself, characteristics of the industry in which the firm competes, and the financial and economic environment in which the firm operates.

Characteristics of the firm's founder and/or owner that have been found to be important are that person's age, education, financial endowment, management experience, attitude toward risk, access to credit and credit quality, previous experience in starting a new firm, gender, and race. Firm characteristics found to be important include financial ratios, age, size, access to credit and credit quality, organizational form, and geographic location. Industry characteristics that are often considered are broad categories of the type of

20. Many of the concepts used in this methodology have been controversial for years. See Kwast, Starr-McCluer, and Wolken (1997).

21. While we cannot review this entire literature here, we do want to place our work within its context. Recent reviews appear in Mach and Wolken (2012) and Balcaen and Ooghe (2006). Other interesting and relatively recent work includes Cole and Sokolyk (2013, 2014), Hunter (2011), Liao, Welsch, and Moutray (2008), Ooghe and de Prijcker (2008), Strotmann (2007), Cressy (2006), Headd (2003), Honjo (2000), and Everett and Watson (1998).

industry (e.g., retail, manufacturing, and service), overall growth rates in the industry, the degree of competition, and the size of the industry.

While each of these factors has been considered in one or more studies, no study has considered all of the factors. Ours is no exception. However, unlike most previous work, we are able to include variables in each of the first three categories in our examination of the probability that a small business survived the crisis. For example, we include the owner's age, education, net worth, and attitude toward risk, as well as a variety of firm and industry characteristics.

7.2   Small Businesses in the Surveys of Consumer Finances

This chapter uses information from the cross-sectional SCFs in 2007 and 2010 and from the panel reinterview in 2009 with participants in the 2007 survey.[22] The SCF is distinguished from other US household surveys by its focus on wealth measurement and inclusion of an oversample to provide adequate coverage of very wealthy households. These characteristics have special utility for this chapter. The SCF collects detailed information on all aspects of wealth, including the closely held businesses that are the subject of this chapter, along with supporting information on sources and uses of income, use of financial services, and other demographic and attitudinal characteristics. This information allows us not only to examine important details of businesses, but also to look closely at the relationship between some key dynamics of businesses and important aspects of the financial situation of the business owners.

The high-wealth oversample helps to provide a better representation of some of the more financially successful business owners. For example, in 2010, 13.3 percent of households overall had some type of closely held business investment, while the corresponding figure for the wealthiest 1 percent of households was 75.3 percent. For households outside the wealthiest 1 percent, the share of business wealth in total household net worth was 12.1 percent, while among the wealthiest 1 percent the figure was 37.7 percent. Thus, inadequate coverage of the wealthiest households would be likely to have adverse effects on the ability to analyze personal businesses.

7.2.1   Limitations of the SCF Small Business Data

While the SCF is a rich source of information, its design imposes limitations on our analysis. For example, the 2007 and 2010 surveys used a lengthy questionnaire to cover the affairs of each sample household at a relatively fine level of detail. However, a variety of concerns required shortening the length of the 2009 reinterview. Consequently, much of the detail

---

22. For additional background on these surveys, see Bucks et al. (2009), Bricker et al. (2011), and Bricker et al. (2012).

in the regular cross-sectional surveys was suppressed, while the higher-level architecture framing the questions was retained. For the section of the survey covering businesses, this meant collapsing the information on all actively managed businesses to a total of the values of the businesses and the loans of the businesses to, from, or sponsored by the household. We offset this limitation of the 2009 survey somewhat by adding new elements to the panel questionnaire to obtain information relevant to understanding the effects of the financial crisis. For example, whenever a business had been reported in the 2007 survey and the 2009 respondent no longer reported a business, the respondent was asked what had become of the business. Thus, we can study factors that affected the survival or failure of these businesses. Conversely, we can identify when a business appears on the 2009 survey but not on the 2007 SCF. Thus, we can study factors that affected a household's decision to create a small business during this period. In addition, questions were added in 2009 on recent credit experiences and expectations of credit availability. The 2010 SCF incorporated these credit-related questions and added more detailed questions on the use of financial services by businesses.

The survey design also affects the scope of entities that can be considered in our analysis. First, not all assets treated as businesses for tax purposes may be reported by SCF respondents as a business. The only nonnegligible exception of this sort in the SCF is investment real estate. Because some households appear to report such assets as businesses and some do not, researchers sometimes combine such information to produce a more uniform measure of businesses. However, because the information collected in the survey for real estate investments differs in important ways from that collected for businesses in the SCF, we do not include such real estate holdings in our analysis.

Households reporting that they own one or more businesses may have an active interest in running their business or a passive one. It is a reasonable assumption that the active owner would be more knowledgeable about the operations of its business. As a result, the SCF collects more detailed information on businesses in which the household has an active management role. To take advantage of this information, we focus on the set of actively managed businesses and their owners. In 2010, 12.5 percent of households had at least one business with an active management role and 1.3 percent had at least one with a more passive management role (0.5 percent had both).

There is often not a clear distinction between self-employment and business ownership. Some types of self-employment may not be associated with assets or liabilities that survey respondents would consider a business. In both the 2007 and 2010 surveys, when respondents who did not report a personal business answered later in the interview that they were self-employed, they were asked whether their self-employment was associated with a business with any net value. This follow-up captures some additional businesses, but it does not address business structures that have no significant net value.

Moreover, the check on the data is not symmetric in that there may be businesses reported directly that have no significant net value. In 2007, 74.3 percent of households that reported self-employment activity by the household head or that person's spouse or partner also reported owning a personal business; in 2010, the proportion dropped to 70.6 percent.

In principle, the 2007 SCF collected detailed information on up to three actively managed businesses and the 2010 survey collected such information for as many as two; any remaining actively managed businesses were recorded as summary information. In practice, it appears that it was common in both surveys for respondents to combine multiple businesses effectively operated as a single business but that retained a degree of legal separation for tax or other reasons. The interview questionnaire instructions allow this way of reporting. The advantage of this approach is that the business as reported is more likely to reflect the business in a functional sense; the disadvantage is that the business described may not be a single legal entity. It is impossible to give a precise estimate of the extent to which multiple businesses might be combined in this way in the SCFs.

Some closely held businesses are large, sometimes as large as well-known publicly traded firms. Such large firms almost surely look and behave differently from smaller and more entrepreneurial firms. To avoid potential biases and sharpen the focus of this study, we restrict the set of businesses considered to those with fewer than 500 employees. In the 2010 SCF, only 0.8 percent of primary businesses were larger than this size.

We adopt one other restriction on the set of businesses considered. The SCF includes farm businesses along with other types of businesses, but when a farmer also lives on some part of the property farmed, which is often the case, the information available is less straightforward to use than is the case for other types of business. For example, separating the value of land farmed from the associated residence and its mortgages or loans typically requires strong assumptions about what should be attributed to services purely related to housing. An even more difficult problem is the proper treatment of financing options and government incentives that apply entirely or largely to farmers. Our view is that combining farms with other types of businesses in the SCF would risk substantially reducing the clarity of our results. We therefore do not include as a business any farm that is also the primary residence of the household. In 2010, 0.8 percent of the SCF households had a farm business on a property where they lived.

Perhaps the most important limitation of the SCF for business analysis is that while the survey is designed to gather data on the businesses owned by households, it is not designed to be representative of the population of businesses. Only in the case of ownership of a sole proprietorship or other business with no owners outside the survey household do the household and business units coincide statistically. To realign the survey to represent the universe of privately held businesses, it would be necessary to adjust the household weight associated with each business owner, accounting for the business ownership share. In addition, this adjustment would need to be performed separately for each business a household owned. Unfortunately, such an adjustment is not possible for the SCF, because ownership shares are only collected for the set of actively managed businesses and only on the first three (two) businesses for which detailed information was collected in 2007 (2010). To address this limitation, this study focuses on the first actively managed business reported by respondents in the 2007 and 2010 surveys, which should be the largest or most important one for the household. Among this set of "primary businesses," 80.2 percent were fully owned by the household and 7.2 percent were half-owned. In addition, our set of primary businesses includes 72.4 percent of the total value of small businesses in the 2007 SCF, and 68.9 percent of the total value in 2010.

For all these reasons, the results reported here do not describe the full universe of closely held businesses, but rather the universe of primary, actively managed, nonfarm business interests, weighted by the population of owners. However, as is discussed below, the available data suggest that this more limited approach should be highly representative of the larger universe.

7.2.2   Comparing SCF and US Census Data

Estimates of the US Bureau of the Census reported in the Statistics of US Businesses (SUSB) and a series on nonemployer businesses provide some basis for examining the degree of coverage of the universe of all small businesses using the definition of small businesses we have developed from the SCF for this chapter. According to the census, there were about 27.8 million nonemployer (no employee) businesses in 2007. Estimates based on our definition derived from the principal business owned by the household indicate that there were only about 5.5 million such businesses because of our more narrowly focused approach.

Several factors may explain the large difference. First, as noted earlier, many self-employed people do not report in the SCF that they own a business. If all households with a self-employed head or spouse/partner and no reported business are treated as having a nonemployer business, the SCF estimate rises to about 10.8 million. Second, as noted earlier, some households have real estate holdings that are formally organized as a business, but reported as directly owned real estate in the SCF. Including all of the properties from which the household is known to have received any income as nonemployer businesses raises the total to about 18.8 million. However, this augmentation with real estate holdings almost surely overstates the possible number of unreported nonemployer businesses in the SCF, not least because ownership of income-producing real estate is often shared and thus may be double counted. Third, and possibly most important, the census estimate of nonemployer businesses is based on business tax returns filed at any point during the year. If there is significant flux in the existence of this smallest category of business, the wider window of the census estimate would capture more short-lived businesses than the SCF, which is based on the state of the household's assets as of the time of the interview.

The SUSB estimates of the number of employer (one or more employees) businesses are made using the Census Business Registry, which purports to be a list of all existing US businesses with employees. The census estimates that there were about 6 million employer businesses with fewer than 500 employees in 2007. Estimates with our definition indicate that there were about 8.1 million households with such businesses as their primary business. Part of the difference in these estimates may be the result of the inclusion of more than one household member among the total number of people working for the business. Assuming that any household head or spouse/partner who works in the household's business is not an employee, the SCF estimate of the total number of employer businesses with fewer than 500 employees falls to about 6.9 million. Adjusting the SCF estimate for the share of the business that each household owns reduces the number of household businesses with fewer than 500 employees to about 6.1 million.

On balance, these comparisons indicate that while—for a variety of logical reasons—the SCF and census data do not match well for no-employee small businesses, the two data sources compare closely with respect to numbers of employer firms. For this reason, much of our analysis separates no-employee small businesses from firms with at least one employee.

Tables 7B.7 and 7B.8 in appendix B further compare the distribution of SCF employer businesses by our definition with SUSB data by industrial sector and by firm size for 2007. Given the small sample size of the SCF, there are some differences in the patterns shown by the two sources. Overall, however, the distributions are similar.

7.2.3   Adjustments for Statistical Concerns

Like any survey, the SCF is subject to potential error because of the small sample of the population interviewed. In addition, some households selected into the survey do not participate, making it possible that the characteristics of participants might differ from those of nonrespondents in ways that induce bias in the statistics we report. The SCF addresses these problems through weighting. Nonresponse adjustments tailored to the survey help to mitigate the effects of nonresponse. A replication method is used to estimate variability caused by sampling; many pseudo-samples are selected from the set of completed cases, and the full set of weighting adjustments is made for each such pseudo-sample. The variability of estimates across calculations using each of the replicate weights serves as an estimate of the range of variability of estimates as a result of sampling.

In addition to the nonrespondents, some respondents fail to give answers to all the questions asked. The SCF uses a multiple imputation to estimate the distribution of the missing data. Under this method, multiple values for a missing item are randomly drawn from the distribution of the value, conditional on the observed information. Variability of estimates across different sets of such draws represents the added uncertainty as a result of having missing information.

7.3   Small Businesses in 2007 and 2010

This section uses variables available on the 2007 and 2010 SCFs to examine small businesses and the households that own and actively manage them before and just after the financial crisis and the Great Recession. In addition to analyzing separately 2007 and 2010, we follow the literature's convention of distinguishing established from new small businesses.[23] As noted in the previous section, we also distinguish firms with no employees from those with at least one employee.[24] While we only report and analyze multivariate results here, appendix B (Univariate Analysis) provides our univariate results. This section also describes some key characteristics of SCF small businesses not discussed in section 7.2.

7.3.1   Households that Own and Actively Manage a Small Business

Tables 7.1A and 7.1B provide the results of multivariate logit regressions that estimate the probability that a household owns and actively manages a small business.[25] Table 7.1A separates households into those with an established small business (left panels) and those with a new small business (right panels) in a given year, 2007 and 2010. Table 7.1B separates households into those whose small business had no employees (left panel) from those with at least one employee (right panel), again by 2007 and 2010. The right-hand-side variables in the regressions reported in the (1) columns of both tables are the same as those in our univariate analysis, with three exceptions. Only income including that from the small business and net worth including small business equity are included. In addition, the ratio of home equity to total net worth, which also proxies for home ownership, is included.[26] The additional specifications presented in the (2) columns will be discussed shortly. In all cases, the reported coefficients are marginal effects.

23. Established businesses are defined as small businesses that are more than three years old or that were acquired by the household more than three years previously. While there is no standard definition of a new small business, many studies use between two and four years, and thus our choice of three years seemed reasonable (see Everett and Watson 1998). Moreover, the triannual nature of the SCF means that there is negligible overlap in the population of our new small businesses. In 2007, in our sample of 1,137 small businesses, 82 percent of the SCF's small businesses met this definition of established and 18 percent were new; in 2010, of a total sample of 1,536 small businesses, the percentages were 85 percent and 15 percent, respectively.

24. Sample size limits prevent us from combining the two concepts.

25. All data analyses in this study use SCF analysis weights as described in section 7.2.3.

26. Inclusion of both this ratio and a home ownership indicator variable led to substantial multicollinearity. All dollar values enter in log form in these and subsequent regressions. As explained in more detail in appendix B, all dollar values are in 2007 dollars.

Table 7.1A Probability of owning and actively managing a small business (SB)

	Established versus no small business				New versus no small business			
	2007		2010		2007		2010	
Variable	(1)	(2)	(1)	(2)	(1)	(2)	(1)	(2)
Log(HH income)	-0.093	-0.068	-0.136***	-0.146***	-0.086	-0.192**	-0.064	-0.055
	(0.064)	(0.072)	(0.037)	(0.037)	(0.105)	(0.079)	(0.100)	(0.114)
HH age	-0.024***	-0.025***	-0.004	-0.003	-0.034***	-0.033***	-0.032***	-0.038***
	(0.005)	(0.006)	(0.005)	(0.005)	(0.007)	(0.009)	(0.006)	(0.008)
HH educ.	-0.061**	-0.064**	-0.015	0.001	0.157***	0.125**	0.144***	0.101**
	(0.029)	(0.032)	(0.026)	(0.027)	(0.049)	(0.055)	(0.042)	(0.049)
Log(HH net worth)	0.698***	1.033***	0.437***	0.469***	0.112*	0.079	0.084**	0.097
	(0.068)	(0.112)	(0.068)	(0.145)	(0.064)	(0.106)	(0.038)	(0.061)
Home to net worth	-1.153***		-1.157***		-0.328		-0.322	
	(0.111)		(0.196)		(0.310)		(0.275)	
Log(house)		-0.448***		0.154		0.151		0.049
		(0.127)		(0.162)		(0.187)		(0.173)
Log(mortgage)		0.059***		0.044***		0.094**		0.027
		(0.019)		(0.016)		(0.047)		(0.031)
HH partnered	0.393**	0.614***	0.664***	0.725***	1.054***	0.766**	0.791***	0.574**
	(0.159)	(0.197)	(0.131)	(0.152)	(0.271)	(0.300)	(0.220)	(0.272)
HH cred. access	0.264**	0.105	0.685***	0.429***	0.637***	0.131	0.263	0.046
	(0.135)	(0.176)	(0.112)	(0.151)	(0.235)	(0.299)	(0.192)	(0.299)
Riskpref	-0.117	-0.159	-0.106	-0.080	-0.268**	-0.279**	-0.404***	-0.380***
	(0.094)	(0.104)	(0.071)	(0.079)	(0.114)	(0.129)	(0.095)	(0.122)
Pseudo R²	0.28	0.25	0.24	0.20	0.15	0.14	0.12	0.11
N	4,073	4,073	6,106	6,106	3,334	3,334	5,261	5,261

Note: Marginal effects of logistic regressions of a 2007 and 2010 SB ownership dummy on contemporaneous HH variables. Variables may be endogenous to SB ownership and should be interpreted as conditional correlations only. Standard errors in parentheses.

***Significant at the 1 percent level.

**Significant at the 5 percent level.

*Significant at the 10 percent level.

Table 7.1B Probability of owning and actively managing a small business (SB)

| | No employee versus no small business | | | | Employee versus no small business | | | |
| | 2007 | | 2010 | | 2007 | | 2010 | |
Variable	(1)	(2)	(1)	(2)	(1)	(2)	(1)	(2)
Log(HH income)	0.041	-0.076	-0.163***	-0.180***	-0.106	-0.094	-0.105**	-0.115***
	(0.125)	(0.089)	(0.048)	(0.049)	(0.068)	(0.068)	(0.041)	(0.040)
HH age	-0.012*	-0.013*	-0.004	-0.005	-0.035***	-0.040***	-0.013**	-0.015**
	(0.006)	(0.007)	(0.004)	(0.005)	(0.006)	(0.007)	(0.006)	(0.006)
HH educ.	0.115***	0.102***	0.064**	0.035	-0.074**	-0.100***	0.013	0.015
	(0.040)	(0.042)	(0.032)	(0.037)	(0.037)	(0.035)	(0.031)	(0.031)
Log(HH net worth)	0.152**	0.037	0.136***	0.122**	0.728***	1.300***	0.435***	0.572***
	(0.066)	(0.075)	(0.040)	(0.056)	(0.106)	(0.109)	(0.081)	(0.172)
Home to net worth	-0.134		-0.608***		-1.473***		-1.107***	
	(0.266)		(0.218)		(0.297)		(0.237)	
Log(house)		0.297**		0.238*		-0.674***		0.037
		(0.140)		(0.129)		(0.125)		(0.183)
Log(mortgage)		0.009		0.052**		0.092***		0.036*
		(0.025)		(0.022)		(0.022)		(0.019)
HH partnered	0.480**	0.562**	0.554***	0.513***	0.697***	0.743***	0.882***	0.845***
	(0.207)	(0.237)	(0.158)	(0.185)	(0.184)	(0.223)	(0.156)	(0.183)
HH cred. access	0.059	-0.042	0.748***	0.426**	0.615***	0.244	0.445***	0.268
	(0.164)	(0.218)	(0.154)	(0.210)	(0.163)	(0.214)	(0.125)	(0.175)
Riskpref	-0.221*	-0.311**	-0.210**	-0.189*	-0.123	-0.104	-0.215***	-0.137
	(0.114)	(0.126)	(0.084)	(0.098)	(0.091)	(0.104)	(0.077)	(0.089)
Pseudo R²	0.09	0.09	0.10	0.09	0.31	0.30	0.24	0.21
N	3,402	3,402	5,389	5,389	4,005	4,005	5,979	5,979

Note: Marginal effects of logistic regressions of a 2007 and 2010 SB ownership dummy on contemporaneous HH variables. Variables may be endogenous to SB ownership and should be interpreted as conditional correlations only. Standard errors in parentheses.

***Significance at the 1 percent level.
**Significance at the 5 percent level.
*Significant at the 10 percent level.

We use the conventional definition of a marginal effect: the impact of a unit change in a right-hand-side variable on the estimated probability when all right-hand-side variables are measured at their mean.

Looking first at the (1) columns for households with an established small business (versus those with no small business) in 2007, all but two of the right-hand-side variables are statistically significant at the 5 percent level or better. Interestingly, neither the household's income nor its risk preference variable is significant.

The results for 2010 are similar but not quite the same. In 2010 a household's age, education, and risk preference were insignificant, but now its income was significantly negative. Thus, ceteris paribus, in both years a household was more likely to have an established small business if it had higher net worth, if less of its net worth were in home equity, if it were partnered, and if it had access to credit.[27] In 2007, younger and less educated households were more likely to own and actively manage an established small business, but these variables were not significant in 2010.

Results for households with a new small business (right panel of table 7.1A) are similar to, but also differ in interesting ways, from those for households with an established small business. Thus, ceteris paribus, and as was the case for households with an established small business, in both years a household was more likely to have a new small business if it had higher net worth, if it were partnered, and if it had access to credit (although the level of significance in 2010 is a very weak 12 percent). However, in contrast to households with an established firm, in both years a household was more likely to have a new small business if it were younger, more educated, and if it were less risk averse. On balance, these results support our and the literature's emphasis on separating established and new small businesses. It is interesting that in both years the household's income and the ratio of its home equity to total net worth were not correlated with the probability of owning and actively managing a new small business.

Turning to table 7.1B, we again focus initially on results in the (1) columns. Overall, the logits that separate households into those firms that have no employees versus those that have some employees are much more consistent across the two groups and across both years than were the regressions that separated households with established versus new firms. Thus, ceteris paribus, in both groups and both years, a household was significantly more likely to have either a small business with no or some employees if it were younger, had greater net worth, a smaller ratio of home equity to net worth (except no-employee households in 2007), were partnered, had access to credit (again except no-employee households in 2007), and if it were less risk averse (except employee households in 2007). As was true in table 7.1A, a

---

27. We use a conservative definition of credit access. The household must have a loan from an insured depository other than a credit card or an educational loan.

household's income was either negatively correlated or uncorrelated with the probability that it has a small business. Interestingly, the fact that all of the negative correlations with income in both tables occur in 2010 may suggest some causal impact of the recession, a topic we will discuss in more detail. In addition, the disparate correlations of education with the probability of owning a small business suggest an important distinction. More education increased the probability of owning a new small business or a firm with no employees, but it was either unrelated or negatively correlated with the probability of owning an established small business or a firm with employees.

On balance, the results of the two tables suggest that while separating households into those with established versus new firms is generally critical for researchers (and policymakers), distinguishing households whose firms have no employees versus some employees may be less critical.

The statistically negative or zero correlation of household income with the probability of having an established or a new small business or one with no or some employees is unexpected and inconsistent with our univariate results. A straightforward interpretation is that once we control for other important factors, such as net worth, income fades in importance for understanding which households own and actively manage a small business.[28] Alternatively, it may be that a household that started a small business had relatively unstable income. It may also be that important conceptual differences between the income of households with no small businesses (e.g., relatively more wages) and the income of those with a small business (e.g., relatively more unrealized capital gains) confuse the interpretation of the income coefficient. In addition, Slemrod (2007) provides strong evidence that underreporting of business income for tax purposes is substantial among households that own small businesses.[29] Thus, our multivariate results for household income may in part reflect the underreporting of income by survey households. On balance, while all these factors probably play some role, we lean toward emphasizing the effects of the Great Recession, subject to the caveat that our income results seem worthy of additional research.

The generally negative correlation of a household's ratio of its home equity to total net worth with the probability that it owns and actively manages a small business is interesting and provocative, especially because previous studies have been unable to construct such a variable. On the one hand, our results may merely reflect the conventional wisdom that households with a small business tend to use home equity as collateral for mortgage loans that support their business, thereby driving down their ratio of home equity to net worth. On the other hand, our results may also suggest the new and perhaps provocative suggestion that, ceteris paribus, a dollar of net worth

---

28. The negative coefficient on income is robust to a variety of model specifications.
29. Households are encouraged to use tax records to assist their responses to the SCF.

in home equity may be less valuable to a household that has a small business than is a dollar in other, possibly more liquid, forms of net worth.

To test these possibilities, we estimated logit models, reported in the (2) columns of tables 7.1A and 7.1B, that substitute two new right-hand-side variables for the ratio of home equity to net worth. "House" is the log dollar value of a household's housing assets, and "mortgage" is the log dollar value of any mortgages for which those housing assets are the collateral. The column (2) results for these variables are generally strongest for households with established firms and those whose small business has some employees. These estimations suggest that (a) conditional on having housing assets, tapping into home equity via any type of mortgage is positively associated with the probability of having a small business; but that (b) conditional on the amount of those mortgages, holding a larger proportion of total net worth in housing may be either a negative or neutral signal of small business ownership.[30] The first result is consistent with the conventional wisdom that many small business owners use their home as collateral for loans that support their business. However, the second result is consistent with our new conjecture that other forms of net worth at the margin may be more valuable to the small business owner. In either case, we believe these results warrant further research on the interdependencies and interconnections between home ownership and small business finance.

7.3.2   Key Characteristics of SCF Small Businesses

Turning to the small businesses themselves, tables 7.2A and 7.2B display six key characteristics of small businesses owned and actively managed by households in 2007 and 2010. Table 7.2A separates established from new firms, while table 7.2B distinguishes between small businesses with no employees and those with a least one employee. Because it is clear that the means of the variables are often strongly affected by observations in the upper tail of a given distribution, most of our discussion will focus on the median of a given variable.

Each of the four measures of size in table 7.2A suggests that the established small businesses in the SCF are quite small. In both years, the median number of employees is only one and even the 90th percentile is a modest fourteen employees. Median annual income (profits) in 2007 is only $41,000 based on median sales (revenues) of $119, 000, and the median value of the firm is just $110,000. In addition, it is clear that the Great Recession had a substantial effect, with median real income (business income) falling 51 percent and median total revenues (business sales) by 33 percent between 2007 and 2010.

Except for the median number of employees (one), the size measures of

---

30. This interpretation is supported by all of the results except those for households in 2007 and 2010 whose small businesses have no employees.

Table 7.2A   **Key characteristics of primary SBs actively managed by HHs**

	2007				2010			
	Mean	Median	P25	P90	Mean	Median	P25	P90
Established SB								
No. employees	8.3	1	0	14	8.6	1	0	14
Bus. income	523	41	13	500	417	20	2	300
Bus. sales	2,029	119	31	2,000	6,294	80	23	2,100
Bus. value	2,841	110	15	3,846	2,267	72	10	2,433
HH bus. loan	0.131				0.129			
Amt. (% of sales)	1.28[a]	0.145	0.03	2.24	6.38	0.227	0.067	5.4
New SB								
No. employees	5.3[a]	1	0	9	1.5[b]	1	0	4
Bus. income	124[b]	3.5	0	100	41[b]	0.5	0	65
Bus. sales	968	15	1	406	217	7	0	200
Bus. value	623[b]	22	2	699	659[b]	21	1	391
HH bus. loan	0.217[b]				0.193[b]			
Amt. (% of sales)	2.10[a,b]	0.6	0.210	5.21	172.7[b]	0.5	0.30	4.5

[a]Mean significantly different from 2010 at 5 percent or greater.
[b]Mean significantly different from HHs with established SB at 5 percent or greater.

Table 7.2B   **Key characteristics of primary SBs actively managed by HHs**

	2007				2010			
	Mean	Median	P25	P90	Mean	Median	P25	P90
No emp. SB								
Age	10.2	7	2	24	10.6	9	3	28
Bus. income	244	11	2	90	269	10	0	70
Bus. sales	497	119	31	2,000	8,124	24	3	160
Bus. value	162	8	0	250	124	19	3	190
HH bus. loan	0.119[a]				0.053			
Amt. (% of sales)	3.64[a]	0.586	0.076	4.81	20.8	0.481	0.143	18.8
Emp. SB								
Age	11.9[a,b]	9	3	28	13.4	10	4	31
Bus. income	505	52	9	700	356	17	0	400
Bus. sales	2,523[b]	167	45	2,880	2,449	112	24	266
Bus. value	949[a,b]	122	34	2,000	730[b]	95	19	1,283
HH bus. loan	0.185[b]				0.209[b]			
Amt. (% of sales)	0.822[a,b]	0.250	0.033	2.00	44.2	0.302	0.077	4

[a]Mean significantly different from 2010 at 5 percent or greater.
[b]Mean significantly different from HHs with no employee SB at 5 percent or greater.

new businesses are, as expected, much smaller than those of established firms. In 2007, median profits at new small businesses were a mere $3,500, median total revenues (business sales) only $15,000, and the median value of the firm (business value) was only $22,000. The first two numbers decline to a tiny $500 and $7,000 in 2010, although reported median firm value holds fairly steady at $21,000. Moreover, while the numbers of employees at the 25th and 50th percentiles were unchanged across the two years, the number of employees at the 90th percentile declined by 56 percent. Taken together, these patterns indicate that the recession produced a shift toward smaller firms among new small businesses, a pattern not so evident among the established firms, where the number of employee measures remained unchanged. This result for new firms is consistent with the view that many workers who lost their jobs during the recession formed their own small businesses, a hypothesis we investigate more deeply in section 7.4.

The last two rows of each panel of table 7.2A provide our first glimpse of the interdependencies between small business and household finance. In both years, the indicator for whether a household has either made or guaranteed a loan to its small business is significantly smaller at the established small businesses than at the new firms. Moreover, the percentages are stable across the two years at both sets of small businesses. On average across both years, about 13 percent of established small businesses had either a loan from or a loan guaranteed by the owner-household, while about 20 percent of new small businesses had such a loan or guarantee. In another sign of the recession's effects (here lower sales for most of the distribution), the ratio of the value of this loan or guarantee, when one existed, to the firm's total sales rose substantially from 2007 to 2010 across all four measures of this ratio's distribution at the established small businesses.

The data in table 7.2B reinforce the impressions provided in table 7.2A. The three size measures continue to show that the small businesses in the SCF are typically small, and the declines in median income and sales between 2007 and 2010 were mostly severe. In both years, firms with some employees were significantly more likely to have a loan or a loan guarantee from their owner-manager household. This likelihood remained constant from 2007 to 2010 at the small businesses with employees, but fell significantly at the firms with no employees. Last, all of the firm age measures remained stable across the two years, indicating that, at least along this dimension, the two cross sections were similar.

Table 7.3 categorizes established and new small businesses (top panel) and firms with no employees versus some employees (bottom panel) into six broad industry classifications. This and the subsequent tables in this section separate firms into three groups based on the number of employees. The boundaries of the groups were defined to reflect substantive differences in the sample (e.g., the large proportion of businesses with no employees) and to ensure a substantial number of firms in each employee group.

Table 7.3   **Industry classifications (percent primary SBs actively managed by HHs)**

	2007		2010	
	Established	New	Established	New
Agricultural	7.7	2.2	7.0	5.8
Mining	21.5	11.6	14.2	11.5
Manufacturing	7.1	6.4	5.8	8.9
Wholesale/retail	11.6	20.8	15.3	14.3
Lower-tech service	13.5	19.8	17.2	11.8
Prof. services	38.7	39.2	40.6	47.7

	2007			2010		
	No employee	Employee = 1,2	Employee ≥ 3	No employee	Employee = 1,2	Employee ≥ 3
Agricultural	7.0	4.1	6.2	7.7	7.5	8.4
Mining	16.5	21.9	18.1	13.7	14.2	9.0
Manufacturing	6.7	5.9	7.8	7.0	6.0	4.9
Wholesale/retail	13.8	16.1	14.0	14.1	14.0	14.0
Lower-tech service	14.1	16.5	16.2	13.3	19.2	12.8
Prof. services	42.0	35.5	37.69	44.2	39.1	50.8

It is clear that for both established and new small businesses, for all three size classes and for both years, the "professional services" category dominates with between 36 percent and 51 percent of the firms. Indeed, among all five categories of firms, the sum of the "professional services" and the "lower technical services" categories is over 50 percent of the firms in all of the ten possible cells. Thus, service industries dominate the sample. Still, there are substantial percentages in all of the industrial classifications, including the heavier industries of mining and manufacturing. Put differently, the SCF samples represent a broad cross section of American small businesses. Overall, the data suggest a move toward professional services from 2007 to 2010. This perhaps reflects in part the relatively high rate of job loss by certain white-collar workers during the recession, a suggestion we investigate more deeply in section 7.4.[31]

Table 7.4 categorizes the small businesses by ownership structure, using the same panel structure as table 7.3. In both years, sole proprietorships dominate all categories except the largest firms in 2010, where Subchapter S is the most oft-chosen organizational structure. Sole proprietorships are especially prevalent among smaller firms and their percentage is about the

31. Autor (2010, 2) documents that job losses during the Great Recession "have been far more severe in the middle-skilled white- and blue-collar jobs than in either high-skill, white-collar jobs or in low-skill service occupations."

Table 7.4   SB ownership structure (percent of primary SBs actively managed by a HH)

	2007		2010	
	Established	New	Established	New
Sole proprietor	46.7	50.1	49.7	50.0
Subchapter S	17.4	12.2	17.0	5.2
LLC/LLP	13.8	23.9	19.4	14.9
Partnership	12.7	8.6	6.5	29.9
Other	9.4	5.2	7.5	4.0

	2007			2010		
	No employee	Employee = 1,2	Employee ≥ 3	No employee	Employee = 1,2	Employee ≥ 3
Sole proprietor	68.6	46.9	23.2	72.9	46.5	19.1
Subchapter S	11.2	13.0	23.7	5.6	11.5	29.4
LLC/LLP	14.9	16.1	19.8	16.1	26.5	25.8
Partnership	2.5	17.9	17.4	1.8	11.5	10.7
Other	2.9	4.5	15.9	3.2	3.6	15.0

same in both years across new and established small businesses. As firms grow but not necessarily become more established, corporate and partnership structures become more common. Despite these broad patterns, it is clear that small businesses chose a variety of ownership structures.

7.3.3   How Households Acquire Their Small Business

The final table in this section describes small businesses owned and actively managed by households according to how they were acquired by the household. The data in table 7.5 indicate that the vast majority of small businesses, typically over 75 percent, were started de novo by the household. However, substantial percentages of small businesses, especially those with three or more employees, were purchased by the household. Relatively few—typically less than 5 percent—were inherited.

Given the interest in the role of inheritances in the small business literature, we looked closely at the characteristics of households (and their small business) that inherited their established small business versus households that acquired their established business in another way.[32] On average, households that inherited their business had greater net worth (including equity in the small business), higher income (including business income), a smaller percent of their total net worth in home equity, and a higher level of risk aversion. In addition, small businesses that were inherited tended to be larger and less likely to have a loan that came from or was guaranteed by

32. These results are not shown in a table, but are available on request from the authors.

Table 7.5   Methods of acquiring a SB (percent of primary SBs actively managed by a HH)

	2007		2010	
	Established	New	Established	New
Bought/invest	14.5	17.5	14.6	11.1
Started	73.7	75.8	76.3	81.8
Inherited	5.9	2.5	4.0	3.2
Join/promote	5.9	4.2	5.2	3.9
	2007			2010		
	No employee	Employee = 1,2	Employee ≥ 3	No employee	Employee = 1,2	Employee ≥ 3
Bought/invest	6.3	15.0	26.9	8.8	11.2	23.8
Started	86.9	80.0	54.7	86.8	80.6	60.6
Inherited	4.7	0.8	8.2	2.6	4.2	4.9
Join/promote	2.1	4.3	10.2	1.7	3.9	10.5

its owner-household. While most of these differences between the two sets of households and the two sets of small businesses seem unsurprising and reasonable, they suggest that the role of inheritances remains an interesting area for future research.

7.4   Small Business Survival, Failure, and Creation from 2007 through 2009

This section uses the 2007 SCF and its 2009 panel reinterview to examine differences between small businesses that survived and those that failed during the financial crisis and the subsequent Great Recession and to attempt to identify the key characteristics of households that started a small business during this period. As was the case in section 7.3, we present and analyze multivariate tests here; supporting univariate tables and discussion are given in appendix B.

7.4.1   Survival and Failure

The definition of small business failure is not straightforward. According to Everett and Watson (1998), the literature has used five basic measures: (a) discontinuance of ownership of the business, (b) discontinuance of the business itself, (c) bankruptcy, (d) businesses that were sold or liquidated to prevent further losses, and (e) businesses that simply could not "made a go of it."[33] The 2009 SCF asks a household if its small business "went out of business" between 2007 and the survey and the reinterview date. In

33. Everett and Watson (1998, 374).

addition, the survey allows us to exclude from this definition businesses that were sold, went public, or were transferred to another family member. Thus, our definition of failure most closely resembles the idea of failure as discontinuance of the business, not simply a change of ownership or limited only to bankruptcy.[34]

7.4.2   The Probability of Survival

Table 7.6 presents logit regression results that estimate the marginal effects of a wide array of right-hand-side variables on the probability that a firm would survive from 2007 to 2009. The independent variables are based on factors identified in the literature (see section 7.1) and discussed in appendix B. The table reports separate regressions for the pooled sample of all small businesses, and for established, new, no-employee, and firms with at least one employee. In each case, the logits estimate the relationship of variables whose values were observed in 2007 with the probability that a small business would have continued to survive in 2009.

Our primary conclusion from table 7.6 is that the factors correlated with the probability of small business survival are at best poorly understood, at least for the recent crisis and the Great Recession.[35] Very few of the marginal effects are statistically significant, even in the regressions with the largest number of observations. On balance, these results are a challenge to several conventional views of what determines small business survival or failure and thus strongly suggest that this is an area that warrants additional research.

That being said, clues to where research is most needed, and where it is less so, can be gleaned from an attempt to extract patterns from the results for this period. A household's net worth is the variable most consistently correlated with the probability of a firm's survival. As in previous studies, ceteris paribus, higher net worth was generally correlated with an increased probability of survival. Older owner-managers were sometimes associated with increased chances of survival, although the under thirty-five years of age indicator variable has the strongest positive marginal effect of the three age indicators that are significant. There is evidence that a partnered household was helpful, especially for new firms. Ceteris paribus, larger businesses appear to have had a greater chance of survival, although the distinction between no-employee and some employees firms does not seem to be important in this regard. Established firms with a loan or a loan guarantee from the household may have had a higher probability of survival (again reinforcing the importance of household and small business finance interdependencies), as did a firm with employees that was over five years old. And, new businesses and firms with employees that were not part of either the "profes-

---

34. Of the total number of business terminations in the 2009 SCF, 83 percent met our definition, 15 percent were sold or went public, and 2 percent disappeared for other reasons such as a divorce settlement.

35. In contrast, the univariate comparisons in appendix B suggested stronger conclusions.

Table 7.6 **Probability of survival 2007–2009**

Variable	Pooled	Established	New	No employee	Employee
Log(HH income)	–0.085	0.027	–0.870**	–0.321**	0.030
	(0.072)	(0.072)	(0.401)	(0.130)	(0.081)
Log(HHnetworth)	0.106**	0.064	0.320***	0.109	0.173***
	(0.044)	(0.062)	(0.104)	(0.071)	(0.064)
Homeowner	–0.008	0.382	0.553	0.104	0.794
	(0.442)	(0.831)	(1.086)	(0.715)	(1.421)
Age1	–0.225	14.973***	–1.167	–0.073	0.445
	(0.442)	(0.835)	(0.896)	(0.699)	(0.859)
Age2	0.513	0.994**	0.693	1.068**	0.161
	(0.337)	(0.450)	(0.713)	(0.461)	(0.577)
Educ.	–0.031	–0.108	0.157	0.076	–0.059
	(0.083)	(0.112)	(0.150)	(0.105)	(0.141)
HHpartner	0.720*	0.445	1.754**	0.583	0.401
	(0.434)	(0.593)	(0.870)	(0.613)	(0.977)
HHcredaccess	–0.235	–0.388	0.486	–0.164	0.112
	(0.595)	(0.638)	(1.470)	(0.672)	(1.041)
Riskpref	–0.210	0.093	–0.744	0.026	–0.778*
	(0.257)	(0.354)	(0.634)	(0.324)	(0.422)
Log(businncome)	0.039	0.104*	–0.009	0.085	–0.019
	(0.036)	(0.062)	(0.071)	(0.052)	(0.070)
Log(busvalue)	0.052	0.102*	–0.019	0.053	0.094
	(0.035)	(0.058)	(0.061)	(0.046)	(0.089)
Emp.	0.944**	0.960	1.215		
	(0.451)	(0.795)	(0.913)		
HHbusloan	0.314	1.296*	0.178	0.817	0.185
	(0.396)	(0.782)	(0.807)	(0.543)	(0.593)
Corp	0.306	0.730	–0.024	0.188	0.311
	(0.348)	(0.632)	(0.648)	(0.522)	(0.536)
Busage5	–0.351			0.146	–1.328**
	(0.372)			(0.468)	(0.545)
Industry dummies	Y	Y	Y***	Y	Y*
Pseudo R²	0.26	0.28	0.54	0.36	0.27
N	1,018	835	183	239	777

Notes: Logistic regressions of a 2007–2009 survival dummy on 2007 household and business variables. Industry dummies are deemed significant if at least one of the industry dummies is significantly different at the indicated level from the professional services industry (excluded dummy). Survival is defined as the continued ownership of the business by the household. Failed is defined as a termination of the business itself: "went out of business" to P09502 in the 2009 SCF. Marginal effects reported. Standard errors in parentheses.

***Significant at the 1 percent level.

**Significant at the 5 percent level.

*Significant at the 10 percent level.

sional services" or the "mining and construction" industry appeared more likely to survive. Higher-income households were associated with a lower probability of survival at new and no-employee small businesses. This curious result reinforces our earlier suggestion that the role of household income in understanding small business finance deserves further research.

Perhaps the variables that are never correlated with the probability of survival are as interesting as those that are correlated sometimes. Home ownership, education, access to credit, and organizational form are never significant. In addition, a household's degree of risk preference is only significant in the employee regression, where lower risk aversion is associated with an increased probability of survival. All of these results challenge either the conventional wisdom or the existing literature.

7.4.3   Creation

Our discussion of some of the characteristics of small businesses in the SCF conjectured that workers who lost their jobs during the recession may have responded in part by starting their own small business. We now pursue this hypothesis more deeply using the 2007 SCF and its 2009 panel reinterview. Using the two surveys, we can identify households that did not have a business in 2007 but started a business between these two years that survived at least until 2009. We compare their characteristics with those of households that neither started nor owned a business during the same period.

The Probability of Creation

Table 7.7 presents the results of two sets of logit regressions. The first set, contained in the "panel" column, relates the probability that a household would start a new small business between 2007 and 2009 to the variables in univariate table 7B.6. With the exception of the "Unemp. 12 mo. 2009" variable, all of the right-hand-side variables are 2007 values of a given variable. Thus, this logit is "forward looking" in that it estimates the relationship between the current values of the right-hand-side variables and *future business creation* by the household. The second set, contained in the next two columns, replicates as well as we can the cross-section regressions for new small businesses reported in the (1) columns of table 7.1A. Thus, these logits are "backward looking" in that they estimate the relationship between the current values of the right-hand-side variables and *past business creation* by the household. Put differently, both sets of regressions investigate what household characteristics are associated with the probability that a household will start a small business, but each approaches the issue from a different direction.

Looking first at the forward-looking panel regression, households were, ceteris paribus, more likely to start a small business during the heart of the crisis and the Great Recession if in 2007 they were more educated, had higher income, had access to credit, and if the head of the household had

Table 7.7   Probability of starting new small business during crisis (given no SB in 2007)

Variable	Panel	Cross section 2009	Cross section 2007
HH educ.	0.285**	0.475***	0.229***
	(0.128)	(0.158)	(0.089)
Log(HH income)	0.946**	0.219	−0.039
	(0.368)	(0.434)	(0.208)
Age	−0.006	−0.046**	−0.053***
	(0.021)	(0.020)	(0.012)
Riskpref	−0.558	−0.820**	−0.333*
	(0.348)	(0.370)	(0.194)
HH partner	0.503	2.038***	1.675***
	(0.610)	(0.768)	(0.470)
Log(networth)	−0.029	0.255**	0.268
	(0.097)	(0.120)	(0.163)
Home to networth	0.027	−1.649*	−0.812
	(0.928)	(0.965)	(0.588)
HH cred. access	1.577*		
	(0.881)		
Unemp. 12 mo. 2007	−0.361	−0.223	0.578
	(0.824)	(0.992)	(0.499)
Unemp. 12 mo. 2009	2.241***	1.679**	
	(0.627)	(0.826)	
Pseudo R^2	0.10	0.11	0.14
N	2,712	2,919	3,284

Notes: The first column reports the results of a logistic regression of a 2007–2009 SB creation dummy on 2007 household characteristics and a 2009 dummy for unemployment for the HH in the previous twelve months from the time of the 2009 interview. Sample is limited to only those HHs that did not own a SB in 2007. The second column reports the results of a logistic regression of 2009 ownership of a new SB on contemporaneous 2009 household characteristics. In this case SB = 1 if the household owns a SB two years or younger and SB = 0 if the household does not own a SB in 2009. Due to data limitations, HH Cred Access cannot be constructed in 2009. The third column reports a regression comparable to the second column using 2007 variables. In percentage probability terms, not decimal. Standard errors in parentheses.
***Significant at the 1 percent level.
**Significant at the 5 percent level.
*Significant at the 10 percent level.

been unemployed at any time in the twelve months before the 2009 SCF. However, none of the other right-hand-side variables are statistically significant, including, perhaps most notably, a household's net worth.

Turning to the backward-looking cross-section regressions, our first observation is that, using the 2009 reinterview data, we cannot replicate the regressions reported in table 7.1A. This is because, as was discussed in section 7.2, the 2009 SCF did not collect all of the data collected in 2007 and 2010. However, we can come close: the first seven right-hand-side variables given in table 7.7 also appear in table 7.1A.

Of the fourteen coefficients listed for these variables in the two cross-section regressions, twelve are both the same sign and statistically significant as in table 7.2A. Thus, the cross-section regressions in table 7.13 tell essentially the same story as the cross-section regressions of table 7.2A.

When we compare the panel and cross-section results, the consistency between the two approaches is seen to be problematic. Of the seven variables common to all three regressions, only education is the same sign (positive) and statistically significant in all three.

A household's income is positive and significant in the panel regression of table 7.7, but insignificant in both cross sections. On the one hand, this asymmetry may reflect the logical possibility that ex ante households with more income are more likely to start a small business because they have the cash flow to do so, but realized income is irrelevant for households that have started a small business in the previous two or three years. On the other hand, the asymmetry may merely reflect tax avoidance or the fact that we do not understand the interrelationships between a household's income and its willingness to start a small business. Given the difficulty we have had in this study interpreting the role of income, we think these results deserve more research in this area.

Perhaps the most interesting new results in table 7.7 are those for the unemployment history variables. Unemployment by the head of household in the twelve months before the crisis (2007) is uncorrelated with the probability that the household will start a small business in all three regressions. However, a household head's unemployment status in the twelve months prior to the 2009 SCF is, ceteris paribus, positively correlated with its probability of starting a small business in both the panel and the 2009 cross-section regressions. Thus, both sets of regressions support our conjecture that unemployment during the crisis and the Great Recession prompted some households to start a small business. The fact that unemployment prior to the crisis is irrelevant in the 2007 cross section suggests that the role of unemployment in small business creation may have been unusually strong during the crisis and the Great Recession. However, before reaching this conclusion, more research is warranted.

Our comparisons of these two sets of model results lead us to one more conclusion: both cross-section and panel data are highly valuable for analyzing these types of issues and other topics in household and small business economics. The 2009 panel SCF was collected as a result of a financial crisis and the ensuing Great Recession, but we believe the analyses presented here have more than proved that panel data should be collected on a more regular basis. Only panel data offer a reasonable hope of distinguishing changes as a result of changed circumstances from changes caused by composition effects or shifts within groups.

7.5   Small Business Finance in 2009 and 2010

This section uses the expanded small business data collected on the 2010 SCF and the smaller number of equivalent items included in the 2009 reinterview to investigate small business finance topics during these years. We begin by discussing small business access to credit in 2009 and 2010, and conclude by describing the types of financial institutions and broader financial services used by small businesses using data available only in 2010.

7.5.1   Access to Credit

Table 7.8 characterizes established and new (top panel) and no-employee and some employees (bottom panel) small businesses according to a broad definition of their access to credit in 2009 and 2010. Each panel contains five measures of credit availability. The first row gives the percent of small businesses that applied for credit, and the second the percent of these firms either fully or partly denied credit. The combination of these rows provides a conventional view of credit availability. The third row provides a less conventional perspective by showing the percent of small businesses that wanted credit but did not apply because they *expected to be denied*, even though they had not been denied credit in the previous five years.[36] The fourth measure is the sum of rows 1 and 3, and provides a measure of total demand, that is, the percent of small businesses that wanted credit whether or not they applied. Row 5 gives the percent of row 4 small businesses (i.e., those that wanted credit) whose credit needs were not fully met.

Starting again with established firms and first looking at rows 1 and 2, the conventional measures of credit access, while the percent of firms that applied for credit is remarkably stable across 2009 and 2010, the percent that were denied rose substantially in 2010 (from 11 percent to 20 percent). However, the other measures of credit access suggest that credit conditions did not change much for established small businesses between the two years. The percent of firms that wanted credit but did not apply because they expected to be denied actually fell slightly. Meanwhile, the percentage of small businesses wanting credit and the percentage of small businesses that had unfulfilled credit needs increased by small amounts.

Turning to the new firms, it is clear that credit supply constraints were more severe for new than for established small businesses, especially in 2009. For example, in 2009 60 percent of new firms said their credit needs were unfulfilled while 36 percent of established businesses said this was the case. This difference narrowed in 2010, but this percentage was still substantially larger at the new firms. However, the percent of new firms that were fully or partly denied fell by almost 16 percentage points between 2009 and 2010. Total demand for credit (line 4) fell from 40 percent to 25 percent of firms, and the percent of firms that said their credit needs were unfulfilled fell from 60 percent to 46 percent. On balance, these data suggest that credit access for new firms actually improved between 2009 and 2010.

---

36. Thus we exclude from this measure small businesses that might not be considered creditworthy because they had been denied credit in the recent past.

Table 7.8   Access to credit in 2009 and 2010 (percent of primary SBs actively managed by a HH)

	2009		2010	
	Established	New	Established	New
1. Applied for credit	21.9	26.8	25.3	17.7
2. Applied, but fully or partially denied	11.3	41.0	19.8	25.4
3. Wanted credit but did not apply b/c expected denial	8.3	12.8	7.9	6.9
4. Wanted credit	30.2	39.6	33.2	24.6
5. Credit needs unfulfilled	35.7	60.0	38.9	46.3

	2009			2010		
	No employee	Employee =1,2	Employee ≥ 3	No employee	Employee =1,2	Employee ≥ 3
1. Applied for credit	9.9	21.9	38.4	10.5	21.5	44.7
2. Applied, but fully or partially denied	27.5	17.3	20.8	19.7	25.0	19.0
3. Wanted credit but did not apply b/c expected denial	7.6	6.8	13.8	4.9	8.9	10.2
4. Wanted credit	17.5	28.7	52.2	15.4	30.4	54.9
5. Credit needs unfulfilled	59.0	36.9	41.7	45.3	47.0	34.0

A different perspective is provided in the bottom panel of table 7.8. The percent of firms applying for credit increased substantially with firm size in both years while the percent of these firms that were fully or partially denied hovered around 20–25 percent for all size classes in both years. The percent of firms that wanted credit but did not apply because they expected to be denied increased with firm size in both years. Thus, total demand for credit (line 4) increased substantially with firm size, consistent with the partial demand reflected in line 1. Importantly, the percent of small businesses that said their credit demands were unfulfilled declined substantially with firm size in both years. Thus, credit conditions were unsurprisingly tighter for the smallest firms. However, credit conditions appeared to improve, especially for the smallest firms, in 2010. The percent of no-employee firms that said their credit needs were unfulfilled fell from 59 percent in 2009 to 45 percent in 2010.

7.5.2   Reasons Given for Actual or Expected Credit Denial

Both the 2009 and 2010 SCFs asked respondents to identify the reasons for either being denied (given the small business applied for credit) or expecting to be denied credit (given the small business did not apply for credit). Since owner-managers were not prompted with possible reasons, the survey recorded a large variety of open-ended responses that were classified using a common coding framework. However, respondents were allowed to give only one, and presumably the most important, reason for actual or expected denial. We have further aggregated the reasons given into eight categories, and the percentages of small businesses identifying a reason in each of these categories are displayed in table 7.9. In both years, the reasons given range from primarily internal factors such as credit history and a poor balance sheet to external causes such as a weak economy and government regulation. Because of sample size limitations, table 7.9 does not separate firms into established, new, or by size.

Several interesting patterns emerge from table 7.9. In both years, some type of "credit history" issue is typically the dominant reason given for either the denial or expected denial of credit.[37] Credit history is closely followed by reasons associated with the type or size of the business[38] or business viability (especially in 2009) for why credit was denied. However, in both years a "poor balance sheet" is also a major reason given for the actual and the expected denial of credit. Indeed, except for a "weak economy," cited somewhat frequently for the expected denial of credit in both years, the other

37. Small business owners appear to have difficulty separating business from personal credit history and thus we combine these reasons into one generic credit history category. The evident difficulty of separating business and personal credit history supports the view that for many business owners, household and business finance are closely intertwined.
38. This included reasons such as the small business was too small, a "bad fit," or the "wrong type."

Table 7.9   **Reasons credit either was or was expected to be denied in 2010 (percent of responses)**

	2009		2010	
	Denied	Expected denied (given not denied)	Denied	Expected denied (given not denied)
Poor balance sheet	9.8	26.6	36.0	25.3
Credit history	28.1	39.4	38.9	32.1
Type/size of business	21.3	7.9	14.2	10.0
Viability of business	33.7	5.6	10.8	16.4
Informational problems	0.0	0.0	0.0	4.5
Weak economy	4.5	19.8	0.0	10.4
Government regulation	2.0	0.6	0.0	0.6
Other	0.6	0.1	0.0	0.8

reasons listed in table 7.9 are of minor importance compared with the first four reasons. For example, "government regulation" is rarely cited as a reason. On balance, the data in table 7.9 suggest that reasons primarily internal to the firm are by far the most common factors cited by small businesses for their actual or expected denial of credit over these two years.

7.5.3   Relationship Finance

As discussed in our literature review, the relationship between a small business and its financial institutions, especially its commercial bank(s), has been a core concern of small business finance research. In addition, some of the primary issues in relationship finance, such as the role of commercial banks versus other financial intermediaries and the importance of local versus nonlocal banks, are central to the methodology used by federal agencies in their antitrust analysis. The 2010 SCF allows us to examine some of the most important issues identified in this research and relevant to policy analysis.

Table 7.10 provides several perspectives on the importance of credit relationships in 2010 for established versus new small businesses (top panel) and firms with no employees versus those with some employees (bottom panel). The first four rows of each panel provide a short-run view by focusing on relationships that existed over the previous year. Rows 5 through 8 provide an intermediate-run perspective by examining relationships over either the previous five years or since the business came into existence.

The short-run importance of credit relationships with commercial banks, often viewed as having a comparative advantage in supplying credit to small businesses, is explored in rows 1 and 2 of each panel. The first row reports the percent of the "primary" small businesses owned and actively managed by a household that at some point over the previous year had a business loan, a business line of credit, or a personal loan used for business purposes with a

Table 7.10   **Credit relationships of SBs 2010 (percent of primary SBs actively managed by a HH)**

	Established	New
1. Bank credit (ex. CC)	19.8	16.8
2. Bank credit (in CC)	38.6	34.6
3. Credit relation (ex CC)	23.8	24.0
4. Credit relation (in CC)	39.8	37.2
5. Cred. rel. or bus. appl. for cred. in prev. five yrs. (ex CC)	36.0	32.9
6. Cred. rel. or bus. appl. for cred. in prev. five yrs. (in CC)	47.6	43.2
7. Cred. rel. or bus./HH appl. for cred. in prev. five yrs. (ex CC)	79.9	86.2
8. Cred. rel. or bus./HH appl. for cred. in prev. five yrs. (in CC)	83.6	88.1

	No employee	Employee = 1,2	Employee ≥ 3
1. Bank credit (ex. CC)	8.8	16.7	35.1
2. Bank credit (in CC)	27.0	36.0	55.1
3. Credit relation (ex CC)	12.2	24.5	40.3
4. Credit relation (in CC)	27.4	38.4	57.5
5. Cred. rel. or bus. appl. for cred. in prev. five yrs. (ex CC)	18.9	36.6	57.9
6. Cred. rel. or bus. appl. for cred. in prev. five yrs. (in CC)	31.2	46.9	67.1
7. Cred. rel. or bus./HH appl. for cred in prev. five yrs. (ex CC)	78.5	80.6	87.0
8. Cred. rel. or bus./HH appl. for cred in prev. five yrs. (in CC)	82.4	83.4	89.6

Notes: 1. Reflects the presence of a personal bank loan used for business purposes, business bank loan, or business line of credit in questions regarding services used at the primary financial institution or sources of external finance for the ongoing operation or expansion of the SB in the previous year; 2. reflects 1. plus the use of a credit card; 3. reflects 1. plus the use of an "other" credit relationship for external financing of the SB; 4. reflects 3. plus credit cards; 5. reflects 3. plus any SBs that applied for credit in the lesser of the previous five years or since existence; 6. reflects 5. plus credit cards; 7. reflects 5. plus any SBs where the owner/manager HH applied for credit in the lesser of the previous five years or since existence; 8. reflects 7. plus credit cards.

commercial bank, in all cases excluding credit cards. Looking first at the top panel, almost 20 percent of the established firms and 17 percent of the new firms had such a bank credit relationship in 2010. Adding credit cards (CC in table 7.10) to the mix essentially doubles these percentages for both groups. Turning to the bottom panel, it is clear that the importance of bank credit relationships increases with firm size. Some 35 percent of the largest firms report such a relationship, but only 9 percent of the no-employee firms do. Credit cards appear more important for the smallest firms—the percentage reporting a credit relationship triples for no-employee firms but only rises by a factor of 0.6 percent at the largest small businesses.

While our results indicate that business credit cards are an important part of a small business' banking relationship, we cannot tell if they are used primarily for credit or transactions purposes. However, using the Kauffman Firm Survey, Robb and Robinson (2012) found they are very important for transaction purposes, much less so as a source of credit. Using the National Survey of Small Business Finances, Mach and Wolken (2006) found that while a substantial percent of small businesses use credit cards, it is unclear how important they are as a source of credit. Whatever the primary role of credit cards for small businesses, our results are consistent with the conventional wisdom that commercial banks are an important source of credit for small businesses.

Rows 3 and 4 add "other" external sources of credit to the definition of a credit relationship. Such sources include other types of insured depositories (e.g., savings banks and credit unions) and nonbank financial institutions (e.g., finance companies and mortgage banks). Comparing rows 1 and 3 in both panels shows that while nonbank sources contribute to the supply of credit for small businesses, on balance nonbanks appear (consistent with the conventional wisdom) to be a modest source of funds. For example, among the established firms, the percent reporting a credit relationship rises from 20 percent to 24 percent, and among the largest firms the percent rises from 35 percent to 40 percent. Consistent with the life cycle theory of small business finance, the role of nonbank sources at new businesses is more substantial than at the established businesses. Row 4 in the bottom panel reinforces the increasing importance of credit relationships as a firm grows. Some 58 percent of the largest firms report a short-term credit relationship, but only 27 percent of the no-employee businesses do so.

Rows 5 through 8 give some insight into the importance of intermediate-run credit relationships. Because the questions behind these tabulations do not distinguish bank from nonbank sources of funds, the responses build on the bank and nonbank relationships as defined in row 3. Comparing rows 5 and 3 in both panels, it is clear that a longer-run perspective increases the importance of credit to small businesses. For example, among the established firms, the percent reporting a credit relationship jumps from 24 percent in the short run to 36 percent in the intermediate run, and among the largest firms, the percent rises from 40 percent to 58 percent. Row 6 adds credit cards and the data continue to support the importance of credit cards, but they play a smaller role in the intermediate run than in the short run. This suggests that credit cards are perhaps used more for transactions purposes than as a permanent source of credit.

Rows 7 and 8 of table 7.10 add to the numerator used in rows 5 and 6 the number of households owning and actively managing a small business in 2010 that applied for credit as a household. While such credit may not have been used for business purposes, we include this calibration because the often close and complex interdependencies between household and small business finance suggest "credit independence" is not necessarily the case. Put differently, the calculations shown in rows 7 and 8 give the broadest possible indication of the importance of credit to small businesses that the SCF can provide. These data show that credit access is important to the vast majority of small businesses and the households that own and manage them. All of the cells in rows 7 and 8 of both panels are over, and typically well over, 75 percent.

Table 7.11   **Primary financial institution of a SB in 2010 (percent of primary SBs actively managed by a HH)**

	Established	New	
Commercial bank	76.7	76.5	
Savings bank	7.5	5.2	
Credit union	5.4	8.9	
Fin./loan co.	0.8	0.5	
Brokerage	0.2	0.2	
Mortgage co.	0.3	0.0	
Other	0.0	0.0	
None	8.7	8.8	
	No employee	Employee = 1,2	Employee ≥ 3
Commercial bank	70.4	78.3	84.1
Savings bank	3.1	7.0	6.8
Credit union	11.3	7.5	2.7
Fin./loan co.	1.0	0.4	0.7
Brokerage	0.4	0.1	0.0
Mortgage co.	0.1	0.7	0.0
Other	0.0	0.0	0.0
None	13.6	6.1	4.5

7.5.4   Primary Financial Institution

Table 7.11 shows the percentages of small businesses that identified various types of financial institutions as their "primary financial institution" in 2010. As with previous similar tables, established versus new firms are shown in the top panel and no-employee versus some employees firms are given in the bottom panel. Overwhelming majorities of both established and new small businesses and businesses across all size classes identified a commercial bank as their primary financial institution. At the low end of the spectrum, 70 percent of the smallest new businesses said a commercial bank was their primary financial institution. At the top end, 84 percent of the largest new firms did so. When we add the percentages for savings banks and credit unions to the commercial bank percentages, the percentages jump to between 85 percent and 94 percent. Having said this, it is noteworthy that almost 9 percent of both established and new small businesses and almost 14 percent of the no-employee businesses did not identify any financial institution type as their primary financial institution (the last row in each panel). Around 5 percent of the other size classes responded similarly. Still, it is clear that insured depositories, and especially commercial banks, are by far the most important financial institutions for the vast majority of small businesses.

7.5.5   Key Financial Services

Table 7.12A identifies the most important financial services used by a small business at its primary financial institution (almost always a com-

Table 7.12A   **Financial services used by a SB at its primary financial institution in 2010 (percent of primary SBs actively managed by a HH)**

	Established	New	
Business checking	83.4	76.2	
Business savings	24.4	26.0	
Business line of credit	16.0	13.9	
Business mortgage	5.7	1.8	
Business credit card	19.2	16.3	
Business payroll	14.5	22.3	
None	3.7	6.9	

	No employee	Employee = 1,2	Employee ≥ 3
Business checking	73.2	84.3	90.9
Business savings	17.9	22.5	37.6
Business line of credit	7.1	12.3	31.7
Business mortgage	1.8	5.9	7.7
Business credit card	12.6	16.4	29.7
Business payroll	14.6	17.2	18.3
None	7.2	3.2	1.9

mercial bank), and table 7.12B examines whether small businesses tend to bundle, or cluster, their use of financial services at these institutions. Looking at table 7.12A, it is clear that the vast majority (over 75 percent) of both established and new firms use a business checking account at their primary institution. In addition, the incidence of use increases with business size, with 73 percent of even the smallest firms saying they use a business checking account. Indeed, use of each service increases with firm size. Business savings accounts are cited much less often than checking accounts, but still relatively frequently by all of the six groupings of small businesses. On balance, it is clear that the supply of deposit services is a central function of financial intermediaries for small businesses.

The data in table 7.12A reinforce the importance of credit services to small businesses. For both established and new firms, business lines of credit and (as in table 7.10) business credit cards appear to be the most important credit services. This impression is reinforced when the data are arrayed by firm size. For example, 32 percent of the largest firms and 7 percent of the smallest firms report having a business line of credit. Business credit cards are used by 30 percent of the largest small businesses and 13 percent of the smallest firms. In contrast, business mortgages are used by very few new and no-employee firms, although their use increases to almost 6 percent by established firms and to almost 8 percent by the largest small businesses.[39]

In addition to deposit and credit services, the data in table 7.12A indicate that business payroll services, a type of payments service, are important

39. A business mortgage is any mortgage owed by the small business.

Table 7.12B   Number of financial services used by a SB at its primary financial institution in 2010 (given at least 1)

	Established	New
1 service	41.7	34.4
2 services	35.3	35.3
> 2 services	23.0	30.4
At least 1 credit and 1 deposit service	33.7	38.5

	No employee	Employee = 1,2	Employee ≥ 3
1 service	47.3	40.0	37.9
2 services	33.1	35.9	33.1
>2 services	19.1	24.1	29.0
At least 1 credit and 1 deposit service	30.4	59.8	41.0

to some small businesses, and more important to new than to established firms. In addition, 15 percent of the smallest firms report using business payroll services, a proportion that rises only to 18 percent at the largest small businesses.

The data in table 7.12B are somewhat ambiguous regarding whether small businesses tend to cluster their use of financial services at their primary financial institution. In this sense, these data are not a strong reinforcement of the importance of relationship finance. For example, only 23 percent of established firms and 30 percent of new businesses say they use more than two services at their primary institution, while 42 percent of established and 34 percent of new firms say they use only one service. When firms are arrayed by size, the data remain ambiguous. Thus, the extent of clustering of financial services and its importance for relationship finance and antitrust analysis warrants future research.[40]

7.5.6   Local Banking Offices

Table 7.13 addresses the final small business finance issue to which this chapter contributes: the importance of local banking offices to small businesses. The table gives the mean, median, and 25th and 90th percentiles of the distribution of miles between a small business and the nearest office of its primary financial institution in 2010, once again separating the firms into six groups.[41] It is clear that, according to this metric, local banking offices remain highly important to both established and new small businesses and

40. Bank antitrust analysis at the US Department of Justice and the banking agencies assumes small businesses consume a cluster of services at their geographically local depository institution.
41. We cannot say if the primary financial institution is a small, medium, or large firm. However, as already discussed, we can say the primary financial institution is almost always a commercial bank.

Table 7.13   **Distance (miles) to primary financial institution from SB in 2010**

	Mean	Median	P25	P90
		2010		
Established	5.04	2	0	12
New	6.13	3	0	15
0 employees	5.06	2	0	12
1,2 employees	5.08	2	0	11
≥ 3 employees	5.91	2	0	15

Note: Differences not significant at $p < 0.10$.

across all size classes of firms. For example, the median distance across all the groupings of small businesses is never more than three miles, and the mean distance ranges from a low of five miles (for established and the two smallest size classes) to a maximum of six miles (for new and the largest small businesses). Even the 90th percentile distances only range from twelve to fifteen miles.

7.6 Summary

This section summarizes our most important findings within the context of a unified narrative of the experiences of small businesses owned and actively managed by households over the financial crisis and the Great Recession. It also suggests key areas needing further research and recommends additions and revisions to existing data.

7.6.1 The SCFs are a Rich Source of Small Business Data

The SCFs are rich and underused sources of information on small businesses and the households that own and actively manage them. Indeed, SCF data are unique in several important ways, including:

1. Having three surveys conducted between 2007 and 2010, one of which is a panel;
2. containing extensive data on the close association between small business and household finance;
3. including households that do not own a small business; and
4. collecting a substantial amount of information on small businesses' use of financial institutions and services.[42]

While it is difficult to benchmark precisely the SCF data with US Census data on small businesses, it is clear that the small businesses in the SCF represent a broad cross section of firms with regard to size, age, industrial clas-

42. Of course, the 2013 and subsequent SCFs will also have many of these advantages.

sification, ownership structure, and method of acquisition by the household. The SCF and census data appear to coincide well for small businesses with at least one employee, but diverge for firms with no employees.

7.6.2   The Financial Crisis and Great Recession Hurt Small Businesses

Our examination of the SCF data over the period just before, during, and just after the financial crisis and the ensuing Great Recession revealed a complex picture of small businesses and their owner-managers. The financial crisis and the Great Recession severely affected the vast majority of both established and new small business. For example, between 2007 and 2010, median real revenues and profits fell by 33 percent and 51 percent, respectively.

The 2009 and 2010 SCFs indicate that while during the crisis and the Great Recession credit supply conditions were a concern for both established and new small businesses, constraints were much more severe at new firms. For example, in 2009 60 percent of new firms said their credit needs were unfulfilled while 36 percent of established firms said this was the case. In addition, credit conditions were tighter for the smallest firms. Credit supply improved by 2010 for both established and new firms and for both small businesses with no employees and those with at least one employee.

Households gave a variety of reasons for their small business either being denied credit or expecting it to be denied credit. In general, reasons primarily internal to the firm were the most common factors cited for their actual or expected denial of credit. For example, in both 2009 and 2010, some type of credit history issue was typically the dominant reason given for either the denial or expected denial of credit. Reasons associated with the type or size of the business or its poor balance sheet were also cited frequently. Mostly external factors, such as a weak economy or government regulation, were given much less often.

7.6.3   Small Business and Household Finance are Intimately Connected

The interdependencies and other interactions between the finances of small businesses and their owner-manager households are numerous and complex and continue to be an important area for research. The vast majority of small businesses in the SCFs, typically over 75 percent, were started by the household, and relatively few were inherited. In addition, substantial percentages of households made or guaranteed a loan to their small business. These percentages were stable across 2007 and 2010 and were more important for new small businesses than for established firms. On average, about 20 percent of new small businesses and 13 percent of established businesses had such a loan or guarantee. Established firms had a higher probability of survival over 2007–2009 if they had such a loan or guarantee. In addition, households that had access to credit were more likely to start a small business over this period.

Multivariate statistical tests show the importance of distinguishing between established and new firms when trying to identify the characteristics of households that have a small business. For example, in both 2007 and 2010, a household was more likely to have an established small business if it had (a) higher net worth, (b) less of its net worth in home equity, (c) a partner, and (d) access to credit.

In contrast, while factors (a), (c), and (d) were also significantly correlated in both years with the probability a household had a new firm, in both years a household was also more likely to have a new small business if it were (a) younger, (b) more educated, and (c) less risk averse.

While all of these results are interesting, many reinforce the existing literature (e.g., the importance of household net worth and access to credit, and personal characteristics such as age, education, and risk attitude) and some deserve further investigation (e.g., the consistently negative or zero correlation of household income with the probability of having a small business and the positive correlation of being partnered), the home equity correlations are especially intriguing and are uniquely well suited to being examined using the SCF. Our research is consistent with the simultaneous existence of two interpretations of the data. First, conditional on having housing assets, we find that tapping into home equity via any type of mortgage is positively associated with having a small business. This result is consistent with the conventional wisdom that many small business owners use their home as collateral for loans that support their business. Second, conditional on the amount of the mortgages supported by a home, we find that holding a larger proportion of total net worth in housing is a negative signal of small business ownership. This suggests the new conclusion that nonhousing forms of net worth may, at the margin, be more valuable to the small business owner, perhaps because they are more liquid.

7.6.4   Laid-Off Workers Responded in Part by Starting Small Businesses

Our results indicate that workers who lost their jobs during the Great Recession often started their own small business. Multivariate tests using the 2007–2009 panel SCFs show that households were more likely to start a small business during the heart of the crisis and the Great Recession if in 2007 they had (a) higher income, (b) access to credit, (c) more education, and (d) the head of household had been unemployed sometime in the year before the 2009 reinterview. In addition, the relatively high rate of job loss by certain segments of white-collar workers during the Great Recession is consistent with SCF data that indicate a trend between 2007 and 2010 toward the creation of small businesses in the professional services industrial classification.

In contrast to our analysis of new small businesses formation using backward-looking cross-section data, the forward-looking estimations using the 2009 panel reinterview of 2007 SCF respondents find no correlation of household small business creation with the household's net worth, ratio of home equity to net worth, risk preferences, partnership status, and age. However, both panel and cross-section results identify a positive correlation for education and unemployment status in the twelve months before 2009. While the reasons for the asymmetries between the panel and the cross-section results are not always clear, we believe our analyses of both strongly indicate that both types of information are highly valuable for researching the topics addressed in this chapter and many other issues in household and small business economics.

7.6.5   Small Business Survival Factors are Poorly Understood

Once again exploiting data from the 2007 SCF and its 2009 panel reinterview, we examined what variables 2007 values correlate with the probability that the business would survive from 2007 through the reinterview. While a variety of variables are sometimes correlated with the probability of survival, our primary conclusion is that the factors correlated with the probability of small business survival are at best poorly understood, at least for the recent crisis and Great Recession. As has been found in previous studies, higher household net worth was generally (but not in all models) correlated with increased chances of survival. This is an area in need of additional research.

7.6.6   Relationship Finance Remains Important for Small Businesses

This study reinforces the importance of relationship finance to both established and new small businesses. Indeed, access to credit is consistently significant in our multivariate tests. The SCF data for 2010 indicate that these relationships are heavily focused on commercial banks. Small businesses use deposit, credit, and sometimes payments services at their primary financial institution, institutions that are almost always a commercial bank. Business checking and savings accounts are the most important deposit services.

With respect to credit services, our research indicates that business lines of credit, business loans, and possibly bank credit cards are the most important credit services. In contrast, business mortgages are used by a small share of established small businesses and by even smaller proportions of new businesses. While access to credit is important even for some of the smallest (no-employee) firms, the incidence of credit relationships increases substantially with business size. In addition, credit relationships tend to increase in importance over time for both established and new firms and for both smaller and larger businesses.

Local banking offices remain highly important to both established and new small businesses and to small businesses of all sizes. For example, the median distance between a small business and the nearest office of its primary financial institution in 2010 across all of the groupings of small businesses used in this chapter is never more than three miles, and other moments of this distribution are consistent with our conclusion. This is consistent with the use of local markets for small business financial services in bank antitrust analysis. However, our results suggest that continuing to assume that small businesses cluster their use of financial services at their primary financial institution is more problematic.

7.6.7   Recommendations for Future Research and Improved Data

Throughout this chapter, we have identified topics that we believe are especially in need of further research. Key topics include deeper understanding of the

1. interdependencies and interconnections between household and small business finance, including the roles of home equity and household income;
2. factors that affect the creation of small businesses, including the roles of employment history and education;
3. factors that affect small business survival; and
4. factors that affect small business credit availability and their choices of financial institutions and services.

In addition, we have not investigated a number of topics that could be studied with the SCF, such as the roles of gender and race in small business finance, creation, and survival.

All of these topics, and others, require high-quality data. With respect to the future conduct of the SCF, we make three recommendations.

First, we recommend conducting future panel reinterviews. This research was aided greatly by the availability of the 2009 panel reinterview of the 2007 SCF. This was the first panel reinterview of SCF respondents since the major redesign of the survey in 1989, and was done primarily in response to the financial crisis. The costs of such efforts could be made manageable by not conducting the reinterview with the same frequency as the triannual cross-section SCF, but often enough to provide data over the full economic cycle, or by alternating cross-section and panel reinterviews.

Second, existing questions could be clarified, and perhaps augmented, to focus on how households get financing for creating their small business, how this financing evolves over time, and what types of collateral are used. As a corollary, it would be highly desirable to get a clearer picture of the criteria small businesses use to choose their primary financial institution and when in the life cycle of their business they make and may revise that decision. We understand the difficulties of adding more questions to an already long survey, but we believe significant benefits could be achieved from the combination of a small number of additional questions, some culling of less useful inquiries, and some clarification of existing questions.

Last, we recommend expansion of the sample size to as large a sample as budget realities will allow. The SCF is a unique data source for many topics of intense interest to policymakers, researchers, industry participants, and the general public that go far beyond small business finance. However, analysis of many of these topics is often limited by the small number of observations that occur as the researcher drills down in the data to gain a deeper understanding of the subject under investigation.

Appendix A
Variable Definitions

Table 7A.1   Variable definitions

HH income	Total household (HH) income
Non bus. HH income	Total HH income less income from small business (SB) and rental income
HH age	Age in years
HH educ.	Years of education
Non bus. net worth	HH net worth less value of SB
Net worth	Total HH net worth (including SB)
Homeowner	Dummy = 1 if HH owns a home
HH partnered	Dummy = 1 if HH is married or has a partner
HH cred. access	Dummy = 1 if HH has a loan from an insured depository institution (other than credit cards [CC] or educational loans)
Home to net worth	Fraction of net worth held in home equity (bounded to [0,1])
Risk prefs	Subjective self-assessment of riskiness 1–4 (larger is more risk averse)
No. employees	Number of employees at SB, including self
Bus. income	Profits of SB
Bus. sales	Sales of SB
Bus. value	Total value of SB (irrespective of HH's share)
Bus. age	Calendar year age of business
HH bus. loan	Dummy = 1 if the HH made loan to SB
Amt. (% of sales)	Given HHBusLoan = 1, the fraction of loan to bus. sales
Age1	Dummy = 1 if HH age < 35
Age2	Dummy = 1 if 35 < = HH age < 62
Emp.	Dummy = 1 if no. employees > = 3
Corp.	Dummy = 1 if SB is a limited liability corporation or S corp.
BusAge5	Dummy = 1 if business < = 5 years old
Unemp. 12 mo. 2007	Dummy = 1 if head of HH was unemployed at any time in 12 months before 2007 SCF
Unemp. 12 mo. 2009	Dummy = 1 if head of HH was unemployed at any time in 12 months before 2009 SCF
SB	Dummy = 1 if HH owns and actively manages a SB and their primary business is a nonfarm with less than 500 employees. Dummy = 0 if HH is a nonfarm HH that does not have a SB with greater than 500 employees
NEW	SB less than or equal to 3 calendar years old
ESTABLISHED	SB greater than 3 calendar years old
Survival	Dummy = 1 if SB = 0 in 2007 and the SB went out of business, = 1 if business survived until 2009 or was sold
Started SB	Dummy = 1 if SB = 0 in 2007 and SB = 1 in 2009
House	Value of all residential houses owned by HH
Mortgage	Value of all HH debt collateralized by residential housing

Note: All dollar values expressed in thousands of 2007 dollars.

Appendix B
Univariate Analysis

This appendix provides univariate results that help to form the basis for the multivariate logit regressions discussed in the text.

Households That Own and Actively Manage a Small Business

Tables 7B.1A and 7B.1B compare three sets of households with each other, between 2007 and 2010, across four dimensions. The top panel of each table provides key characteristics of households that do not own and actively manage a small business (non-SB owners) in each of the years. The middle panel of 7B.1A shows the same variables for households that own and actively manage an established small business (est. SB), and the middle panel of table 7B.1B displays the same variables for households with a small business that has no employees (no emp. SB). Similarly, the bottom panel of table 7B.1A provides comparable data for households that own and actively manage a new small business (new SB), and the bottom panel of table 7B1.B displays data for households with a small business that has at least one employee (emp. SB).[43] The number of observations is provided in each cell. Because many distributions in the SCF (and other household and small business surveys) are highly skewed, each continuous variable's mean plus its median (P50), 25th (P25), and 90th (P90) percentile values are shown.[44] For small business owners, two measures of income and net worth are provided: one includes business income or the value of the business, as appropriate, and the other does not.[45] In addition, for all three groups of households, the ratio of home equity to total net worth (including small business equity where applicable) is given. To our knowledge, this is the first study of small business owners to separate home equity from other components of net worth, a potentially important analytical advantage and a major benefit of using the SCF. Separate compilations are provided for established, new, no-employee and employee small businesses, but the concepts are not combined in order to maintain sufficient sample size. Last, when comparing variables across the two years, it is important to remember that the samples are two separate cross sections of households, not a panel of the same households.

---

43. To preserve consistency with the groups of households that own a small business, the non-SB owners grouping of households also excludes farmers as defined in the main text.

44. See, for example, Cole and Sokolyk (2013), Bricker et al. (2012), and Mach and Wolken (2006).

45. In this and all tables here and in the text dollar values are given in 2007 dollars. Our inflation deflator is the annual average of the all items Consumer Price Index Research Series Using Current Methods for urban households (CPI-U-RS), computed by the US Bureau of Labor Statistics.

Table 7B.1A   **Characteristics of HHs that own and actively manage small businesses and those that do not**

	2007				2010			
	Mean	P50	P25	P90	Mean	P50	P25	P90
Non SB owners	$N = 3{,}135$				$N = 5{,}031$			
HH income	65[a,b,c]	40	21	120	60[a,b]	38	21	114
HH age	50.2[a,b]	49	36	77	50.4[a,b]	49	36	76
HH educ.	13.1[a,b,c]	13	12	17	13.3[a,b]	13	12	17
HH net worth	345[a,b,c]	95	10	693	289[a,b]	57	6	606
Homeowner	0.61[a,b]				0.60[a,b]			
Home to net worth	0.46[a,b,c]	0.43	0	1	0.42[a,b]	0.33	0	1
HH partnered	0.55[a,b]				0.54[a,b]			
HH cred. access	0.66[a,b,c]				0.45[a,b]			
Risk prefs	3.2[a,b,c]	3	3	4	3.3[a,b]	4	3	4
Est. SB	$N = 938$				$N = 1{,}306$			
HH income	214[c]	91	58	394	168	75	44	356
Non bus. HH income	121[c]	51	13	230	101	48	13	225
HH age	51.5[c]	51	43	66	54.0	55.0	46.0	70.0
HH educ.	14.3	14	12	17	14.4	15.0	12.0	17.0
Non bus. net worth	1,433[c]	652	225	5,723	1,249	529	149	4,225
Net worth	2,405[c,(z)]	807	284	7,645	1,960	615	190	5,456
Homeowner	0.89				0.88			
Home to net worth	0.29[c]	0.23	0.10	0.71	0.26	0.19	0.05	0.66
HH partnered	0.78				0.81			
HH cred. access	0.64[c]				0.73			
Risk prefs	2.7[c]	3	2	4	2.8	3	2	4
New SB	$N = 199$				$N = 230$			
HH income	115[b]	73	43	186	107[b,(z)]	64	39	193
Non bus. HH income	91[b]	54	30	162	93	51	25	180
HH age	42.6[b]	41	34	60	42.8[b]	43	32	60
HH educ.	14.7[b]	16	13	17	14.6	16	12	17
Non bus. net worth	562[b,c]	243	107	1,394	631[b]	158	47	1,992
Net worth	802[b]	289	123	2,074	855[b]	215	64	2,362
Homeowner	0.79[b,c]				0.70[b]			
Home to net worth	0.35[b]	0.25	0.07	1	0.29	0.15	0	1
HH partnered	0.83				0.77			
HH cred. access	0.70[b,c]				0.63			
Risk prefs	2.7	3	2	4	2.8[b]	3	2	4

Note: Comparison for income and net worth measures are made in both logs and levels. Log statistical comparisons are made to mitigate the effect of outliers; (z) indicates significant for levels only and (y) indicates significant in logs only. All dollar values expressed in thousands.

[a]Mean significantly different from new SBs at 5 percent or greater.

[b]Mean significantly different from established SBs at 5 percent or greater.

[c]Mean significantly different from 2010 at 5 percent or greater.

Table 7B.1B   **Characteristics of HHs that own and actively manage small businesses and those that do not**

	2007				2010			
	Mean	P50	P25	P90	Mean	P50	P25	P90
Non SB owners	$N = 3{,}135$				$N = 5{,}031$			
HH income	65^{a,b,c}	40	21	120	60^{a,b}	38	21	114
HH age	50.2^{a,b}	49	36	77	50.4^{a,b}	49	36	76
HH educ.	13.1^{a,b,c}	13	12	17	13.3^{a,b}	13	12	17
HH net worth	345^{a,b,c}	95	10	693	289^{a,b}	57	6	606
Homeowner	0.61^{a,b}				0.60^{a,b}			
Home to net worth	0.46^{a,b,c}	0.43	0	1	0.42^{a,b}	0.33	0	1
HH partnered	0.55^{a,b}				0.54^{a,b}			
HH cred access	0.66^{a,b,c}				0.45^{a,b}			
Risk prefs	3.2^{a,b,c}	3	3	4	3.3^{a,b}	4	3	4
No emp. SB	$N = 267$				$N = 358$			
HH income	114	74	42	172	103	63	34	201
Non bus. HH income	82	47	18	135	73	42	12	160
HH age	48.2^c	48	38	63	50.3	51	41	67
HH educ.	14.5	15	13	17	14.2	14	12	17
Non bus. net worth	709^c	205	64	1,390	642	153	34	1,709
Net worth	910$^{c,(z)}$	263	88	1,926	786	217	70	1,971
Homeowner	0.81				0.80			
Home to net worth	0.39^c	0.32	0.13	1	0.32	0.22	0.01	0.86
HH partnered	0.74				0.73			
HH cred. access	0.57^c				0.70			
Risk prefs	2.8^c	3	2	4	3.0	3	2	4
Emp. SB	$N = 870$				$N = 948$			
HH income	230^{b,c}	100	60	450	186^b	82	48	395
Non bus. HH income	132^b	56	19	254	117^b	54	20	263
HH age	49.1^{b,c}	49	39	65	51.8^b	52	43	69
HH educ.	14.3	15	12	17	14.6^b	16	12	17
Non bus. net worth	1,474^b	379	128	3,506	1,404^b	385	87	3,437
Net worth	2,592^{b,c}	699	237	6,402	2,298^b	592	154	5,316
Homeowner	0.89^b				0.86^b			
Home to net worth	0.35^b	0.20	0.09	0.77	0.26^b	0.18	0.06	0.68
HH partnered	0.83^b				0.84^b			
HH cred. access	0.72^b				0.70			
Risk prefs	2.8^c	3	2	4	2.9^b	3	2	4

Note: Comparison for income and net worth measures are made in both logs and levels. Log statistical comparisons are made to mitigate the effect of outliers; (z) indicates significant for levels only and (y) indicates significant in logs only. All dollar values expressed in thousands.

[a]Mean significantly different from emp. SBs at 5 percent or greater.

[b]Mean significantly different from no emp. SBs at 5 percent or greater.

[c]Mean significantly different from 2010 at 5 percent or greater.

Households with an Established or New Small Business

The univariate comparisons in table 7B.1A suggest several broad but preliminary conclusions. First, households with established or new small businesses differ in several statistically and economically significant ways from households that do not own a small business. Indeed, the means of all of the variables listed in the top panel are significantly different at the households with established or new small businesses from the means at the non-SB owners. On average, households with either type of small business have statistically and substantially higher incomes, over a year more education, much higher net worth by either measure shown, a higher percentage of home ownership, a lower percentage of their net worth in housing if they own a home, are more likely to have a spouse or other personal partner, and lower levels of professed risk aversion. All of these differences in means exist in both 2007 and 2010. Moreover, where relevant, virtually all of these impressions hold up to comparisons of medians and the two other percentiles shown. The average age of non-SB owners in both years is statistically (but only slightly) less than that of the average owner of an established SB, but statistically higher by a little over seven years than the mean age of the owner of a new small business. However, these age results do not necessarily hold up across the three percentiles of the distribution. Last, while prior to the crisis (2007) the percent of households with access to credit is about the same across all three groups, postcrisis (2010) the percent is significantly smaller at the non-SB households.

Second, while the means of most of the variables differ in expected and significantly different ways between households with established small businesses and those with new small businesses, there are some interesting exceptions. In 2007, households owning an established business had statistically higher mean incomes than households with a new small business, and this result holds in 2010 if business income is included. However, when business income is excluded, in 2010 both sets of households have comparable average incomes. Moreover, P25 and median values of this latter measure of income are lower at established firms in both years. Clearly, households with established firms rely relatively more on income from their firms than do households owning a new business. In addition, the mean net worth of households with established firms is significantly larger than that of households with a new firm in both years across both definitions of net worth, and this result holds across the other moments of the distribution shown in table 7B.1A. The heads of households with established small businesses tended to be older, to have slightly less education, and to be more likely to own a home than the heads of households with new small businesses, but there is no difference in their probability of being partnered or their mean risk preference. When a home was owned, in 2007 the percent of total net worth held in the home was higher at households with a new small business, but this was not the case in 2010. Moreover, in both years a similar pattern is observed in the medians of this ratio. Last, before the crisis, households with an established small business were significantly less likely to have access to credit than were households with a new small business, but this (statistical) difference disappears in 2010.

The third broad impression provided by the data in table 7B.1A is that the financial crisis and the ensuing recession significantly and adversely affected both households that did not have a small business and those with an established firm. Looking first at the non-SB owners, in 2010 such households had, on average, significantly lower real income (down 8 percent) and less net worth (down 16 percent), and tended to have slightly more education and to be a little more risk averse than the comparable cross section in 2007. In addition, consistent with a steep decline in home values, the ratio of home equity to total net worth fell, as did the percent of households with access to credit.

Turning to households owning an established firm and using the income and net worth measures that include small businesses, we find that households with established small business also lost income (down 21 percent) and net worth (down 24 percent). Means of household income and net worth, excluding small business income and equity, fell 17 percent and 19 percent, respectively. The group of such households was slightly more risk averse in 2010 than in 2007, their average age increased and their mean years of education remained unchanged. Neither households with an established nor those with a new business experienced significant changes in either average home ownership or partnership rates. However, for both groups, the average ratio of home equity to total net worth (including equity in the small business) fell, and the percent of households reporting access to credit increased.

The fourth general impression from table 7B.1A is that, in contrast to the non-SB owners and the established small business household groups, many of the mean characteristics of households that successfully started a new small business in the three years before either 2007 or 2010 were little changed between those years. This result is perhaps surprising, given the differences found for the other two household groups and the obvious differences between the three years prior to 2007 versus 2010. Statistical tests of the difference in means indicate that only the level of real net worth (excluding the value of the small business) and the percentages of households that were homeowners or used bank credit changed significantly. Interestingly, the non-small business components of net worth increased by 7 percent. Less surprisingly, the percent of households owning a home declined from 79 percent in 2007 to 70 percent in 2010 and the percent reporting access to credit also declined significantly. These patterns are consistent with the view that while the financial endowment needed to start a small business rose during the crisis period, perhaps because of increased credit constraints, the ability of housing net worth to provide that endowment declined, consistent with a precipitous decline in housing prices and the overall decline in home ownership.

Comparisons of the intertemporal patterns of the medians and other percentiles of the distributions of households that started a new small business in the three years before either 2007 or 2010 suggest a more complex and perhaps less surprising story than that provided by the means. While the head of household's age and years of education remain essentially constant within the group across the two surveys, median and P25 values of both measures of household income and both measures of net worth all declined substantially from 2007 to 2010, and only increased at the 90th percentile. Thus, as was the case for the "non-SB owners" and the owners of established small businesses, it is clear that the owners of new small businesses in the lower portions of these distributions were typically much worse off in 2010 than the comparable group in 2007.

Households Whose Small Business had No or Some Employees

As was true in table 7B.1A, the univariate comparisons of table 7B.1B suggest several broad but preliminary conclusions that in most cases need to be subjected to multivariate tests. First, both no-employee and households whose small business has one or more employees differ in several statistically and economically significant ways from households that do not own a small business. Indeed, once again the means of all of the variables listed in the top panel are significantly different at the households with either type of small business than the means at the non-SB owners. On average and in both 2007 and 2010, households with either type of small business had higher incomes, more education, and greater net worth were more likely to own a home, had a lower ratio of home equity to total net worth if they owned a home, were more likely to be partnered, and had lower levels of professed risk aversion. Where relevant, virtually all of these impressions hold up to comparisons of medians and the two other percentiles shown. In 2007, households with a small business were slightly younger than households that did not own a small business, but this was not necessarily the case in 2010. In addition, in 2007 credit access did not present a uniform pattern across the household groups, but in 2010 households with a small business consistently were more likely to have access to credit.

Second, in both years the households whose small business had no employees generally differed significantly from households whose small business had at least one employee. On average in both years, households whose small business had at least one employee had higher incomes using both measures of income, were older, had higher net worth using both measures of net worth, were more likely to own a home, had a lower ratio of home equity to total net worth if they owned a home, and were more likely to be partnered. Interestingly, in 2007 the mean education level of the two groups was the same and households whose small business had at least one employee were much more likely to have credit access. However, by 2010 households with at least one employee had (slightly) more education but were no more likely to have access to credit. In both years there is little or no difference in reported risk preference between the two groups. All of these impressions are supported by the other moments of the distributions shown.

Comparisons between 2007 and 2010 of the two groups of households that owned and actively managed a small business indicate that the financial crisis and recession severely affected both groups, especially households at or below the median level of a given variable. Thus, mean real total income of households whose small business had at least one employee fell by 19 percent, and their real total net worth declined by 11 percent. Households whose small business had no employees showed no statistically significant decline in either average income measure, but both mean measures of real net worth fell significantly and substantially. The average age of both groups of households increased, and both groups reported slightly higher levels of risk aversion. Reported access to credit increased for households whose small business had no employees, but remained statistically unchanged for households whose business had at least one employee.

Small Business Survival and Failure

Table 7B.2 compares key characteristics in 2007 of small business-owning households whose firms would survive from 2007 to 2009 (top panel) with those of households whose firms would fail (bottom panel) over that period. The data in this and the next section in this appendix use the panel of households provided by the 2007 and 2009 SCFs.

In 2007, households with small businesses that would survive had higher levels of real income (both including and excluding income from the small business) and real net worth (excluding the value of the small business) than households whose firms would fail. Median household income (including income from the small business) was 43 percent greater and median nonbusiness net worth 209 percent larger at the households whose firms survived. Households whose firms would survive were 18 percentage points more likely to own a home, but the mean value of their ratio of home equity to total net worth was not significantly different from that of households whose small business failed. Also, there were no statistically significant differences in the means between the two sets of households with respect to the heads of household's age, years of education, partnership status, access to credit, and degree of risk preference.

Turning to the small businesses themselves, table 7B.3 compares key characteristics in 2007 of small businesses that would survive from 2007 to 2009 (top panel) with those of small businesses that would fail (bottom panel). Mean values of all seven characteristics shown differ significantly across the two groups, and these differences hold up across the three percentile points

Table 7B.2   Characteristics of HHs that actively manage a SB (by survival status
                    2007–2009)

	2007			
	Mean	Median	P25	P90
Survived 07–09, N = 923				
HH income	205	90	55	383
Non bus. income	121	54	17	227
HH age	49.3	49	40	65
HH educ.	14.5	16	12	17
Non bus. net worth	2,237	557	198	5,514
Home to net worth	0.31	0.23	0.10	0.92
Partnered	0.82			
HH credit access	0.89			
Homeowner	0.88			
Risk prefs	2.78	3	2	4
Failed 07–09, N = 65				
HH income	86[a]	63	48	147
Non bus. income	70[a]	50	30	135
HH age	45.9	42	35	65
HH educ.	14.6	15	12	17
Non bus. net worth	515[a]	180	34	921
Home to net worth	0.40	0.32	0.10	1
Partnered	0.74			
HH credit access	0.89			
Homeowner	0.70[a]			
Risk prefs	2.92	3	2	4

[a]Mean significantly different from open SBs at 5 percent or greater.

given. More specifically, in 2007 all four measures of firm size—number of employees, business income, total sales, and business value—are substantially larger at the businesses that would survive the next two years. In addition, the firms that would survive were older—on average by about five years—than the firms that would fail. Small businesses that would survive were slightly more likely to have a loan or financial guarantee from their owner-manager household than were the small businesses that would fail. However, consistent with the data in tables 7.2A and 7.2B, well under 25 percent of firms in either group had such a financial relationship with their owner-manager household. When such a loan or guarantee did exist, the combination of the two was a much smaller percentage of sales in 2007 (on average about one-fifth as great) at the firms that would survive.

Table 7B.4 separates the surviving and failed firms as of 2007 according to the same industry classifications used in table 7.3. While the percentages clearly differ between the two groups, only the "wholesale/retail" and the "lower-tech services" classifications appear noteworthy. Both of these

Table 7B.3   **Characteristics of 2007 primary SBs actively managed by HHs (by survival status 2007–2009)**

	2007			
	Mean	Median	P25	P90
Survived 07–09				
No. employees	8.47	1	0	14
Bus. income	501	30	5	500
Bus. sales	1,912	92	23	1,800
Bus. value	2,717	102	14	4,000
Business age	12.1	9	3	28
HH bus. loan	0.17			
Amt. (% of sales, given loan)	1.19	0.21	0.033	1.88
Failed 07–09				
No. employees	1.74[a]	0	0	2
Bus. income	28[a]	2	0	68
Bus. sales	79[a]	9	1	200
Bus. value	120[a]	10	0.2	331
Business age	7.5[a]	4	1	20
HH bus. loan	0.15[a]			
Amt. (% of sales, given loan)	5.52[a]	1.32	0.6	8.33

[a]Mean significantly different from HHs with open SBs at 95 percent or greater.

Table 7B.4   **Surviving versus failed 2007 SBs by industry (percent of primary SBs actively managed by a HH)**

	2007
Surviving SB	
Agricultural	6.4
Mining	18.6
Manufacturing	7.1
Wholesale/retail	14.2
Lower-tech service	12.7
Prof. services	41.0
Failing SB	
Agricultural	4.0
Mining	14.9
Manufacturing	3.2
Wholesale/retail	20.0
Lower-tech service	21.7
Prof. services	36.1

Table 7B.5   Surviving versus failed 2007 SBs by ownership structure

	2007
Survived 07–09	
Sole proprietor	43.4
Subchapter S	17.9
LLC/LLP	16.7
Partnership	12.5
Other	9.3
Failed 07–09	
Sole proprietor	63.2
Subchapter S	4.6
LLC/LLP	21.1
Partnership	6.8
Other	4.2

categories are substantially smaller among the businesses that would survive. Indeed, only about 27 percent of the firms that would survive belong to one of these categories, as compared with almost 42 percent of the businesses that would fail.

Small businesses that would survive or fail are classified by their 2007 ownership structure in table 7B.5. The two structures that clearly stand out as differing between the two groups are "sole proprietor" and "Subchapter S." Forty-three percent of the firms that would survive over 2007–2009 were sole proprietorships in 2007, but 63 percent of those that would fail had adopted this ownership form. In contrast, almost 18 percent of the firms that would survive were subchapter S corporations in 2007, compared with not quite 5 percent of the firms that would fail.

As was true in the first section of this appendix, the univariate comparisons in this section suggest several broad but preliminary conclusions. In 2007, households with small businesses that would survive the next two years generally had higher levels of income and nonbusiness net worth and were more likely to own a home than were households whose firms would fail. Firms that would survive were generally larger across several measures of size and tended to be older. Firms that survived were slightly more likely to have a loan or financial guarantee from their owner-manager household. When such a loan or guarantee existed, it was usually a much smaller percentage of sales at firms that would survive. While industry classifications generally did not appear to differ much between the two classes of firms, notable exceptions are the "wholesale/retail" and "lower-tech services" groups, both of which had substantially smaller percentages of firms that survived. Last, sole proprietorships were greatly underrepresented and subchapter S corporations were substantially overrepresented in the group of small businesses that would survive.

Small Business Creation

Table 7B.6 compares selected characteristics of households that started a small business in the 2007–09 period (top panel) with those who did not (bottom panel). It is apparent that, with only the two exceptions of the ratio of home equity to net worth and the household head's unemployment status in the twelve months prior to the 2007 survey, the means of all of the variables shown are statistically different between households that started a new business and households that did not. Moreover, where relevant, most of these differences are sustained across the other moments of the distributions shown. Thus, the heads of households that started a small business during the crisis and the Great Recession tended in 2007 to have higher income and greater net worth, to be younger, to have more education, to be more likely to be partnered, to be less risk averse, and to be more likely to have access to credit than the heads of households who did not start a small business. Some of these characteristics (e.g., income, net worth, and education) would seem to describe white-collar workers more than other types of employees.

Table 7B.6　　　　Characteristics of HHs that started a SB during crisis (2007–2009)

	2007			
	Mean	Median	P25	P90
Started SB 07–09, $N = 131$				
Income	97[a]	70	43	163
HH age	45.2[a]	46	34	63
HH educ.	14.5[a]	15	12	17
Net worth	641[a]	166	39	1,398
Home to net worth	0.46	0.39	0.09	1
Partnered	0.69[a]			
HH credit access	0.56[a]			
Risk prefs	2.84[a]	3	2	4
Unemp. 12 mo. 2007	0.11			
Unemp. 12 mo. 2009	0.29[a]			
Did not start SB 07–09, $N = 2,464$				
Income	60	40	22	116
HH age	50	48	35	75
HH educ.	13.1	13	12	16
Net worth	294	88	10	657
Home to net worth	0.47	0.46	0	1
Partnered	0.55			
HH credit access	0.43			
Risk prefs	3.2	3	3	4
Unemp. 12 mo. 2007	0.11			
Unemp. 12 mo. 2009	0.16			

[a]Mean significantly different from HH that did not start a SB 2007–2009 at 5 percent or greater.

The last two variables in each panel of Table B6 provide important details regarding the employment history of the two household groups. The indicator variables for "Unemp. 12 mo. 2007" and "Unemp. 12 mo. 2009" give the percentage of heads of household who were unemployed at any time in the twelve months before the 2007 and 2009 surveys, respectively. Thus, in the prerecession year of 2007, the same percentage (11 percent) of heads of household had been unemployed sometime in the previous twelve months in both household groups. However, by 2009, 29 percent of the household heads where a new business was started had been unemployed in the previous year, but this was true at only 16 percent of the households that did not start a business. Thus, these data support the conjecture that the sharp rise in unemployment during the Great Recession was an important driver in the creation of new small businesses during that period.

Comparing SCF and US Census Data

Tables 7B.7 and 7B.8 compare the distribution of SCF data for firms with at least one employee with the distribution for comparable firms as reported in the US Census Bureau's Statistics of US Businesses (SUSB), all in 2007. Table 7B.7 separates firms into twenty industrial categories, and table 7B.8 divides businesses into five groups based on the number of employees. As reported in section 7.2 of the main text, it is clear that the SCF and census distributions are similar.

Table 7B.7   Employer small businesses by industrial category, percent (2007)

Industry	SUSB	SCF
Forestry, fishing, hunting, and agriculture support	0.4	3.1
Mining	0.3	0.2
Utilities	0.1	0.2
Construction	13.1	19.4
Manufacturing	4.7	5.9
Wholesale trade	5.5	3.5
Retail trade	11.7	7.6
Transportation and warehousing	2.8	2.4
Information	1.2	1.6
Finance and insurance	4.3	4.5
Real estate and rental and leasing	4.9	6.1
Professional, scientific, and technical services	12.9	17.6
Management of companies and enterprises	0.3	0.0
Administrative and support and waste management and remediation services	5.3	7.1
Educational services	1.2	1.1
Health care and social assistance	10.1	6.3
Arts, entertainment, and recreation	1.9	2.2
Accommodation and food services	7.8	4.1
Other services (except public administration)	11.1	7.3
Unclassified	0.2	0.0

Number of employees	SUSB	SCF
< 5	61.4	58.7
5–9	17.6	16.9
10–19	10.7	11.6
20–99	8.8	9.9
100–499	1.5	3.0

Table 7B.8   Employer small businesses by number of employees, percent (2007)

References

Autor, D. 2010. "The Polarization of Job Opportunities in the US Labor Market."
  Working Paper, Center for American Progress and The Brookings Institution's
  Hamilton Project, April. http://economics.mit.edu/files/5554.
Avery, R. B., R. W. Bostic, and K. A. Samolyk. 1998. "The Role of Personal Wealth
  in Small Business Finance." *Journal of Banking and Finance* 22:1019–61.
Balcaen, S., and H. Ooghe. 2006. "35 Years of Studies on Business Failure: An
  Overview of the Classic Statistical Methodologies and their Related Problems."
  British Accounting Review 38:63–93.
Berger, A. N., N. H. Miller, M. A. Petersen, R. G. Rajan, and J. C. Stein. 2005. "Does
  Function Follow Organizational Form? Evidence from the Lending Practices of
  Large and Small Banks." *Journal of Financial Economics* 76:237–69.
Berger, A. N., and G. F. Udell. 1995. "Relationship Lending and Lines of Credit in
  Small Firm Finance." *Journal of Business* 68 (3): 351–81.
———. 1998. "The Economics of Small Business Finance: The Roles of Private
  Equity and Debt Markets in the Financial Growth Cycle." *Journal of Banking
  and Finance* 22:613–73.
———. 2006. "A More Conceptual Framework for SME Finance." *Journal of Bank-
  ing and Finance* 30:2945–66.
Black, S. E., and P. E. Strahan. 2002. "Entrepreneurship and Bank Credit Avail-
  ability." *Journal of Finance* 57 (6): 2807–33.
Brevoort, K. P., and T. H. Hannan. 2006. "Commercial Lending and Distance: Evi-
  dence from Community Reinvestment Act Data." *Journal of Money, Credit and
  Banking* 38 (8): 1991–2012.
Brevoort, K. P., J. A. Holmes, and J. D. Wolken. 2009. "Distance Still Matters: The
  Information Revolution in Small Business Lending and the Persistent Role of
  Location, 1993–2003." Finance and Economics Discussion Series no. 2010-08,
  Board of Governors of the Federal Reserve System, December.
Bricker, J., B. K. Bucks, A. B. Kennickell, T. L. Mach, and K. B. Moore. 2011. "Sur-
  veying the Aftermath of the Storm: Changes in Family Finances from 2007 to
  2009." Finance and Economics Discussion Series no. 2011-17, Board of Gover-
  nors of the Federal Reserve, March.
Bricker, J., A. B. Kennickell, K. B. Moore, and J. Sabelhaus. 2012. "Changes in US
  Family Finances from 2007 to 2010: Evidence from the Survey of Consumer
  Finances." *Federal Reserve Bulletin* 98 (2): 1–78.
Bucks, B. K., A. B. Kennickell, T. L. Mach, and K. B. Moore. 2009. "Changes in
  US Family Finances from 2004 to 2007: Evidence from the Survey of Consumer
  Finances." *Federal Reserve Bulletin* 95:A1–56.
Cole, R., and T. Sokolyk. 2013. "How Do Start-Up Firms Finance Their Assets?

Evidence from the Kauffman Firm Surveys." Working Paper, DePaul University and Brock University.
———. 2014. "Debt Financing, Survival, and Growth of Start-Up Firms." Working Paper, DePaul University and Brock University.
Cressy, R. 2006. "Why Do Most Firms Die Young?" *Small Business Economics* 26:103–16.
Decker, R., J. Haltiwanger, R. Jarmin, and J. Miranda. 2014. "The Role of Entrepreneurship in US Job Creation and Economic Dynamism." *Journal of Economic Perspectives* 28 (3): 3–24.
DeYoung, R., D. Glennon, and P. Nigro. 2008. "Borrower-Lender Distance, Credit Scoring, and Loan Performance: Evidence from Informational-Opaque Small Business Borrowers." *Journal of Financial Intermediation* 17:113–43.
Elyasiani, E., and L. G. Goldberg. 2004. "Relationship Lending: A Survey of the Literature." *Journal of Economics and Business* 56:315–30.
Evans, D. S., and B. Jovanovic. 1989. "An Estimated Model of Entrepreneurial Choice under Liquidity Constraints." *Journal of Political Economy* 97 (4): 808–27.
Everett, J., and J. Watson. 1998. "Small Business Failure and External Risk Factors." *Small Business Economics* 11:371–90.
Haltiwanger, J., R. S. Jarmin, and J. Miranda. 2013. "Who Creates Jobs? Small Versus Large Versus Young." *Review of Economics and Statistics* 95 (2): 347–61.
Headd, B. 2003. "Redefining Business Success: Distinguishing between Closure and Failure." *Small Business Economics* 21:51–61.
Holtz-Eakin, D., D. Joulfaian, and H. S. Rosen. 1994. "Entrepreneurial Decisions and Liquidity Constraints." *Rand Journal of Economics* 25:334–47.
Honjo, Y. 2000. "Business Failure of New Firms: An Empirical Analysis Using a Multiplicative Hazards Model." *International Journal of Industrial Organization* 18:557–74.
Hunter, M. G. 2011. "Understanding the Common Causes of Small Business Failures: A Qualitative Study." *Journal of Applied Management and Entrepreneurship* 16 (1): 86–103.
Hurst, E., and A. Lusardi. 2004. "Liquidity Constraints, Household Wealth, and Entrepreneurship." *Journal of Political Economy* 112 (2): 319–47.
———. 2008. "Do Household Savings Encourage Entrepreneurship? Household Wealth, Parental Wealth, and the Transition in and out of Entrepreneurship." In *Overcoming Barriers to Entrepreneurship in the United States*, edited by Diana Furchtgott-Roth. Lanham, MD: Rowman and Littlefield, Lexington Books.
Kerr, W. R., and R. Nanda. 2009. "Democratizing Entry: Banking Deregulations, Financing Constraints, and Entrepreneurship." *Journal of Financial Economics* 94:124–49.
Kroszner, R. S. 2008. "Effects of the Financial Crisis on Small Business." Governor, Board of Governors of the Federal Reserve System, testimony before the Committee on Small Business, US House of Representatives, November 20. https://www.federalreserve.gov/newsevents/testimony/kroszner20081120a.htm.
Kwast, M. L., M. Starr-McCluer, and J. D. Wolken. 1997. "Market Definition and the Analysis of Antitrust in Banking." *Antitrust Bulletin* Winter:973–95.
Liao, J., H. Welsch, and C. Moutray. 2008. "Start-Up Resources and Entrepreneurial Discontinuance: The Case of Nascent Entrepreneurs." *Journal of Small Business Strategy* 19 (2): 1–15.
Mach, T. L., and J. D. Wolken. 2006. "Financial Services Used by Small Businesses: Evidence from the 2003 Survey of Small Business Finances." *Federal Reserve Bulletin* October:A167–95.
———. 2012. "Examining the Impact of Credit Access on Small Firm Survivability."

Finance and Economics Discussion Series no. 2012-10, Board of Governors of the Federal Reserve System, Washington, DC, October. https://www.federalreserve.gov/pubs/feds/2012/201210/201210pap.pdf.

Neumark, D., B. Wall, and J. Zhang. 2011. "Do Small Businesses Create More Jobs? New Evidence for the United States from The National Establishment Time Series." *Review of Economics and Statistics* 93 (1): 16–29.

Ooghe, H., and S. De Prijcker. 2008. "Failure Processes and Causes of Company Bankruptcy: A Typology." *Management Decision* 46 (2): 223–42.

Petersen, M. A., and R. G. Rajan. 1995. "The Effect of Credit Market Competition on Lending Relationships." *Quarterly Journal of Economics* May:407–43.

———. 1994. "The Benefits of Lending Relationships: Evidence from Small Business Data." *Journal of Finance* 49 (1): 3–37.

———. 2002. "Does Distance Still Matter? The Information Revolution in Small Business Lending." *Journal of Finance* 57 (6): 2533–70.

Robb, A. M., and E. J. Reedy. 2011. "An Overview of the Kauffman Firm Survey: Results from 2009 Business Activities." Kauffman Foundation, March. http://www.kauffman.org/what-we-do/research/kauffman-firm-survey-series.

Robb, A. M., and D. T. Robinson. 2012. "The Capital Structure Decisions of New Firms." *Review of Financial Studies* 1 (1): 1–27.

Schenone, C. 2010. "Lending Relationships and Information Rents: Do Banks Exploit Their Information Advantages?" *Review of Financial Studies* 23 (3): 1149–99.

Schmalz, M. C., D. A. Sraer, and D. Thesmar. 2013. "Housing Collateral and Entrepreneurship." NBER Working Paper no. 19680, Cambridge, MA.

Slemrod, J. 2007. "Cheating Ourselves: The Economics of Tax Evasion." *Journal of Economic Perspectives* 21 (1): 25–48.

Strotmann, H. 2007. "Entrepreneurial Survival." *Small Business Economics* 28 (1): 87–104.

Udell, G. F. 2008. "What's in a Relationship? The Case of Commercial Lending." *Business Horizons* 51:93–103.

8

Does Unemployment Insurance Change the Selection into Entrepreneurship?

Johan Hombert, Antoinette Schoar, David Sraer, and
David Thesmar

Between 2003 and 2005, the pace of new firm creations rose by about 25 percent in France (see figure 8.1). This increase was induced by a major reform of the French unemployment insurance (UI) system, which led to greater protection against downside risk for unemployed people who became entrepreneurs. Such protection was introduced via two changes to the Plan d'Aide au Retour à l'Emploi (PARE). First, unemployed people who become entrepreneurs could retain their rights to unemployment insurance in case of failure for up to three years. Before, they would have lost all future claims to UI if they started a business. Second, unemployed entrepreneurs were allowed to keep their unemployment benefits *while* starting their own firm and complement entrepreneurial income with up to 70 percent of their pre-unemployment income. This reform led to massive entry of unemployed people into entrepreneurship in France (Hombert et al. 2014).

However, some observers have pointed out that these reforms may change the composition of firms. In particular the concern was that greater downside insurance, which means reduced failure risk, might lead to an increase

Johan Hombert is associate professor of finance at HEC Paris. Antoinette Schoar is the Michael Koerner '49 Professor of Entrepreneurial Finance at MIT Sloan School of Management, a research fellow of the Centre for Economic Policy Research, and a research associate and director of the Entrepreneurship Working Group at the National Bureau of Economic Research. David Sraer is an associate professor at the Haas School of Business and the Department of Economics at the University of California, Berkeley, a research fellow of the Centre for Economic Policy Research, and a faculty research fellow of the National Bureau of Economic Research. David Thesmar is professor of finance at MIT Sloan School of Management and a research fellow of the Centre for Economic Policy Research.

We are grateful to Mark Roberts for his discussion of our chapter. We also thank Jorge Guzman, Pat Kline, and other conference participants for their comments. For acknowledgments, sources of research support, and disclosure of the authors' material financial relationships, if any, please see http://www.nber.org/chapters/c13500.ack.

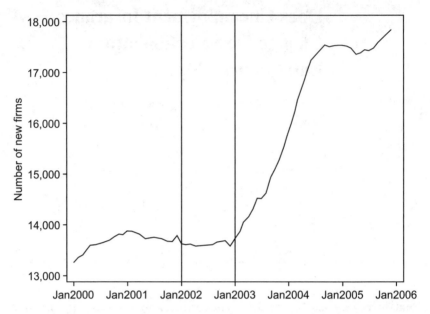

Fig. 8.1   Number of new firms created in France
Source: Hombert et al. (2014).

in "subsistence" entrepreneurship (small firms with no ambition to grow) or less competent entrepreneurs starting a firm as opposed to "transformational" entrepreneurs (Schoar 2010). The implicit assumption in many of these arguments is that greater risk tolerance might be positively correlated with competence level or the ability to generate high returns. While the correlation ex ante could take on any sign, it is important to understand this selection criterion. The effect of making entrepreneurship safer is a priori ambiguous. If entrepreneurs *know* their ability, more insurance leads to more entry of less "able" entrepreneurs (this is the basic force in the model by Lucas [1978]). If entrepreneurs *do not know* their ability, more insurance leads to more entry but no change in composition (Jovanovic 1982). Because of its large scale, this reform may have visibly changed the composition of the entrepreneurial pool along many dimensions such as ability (Lucas 1978), risk tolerance (Kihlstrom and Laffont 1979), private benefits of being "one's own boss" (Moskowitz and Vissing-Jørgensen 2002), optimism (Landier and Thesmar 2009), or ambition (Hurst and Pugsley 2011). In previous work (Hombert et al. 2014), we look at observable measures of entrepreneurial ability and measures of short-term performance.

In this chapter, our goal is to build on the prior analysis to investigate the effect of the reform on the likelihood that the newly created firms will become "big" as opposed to an effect of whether the new firms have the same chance of surviving or creating one job. This is unfortunately impossible to do directly in the context of the PARE reform, because our accounting data stop in 2007, giving us too little perspective on the postcreation growth of these firms. To deal with this problem, we start by building a predictor of long-term success on an older cohort of firms—created in 1994—for which we have detailed firm-level information (entrepreneur's background, ambition, education, etc.). We then check in which direction these success-predicting characteristics changed before and after the PARE reform. To investigate this, we use the same methodology as in Hombert et al. (2014): We compare industries that are the most exposed to the reform to industries that are the least exposed.

We also investigate the equilibrium implications of the reform, which is large enough to shift the industry equilibrium. Our methodology rests on a difference-in-differences estimation strategy: We compare industries in which the typical new firm that is started is small (the treated group) to industries in which new start-ups are typically larger (the control). The idea is that industries where the natural firms' size at start is small are more affected by the reform, since entrepreneurs who were previously unemployed tend to start smaller firms.

We show that the PARE reform had a stronger impact in treated industries than in control sectors. We then look at whether average "quality" of new start-ups was any different between most exposed and less exposed industries, where quality is measured with metrics of firm survival and growth. We find that the propensity of new start-ups to hire or to survive in the first two years did not decline more in treated sectors. New entrepreneurs were not less educated or ambitious; the new firms appeared to have the same quality as the previously created ones. At the industry level, we found that the new jobs created by the reform crowded out job creation among incumbents, but there was a gain in efficiency as the newly created firms are more productive than the incumbents they displaced and also pay higher wages to workers.

The chapter follows the structure of our two-step methodology. In section 8.1, we rapidly survey the existing literature showing that entrepreneurial characteristics predict firm performance. In section 8.2, we focus on the cohort of firms created in 1994, and show which characteristics predict the probability of becoming big. In section 8.3, we investigate whether these characteristics changed around the PARE. Section 8.4 concludes.

8.1   Entrepreneurial Characteristics and Firm Performance: Literature Review

Our analysis relies on our ability to predict firm performance based on entrepreneurial characteristics. In doing so, this chapter relies on a large literature that documents the link between characteristics and firm performance. This section is a brief review of this literature.

One important dimension that has been shown to have strong predictive power on a person's propensity to start a business is wealth of the founder or shocks to the wealth of the founder (see, for example, Evans and Jovanovic 1989; Holtz-Eakin, Joulfaian, and Rosen 1994a, 1994b). In a world where people are credit constrained, wealth shocks are also correlated with a relaxation of credit constraints. While the two interpretations similarly predict that wealth correlates with entry rate, they have opposite predictions regarding entrepreneurial success. Under the financing constraints hypothesis, wealthy entrepreneurs are able to invest more and thus to grow faster. In contrast, a pure wealth effect would lead people to start lower-quality firms and the luxury good hypothesis predicts that wealthy individuals start lower-quality firms. The evidence is mixed. In support of the financing constraints hypothesis, Adelino, Schoar, and Severino (2013) and Schmalz, Sraer, and Thesmar (2013) find that positive shocks to real estate prices lead to more entry and higher postentry growth, and Fracassi et al. (2016) show that positive shocks to debt supply have similar effects. In contrast, Hurst and Lusardi (2004) find that wealthy entrepreneurs are more likely to start less capital-intensive businesses and Nanda (2008) shows that these wealthy entrepreneurs have low quality and are less likely to be profitable. Similarly, Andersen and Nielsen (2012) show that exogenous wealth shocks lead to the entry of low-quality entrepreneurs. This latter set of evidence is consistent with the view that some entrepreneurs start up because they derive nonpecuniary benefits from running a business (Moskowitz and Vissing-Jørgensen 2002). Consistent with this, Hurst and Pugsley (2011) show that the majority of business owners state they became entrepreneurs for nonpecuniary reasons and that these nonpecuniary motives predict low growth.

A second dimension is the effect of entrepreneurial skills. Entrepreneurs might be more successful if they have higher education (Van Der Sluis, Van Praag, and Vijverberg 2008) and if they have higher cognitive and social skills (Hartog, Van Praag, and Van Der Sluis 2010). Lazear (2005) also argues that entrepreneurs are jacks-of-all-trades rather than specialists. Consistent with this, Hartog, Van Praag, and Van Der Sluis (2010) show that entrepreneurs with a balanced portfolio of skills perform better.

A third dimension is the role of preferences and beliefs. Theory suggests that risk-tolerant (Kihlstrom and Laffont 1979) and optimistic individuals (De Meza and Southey 1996) are more likely to become entrepreneurs and, conditional on entry, are of lower average quality. Consistent with this, Hvide and Panos (2014) find that more risk-averse individuals are more likely to become entrepreneurs and less likely to survive, and Landier and Thesmar (2009) show that optimistic entrepreneurs choose more risky capital structures. On the other hand, access to information can assuage optimism: Lerner and Malmendier (2013) show that individuals exposed to previous entrepreneurs are less likely to start low-quality ventures.

Finally, there is a literature that investigates the effect of family ownership on firm behavior (Bertrand and Schoar 2006). In particular, it finds that businesses are more profitable when they are run by their founders (Adams, Almeida, and Ferreira 2009) whereas they are less profitable when they are run by heirs of the founder (Pérez-González 2006; Bennedsen et al. 2007; Bertrand et al. 2008). However Sraer and Thesmar (2007) show that family firms are more profitable because they can honor implicit labor contracts and pay lower wages.

8.2   Forecasting Long-Term Performance

8.2.1   Empirical Strategy and Data

Statistical Framework

Our goal in this section is to lay out the framework for how we predict the long-term success of a firm using some of its characteristics at birth. We simply seek to run a regression of the following form:

$$(1) \qquad\qquad Y_i = X_i\beta + \varepsilon,$$

where i indexes the firm; Y_i is our measure of long-term success and X_i is the set of characteristics. To ease readability, we present in this chapter the results of linear regressions, but have verified that a logistic specification does not give qualitatively different results. The idea is to establish correlations between long-term success and certain observable characteristics of the firm and the founder. We are not trying to argue that these characteristics are causally driving the long-term outcome at the exclusion of other variables, but we believe that they might be an indicator of some underlying fundamental difference of successful start-ups.

We focus on the cohort of French firms started in 1994, for which we have long-term performance data (until 2007) and for which we can obtain founder characteristics using a separate survey.

Firm Characteristics

To measure the characteristics, X_i, we rely on a large-scale survey run by the National Institute of Statistics and Economic Studies (INSEE), the French statistical office, every four years starting in 1994 (see Landier and Thesmar [2009] for an extensive description of this survey). This survey samples approximately one-third of all new firms registered in the country during the first semester of a given year. To achieve maximum representativeness it uses stratified sampling, where the strata are the headquarters' region and the two-digit industry code of the firm. The New Enterprise Information System (SINE) survey has been run in 1994, 1998, 2002, 2006, and 2010. Each time the coverage is high because filling in the questionnaire is compulsory: The response rate is typically around 85 percent. This survey contains a firm-level identifying number, which allows it to be matched with accounting data (see below).

In the 1994 wave of the SINE survey, we have 26,674 different new firms. As predictors of long-term success, we use variables that relate both to characteristics of the project and of the entrepreneur. These variables are selected because they have been shown in other studies to be predictors of the upside potential of a new venture. They are:

- **New idea.** This variable is a dummy equal to 1 if the motivation of the entrepreneur was to "implement a new idea" as opposed to "seizing an opportunity," "not being able to find a job," or "be autonomous." Landier and Thesmar (2009) have shown that this variable correlates very strongly with measures of entrepreneurial optimism, a finding consistent with the behavioral literature.
- **Local market.** This variable is equal to 1 if, at the moment of the survey, the entrepreneur declares that his clientele is "local" as opposed to "international," "cross-border," "national," or "regional." In contrast to "new idea," we expect firms addressing a local clientele to have, a priori, less upside potential.
- **Subsidized.** This variable is equal to 1 if the entrepreneur declares that he receives at least one subsidy. During the 1990s, a popular state-funded subsidy was given under the ACCRE program, which gives a lump sum to unemployed people who became entrepreneurs. Regions and municipalities also subsidize entrepreneurship through cash transfers or in-kind support. These subsidies are typically small, and should not make a difference for a truly ambitious entrepreneur unless he is credit constrained.
- **Ambition.** We use two separate questions: one about hiring plans and one about growth expectations. Both of these questions are intended to measure the entrepreneur's ambition to grow, that is, his belief in the upside potential of the firm. The first question specifically asks the entrepreneur, during the year when the firm was founded (here, in 1994), whether the entrepreneur plans to hire one or more employees in the coming year. The entrepreneur can reply: "Yes," "No," or "Don't Know." We set the "hiring plans" dummy to 1 if the entrepreneur answers "Yes." The second question is formulated the following way: "What do you think will happen to your start-up over the next six months? (a) it will grow, (b) it will keep steady, (c) I will have to turn around a difficult situation, (d) I will shut down the firm, or (e) don't know." We code the "growth plans" dummy to 1 if the answer is (a).
- **Serial entrepreneur.** This dummy is equal to 1 if the entrepreneur declares that the present start-up is not his first.
- **Former manager.** This dummy is equal to 1 if the entrepreneur is a for-

mer executive. It is intended to measure both entrepreneurial ability and outside options on the salaried labor market. The question allows the surveyed entrepreneur to select within broad categories of the French job classification: independent (shopkeepers, lawyers), entrepreneur, executive, supervisor/middle manager, white- and blue-collar worker, student, or inactive.

- **College education.** This dummy is equal to 1 if the entrepreneur declares to have a college degree. It is related to the "former manager" dummy in that it measures both outside options and potentially entrepreneurial ability. The options in this question are: no high school degree, high school degree below high school graduation, high school graduate, short college degree (two years), college graduate, or engineering degree. We take all college degrees (short, long, engineering) into our dummy.

We report summary statistics for these variables in table 8.1. For comparison, we tried as much as possible to reconstruct the same variables for other waves of the SINE survey (1998, 2002, 2006). It was not always possible to do it exactly, as the phrasing of some questions changed somewhat.

We report these numbers to discuss robustness only. In our subsequent analysis of 1994 data, about half of the entrepreneurs were selling to local clients and just over 30 percent took a subsidy in one form or another. About our "ambition measure": about 40 percent of the entrepreneurs expect further growth and 20 percent plan on hiring at least an additional person. About 20 percent of entrepreneurs are former executives and about 30 percent have a college degree (short, long, or engineering). This makes the average entrepreneur significantly more skilled than the average person

Table 8.1   **The characteristics of French entrepreneurs**

	Wave of the SINE survey			
	1994	1998	2002	2006
Motivation: Implementing a new idea (%)	8.3	14	20	2.8
Most clients local (%)	50	55	55	58
Took subsidy (%)	31	27	28	43
Plans to grow (%)	43	48	47	55
Plans to hire (%)	21	24	24	24
Serial entrepreneur (%)	6.4	12	13	12
Former executive (%)	18	15	22	27
College diploma (%)	36	33	30	33
Average number of observations	30,778	30,067	47,668	48,597

Note: These numbers are obtained using four different waves of the SINE survey (firms created in 1994, 1998, 2002, and 2006). The bottom line is the average number of observations across variables (some variables are not defined on the entire sample due to missing values). Definitions for 1994 are described in the main text. Questions change slightly from year to year; we tried to harmonize the variable definition across cohorts as much as possible.

in the labor force. For instance, Schmalz, Sraer, and Thesmar (2013) report that in the general population age twenty to sixty-five in France, on average from 1990 to 2002, approximately 16 percent have a college degree (see their table 3).We make one more change to ease readability. In our regressions, we invert the sign of the two variables "local markets" and "subsidized" so that all characteristics in our list are expected to have a positive impact on long-term growth.

Accounting Data

Accounting data come from tax files made available by INSEE to researchers (see Bertrand et al. [2007] for a more detailed description). Besides detailed accounting information, the tax files also provided us with the number of employees. They cover all firms subject to the regular corporate tax regime (*Bénéfice Réel Normal*) or to the simplified corporate tax regime (*Régime Simplifié d'Imposition*), which together represent 55 percent of newly created firms during our sample period. Small firms with annual sales below €32,600 (€81,500 in retail and wholesale trade) can opt out and choose a special microbusiness tax regime (*Micro-Enterprise*), in which case they do not appear in the tax files. Since expenses, and in particular, wages cannot be deducted from taxable profits under the microbusiness tax regime, firms opting for this regime are likely to have zero employees. For this reason, in the empirical analysis we will assume that firms that do not appear in the tax files do not have employees.

Besides accounting and employment information, tax files include the same firm identifying number as the SINE survey. We thus use it to merge the two data sets. We show in figure 8.2 the product of this operation. For each date t, we plot in this figure the number of firms present in the 1994 SINE survey that are also found in the tax files at date t. Figure 8.2 shows that the matching procedure is quite efficient, as about 18,000 firms—out of some 31,000—from the SINE survey reported accounts to the tax authorities in 1995—the number is slightly smaller in 1994 because firms are not mandated to report accounts after their first year of activity. The firms not present in the tax files have either exited or do not generate enough annual turnover to make it into the regular corporate tax regime. The other lesson of figure 8.2 is that there is significant attrition, as expected in the demographics of young firms: starting from 18,000 in 1995, the number of firms still alive shrinks to about 12,000 in 2000, which corresponds to a five-year attrition rate of about 33 percent.We use the tax files to compute several measures of "long-run success" of the firm, Y_i. Our main measure is a dummy equal to one if the firm has more than fifty employees in 2007 (after twelve years). We set this dummy equal to missing if the firm exits the sample before its twelfth anniversary, so our main measure of long-term success jointly measures growth *conditional* on survival. In figure 8.3, we plot the fraction of surviving firms from the 1994 SINE survey that have reached at least fifty employees. This

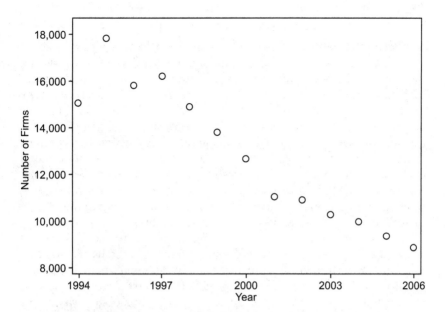

Fig. 8.2 Attrition in the 1994 cohort of firms present in both SINE and the tax files

Note: To draw this figure, we start with the initial sample of all firms present in the SINE survey in 1994. For each year t, we then plot the number of firms from this sample that are present in the tax files. For instance, about 18,000 firms from the 1994 SINE survey are found in the tax files.

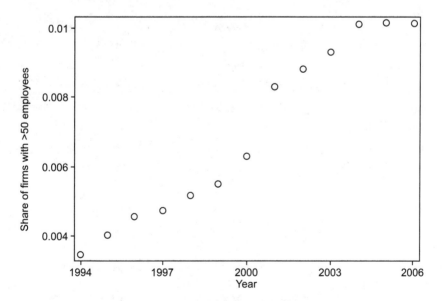

Fig. 8.3 Fraction of firms created in 1994 with more than fifty employees

Note: To draw this figure, we start with the initial sample of all firms present in both the tax files and the SINE survey in 1994. In year t, we compute the fraction of firms in the initial sample that are still in tax files at date t and have more than fifty employees.

number doubles between 1994 and 2007, from less than 0.4 percent to about 1 percent at the end of the period. This both reflects the fact that surviving firms grow and cross the fifty-employee threshold and that the total number of firms decreases over time, as shown in figure 8.2. Note that 1 percent of firms surviving up to 2007 corresponds to about ninety firms. While the number of "large" firms is not very big, it is not surprising that these firms account for a large share of all jobs. In figure 8.4, we illustrate this skewness effect by reporting, for each year t after 1994, the fraction of the cohort's total employment coming from members of this cohort that employ more than fifty workers. This number goes up over time, as expected, given the rising fraction of large firms shown in the previous figure, and it is in the vicinity of 20 percent toward the end of the period. Hence, the job-creation potential of, cohort of firms after a few years is greatly affected by the contribution of the best performers. We have experimented with alternative measures of long-term growth such as, for instance, a dummy equal to one if the firm grows its workforce by at least 600 percent in the first ten years, and zero else (including if the firm exits). Another alternative measure was simply the log of one plus the number of employees ten years after creation, and

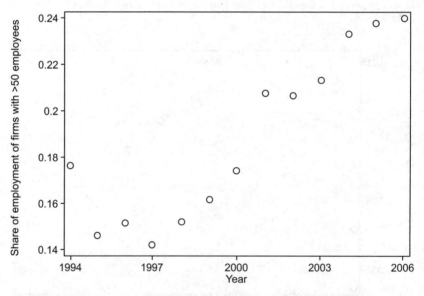

Fig. 8.4   Fraction of employment of the 1994 cohort that is accounted for by "large" firms

Note: For each date t we compute the total employment of firms present in the 1994 SINE survey and still present in the tax files. Out of this total employment, we calculate the share of employment that comes from firms born in 1994, present in the SINE survey, and still present in the tax files. For example, in 2001 about 21 percent of the employment of the 1994 cohort was accounted for by firms hiring at least fifty employees.

zero if the firm exits before ten years. These alternative measures give similar results, which we choose not to report to save space. Finally, to analyze risk taking we create a dummy variable equal to one if a firm from our cohort present in tax files at date t is not in the tax files at date $t + 1$. Thus, we study the propensity to exit on the panel of all firms in the 1994 SINE survey, tracked from 1994 to 2007. Our contention is that characteristics that predict long-term growth are characteristics that also predict failure, since we expect transformational entrepreneurs to both "aim bigger" and take more risk.

8.2.2   Results

We regress various specifications of equation (1) and report the results in table 8.2. Significant or not, we find that all variables predict long-term success in the expected direction. When we focus on statistically significant variables, we find that the main predictors of long-term success are not the obvious measures of intrinsic ability (such as education or past work experience), but variables related to the "seriousness" of the project: ambition, serial entrepreneurs, and new idea motivation. We estimate linear probability models, so the coefficients receive direct interpretations. We find pretty large effects. For instance, entrepreneurs motivated by new ideas are 1 percentage point more likely to become large. This is a large effect, given that the probability of being large conditional on survival up until 2007 is equal to 1 percent (see figure 8.3), so the fact is that the new idea motivation doubles the probability of success. Another very strong predictor of success is our ambition measure, in particular the fact that the entrepreneur declares hiring plans a few months after creation. Given the rigidity of French labor laws, hiring is a major decision for a small firm, and it is not entirely surprising that it has predictive power over long-term growth. When the entrepreneur plans to grow in the year of creation, the probability of eventual success increases by about 50 basis points (bp), which corresponds to an increase by 50 percent. Last, a serial entrepreneur is approximately 1 percentage point more likely to succeed conditionally on survival, which again corresponds to a doubling of the average probability. We then find evidence weakly consistent with the idea that the entrepreneurs more likely to achieve long-term success are also the ones that take more risk. To show this, we regress the exit dummy on entrepreneurial characteristics, and report the result of this investigation in table 8.3. Again we estimate a very simple ordinary least squares (OLS) regression to ease readability. Some of the variables that predict long-term success also correlate with exit probability. For instance, a serial entrepreneur is 1 percentage point more likely, every year, to exit from the tax files—to be compared to an average exit rate of about 8 percent per year. A new idea-driven entrepreneur is about 60 bps more likely to exit every year. An entrepreneur still forecasting business growth a few months after creation is about 40 bps more likely to exit every year. Some other variables that do not strongly predict long-term success

Table 8.2   Predicting the probability of exiting the data in the following year

	(1)	(2)	(3)	(4)	(5)	(6)	(7)	(8)	(9)
	\= 1 if > 50 empl. in 2007								
Percent new-idea driven	.01*** (.0029)								.008*** (.003)
Percent nonsubsidized		.0016 (.0022)							.00094 (.0017)
Percent selling globally			.0073*** (.0022)						.0018 (.0017)
Percent serial entrepreneurs				.0097*** (.0033)					.0072** (.0034)
Percent managers					.0066*** (.002)				.0041* (.0021)
Percent college grads						.0013 (.0019)			.00033 (.0019)
Percent growth plans							.01*** (.0021)		.0028 (.0017)
Percent hiring plans								.016*** (.0025)	.0056*** (.0021)
Observations	7,672	8,583	8,583	7,716	7,672	7,672	8,520	8,520	7,610
R-squared	.017	.026	.027	.016	.017	.016	.029	.031	.021
Industry fixed effects	Yes	Yes	Yes	Yes	Yes	Yes	Yes	Yes	Yes

Note: The OLS regression results with two-digit industry fixed effects. In all regressions, the LHS variable is a dummy equal to 1 if the firm created in 1994 (a) is still present and (b) has more than fifty employees in 2007. Columns (1)–(8) only include one potential project-entrepreneur characteristic, while column (9) includes them all together.

***Significant at the 1 percent level.
**Significant at the 5 percent level.
*Significant at the 10 percent level.

Table 8.3   Predicting the long-term success probability

				= 1 if firm at *t* disappears from data in *t* + 1				
	(1)	(2)	(3)	(4)	(5)	(6)	(7)	(8)	(9)
Percent new-idea driven	.0049* (.0027)								.0036 (.0027)
Percent nonsubsidized		-.0044*** (.0015)							-.0047*** (.0016)
Percent selling globally			.004*** (.0014)						.0046*** (.0015)
Percent serial entrepreneurs				.0088*** (.0029)					.012*** (.003)
Percent managers					-.0058*** (.0019)				-.0087*** (.0019)
Percent college grads						.0078*** (.0017)			.0083*** (.0017)
Percent growth plans							.0024* (.0014)		.0025 (.0016)
Percent hiring plans								.002 (.0017)	.0019 (.0019)
Observations	144,526	161,038	161,038	145,391	144,526	144,526	160,076	160,076	143,604
R-squared	.0096	.0095	.0095	.0097	.0096	.0097	.0091	.0091	.0097
Year fixed effects	Yes	Yes	Yes	Yes	Yes	Yes	Yes	Yes	Yes
Industry fixed effects	Yes	Yes	Yes	Yes	Yes	Yes	Yes	Yes	Yes

Note: The OLS regression results with two-digit industry and year fixed effects. In these regressions we focus on firms present in the 1994 wave of the SINE survey, and use all observations from 1994 to 2007. In all regressions, the LHS variable is a dummy equal to 1 if the firm present in year *t* exits from tax files in year *t* + 1. Columns (1)–(8) only include one potential project-entrepreneur characteristic, while column (9) includes them all together.

***Significant at the 1 percent level.

**Significant at the 5 percent level.

*Significant at the 10 percent level.

also predict failure: college graduates are more likely to fail (1.1 percentage points). Nonsubsidized businesses are also more likely to fail.

8.3   Did the PARE Reform Alter the Fraction of High-Potential Start-Ups?

Our goal in this section is to look at whether characteristics that predict long-term success change around the 2002 PARE reform, which drew many unemployed individuals into the entrepreneurship pool. First, we describe the empirical methodology and the data. Then, we discuss our results.

8.3.1   Methodology and Data

Methodology

In this section, we follow the methodology developed in Hombart et al. (2014). We look at the evolution of entrepreneurial characteristics in industries that are the most exposed to the PARE reform *compared* to the evolution in the sectors that were the least exposed to the reform. In mathematical terms, this amounts to running the following regression:

$$(2) \qquad X_{ist} = a_s + \sum_{k=1}^{4} b_k \mathrm{POST}_t \times T_{s,k} + \sum_{k=1}^{4} \mathrm{POST}_t \times Z_s + \varepsilon_{ist},$$

where X_{ist} is a start-up/entrepreneur characteristic; X_{ist} corresponds to the predictors of long-term success that we have identified in the previous section such as new idea, serial entrepreneurs, or initial ambition. We also look at the "predicted probability of long-term success" estimated in equation (1) as the linear combination of all entrepreneurial/firm characteristics that optimally predicts long-term success; $T_{s,k}$ is a treatment variable, which is equal to 1 if the firm is in the kth quartile of exposure to the PARE reform. We will measure exposure to PARE as a "small-scale" industry, that is, an industry where it is easy to start small (see below). Thus, if the reform has a clean, identifiable effect on the entrepreneurial composition, the coefficient b_k should be monotonically increasing or decreasing in k. Finally, Z_i stands for a set of observable controls, which may explain changes in the composition of entrepreneurs independently of the reform.

Measuring Treatment

To construct the sector-level treatment variable, $T_{s,k}$, we follow Hombert et al. (2014) and compute the fraction of firms created as sole proprietorships in each industry. To do this, we exploit the French registry of firms. The registry contains the universe of firms that are registered each month in France. This is a monthly data set, and it is available from 1993 to 2008. Each newly created firm includes the number of employees at creation and the industry in which the firm operates, using a four-digit classification system similar to the four-digit North American Industry Classification System (NAICS). It also provides the firm's legal status (sole proprietorship, limited liability corporation, or corporation). For each four-digit sector, we compute the fraction of sole proprietorships among newly created firms from 1999 to 2001, and then sort industries into quartiles of the treatment intensity. This leads to the four treatment variables $T_{s,k}$ for $k \in \{1,2,3,4\}$. In Hombert et al. (2014), we show that sectors in the high-treatment group are those one would expect: business consultants, contractors, hairdressers, taxi drivers, and so forth.

Characteristics

The industry controls, Z_s, are computed using the tax files described previously. We use two variables that are defined in the prereform period. The average fixed asset to employment ratio of all firms in sector s over the period 1999–2001 is $(K / L)_s$; Salesgr$_s$ is the average annual sales growth of all firms over the same period. These two industry variables are designed to pick up any change in characteristics that is due to differential industry exposure to the business cycle. They turn out to be statistically insignificant. The characteristics X_{ist} on the LHS of equation (2) are obtained from the SINE survey described in the Firm Characteristics section. We use two waves of the survey: 2002 (before the PARE reform) and 2006 (after the PARE reform), so we only have two observations per industry s. We report averages of the characteristics in the two periods in table 8.1: Some variables receive the exact same definitions as in the Firm Characteristics section. These are cases where the phrasing of the question is identical (local clients, ambition variables, serial entrepreneur, former executive, and college graduates). Two variables (new idea and subsidy) exhibit significant breaks, however, because the alternatives provided in the questions differ a bit. This means that it is difficult to interpret the aggregate change in characteristics directly, but our difference-in-differences framework will help somewhat. The assumption here is that the change in variable coding between 2002 and 2006 is orthogonal to whether an industry is small scale or not. Finally, we construct the expected probability of success of a venture using the coefficients on characteristics estimated in the previous section for the 1994 cohort. We use a dummy equal to 1 if the firm reaches at least fifty employees twelve years after creation, and the coefficients estimated in column (9) of table 8.2. The underlying assumptions here are that (a) the relationship between characteristics X and long-term success probability is stable over time, including for the 2002 and 2006 cohort, and (b) that the noise introduced by the changes in the exact definitions of characteristics is uncorrelated with our treatment variables. Using this technique to estimate, at the start-up level the predicted probability of success, we find that the average (median) is equal to 1 percent

(0.5 percent) in 2002 and 1.3 percent (0.5 percent) in 2006. It thus remains to be seen whether such an estimated probability increases more in exposed industries, which is the goal of the next section.

8.3.2   Empirical Results

We estimate equation (2) and report the results in table 8.4. We find that, if anything, the share of entrepreneurs with characteristics predicting success in the long-run increases more in exposed industries. The fraction of entrepreneurs motivated by the implementation of a new idea increases by 11 percentage points more in exposed industries than in less exposed ones. This difference is significant at 1 percent and large given that the fraction of such entrepreneurs in the 2002 sample is only 20 percent. A similarly big effect can be found for the frequency of serial entrepreneurs, which increases by 7 percentage points more in exposed sectors (while the sample frequency in 2002 is 13 percent). Finally, the fraction of ambitious entrepreneurs also grows significantly more in treated sectors, but the effect is smaller economically: the fraction of entrepreneurs who expect to grow increases by 2.5 percentage points, only one-tenth of the sample frequency in 2002 (24 percent). One variable, however, goes in the opposite direction: the fraction of former executives, which drops by 14 percentage points, almost half of the sample mean of 30 percent in 2002. We then aggregate all of these variables into a single predicted success probability, and check in column (9) how this predicted success is affected by the reform. We do not find much statistical action here. The decrease in the fraction of former executives among entrepreneurs fully compensates the increase in the fraction of entrepreneurs endowed with new ideas, serial entrepreneurs and ambitious ones, so that the impact on the average probability is marginally negative. To further highlight the role of the "former executive" dummy, we use in column (10) a predicted probability computed using all the coefficients from column (9), in table 8.2, *except* the coefficient on "former executive," which we set to zero. If we remove this effect, the proportion of potential successful start-ups actually *rises* by 0.6 percentage points (for a sample mean of 1 percent) in the most exposed industries. All in all, given that the "former executive" is not a very precisely estimated predictor of long-term success (it is statistically significant at 10 percent only in table 8.2), we conservatively conclude that the PARE reform has little effect on the long-term potential of new ventures.

8.4   Conclusion

The French Reform of 2003, documented in Hombert et al. (2014), led to a massive increase in the supply of entrepreneurs. The question we investigate in this chapter is whether it led to a significant reduction in the potential for long-term success of new ventures, since the reform might have drawn in people with different competence levels or ambitions to grow their firms. We

Table 8.4   Predicting the long-term success probability

	New idea (1)	Nonsubsidized (2)	Global market (3)	Serial entrepreneur (4)	Former manager (5)	College graduate (6)	Wants to grow? (7)	Wants to hire? (8)	Predicted success I (9)	Predicted success II (10)
					Entrepreneur/project characteristics					
POST	-.26***	-.15***	-.0097	-.07***	.29***	.0095	.059**	-.03	.0041**	-.0075***
	(-6.5)	(-6)	(-.32)	(-4.2)	(3.5)	(.28)	(2.3)	(-1.6)	(2.5)	(-5.3)
POST x Q2	-.008	-.028	-.0089	.032***	.0081	-.012	.011	-.016	-.00069	.0021**
	(-.27)	(-1.5)	(-.42)	(2.7)	(.16)	(-.63)	(.6)	(-1)	(-.55)	(2.1)
POST x Q3	.042	-.019	-.0048	.052***	-.013	.002	.01	.0066	-.00067	.0042***
	(1.4)	(-1.2)	(-.29)	(4.8)	(-.22)	(.11)	(.75)	(.58)	(-.55)	(4.6)
POST x Q4	.11***	-.0023	.0091	.071***	-.14***	.0044	.045***	.025**	-.002*	.0063***
	(4.1)	(-.14)	(.61)	(6.5)	(-2.9)	(.25)	(3.3)	(2.2)	(-1.7)	(7.1)
POST x K/L	.014	.01	-.0068	.0037	-.077**	.01	-.0043	.0088	.00036	.00048
	(1.3)	(1.3)	(-.72)	(.75)	(-2.3)	(.82)	(-.52)	(1.5)	(.8)	(1.1)
POST x Salesgr	-.027*	-.029**	-.02	-.0055	.063	.008	.003	-.014*	-.00072	-.00079
	(-1.7)	(-2.4)	(-1.6)	(-.74)	(1.1)	(.5)	(.25)	(-1.8)	(-1.1)	(-1.3)
Observations	89,670	87,816	87,498	87,993	70,364	88,026	89,670	87,526	69,967	87,247
R^2	.11	.067	.17	.025	.11	.25	.034	.057	.032	.035

Note: In this table, we estimate equation (2) using the 2002 and 2006 waves of the SINE survey. POST = 1 in 2006 and 0 in 2002; Q2–Q4 are quartile of intensity of exposure to the PARE reform; Q4 is equal to 1 for sectors in the top quartile of the fraction of firms started as sole proprietorships. Columns (1)–(8) use as LHS each of the characteristics investigated in tables 8.2 and 8.3. Column (9) uses as LHS the predicted probability of having at least fifty employees twelve years after creation, using the coefficients in column (9) of table 8.2. In column (10), we use an alternative measure of predicted probability that uses all the coefficients of column (9) of table 8.2, *except* the "former executive" coefficient that we set to zero.

***Significant at the 1 percent level.

**Significant at the 5 percent level.

*Significant at the 10 percent level.

proceed in two steps. First, we show that some entrepreneurial and project characteristics, which we can measure using a large-scale survey, significantly predict the probability that newly founded firms succeed in the long run. We show that firms started by entrepreneurs who plan on growing, have already had entrepreneurial experience, and are motivated by new ideas are significantly more likely to employ at least fifty persons after twelve years. We then use this relationship to see if the success potential of start-ups was significantly deteriorated by the 2003 reform. We find that it was not. A caveat of our analysis is that we observe few very successful firms, and that we have to content ourselves with the fifty-employees threshold as a measure of success. A possible route for improvement in our methodology would be to estimate Pareto coefficients for the tail of the distribution of long-term firm size.

References

Adams, Renée, Heitor Almeida, and Daniel Ferreira. 2009. "Understanding the Relationship between Founder–CEOs and Firm Performance." *Journal of Empirical Finance* 16 (1): 136–50.
Adelino, Manuel, Antoinette Schoar, and Felipe Severino. 2013. "House Prices, Collateral and Self-Employment." NBER Working Paper no. 18868, Cambridge, MA.
Andersen, Steffen, and Kasper Meisner Nielsen. 2012. "Ability or Finances as Constraints on Entrepreneurship? Evidence from Survival Rates in a Natural Experiment." *Review of Financial Studies* 25 (12): 3684–710.
Bennedsen, Morten, Kasper M. Nielsen, Francisco Pérez-González, and Daniel Wolfenzon. 2007. "Inside the Family Firm: The Role of Families in Succession Decisions and Performance." *Quarterly Journal of Economics* 122 (2): 647–91.
Bertrand, Marianne, Simon Johnson, Kislert Samphantharak, and Antoinette Schoar. 2008. "Mixing Family with Business: A Study of Thai Business Groups and the Families behind Them." *Journal of Financial Economics* 88 (3): 466–98.
Bertrand, Marianne, and Antoinette Schoar. 2006. "The Role of Family in Family Firms." *Journal of Economic Perspectives* 20 (2): 73–96.
Bertrand, Marianne, Antoinette Schoar, and David Thesmar. 2007. "Banking Deregulation and Industry Structure: Evidence from the French Banking Reforms of 1985." *Journal of Finance* 62 (2): 597–628.
De Meza, David, and Clive Southey. 1996. "The Borrower's Curse: Optimism, Finance and Entrepreneurship." *Economic Journal* 106 (435): 375–86.
Evans, David S., and Boyan Jovanovic. 1989. "An Estimated Model of Entrepreneurial Choice under Liquidity Constraints." *Journal of Political Economy* 97 (4): 808–27.
Fracassi, Cesare, Mark J. Garmaise, Shimon Kogan, and Gabriel Natividad. 2016. "Business Microloans for US Subprime Borrowers." *Journal of Financial and Quantitative Analysis* 51 (1): 55–83.
Hartog, Joop, Mirjam Van Praag, and Justin Van Der Sluis. 2010. "If You Are So Smart, Why Aren't You an Entrepreneur? Returns to Cognitive and Social Ability: Entrepreneurs versus Employees." *Journal of Economics & Management Strategy* 19 (4): 947–89.

Holtz-Eakin, Douglas, David Joulfaian, and Harvey S. Rosen. 1994a. "Entrepreneurial Decisions and Liquidity Constraints." *RAND Journal of Economics* 25 (2): 334–47.
———. 1994b. "Sticking It Out: Entrepreneurial Survival and Liquidity Constraints." *Journal of Political Economy* 102 (1): 53–75.
Hombert, Johan, Antoinette Schoar, David Sraer, and David Thesmar. 2014. "Can Unemployment Insurance Spur Entrepreneurial Activity?" NBER Working Paper no. 20717, Cambridge, MA.
Hurst, Erik, and Annamaria Lusardi. 2004. "Liquidity Constraints, Household Wealth, and Entrepreneurship." *Journal of Political Economy* 112 (2): 319–47.
Hurst, Erik, and Benjamin Wild Pugsley. 2011. "What Do Small Businesses Do?" *Brookings Papers on Economic Activity* 43 (2): 73–142.
Hvide, Hans K., and Georgios A. Panos. 2014. "Risk Tolerance and Entrepreneurship." *Journal of Financial Economics* 111 (1): 200–23.
Jovanovic, Boyan. 1982. "Selection and the Evolution of Industry." *Econometrica* 50 (3): 649–70.
Kihlstrom, Richard E., and Jean-Jacques Laffont. 1979. "A General Equilibrium Entrepreneurial Theory of Firm Formation Based on Risk Aversion." *Journal of Political Economy* 87 (4): 719–48.
Landier, Augustin, and David Thesmar. 2009. "Financial Contracting with Optimistic Entrepreneurs." *Review of Financial Studies* 22 (1): 117–50.
Lazear, Edward P. 2005. "Entrepreneurship." *Journal of Labor Economics* 23 (4): 649–80.
Lerner, Josh, and Ulrike Malmendier. 2013. "With a Little Help from My (Random) Friends: Success and Failure in Post-business School Entrepreneurship." *Review of Financial Studies* doi: 10.1093/rfs/hht024.
Lucas, Robert E. 1978. "On the Size Distribution of Business Firms." *Bell Journal of Economics* 9 (2): 508–23.
Moskowitz, Tobias J., and Annette Vissing-Jørgensen. 2002. "The Returns to Entrepreneurial Investment: A Private Equity Premium Puzzle?" *American Economic Review* 92 (4): 745–78.
Nanda, Ramana. 2008. "Cost of External Finance and Selection into Entrepreneurship." Harvard Business School Working Paper no. 08–047, January. Harvard Business School, Harvard University.
Pérez-González, Francisco. 2006. "Inherited Control and Firm Performance." *American Economic Review* 122 (2): 647–91.
Schmalz, Martin, David Sraer, and David Thesmar. 2013. "Housing Collateral and Entrepreneurship." NBER Working Paper no. 19680, Cambridge, MA.
Schoar, Antoinette. 2010. "The Divide between Subsistence and Transformational Entrepreneurship." In *Innovation Policy and the Economy*, vol. 10, edited by Josh Lerner and Scott Stern, 57–81. Chicago: University of Chicago Press.
Sraer, David, and David Thesmar. 2007. "Performance and Behavior of Family Firms: Evidence from the French Stock Market." *Journal of the European Economic Association* 5 (4): 709–51.
Van Der Sluis, Justin, Mirjam Van Praag, and Wim Vijverberg. 2008. "Education and Entrepreneurship Selection and Performance: A Review of the Empirical Literature." *Journal of Economic Surveys* 22 (5): 795–841.

9
Job Creation, Small versus Large versus Young, and the SBA

J. David Brown, John S. Earle, and Yana Morgulis

9.1 Introduction

One of the few areas of recent consensus across all major political groups in the United States is the supposedly important role played by small businesses in job creation. The initiatives justified by this conviction include a variety of small business loan and support programs, largely through the Small Business Administration (SBA), as well as preferential treatment of small businesses in contracting and regulatory requirements.[1] The empirical basis for the belief goes back to Birch (1987), although the underlying methods and data were questioned by Davis, Haltiwanger, and Schuh (1996). More recently, Neumark, Wall, and Zhang (2011) have reconfirmed the Birch conclusion with improved data and methods, but Haltiwanger, Jarmin, and Miranda (2013; hereafter HJM) have shown that the size-growth relationship is not robust to controlling for age (as had Evans [1987] for a much smaller data set on manufacturing industries). Indeed, HJM find that

J. David Brown is a senior economist at the US Census Bureau. John S. Earle is a professor at the Schar School of Policy and Government at George Mason University and at the Central European University, and a research fellow of the Institute for the Study of Labor (IZA). Yana Morgulis is a consultant at The Boston Consulting Group.

We thank the SBA for providing the list of loans we use in the analysis and Manuel Adelino, Julie Cullen, Javier Miranda, and participants in the 2013 CAED Conference and the 2014 NBER/CRIW Conference on Measuring Entrepreneurial Businesses for comments. John Earle's research on this project was supported by the National Science Foundation (NSF Grant no. 1262269 to George Mason University). Any opinions and conclusions expressed herein are those of the authors and do not necessarily reflect the views of the US Census Bureau. All results have been reviewed to ensure that no confidential information on individual firms is disclosed. For acknowledgments, sources of research support, and disclosure of the authors' material financial relationships, if any, please see http://www.nber.org/chapters/c13497.ack.

1. A recent example is the JOBS Act, which loosens regulations on financing.

the relationship may even reverse signs, so that larger firms contribute more to job creation, once age is taken into account.

This research has attracted considerable attention both from scholars and journalists, and it is very useful as an empirical description of the economy, laying out the "facts" that may be juxtaposed against theories of firm and industry dynamics. Haltiwanger, Jarmin, and Miranda (2013, 360) infer from their results that "to the extent that policy interventions aimed at small businesses ignore the important role of firm age, we should not expect much of an impact on the pace of job creation." Strictly speaking, this inference requires the assumption that the patterns of responsiveness of employment to interventions across different categories of firms (defined by age and size) mimic the empirical regularities of employment dynamics in these categories more generally. While it could be the case that the categories with the strongest record of job creation also respond the most to a given intervention, it is also possible that there is no relationship. Potentially, the types of firms that typically create the fewest jobs might even benefit the most from supportive measures. More generally, empirical regularities have no necessary implications for the design of effective interventions.

Several studies provide indirect evidence that financial constraints on growth vary with firm size and age. Fort et al. (2013) suggest that financial constraints have the greatest impact on smaller, younger firms' growth, finding that their employment dynamics are more sensitive to housing price shocks. They state this could be due to such firms' greater dependence on home equity financing than other firms that can more easily obtain commercial loans. Adelino, Ma, and Robinson (2014) show that start-ups' higher responsiveness to investment opportunities is accentuated in local areas with better access to small business finance, implying that start-up job creation is curbed by financing constraints. Levenson and Willard (2000) supply survey evidence suggesting that younger, smaller US firms are more likely to be denied credit, and Canton et al. (2013) also report that younger, smaller firms across the European Union are more likely to perceive that bank loan accessibility is low. Note, however, that inability to obtain a bank loan does not by itself mean the firm's growth is constrained; the firm may not intend to use the loan for expansion. Hurst and Pugsley (2011) report that most small firms grow very little, entering at low employment levels and tending to remain small; survey evidence suggests the majority do not desire to grow, with the implication that they would not grow even if they had better financial access.[2]

This chapter more directly tests the variation by age and size in the association between financial access and firm growth, using the SBA's 7(a) and 504 loan guarantee programs. For this purpose, we have linked a complete list of

---

2. An alternative possibility is that small, mature firms are small due to lack of access to finance in the past, in which case they may benefit even more from SBA loans than other firms.

SBA 7(a) and 504 loans to the Census Bureau's employer and nonemployer business registers and to the Longitudinal Business Database (LBD), which tracks all firms and establishments in the US nonfarm business sector with paid employees on an annual basis in 1976–2012. We restrict the analysis to recipients of loans in 1991–2009 and their matched controls.

While our chapter is inspired to some extent by HJM, and we use some of the census data they developed, our question and therefore our methods are different. While HJM measure year-to-year growth in employment, our focus is the change in employment from the period before the SBA loan to the period after the loan is received, as well as on firm survival after loan receipt. Our estimation method involves construction of a control sample of firms based on age, industry, year, size in the year prior to loan receipt, and several years of growth history.

The estimation results suggest that both job creation and survival effects of a $1 million loan decrease in age, controlling for size. Survival effects also decrease in size, but the association of size and job creation from loans is positive with or without age controls. This contrasts somewhat with HJM, who find positive size effects on job creation only when controlling for age. The fact that the job creation effect from loans is stronger in firms growing faster prior to loan receipt can help explain the positive association between the job creation effect from loans and size. Survival effects are strongest in the age-size categories most vulnerable to exit.

An important caveat to bear in mind when interpreting these estimates is the possibility of a contemporaneous shock to demand, costs, or productivity that could raise both the amount (or probability) of an SBA loan and the growth of employment. Our matching can only control for preloan growth and time-invariant characteristics. On the other hand, if the correlations of such shocks with loan probability and employment growth are similar across size and groups, then the relative magnitudes of the loan effects would also be similar.

The rest of the chapter is structured as follows. Section 9.2 describes the SBA programs we analyze. Section 9.3 describes the data, including the matched control samples. Section 9.4 outlines our methodology. Section 9.5 provides estimation results, and section 9.6 concludes.

9.2   SBA Loan Programs

The SBA has several small business loan guarantee programs. In this chapter, we focus on the largest two groups of programs, 7(a) and 504, and this section describes the programs' current characteristics.[3] Small businesses seeking financing apply to private lenders (generally not for SBA

3. SBA (2015) is the primary source for our description, and it contains further details. Brown and Earle (forthcoming) estimate separate job creation effects for 7(a) and 504 loans, finding similar magnitudes. In this chapter we do not distinguish separate effects by loan type.

loans in particular, but for any type of loan). The lenders then decide which applicants are denied, which receive conventional loans, and which of them are both eligible and good candidates for SBA loans. For subprograms where the SBA makes the final credit decision, the lender sends an application for a SBA loan to the SBA on behalf of the applicant, while for other subprograms the lender makes the final credit decision. Not all firms meeting program eligibility requirements receive loans—for example, the lender or the SBA could deny an application based on credit risk just as with conventional loans.

Most 7(a) loans (aside from special subprograms) have a $5 million maximum amount, with an 85 percent maximum SBA guarantee rate for loans up to $150,000 and 75 percent for higher amounts. Loans for working capital and machinery usually have a maturity of up to ten years, while the term for loans for purchase of real estate can be as long as twenty-five years. The SBA sets maximum loan interest rates, which decrease with loan amount and increase with maturity. To qualify, a business must be for-profit; meet SBA size standards;[4] show good character, management expertise, and a feasible business plan; not have funds available from other sources; and be an eligible type of business.[5] The SBA itself makes the final credit decisions for most of these loans.

Some 7(a) programs are more streamlined. In the Preferred Lender Program (PLP) the SBA delegates the final credit decision and most servicing and liquidation authority to PLP lenders, while the SBA's role is to check loan eligibility criteria. The SBA grants lenders PLP status based on their past record with the SBA, including proficiency in processing and servicing SBA-guaranteed loans. The PLP lender agrees to liquidate all business assets before asking the SBA to honor its guaranty in payment default cases. In the 7(a) Certified Lender Program (CLP), the SBA promises a loan decision within three working days on applications handled by CLP lenders. The SBA conducts a credit review, relying on the credit knowledge of the lender's loan officers rather than ordering an independently conducted analysis. Lenders with a good performance history may receive CLP status.

The express loan program is a final large category of 7(a). These have a 50 percent maximum SBA guaranty and a $350,000 maximum loan amount. Interest rates can be higher than on other 7(a) loans, but the SBA promises a decision on approval within thirty-six hours. The PLPs also have an advantage here, as they may make eligibility determinations on their own.

Depending on the type of business, the 504 Loan Program offers loan guarantees up to $5.5 million. Typically a lender covers 50 percent of the

4. The size standards vary by industry, with the criterion sometimes employment, sometimes revenue, and sometimes assets.
5. This includes engaging in business in the United States; possessing reasonable owner equity to invest; and using alternative financial resources, including personal assets, before seeking financial assistance.

project costs, a Certified Development Company (CDC) certified by the SBA provides up to 40 percent of the financing (100 percent guaranteed by an SBA-guaranteed debenture), and the borrower contributes at least 10 percent (the borrower is sometimes required to contribute up to 20 percent). The CDCs are nonprofit corporations promoting community economic development via disbursement of 504 loans. Proceeds may be used for fixed assets or to refinance debt in connection with an expansion of the business via new or renovated assets.[6] The 504 loan eligibility requirements are similar to those listed for 7(a) loans above.

Lenders must pay a guaranty fee that increases with maturity and guaranteed amount for 7(a) loans. For both programs they must sign the "Credit Elsewhere Requirement," which states "Without the participation of SBA to the extent applied for, we would not be willing to make this loan, and in our opinion the financial assistance applied for is not otherwise available on reasonable terms." This requirement, also called the "Credit Elsewhere Test," must be accompanied by a detailed explanation of why the loan would be unavailable on conventional terms.[7] Both the requirement and the fee create costs of using SBA loan guarantees. In addition, there are administrative costs to the lender, including the specific bureaucratic formulae for loan application and SBA monitoring of lenders participating in the program. The SBA loans tend to be concentrated in a relatively small number of lenders (especially PLP lenders), probably because of scale economies in these costs.[8]

9.3 Data

We identify loan recipients, dates, and amounts with a confidential database on all 7(a) and 504 loans guaranteed by the SBA from the fourth quarter of 1990 through the third quarter of 2009. We reset the loan year to be on a fiscal year basis (October of the previous calendar year through September of the current calendar year), using the date the SBA approved the loan so that the loan year is roughly centered on the Census Bureau's LBD (described below) employment measure, which is the number of employees in the pay period including March 12. As shown in table 9.1, loans to firms in US territories are excluded because of uneven coverage of other

6. The SBA loan data for 2006–2009 contain the amount of loan receipts devoted to each category of loan use. The shares of loans going to different uses vary by age and size, but not in a way that can help explain the job creation and survival effect patterns.

7. Examples of acceptable factors are that the business needs a larger loan or longer maturity than the lender's policy permits, or the collateral does not meet the lender's policy requirements.

8. As shown by Brown and Earle (forthcoming), PLP lender branches are not evenly distributed across the country, raising the potential concern that they may locate in areas with higher growth potential. Using a nearly identical sample to this chapter, Brown and Earle (forthcoming) find that the job creation effects of SBA loans are robust to the inclusion of a control for county-industry employment growth over the analyzed period.

Table 9.1   Path from full SBA loan data set to treated firms in final matched
               regression sample

	Number
Total SBA loans in 1991–2009	1,141,200
Except US territories	1,124,900
Except cancelled loans	979,600
After consolidating loans to the same borrower in the same year	947,300
Except loans not matched to any business register	824,200
Except loans matched to nonemployer business register	760,000
Except loans matched to a business register but not matched to the LBD firm data	701,500
Except SBA 7(a)/504 loans in years after the first loan year in the 1991–2009 period	518,200
Except firms with first SBA loan before 1991 or a SBA disaster loan at any time	486,200
Except firms with missing exact matching variables (employment in year before loan receipt, industry, or state [sample for control matching process])	459,600
Except firms without matched controls for three-year employment growth with exit zeroes	310,400
Except firms with greater than 249 employees in $t-1$ (regression sample for tables 9.16 and 9.17)	309,700
Except firms missing three-year employment growth without exit	222,300
Except firms without matched controls for three-year employment growth without exit (regression sample for tables 9.8 and 9.9)	215,000

Note: Numbers are rounded to the nearest 100 for disclosure avoidance.

data sources. Since cancellations may occur at the initiative of the borrower, canceled loans are excluded. We aggregate loan amounts when borrowers receive multiple SBA loans in the same year.[9] We drop loans received in subsequent years to focus on the effects of the first treatment.

We match the confidential SBA 7(a) and 504 data and publicly available 7(a), 504, and disaster loan data covering loans since the inception of these programs to the Census Bureau's employer and nonemployer business registers.[10] We first link by Employer Identification Numbers (EINs) and Social Security Numbers (SSNs).[11] For confidential 7(a) and 504 records that can-

9. Our loan amount variable is the amount disbursed, converted to real 2010 prices using the annual average Consumer Price Index. We use the total amount from loan financing, not just the amount guaranteed by the SBA. For 504 loans we impute the total loan amount based on the guaranteed amount specified in the database, using the 504 program guidelines. The SBA-guaranteed portion is 40 percent, the equity share is 10 percent plus an additional 5 percent if a new business and/or an additional 5 percent if special use property, and the residual is a nonguaranteed bank loan. We are unable to observe if the project is for special use property; our imputations assume there is none. The database includes a third-party loan amount, but it contains many implausibly high values.

10. The SBA has a separate disaster loan program, and we have names and addresses for the recipients from 1953 through March 31, 2011. We have chosen to focus the analysis on 7(a) and 504 loans in the confidential database because the match rate to census data is much higher due to the presence of EINs and SSNs.

11. About three-fourths of the linked records are linked via EIN or SSN.

not be linked by EIN or SSN, and for the publicly available data without EINs or SSNs, we probabilistically link records by different combinations of business name, street address, and ZIP Code. Table 9.1 shows that 87 percent of the confidential loan records are linked to a business register. Of these, 7.8 percent are linked only to a nonemployer business register (i.e., they are self-employed and have no payroll employment). We exclude firms receiving a disaster loan before their first 7(a) or 504 loan, as well as firms receiving a 7(a) or 504 loan prior to 1991. Firms require an industry code, state (for those with nineteen or fewer employees), and employment in the year prior to loan receipt to be included in the matching process with LBD control firms, as described in the next section. Of these, we could not find any control firms meeting our matching criteria (discussed in the next section) for 32 percent of them. About 87,000 treated firms do not have employment in each of the next three years following loan receipt, which is necessary for the dependent variable in the main employment regression samples. About 7,300 additional treated firms cannot be included in the main regression sample because none of their matched controls has employment in each of the next three years after the treated firm's loan receipt.[12]

The LBD is built from longitudinally linked employer business registers (Jarmin and Miranda 2002) tracking all firms and establishments with payroll employment in the US nonfarm business sector on an annual basis in 1976–2012. The SBA loan match to employer business registers allows us to link the SBA data to the entire LBD. The LBD contains employment, annual payroll, establishment age (based on the first year the establishment appears in the data set), state, county, ZIP Code, industry code, and firm ID. The industry code is a four-digit Standard Industrial Classification (SIC) code through the year 2001 and a six-digit North American Industry Classification System (NAICS) code in 2002–2012.

We aggregate the LBD to the firm level by assigning each firm the location of its largest establishment by employment and its modal industry code. Following HJM, we set the firm birth year to be the earliest birth year among establishments belonging to the firm when it first appears in the LBD, and the firm exit year is the latest exit year among establishments belonging to the firm in the last year the firm appears in the LBD.

Our firm employment measure aggregates establishment employment in a way that focuses on organic job creation.[13] Employment in $t - 1$, the year prior to the treatment year (defined for control firms as the matched treated firm's treatment year), is the base year (unadjusted) for treated firms and their matched controls. The employment of the acquired establishments

12. Brown and Earle (forthcoming) provide comparisons between the matched and unmatched samples of firms receiving loans after start-up based on characteristics in the SBA loan recipient data.

13. Our method of calculating organic growth builds on HJM, but is more complicated because HJM consider growth only over one-year periods, while we estimate for several years before and after the loan.

as of the year of the merger is included in the firm's employment in all years prior to any mergers or acquisitions occurring before the base year, as if the establishments were always together. The employment of divested establishments is not included in the firm's employment prior to divestment, as if the establishments were never together, if a divestiture occurs before the base year. If a merger, acquisition, or divestiture occurs after the base year, employment of divested establishments measured in the year prior to divestment is included in all subsequent years, while that of the acquired establishments is not.[14]

Following HJM and other analyses of age-size variation in firm growth, we form age-size categories. Only a tiny fraction of SBA loan recipients have more than 249 employees in the year prior to loan receipt,[15] so we restrict attention to firms up to this threshold, with the following groupings: 1–4, 5–19, 20–49, 50–99, and 100–249 employees. As we show below, SBA recipients also tend to be young firms, and we group years of age as follows: zero (start-up), one to three, four to ten, and eleven or older.[16] We estimate separate effects for the sixteen age-size groups defined as the intersection of these categorizations. As discussed in the next section, start-ups require a separate matching process (because of the lack of available history for matching), but they are also of special interest in light of the HJM findings on their great importance in job creation. Among the fifteen non-start-up groups, the one- to three-year-old age category is of particular interest, representing the "valley of death"—the period of high mortality among firms in their first few years. The eleven or older age category corresponds to "mature" firms.

We next turn to a description of the SBA loan recipients by age, size, and growth in comparison to nonrecipients in the LBD. As discussed in Brown and Earle (forthcoming), remarkably little is known about what types of firms get SBA loans and how recipients compare to nonrecipients, so these results may be of broader interest to anyone studying SBA programs.

Table 9.2 shows the number of loan recipients in the LBD that fall into each of the sixteen age-size categories. The numbers decline in size for the youngest continuers, while the most numerous size category is five to nineteen employees for the older age groups. The youngest continuers (age one to three) in the largest size (100–249 employees) group are a particularly small cell, suggesting caution in the interpretation of the results for this group.

How does the age-size distribution of recipients compare with nonrecipients? Table 9.3 shows the empirical probability of receiving an SBA loan in

14. For acquisitions prior to the base year and divestitures after the base year, we use a single employment value applied to all preacquisition years and postdivestment years, respectively, to avoid including employment changes occurring under other firms' ownership.

15. Among SBA loan recipients otherwise able to be in the regressions in tables 9.8 and 9.9, 0.3 percent have more than 249 employees in the year prior to loan receipt.

16. Start-up is defined as entry into the LBD, implying positive employment, and therefore employment in start-up firms is by definition zero in the year prior to start-up. We do not divide start-ups into size categories.

Table 9.2   **Number of SBA loan recipients in LBD by age and size**

	Employment in year $t-1$					
Age	1–4	5–19	20–49	50–99	100–249	Total
0						65,600
1–3	55,300	40,800	7,700	1,500	400	107,700
4–10	37,500	52,900	14,400	3,300	1,000	111,800
11+	20,700	40,200	16,600	5,500	2,300	86,700
Total	113,400	133,900	38,800	10,300	3,700	373,500

Notes: This sample includes SBA loan recipients with and without matched controls that either received a loan at start up or had 249 employees or fewer in $t-1$. The numbers are rounded to the nearest 100 for disclosure avoidance. Age is measured in the loan receipt year, and size is employment in the year prior to loan receipt.

Table 9.3   **SBA loan recipients as percent of all LBD firm years in 1991–2009**

	Employment in year $t-1$					
Age	1–4	5–19	20–49	50–99	100–249	Total
0						0.69
1–3	0.44	0.78	0.88	0.69	0.45	0.55
4–10	0.26	0.60	0.82	0.71	0.48	0.42
11+	0.13	0.29	0.42	0.40	0.30	0.23
Total	0.26	0.48	0.59	0.50	0.34	0.40

Notes: This sample includes SBA loan recipients with and without matched controls. The SBA loan recipients in the numerator are counted once. All SBA loan recipient and nonrecipient firm years are included in the denominator. Age is measured in the loan receipt year and size is employment in the year prior to loan receipt.

a particular year. For the sample as a whole the probability is 0.40 percent, and for start-ups the probability is 0.69 percent. Probabilities decline in age overall and for the size categories with up to forty-nine employees, while the age four to ten group has the largest probability for the two largest-size categories. The relationship with size is inverse-U shaped, with the twenty to forty-nine employee category having the highest probabilities. For every age group, the probability of receiving an SBA loan is higher for the 100–249 size group than for the one to four employee group. Thus, from a probability of receipt standpoint SBA loans are, in practice, allocated toward start-ups and younger firms but not toward the smallest size groups among the more mature small- to medium-sized firms that receive the loans. Nonetheless, a substantial share of all SBA loans goes to very small, mature firms.

Brown and Earle (forthcoming) report that SBA recipients' preloan growth rates tend to differ systematically from that of typical firms described

Table 9.4   **Mean employment growth between four years before and one year before loan receipt for SBA loan recipients by age and size**

	Employment in year $t-1$					
Age	1–4	5–19	20–49	50–99	100–249	Total
4–10	0.041	0.336	0.451	0.516	0.564	0.222
11+	−0.072	0.092	0.145	0.174	0.198	0.054
Total	0.003	0.232	0.288	0.305	0.306	0.150

Notes: This sample includes SBA loan recipients with and without matched controls. Growth is calculated using the Davis-Haltiwanger method $\{[2 \times (emp_{t-1} - emp_{t-4})] / (emp_{t-4} + emp_{t-1})\}$. Age is measured in the loan receipt year and size is employment in the year prior to loan receipt.

by Hurst and Pugsley (2011). Eslava and Haltiwanger (2014) show that young Colombian manufacturing firms that are also larger (often meaning they grew faster since birth) experience higher growth rates. One explanation for this pattern is that young firms with drive, managerial talent, and ambition grow faster from birth, and these factors persist in affecting growth rates later on.[17] Table 9.4 tabulates average employment growth rates from four years before the loan to one year prior to the loan for the SBA recipient sample by age-size categories, restricting attention to firms at least four years old. For comparison, table 9.5 contains the analogous computation for all nonrecipients in the LBD. The mean three-year preloan growth rate is higher among SBA recipients than nonrecipients in all age-size groups except very small, mature firms (age eleven or older with one to four employees). Mean three-year growth among SBA recipients is 0.150 compared to 0.019 among nonrecipients. Thus, while these results support Hurst and Pugsley's (2011) findings about the growth of typical small firms, they imply that many SBA firms belong to the atypical subset of small firms (including gazelles) that tend to grow strongly, even prior to loan receipt. Together with the other factors differentiating recipients and nonrecipients, this result highlights the importance of conditioning on prior growth. Below, we outline a matching approach to estimation where comparisons are carried out with controls experiencing similar past growth histories.

The analysis above is conditional on survival. But SBA loan receipt may also affect survival, which we discuss in a separate subsection below.

Finally, all of this analysis so far has implicitly treated SBA loan receipt as a binary treatment. The SBA loan amounts vary substantially, however. Table 9.6 displays mean loan amounts by age-size categories. Loan amounts increase monotonically in both age and size, except that start-ups receive slightly larger loans than one to four employee non-start-ups. While the

17. To the extent that initial success is due to luck or other transient factors, however, there could be reversion to the mean.

Table 9.5   **Mean pretreatment employment growth for all non-SBA LBD firms present in year *t* in 1991–2009 by age and size**

| Age | Employment in year $t-1$ | | | | | |
	1–4	5–19	20–49	50–99	100–249	Total
4–10	0.007	0.267	0.342	0.382	0.421	0.066
11+	−0.064	0.072	0.104	0.122	0.135	−0.015
Total	−0.031	0.147	0.176	0.186	0.191	0.019

Note: Growth is calculated using the Davis-Haltiwanger method $\{[2 \times (emp_{t-1} - emp_{t-4})] / (emp_{t-4} + emp_{t-1})\}$. Age is measured in the loan receipt year and size is employment in the year prior to loan receipt.

Table 9.6   **Mean SBA loan size (2010 $US) with and without matched controls**

| Age | Employment in year $t-1$ | | | | | |
	1–4	5–19	20–49	50–99	100–249	Total
0						259,362
1–3	220,059	389,783	648,111	895,688	902,995	327,228
4–10	250,075	471,787	800,836	1,008,725	1,116,431	456,831
11+	253,158	505,480	902,777	1,204,657	1,314,167	584,643
Total	236,005	456,907	814,098	1,096,969	1,219,093	445,995

Notes: This sample includes SBA loan recipients with and without matched controls that either received a loan at start up or had 249 employees or fewer in $t-1$. The numbers are rounded to the nearest 100 for disclosure avoidance. Age is measured in the loan receipt year and size is employment in the year prior to loan receipt.

grand mean across all SBA loans is $445,995 (in 2010 USD), the mean amount for the smallest-size group is about half that, and it is three times bigger for the largest-size group. This suggests that the treatments are very different across age-size groups, and the analysis allows for this variation by using loan amount rather than a simple treatment dummy.

9.4   Estimation Strategy

Our attempt to estimate the causal effect of SBA loan receipt on employment and survival faces typical identification challenges. Let $TREAT_{it} \in \{0,1\}$ indicate whether firm i receives an SBA loan in year t, and let y_{it+s}^1 be employment at time $t + s$, $s \geq 0$, following loan receipt. The employment of the firm if it had not received a loan is y_{it+s}^0. The loan's causal effect for firm i at time $t + s$ is defined as $y_{it+s}^1 - y_{it+s}^0$. The value of y_{it+s}^0 is not observable, however. We define the average effect of treatment on the treated as $E\{y_{it+s}^1 - y_{it+s}^0 \mid TREAT_{it} = 1\} = E\{y_{it+s}^1 \mid TREAT_{it} = 1\} - E\{y_{it+s}^0 \mid TREAT_{it} = 1\}$. A counterfactual of the last term, that is, the average employment outcome of loan recipients had they not received a loan, can be estimated using the average employment of nonrecipients, $E\{y^0_{it+s} \mid \text{TREAT}_{it} = 0\}$. This approximation is valid as long as there are no uncontrolled contemporaneous effects correlated with loan receipt. To help control for such contemporaneous effects, we use matching techniques to select a comparison group.

For this purpose, we have taken the following steps. As mentioned in section 9.3, we limit our treated sample to firms in the LBD receiving their first SBA 7(a) or 504 loan in 1991–2009 and those not receiving a SBA disaster loan prior to their first 7(a) or 504 loan. To be eligible to be a candidate control firm for a particular treated firm, a firm can never have received an SBA 7(a), 504, or disaster loan at any time between 1953 and 2009; it must be in the same four-digit industry in the treated firm's loan receipt year and be in the same firm-age category (one to two years old, three to five years old, six to ten years old, and eleven years or older) in the treated firm's loan receipt year and in the same employment category (one employee, two to four employees, five to nine employees, ten to nineteen employees, twenty to forty-nine employees, fifty to ninety-nine employees, and one hundred or more employees) in the year prior to loan receipt. For non-start-ups, the control must have nonmissing employment in the year prior to the treated firm's loan receipt. Among firms with nineteen or fewer employees in the previous year and start-ups, we also require the candidate control firm to be located in the same state (firms with one to nineteen employees are much more numerous than ones with more than nineteen employees, so we can afford to impose more restrictions on this group).[18] In addition, for non-start-ups we impose a restriction that the ratio of the treated firm's employment in the previous year to the control firm's previous year employment be greater than 0.9 and less than 1.1. This means that among firms with nine or fewer employees, employment must match exactly.

For the non-start-ups, we would also like to match on variables representing the growth history prior to treatment year, but it is difficult to design matching thresholds for each variable separately, so we reduce this dimensionality problem with propensity score matching. We estimate separate probit regressions using the sample of treated firms and their candidate controls (according to the exact-matching criteria) for different age-size categories (defined in the exact matching above).[19] The probit regresses a dummy for SBA loan receipt on cubic functions of the preloan year logs of employment, revenue, and assets, and their annual growth rates back four years prior to the loan; the log of payroll/number of employees in the preloan year; firm

18. Larger firms may well be in national markets, in which case matching on state would not be appropriate. Matching on geography below the state level even for the smallest firm categories would result in a large number of treated firms being left out of the analysis, potentially biasing the results.
19. Treated firms with no candidate controls are dropped at this point.

age; firm age squared; a multiunit firm dummy; and year dummies. For the lagged employment growth variables, all revenue and assets variables, and for the log of payroll/number of employees in the year prior to the treated firm's loan receipt, we also impute zeroes in place of missing values and include dummies for such cases. Conditioning on four years of lagged employment, revenues, and assets is intended to create a control group with very similar histories to the treated firms.

The treated firm observations in the probit regressions are each assigned a weight of $(N - R) / R$, where N is the total number of firms in the regression and R is the number of treated firms in the regression. The nontreated firms are assigned a weight of 1. This equalizes the total weight of the treated firm and nontreated firm groups. The purpose of this weighting is to produce propensity scores that span a wider range, centered around 0.5 rather than near zero.

We limit the treated and nontreated firms in the employment and survival regression analysis to those within a common support, meaning that no propensity score of a treated (nontreated) firm that we use is higher than the highest nontreated (treated) firm propensity score, and no propensity score of a treated (nontreated) firm that we use is lower than the lowest nontreated (treated) firm propensity score. A nontreated firm is included as a control for a particular treated firm if the ratio of the treated to the nontreated firm's propensity score is at least 0.9 and not more than 1.1. Treated firms with no controls meeting all these criteria are not included in the employment and survival regression analysis. Nontreated firms appear in the regressions as many times as they have treated firms to which they are matched (i.e., this is matching with replacement). Kernel weights are applied to the controls.[20] In the employment and survival regressions, each control is assigned a final weight of their kernel weight divided by the sum of the kernel weights for all controls for a particular treated firm, and the treated firm is given a weight of 1. As a result, the treated firm and all its control firms together receive equal weight.

Propensity score matching relies on a strong assumption of "selection on observables." Since our data are longitudinal, for the non-start-ups we are also able to eliminate unobserved, time-invariant differences in employment through difference-in-differences (DID) regression specifications. This estimation strategy does not control for possible time-varying unobservables, such as systematically different demand, productivity, or cost shocks received by treated and control firms during the treatment year. Brown and Earle (forthcoming) address this possibility by using an instrumental variable (IV) strategy in addition to the ordinary least squares (OLS) strategy

---

20. The kernel weight is $1 - \{abs[(\text{propensity score}_{tr} / \text{propensity score}_{ntr}) - 1] / 0.1\}^2$ where tr is a subscript for the treated firm, and ntr is a subscript for the nontreated firm. See Imbens and Wooldridge (2009) for discussion of kernel weighting.

employed here. They estimate slightly stronger employment effects in IV specifications than in OLS specifications like those used here. We do not estimate IV specifications here, because the instrumental variables suffer from weak first-stage power in thin age-size cells.

For firms receiving an SBA loan at start-up (during the first year of positive employment in the LBD), the matching procedures involve exact matching on industry, year, age (start-ups are matched only with start-ups), state, but not propensity score matching. We do not exact match on start-up employment because that is influenced by the treatment. Without propensity score matching on growth history and exact matching on preloan employment level, treated and control start-ups may thus be less closely matched on observables than non-start-ups.

Our analysis focuses on the first SBA loan, as subsequent loan receipt (approximately 20–25 percent of the loan sample is subsequent loans) may be influenced by the outcome of the first one. Also, given our long time series, we find it useful to constrain the time frame around which we calculate employment growth to focus on the short- and medium-term effects of the loan. This puts all of the loan cohorts on an equal footing so that each counts equally rather than having longer time series for the early cohorts and shorter series for the later ones. The basic form of the regression, therefore, uses the change in employment as the dependent variable as follows:

$$\Delta E_{ijt} = \alpha_j + X_{ijt}\beta + \theta_i\delta + u_{ijt},$$

where ΔE is the change in the number of employees over some period, i indexes firms from 1 to I, j indexes from 1 to J the treated firms to which the firm is a control (for treated firms $i = j$), and t indexes the loan years from 1 to T; α_j is a fixed effect for each group of treated firms and its matched controls (the "treatment-control-group"), X_{ijt} is a set of other variables including firm age and age squared (only for the specifications used in figure 9.1); u_{ijt} is an idiosyncratic error; θ_i is the amount of the SBA loan (which equals 0 for nontreated firms) received in year t, and δ is the loan effect of interest.

The dependent variable is defined in one specification as change in average employment from three years before to three years after the loan: $\Delta E_{ijt} = E_{ij.post} E_{ij.pre}$, with $E_{ij.post} = (E_{ijt+1} + E_{ijt+2} + E_{ijt+3}) / 3$, and $E_{ij.pre\_t} = (E_{ijt-1} + E_{ijt-2} + E_{ijt-3})/3$.[21] In survival regressions the dependent variable is a dummy for survival through a particular year after the treated firm's loan receipt.

The reliability of propensity score matching depends on whether, conditional on the propensity score, the potential outcomes y^1 and y^0 are independent of treatment incidence. The assumption of independence conditional on observables depends on the pretreatment variables being balanced between the treated and control groups. We assess this in two ways—by

21. In cases of missing values in years prior to loan receipt, we average employment during the available years $t-3$, $t-2$, and $t-1$.

Table 9.7   Bias before and after propensity score matching

	All nontreated	All treated	Control sample	Treated sample	Final standardized difference	Bias reduction (%)
Log emp$_{t-1}$	1.761	1.902	1.999	1.997	−0.143	98.69
Log (emp$_{t-1}$ / emp$_{t-2}$)	0.017	0.071	0.073	0.075	0.565	95.48
Log (emp$_{t-2}$ / emp$_{t-3}$)	0.024	0.072	0.070	0.073	0.735	93.57
Log (emp$_{t-3}$ / emp$_{t-4}$)	0.027	0.070	0.067	0.070	0.660	93.75
Log rev$_{t-1}$	6.396	6.611	6.710	6.691	−1.278	91.19
Log (rev$_{t-1}$ / rev$_{t-2}$)	0.031	0.091	0.093	0.111	3.892	70.13
Log (rev$_{t-2}$ / rev$_{t-3}$)	0.041	0.095	0.099	0.109	2.308	81.48
Log (rev$_{t-3}$ / rev$_{t-4}$)	0.052	0.098	0.094	0.102	2.076	82.03
Log assets$_{t-1}$	4.867	5.107	5.220	5.100	−6.533	50.22
Log (assets$_{t-1}$ / assets$_{t-2}$)	0.017	0.116	0.096	0.121	4.040	74.21
Log (assets$_{t-2}$ / assets$_{t-3}$)	0.030	0.073	0.077	0.088	1.803	74.87
Log (assets$_{t-3}$ / assets$_{t-4}$)	0.038	0.076	0.074	0.084	1.784	72.62
Log wage	3.042	3.048	3.079	3.088	1.074	−42.39
Age	10.706	8.324	8.863	8.773	−1.080	96.21
Multiunit	0.044	0.051	0.050	0.050	−0.381	88.90

Notes: For a given variable, say age, the standardized difference (percent bias) is $SDIFF$(age) = $\{100(1 \ / \ N) \ \Sigma_{i \in A}[\text{age}_i - \Sigma_{j \in C} \ g(p_i, p_j)\text{age}_j]\} \ / \ \sqrt{[Var_{i \in A}(\text{age}) + Var_{j \in C}(\text{age})] \ / \ 2}$. The group before propensity score matching is treated and control firms satisfying exact matches on employment, treatment year age category, industry, year, and state (if it has nineteen or fewer employees in the prior year). Firms in the group after propensity score matching satisfy the propensity score bandwidth criterion, the common support criterion, and are in the regression samples for tables 9.8 and 9.9. The samples do not include firms receiving loans at start-up or their controls.

performing a standardized difference (or bias) test for the main variables included in the matching probit regressions, and by analyzing the pretreatment event-time dynamics. Table 9.7 reports the means of the main variables included in the matching probit regressions for four different samples: all treated firms, all nontreated firms, treated firms included in the employment regressions in tables 9.8 and 9.9, and controls included in those employment regressions. Treated firm employment is larger and age is younger than for nontreated firms prior to matching, and treated firms experience more employment growth in the four years prior to treatment. After matching, these differences are negligible. The standardized difference measures confirm this: employment, employment growth, and age biases are reduced by over 93 percent.[22] None of the biases are close to being large after matching.[23] Appendix table 9A.1 shows the means and percent bias after matching by age-size categories. Though none of the biases are large, the biggest ones are for larger young firms (the age one to three categories with fifty or more employees), which are the groups with the smallest loan recipient counts.

22. The mean age is very similar in the total treated and total nontreated samples, leaving little scope for improvement through matching.
23. Rosenbaum and Rubin (1985) consider a value of 20 to be large.

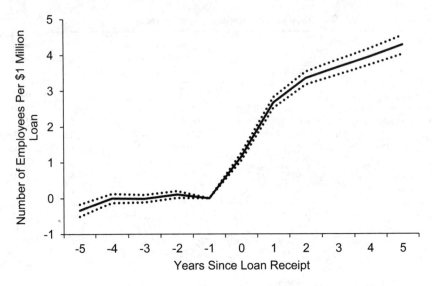

Fig. 9.1   Dynamics for number of employees per $1 million loan, firms receiving loans after start-up

Notes: These are loan amount coefficients from kernel-weighted OLS regressions with a dependent variable of the firm's employment in the respective year minus employment in year $t - 1$. Loan amount is in millions of 2010 dollars. Treatment year age, age squared, and treated firm-control fixed effects are included in the regressions. The sample is the same in the regressions in years t, $t + 1$, $t + 2$, $t + 3$, $t + 4$, and $t + 5$. To be in the samples for the pretreatment years, treated firms and at least one control must have positive employment in the respective year, as well as in $t - 1$ through $t + 5$. The dotted lines are the bounds of the 99 percent confidence interval, based on standard errors clustered by firm.

These tests suggest the matching has achieved reasonable balance within each age-size category; treated firms are matched with controls that have had similar growth in the past.

The second test for how effectively the matching process has achieved balance between the treated and control groups uses estimates of the dynamic effects of SBA loan receipt on employment in our sample of non-start-up firms as a "preprogram test" in the sense of Heckman and Hotz 1989, or a "pseudo-outcome" test in the sense of Imbens and Wooldridge (2009). We define t as the loan year, and use the year prior to the loan, $t - 1$, as the base year, computing employment differences for each year from five before to five after the loan, so that $\Delta E_{ijt} = E_{ijt+s} - E_{ijt-1} (s = -5, -4, \ldots 4, 5)$. Figure 9.1 shows that pretreatment growth differences between future treated and control firms are negligible, so the matching appears to be effective at eliminating growth differences prior to $t - 1$. Non-start-up SBA loan recipient employment grows significantly more than that of controls starting in the loan year, and the gap steadily grows to 4.3 extra jobs per $1 million loan by five years after loan receipt.

Table 9.8   **Size effects on employment growth per $1 million loan by size categories, age categories**

	Loan amount coefficient	Number of observations	Number of treated firms
Emp. 1–4	2.434	1,284,000	59,700
	(0.061)		
Emp. 5–19	2.173	737,700	67,800
	(0.043)		
Emp. 20–49	3.115	2,517,600	28,400
	(0.066)		
Emp. 50–99	3.946	286,800	6,900
	(0.206)		
Emp. 100–249	5.873	56,900	2,400
	(0.635)		
Age 0	5.336	7,556,800	49,800
	(0.195)		
Age 1–3	3.130	1,282,100	53,100
	(0.128)		
Age 4–10	2.960	1,108,400	57,400
	(0.100)		
Age 11+	3.015	2,492,400	54,700
	(0.081)		

Notes: These are kernel-weighted OLS regressions, run separately for each size and age category. The dependent variable is average employment in $t + 1$ through $t + 3$ minus average employment in $t - 3$ through $t - 1$, including only firms that have positive employment in each of those years. Loan amount is in millions of 2010 dollars. Treated firm-control fixed effects are also included in the regressions. Standard errors, cluster-adjusted by firm, are in parentheses. The number of observations and SBA firms are rounded to the nearest 100 for disclosure avoidance.

9.5   Results

9.5.1   Employment Growth Estimates

We present estimates considering heterogeneity separately by size and age groups (table 9.8), followed by effects across age-size groups (table 9.9 and figures 9.2 and 9.3), to see how the effects differ with and without age-size interactions. For a decisionmaker interested in allocating loans to maximize the impact, an important question concerns the observability of variables used in targeting. Decisionmakers may have more reliable information on firm size than age (because age is more easily manipulated), so it is useful to know whether conditioning loans only on size reduces the efficiency of loan allocation.[24] The question is similar to HJM's analysis of the size-growth

24. Observed firm age might be easily manipulated, for example, by renaming and reregistering what is essentially the same company. Firm size might be manipulated through hiring decisions on the margin, but large changes in firm size are more difficult, although splitting up a large firm to make it eligible for small business preferences is hardly unheard of. If age

Table 9.9   Employment growth regressions by age-size categories

	Loan amount coefficient	Number of observations	Number of treated firms
Age 0	5.336	7,556,800	49,800
	(0.195)		
Age 1–3, emp. 1–4	3.356	622,500	28,500
	(0.113)		
Age 1–3, emp. 5–19	2.606	163,800	18,500
	(0.130)		
Age 1–3, emp. 20–49	3.738	467,400	5,000
	(0.280)		
Age 1–3, emp. 50–99	2.127	26,600	800
	(0.876)		
Age 1–3, emp. 100–249	8.712	1,800	200
	(4.739)		
Age 4–10, emp. 1–4	1.783	313,800	19,500
	(0.067)		
Age 4–10, emp. 5–19	2.244	201,100	25,100
	(0.069)		
Age 4–10, emp. 20–49	3.260	547,600	10,300
	(0.119)		
Age 4–10, emp. 50–99	4.587	41,000	1,900
	(0.539)		
Age 4–10, emp. 100–249	6.932	4,700	500
	(2.131)		
Age 11+, emp. 1–4	1.644	347,700	11,700
	(0.120)		
Age 11+, emp. 5–19	1.879	372,700	24,200
	(0.047)		
Age 11+, emp. 20–49	2.871	1,502,400	13,100
	(0.072)		
Age 11+, emp. 50–99	3.969	219,200	4,200
	(0.217)		
Age 11+, emp. 100–249	5.504	50,400	1,700
	(0.625)		

Notes: These are kernel-weighted OLS regressions, run separately for each age-size category. The dependent variable is average employment in $t + 1$ through $t + 3$ minus average employment in $t - 3$ through $t - 1$, including only firms that have positive employment in each of those years. Loan amount is in millions of 2010 dollars. Treated firm-control fixed effects are also included in the regressions. Standard errors, cluster-adjusted by firm, are in parentheses. The number of observations and SBA firms are rounded to the nearest 100 for disclosure avoidance.

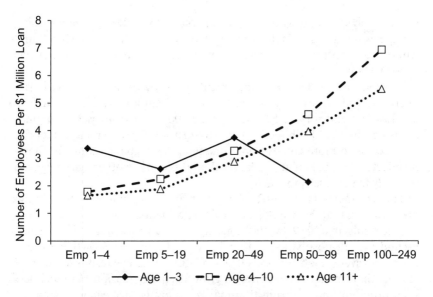

Fig. 9.2   Size effects on employment growth per $1 million loan for each age category

Note: These are plots of non-start-up firm loan amount coefficients reported in table 9.9, including only coefficients significant at the 5 percent level.

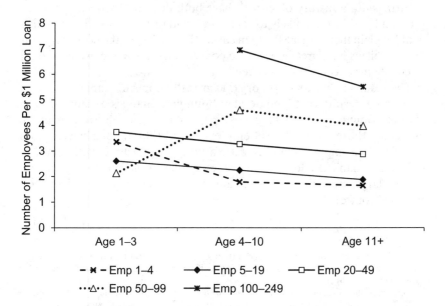

Fig. 9.3   Age effects on employment growth per $1 million loan for each size category

Note: These are plots of non-start-up firm loan amount coefficients reported in table 9.9, including only coefficients significant at the 5 percent level.

relationship with and without age controls; HJM report that controlling for age essentially eliminates the negative size-growth relationship found without age controls, and we can carry out a similar analysis for the effects of SBA loans.

Table 9.8 shows that the employment effects of the loans generally rise in size, varying from 2.2 jobs per $1 million loan for the five to nineteen employment category to 5.9 jobs for the 100–249 category. This pattern holds despite the likelihood that control firms in the larger size categories have access to more conventional financing than smaller controls. Start-up effects (5.3 jobs) are much larger than those in the other age categories (roughly flat at three jobs each).

The size analysis for non-start-ups with and without age controls in figure 9.4 shows that the size effects are virtually identical either way. Comparing the results in table 9.9 with the average preloan growth rates in table 9.4, we find a strong positive association between average past growth in the category and average job creation effects of SBA loans. The results in table 9.9 suggest that smaller, older firms do grow after loan receipt, but much less than other groups. Firms in the smaller, older age-size categories have a much lower propensity to receive SBA loans than other age-size categories (table 9.2),[25] but they still represent a significant fraction of total SBA loans (the three categories with fewer than two created jobs per $1 million loan represent 26 percent of all SBA loans).

Firms with a history of growth have both demonstrated the ability to grow and may be more likely to want to expand further in the future, which could explain their larger SBA loan effects. This is despite the possibility that growing firms have greater access to conventional financing, which should attenuate the effect of SBA-backed loans.[26]

The results above focus on organic growth. Appendix tables 9A.2 and 9A.3 show results that include firm boundary changes as employment changes. Boundary changes are most frequent in larger, more mature firms, especially those with 100–249 employees and that are age eleven years or older. The employment effects are a bit higher for firms with 100–249 employees than the effects solely using organic employment growth, suggesting larger treated firms are expanding more via acquisition than their matched controls.

---

is therefore less easily or reliably observed than size, then an important question is whether using information on size alone is at all useful, or if age is a crucial piece of information for targeting types of firms.

25. This could reflect either less need/desire for a loan or lower-quality loan applications.

26. The control firms in the age-size categories with higher past growth rates are more likely to receive conventional financing than controls in other categories, dampening the treatment effects if finance facilitates growth.

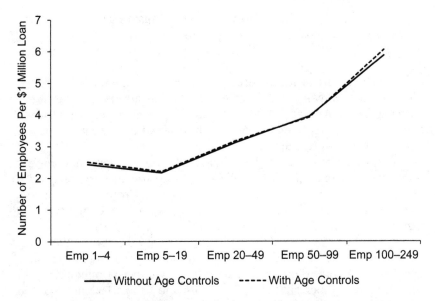

Fig. 9.4   Size effects on employment growth per $1 million loan, with and without age controls

Notes: These are plots of loan amount coefficients for non-start-up firms reported in tables 9.8 and 9.9. The numbers with age controls are averages of the coefficients for the size category across age categories, weighted by the number of treated firms in each cell.

9.5.2   Survival Estimates

The analysis so far assumes no differences in survival rates between treated firms and controls, although the SBA frequently refers to business survival as a performance measure, and access to loans may well affect survival. The direction of the effect is not certain, however, because while more finance may help a business through hard times, increased leverage and possible overextension could create greater vulnerability. Nor is the measurement of survival unambiguous, and any disappearance from the database is classified as an exit. Though great effort has been made to link establishments across time in the LBD, we cannot always distinguish bankruptcy and other genuine shutdowns from buy-outs or reorganizations that lead to a change in the identifying code in the LBD. As some of these outcomes represent business failure, others reflect success, and some level of exit is a normal feature of a dynamic economy, the analysis of exit is thus also not as clear normatively as our analysis of employment effects.

With these qualifications in mind, we are nonetheless interested to ascertain how SBA loan receipt affects firm survival. In this section we estimate these effects using linear probability model (LPM) regressions for shorter-

(three-year) and longer-run (ten-year) survival. Again we examine the heterogeneity by age-size categories. Other than the dependent variable, the regressions are identical to the employment regressions in the previous section.

We include only firm exits occurring within the examined time period that have no surviving establishments (establishment sales to other firms) postexit. Firms that exit via sale of their establishments are ambiguous from a performance perspective—some may be cases where the entrepreneur is cashing in on a successful venture.

To provide a baseline for the estimated effects, the three- and ten-year survival rates in the regression sample for each age-size category are reported in tables 9.10 and 9.11. Average survival rates generally increase with both age and size, but for within age groups there is little difference in survival for size groups of five employees and greater.

Tables 9.12 and 9.13 and figures 9.5, 9.6, and 9.7 display the three-year survival regression results. The effects are sharply declining in age, ranging from a 14 percent higher propensity to survive per $1 million loan for start-ups to –1.2 percent for mature firms, and this pattern holds across all size classes (figure 9.6). The effects for non-start-ups vary little across employment categories, with the exception of a higher effect for the smallest firms (one to four employees), and this pattern holds with or without age controls (figure 9.7). The firms least likely to want to grow (small, mature firms) actually exhibit negative survival effects from loan receipt.

The ten-year survival effect (tables 9.14 and 9.15 and figures 9.8, 9.9, and 9.10) is much stronger for firms with nineteen or fewer employees than the three-year effect, while it is very similar for larger firms, resulting in a sharper decline of the effect with size. Loans have a larger effect on shorter-run than longer-run survival for start-up firms, suggesting that the loans are particularly beneficial while they are in the "valley of death." The effects are higher over the longer period for the other age categories, though. Across age-size

Table 9.10   Three-year survival rates in survival regression samples (percent)

	Employment in year prior to SBA loan					
Age	1 to 4	5 to 19	20 to 49	50 to 99	100 to 249	Total
0						62.27
1–3	68.17	72.50	71.80	71.88	71.00	70.00
4–10	74.57	80.31	80.86	79.76	79.47	78.26
11+	76.78	83.60	85.18	85.57	86.51	82.54
Total	71.76	79.05	80.95	81.97	83.44	72.90

Note: These numbers are calculated from the full survival regression samples for loans issued in 1991–2009, including both treated and control firms.

Table 9.11 **Ten-year survival rates in survival regression samples**

	Employment in year prior to SBA loan					
Age	1 to 4	5 to 19	20 to 49	50 to 99	100 to 249	Total
0						30.79
1–3	36.31	40.85	39.31	37.33	34.79	38.28
4–10	43.56	49.78	49.92	49.02	46.80	47.80
11+	45.83	56.13	58.47	57.82	58.53	54.99
Total	40.46	49.37	51.83	52.76	54.20	43.13

Note: These numbers are calculated from the full survival regression samples for loans issued in 1991–2002, including both treated and control firms.

Table 9.12 **Three-year survival regressions by size categories, age categories**

	Loan amount coefficient	Number of observations	Number of treated firms
Emp. 1–4	0.026	2,832,100	95,100
	(0.002)		
Emp. 5–19	0.007	1,220,600	94,900
	(0.001)		
Emp. 20–49	0.010	4,221,500	37,000
	(0.001)		
Emp. 50–99	0.012	423,400	8,900
	(0.002)		
Emp. 100–249	0.012	77,200	3,100
	(0.003)		
Age 0	0.140	24,686,200	83,400
	(0.002)		
Age 1–3	0.055	3,057,100	85,100
	(0.002)		
Age 4–10	0.020	1,953,200	81,700
	(0.001)		
Age 11+	−0.0124	3,764,600	72,200
	(0.0009)		

Notes: These are kernel-weighted OLS regressions, run separately for each size and age category. The dependent variable is a dummy for survival through $t + 3$. Loan amount is in millions of 2010 dollars. Treated firm-control fixed effects are also included in the regressions. Standard errors, cluster-adjusted by firm, are in parentheses. The number of observations and SBA firms are rounded to the nearest 100 for disclosure avoidance.

Table 9.13   **Three-year survival regressions by age-size categories**

	Loan amount coefficient	Number of observations	Number of treated firms
Age 0	0.140	24,686,200	83,400
	(0.002)		
Age 1–3, emp. 1–4	0.067	1,638,900	47,700
	(0.004)		
Age 1–3, emp. 5–19	0.052	350,000	28,600
	(0.003)		
Age 1–3, emp. 20–49	0.042	1,012,900	7,300
	(0.004)		
Age 1–3, emp. 50–99	0.069	51,600	1,200
	(0.007)		
Age 1–3, emp. 100–249	0.036	3,800	300
	(0.022)		
Age 4–10, emp. 1–4	0.017	608,900	30,100
	(0.004)		
Age 4–10, emp. 5–19	0.013	331,700	34,800
	(0.002)		
Age 4–10, emp. 20–49	0.025	939,300	13,400
	(0.002)		
Age 4–10, emp. 50–99	0.026	65,700	2,600
	(0.005)		
Age 4–10, emp. 100–249	0.023	7,600	700
	(0.009)		
Age 11+, emp. 1–4	−0.044	584,300	17,300
	(0.005)		
Age 11+, emp. 5–19	−0.026	538,900	31,500
	(0.002)		
Age 11+, emp. 20–49	−0.010	2,269,300	16,200
	(0.001)		
Age 11+, emp. 50–99	−0.0003	306,200	5,100
	(0.0020)		
Age 11+, emp. 100–249	0.0078	65,800	2,100
	(0.0032)		

Notes: These are kernel-weighted OLS regressions, run separately for each age-size category. The dependent variable is a dummy for survival through $t + 3$. Loan amount is in millions of 2010 dollars. Treated firm-control fixed effects are also included in the regressions. Standard errors, cluster-adjusted by firm, are in parentheses. The number of observations and SBA firms are rounded to the nearest 100 for disclosure avoidance.

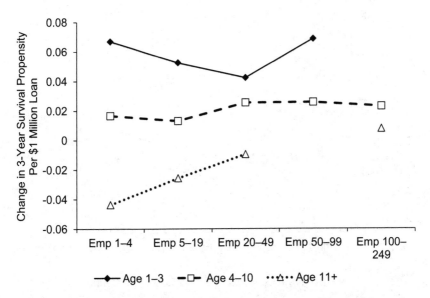

Fig. 9.5 Size effects on three-year survival propensity per $1 million loan for each age category

Note: These are plots of non-start-up firm results reported in table 9.13, including only coefficients significant at the 5 percent level.

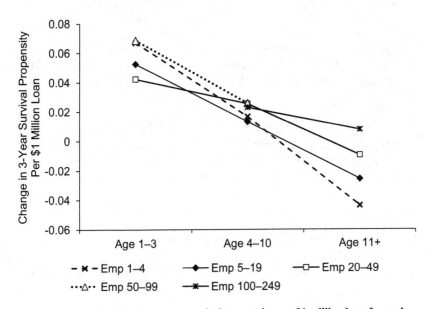

Fig. 9.6 Age effects on three-year survival propensity per $1 million loan for each size category

Note: These are plots of non-start-up firm results reported in table 9.13, including only coefficients significant at the 5 percent level.

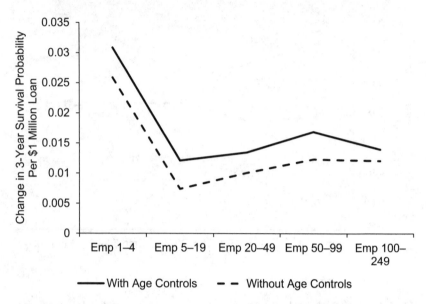

Fig. 9.7   Size effects on three-year survival propensity per $1 million loan, with and without age controls

Note: These are plots of results for non-start-up firms reported in tables 9.12 and 9.13. The results with age controls are averages of the coefficients for the size category across age categories, weighted by the number of treated firms in each cell.

groups, the estimated survival effects are strongly negatively correlated with average survival rates in the corresponding subpopulations, suggesting SBA loans have the greatest survival benefits for firms that are particularly vulnerable to exit.

9.5.3   Employment Growth Estimates Incorporating Exit

If we assume exit represents job loss, the significant survival effects from SBA loan receipt suggest the employment growth analysis focusing on surviving firms in section 9.5.1 may be biased. We investigate this by imputing zero values for employment following exit and reestimating.[27] The patterns are somewhat sensitive to whether exit is taken into account: the estimates incorporating exit, shown in tables 9.16 and 9.17 and figures 9.11, 9.12, and 9.13, result in a stronger positive association between size and the employment effect, and the effect now declines with age: relative to their matched controls, fewer treated firms going through the "valley of death" destroy jobs via exiting.

---

27. Exit effects could be incorporated in many ways, as it is not conceptually clear how many years of zeros to impute postexit. These results can thus be viewed as giving an indication of the direction the exit effect exerts on employment estimates rather than some exact magnitude.

Table 9.14   Ten-year survival regressions by size categories, age categories

	Loan amount coefficient	Number of observations	Number of treated firms
Emp. 1–4	0.072	1,105,000	40,000
	(0.004)		
Emp. 5–19	0.035	659,900	48,400
	(0.003)		
Emp. 20–49	0.011	2,697,500	22,400
	(0.002)		
Emp. 50–99	0.012	286,500	5,600
	(0.004)		
Emp. 100–249	0.013	43,000	1,800
	(0.006)		
Age 0	0.117	8,729,600	37,700
	(0.003)		
Age 1–3	0.079	1,405,200	38,000
	(0.004)		
Age 4–10	0.046	1,197,300	42,100
	(0.003)		
Age 11+	–0.008	2,189,400	38,200
	(0.002)		

Notes: These are kernel-weighted OLS regressions, run separately for each size and age category. The dependent variable is a dummy for survival through $t + 10$. Loan amount is in millions of 2010 dollars. Treated firm-control fixed effects are also included in the regressions. Standard errors, cluster-adjusted by firm, are in parentheses. The number of observations and SBA firms are rounded to the nearest 100 for disclosure avoidance.

These patterns are again highly correlated with mean past growth rates in the age-size groups, consistent with the idea that firms demonstrating past growth are more likely to want to grow in the future and thus to use the loan for expansion.

9.5.4   Variation by Pretreatment Growth

The fact that the job creation loan effects are larger by size categories suggests there may be an association between pretreatment growth and the employment response to loan receipt, since there is a mechanical relationship between past growth and size. If so, then past employment growth could be used to inform loan allocation. A similar argument applies to survival: if past growth reflects not only a demonstrated desire to grow in the future, but also firm quality, then it should be associated with survival. We may test this directly by interacting pretreatment employment growth and loan amount in regressions by age categories (except start-ups).[28]

28. For firms with positive employment in both $t-4$ and $t-1$, pretreatment growth is the difference between employment in $t-1$ and $t-4$, divided by three so as to annualize it. If a firm does not have employment in $t-4$, but has it in $t-3$, pretreatment growth is the difference between employment in $t-1$ and $t-3$, divided by two. Firms without positive employment in $t-4$

Table 9.15   Ten-year survival regressions by age-size categories

	Loan amount coefficient	Number of observations	Number of treated firms
Age 0	0.117	8,729,600	37,700
	(0.003)		
Age 1–3, emp. 1–4	0.094	563,600	19,400
	(0.007)		
Age 1–3, emp. 5–19	0.081	171,900	13,700
	(0.006)		
Age 1–3, emp. 20–49	0.065	635,500	4,100
	(0.006)		
Age 1–3, emp. 50–99	0.089	32,200	700
	(0.014)		
Age 1–3, emp. 100–249	0.002	2,000	100
	(0.034)		
Age 4–10, emp. 1–4	0.066	287,800	13,200
	(0.008)		
Age 4–10, emp. 5–19	0.044	197,100	18,600
	(0.005)		
Age 4–10, emp. 20–49	0.036	661,400	8,200
	(0.004)		
Age 4–10, emp. 50–99	0.057	46,100	1,600
	(0.008)		
Age 4–10, emp. 100–249	0.069	5,000	400
	(0.018)		
Age 11+, emp. 1–4	0.039	253,600	7,400
	(0.009)		
Age 11+, emp. 5–19	0.00002	290,900	16,200
	(0.00444)		
Age 11+, emp. 20–49	−0.020	1,400,700	10,100
	(0.003)		
Age 11+, emp. 50–99	−0.014	208,200	3,300
	(0.004)		
Age 11+, emp. 100–249	0.002	36,000	1,300
	(0.007)		

Notes: These are kernel-weighted OLS regressions, run separately for each age-size category. The dependent variable is a dummy for survival through $t + 10$. Loan amount is in millions of 2010 dollars. Treated firm-control fixed effects are also included in the regressions. Standard errors, cluster-adjusted by firm, are in parentheses. The number of observations and SBA firms are rounded to the nearest 100 for disclosure avoidance.

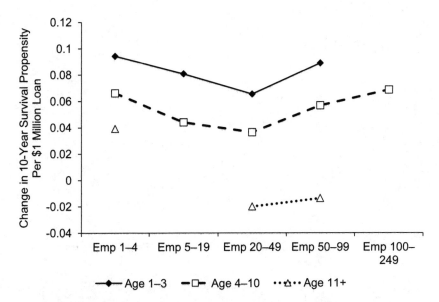

Fig. 9.8 Size effects on ten-year survival propensity per $1 million loan for each age category

Note: These are plots of non-start-up firm results reported in table 9.15, including only coefficients significant at the 5 percent level.

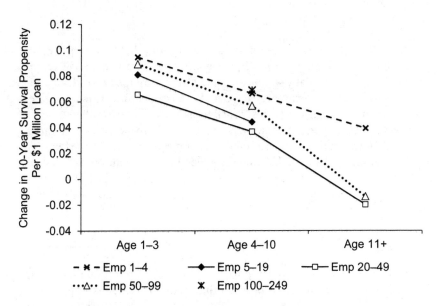

Fig. 9.9 Age effects on ten-year survival propensity per $1 million loan for each size category

Note: These are plots of non-start-up firm results reported in table 9.15, including only coefficients significant at the 5 percent level.

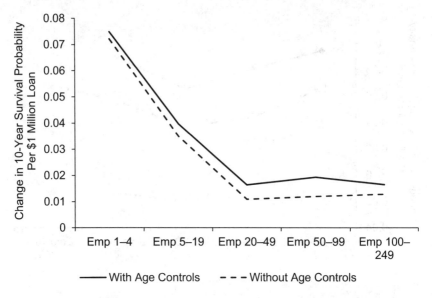

Fig. 9.10   Size effects on ten-year survival propensity per $1 million loan, with and without age controls

Notes: These are plots of results for non-start-up firms reported in tables 9.14 and 9.15. The results with age controls are averages of the coefficients for the size category across age categories, weighted by the number of treated firms in each cell.

Table 9.18 shows that the estimated relationship between pretreatment growth and the loan amount impact is positive for all three age groups, although it is statistically significant only for firms in the two older age categories, when exiting firms are excluded. When exit zeroes are incorporated, all three categories have positive associations and are statistically significant. The estimates suggest job creation per $1 million loan increases by about 0.1 for each additional employee added in the three years prior to the loan. The effects on survival are weaker, and the effect on longer-run survival is statistically insignificant for all three age categories. These results are consistent with pretreatment growth partly reflecting firm quality and partly a desire to expand further in the future.

9.6   Conclusion

Research on measures to support small businesses has been preoccupied with examining the basic proposition that small firms are disproportionate

---

and $t-3$, but with it in $t-2$, have pretreatment growth of the difference between employment in $t-1$ and $t-2$, and those only with positive employment in $t-1$ have pretreatment growth of employment in $t-1$ (since employment prior to that is assumed to be zero).

Table 9.16   **Employment growth regressions by size categories, age categories, accounting for exit**

	Loan amount coefficient	Number of observations	Number of treated firms
Emp. 1–4	2.094	2,633,400	90,700
	(0.050)		
Emp. 5–19	1.892	1,176,000	92,000
	(0.038)		
Emp. 20–49	2.995	4,036,100	35,800
	(0.067)		
Emp. 50–99	4.137	409,100	8,600
	(0.214)		
Emp. 100–249	6.947	73,800	2,900
	(0.702)		
Age 0	6.278	22,887,400	79,600
	(0.122)		
Age 1–3	3.537	2,860,300	81,500
	(0.113)		
Age 4–10	2.995	1,850,000	78,500
	(0.104)		
Age 11+	2.585	3,618,100	70,100
	(0.085)		

Notes: These are kernel-weighted OLS regressions, run separately for each size and age category. The dependent variable is average employment in $t + 1$ through $t + 3$ minus average employment in $t - 3$ through $t - 1$, including zeros for employment in years after exit. Loan amount is in millions of 2010 dollars. Treated firm-control fixed effects are also included in the regressions. Standard errors, cluster-adjusted by firm, are in parentheses. The number of observations and SBA firms are rounded to the nearest 100 for disclosure avoidance.

job creators. Although the proposition is practically an article of faith for many, HJM have recently shown that firm size and growth are essentially uncorrelated once the analysis accounts for firm age, and systematically larger job creation only comes from new entrants and very young firms. Whatever the nature of the firm age-size-growth relationships, however, the existing research does not address the question of whether and how job creation and survival per dollar of financing backed by the government varies across firms by size and age.

Our analysis matches firms with fewer than 250 employees receiving loans in the two largest loan guarantee programs of the Small Business Administration (the 7[a] and 504 programs) to nonrecipients that are essentially identical along every observable: preloan size, age, industry, year, and preloan growth history. For the results to be interpreted as causal, one must assume that there are no systematic time-varying differences between the loan recipients and control firms, such as differential demand, productivity, or cost shocks at the time of loan receipt. This is a potentially important caveat, as it is not difficult to imagine such shocks as the very motivation for

Table 9.17   **Employment growth regressions by age-size categories, accounting for exit**

	Loan amount coefficient	Number of observations	Number of treated firms
Age 0	6.278	22,887,400	79,600
	(0.122)		
Age 1–3, emp. 1–4	2.984	1,510,600	45,400
	(0.087)		
Age 1–3, emp. 5–19	2.643	334,400	27,600
	(0.368)		
Age 1–3, emp. 20–49	4.369	962,900	7,000
	(0.246)		
Age 1–3, emp. 50–99	5.362	48,800	1,200
	(0.907)		
Age 1–3, emp. 100–249	16.587	3,600	300
	(3.777)		
Age 4–10, emp. 1–4	1.554	567,100	28,700
	(0.058)		
Age 4–10, emp. 5–19	2.035	318,500	33,700
	(0.061)		
Age 4–10, emp. 20–49	3.400	894,600	13,000
	(0.116)		
Age 4–10, emp. 50–99	5.403	62,700	2,500
	(0.513)		
Age 4–10, emp. 100–249	7.488	7,200	700
	(2.329)		
Age 11+, emp. 1–4	1.143	555,700	16,700
	(0.115)		
Age 11+, emp. 5–19	1.301	523,100	30,700
	(0.046)		
Age 11+, emp. 20–49	2.341	2,178,600	15,800
	(0.081)		
Age 11+, emp. 50–99	3.516	297,700	4,900
	(0.232)		
Age 11+, emp. 100–249	6.232	63,100	2,000
	(0.678)		

Notes: These are kernel-weighted OLS regressions, run separately for each age-size category. The dependent variable is average employment in $t + 1$ through $t + 3$ minus average employment in $t - 3$ through $t - 1$, including zeros for employment in years after exit. Loan amount is in millions of 2010 dollars. Treated firm-control fixed effects are also included in the regressions. Standard errors, cluster-adjusted by firm, are in parentheses. The number of observations and SBA firms are rounded to the nearest 100 for disclosure avoidance.

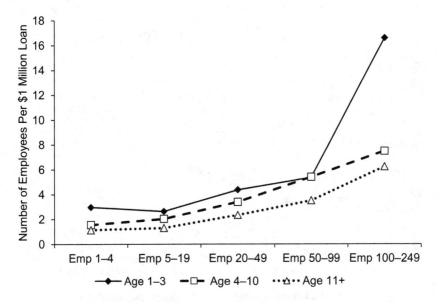

Fig. 9.11   Size effects on employment growth (accounting for exit) per \$1 million loan for each age category

Note: These are plots of non-start-up firm results reported in table 9.17, including only coefficients significant at the 5 percent level.

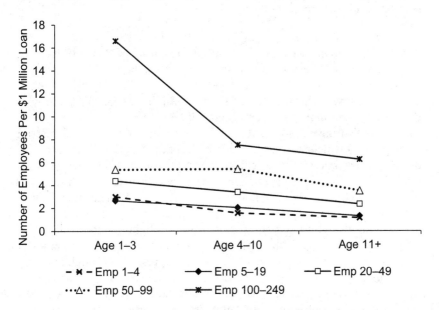

Fig. 9.12   Age effects on employment growth (accounting for exit) per \$1 million loan for each size category

Note: These are plots of non-start-up firm results reported in table 9.17, including only coefficients significant at the 5 percent level.

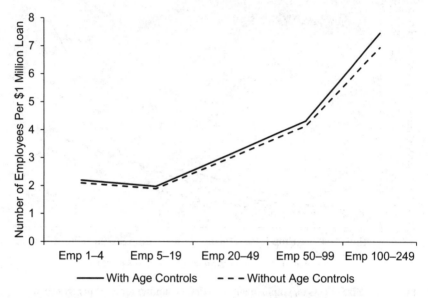

Fig. 9.13   Size effects on employment growth (accounting for exit) per $1 million loan, with and without age controls

Note: These are plots of results for non-start-up firms reported in tables 9.16 and 9.17. The results with age controls are averages of the coefficients for the size category across age categories, weighted by the number of treated firms in each cell.

applying for a loan. On the other hand, if the nature of this bias does not vary systematically across size and age groups, then the relative magnitudes of the loan effects would be unchanged.

Consistent with HJM's findings for overall job creation rates and with the literature on loan access and financial constraints on growth by firm age, we find strong employment and survival effects for start-up firms and both the employment and survival effects decline in age. Survival effects also decline in size, but within age categories employment effects increase with size. Unlike HJM, however, the employment effects increase with size even without age controls. We also find that the categories of firms most vulnerable to exit experience the largest survival effects from loan receipt. The loans are particularly helpful to young firms coping with the "valley of death."

The finding that small, mature firms expand the least and experience lower survival rates in response to SBA loan receipt suggests that though they may have difficulty obtaining loans (as suggested by the literature on loan access by firm size), their financial constraints only weakly affect growth. An interpretation of this result, consistent with Hurst and Pugsley's (2011) contention that most such firms are not motivated to grow, is that government support for them may therefore have a smaller impact. Though small, mature firms exhibit the lowest probability of receiving an SBA loan among all age-size categories and they still account for a substantial fraction of all SBA loans.

Table 9.18   **Regressions with pretreatment growth interactions by age categories**

	Loan amount	Pretreatment growth	Loan amt.* pretreatment growth	Number of obs.	Number of treated firms
		Employment growth			
Age 1–3	3.080	0.102	0.012	1,282,100	53,100
	(0.150)	(0.019)	(0.021)		
Age 4–10	2.611	0.060	0.120	1,108,400	57,400
	(0.107)	(0.035)	(0.034)		
Age 11+	2.786	0.210	0.093	2,492,400	54,700
	(0.078)	(0.024)	(0.021)		
		Employment growth with exit zeros			
Age 1–3	2.896	0.068	0.090	2,860,300	81,500
	(0.156)	(0.017)	(0.023)		
Age 4–10	2.696	0.114	0.102	1,850,000	78,500
	(0.115)	(0.030)	(0.038)		
Age 11+	2.406	0.297	0.076	3,618,100	70,100
	(0.082)	(0.027)	(0.018)		
		Three-year survival, 1991–2009 treatments			
Age 1–3	0.052	−0.00168	0.00029	3,057,100	85,100
	(0.002)	(0.00009)	(0.00013)		
Age 4–10	0.019	−0.00011	0.00016	1,953,200	81,700
	(0.001)	(0.00014)	(0.00017)		
Age 11+	−0.013	0.00053	0.00035	3,764,600	72,200
	(0.001)	(0.00010)	(0.00009)		
		Ten-year survival, 1991–2002 treatments			
Age 1–3	0.077	−0.0018	0.00015	1,405,200	38,000
	(0.004)	(0.0001)	(0.00022)		
Age 4–10	0.045	−0.0006	0.00029	1,197,300	42,100
	(0.003)	(0.0002)	(0.00039)		
Age 11+	−0.008	0.0007	−0.00001	2,189,400	38,200
	(0.002)	(0.0002)	(0.00020)		

Notes: These are kernel-weighted OLS regressions, run separately for each age category. The dependent variable for employment growth is average employment in $t+1$ through $t+3$ minus average employment in $t-3$ through $t-1$, including only firms that have positive employment in each of those years. The dependent variable for employment growth with exit zeros is average employment in $t+1$ through $t+3$ minus average employment in $t-3$ through $t-1$, including zeros for employment in years after exit. The dependent variable for three-year survival is a dummy for survival through $t+3$. The dependent variable for ten-year survival is a dummy for survival through $t+10$. Loan amount is in millions of 2010 dollars. Treated firm-control fixed effects are also included in the regressions. For firms with positive employment in both $t-4$ and $t-1$, pretreatment growth is the difference between employment in $t-1$ and $t-4$, divided by three so as to annualize it. If a firm does not have employment in $t-4$, but has it in $t-3$, pretreatment growth is the difference between employment in $t-1$ and $t-3$, divided by two. Firms without positive employment in $t-4$ and $t-3$, but with it in $t-2$, have pretreatment growth of the difference between employment in $t-1$ and $t-2$, and those only with positive employment in $t-1$ have pretreatment growth of employment in $t-1$ (since employment prior to that is assumed to be zero). Standard errors, cluster-adjusted by firm, are in parentheses. The number of observations and SBA firms are rounded to the nearest 100 for disclosure avoidance.

Appendix

Table 9A.1   **Bias after propensity score matching by age-size category**

	Control sample	Treated sample	Standardized difference
Age 1–3, emp. 1–4			
Log emp$_{t-1}$	0.703	0.703	0.000
Log (emp$_{t-1}$ / emp$_{t-2}$)	0.045	0.055	2.257
Log (emp$_{t-2}$ / emp$_{t-3}$)	0.136	0.135	−0.231
Age 1–3, emp. 5–19			
Log emp$_{t-1}$	2.099	2.097	−0.138
Log (emp$_{t-1}$ / emp$_{t-2}$)	0.281	0.277	−0.867
Log (emp$_{t-2}$ / emp$_{t-3}$)	0.311	0.301	−2.343
Age 1–3, emp. 20–49			
Log emp$_{t-1}$	3.331	3.328	−0.236
Log (emp$_{t-1}$ / emp$_{t-2}$)	0.345	0.358	2.881
Log (emp$_{t-2}$ / emp$_{t-3}$)	0.413	0.437	5.740
Age 1–3, emp. 50–99			
Log emp$_{t-1}$	4.155	4.153	−0.126
Log (emp$_{t-1}$ / emp$_{t-2}$)	0.368	0.384	3.740
Log (emp$_{t-2}$ / emp$_{t-3}$)	0.492	0.547	12.913
Age 1–3, emp. 100–249			
Log emp$_{t-1}$	4.947	4.945	−0.102
Log (emp$_{t-1}$ / emp$_{t-2}$)	0.481	0.518	8.626
Log (emp$_{t-2}$ / emp$_{t-3}$)	0.586	0.598	2.774
Age 4–10, emp. 1–4			
Log emp$_{t-1}$	0.833	0.833	0.000
Log (emp$_{t-1}$ / emp$_{t-2}$)	−0.039	−0.038	0.161
Log (emp$_{t-2}$ / emp$_{t-3}$)	0.008	0.012	1.071
Log (emp$_{t-3}$ / emp$_{t-4}$)	0.042	0.040	−0.564
Age 4–10, emp. 5–19			
Log emp$_{t-1}$	2.163	2.161	−0.118
Log (emp$_{t-1}$ / emp$_{t-2}$)	0.102	0.097	−1.144
Log (emp$_{t-2}$ / emp$_{t-3}$)	0.092	0.091	−0.274
Log (emp$_{t-3}$ / emp$_{t-4}$)	0.127	0.131	0.802
Age 4–10, emp. 20–49			
Log emp$_{t-1}$	3.351	3.347	−0.322
Log (emp$_{t-1}$ / emp$_{t-2}$)	0.143	0.150	1.513
Log (emp$_{t-2}$ / emp$_{t-3}$)	0.143	0.149	1.391
Log (emp$_{t-3}$ / emp$_{t-4}$)	0.188	0.181	−1.683
Age 4–10, emp. 50–99			
Log emp$_{t-1}$	4.169	4.166	−0.230
Log (emp$_{t-1}$ / emp$_{t-2}$)	0.163	0.166	0.664
Log (emp$_{t-2}$ / emp$_{t-3}$)	0.151	0.150	−0.292
Log (emp$_{t-3}$ / emp$_{t-4}$)	0.205	0.206	0.339

(continued)

Table 9A.1   (continued)

	Control sample	Treated sample	Standardized difference
Age 4–10, emp. 100–249			
Log emp$_{t-1}$	4.923	4.923	0.062
Log (emp$_{t-1}$ / emp$_{t-2}$)	0.180	0.209	6.741
Log (emp$_{t-2}$ / emp$_{t-3}$)	0.153	0.157	1.069
Log (emp$_{t-3}$ / emp$_{t-4}$)	0.213	0.204	−2.368
Age 11+, emp. 1–4			
Log emp$_{t-1}$	0.876	0.876	0.000
Log (emp$_{t-1}$ / emp$_{t-2}$)	−0.066	−0.064	0.376
Log (emp$_{t-2}$ / emp$_{t-3}$)	−0.040	−0.032	1.770
Log (emp$_{t-3}$ / emp$_{t-4}$)	−0.022	−0.015	1.766
Age 11+, emp. 5–19			
Log emp$_{t-1}$	2.240	2.237	−0.260
Log (emp$_{t-1}$ / emp$_{t-2}$)	0.030	0.035	1.074
Log (emp$_{t-2}$ / emp$_{t-3}$)	0.021	0.026	1.278
Log (emp$_{t-3}$ / emp$_{t-4}$)	0.019	0.026	1.806
Age 11+, emp. 20–49			
Log emp$_{t-1}$	3.384	3.378	−0.426
Log (emp$_{t-1}$ / emp$_{t-2}$)	0.056	0.061	1.263
Log (emp$_{t-2}$ / emp$_{t-3}$)	0.044	0.052	1.826
Log (emp$_{t-3}$ / emp$_{t-4}$)	0.044	0.046	0.479
Age 11+, emp. 50–99			
Log emp$_{t-1}$	4.201	4.198	−0.232
Log (emp$_{t-1}$ / emp$_{t-2}$)	0.079	0.074	−1.121
Log (emp$_{t-2}$ / emp$_{t-3}$)	0.054	0.055	0.321
Log (emp$_{t-3}$ / emp$_{t-4}$)	0.053	0.055	0.530
Age 11+, emp. 100–249			
Log emp$_{t-1}$	4.962	4.960	−0.180
Log (emp$_{t-1}$ / emp$_{t-2}$)	0.074	0.097	5.295
Log (emp$_{t-2}$ / emp$_{t-3}$)	0.055	0.054	−0.241
Log (emp$_{t-3}$ / emp$_{t-4}$)	0.056	0.071	3.538

Note: For a given variable, say age, the standardized difference (% bias) is $SDIFF(\text{age}) = \{100(1/N)\sum_{i \in A}[\text{age}_i - \sum_{j \in C} g(p_i, p_j)\text{age}_j]\} / \sqrt{[Var_{i \in A}(\text{age}) + Var_{j \in C}(\text{age})]/2}$. These numbers are calculated for the regression samples in table 9.9.

Table 9A.2   **Unadjusted employment growth regressions by size categories, age categories**

	Loan amount coefficient	Number of observations	Number of treated firms	Percent of observations with boundary change
Emp. 1–4	2.431	1,284,000	59,700	0.01
	(0.062)			
Emp. 5–19	2.079	737,500	67,800	0.06
	(0.078)			
Emp. 20–49	3.180	2,516,300	28,400	0.34
	(0.083)			
Emp. 50–99	3.692	286,000	6,900	2.00
	(0.230)			
Emp. 100–249	6.234	55,700	2,400	13.65
	(0.706)			
Age 0	6.022	7,555,600	49,800	0.16
	(0.167)			
Age 1–3	2.978	1,282,100	53,100	0.08
	(0.181)			
Age 4–10	2.975	1,108,300	57,400	0.23
	(0.122)			
Age 11+	3.011	2,489,100	54,700	0.76
	(0.088)			

Notes: These are kernel-weighted OLS regressions, run separately for each size and age category. The dependent variable is average employment in $t + 1$ through $t + 3$ minus average employment in $t - 3$ through $t - 1$, including only firms that have positive employment in each of those years. Employment changes can be due to either organic growth or boundary changes. Loan amount is in millions of 2010 dollars. Treated firm-control fixed effects are also included in the regressions. Standard errors, cluster-adjusted by firm, are in parentheses. The share of observations with boundary changes is kernel weighted. The number of observations and SBA firms are rounded to the nearest 100 for disclosure avoidance.

Table 9A.3   **Unadjusted employment growth regressions by age-size categories**

	Loan amount coefficient	Number of observations	Number of treated firms	Percent of observations with boundary change
Age 0	6.022	7,555,600	49,800	0.16
	(0.167)			
Age 1–3, emp. 1–4	3.340	622,500	28,500	0.01
	(0.114)			
Age 1–3, emp. 5–19	2.158	163,800	18,500	0.03
	(0.339)			
Age 1–3, emp. 20–49	3.714	467,400	5,000	0.15
	(0.293)			
Age 1–3, emp. 50–99	2.168	26,600	800	0.70
	(0.920)			
Age 1–3, emp. 100–249	11.630	1,800	200	6.11
	(5.095)			
Age 4–10, emp. 1–4	1.797	313,800	19,500	0.01
	(0.068)			
Age 4–10, emp. 5–19	2.244	201,100	25,100	0.06
	(0.069)			
Age 4–10, emp. 20–49	3.480	547,900	10,300	0.27
	(0.180)			
Age 4–10, emp. 50–99	3.918	40,900	1,900	1.56
	(0.687)			
Age 4–10, emp. 100–249	6.823	4,700	500	7.85
	(2.255)			
Age 11+, emp. 1–4	1.638	347,700	11,700	0.01
	(0.120)			
Age 11+, emp. 5–19	1.881	372,600	24,200	0.08
	(0.047)			
Age 11+, emp. 20–49	2.857	1,501,100	13,000	0.43
	(0.077)			
Age 11+, emp. 50–99	3.813	218,400	4,100	2.25
	(0.219)			
Age 11+, emp. 100–249	5.852	49,300	1,700	14.47
	(0.712)			

Notes: These are kernel-weighted OLS regressions, run separately for each age-size category. The dependent variable is average employment in $t + 1$ through $t + 3$ minus average employment in $t - 3$ through $t - 1$, including only firms that have positive employment in each of those years. Employment changes can be due to either organic growth or boundary changes. Loan amount is in millions of 2010 dollars. Treated firm-control fixed effects are also included in the regressions. Standard errors, cluster-adjusted by firm, are in parentheses. The share of observations with boundary changes is kernel weighted. The number of observations and SBA firms are rounded to the nearest 100 for disclosure avoidance.

References

Adelino, Manuel, Song Ma, and David T. Robinson. 2014. "Firm Age, Investment Opportunities, and Job Creation." NBER Working Paper no. 19845, Cambridge, MA.

Birch, David L. 1987. *Job Creation in America: How Our Smallest Companies Put the Most People to Work.* New York: Free Press.

Brown, J. David, and John S. Earle. Forthcoming. "Finance and Growth at the Firm Level: Evidence from SBA Loans." *Journal of Finance.*

Canton, Erik, Isabel Grilo, Josefa Monteagudo, and Peter van der Zwan. 2013. "Perceived Credit Constraints in the European Union." *Small Business Economics* 41:701–15.

Davis, Steven, John Haltiwanger, and Scott Schuh. 1996. *Job Creation and Destruction.* Cambridge, MA: MIT Press.

Eslava, Marcela, and John Haltiwanger. 2014. "Young Businesses, Entrepreneurship, and the Dynamics of Employment and Output in Colombia's Manufacturing Industry." Working Paper, Universidad de Los Andes, University of Maryland, May.

Evans, David S. 1987. "The Relationship between Firm Growth, Size, and Age: Estimates for 100 Manufacturing Industries." *Journal of Industrial Economics* 35:567–81.

Fort, Teresa C., John Haltiwanger, Ron S. Jarmin, and Javier Miranda. 2013. "How Firms Respond to Business Cycles: The Role of Firm Age and Firm Size." *IMF Economic Review* 61:520–59.

Haltiwanger, John, Ron S. Jarmin, and Javier Miranda. 2013. "Who Creates Jobs? Small versus Large versus Young." *Review of Economics and Statistics* 95 (2): 347–61.

Heckman, James, and V. Joseph Hotz. 1989. "Choosing among Alternative Nonexperimental Methods for Estimating the Impact of Social Programs: The Case of Manpower Training." *Journal of the American Statistical Association* 84 (408): 862–74.

Hurst, Erik, and Benjamin Wild Pugsley. 2011. "What Do Small Firms Do?" *Brookings Papers on Economic Activity* 43 (2): 73–142.

Imbens, Guido W., and Jeffrey M. Wooldridge. 2009. "Recent Developments in the Econometrics of Program Evaluation." *Journal of Economic Literature* 47 (1): 5–86.

Jarmin, Ronald S., and Javier Miranda. 2002. "The Longitudinal Business Database." CES Working Paper no. 02-17, Center for Economic Studies, US Census Bureau.

Levenson, Alec R., and Kristen L. Willard. 2000. "Do Firms Get the Financing They Want? Measuring Credit Rationing Experienced by Small Businesses in the US" *Small Business Economics* 14:83–94.

Neumark, David, Brandon Wall, and Junfu Zhang. 2011. "Do Small Businesses Create More Jobs? New Evidence for the United States from the National Establishment Time Series." *Review of Economics and Statistics* 93 (1): 16–29.

Rosenbaum, P., and D. B. Rubin. 1985. "Constructing a Control Group Using a Multivariate Matched Sampling Method that Incorporates the Propensity Score." *American Statistician* 39: 33–8.

Small Business Administration (SBA). 2015. *SOP 50 10 5(H), Lender and Development Company Loan Programs.* Effective May 1, 2015. Accessed July 29, 2015. https://www.sba.gov/sites/default/files/sops/SOP_50_10_5_H_FINAL_FINAL_CLEAN_5-1-15.pdf.

III

Data Gaps and Promising Avenues for the Future

Venture Capital Data
Opportunities and Challenges

Steven N. Kaplan and Josh Lerner

10.1 Introduction

Venture capital is a relatively small financial institution. In the five years from 2009 to 2013, the National Venture Capital Association (NVCA 2014) reports that an average of fewer than 1,200 firms received venture capital for the first time annually in the United States. This is a very small fraction— roughly one in 500 or 0.2 percent—of the 600,000 firms (with employees) that are started each year (US SBA 2012). Over the same five-year period, US venture capital partnerships received an average of less than $18 billion in new capital commitments from investors each year. And these figures are for the United States, by far the largest market for venture capital in the world.

So why then does venture capital receive a large amount of theoretical, empirical, policy, and media interest? From a theoretical perspective, venture capital is particularly interesting because it encompasses the extremes of many corporate finance challenges: uncertainty, information asymmetry,

Steven N. Kaplan is the Neubauer Family Distinguished Service Professor of Entrepreneurship and Finance at the University of Chicago Booth School of Business and a research associate of the National Bureau of Economic Research. Josh Lerner is the Jacob H. Schiff Professor of Investment Banking and head of the Entrepreneurial Management unit at Harvard Business School and a research associate and co-director of the Productivity, Innovation, and Entrepreneurship Program at the National Bureau of Economic Research.

This chapter was prepared for the NBER-CRIW Conference on Measuring Entrepreneurial Businesses: Current Knowledge and Challenges. We thank Rick Townsend for very helpful comments. Kaplan and Lerner have consulted to venture capital general partners and limited partners and have invested in venture capital funds. Lerner thanks Harvard Business School's Division of Research for support. Kaplan thanks the Fama-Miller Center at Chicago Booth. All errors and omissions are our own. For acknowledgments, sources of research support, and disclosure of the authors' material financial relationships, if any, please see http://www.nber.org/chapters/c13495.ack.

and asset intangibility. At the same time, from an empirical and policy perspective, venture capital has had a disproportionate impact. Kortum and Lerner (2000) find that venture capital is three to four times more powerful than corporate research and development (R&D) as a spur to innovation. Kaplan and Lerner (2010) find that roughly 50 percent of the "entrepreneurial" initial public offerings (IPOs) in recent years are venture backed, despite the fact that only 0.2 percent of all firms receive venture funding.

But despite the extent of interest in venture capital, substantial misunderstandings about this intermediary persist. This is particularly true in policy circles, which have seen the launch of ill-considered efforts to promote venture activity in many geographies (see Lerner 2009) and media discussions. This reflects the fact that venture capital is a form of private equity, and that one aspect of private equity is that it is indeed private. Unlike mutual funds, venture capitalists are typically exempt from the Investment Company Act of Act of 1940, and typically do not disclose much information to the United States Securities and Exchange Commission (SEC) or other regulators. This has led to a shortage of reliable industry data and to an unappealing setting where industry advocates make sweeping claims about the benefits and critics make broad charges on very shaky empirical foundations.

This lack of a comprehensive data set has also posed challenges to academic research. One of the most important ways that academic research in the social sciences proceeds is by researchers replicating and exploring the limitations of earlier studies. Instead, in venture capital, because the studies often rely on proprietary data sets that are not shared more generally, studies are difficult to replicate or refute. Another unappealing consequence is that dubious or misleading studies can linger for many years without rebuttal.

Sadly, this problem may be getting worse, rather than better. The past decade has seen the rise of "individualized entrepreneurial finance": angels, groups of angels, crowdfunding platforms, and the like. While venture capital remains concentrated in a few metropolitan areas, mostly in the United States, the amount of angel investments appears to be increasing in many nations (Wilson and Silva 2013). Active involvement in the investment and close social ties between angels and entrepreneurs may help to overcome the lack of minority shareholder and legal protections that are important for the development of more institutionalized capital markets. These investors are typically very reluctant to share information about their activities, both for strategic reasons as well as due to a reluctance of personal exposure.

In this chapter, we describe the available data and research on venture capital investments and performance. As we do so, we comment on the challenges inherent in those data and research as well as possible opportunities to do better. We begin by describing the data and research on investments by venture capital funds in portfolio companies. We follow that by describing the data and research on investments (by institutional investors and wealthy individuals) in the venture capital funds.

10.2   Investment Data and Research

10.2.1   Longstanding Databases

Much of the early research into venture capital relied on information available in IPO prospectuses and S-1 registration statements. For the subset of venture-backed firms that eventually go public, voluminous information is available. Investments in firms that do not go public are more difficult to uncover, since these investments are usually not publicized. Unfortunately, because only a relatively modest fraction of venture-backed companies go public, researchers must dig deeper.

There are two longstanding databases that characterize the investments of venture capital funds into portfolio companies, regardless of the investment outcome. VentureXpert (VX), a unit of Thomson Reuters, began collecting data in 1961. Venture Source (VS), a unit of Dow Jones, began collecting data in 1994.

The basic story here is that there are large inconsistencies in both databases and a general problem of incompleteness. Furthermore, qualitatively, both show deterioration in data quality over the past decade. That said, VX has more complete coverage of investments while VS measures outcomes more accurately.

Maats et al. (2011) focus on investments by forty VC funds with vintage years 1993 to 2003. They obtain data about the investments and exits from outside sources and, for two VC funds, from a major limited partner. They then compare the actual data to the data in VS and VX. This follows and expands on an earlier iteration of this research design by Kaplan, Sensoy, and Strömberg (2002).

First, they find that VX has more complete coverage of the investments in the funds. Second, they find that both VX and VS understate the fraction of companies that are defunct, with VX having more incorrect. In fact, VX reports less than 10 percent of investments as defunct when, in fact, more than 20 percent are defunct. Third, VX exit/status coverage has dropped dramatically in recent years, suggesting a lack of investment in collecting new data.

Maats et al. (2011) then do a firm-level comparison for 449 venture-financed firms that are in both VX and VS. Table 10.1 shows that VX appears to have somewhat better coverage. VentureXpert has 40 percent more financing rounds. While VX and VS have postmoney valuations for roughly the same number of firms, VX has roughly 10 percent more postmoney valuations for financing rounds. Table 10.2 provides a round-level comparison for 173 firms that are in both VS and VX. Again, VX has roughly 40 percent more rounds and roughly 10 percent more postmoney valuations.

Maats et al. (2011) also compare the accuracy of the two databases for two specific funds where they obtain data from a limited partner investor in

Table 10.1   Firm-level comparison

	VS	VX
Total firms compared	449	449
Number with postmoney valuations	285	286
Rounds with postmoney valuations	693	764
Number with same number of valued rounds in VS and VX	85	85
Count of investors	3,485	3,405
Number with same number of investors in VS and VX	107	107
Average investment per company ($M)	43.9	52.0
Number with same[a] investment amount in VS and VX	113	113
Count of rounds	1,507	2,145
Number with same round count	134	134

Source: Maats et al. (2011).
[a]Within $1 million.

Table 10.2   Round-level comparison

	VS	VX
Total firms compared	173	173
Count of rounds	592	857
Number with investment date	591	857
Rounds with same date in VS and VX	190	190
Number with postmoney valuation	262	288
Number with same[a] postmoney valuation in VS and VX	95	95
Number with same number of investors in VS and VX	203	207
Number of rounds with investment amount	570	857
Average investment per company ($M)	7.8	8.6
Number with same[a] investment amount in VS and VX	248	258
Number with same[a] date, amount, investor count, and valuation	13	13

Source: Maats et al. (2011).
[a]Within $1 million.

the two funds. VentureXpert does a much better job of including firms in the database that the funds actually invested in. The funds that VS excludes tend to be predominantly funds that failed, leading to a likely upward performance bias in VS.

The earlier comparison by Kaplan, Sensoy, and Strömberg (2002) had suggested some valuation advantages for VS. They compared the actual valuations in 143 financings to their reported values in VS and VX (prior to 2000). They found that VS included almost twice as many valuations as VX and the average absolute error of those valuations was only 60 percent of those in VX.

There is an important additional caveat in measuring valuations. They do not reflect the impact of transaction terms, instead simply reporting the "pre" or "most-money" valuation, which are defined as the product of the nominal price per share paid in transaction times the number of shares outstanding (typically, assuming all shares are converted into common stock) before and after the transaction. In other words, these calculations ignore the implicit call and put options associated with these securities. See Kaplan and Stromberg (2003) for a catalog of these features.

Liquidation preferences, in particular, can have a large impact on values. Metrick and Yasuda (2010) provide examples where valuations change by 75 percent when deal terms are properly analyzed. To correctly analyze valuations across different investments, it is necessary to have access to the actual deal terms. This requires access to the underlying deal documents, which are not easy to obtain.

There is one other difficulty in both databases—firm name changes. Both databases only index on the current (or latest) portfolio company name. The recording of former names is desultory at best. Of course, this makes matching to historical records challenging.

Finally, the results in Maats et al. (2011)—as well as anecdotal accounts— suggest that there has been substantial subsequent deterioration in the quality of both databases. In particular, the initial focus by VS on valuations seems to have been largely abandoned. In part, this may reflect the challenges associated with the reliance on commercial data providers, who may decide on an investment in ensuring data quality that, while profit maximizing, is less than an academic financial economist would prefer.

10.2.2   More Recent Alternatives

There are a number of recent alternatives to VX and VS. Several databases that focus on tracking private equity (buyout) funds and transactions also include some VC funds and deals. These databases are typically based on disclosures from limited partners, filings with the SEC, and other public (but often difficult to access) sources. Examples include Capital IQ, Pitchbook, and Preqin. VCExperts is a newer database that specializes in VC deals and is sourced from state and federal regulatory filings by private companies.

The SEC maintains Form D filings of private financings, but these provide only the amount of funding and not the names of investors.

There are some websites that track venture capital financings. Crunchbase, by Tech Crunch, is the best known. While many of these newer databases are promising, they have not gotten the kind of scrutiny that VS and VX have. Thus, their ability to support academic research is still to be fully determined.

10.2.3   The Bottom Line on Portfolio Company Data

As mentioned above, the basic story on portfolio company data is not a great one. There are large inconsistencies in the two major existing databases,

VX and VS, and a general problem of incompleteness. Furthermore, qualitatively, both show deterioration in data quality over the past decade. As we will discuss in the conclusion, there is an opportunity for a new provider—whether for-profit or nonprofit—to significantly improve on these data.

It also seems possible that the fund performance data providers described in the next section, particularly Burgiss, Cambridge Associates, and Preqin, will be able to augment their fund data with data on individual portfolio companies.

10.3   Performance Data

There are currently three major providers of data on VC (and private equity) performance—Burgiss Private I, Cambridge Associates (CA), and Preqin. Pitchbook is a fourth newer entrant with more of a focus on private equity performance. Until recently, there was a fifth, Thomson Venture Economics (TVE). For reasons likely related to poor quality data that we describe below, TVE decided to discontinue its database and, instead, make CA available on TVE's platform.

As with the data on VC firm investments in portfolio companies, VC fund performance data are also potentially subject to biases:

- First, the data from any one provider may be incomplete. For instance, a number of leading venture capital funds have pressured pension funds not to post online or to report their performance to data providers such as Preqin. Some have gone as far as to drop institutions that cannot make such commitments as limited partners (Lerner, Leamon, and Hardymon 2011). Given the highly skewed nature of performance in venture capital, even a handful of omissions can have a substantial impact on reported performance figures.
- Second, it is possible there is a backfill bias in that the databases report positive past returns for funds that are newly added to the database. Many first-time funds do not have any institutional investors and may not be captured by commercial data providers unless they successfully raise a second fund.
- Third, to the extent that the databases rely on data directly reported by the general partners (GPs), it is possible that poorly performing funds stop reporting or never report at all.
- Fourth, to the extent that database providers rely on information from GPs—or the limited partners (LPs) report data from GPs without adjustment—the quality of the information can suffer from deliberate distortions of the valuations. One example is the valuation of still private companies in the venture capitalists' portfolios. Particularly with early stage companies, valuations assigned by venture firms to

their own portfolio of investments are often based not on quantitative metrics (such as price-to-earnings or discounted cash flow) because the company may not have any prior earnings or reliable projections. Instead, the partners rely on complex, frequently subjective assessments of a venture's technology, expected market opportunity, and its management team's prowess. Less established groups, or those seeking to raise new funds in the near future, may be tempted to shade these valuations upward. Similar concerns have been raised by stock distributions to LPs, a technique often employed by venture funds to unwind large positions in recently public (and often thinly traded) firms. While venture groups may value these distributions at the price prior to the distribution, the sales that ensue after the distribution often mean that the realized price is substantially lower. Again, because many LPs do not adjust the GPs' data, these inflated valuations may find their way into databases.

- Finally, the commercial platforms use different data definitions that complicate cross-platform comparisons. For example, funds are generally grouped by vintage year—the year they began. However, the different platforms define beginning differently. Burgiss groups funds by the year in which the year the fund first takes down money from investors. Cambridge Associates groups funds by the year the fund is legally formed. Preqin groups funds by the year the fund makes its first investment in a company. While these three definitions will often coincide, they do not always do so.

In addition, some funds make investments not only in venture capital/early-stage companies, but also in growth-stage companies and in buyouts. Indeed, it is frequently difficult to define where early-stage investing ends and later-stage transactions begin. While traditional buyout groups such as TPG have increasingly taken part in the later rounds of social media companies, many venture funds have undertaken growth investments in traditional manufacturing firms in markets such as India and China. In some cases, one commercial platform will classify a multiasset class investor as a VC fund while a different platform will classify the same investor as a buyout fund.

In the rest of this section, we describe the coverage of the major platforms and their advantages and disadvantages.

10.3.1 Coverage

Figure 10.1 presents data on fund coverage by four of the commercial platforms as of the first quarter of 2011 using data from Harris, Jenkinson, and Kaplan (2014). Thomson Venture Economics (TVE) had the highest number of funds in the 1980s and the 1990s. In the first decade of the

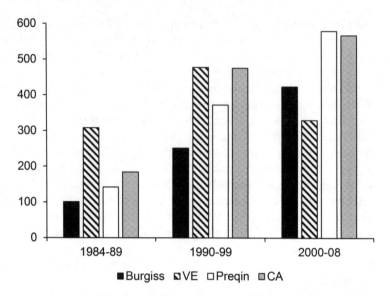

Fig. 10.1   Number of VC funds in database
Source: Harris, Jenkinson, and Kaplan (2014).

twenty-first century, however, TVE declined to the lowest coverage with
Preqin and CA moving to the highest number of funds represented. Though
not illustrated in the graphs above, Burgiss had increased its representation
for the most recent vintage years, 2006 to 2008, to roughly the same coverage
as Preqin and CA. In its most recent release, the second quarter of 2014,
Burgiss' coverage had increased markedly to 538 VC funds with vintage
years from 2000 to 2008, up from the 423 funds in 2011.

   Figure 10.2 presents total capital commitments represented in the commercial platforms as a proportion of total capital committed to VC, using
the data in Harris, Jenkinson, and Kaplan (2014) as of 2011 Q1. Total committed capital is taken from the annual totals provided by the Private Equity
Analyst. Burgiss and Preqin have a higher proportion of total commitments
from 2000 to 2008. Capital commitments for CA funds were not available
for the study.

   As with the number of funds, TVE had strong coverage in the 1980s and
1990s with over 100 percent of committed capital in the 1980s and almost
80 percent in the 1990s. In the first decade of the twenty-first century, TVE
dropped off. Preqin had performance data on funds with roughly 70 percent
of committed capital; Burgiss had performance data on funds with 60 percent of committed capital.

   In its most recent release, 2014 Q2, Burgiss has coverage of 72 percent of
committed capital for 2000 to 2008 vintages. Its coverage reaches 89 percent
of committed capital for vintages from 2006 to 2013.

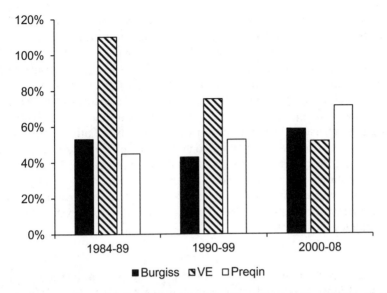

Fig. 10.2   VC capital commitments represented, estimated proportion of total universe
Source: Harris, Jenkinson, and Kaplan (2014).

10.3.2   Commercial Platforms

Burgiss Overview

The data are derived from LPs for whom Burgiss' systems provide recordkeeping and performance-monitoring services. The Burgiss data are sourced exclusively from a diverse array of LPs for whom Burgiss provides recordkeeping and performance-monitoring services. This includes a complete transactional and valuation history between the LPs and fund investments. As a result, Burgiss is able to record exact cash outflows/investments made by LPs to GPs and distributions from GPs back to LPs. Burgiss also cross-checks across investors in the same fund. This feature results in investment histories that are free from any reporting bias. For instance, Burgiss has the complete investment history of LPs who allow Burgiss to aggregate their data. In addition, the Burgiss data are current because Burgiss' LPs receive their data currently from GPs, and Burgiss uses the quarterly reporting used by most investors.

Harris, Jenkinson, and Kaplan (2014) report that their data come from over 200 institutional investors representing over $1 trillion in committed capital. Two-thirds of the LPs have private equity (PE) commitments of over $100 million. Of these, 60 percent are public/private pensions and 20 percent are endowments or foundations.

Over time, the number of funds in the Burgiss database has increased as

Burgiss has gained permission to access the investment performance of an increasing number of LPs. The one potential bias in the Burgiss data is that the LPs who allow access are selected. In particular, it is possible that the LPs who allow access, as a group, have tended to invest in above average funds and, therefore, exclude some below average funds. For this bias to be in the data, however, (a) there would have to be a group of institutional investors who invested in the worst VC funds, had poor performance, and do not use Burgiss to measure their fund performance; and (b) no other institutional investors who do use Burgiss invested in those same VC funds, so the poorly performing PE funds do not show up in the data set. Given the size of the Burgiss data set, this seems unlikely. Furthermore, the fact that Burgiss covers almost 90 percent of the total capital committed to venture capital in post-2005 vintages suggests that this bias, even if it were to exist, is likely to be small for those vintages.

Preqin

Preqin's performance data are sourced primarily from public filings by pension funds, from Freedom of Information Act (FOIA) requests to public pension funds, and voluntarily from GPs (about 60 percent of performance data) and LPs.

Preqin (and Pitchbook) are the only major data sources that identify GPs by fund name. This means that the Preqin data are transparent and can be verified/corrected. The authors know GPs who have voluntarily contacted Preqin to correct erroneous data for their funds.

At the same time, Preqin has at least three potential biases. First, Preqin may miss some high-performing funds that do not have public pension fund investors or have reporting restrictions. Notably, Preqin does not have performance data for a number of funds raised by very high-performing VCs like Sequoia and Accel.

Second, because Preqin relies on voluntary reporting, Preqin often has somewhat stale data because of tardy responses.

Third, Preqin reports performance for a number of funds for which it does not have the granular cash flow data. In other words, some LPs simply report internal rates of return (IRRs) and multiples without reporting the cash flows that generated them.

Cambridge Associates (CA)

Cambridge Associates sources its data from voluntary disclosures by LPs and by GPs who have raised or are trying to raise capital. Because GPs typically do not try to raise a new fund if their performance is poor, CA may have a bias toward successful GPs. Also favoring this bias is CA's traditional orientation to providing services to endowments, who appear to have (historically at least) selected the most successful venture capital LPs with which to invest (Lerner, Schoar, and Wongsunwai 2007).

Whatever its other strengths and weaknesses, CA also is the least transparent of the commercial platforms.

Thomson Venture Economics (TVE)

Thomson Venture Economics has traditionally sourced its data from both LPs and GPs in a manner similar to that used by CA. The major issue with TVE was that it appeared to stop updating performance on roughly 40 percent of the venture capital and private equity funds in the VE sample. Stucke (2011) finds that of 488 buyout funds with 1980–2005 vintage years, 43 percent have constant net asset values (NAVs) and no cash flow activity for at least two years prior to December 2009. Phalippou and Gottschalg (2003) find that 300 of 852 sample funds are inactive for over three years, with most for six or more years.

Stucke (2011) compares the performance of individual buyout funds in TVE to the actual performance of those funds provided by a large LP in those funds. He finds a substantial downward bias in the TVE data. While he does not study VC funds, it seems likely that the VC performance data had a similar downward bias.

Consistent with such a downward bias, Harris, Jenkinson, and Kaplan (2014) find that VC fund performance in the TVE data is lower than that in Burgiss, CA, and Preqin. Also strongly consistent with data problems, in March 2014, TVE decided to discontinue its benchmark data and, instead, contracted with CA to provide CA's private equity benchmarking data to TVE subscribers.[1]

10.3.3   Performance Results

Harris, Jenkinson, and Kaplan (2014) present VC (and PE) performance data from the major commercial databases as of the first quarter of 2011. Harris, Jenkinson, and Kaplan (forthcoming) present performance data updated to the second quarter of 2015. They find that venture capital (VC) funds outperformed public markets (as measured by the S&P 500) substantially until the vintages of the late 1990s. Coinciding to some extent with the tech bust, vintages from 1999 to 2003 underperformed public markets. Vintages from 2004 to 2010 have rebounded, performing better than or equal to public markets. That performance has likely further improved since then. This performance contrasts with the view held by some that VC has been a poorly performing asset class as a whole in this century.

Harris, Jenkinson, and Kaplan (2014) also find that Burgiss, Cambridge Associates, and Preqin yield qualitatively and quantitatively similar performance results. Tables 10.3A and 10.3B reproduce these results from

---

1. See, "Thomson Reuters Partners with Cambridge Associates on Benchmark Data," March 2014. Available at https://www.pehub.com/2014/03/thomson-reuters-partners-with-cambridge-associates-on-benchmark-data/.

Table 10.3A   Venture capital multiples from commercial databases

Vintage	Weighted average multiples			Average multiples				Median multiples		
	Burgiss	Venture Economics	Preqin	Burgiss	Venture Economics	Preqin	Cambridge Associates	Burgiss	Venture Economics	Preqin
1984	1.73	1.59	2.74	1.78	1.57	2.35	1.70	1.71	1.37	1.99
1985	1.93	2.08	2.24	1.96	2.02	2.59	2.61	1.81	1.84	2.15
1986	1.82	2.79	2.19	1.83	1.72	1.85	1.83	1.93	1.54	1.67
1987	2.77	2.39	2.54	2.70	2.02	2.51	2.56	2.35	1.65	2.22
1988	2.88	2.59	2.98	2.45	2.04	2.58	2.15	2.55	1.86	2.57
1989	3.09	2.42	2.80	2.92	2.13	2.55	2.44	2.41	1.89	2.27
1990	3.30	2.82	2.81	2.96	2.32	2.50	2.74	2.48	1.81	2.22
1991	2.92	3.26	2.95	3.11	2.47	4.41	3.07	2.70	2.23	2.75
1992	2.72	3.45	2.84	2.69	3.46	3.26	3.54	2.07	2.18	2.07
1993	6.34	3.31	3.38	6.65	2.92	3.86	3.49	3.28	1.67	2.58
1994	6.58	4.65	7.19	5.27	3.32	3.98	3.83	3.05	2.23	2.08
1995	3.55	4.16	6.33	3.64	3.83	5.16	5.20	2.50	2.43	1.89
1996	6.33	4.78	2.81	5.92	4.68	3.49	4.51	2.06	2.14	1.87
1997	3.28	2.38	2.83	3.03	2.49	2.69	2.52	1.87	1.63	1.52

1998	1.60	1.74	1.77	1.55	1.68	1.67	1.51	0.93	1.10	1.08
1999	0.94	0.74	0.87	0.81	0.84	0.93	0.93	0.73	0.72	0.81
2000	0.97	1.06	1.04	0.91	0.94	1.14	0.90	0.88	0.88	0.99
2001	1.01	1.21	1.19	0.97	1.11	1.08	1.09	0.87	1.00	1.04
2002	1.07	0.96	1.12	1.01	0.98	0.98	1.06	0.99	0.93	0.96
2003	1.11	1.16	1.07	0.99	1.13	1.01	1.08	1.00	1.06	1.02
2004	1.07	1.08	1.19	1.01	1.04	1.22	1.36	0.97	0.99	0.98
2005	1.31	1.14	1.11	1.37	1.13	1.04	1.06	1.02	0.98	1.04
2006	1.04	1.01	1.05	1.01	0.93	1.02	1.03	0.95	0.96	0.98
2007	1.09	1.01	1.06	1.06	1.05	1.12	1.22	1.06	0.96	1.01
2008	0.97	0.94	1.00	0.99	0.93	1	1.06	0.98	0.92	0.95
Average	**2.46**	**2.19**	**2.36**	**2.34**	**1.95**	**2.24**	**2.18**	**1.73**	**1.48**	**1.63**
Average 2000s	1.07	1.06	1.09	1.03	1.03	1.07	1.10	0.97	0.96	1.00
Average 1990s	3.76	3.13	3.38	3.56	2.80	3.20	3.13	2.17	1.81	1.89
Average 1980s	2.37	2.31	2.58	2.27	1.92	2.41	2.22	2.13	1.69	2.15

Source: Harris, Jenkinson, and Kaplan (2014).

Table 10.3B Venture capital IRRs from commercial databases

Vintage	Weighted average IRR				Average IRR				Median IRR			
	Burgiss	Venture Economics	Preqin	Cambridge Associates	Burgiss	Venture Economics	Preqin	Cambridge Associates	Burgiss	Venture Economics	Preqin	Cambridge Associates
1984	7.9	6.0	16.7	8.1	8.2	5.0	14.7	7.7	6.9	3.6	12.8	6.3
1985	7.1	9.2	14.6	12.4	5.5	8.2	10.4	11.6	8.7	8.6	13.5	12.7
1986	9.4	11.9	14.3	13.2	9.0	7.3	13.6	8.8	9.3	6.3	8.9	9.4
1987	20.2	12.9	12.4	17.9	15.8	7.6	23.7	14.5	16.7	7.2	14.9	15.7
1988	24.4	19.8	28.6	18.6	17.9	12.3	21.5	14.3	21.6	9.5	23.1	11.9
1989	25.7	16.4	25.8	18.1	20.5	13.0	16.7	17.1	15.3	10.9	14.7	13.3
1990	29.5	24.8	20.3	31.4	25.3	18.5	55.7	24.3	21.7	14.3	19.3	21.9
1991	28.5	28.9	36.5	23.5	28.1	18.7	26.7	23.0	24.4	17.8	28.7	18.6
1992	24.8	31.5	25.1	24.9	21.0	27.8	33.3	28.7	14.2	13.4	21.5	21.0
1993	51.9	28.5	44.2	37.6	47.1	21.7	29.9	29.5	40.9	12.4	36.5	18.8
1994	41.4	42.9	47.0	47.2	41.7	26.9	55.9	34.6	31.8	23.7	27.1	26.5
1995	46.4	56.6	59.6	65.0	49.2	44.4	35.8	56.8	28.9	19.3	20.0	42.9
1996	76.7	61.2	22.7	71.4	64.5	67.0	48.6	61.1	25.2	28.2	14.8	37.1
1997	76.1	44.1	58.1	69.3	65.9	48.5	26.1	52.8	26.3	19.9	22.8	8.9

1998	15.5	24.4	19.8	13.2	16.3	25.8	-4.2	18.3	-1.2	2.0	4.9	0.4
1999	-4.5	-6.5	-4.4	-3.6	-7.4	-4.6	-0.2	-3.6	-5.6	-5.9	-4.9	-4.4
2000	-1.3	0.4	-0.4	-1.5	-2.7	-1.5	-1.0	-3.7	-2.1	-2.0	-0.5	-3.3
2001	-0.7	4.6	4.0	1.0	-1.7	2.0	-2.8	-1.5	-2.4	0.0	1.2	-0.7
2002	0.6	-0.8	2.1	-0.1	-1.1	-0.7	-1.5	0.7	-0.2	-1.2	-0.6	0.4
2003	0.9	3.6	1.7	2.8	-2.1	3.1	1.5	0.6	0.1	1.3	0.1	0.5
2004	0.3	1.9	2.3	2.6	-1.5	0.7	-0.5	2.0	-1.0	-0.3	-0.2	0.9
2005	3.3	2.9	2.0	1.0	2.2	2.5	-1.6	-1.1	0.5	-0.4	0.8	1.0
2006	0.6	0.0	1.1	2.9	-1.3	-3.7	3.8	-0.2	-2.4	-1.9	-1.4	0.3
2007	3.2	-0.9	3.9	4.1	1.7	1.3	-1.3	7.1	2.6	-1.7	1.5	3.9
2008	-4.5	-5.2	-2.7	3.7	-2.8	-7.1		1.6	-1.6	-6.5	-3.9	1.1
Average	**19.3**	**16.8**	**18.2**	**19.4**	**16.8**	**13.8**	**16.9**	**16.2**	**11.1**	**7.1**	**11.0**	**10.6**
Average 2000s	0.3	0.7	1.6	1.8	-1.0	-0.4	-0.4	0.6	-0.7	-1.4	-0.3	0.5
Average 1990s	38.6	33.6	32.9	38.0	35.2	29.5	30.8	32.5	20.7	14.5	19.1	19.1
Average 1980s	15.8	12.7	18.7	14.7	12.8	8.9	16.8	12.3	13.1	7.7	14.7	11.5

Source: Harris, Jenkinson, and Kaplan (2014).

Harris, Jenkinson, and Kaplan (2014). There is little reason to believe that the Burgiss and Preqin data sets, in particular, suffer from performance selection biases in the same direction. At the same time, consistent with Stucke (2011), they find that performance is lower in the Venture Economics data (particularly for buyout funds).

Kaplan and Sensoy (forthcoming) provide a broader summary of the performance of PE and VC funds. Other research is broadly consistent with the results in Harris, Jenkinson, and Kaplan (2014, forthcoming).

10.3.4   The Bottom Line on Performance Providers

Based on the research done to date, Burgiss is likely the best of the commercial data providers. The data it has are current and do not appear to be selected. Given the similar results in Preqin and CA, it is unlikely there is any appreciable bias across these databases. The fact that Burgiss now covers performance for almost 90 percent of the total capital committed to venture capital in post-2005 vintages suggests that the ability to do research on venture capital funds will continue to improve over time. This is particularly encouraging given that Burgiss makes its data available to researchers through proposals to the PERC (Private Equity Research Consortium). Kaplan serves on PERC's academic advisory board.

While Preqin (and Pitchbook) have potential selection biases, they are also powerful and valuable because they identify the performance of individual funds. This allows a better fix on the potential selection biases at work.

Thomson Venture Economics (TVE) should not be used. Its database has been discontinued. Results in past work using TVE should be viewed with caution.

It is also worth noting that this is a dynamic field, with a number of new entrants. Examples include eFront and State Street Bank, which have gathered data as part of their work with general and limited partners, and analytics solutions providers such as Bison. While it is still early to evaluate many of these efforts, the promise of more and higher quality data augurs well for future research opportunities.

A "horse of a different color" is the Private Capital Research Institute, in which both of the authors are involved (Kaplan as an academic advisory board member and Lerner as director). This foundation-supported non-profit is in the process of developing a database exclusively for academic research, modeled after the architecture for compiling confidential information employed by the US government. By restricting the data use to these applications, it is hoped that a broader swath of the industry will consent to the utilization of their data.

The heart of the PCRI effort is high-quality data about private capital investments. While commercial data vendors typically piece this together from a variety of sources, including security filings and disclosure statements by institutional investors, frequently the information is incomplete and inconsistent.

The vision of the PCRI is to focus very much on obtaining data from the private equity firms themselves. To date, over 40 of the 100 largest private equity firms worldwide have provided data to the PCRI, or are in the process of doing so. It might be plausibly wondered why private equity firms would be willing to share data with the PCRI when the commercial databases have often struggled to get data from these institutions. The answers are several:

1. The constraints the PCRI places on the use of the data. In particular, the PCRI is designed to be a project run by academics and for academics. The information is used exclusively for academic research, rather than for any commercial purpose.

2. The research protocol simultaneously allows academics to undertake high-quality research while protecting the confidentiality of the data being provided by the private equity firms. In particular, following the model employed by the United States Bureau of the Census when making available information that it and the United States Internal Revenue Service collect, academics can undertake detailed cross-tabulated analyses but not download or view individual data entries. Essentially, the academics would be able to upload queries and download results without "touching" the individual data entries.

3. A third reason for the success of the PCRI in generating participation in the private equity community has to do with the fact that the industry itself is under much greater scrutiny. In particular, in the aftermath of the financial crisis there has been much greater attention to institutions such as hedge funds and private capital groups that traditionally were exempt from most regulatory oversight in the United States and Europe. As a result of these pressures, industry leaders have increasingly appreciated the need for high-quality independent research.

Gathering information from the private equity firms has limitations. Even if every active group chose to participate, there would still be a number of groups that have gone out of business. As a result, the PCRI is complementing the data gathered from the private equity firms with data from commercial sources. In addition, the PCRI is working with a commercial group that has developed an extremely efficient and cost-effective manner to collect the cash flow data of private equity funds from public regulatory and disclosure filings. As regulations push private equity groups to undertake more and more security filings, this will likely be an increasingly fruitful methodology. This relationship will allow us to gain more experience with the harvesting of such data. Thus, the use of commercial data sources allow the PCRI to get a more holistic picture of the activity in the private capital industry, as well as to quantify any potential biases that may affect rigorous scientific analysis.

In addition to our own efforts to acquire data for the PCRI, the support of the institutional investor community has proved valuable. Because there are ambiguities about whether institutional investors can share data on existing funds, the PCRI initially did not ask them for data directly. Nonetheless, a number of institutional investors—including some formally on our practitioner board—have been very helpful in encouraging the private capital firms in which they have invested to share data with the PCRI.

10.4 Conclusions

Venture capital is an increasingly important intermediary, able to transform capital into new firms and innovations in an apparently highly productive manner. This intermediary is attracting increasing interest by policymakers and investors, but the availability of data as well as the consistency of the academic findings using these data are still lacking.

This chapter attempted to take a careful look at the availability of information about this intermediary. Several conclusions emerge from our review of the major data sources for venture capital investments and funds:

- Reflecting the relative lack of disclosure and the substantial information asymmetries surrounding venture capital, it is difficult to paint in definitive terms the level of investment activity and fund performance.
- Existing databases differ in methodologies, and analyses frequently produce discrepancies and varying conclusions. These problems are particularly prevalent when it comes to transaction-level data.
- That being said, the venture data space has seen substantial entry, particularly in regard to performance measurement. As a result, the quality of information available has increased in recent years and can be expected to continue to do so going forward.

References

Harris, R., T. Jenkinson, and S. Kaplan. 2014. "Private Equity Performance: What Do We Know?" *Journal of Finance* 69 (5): 1851–82.
———. Forthcoming. "How Do Private Equity Investments Perform Compared to Public Equity?" *Journal of Investment Management*.
Kaplan, S., and J. Lerner. 2010. "It Ain't Broke: The Past, Present, and Future of Venture Capital." *Journal of Applied Corporate Finance* 22 (2): 36–46.
Kaplan, S., and B. Sensoy. Forthcoming. "Private Equity Performance: A Survey." *Annual Review of Financial Economics*.
Kaplan, S., B. Sensoy, and P. Strömberg. 2002. "How Well Do Venture Capital Databases Reflect Actual Investments?" Working Paper, University of Chicago.
Kaplan, S., and P. Strömberg. 2003. "Financial Contracting Theory Meets the Real World: Evidence from Venture Capital Contracts." *Review of Economic Studies* 70:281–315.

Kortum, S., and J. Lerner. 2000. "Assessing the Contribution of Venture Capital to Innovation." *Rand Journal of Economics* 31:674–92.

Lerner, J. 2009. *The Boulevard of Broken Dreams: Why Public Efforts to Boost Entrepreneurship and Venture Capital Have Failed—and What to Do About It.* Princeton, NJ: Princeton University Press.

Lerner, J., A. Leamon, and F. Hardymon. 2011. *Private Equity, Venture Capital, and the Financing of Entrepreneurship: The Power of Active Investing.* New York: John Wiley & Sons.

Lerner, J., A. Schoar, and W. Wongsunwai. 2007. "Smart Institutions, Foolish Choices: The Limited Partner Performance Puzzle." *Journal of Finance* 62:731–64.

Maats, F., A. Metrick, A. Yasuda, B. Hinkes, and S. Vershovski. 2011. "On the Consistency and Reliability of Venture Capital Databases." Working Paper, University of California at Davis.

Metrick, A., and A. Yasuda. 2010. *Venture Capital and the Finance of Innovation.* New York: John Wiley & Sons.

National Venture Capital Association. 2014. *Venture Capital Yearbook.* Washington, DC: National Venture Capital Association.

Phalippou, L., and O. Gottschalg. 2003. "The Performance of Private Equity Funds." *Review of Financial Studies* 22 (4): 1747–76.

Stucke, R. 2011. "Updating History." Working Paper, Oxford University. Available at http://papers.ssrn.com/sol3/papers.cfm?abstract_id=1967636.

US Small Business Administration (SBA). 2012. *The Small Business Economy.* Washington, DC: Government Printing Office.

Wilson, Karen, and Filipe Silva. 2014. "Policies for Seed and Early Stage Finance." Science, Technology and Innovation Directorate Policy Paper no. 9, Organisation for Economic Co-operation and Development.

11

The Promise and Potential of Linked Employer-Employee Data for Entrepreneurship Research

Christopher Goetz, Henry Hyatt, Erika McEntarfer, and Kristin Sandusky

11.1 Introduction

Linked employer-employee data fill an important gap in the set of data used to study entrepreneurship, shedding light on questions that cannot be addressed using firm- or individual-level data alone. For researchers interested in start-up firms and their founders, data identifying the transition of the entrepreneur from the workforce to founding a new firm is of inherent interest. How workers move from being employees to entrepreneurs, whom they recruit for start-up teams, and what predicts starts, successes, and failures is key to understanding the dynamics of entrepreneurial activity in the United States. Policymakers are interested in entrepreneurship in part because they are interested in job growth. Linked employer-employee data show who works for new firms and whether these firms are creating "good" jobs. Labor market agglomeration effects are widely acknowledged to be important in the spatial clustering of technological or innovative industries. Yet labor market flows across firms are difficult to understand with existing business- or household-level data sets.

In this chapter, we discuss the potential of linked employer-employee

Christopher Goetz, Henry Hyatt, Erika McEntarfer, and Kristin Sandusky are research economists at the Center for Economic Studies (CES) at the US Census Bureau.

We thank Rajshree Agrawal, Hubert Janicki, Shawn Klimek, and participants in the NBER-CRIW Entrepreneurship Conference for very helpful comments on this chapter. We also thank Douglas Walton and Alexandria Zhang for assistance in preparing some of the tabulations. Any opinions and conclusions expressed herein are those of the authors and do not necessarily represent the views of the US Census Bureau. While most of the figures and tables in this chapter are calculated from public-use data, some tables use confidential Census Bureau microdata. All such tables and figures have been reviewed to ensure that no confidential information is disclosed. For acknowledgments, sources of research support, and disclosure of the authors' material financial relationships, if any, please see http://www.nber.org/chapters/c13494.ack.

data for the study of entrepreneurship, and provide a road map for researchers interested in using these data. We will discuss both the confidential microdata and public-use data derived from linked employer-employee data. Linked employer-employee microdata for the United States are currently available to approved researchers working in restricted data centers. However, the Census Bureau has recently stepped up efforts to create new public-use data about young firms using linked employer-employee data as part of the Longitudinal Employer-Household Dynamics (LEHD) program. The result is new public-use data on workforce composition, hiring, turnover, and earnings paid to workers at young firms. Because these new statistics are sourced from administrative data, they are available at much finer geographic and industry detail than is usually available in public-use statistics. While lacking the flexibility of the confidential microdata, these new statistics bring many of the benefits of the linked employer-employee data into the public domain for easier research access.

Specifically, our goals in this chapter are threefold:

1. To familiarize researchers with the US linked employer-employee data and how it can be used in entrepreneurship research;

2. to describe newly available public-use statistics derived from linked employer-employee data and provide examples of how they can be used to study entrepreneurship; and

3. to outline future plans to expand the set of available data to study entrepreneurship by linking in new administrative data sources on self-employment and partnerships, as well as identifying the employment history and human capital formation of entrepreneurs themselves.

This chapter begins with a brief overview of the current landscape of data available for empirical research on entrepreneurship. We then describe the linked employer-employee microdata in more detail, and provide information on how to access the data. Subsequent sections describe new public-use statistics tabulated from the linked employer-employee data, and provide specific examples of how they can be used to study workforce and earnings dynamics in new firms. Section 11.5 of the chapter outlines a vision for future work to build a new statistical infrastructure from linked administrative data to support entrepreneurship research. Section 11.6 concludes.

11.2 An Overview of Available Data for Entrepreneurship Research

Entrepreneurship has long been acknowledged to play an important role in modern economies by spurring innovation, creating jobs, and enhancing productivity. However, only in the last few decades has entrepreneurship flourished as a research area within economics. Data on entrepreneurial activity are necessary for any empirical research on the determinants of entrepreneurship and the impact of entrepreneurship on the economy. Yet the existing statistical infrastructure is in many ways inadequate to investigate questions around business formation and innovative activity. Despite several new data sources made available in the last decade, many important data gaps remain.

Currently available data to study entrepreneurship include firm-level or owner-level microdata, as well as published aggregate statistics. Table 11.1 details the most commonly used publically available data in entrepreneurship research. Information on entrepreneurs typically comes from household- or business-level surveys, mostly as cross-sectional snapshots, although a few smaller panel data sets are available. The Current Population Survey (CPS), the Survey of Consumer Finance (SCF), the Panel Study of Income Dynamics (PSID), the National Longitudinal Surveys (NLS), and the other household surveys listed here ask a similar small set of questions concerning self-employment and business ownership.[1] Data on both founders and their businesses are available in the Census Bureau's Survey of Business Owners (SBO), and the Kauffman Firm Survey (KFS). With regard to business-level data on new firms, statistics on start-ups and established firms are available in the Business Dynamics Statistics (BDS) and the Business Employment Dynamics (BED). The creation of the BDS and BED has led to a growth of research documenting the importance of new businesses for job creation and economic growth. The Quarterly Workforce Indicators (QWI), derived from LEHD microdata, are a relatively recent addition to this list, which we will describe in greater detail later in this chapter.

Most existing data sources are limited in their ability to depict the interaction between start-ups and their human assets, including owner, founding team members, and early employees. The omission of human capital, which can strongly influence both the nature and the success of a new business, increasingly leaves researchers of entrepreneurship at a disadvantage as the US economy becomes more service oriented and knowledge based. Data that contain information on owners or workers are typically unable to follow the business over time, or else only provide dynamic information on a limited sample of business entrants. These shortcomings make it difficult to study the impact of factors such as owner characteristics and experience on the outcomes of start-ups, and measure the potentially changing effects over time.

The scope of entrepreneurship research is broad, but there are many research questions for which longitudinally linked employer-employee data are especially useful. Table 11.2 lists some of the overarching questions in the field of entrepreneurship research (with a selection of representative studies), along with some specific examples of how linked employer-employee data can be employed in the study of these topics. For instance several researchers have noted that young firms typically hire younger workers (e.g., Ouimet and Zarutskie 2014), spawning wider interest in exploring how

---

1. For a summary of studies using the National Longitudinal Survey of Youth 1979 (NLSY79) to study entrepreneurship, see Fairlie (2005).

Table 11.1   Public-use data to study firm dynamics and entrepreneurship

Data set(s)	Sampling unit or frame	Key variables	Frequency	Level of detail	Strengths
Business Dynamics Statistics (BDS)	Establishment	Employment, job creation, and destruction by firm age and size.	Annual: 1978–current. Two-year lag.	Industry sector (SIC), national, state, and MSA.	Long time series on employment, job creation, and destruction trends for young firms.
Business Employment Dynamics (BED)	Establishment	Job gains from new and expanding establishments and jobs lost from downsizing and closing establishments.	Quarterly: 1992–current. Nine-month lag.	National and state by NAICS sector; three-digit NAICS available nationally. Firm age categories at state level, firm size at national level.	Quarterly frequency and relatively current data on start-ups and new establishments.
Quarterly Workforce Indicators (QWI)	Job (worker-establishment pair)	Employment, job creation and destruction, hires and separations, earnings and starting earnings by firm age or size.	Quarterly: 1990 (start year varies by state) current. Nine-month lag.	National-, state-, CBSA-, and county-level data. Industry detail up to four-digit NAICS. Worker age, sex, education, race/ethnicity.	Provides worker demographics, earnings, and turnover as well as job creation and destruction at young firms. Available at very detailed geography and industry. High frequency and relatively current.
Kauffman Firm Survey (KFS) Microdata, Dun & Bradstreet Market Identifier Data (D&B)	KFS: New firms in 2004. D&B: Around 50 million establishments since 1990.	Business characteristics, with info on strategy, credit, and financing. Kauffman includes demographics of the principals.	Annual. Kauffman survey stopped in 2011.	Firm or establishment level. Confidential version of KFS contains more industry and geographic detail.	Wealth of information on the firm level, although samples are not representative of universe.

Data source	Unit	Variables	Frequency	Geography	Notes
Household surveys: Current Population Survey (CPS), National Longitudinal Surveys (NLS/NLSY), Survey of Income and Program Participation (SIPP), Panel Study of Income Dynamics (PSID), Survey of Consumer Finance (SCF)	Household	Detailed job and earnings histories of potential entrepreneurs, self-employment entry and exit.	Varies	Individual level. Confidential and restricted versions with more detail often available through application process.	Wide variety of information on potential entrepreneurs, although samples are often small.
Census Business Register Statistics: County/ZIP Code Business Patterns, Nonemployer Statistics, Statistics of US Businesses (SUSB)	Establishment	Establishment counts, employment and payroll by establishment, and enterprise-size class.	Annually since the late 1990s	Statistics for industry sectors generally available at the county level and above.	Establishment counts of small businesses at fine levels of geography, and ability to distinguish nonemployers
Survey of Business Owners (SBO)/Characteristics of Business Owners (CBO)	Business owner	Owner demographics, geography, industry, firm receipts and employment size, detailed information on financing and revenues.	Every five years since 2007	SBO: National, state, and county by NAICS two-through six-digit industry for selected geographies. CBO: National by industry.	Rich set of variables describing the individual owners and their business finances.

Table 11.2   Questions in entrepreneurship research

Question	Selected empirical papers	Selected data sets used	Potential value added
What are the dynamics of new business formation and growth?	Birch (1979); Dunne, Roberts, and Samuelson (1989); Acs and Mueller (2008); Davis and Haltiwanger (2014)	Dun and Bradstreet microdata, Census of Manufactures microdata, Longitudinal Estab. and Ent. Microdata (LEEM), Quarterly Workforce Indicators	QWI and J2J: Ability to observe labor dynamics at firms zero to one year old, stratified by a variety of observable characteristics
How does entrepreneurship interact with the business cycle?	Gertler and Gilchrist (1994); Carree (2002); Congregado, Carmona, and Golpe (2010); Fort et al. (2013)	Quarterly Financial Report—Manufacturing, County Business Patterns, Current Population Survey, Business Dynamics Statistics	QWI and J2J: Time-series measures of hiring, separations, and poaching at young firms versus established firms
How does entrepreneurship depend on the available labor force?	Combes, Duranton, and Gobillon (2008); Doms, Lewis, and Robb (2010); Ouimet and Zarutskie (2014); Figueiredo, Guimarães, and Woodward (2014)	French microdata, Kauffman Firm Survey, Decennial Census, LEHD microdata, Portuguese Administrative microdata	QWI and J2J: Observe demographics of the labor force at young firms such as age, sex, race, and education
How and why are geographic and industrial clusters formed?	Ellison and Glaeser (1997); Rosenthal and Strange (2003); Glaeser, Kerr, and Ponzetto (2010); Kerr and Kominers (2010)	Census of Manufactures, Dun and Bradstreet Marketing Indicators, Longitudinal Business Database, US Patent Office microdata	QWI and J2J: Statistics available at fine levels of geography and industry detail
How are spin-offs created?	Klepper (2001); Franco and Filson (2006); Chatterjee and Rossi-Hansberg (2012); Agarwal et al. (2013)	Business Employment Dynamics, Disk/Trend Industry Data, Statistics of US Businesses, LEHD Microdata	J2J: Ability to detect flows within an industry and geographic location
Where do entrepreneurs come from?	Evans and Leighton (1989); Hurst and Lusardi (2004); Lazear (2005); Hurst and Pugsley (2011)	Current Population Survey, NLSY, Panel Study of Income Dynamics, Data Set of Stanford Alumni, Statistics of US Businesses	Future Business Owner Statistics: Info on previous employment status and industry experience of business owners
How do entrepreneurs fare in their outcomes?	Bates (1990); Holtz-Eakin, Joulfaian, and Rosen (1994); Hamilton (2000); Moskowitz and Vissing-Jørgensen (2002)	Characteristics of Business Owners, Internal Revenue Service microdata, Survey of Income and Program Participation, Survey of Consumer Finances	Future Business Owner Statistics: Ability to measure earnings and year-to-year survival of sole-proprietor businesses

labor-related factors can influence the success of new ventures. Detailed data on labor market flows across firms are well suited for investigating subjects like agglomeration economies, labor market spillovers, and spin-off firms (e.g., Agarwal et al. [2013], using LEHD microdata). Highly spatial public-use data on young firms by detailed industry can help explain why regional growth appears to be correlated with the presence of many small/ young firms (e.g., Glaeser, Kerr, and Ponzetto 2010). Data linking business owners and their employment histories can help identify the determinants of entrepreneurship and new business success, a large literature that includes the work of Evans and Leighton (1989), Hurst and Lusardi (2004), and Hamilton (2000). Planned integration of self-employment data with linked employer-employee data would enable further investigation into the distinction between types of entrepreneurship. As only a small subset of entrepreneurs starts new businesses with an intent to grow, identifying potential high-growth entrepreneurs is of great economic and policy interest (e.g., Hurst and Pugsley 2011; Chatterjee and Rossi-Hansberg 2012).

11.3   The Longitudinal Employer-Household Dynamics (LEHD) Data

The Longitudinal Employer-Household Dynamics (LEHD) program at the US Census Bureau has built over the last decade a comprehensive linked employer-employee data set for the United States. The result of this effort is a comprehensive longitudinal database covering over 95 percent of US private-sector jobs and most public-sector employment.

The LEHD data system is extraordinarily complex, linking data across multiple agencies, blending administrative and survey data, and filling data gaps with additional source data whenever possible. The LEHD job-level data come primarily from quarterly worker-level earnings submitted by employers for the administration of state unemployment insurance (UI) benefit programs. Information on federal jobs (not covered by state UI programs) is provided to the census by the Office of Personnel Management (OPM).[2] These job-level records are linked to establishment-level data collected for the Bureau of Labor Statistics' Quarterly Census of Employment and Wages (QCEW) and Census Bureau's Longitudinal Business Database (LBD) data to obtain further information about the employer. Demographic information about individual workers is obtained via links to census surveys and Social Security administrative data. Residential information on workers comes primarily from Internal Revenue Service (IRS) address data. Ongoing work to integrate administrative data on self-employed workers is described later in this chapter.

As is evident from the description above, the LEHD data rely on data-

---

2. State UI covers most private employment, as well as state and local government employment. There are notable exceptions to coverage, namely most small agricultural employers, religious institutions, and much of the nonprofit sector. Office of Personnel Management federal employment data includes the civilian workforce, but not the armed forces or the postal service.

sharing agreements with multiple state and federal agencies to provide critical inputs to the linked employer-employee data. Key among these are data-sharing agreements between state governments and the Census Bureau through the Local Employment Dynamics (LED) partnership. State agencies provide the principal job-level data (state UI records of employee-specific total quarterly wage and salary payments) as well as QCEW data. As of this writing, all fifty states, the District of Columbia, Puerto Rico, and the Virgin Islands have provided data to the LEHD program through this partnership. Because states joined the partnership at different times with different amounts of data archived, the set of available states in the LEHD data varies by year; states with the longest panels have data that begins in the early 1990s and the last state, Massachusetts, enters in 2010.

These noncompulsory data-sharing agreements make LEHD unique among statistical programs. While the LEHD program has been enormously successful in bringing together multiple agencies to share data to create universe-level data on jobs in the United States, the voluntary nature of these agreements (state and federal partners receive no compensation for participation in the program) is a great risk to the long-term viability of the data program. Withdrawal of data-sharing partners from the program risks the integrity of many of the products provided from the LEHD data and the usability of the data for research. These data-sharing agreements also have implications for researcher access to the confidential microdata, outlined in the next section.

The ability to identify firm age is a recent enhancement to the LEHD data, a highly valuable additional characteristic for researchers interested in entrepreneurship. Firm age is obtained via links to the microdata that underlie the Longitudinal Business Database (LBD), which also serves as the source data for the Census Bureau's Business Dynamics Statistics (BDS). As in the BDS, firm age is defined as the age of the oldest establishment in the national firm. An establishment is age zero in the first year that it reports any positive payroll, and ages chronologically thereafter. Firm age is robust to ownership changes such as mergers, spin-offs, and ownership changes. For example, a new legal entity spun off as a result of merger and acquisition activity will not be considered a new firm; instead, it is assigned the age of its oldest establishment at the time of its formation.

A comprehensive description of the LEHD data is available in Abowd et al. (2009). A detailed discussion of the methodology used to add firm age to the LEHD data is provided in Haltiwanger et al. (2014).

11.3.1   Researcher Access to LEHD Microdata

Researchers can apply for access to LEHD microdata by submitting a research proposal through the Federal Research Data Center (FRDC) network. Applications for microdata access for research undergo a formal approval process that includes review of the proposal by the Census Bureau as well as by state and federal agencies that have supplied worker and firm data to the LEHD program. Projects approved to use the confidential microdata are conducted in a secure research data center with all output undergoing a formal disclosure review process before being permitted for dissemination outside the secure facilities.[3]

The proposal review process for LEHD confidential data access is complicated by the many data-sharing agreements between data partners and the US Census Bureau. Any FRDC proposal requesting access to IRS data must be approved by the IRS (whether a proposal using LEHD data needs IRS approval depends on the data requested, but firm age, likely of critical interest to entrepreneurship researchers, is sourced from IRS data). State agreements vary, with some states choosing to allow their state data in pooled multistate research samples for research projects approved by the Census Bureau. Other state partners choose to review proposals and approve or deny data access on a project-by-project basis.[4]

In short, acquiring confidential LEHD microdata access for entrepreneurship research can be classified as a "high-cost/high-reward" activity. The scope of research projects that benefit from such rich microdata is vast. This is particularly true in the interdisciplinary field of entrepreneurship research, where many topics deal with the fundamental interactions between workers and firms. For instance, LEHD data allow identification of spinoff firms and the employment history of their start-up teams. Employment with start-up firms is considered a risky but potentially high-reward career strategy—linked employer-employee data can measure both the risks and the long-term earnings benefits of joining a start-up team. Acquiring talented employees is critical for start-up success—better understanding of how labor market agglomeration effects spur industry growth would help policymakers interested in encouraging local entrepreneurship efforts. These examples obviously represent only a handful of possible topics for research using linked employer-employee data. Additionally, the LEHD microdata can be linked to other person and firm-level data, expanding the set of possible research questions even further.

Although LEHD microdata access offers the broadest possibilities for projects in entrepreneurship research, the relatively high cost of obtaining access to the data (writing a successful proposal, obtaining necessary approvals, possible travel to a research data center) is prohibitive for many researchers. This is especially true for younger researchers (e.g., graduate

---

3. More information on how to apply for confidential microdata research access through the FRDC network is available on the Center for Economic Studies website: https://www.census.gov/ces/.

4. Under all LED data-use agreements, any state or substate tabulation or estimate released from LEHD data must be approved by the state partner. Tables and estimates in research papers must have a minimum of three states contributing to the estimate or cell to avoid this requirement.

students, junior faculty). Policymakers and journalists interested in entrepreneurship often need quick answers to immediate questions. Thus, in the next few sections of this chapter we focus primarily on new public-use statistics on young firms created from the LEHD data, which can be accessed by the broader research and policy community.

11.3.2   LEHD Public-Use Data for Entrepreneurship Research

In this section, we briefly describe three public-use data products derived from LEHD microdata, with a focus on new data on firm age. In the following section, we illustrate the value of these statistics for entrepreneurship research by means of examples. Table 11.3 provides an overall summary of this new data, including variables, frequency, and stratification levels, also highlighting the strengths of these statistics relative to other available data.

The Quarterly Workforce Indicators (QWI)

The Quarterly Workforce Indicators (QWI) are a set of thirty-two economic indicators providing employment, hires and separations, business expansion and contraction, as well as earnings for the universe of UI-covered employment in the United States. Data are available by worker demographics (sex, age, education, as well as race and ethnicity) and firm characteristics (firm age, size) as well as at fine levels of detail by workplace geography (county and Workforce Investment Board area) and industry (highly detailed four-digit North American Industry Classification System [NAICS] codes).

The QWI statistics by firm age are quite new (the first release was in 2013), made possible by the recent enhancements to the LEHD microdata discussed earlier in this chapter. The QWI provide data for five firm-age tabulation levels, with the youngest firm category being firms less than two years old. While the ability to examine employment growth at young firms is not a unique feature of the QWI, several indicators are uniquely available in the QWI: earnings at start-ups, earnings of new hires at start-ups, hires, separations, and turnover.[5] Moreover, the QWI are tabulated for new businesses down to the county level, a level of geographic detail not widely available in other statistics. Finally, as we show in a later example, the QWI are unique in allowing the composition of the start-up workforce to be examined: for example, the share of young workers, of women, of racial minorities, or of highly educated workers employed at start-ups.

LEHD Origin Destination Employment Statistics (LODES)

LEHD Origin Destination Employment Statistics (LODES) provide employment data by both place of work and place of residence at block-level

---

5. Job creation and destruction for young firms and establishments can also be analyzed with the BDS and the BED.

Table 11.3   Newly available data on firm dynamics and entrepreneurship from LEHD

Variable	Available in	Frequency	Most granular geographic detail	Most granular industry detail	Worker demographics	Fills a gap in public-use statistics by allowing researchers to	Also available in (most granular level of detail)
Employment by firm age	QWI	Quarterly	County	NAICS4	Age, sex, education, race/ethnicity	Examine demographics of workers at young firms and within detailed industries. Map detailed substate geographic industry clusters	BDS (MSA-year-industry sector)
Employment by firm age	LODES	Annual	Census block	All industries	All demographic groups	Map clusters of young firms at very detailed geographies	BDS (MSA-year-industry sector)
Hires/separations by firm age	QWI	Quarterly	County	NAICS4	Age, sex, education, race/ethnicity	Examine churn at young firms within detailed industries/geographies	None
Earnings and starting earnings by firm age	QWI	Quarterly	County	NAICS4	Age, sex, education, race/ethnicity	Examine earnings at young firms by worker demographics	None
Job-to-job moves by firm age	J2J	Quarterly	State	Industry sector	All demographic groups	Examine where early start-up employees are coming from and going to after separating	None
Hires/separations to nonemployment by firm age	J2J	Quarterly	State	Industry sector	All demographic groups	Decompose worker churn at young firms into workers moving to and from other jobs versus moving in and out of nonemployment	None

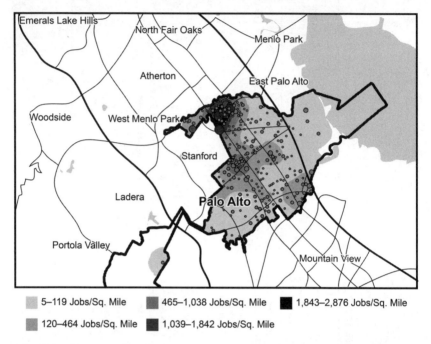

Fig. 11.1   Concentration of start-up employment near Stanford University and Palo Alto, CA

Notes: LEHD Origin-Destination Employment Statistics (LODES), 2013. Only employment in firms less than two years old is shown in map.

geography. The ability to analyze employment by both place of residence as well as place of work is critical for identifying regional labor markets and understanding the interconnectedness of geographic areas that lie across state and metro area boundaries. A combination of noise infusion (similar to QWI) and synthetic data methods is used to protect worker and firm characteristics, including residential location. A web-based mapping application, OnTheMap, provides an easy-to-use interface for mapping small-area workforce characteristics. The application also provides tabulations to accompany the workforce maps on employer and worker characteristics, and allows users to create custom analyses of geographies. For researchers interested in entrepreneurship, a key feature of interest is highly detailed block-level data of employment at new firms. For example, figure 11.1 uses LODES data in OnTheMap to show the spatial concentration of new firms near the Stanford University campus in Palo Alto, California.

Job-to-Job Flows (J2J)

Job-to-Job Flows (J2J) is a brand new data product from the Census Bureau on the flows of workers between employers, with data first released in December of 2014. Job-to-Job Flows is the first public-use data product that exploits the ability of the linked employer-employee microdata to follow workers across firms, across industries, and across labor markets.

The J2J statistics and the underlying microdata should prove particularly valuable to researchers of entrepreneurship. A unique feature of the database is its ability to provide a dynamic view of the workforce in the early years of a business, permitting examination of the role that gender, age, industry experience, and experience working at other new businesses plays in the success or failure of new firms. Additionally, the potential to study start-up teams as groups of workers moving from their previous employers to the newly established firm is also unique to linked employer-employee data. While there is no information about each individual's role or title in the company, strategies have been employed to identify founders (see Agarwal et al. 2013) using LEHD microdata. Finally, the ability to identify coworkers and network effects from working in new technologies may also be interesting to researchers studying agglomeration economies and their role in forming industrial clusters.

As of this writing, the J2J data are in beta stage, with more detailed tabulations planned for later releases. A full description of the methodology used for deriving the worker flow estimates from the LEHD data is available in Hyatt et al. (2014).

11.4   Some Examples of Analysis Using the Quarterly Workforce Indicators and Job-to-Job Flows

In this section, we provide some specific examples of how the public-use QWI and J2J data can be used to answer questions of interest to researchers studying entrepreneurship.

11.4.1   Who Works at Start-Ups?

We begin by presenting simple descriptive statistics from the QWI on the population of workers employed at start-ups. Table 11.4 compares the workforce composition of start-ups to that of more established businesses, where start-ups are defined as businesses of age zero to one year and established businesses are grouped into two age categories, two to ten years old and older than ten years.

Comparing the percentages across the columns in table 11.4, we see that start-ups disproportionately employ more young workers, with workers age fourteen to twenty-four representing 20.2 percent of the workforce at start-ups (versus 14.5 percent overall). Employment at younger firms also skews toward females (51.0 percent) and the less educated. Young firms are also more likely to employ Asian and Hispanic workers. Obviously, some of the differences in demographics across young and old firms are driven by industry composition (e.g., leisure and hospitality firms are overrepresented

Table 11.4   Demographics of the workforce at young versus established firms

	All firms (%)	0–1 year (%)	2–10 years (%)	11+ years (%)
By age				
Age 14–24	14.5	20.2	17.6	13.6
Age 25–44	43.4	45.0	46.2	42.7
Age 45–64	37.2	30.5	32.6	38.6
Age 65–99	4.9	4.3	4.5	5.0
By sex				
Men	52.0	49.0	51.2	52.3
Women	48.0	51.0	48.8	47.7
By education				
Less than high school	12.2	14.7	13.5	11.8
High school	23.9	22.3	23.0	24.2
Some college	26.9	24.2	25.5	27.4
Bachelor's degree or higher	22.4	18.6	20.9	23.0
Education not available (age 24 or less)	14.5	20.2	17.0	13.6
By race				
White alone	79.4	76.6	78.9	79.6
Black or African American alone	12.3	11.7	11.0	12.6
American Indian or Alaska Native alone	0.9	1.1	1.1	0.9
Asian alone	5.5	8.3	6.9	5.0
Native Hawaiian or other Pacific Islander alone	0.3	0.3	0.3	0.2
Two or more race groups	1.6	2.0	1.9	1.6
By ethnicity				
Not Hispanic or Latino	86.1	83.3	84.2	86.7
Hispanic or Latino	13.9	16.7	15.8	13.3
Total all workers	100.0	3.5	16.9	79.5

Source: Authors' calculations from Census Quarterly Workforce Statistics (QWI), using private-sector employment counts in 2013:Q3 for all US states (except Massachusetts) and the District of Columbia.

among young firms). These same statistics are available within detailed industries, so users can measure how the demographics of new firms in a given industry compare to more established firms.

11.4.2   Did Changing Demographics Contribute to the Decline in Start-Ups?

Next, we use the QWI to explore whether the composition of firms or the workforce can account for changes in certain economic indicators that we care about. Specifically, we turn to the important question of what has caused the documented decline in employment at start-ups.[6] We begin the

6. This topic is discussed in a number of recent papers including Haltiwanger, Jarmin, and Miranda (2012), Hyatt and Spletzer (2013), Decker (2014), Decker et al. (2014a, 2014b), Davis and Haltiwanger (2014), Pugsley and Sahin (2014), and Dinlersoz, Hyatt, and Janicki (2015).

analysis in the year 2000, after which the employment share of start-ups began to decline and the earnings paid by new firms eroded.[7] We consider the share of employment at start-ups, the trend in the earnings differential between start-ups and established firms, as well as measures of employment reallocation: job creation, job destruction, hires, and separations.

We begin by describing the trends over time, although the decompositions that follow will only pertain to the endpoints of the trends plotted in these figures, which span from 2000Q2 to 2012Q2. Figures 11.2A and 11.2B present the trends in employment and earnings for two age categories: "start-up" firms, those age zero to one, and all other firms, that is, those age two or older. Figure 11.2A shows that the employment share at young firms has declined throughout the first decade of the twenty-first century, consistent with the evidence in the literature referenced above. The earnings series in figure 11.2B shows divergent trends for young and old firms. Consistent with the evidence first documented by Brown and Medoff (2003), earnings at young firms are lower than earnings at older firms. The average earnings of workers at the youngest firms have declined in real terms throughout the first decade of the twenty-first century, but the earnings at older businesses have shown a modest increase, consistent with the findings of Haltiwanger et al. (2012) and Dinlersoz. Hyatt, and Janicki (2015).

Information on the composition of the workforce by firm age can be used to answer questions related to the decline of start-ups and of business and employment dynamics more generally, a much discussed topic. Following Hyatt and Spletzer (2013), we will measure the effect of compositional changes using a standard decomposition technique to separate between-group differences from trends within groups for employment shares and earnings at start-ups (age zero to one) and all other businesses (age two or older). In such a shift-share analysis, an aggregate Y_t can be written as $\sum_i Y_{it} S_{it}$, where i indexes groups of the workforce or businesses (such as worker age or industry sector), and S_i is the share of the population that the group represents. We then decompose the difference $\Delta Y_t = Y_t - Y_{t-1}$ according to:

$$(1) \qquad \Delta Y_t = \sum_i \Delta Y_{it} S_{i\cdot} + \sum_i Y_{i\cdot} \Delta S_{it},$$

where $Y_{i\cdot}$ denotes the mean such that $Y_{i\cdot} = (Y_{it} + Y_{it-1}) / 2$, and likewise $S_{i\cdot}$. In other words, the decline in employment dynamics is equal to the change in

---

7. Another reason for starting in 2000 is that most of the states in the statistics above had entered the program as of that time, thus the analysis can be conducted on a balanced panel. Different states enter the LEHD data at different times. The year 2000 was chosen as a starting point because most of the country is in the scope of the data set by that year. The states included are AK, CA, CO, CT, DE, FL, GA, HI, ID, IL, IN, IL, IN, IA, KS, LA, ME, MD, MN, MO, MT, NE, NV, NJ, NM, NY, NC, ND, OH, OK, OR, PA, RI, SC, SD, TN, TX, UT, VT, VA, WA, WY, and WI. Comparisons are between 2000:Q2 and 2012:Q2. The year 2000 corresponds to the start of the job-to-job flows data, as described below. Furthermore, the year 2000 is a good starting point to consider the decline in entrepreneurial employment (see Dinlersoz, Hyatt, and Janicki 2015).

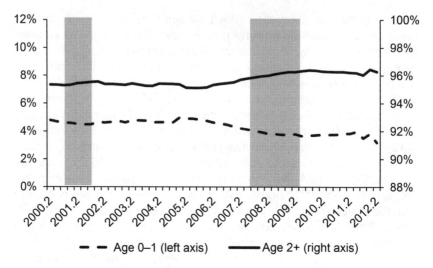

Fig. 11.2A   Employment shares by firm age

Notes: Authors' calculation of the Quarterly Workforce Indicators. All data are seasonally adjusted.

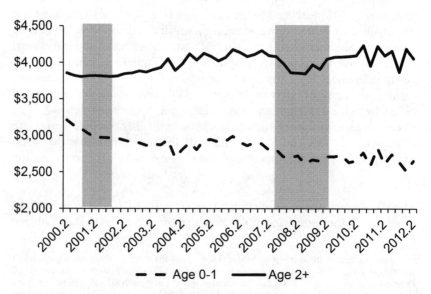

Fig. 11.2B   Real quarterly earnings by firm age

Notes: Authors' calculation of the Quarterly Workforce Indicators. All data are seasonally adjusted.

Table 11.5   **Employment composition on differences in employment and earnings (2000:Q2 vs. 2012:Q2)**

	Employment (%)	Start-up earnings penalty (%)
Sex	0.1	3.5
Age	9.4	11.1
Education	−0.3	15.4
Race	0.0	0.8
Ethnicity	−1.2	2.3
Industry	−10.9	33.4

Source: Authors' calculations of the Quarterly Workforce Indicators.
Note: Employment shares and comparisons are of those age zero to one in the Quarterly Workforce Indicators versus those age two or older. See text for exact formulas.

the dynamics of each group weighted by the group's average employment share (the within effect), plus the change in each group's employment share weighted by the group's average measure of dynamics (the composition effect).

The first column of table 11.5 contains the results of this shift-share analysis for the change in the employment at young firms relative to old firms between 2002Q2 and 2012Q2. Letting Y_t be the share of employment at start-ups, each row reports the percentage of ΔY_t that is attributable to the composition effect of a given group ($\Sigma_i Y_i \Delta S_{it}$). The intuition for this analysis is that different types of workers may be different inputs to the production process, or that the demands for the output of different industries may lead to the shifts in business entry/exit rates for those industries. For example, younger workers may be more productive at start-ups, as in Ouimet and Zarutskie (2014) and Acemoglu, Akcigit, and Celik (2014), or have fewer resources to wait for a higher wage offer from an older firm as in Dinlersoz, Hyatt, and Janicki (2015). However, as shown in table 11.5, most of the changes in composition should have in fact *increased* the share of start-ups, not decreased it, although the effects of changes in industry composition and worker demographics are fairly small. The main exception to this is the aging of the US workforce, a demographic trend that does appear tied to the decline in employment share at start-ups. The increase in the share of older workers, and their tendency to work at established businesses, explains 9.4 percent of the decrease in the share of employment at start-ups.

Figure 11.2B shows the average real earnings for workers who worked the entire quarter at start-ups and established firms between 2000 and 2012. As can be seen in the graph, earnings at established firms are rising over this period, while earnings at start-ups are falling. In the second column of table 11.5, we decompose the rising earnings premium at established firms by observable characteristics of firms and workers in the QWI. The formula for this composition change is slightly different, as it compares changes in two groups with each other. We calculate the percentage that the changes in the shares in each of the two categories explain, given the average earnings for the categories, as follows:

$$(2) \qquad \frac{\sum \Delta \text{Share}_{\text{Old},x} * \overline{\text{Earn}}_x - \sum \Delta \text{Share}_{\text{Young},x} * \overline{\text{Earn}}_x}{\Delta \text{Earn}_{\text{Old}} - \Delta \text{Earn}_{\text{Young}}}.$$

This provides a measure of how the change in a share for a subset of the population defined by a characteristic (x), as well as in the average earnings for that particular characteristic, is related to the change in earnings at young firms relative to old firms. Unlike our results for employment shares at start-ups, changes in industry composition and worker demographics explain a considerable part of the apparent increased earnings premium for working at an established firm. For example, changes in the industry composition across young and older firms explains about one-third of the decline in relative earnings at start-ups. Workers at established firms are also trending toward the older and more educated, relative to younger firms. However, since these effects are measured independently of the change in the industry distribution, they may in fact be interrelated, and thus their impacts are not necessarily additive.

In turn, table 11.6 shows how the change in the composition of employment by firm age explains the decline in four employment dynamics measures: hires, separations, job creation, and destruction. These measures exploit the dynamic aspect of the LEHD data: workers and business size are linked longitudinally to create these measures. This decomposition is again computed according to equation (2) above. Results show that the shift away from entrepreneurship explains a substantial portion in the decline of such dynamics, due to the fact that start-ups are more volatile in terms of employment dynamics. The table shows that the decline in start-ups explains 9.3 percent of the decline in hires and 6.8 percent of the decline in separations.[8] These results are similar to what Hyatt and Spletzer (2013) found using the LEHD microdata.

The above examples show how the demographic and industrial detail of the QWI can be used to study the composition of start-up employment and its effects on economic dynamics. However, note that these exercises only scratch the surface of what can be learned from these statistics. All of the measures used here can be cross-tabulated on multiple levels, and are also available at narrow geographic detail, allowing for much more complex analyses.

---

8. Additionally, the decline in start-ups explains 25.8 percent of the decline in job creation, but only 9.5 percent of the decline in job destruction. These results are similar to what Decker et al. (2014b) found using the BDS.

Table 11.6	Change in employment dynamics due to decline in start-ups (2000–2012)			
	Hires (%)	Separations (%)	Job creation (%)	Job destruction (%)
2000:Q2	30.0	27.1	8.6	5.7
2012:Q2	20.5	17.4	7.1	4.0
Change	−9.5	−9.7	−1.5	−1.7
Percent of change explained firm age:	9.3	6.8	25.8	9.5

Source: Authors' calculations from the Quarterly Workforce Indicators. See text for formulas.

11.4.3   Where Do Early Employees Come From?

The new Job-to-Job Flows (J2J) data allow us to identify movements of workers into start-up firms from other employers. Figures 11.3A, 11.3B, and 11.3C show a comparison of worker flows across three classes of employers: young firms (less than two years), established firms (more than eleven years), and small firms of all ages (less than twenty employees). Employment growth in each employer class is the sum of net employment flows (i.e., hires of nonemployed workers minus separations to nonemployment) and new worker reallocation (i.e., hires of workers away from other firms minus separations employees to other firms). This decomposition allows us see how firms grow, either through the poaching of workers from other firms or through net employment flows.

Figure 11.3A depicts the hire and separation rates at start-up firms from 2000 to 2013. As can be seen in the figure, new firms obtain a significant share of their early employment growth by poaching workers away from more established firms. Flows into new firms from established firms are much higher than separations from new firms to more established employers. Poaching hires were highest during the 2000–2002 period, when half of new firm hires were of workers moving from other jobs. Overall, this decomposition shows the importance of worker moves from more established firms as a critical input to early firm growth.

As a comparison, figure 11.3B shows this decomposition for established firms. In contrast to start-ups, net employment growth at established firms is much smaller, and occurs exclusively via net employment flows. We find in other analyses (not shown) that the high contribution of job-to-job flows to employment growth at young firms disappears by the time firms are two to three years old. This may suggest that the high growth rate from worker reallocation at the youngest firms is driven by start-up teams transitioning from their previous jobs at older firms to the new firm.

As an additional comparison, we show the flows at businesses (of all ages) with fewer than twenty employees in figure 11.3C. This decomposition for small businesses looks more like that for older established firms

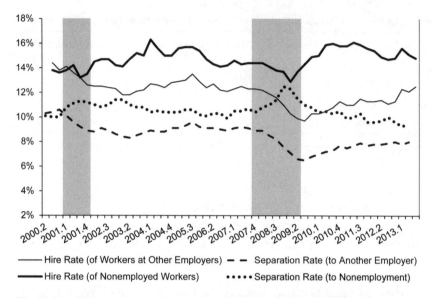

Fig. 11.3A   Hires and separations at young firms (0–1 year old), 2000–2013

Notes: Authors' calculations from national Job-to-Job Flows data, beta 2014:Q1 release. All data are seasonally adjusted.

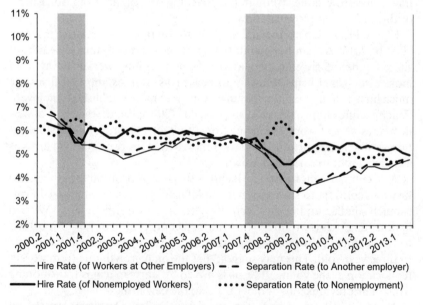

Fig. 11.3B   Hires and separations at established firms (11+ years old), 2000–2013

Notes: Authors' calculations from national Job-to-Job Flows data, beta 2014:Q1 release. All data are seasonally adjusted.

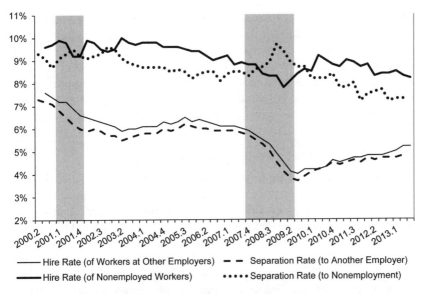

Fig. 11.3C   **Hires and separations at small firms (<20 employees), 2000–2013**

Notes: Authors' calculations from national Job-to-Job Flows data, beta 2014:Q1 release. All data are seasonally adjusted.

than for younger firms. Net worker reallocation to small firms from larger firms is low, although very slightly positive.[9] Haltiwanger, Jarmin, and Miranda (2013) find that, controlling for age, it is young firms rather than small firms that disproportionately drive job creation. Here we find that a pattern of employment growth through worker relocation (workers voting with their feet) characterizes new firms but not small firms, generally. That workers are willing to move from established (and presumably more stable and higher-paying) employers to start-ups suggests that for early employees, working at a new firm offers opportunities for advancement and career growth not available to them at more established firms.

At press time, the J2J data are quite new, and do not yet provide as many tabulation levels as the QWI. The possibilities for analysis will only expand as the J2J statistics release more detailed tabulations.

11.5   Looking Forward: The Potential for New Data on Entrepreneurship

While substantial progress has been made in the last few years making linked employer-employee data more useful and accessible for entrepreneur-

---

9. Haltiwanger, Hyatt, and McEntarfer (2015) point out that the fact that worker relocation does *not* in fact redistribute workers away from small firms to large firms is inconsistent with a number of important labor market models, particularly Burdett and Mortensen (1998).

ship research, the work we have described so far represents only a fraction of possible ways to expand the frontier of data available for research. In particular, linking in additional data on business owners and creating new measures of the dynamics of entrepreneurship would be an important advance in the statistical infrastructure for studying new business formation. In this section, we discuss the potential for including more information on entrepreneurs and their firms from linked employer-employee data, and discuss some results from work-to-date on integrating these new sources of data.

11.5.1   Linking Data on Business Owners

Efforts are currently underway to enhance the set of available data on business owners and the self-employed by integrating data on sole proprietors and partnerships into the LEHD data infrastructure. A prototype microdata file is being created that covers the universe of active US sole proprietorships and partnerships, both with and without employees, from 2002 through 2013. The Census Bureau is undertaking research into using these data for new public-use statistics on the dynamics of business ownership.[10]

The universe of this data set encompasses all unincorporated businesses owned and run by one or more individuals. The data that we integrate originate primarily from individual federal income tax returns, such as income filings from Schedules C and K1, payroll tax records for employers (Form 941), and applications for an Employer Identification Number (EIN) for employers (Form SS-4). The scope of our data includes owners of sole proprietorships, partnerships, and Subchapter S corporations. Owners of limited liability companies (LLCs) and the like are included as long as they do not elect to be taxed by the IRS as a corporation. The individual business owners can then by linked via a personal identifier to the LEHD job-level database, thus providing an employment history for each owner. More details on how the data are constructed are provided in Garcia-Perez et al. (2013).

This linking of information on business ownership and employment status joins information in a way that is not available in other data sources, permitting a unique view of the path to entrepreneurship. Individuals starting businesses bring with them a preexisting stock of human capital through their past experience, both in the labor market and also as prior business owners. The potential statistics derived from this unique data source will allow researchers to study the intersection of these two employment spheres, which has been little explored up to this point.

One challenge in the study of entrepreneurship is the lack of a cleanly defined measure of entrepreneurial activity. Measurement aside, there is, in fact, no consistent definition in the literature of what entrepreneurship

---

10. This builds on previous work integrating the employer and nonemployer business data (see Davis et al. 2009).

is. At its narrowest, entrepreneurs have been identified as the founders of innovative new businesses that grow rapidly in both employment and output and thus drive national measures of economic growth. More broadly, the word entrepreneur has at its root "one who starts" and thus can refer to the founder of any business regardless of size or outcome.

More broadly still, entrepreneurial activity is associated with business ownership of any kind (with or without employees) and with self-employment, which is in turn equally hard to define. In fact, for tax purposes in the United States, contract and contingent workers are defined as self-employed and their earnings treated as self-employment earnings.

Taken independently, each of these varied concepts of entrepreneurial activity has value and each measure reveals a different facet of the economy. Rises and falls among innovative, high-growth businesses have obvious implications for national employment and output. The set of all business starts with or without employees tells us, at a minimum, about the economy's capacity to support such efforts. The set of small self-owned businesses without employees combined with the pool of contract or contingent workers serves as an alternative measure of employment in a changing economy. This count may also measure what the development literature calls the informal labor market.

To better understand the implications of a rise or fall in these varied measures of entrepreneurial activity, we must recognize that each of these events, the start of a new business (with or without employees) or the transition to contingent work, reflects a choice made by the owner. These choices are in turn influenced by the owner's personal preentry economic environment. In addition, trends in the varying concepts of entrepreneurship likely are interrelated. For example, ownership of a business without employees in many cases precedes the "birth" of an employer business. Thus, our ability to extract information from these trends is greatly enhanced by placing them in a broader context.

The linked employer-employee data constructed by the LEHD program have the potential to provide this context. Specifically, statistics released from these data may improve our understanding of entrepreneurial dynamics in three ways. First, as noted, it is the use of federal tax filings by sole proprietorships, partnerships, and Subchapter S corporations that gives the LEHD program its ability to identify business owners. Knowledge of the type of originating tax form combined with the presence or absence of employees allows us to disentangle these varied types of entrepreneurship and to separately examine trends in each. Second, by combining administrative data on the universe of individual business owners with the universe of covered wage and salary work, the resulting data set permits us to observe an owner's preownership wage and salary work history, and thus to potentially generate statistics based on prior employment, earnings, and industry experience. Third, we can follow individuals as they transition between ownership of businesses without employees, employer businesses, and traditional work, and explore the interconnection between these spheres. In short, by identifying differing types of business ownership and by integrating each with employment and earnings history and prior ownership experience for the owner, the program has the potential to release a set of statistics that gives insight into what each of these measures may be telling us about the vitality of the economy.

We will next describe the type of statistics the program has the ability to create to measure conventional self-employment, as well as self-employment as an alternate form of employment (what the literature has termed the "gig economy"). We follow with a more developed discussion of how linked employer-employee-owner data may further our knowledge of entrepreneurship by tracking the events that precede and follow the birth of a business.

11.5.2   Self-Employment and the "Gig Economy"

The vast majority of businesses that report earnings have no employees. While self-employment counts have stagnated in survey reports in recent years, the count of these nonemployer sole-proprietor businesses have continued to rise.[11] This count includes any person who receives income as a statutory employee or contingent worker or who operates a business or practice for profit with regularity and continuity.[12] Internet businesses, freelancers, contract workers, consultants, and so forth, all are included in this measure.

The rise in employment arrangements of this type is linked in part to technology, which has significantly lowered the entry cost for these businesses. The US economy has become much more service oriented and thus the capital requirements associated with business entry are low. The pros and cons of this trend have been widely discussed and can be viewed from the perspective of the employer, the worker, or the economy as a whole. From an employer's perspective, the availability of an on-demand workforce lowers labor costs and provides flexibility. From the worker's perspective, a less formal work arrangement often precludes other benefits of employment such as stability and health insurance coverage, yet does provide an alternative to conventional work when faced with unemployment or underemploy-

11. In a recent interview, Laurence Katz described preliminary work with Alan Krueger to investigate the discrepancy between steady trends in self-employment in survey data and increases in self-employment suggested by tax data. Rob Wile, "There are probably way more people in the 'gig economy' than we realize." July 27, 2015, Fusion.net.

12. Data on nonemployer sole proprietors originate from filings of IRS 1949 Schedule C. The Schedule C instructions state "use Schedule C (Form 1040) to report income or loss from a business you operated or a profession you practiced as a sole proprietor. An activity qualifies as a business if your primary purpose for engaging in the activity is for income or profit and you are involved in the activity with continuity and regularity. For example, a sporadic activity or a hobby does not qualify as a business. Also use Schedule C to report (a) wages and expenses you had as a statutory employee, (b) income and deductions of certain qualified joint ventures, and (c) certain income shown on Form 1099-MISC, Miscellaneous Income."

ment. For the economy as a whole, a rise in unemployment is one of the mechanisms through which the economy is theorized to self-correct during recessions. Thus, unlike a rise in conventional entrepreneurship, which is viewed as a driving force of economic growth, it is not clear whether we should regard the rise in the numbers of nonemployer sole proprietors as a sign of economic strength.

Linked employer-employee-owner data have the potential to create statistics that provide more insight into these trends. For each new nonemployer, we observe their employment and earnings status in time periods preceding self-employment entry. The data thus give us some ability to distinguish those new nonemployers pushed into self-employment by lack of economic opportunity from those lured into self-employment by higher anticipated returns. We can identify those entrants with no wage and salary earnings, those with broken spells of employment, those previously working at a downsizing employer, or those employed but earning significantly less than comparable workers. Similarly, we can identify those entrants with high, above average, or rising wage and salary earnings. An understanding of the forces that influence self-employment entry may help economists understand the rise of business ownership of this type.

11.5.3 Measuring Business Ownership Dynamics

The determinants of entrepreneurial success are a much-studied topic, but many of these factors are determined prior to the beginning of a business. The human capital and prior experience that an entrepreneur brings to a new venture are clearly important, and may not be possible to fully encapsulate in measures such as education level. Moreover, many business starts and business failures occur before the firm hires its first employees. Such small owner-operated businesses are not included in statistics such as the BDS and QWI, where business birth is defined as the moment the firm hires its first worker. In order to identify the characteristics of successful entrepreneurs, and to answer questions like why the rate of entrepreneurship is declining, it may be important to observe these potential job creators at their earliest stages.

Such a link should prove enlightening in the context of the well-documented decline in US start-ups, which has sparked much interest in the underlying causes and implications of this slowdown. Although the overall trend in start-ups may be downward, in reality the composition of new business owners is constantly in flux, with certain types of individuals exhibiting differing and perhaps offsetting trends. To understand the decrease in start-ups requires knowledge of the factors that precede a business and an understanding of how these factors influence the odds of a successful start-up. For example, the self-employment literature recognizes that some are pushed into self-employment by lack of economic opportunity while others are pulled into entrepreneurship by means of comparative advantage or innovative idea. Statistics derived from linked sole-proprietor and LEHD data will offer a way to help parse such differences in the paths of potential entrepreneurs.

11.5.4   Don't Quit Your Day Job: A Look at Self-Employment Dynamics

Researchers are interested in identifying successful transitions to entrepreneurship. One measure of success is the owner's ability to create a primary source of earnings for themselves from the business. The combined owner-work history data are well suited to explore the following question: What share of self-employed businesses grow enough to allow the owner to leave wage and salary employment?

The left-hand panel of table 11.7 shows the percentage of sole proprietors in 2009 who are engaged in wage and salary work in the same year, as well as in the surrounding years of 2008 and 2010. One of the first facts to stand out is that the majority of self-employed businesses without employees do not in fact grow large enough to supplant the owner's reliance on some form of wage and salary work. Over 50 percent of nonemployer business owners in 2009 have wage and salary income in that year, a share that is higher for new nonemployer business owners (those in the first year of their business), at around 65 percent. For new employers in 2009, defined as businesses with employees who were not employers in 2008, about 40 percent had wage and salary jobs in 2008, 35 percent have such employment in 2009 (the birth year of their employer business), and 30 percent retain it in the following year 2010. For more established business owners with employees, the wage and salary work rate stabilizes at just above 20 percent.

For employer business owners, we can also capture their experience as operators of businesses without paid employees. In the right-hand panel of

Table 11.7   **Employment status of 2009 business owners in years 2008–2010**

Type of 2009 business owner	Percentage with wage and salary income			Percentage with nonemployer income			
	2008 (%)	2009 (%)	2010 (%)	2008 (%)	2009 (%)	2010 (%)	N
New employers	40.5	34.8	29.9	36.3	16.7	24.4	86,011
All employers	21.0	19.9	20.6	17.6	14.9	22.1	721,807
New nonemployers	68.3	65.4	62.3	0.0	100.0	51.7	6,158,104
All nonemployers	53.9	50.7	50.2	65.6	100.0	68.8	17,912,997

Notes: Table reports percentages of sole-proprietor business owners in 2009 of a given type that also have positive income from wage and salary work and/or nonemployer activity in the years 2008–2010. Sample consists of all observed owner-year pairs of a given business type during 2009. "New employers" are defined as owners who have positive income from an employer business in the year 2009, but no such income in year 2008. Similarly "New nonemployers" are those who have nonemployer business income in 2009, but no such income in 2008.

table 11.7, we see that among new employer business owners in 2009, around 36 percent operated a nonemployer business in the previous year. This rate falls by over half to 17 percent during their first year of employer business activity in 2009, suggesting that it may represent the same businesses that are transitioning as they acquire employees. Note that the percentage of new 2009 employers with nonemployer income rises again in 2010 to 24 percent, perhaps indicating that some new employer businesses have shed their employee within one year, but nonetheless maintained the business. Note again that the rate of nonemployer business holding among all employers remains in the 15–20 percent range, meaning that a substantial fraction of owners maintain other sources of business income simultaneous to running an employer business.

This example clearly shows that there is no single path to entrepreneurship, as the relationship between wage and salary work, self-employment, and running an employer business is quite complicated. These data are uniquely suited to studying the interplay between these types of employment, and the future business owner statistics should enable new exploration into the origins of entrepreneurship.

11.6 Conclusion

Linked employer-employee data have enormous potential for empirical research in entrepreneurship. These data allow an ever-growing community of researchers to develop a clearer picture of how new firms come into being, obtain workers, grow, shrink, and exit, and how this dynamic process is related to employment and economic growth. In this chapter, we described the LEHD-linked employer-employee microdata, introduced public-use data on start-ups tabulated from LEHD data, and highlighted how they fill gaps in the set of available data for the study of entrepreneurship. We provided examples that illustrate the power of the new public data to address questions that previously required access to restricted microdata. Work to expand the utility of this data for entrepreneurship research is still ongoing; we also outlined future plans for development of new data products for empirical research on entrepreneurship.

References

Abowd, J., B. Stephens, L. Vilhuber, F. Andersson, K. McKinney, M. Roemer, and S. Woodcock. 2009. "The LEHD Infrastructure Files and the Creation of the Quarterly Workforce Indicators. In *Producer Dynamics: New Evidence from Micro Data*, edited by T. Dunne, J. Jensen, and M. Roberts, 149–230. Chicago: University of Chicago Press.

Acemoglu, D., U. Akcigit, and M. Celik. 2014. "Young, Restless, and Creative: Openness to Disruption and Creative Innovation." NBER Working Paper no. 19894, Cambridge, MA.
Acs, Z., and P. Mueller. 2008. "Employment Effects of Business Dynamics: Mice, Gazelles and Elephants." *Small Business Economics* 30 (1): 85–100.
Agarwal, R., B. Campbell, A. Franco, and M. Ganco. 2013. "What Do I Take with Me? The Mediating Effect of Spin-Out Team Size and Tenure on the Founder-Firm Performance Relationship." Center for Economic Studies Working Paper, US Census Bureau, Washington, DC.
Bates, T. 1990. "Entrepreneur Human Capital Inputs and Small Business Longevity." *Review of Economics and Statistics* 72 (4): 551–59.
Birch, D. 1979. *The Job Generation Process.* Cambridge, MA: MIT Program on Neighborhood and Regional Change.
Brown, C., and J. Medoff. 2003. "Firm Age and Wages." *Journal of Labor Economics* 21 (3): 677–98.
Burdett, K., and D. Mortensen. 1998. "Wage Differentials, Employer Size, and Unemployment." *International Economic Review* 39 (2): 257–73.
Carree, M. 2002. "Does Unemployment Affect the Number of Establishments? A Regional Analysis for US States." *Regional Studies* 36 (4): 389–98.
Chatterjee, S., and E. Rossi-Hansberg. 2012. "Spinoffs and the Market for Ideas." *International Economic Review* 53 (1): 53–93.
Combes, P., G. Duranton, and L. Gobillon. 2008. "Spatial Wage Disparities: Sorting Matters!" *Journal of Urban Economics* 63 (2): 723–42.
Congregado, E., E. Carmona, and A. Golpe. 2010. "Co-Movement and Causality between Self-Employment, Unemployment and the Business Cycle in the EU-12." *International Review of Entrepreneurship* 8 (4): 303–36.
Davis, S., and J. Haltiwanger. 2014. "Labor Market Fluidity and Economic Performance." NBER Working Paper no. 20479, Cambridge, MA.
Davis, S., J. Haltiwanger, C. J. Krizan, J. Miranda, A. Nucci, and L. K. Sandusky. 2009. "Measuring the Dynamics of Young and Small Businesses: Integrating the Employer and Nonemployer Universes." In *Producer Dynamics: New Evidence from Micro Data,* edited by T. Dunne, J. Jensen, and M. Roberts, 329–66. Chicago: University of Chicago Press.
Decker, R. 2014. "Collateral Damage: Housing, Entrepreneurship, and Job Creation." Unpublished Manuscript, University of Maryland.
Decker, R., J. Haltiwanger, R. Jarmin, and J. Miranda. 2014a. "The Role of Entrepreneurship in US Job Creation and Economic Dynamism." *Journal of Economic Perspectives* 28 (3): 3–24.
———. 2014b. "The Secular Decline in Business Dynamism in the US" Unpublished Manuscript, University of Maryland.
Dinlersoz, E., H. Hyatt, and H. Janicki. 2015. "Who Works for Whom? Worker Sorting in a Model of Entrepreneurship with Heterogeneous Labor Markets." CES Working Paper no. 15-08, Center for Economic Studies, US Census Bureau.
Doms, M., E. Lewis, and A. Robb. 2010. "Local Labor Force Education, New Business Characteristics, and Firm Performance." *Journal of Urban Economics* 67 (1): 61–77.
Dunne, T., M. Roberts, and L. Samuelson. 1989. "Plant Turnover and Gross Employment Flows in the US Manufacturing Sector." *Journal of Labor Economics* 7 (1): 48–71.
Ellison, G., and E. Glaeser. 1997. "Geographic Concentration in US Manufacturing Industries: A Dartboard Approach." *Journal of Political Economy* 104 (5): 899–927.

Evans, D., and L. Leighton. 1989. "Some Empirical Aspects of Entrepreneurship." *American Economic Review* 79 (3): 519–35.

Fairlie, R. 2005. Self-Employment, Entrepreneurship, and the NLSY79." *Monthly Labor Review* 128 (2): 40–47.

Figueiredo, O., P. Guimarães, and D. Woodward. 2014. "Firm-Worker Matching in Industrial Clusters." *Journal of Economic Geography* 14 (1): 1–19.

Fort, T., J. Haltiwanger, R. Jarmin, and J. Miranda. 2013. "How Firms Respond to Business Cycles: The Role of Firm Age and Firm Size." NBER Working Paper no. 19134, Cambridge, MA.

Franco, A., and D. Filson. 2006. "Spin-Outs: Knowledge Diffusion through Employee Mobility." *RAND Journal of Economics* 37 (4): 841–60.

Garcia-Perez, M., C. Goetz, J. Haltiwanger, and L. K. Sandusky." 2013. "Don't Quit Your Day Job: Using Wage and Salary Earnings to Support a New Business." CES Working Paper Series no. 13-45, Center for Economic Studies, US Census Bureau.

Gertler, M., and S. Gilchrist. 1994. "Monetary Policy, Business Cycles and the Behavior of Small Manufacturing Firms." *Quarterly Journal of Economics* 109 (2): 309–40.

Glaeser, E., W. Kerr, and G. Ponzetto. 2010. "Clusters of Entrepreneurship." *Journal of Urban Economics* 67 (1): 150–68.

Haltiwanger, J., H. Hyatt, and E. McEntarfer. 2015. "Cyclical Reallocation of Workers across Employers by Firm Size and Firm Wage." NBER Working Paper no. 21235, Cambridge, MA.

Haltiwanger, J., H. Hyatt, E. McEntarfer, and L. Sousa. 2012. "Business Dynamics Statistics Briefing: Job Creation, Worker Churning, and Wages at Young Businesses." Kauffman Foundation Paper Series. http://www.kauffman.org /what-we-do/research/business-dynamics-statistics/business-dynamics-statistics -briefing-job-creation-worker-churning-and-wages-at-young-businesses.

Haltiwanger, J., H. Hyatt, E. McEntarfer, L. Sousa, and S. Tibbets. 2014. "Firm Age and Size in the Longitudinal Employer-Household Dynamics Data." CES Discussion Paper no. 14-16, Center for Economic Studies, US Census Bureau.

Haltiwanger, J., R. Jarmin, and J. Miranda. 2012. "Where Have All the Young Firms Gone?" Kauffman Foundation Paper Series. http://www.kauffman.org /what-we-do/research/business-dynamics-statistics/business-dynamics-statistics -briefing-where-have-all-the-young-firms-gone.

———. 2013. "Who Creates Jobs? Small versus Large versus Young." *Review of Economics and Statistics* 95 (2): 347–61.

Hamilton, B. 2000. "Does Entrepreneurship Pay? An Empirical Analysis of the Returns to Self-Employment." *Journal of Political Economy* 108 (3): 604–31.

Holtz-Eakin, D., D. Joulfaian, and H. Rosen. 1994. "Sticking It Out: Entrepreneurial Survival and Liquidity Constraints." *Journal of Political Economy* 102 (1): 53–75.

Hurst, E., and A. Lusardi. 2004. "Liquidity Constraints, Household Wealth and Entrepreneurship." *Journal of Political Economy* 112 (2): 319–47.

Hurst, E., and B. Pugsley. 2011. "What Do Small Businesses Do?" *Brookings Papers on Economic Activity* 43 (2): 73–142.

Hyatt, H., E. McEntarfer, K. McKinney, S. Tibbets, and D. Walton. 2014. "Job-to-Job (J2J) Flows: New Labor Market Statistics from Linked Employer-Employee Data." *JSM Proceedings 2014*, Business and Economics Statistics Section, 231–45.

Hyatt, H., and J. Spletzer. 2013. "The Recent Decline in Employment Dynamics." *IZA Journal of Labor Economics* 2 (1): 1–21.

Kerr, W., and S. Kominers. 2010. "Agglomerative Forces and Cluster Shapes." NBER Working Paper no. 16639, Cambridge, MA.

Klepper, S. 2001. "Employee Startups in High-Tech Industries." *Industrial and Corporate Change* 10 (3): 639–74.
Lazear, E. 2005. "Entrepreneurship." *Journal of Labor Economics* 23 (4): 649–80.
Moskowitz, T., and A. Vissing-Jørgensen. 2002. "The Returns to Entrepreneurial Investment: A Private Equity Premium Puzzle?" *American Economic Review* 92 (4): 745–78.
Ouimet, P., and R. Zarutskie. 2014. "Who Works for Startups? The Relation between Firm Age, Employee Age, and Growth." *Journal of Financial Economics* 112 (3): 386–407.
Pugsley, B., and A. Sahin. 2014. "Grown-Up Business Cycles." Federal Reserve Bank of New York Staff Report no. 707. https://www.newyorkfed.org/medialibrary/media/research/staff_reports/sr707.pdf.
Rosenthal, S., and W. Strange. 2003. "Geography, Industrial Organization, and Agglomeration." *Review of Economics and Statistics* 85 (2): 377–93.

Contributors

Victor Manuel Bennett
The Fuqua School of Business
Duke University
100 Fuqua Drive
Durham, NC 27708

J. David Brown
Center for Economic Studies
US Census Bureau
4600 Silver Hill Road
Washington, DC 20233

John S. Earle
School of Public Policy
George Mason University
3351 Fairfax Drive, MS 3B1
Arlington, VA 22201

Christopher Goetz
Center for Economic Studies
US Census Bureau
4600 Silver Hill Road
Washington, DC 20233

Jorge Guzman
MIT Sloan School of Management
100 Main Street, E62–343
Cambridge, MA 02139

John Haltiwanger
Department of Economics
University of Maryland
College Park, MD 20742

Johan Hombert
HEC Paris
Finance Department
1 rue de la Liberation
78350 Jouy-en-Josas, France

Erik Hurst
Booth School of Business
University of Chicago
5807 South Woodlawn Avenue
Chicago, IL 60637

Henry Hyatt
Center for Economic Studies
US Census Bureau
4600 Silver Hill Road
ACSD HQ-5K056F
Washington, DC 20233

Ron S. Jarmin
Research and Methodology
US Census Bureau
4600 Silver Hill Road
Washington, DC 20233

Steven N. Kaplan
Booth School of Business
University of Chicago
5807 South Woodlawn Avenue
Chicago, IL 60637

Arthur B. Kennickell
Board of Governors of the Federal
  Reserve System
Washington, DC 20551

Sari Pekkala Kerr
Wellesley College
106 Central Street
Wellesley, MA 02481

William R. Kerr
Harvard Business School
Rock Center 212
Soldiers Field
Boston, MA 02163

Robert Kulick
Department of Economics
University of Maryland
5106 Tydings Hall
College Park, MD 20742

Myron L. Kwast
Division of Insurance and Research
Federal Deposit Insurance
  Corporation
550 17th Street
Washington, DC 20429

Megan Lawrence
Vanderbilt Owen Graduate School of
  Management
Management Hall
401 21st Avenue South
Nashville, TN 37203

Josh Lerner
Harvard Business School
Rock Center 214
Soldiers Field
Boston, MA 02163

Erika McEntarfer
Center for Economic Studies
US Census Bureau
Office: 5K021
4600 Silver Hill Road
ACSD HQ-5K179
Washington, DC 20233

Javier Miranda
US Bureau of the Census
Center for Economic Studies
4600 Silver Hill Road
Washington, DC 20233

Yana Morgulis
The Boston Consulting Group
1735 SEPTA Market-Frankford Line
  # 4100
Philadelphia, PA 19103

Jonathan Pogach
Federal Deposit Insurance
  Corporation
550 17th Street, NW
Washington, DC 20429

Benjamin W. Pugsley
Federal Reserve Bank of New York
33 Liberty Street
New York, NY 10045

Raffaella Sadun
Harvard Business School
Morgan Hall 233
Soldiers Field
Boston, MA 02163

Kristin Sandusky
US Census Bureau
4600 Silver Hill Road
Washington, DC 20233

Antoinette Schoar
MIT Sloan School of Management
100 Main Street, E62–638
Cambridge, MA 02142

David Sraer
Haas School of Business
University of California, Berkeley
545 Student Services Building
Berkeley, CA 94720–1900

Scott Stern
MIT Sloan School of Management
100 Main Street, E62–476
Cambridge, MA 02142

David Thesmar
MIT Sloan School of Management
100 Main Street, E62–635
Cambridge, MA 02142

Tiantian Yang
Department of Sociology
Duke University
268 Soc/Psych Building, Box 90088
Durham, NC 27708–0088

Rebecca Zarutskie
Board of Governors of the Federal
    Reserve System
Mailstop 97
20th Street and Constitution Avenue,
    NW
Washington, DC 20551

Author Index

Subject Index